Peter,

Remember the pioneers who
led the way, and celebrate
the journey.

Ilie H.

QUEER CLERGY

QUEER CLERGY

CLERGY

~

A History of
Gay and Lesbian Ministry in
American Protestantism

~

R.W. HOLMEN

The Pilgrim Press
Cleveland

The Pilgrim Press, 700 Prospect Avenue, Cleveland, Ohio 44115
thepilgrimpress.com
© 2013 by R. W. Holmen

Scripture quotations, unless otherwise noted, are from the New Revised
Standard Version of the Bible, © 1989 by the Division of Christian
Education of the National Council of Churches of Christ in the United
States of America, and are used by permission. Changes have been
made for inclusivity.

Printed in the United States of America on acid-free paper

17   16   15   14   5   4   3   2

Library of Congress Cataloging-in-Publication Data

A catalog record for this book is available from the Library of Congress.

Library of Congress Control Number: 2013919098
ISBN: 978-0-8298-1963-2

Contents

A c k n o w l e d g m e n t s

The subjects of this book have also been its principal sources. The pilgrims from each denomination have shared recollections from the journey toward full inclusion, from the early days to the very recent. Written accounts by the wayfarers in books, articles, newsletters, and other documents have been supplemented by face-to-face interviews, phone conferences, and e-mail correspondence. Iconic veterans of the struggle for full inclusion have also served as fact-checkers who have reviewed the manuscript at various stages and offered correctives when necessary.

From the United Church of Christ, the list begins with perhaps the most iconic figure across denominations: Rev. William R. Johnson, the first openly gay man ordained (in 1972) and who has continued as a pan-denominational gay leader to the present. Rev. Johnson visited with me during the 2012 Coalition Convention at Elmhurst College outside Chicago, and he filled in many details in subsequent e-mails and via a marked-up copy of the manuscript. Another early leader along the UCC journey was Rev. Loey Powell, who visited with me in her office at UCC headquarters in Cleveland and at the same Coalition gathering at Elmhurst, and who provided copies of important Coalition documents. I also visited and corresponded with UCC Executive Michael Schuenemeyer and Coalition Executive Director Andy Lang. The UCC Open and Affirming Program (ONA) has been officially sanctioned by the church since 1985, and Marnie Warner was an early organizer and proponent. I visited with her at the Coalition gathering and subsequently corresponded with her. For two decades, Rev. Ann B. Day and her partner Donna Engberg administered the ONA program and also played leading roles as the welcoming church movement achieved pan-denominational collaboration. Rev. Day provided several packets of documents for my use.

The two principal Episcopal sources have been Dr. Louie Crew and retired Bishop John Shelby Spong. Dr. Crew, through his 1974 newsletter, was the inspiration behind the formation of Integrity USA, the Episcopal LGBT advocacy group, and he has continued to be an Episcopal activist leader to the present. Dr. Crew has shared his own written articles, and he has offered suggestions in phone conversations with and e-mails to me, including commentary following a review of the manuscript.

Though I was familiar with the voluminous writings of Bishop Spong, I had not been aware of his own significant contributions to the Episcopal journey toward full inclusion—from his highly publicized ordination of a gay man in 1989 to his role as principal voice for LGBT issues in the Episcopal House of Bishops during the decade of the nineties. Bishop Spong's autobiography served as a starting point, and subsequent phone conversations and e-mail correspondence clarified and added many details.

A special thanks to Sister Bernadette Barrett, ordained an Episcopal priest as an out lesbian in 1977, who provided a poignant retrospective on her often difficult journey that is reprinted as the coda to the Episcopal section.

The contributors to the Lutheran section of this book are many. Pastor Jim Siefkes, who wrangled a modest appropriation from the American Lutheran Church that facilitated the startup of Lutherans Concerned for Gay People, offered his remembrances from the June 1974 weekend that brought five gay persons together. The insights of those five persons have been preserved by Jeannine Janson in a 2008 booklet that remembered the early days of Lutherans Concerned. Ms. Janson, who has served in various leadership capacities of Lutherans Concerned (now ReconcilingWorks), has also been an indefatigable fact-checker who has offered correctives to succeeding versions of my manuscript. Rev. Ruth Frost, Rev. Phyllis Zillhart, and Rev. Anita Hill made national news and prodded the ELCA through their extraordinary ordinations, and they each shared details of their stories over lunch with me and through e-mails. Rev. Hill has also marked up a copy of the manuscript.

Professor James D. Anderson became involved with Presbyterians for Lesbian and Gay Concerns in the late seventies and served as editor of *More Light Update* for twenty-two years. Dr. Anderson has added to details contained within his own articles through phone conversations and e-mail correspondence with me and over dinner near his home in St. Petersburg. Dr. Anderson provided several boxes of archival issues of *More Light Update* for review, and he later fact-checked the manuscript.

Author Chris Glaser also goes back to the earliest days of the Presbyterian journey. Along with Rev. David Bailey Sindt and Bill Silver, both now deceased, Rev. Glaser was an early mainstay of the Presbyterian Gay Caucus. He was there as an advocate at Presbyterian General Assemblies in the seventies, and he served on an early Presbyterian Task Force, but his own journey to ordination was derailed. Rev. Glaser (finally ordained by the MCC in 2005) has written extensively, and information gleaned from his books and articles has been supplemented through e-mails to me, and he fact-checked the manuscript.

Rev. Scott Anderson became a leader of Presbyterians for Lesbian and Gay Concerns following his outing in 1990. In recent years, Rev. Anderson played an influential role in Presbyterian legislative and judicial wrangling that resulted in the approval of gay ordination, and Rev. Anderson was the first to benefit in a 2011 re-ordination ceremony. Rev. Anderson fact-checked the manuscript.

The greater Chicago area is home to numerous Methodist sources, which was convenient since I resided in the Chicago suburbs as this manuscript unfolded. I first met Steve Webster and his husband, Jim Dietrich, at the 2010 Wisconsin Annual Conference in LaCrosse. Later, I learned that Steve had organized the first gathering of gay Methodists near Northwestern University in 1974, so I arranged lunch with Steve and Jim near their home in Madison, Wisconsin, to hear the story firsthand. I also lunched with Rev. Morris Floyd, an activist from the eighties, on Chicago's north side. Rev. Greg Dell, who was tried and suspended for officiating at a covenant ceremony in the late nineties, joined me for breakfast near his home. I visited recent leaders of Methodist Reconciling

Ministries, Rev. Bonnie Beckonchrist and Rev. Troy Plummer, at their offices. Retired Bishop Joseph Sprague visited with me during a car ride to the O'Hare airport following his speaking engagement in Rockford. Bishop Sprague was arrested, not once but twice, for protesting during the Methodist General Conference in 2000.

Mark Bowman is another of the iconic prophets from the earliest days to the present, and he also resides in Chicago, allowing for several face-to-face visits. Bowman became involved with Methodist Affirmation in 1980 and was the principal person responsible for organizing and administering the Methodist Reconciling Congregations project during its first decades. He was also the long-time editor of the award-winning *Open Hands*, which became a pan-denominational magazine in the nineties. In the last decade plus, Bowman has been the project director of an Internet source entitled The Lesbian, Gay, Bisexual, and Trans-gender Religious Archives Network, which is an online compendium of profiles, oral histories, documents and more. In personal interviews, e-mail correspondence, and as a reviewer of the manuscript, Mark Bowman has been a vital source.

At the 2010 gathering of the Wisconsin Annual Conference, I first met Steve Webster (mentioned above), Rev. Wesley White, and Rev. Amy DeLong, later to be the subject of a nationally publicized ecclesiastical trial. Rev. White and Rev. DeLong have provided insider trial information through phone calls, e-mail correspondence, Rev. DeLong's "Love on Trial" website, and as fact-checkers of the manuscript.

A second species of primary sources are the official documents of the denominations: minutes, resolutions, policy statements, and judicial decisions. Secondary sources from the denominations have been provided by their official news services; in particular, I have utilized releases from the Episcopal News Service, the ELCA News Service, the Presbyterian News Service, and the United Methodist News Service.

Within each denomination, one or more gay-advocacy organizations have evolved and matured over the years, and their websites contain archived press releases, articles and commentary, and selected documents. I am grateful for the support offered by the leaders of these organizations and their permission to freely use the materials on their websites. I note the contributions of the UCC Coalition (www.ucccoalition.org); Episcopal Integrity USA (www.integrityusa.org); the Lutheran Reconciling-Works (www.reconcilingworks.org) and Extraordinary Lutheran Ministries (www.elm.org); More Light Presbyterians (www.mlp.org) and the Covenant Network of Presbyterians (www.covenantpres.org); and Methodist Affirmation (www.umaffirm.org) and the Reconciling Ministries Network (www.rmnetwork.org). I am indebted to the magazines and newsletters associated with these organizations, especially *More Light Update* and *Open Hands* magazine, and also to individual contributors to those publications.

Dr. Heather Rachelle White is currently a visiting professor of religion at New College of Florida. She holds an MDiv degree from Princeton University, and she was also awarded a PhD in philosophy by the Princeton University Department of Religion in 2007. Her doctoral dissertation was entitled "Homosexuality, Gay Communities, and American Churches: A History of a Changing Religious Ethic, 1946–1977." The dissertation is detailed, scholarly, and highly informative and was an invaluable resource for recounting the earliest days of the journey.

Here are snippets about the principal published books that were of great benefit to my research.

For the first eleven years following the creation of the ELCA in 1988, Edward Trexler served as editor of the official ELCA magazine, *The Lutheran*. His book *High Expectations: Understanding the ELCA's Early Years, 1988–2002* chronicles the early ELCA history.

Uncommon Calling, A Gay Christian's Struggle to Serve the Church by the aforementioned Chris Glaser weaves his personal story into the fabric of Presbyterian Church history in the seventies and eighties. *Jesus, the Bible, and Homosexuality* by Rev. Jack Rogers, one time moderator of the Presbyterian General Assembly, also chronicles Presbyterian history and offers a Christ-centered approach to biblical interpretation that rebuts literalistic "proof-texting."

Rev. Julian Rush was a Methodist youth minister and playwright who wrote and directed musicals performed by his youth group. He was outed and lost his church position in the early eighties. His story was told and many of his lyrics reprinted by Lee Hart Merrick in *Julian Rush—Facing the Music: A Gay Methodist Minister's Story*. In the late eighties, Rev. Rose Mary Denman came out to her New England bishop, who chose to put her on trial. Her autobiography, *Let My People In*, tells her story. Rev. Jimmy Creech challenged Methodist strictures against covenant ceremonies in the late nineties, and he paid for his ecclesiastical disobedience when a Methodist court defrocked him. Pastor Creech recounts the details in his autobiography, *Adam's Gift: A Memoir of a Pastor's Calling to Defy the Church's Persecution of Lesbians and Gays*. The Institute on Religion and Democracy, a political organization that sought to influence church policy, is exposed in *Hardball on Holy Ground*, edited by Stephen Swecker.

Finally, Gary David Comstock's pan-denominational work *Unrepentant, Self-Affirming, Practicing: Lesbian/Bisexual/Gay People within Organized Religion* is excellent.

There are many more sources and contributors, to be sure, and I apologize to those not named here. Editorial assistance has been provided by Kristin Firth and Joyce Krauser of EditArts.

Preface

In 1987, my small Lutheran congregation in central Minnesota was in conflict. Church leaders, who could spout chapter and verse, railed against the pending merger that would soon produce the Evangelical Lutheran Church in America (ELCA). Their tone was apocalyptic. The church council voted eleven to one to sever all denominational ties as of January 1, 1988, the date that the apostate ELCA would come into being.

My wife was the sole dissenting vote.

When she came home after midnight in tears, I put on a pot of coffee, and we talked until the eastern sky turned pale yellow. We decided that we would attempt to rally the congregation to support the ELCA, and that marked our baptism into ecclesiastical politics. Somehow, oddly, sex seemed to be at the heart of the anti-ELCA sentiment. During the public meetings that followed, one of our outspoken opponents seemed to take particular delight in mouthing the word "homosexual." Lutheran Social Service was demonized because they used pornographic movies in counseling, or so the argument went.

Eventually, the congregation turned around, and a congregational vote affirmed the relationship with the ELCA. The conservatives bolted and formed their own church. Our congregation experienced a rebirth: new Sunday school teachers stepped up, a fresh council was elected, and the remaining members all dug deeper to keep church finances in the black.

For the next twenty years, I watched with interest as incendiary culture wars threatened to engulf the newly formed ELCA. I attended

numerous synod assemblies as a voting member, my pastor and I participated in a forum at Luther Seminary in St. Paul on a pending human
sexuality statement, and I taught an adult class entitled "What the Bible
really says about homosexuality," but LGBT inclusion was never really
my fight, and I was mostly an observer on the periphery, unaware of the
full depth and breadth of the struggle of many gay and lesbian pioneers.[1]

In the spring of 2009, my novel *A Wretched Man*, a novel of Paul the
Apostle, was in the hands of my publisher awaiting release early the next
year. The novel characterized Paul as a repressed gay man. In the meantime, my publisher suggested I start a blog, and I called it "Spirit of a
Liberal, a blog of progressive, religious themes." Soon, I was blogging
about the upcoming ELCA Churchwide Assembly scheduled for August.
A progressive Human Sexuality Statement and LGBT inclusive ministry
policies were on the agenda amidst widespread anticipation that this
might finally be the year for a breakthrough.

The Assembly would be in Minneapolis, just forty-five minutes up
the freeway from my home in Northfield, Minnesota, and I volunteered
for Goodsoil, a coalition of Lutheran LGBT advocacy groups. There I
was in August wearing a Goodsoil prayer shawl and mingling with folks
in "graceful engagement" in the hallways, over coffee, and during lunch.
I had moved from the periphery and heard myself labeled a "straight
ally." Along with the prayer shawl, the label fit comfortably. As the final
vote totals appeared on the big screens announcing a victory for the cause
of inclusion, I cried and hugged along with many others.

In the months that followed, the blog went viral in Lutheran circles
as I defended the historic ELCA actions and challenged the dissident
organizations: WordAlone, Lutheran CORE, and Lutheran Congregations in Mission for Christ. As bloggers are wont to do, I often spoke
with a sharp tongue. "Thanks for saying what we don't dare to say," a
bishop's assistant whispered later.

As I penned blog posts, I encountered stories of early pilgrims, not
only in my ELCA but across denominations, and I realized there was a
rich narrative of the journey toward full inclusion that hadn't been told.
Despite feeling like an interloper, a straight man writing an LGBT history, I received encouragement as I shared my idea for a book and then
began the process of researching and writing in the spring of 2011. Along

the way, I encountered this comment from a young woman: "I have been thinking a lot these days of our lesbian, gay, and bisexual sisters and brothers and supporters who have gone before us to bring us to this time and place. I wish that I knew more of their names. I wish I knew more of their stories."[2]

It is my hope that this book will help LGBT Christians and straight allies to appreciate our past and to remember the pioneers who have led the church to a place of welcome. To be sure, the journey has been conflicted, but with each victory, great and small, there has been celebration, and part of my motivation is to "shout it from the mountaintops" and to "tell everyone what we have done."

Who speaks for Christians? What is *the* Christian attitude toward LGBT persons? Since the days of Jerry Falwell's "Moral Majority" and the birth of the Christian right, it has been gay-bashing conservatives who have claimed *the* Christian voice. Even within the moderate Protestant denominations, official policy has stigmatized gays and lesbians, and many gays and lesbians perceived Christianity to be hopelessly judgmental and exclusionary and therefore irrelevant to their lives. Many have experienced the church as a source of pain rather than healing.

But recent history has witnessed a groundswell of change within the Christian church, at least within the progressive denominations, and this book is a chronicle of the Damascus-road conversions across entire denominations. Against the strident voices of Bible-thumping, headline-grabbing, self-appointed spokespersons for Christianity, moderate Christians have recently articulated a radically different message, and with words of reconciliation and welcome, the walls have come tumbling down. For many congregations, the slogan "all are welcome" is no longer false advertising.

For our purposes, *full inclusion* implies an attitude of welcome without precondition (all means all) and without limit (not just pew but pulpit).

The LGBT community is not fully included, not fully welcomed, not fully respected, not fully accepted, not fully treated as children of God unless they can participate in all roles, including the offices of ordained ministry. Many of the pilgrims we will encounter seek to answer their call to ordination, but their quest is not merely self-actualization, for they are standard bearers for an entire community. LGBT ordination has been the linchpin, the symbol, the visible sign of inclusivity that sounds: "[t]he message [that] goes out from here to the ears of other gays and lesbians who hear the call to ministry, but even more importantly, to the whole host, the entire LGBT community. Here is a church where you are welcome."[3]

LGBT ordination is about much more than the individuals invited into the pulpit; their presence proclaims a word of affirmation and acceptance to an entire community in a bold, clear voice. If gays and lesbians are welcome in the pulpit, if gays and lesbians can be both guest and host, then and only then is the entire LGBT community fully included in the life of the church. Gays and lesbians in the pulpit are the visible proof of full inclusion; anything short of that betrays a lesser welcome.

Thus, as the visible sign of full inclusion, LGBT ordination has been the terminus, the long-sought end of the journey, the signpost that says that the gay and lesbian pilgrims have arrived at their destination. Accordingly, the quest for inclusive ordination standards will also be the focus of this book.

In 2005, gay New Hampshire Bishop Gene Robinson rode on the Episcopal float in the New York City Pride March along with his daughter, Ella, who later reported,

> I looked over and this guy on the street was kind of cheering, and Dad and he kind of locked eyes, and the guy just burst into tears and said, "Bishop Robinson, thank you, thank you," and just kept saying that as we went past. . . . I was, like, standing there waving my rainbow flag, and I was just dumbstruck. I forget what this means to people, whether they're Episcopalians or have no faith whatsoever. It strikes people on so many different levels. And it reminds me that this is a big thing, and an important thing, for so many people.[4]

The journey toward full inclusion invites a continuing reevaluation of what it means to be church. Do the churches of the Reformation continue to be reforming? How does the church engage in moral deliberation in the late twentieth and early twenty-first centuries? Where are church boundaries and who draws them? Equally profound is the question of Scripture. How is the Bible currently read, interpreted, and applied as authoritative and normative? How shall the church understand the interplay of law and gospel? What are the relative influences of tradition, reason, experience, and Scripture?

Is this an old battle or new?

Traditionalists argue that LGBT inclusion is the crash that followed a long slide down a slippery slope away from immutable, orthodox values, away from biblical authority, and away from the core doctrines—the creeds and confessions—of the church. Such are the gatekeepers who build formidable barriers to preserve the purity and unity of God's holy people; for them, this struggle is merely the latest attack on Christian orthodoxy unleashed centuries ago in the godless Age of Enlightenment. *Sola Scriptura* becomes the rallying cry against the church bodies perceived as too easily swayed by the shifting winds of culture.

Others see a recurrence of the struggle between law and grace. For the modern reformer, the good news of a gracious, redemptive, inclusive God of all creation swirls as a fresh breeze that blows where it will. And then there are the justice-seeking prophets. Along our journey, we will encounter many who answered Jesus' call to *come out* of their tomb-like closets and who reimagined his life-giving cry, *unbind them.*

Though the denominations have long claimed that celibate gays and lesbians could be ordained, just don't fall in love, the LGBT community never accepted the false distinction between being and behavior. At an accelerating pace, progressive denominations have opened the pulpit to LGBT clergy in a relationship. The United Church of Christ first ordained an openly gay man in 1972; bishops of various Episcopal dioceses have ordained gays and lesbians for decades, the Episcopal Diocese of New Hampshire consecrated a gay bishop in 2003, and the Episcopal General Convention in 2009 formally approved LGBT eligibility for all levels of the ordained ministry; the ELCA Churchwide Assembly of 2009 revised its ministry policies to allow LGBT clergy; the Presbyterian Church in 2011 voted to allow gays and lesbians to be ordained as ministers, elders, and deacons; and a United Methodist ecclesiastical court in 2011 rendered token punishment for a lesbian pastor who performed a "holy union" ceremony for a lesbian couple while United Methodist clergy in many regional Conferences signed LGBT-friendly petitions.

These recent policy revisions mark the end of a long and conflicted journey, and this book is a wayfarer's journal, a chronicle of the uncertain path toward full inclusion of gays and lesbians in the life of the church. Along the way, we will encounter many pilgrims who struggled with faith traditions that simultaneously nourished and diminished them, trusting the promise that all are loved by God even when their church betrayed the good news. Although conflict continues, the journey has brought the church to a place of a celebration of gays and lesbians in the pulpit, serving openly and with the full recognition and support of their parishioners in the pews, their leadership councils, and their denominations.

Without meaning to slight the gay and lesbian activists in other faith traditions, and they are legion even though their religious leadership and institutions remain oppressive, the progressive denominations known as mainline Protestant will be the landscape of our journey. Historian David Hollinger suggests replacing the term "mainline" in this context with "ecumenical," and this book will follow his view. "Ecumenical" reflects an outward-looking, nonexclusive view of Christian denominationalism that promotes or tends toward worldwide Christian unity or cooperation; indeed, ecumenism encourages collegiality with other world religions. As an example of ecumenism, the ELCA has formalized relationships with other denominations, including the other four highlighted here, as "full communion partners," which entails a mutual recognition of baptism and a sharing of the Lord's Supper, joint worship, and an exchangeability of members and clergy.

"Evangelical Protestantism," on the other hand, tends toward insularity and exclusivity as well as a more rigid biblicism. Hollinger distinguishes between "ecumenical Protestantism" and "evangelical Protestantism."

> I use ecumenical because it is much more specific historically and analytically than mainstream or liberal. Mainstream is a term that is too general and can cover almost anything. Liberal, too, is a term that you can apply to culture or politics as well as theology. Ecumenical refers to a specific, vital and largely defining impulse within the groups I am describing. It also provides a more specific and appropriate contrast to evangelical. The term

evangelical came into currency in the midcentury to refer to a combination of fundamentalists, Pentecostals, followers of holiness churches and others; ecumenical refers to the consolidation of the ecumenical point of view in the big conferences of 1942 and 1945.[5]

For our purposes, ecumenical Protestantism, which comprises the third largest grouping of United States Christians behind Catholics and Evangelicals, will include these denominations:

- The United Methodist Church (UMC), with more than eight million members.
- The Evangelical Lutheran Church in America (ELCA), with more than four million members. The ELCA came into existence in 1988 as a result of a merger of existing church bodies: the American Lutheran Church (ALC), the Lutheran Church in America (LCA), and the Association of Evangelical Lutheran Churches (AELC).
- The Presbyterian Church USA (PC(USA)), with two million members. The PC(USA) came into existence in 1983 as the result of the merger of the United Presbyterian Church (UPC) and the Presbyterian Church in the USA (PCUSA).
- The Episcopal Church (TEC), with two million members.[6]
- The United Church of Christ (UCC), with more than a million members.

The journey has been blocked by gatekeepers along the way: the opponents of LGBT inclusion that existed in all denominations. While the term "gatekeeper" is potentially pejorative, it is actually borrowed from the writings of one such opponent.[7]

Many now celebrate, but others do not. In response to the LGBT-inclusive actions of ecumenical denominations, many in the pews are roiled up. Some withhold financial support. Some have left altogether, including whole congregations and dioceses. Episcopal dissidents have formed a rival body, the Anglican Church in North America (ACNA), and some Episcopal dioceses have bolted to the conservative ACNA.

The Episcopalians also endure condemnation from many in the world-wide Anglican Communion led by the archbishop of Canterbury. The ELCA also faces rival organizations consisting of dissidents who have departed the ELCA: the WordAlone Ministries, Lutheran Congregations in Mission for Christ (LCMC), Lutheran CORE, and CORE's newly formed denomination called the North American Lutheran Church (NALC), which promises to "reconfigure North American Lutheranism." There are fresh rumblings of a conservative Presbyterian movement called "The Fellowship of Presbyterians"; the Presbyterians already experienced a schismatic reaction to women's ordination four decades ago.

In 1990, CBS television newsman John Blackstone concluded his report on the first Lutheran *extra ordinem* ordinations of gays and lesbians in San Francisco with this question: "Are they out of step with their church or a step ahead?"[8]

With the advantage of historical perspective, this book will consider that question.

NOTES

1. This book will generally prefer the term "gay," "lesbian," or "LGBT" (lesbian, gay, bisexual, transgender), but "homosexual" will be used when the source document or context under discussion uses it. Beverly Wildung Harrison suggests that the term "gayness" implies "a self-affirming and self-respecting person who insists that homoeroticism is good and who wants to live a life of integrity, demanding respect that any person has a moral right to expect." Beverly Wildung Harrison, *Making the Connection* (Boston: Beacon Press, 1975), 142. See Nicholas C. Edsall, *Toward Stonewall* (University of Virginia Press, 2003), 3, for an excellent discussion of the problems of terminology. Also see Jack Rogers, *Jesus, the Bible, and Homosexuality*, rev. exp. ed. (Louisville: Westminster John Knox Press, 2009), 177. Rogers suggests that the gay community may now prefer the term "queer," which is still seen as pejorative by many straight persons. Dr. Carter Heyward, *Keep Your Courage: A Radical Christian Feminist Speaks* (New York: Seabury Press, 2010), 13–17, offers an expansive use of "queer" to include straight allies. "Queerness is

public solidarity in the struggle for sexual and gender justice, of irrepressibly making connections to other struggles for justice, compassion, and reconciliation." Dr. Louie Crew, who played a prominent role in the Episcopal journey and who served as a principal source for the Episcopal section of this book, suggested the use of "Queer" in the title of this book.

2. Susan Kraemer, "Wanderings in Grief and Rage," *More Light Update* (February 1993).

3. Rev. Ruth Frost, press conference preceding the ELCA Rite of Reception of Frost and two others at the Church of the Redeemer, St. Paul, Minnesota, September 18, 2010.

4. Elizabeth Adams, *Going to Heaven: the Life and Election of Bishop Gene Robinson* (Brooklyn: Soft Skull Press, 2006), 265.

5. Amy Frykholm, "Culture Changers: David Hollinger on What the Mainline Achieved," *The Christian Century* 129, issue 14 (July 2, 2012): 26–28. Hollinger refers to gatherings of the Federal Council of Churches (forerunner to the National Council of Churches). In 1942, 375 representatives of 30 communions gathered at Wesleyan University of Ohio to consider a "Just and Durable" peace. The gathering included an impressive list of lay and clergy leaders including chairperson Presbyterian John Foster Dulles, later to be Secretary of State under Eisenhower, Charles Clayton Morrison, editor of *The Christian Century*, industrialist Harvey Firestone, and John R. Mott, Methodist and YMCA international leader and 1946 Nobel Peace Prize winner. Conservatives, and even *Time* magazine, criticized the progressive sentiments of the ecumenical gathering. National Council of Churches website, accessed June 17, 2103, http://www.ncccusa.org/centennial/marchmoment.html.

See also David A. Hollinger, *After Cloven Tongues of Fire* (Princeton, N.J.: Princeton University Press, 2013).

6. Until recently, the initials ECUSA (Episcopal Church of the United States of America) designated the Episcopal Church, but the Church recently began to use the initials TEC (The Episcopal Church), and this book will use that designation even though it is often anachronistic.

7. The metaphor of "gatekeeper" was suggested by James V. Heidinger II, the editor of *Good News*, the publication of the Methodist opposition of the same name, who editorialized that gatekeepers were necessary to protect the church from "those within who would accommodate the church to secular norms or harm the faithful by false doctrine," and he was referring to the LGBT community and their advocates. Stephen Swecker, ed., *Hardball on Holy Ground* (Boston: Wesleyan Press, 2005), 3.

8. "In the Beginning," on the website of Extraordinary Lutheran Ministries, accessed May 28, 2011, http://www.youtube.com/watch?v=PVOz3Z7 t9L0.

※ **I** ※

In the Beginning

The poet laureate of the sixties, Bob Dylan, sang "The Times They Are a-Changin'."

The early years of the decade had witnessed the successes of the civil rights movement—Martin Luther King's "I have a dream speech" in 1963 followed by the Civil Rights Act of 1964. Inspired by the 1963 publication of Betty Friedan's book *The Feminine Mystique*, the women's liberation movement was in full bloom.

But it was a dark decade, too, with thousands dead on the battlefield in the most unpopular war in the nation's history and the assassinations of King and the Kennedy brothers.

As the tumultuous decade rushed to a close, 1969 witnessed the inauguration of Richard Nixon, who later claimed a "silent majority" of support for traditional values; Neil Armstrong walking on the moon and proclaiming "one small step for man, one giant leap for mankind;" flower children sprawled on fields and meadows as Woodstock became the icon of the generation; and the largest antiwar demonstration in U.S. history as more than a quarter million protesters descended on Washington, D.C., in November.

The year was also about Stonewall and the birth of the gay liberation movement.

On June 28, 1969, New York City police raided the Stonewall Inn, a gay bar in Greenwich Village, but their plans went awry; the gay community fought back, and for several days riots and protests filled the streets. One of those arrested reported,

We all had a collective feeling like we'd had enough of this kind of shit. It wasn't anything tangible anybody said to anyone else, it was just kind of like everything over the years had come to a head on that one particular night in the one particular place, and it was not an organized demonstration. It was spontaneous. That was the part that was wonderful.

Everyone in the crowd felt that we were never going to go back. It was like the last straw. It was time to reclaim something that had always been taken from us. It was something that just happened. All kinds of people, all different reasons, but mostly it was total outrage, anger, sorrow, everything combined, and everything just kind of ran its course. It was the police who were doing most of the destruction. We were really trying to get back in and break it free. And we felt that we had freedom at last, or freedom to at least show that we demanded freedom. We didn't really have the freedom totally, but we weren't going to be walking around meekly in the night and letting them shove us around—it's like standing your ground for the first time and in a really strong way, and that's what caught the police by surprise. There was something in the air, freedom a long time overdue, and we're going to fight for it. It took several forms, but the bottom line was, we weren't going to go away. And we didn't.[1]

This book is about the gay rights movement within the church that parallels that of secular society, but the movement toward *full inclusion* in the church was and is more than merely a reaction to popular culture; progressive religious activism actually predated and encouraged Stonewall and its aftermath. Stonewall and the gay liberation movement was closely entwined with concurrent developments within ecumenical Protestantism. To the charge that religious progressives merely exhibited a knee-jerk response to secular cultural trends, the record suggests the opposite—religious leaders were at the forefront, the first small voices crying in the wilderness to prepare the way.

This book shall use the metaphor of a journey, a journey toward full inclusion that slowly meanders across America for over forty years. Along the way, we will encounter numerous brave pioneers, and we will listen to their stories of conflict and celebration.

Before we begin, we must mark our starting point. A journey *toward* full inclusion implies a journey away *from* a situation less than inclusive. Where does our journey start? What was the *status quo ante*, the way things were before the journey?

> Our childhood God despises homosexuals; our church family denies our very existence; our traditional theology openly condemns us; our denominations and churches believe we are sick individuals who choose to alienate ourselves from God by refusing to ask for forgiveness for our sinful ways.
>
> This is my experience, from the heart of a wounded Christian lesbian, unable and unwilling to relinquish my Christianity, looking for an overflowing cup in the midst of a seemingly endless drought.[2]

At mid-century, homosexuality was considered sinful by the church, criminal by society, and disordered by science. For the folks in the pews, homosexuality was an unsavory stew of sin, sickness, and criminality.

And unmentionable. Except for the occasional fire and brimstone sermon that railed against the temptations of the flesh, often with a healthy dose of titillation, discussions of homosexuality were as taboo as the behavior itself. It was "the love that dare not speak its name."[3] Many families had a "funny" uncle, a brother or cousin who disappeared into the debauchery of the metropolis, or a "Bohemian" daughter, but such matters could only be whispered about and never openly discussed. Gays and lesbians in the churches were invisible and closeted, pushed underground by friends, family, and often self-condemnation.

Similarly, congregations and denominations had no stated policies toward homosexuals. None was necessary. Gays were invisible. Gays were nonpersons. Gays had no status and no identity and no existence beyond the demonization of the hellfire sermon. Gays were unknown in the vast majority of congregations; it was only a select few inner-city ministries that encountered gays as real flesh and blood human beings. And it was there that the threads of sin, sickness, and criminality began to unravel.

Upheaval caused by World War II mobilization resulted in gay ghettos in numerous American cities. Gays who received the infamous "blue discharges" from the Navy during the war had clustered in San Francisco where the Navy dumped them—to avoid the embarrassment of returning to small towns but also due to the allure of the burgeoning gay community— "after they've seen Paree"—and all that. Others, mustered out after the war with honorable discharges, lingered in the cities for similar reasons. Other military processing cities included Los Angeles, Seattle, Atlanta, New Orleans, Boston, and New York, whose bohemian Greenwich Village had long been a gay haven.[4]

As post-war America settled into the comfortable culture of Ike, *I Love Lucy*, and the birth of rock and roll, the traditional, unquestioned premise of the church was that homosexuality was sinful; no, it was worse, it was abominable. Homosexuality and Christianity were mutually exclusive terms, and there was a basic incompatibility between being gay and being Christian. Opposites. Oil and water. A wide chasm separated Christianity and homosexuality, Christians and gays. A homosexual chose to indulge in sinful and disgusting sexual behavior and thereby cut himself or herself off from God and from the church. The long tradition of the church was clear; the Bible was unambiguous. Wicked Sodom lent its very name to male penetration of another male. Men who lay with other men were abominations. God's wrath was revealed against shameful lusts, unnatural relations, and indecent acts. The effeminate and the sodomite were lumped together with thieves, adulterers, and drunkards.

So, too, in civil society. Homosexuals were outlaws. Criminal codes included antisodomy laws. Stoked by McCarthy era fears,

> The Federal Bureau of Investigation (FBI) and local police departments cooperated in compiling lists of known or suspected homosexuals, their meeting places and arrest records, even their friends and associates. The postal service kept track of the recipients of questionable material. Shortly after becoming president, Eisenhower signed an executive order officially designating sexual perversion a bar to federal employment.[5]

Local governments routinely harassed the gay community through arrests at gay bars and sweeps of parks and other areas frequented by gays; colleges and universities fired gay educators. In 1955 in a well-pub-licized purge, antigay hysteria swept Boise, Idaho; by its end, dozens of men had lost their jobs, been imprisoned, or been run out of town.[6]

Meanwhile, the scientific community articulated theories of psycho-logical deviance. In the 1940s and 1950s two streams of thought devel-oped within the psychiatric community, both flowing from Sigmund Freud, the father of psychoanalysis. Perhaps the most succinct statement of his views came in a personal letter to the concerned mother of a gay man. "Homosexuality is surely no advantage," he wrote:

> "But it is nothing to be ashamed of, no vice, no degradation, it cannot be classified an illness; we consider it to be a variation of the sexual function produced by a certain arrest of sexual devel-opment. Many highly respectable individuals of ancient and modern times have been homosexuals. . . . It is a great injustice to persecute homosexuality as a crime, and cruelty too. . . . By asking me if I can help, you mean, I suppose, if I can abolish homosexuality and make normal heterosexuality take its place. The answer is, in a general way, we cannot promise to achieve it. In a certain number of cases we succeed in developing the blighted germs of heterosexual tendencies which are present in every homosexual, in the majority of cases it is no more possible, . . . What analysis can do for your son runs in a different line. If he is unhappy, neurotic, torn by conflicts, inhibited in his social life, analysis may bring him harmony, peace of mind, full effi-ciency whether he remains a homosexual or gets changed."[7]

The negative stream of psychoanalysis focused on the notion of "an arrest of sexual development" over against "normal heterosexuality," and the goal of the analyst was to cure, often using extreme measures. Medical theories looked to the home and early childhood to explain the sexual maladjustment of the homosexual. Deficient nurture produced deviant behavior—it was assumed—a pathological hidden fear of the opposite sex that was caused by traumatic parent-child relationships.

Responsible medical journals often published questionable articles that largely went unchallenged. "[S]uffering, unhappiness, limitations in functioning, severe disturbances in interpersonal relationships, and contradictory internal tendencies . . . are all present in the homosexual."[8] In 1952, the American Psychiatric Association classified homosexuality as a "sociopathic personality disturbance," later softened to "a non-psychotic mental disorder" in 1968.[9]

But Freud's views also invited a more progressive attitude, based upon the growing view that homosexuality was immutable, that homosexuals should be seen as victims worthy of compassion rather than punishment, and that appropriate therapy could lead to a well-adjusted life even for the unchanged homosexual. This latter stream that flowed from the Freudian headwaters was largely promoted by religious, especially ecumenical Protestant, counselors.

Liberal Protestantism embraced science, and the postwar emphasis on "pastoral counseling" as a vital role of the minister encouraged the best and latest psychological insights and counseling techniques. In 1943, the founding minister of New York's Riverside Church, Rev. Harry Emerson Fosdick, had been the first clergy leader to suggest that clergy counseling should include concern for homosexuals.[10] Seventeen years later, in 1960, Fosdick noted, "A good minister cannot now escape personal counseling. . . . It is in the air."[11]

Thus, if science said that homosexuals were who they were and did what they did because they were "sick," then for some progressive counselors the appropriate response should be compassionate understanding and treatment rather than punishment. Such counselors were far from questioning the basic assumption of sinfulness, but the notion of disordered sexual development became the scissors to cut the filament between homosexuality and criminality. If homosexuality was developmental, then therapy, not condemnation, was the proper response of counselors. From the vantage of the twenty-first century, this attitude may seem archaic and certainly the science has matured,[12] but the movement from punishment to treatment was an important progressive step.

These early religious counselors were also quick to recognize the corrosive effects of guilt on the emotional well-being of their gay patients, and "clergy, by virtue of their moral authority, held the unique power to absolve homosexual's guilt."[13] As Freud had noted, the prospect of abolishing homosexuality and replacing it with heterosexuality was not likely, and many within the religious counseling community soon moved to accommodation and adjustment without expectation of conversion or cure. The foundation named for George W. Henry and ably managed by executive director Alfred Gross provided the paradigmatic example of a pastoral counseling ministry to the gay community:

> A janitor's closet turned counseling office . . . housed the George W. Henry Foundation. The Henry Foundation was a shoestring operation founded in the late 1940s. At its shaky helm was an aging man named Alfred Gross, who presented himself at various times as a counselor, an Ivy-league trained ethicist, and an ousted Anglican priest. (He was a very interesting guy.) The foundation stayed afloat because of its connection to George W. Henry, a well-known psychiatrist, and by the patronage of prominent supporters, including a number of clergy in the Episcopal Diocese of New York. Gross and his clergy supporters provided counseling services to "men in trouble with themselves or with the law," many of them sent for court-ordered counseling after being charged with sex-related misdemeanors. Most of these clients were gay, and the Henry Foundation was in the business of helping them achieve a "successful adjustment."[14]

Recognizing the practical futility of a cure,

> Gross and other counselors emphasized a "realistic" approach . . . [that] addressed the unhealthy manifestations of homosexuals' guilt and sought to facilitate their change to a discreet homosexual lifestyle that avoided legal and social scrutiny.
>
> In line with its mandate to provide "practical aid," the foundation offered job and housing placement, legal assistance, and limited financial aid in addition to referrals for counseling. Such services were aimed to help with the client's "adjustment," a reference that did not mean that clients would be cured to function as heterosexuals.[15]

A few early Christian books challenged the presumptions of sin, sickness, and criminality. *Homosexuality and the Western Christian Tradition* (1955) by Derrick Sherwin Bailey was followed by UCC pastor Robert Wood's *Christ and the Homosexual* (1960). Leading Christian publications in the seventies included *What about Homosexuality?* (1972) by Episcopal Canon Clinton R. Jones, Catholic Priest John J. McNeill's breakthrough *The Church and the Homosexual* (1976), and *Is the Homosexual My Neighbor?* (1978), a collaboration of Letha Dawson Scanzoni and Virginia Ramey Mollenkott.

After the 1950s witnessed liberal Protestant ministries that treated the homosexual with compassion and dignity through therapy, the raucous 1960s saw progressive religious leaders move into the political arena to advocate for repeal of sodomy laws, elimination of the use of entrapment to arrest homosexuals for solicitation, and arbitrary and indiscriminate arrests for lewd behavior. Such leaders remained a distinct minority within their denominations, but public advocacy by a few caught the attention of the press and the public. In 1964, the Episcopal Diocese of New York supported legislation to repeal New York's sodomy laws.[16] In 1965, an article appeared in the prestigious and influential *Christian Century* that suggested "the law . . . should not penalize private immoralities which cannot be proved contrary to the public good."[17]

Meanwhile, in San Francisco, an ecumenical clergy group met to confer with local gay leaders, and the meeting grew into an organization called the Council on Religion and the Homosexual (CRH). On New Year's Eve, 1964, a benefit ball was scheduled to raise funds, but more importantly, to publicize the new organization to local homosexual communities. Several of the clergy attempted to coordinate with the local chief of police, but they were not well received. The vice squad wanted to know why the clergy were "getting mixed up with a bunch of queers."[18] Finally, the clergy received assurances that the police would not interfere with the event, but they were deceived. At the benefit ball, six persons were arrested, including three lawyers who refused to allow the police to enter. Lutheran pastor Chuck Lewis kept the flashbulbs on his camera popping as he photographed the police, and his assistant Jo Chadwick stashed the film negatives in her bra. The ensuing press and public outrage was a watershed moment in public and religious awareness of official abuse of the gay community. "By serving as witnesses and spokespersons to the abuses suffered by San Francisco's sexual minorities, the churchmen strategically used their moral privilege, granting the legitimacy of the 'cloak of the cloth' to the homophile movement. . . . The ministers' public stand took the conversation out from behind the closed doors of the pastor's study and placed it onto the front pages of morning newspapers."[19]

Historian John D'Emilio stressed the importance of the CRH, which "provided the spark that ignited debate on homosexuality [within the churches. CRH was] able to take advantage of the theological ferment and social activism that infected American religion in the 1960s in order to press for reconsideration of Christian attitudes toward same-sex eroticism."[20] We will encounter CRH again as we journey forward.

The ecumenical Protestant denominations had discovered that gays and lesbians existed beyond the demonized caricatures of hellfire preachers. By the late 1960s or early 1970s, each of our denominations began to wrestle with LGBT issues with halting steps that reflected uncertainty and internal disagreement. Policy statements affirmed human sexuality as a gift from God that enriched the intimacy of relationships and was not solely for procreation. While never quite reaching the point of including LGBT sexuality, the hint was there. All denominations uniformly rejected criminal penalties for gay behavior. The notion of sickness, disease, or arrested sexual development came under question, as it was in the scientific community.

Not surprisingly, the question of sin was always the most controversial element of policy statements, which often questioned, but never quite rejected, traditional moral condemnation of homosexual behavior. That's where the voices in the pews chimed in. When the denominations met in national conventions, their ultimate legislative authorities, resolutions were adopted that restrained or overruled progressive impulses of committees or task forces. Legislative policy statements were laced with traditional, biblical admonitions.

- In 1966, the ALC (Lutheran) national convention approved a statement called "Sexual Integrity in Modern Society." The statement affirmed that "sexuality is God-given and good," but also reiterated the traditional view that homosexuality was "contrary to God's will" while emphasizing that the church should offer "help and healing for warped sexuality."[21]

- In 1967, the Episcopal General Assembly adopted a short statement urging legislative reform of laws relating to homosexuals.[22]

- In 1968, the General Assembly of the UMC (Methodist) similarly urged legislative reform.[23]

- In 1969, the Social Action Committee of the UCC approved a resolution that went further than any other denominational statement, urging the church to: "learn to cherish, and not merely condemn, those whose sexual need and loneliness may prove importunate—though unmarried, unmarriageable, widowed, or homosexual."[24]

- In 1970, soon after Stonewall, the LCA (Lutheran) national convention adopted by an overwhelming voice vote a statement that said, "homosexuality is viewed biblically as a departure from the heterosexual structure of God's creation."[25]

- Finally, a Presbyterian committee issued a statement in 1970 entitled "Sexuality and the Human Community" that suggested that sexual conduct, even if outside the formal marriage bond, might appropriately and responsibly contribute to the intimacy and mutuality of a committed relationship.[26] However, traditional admonitions were affirmed by the next General Assembly. The resolution adopted by the commissioners confirmed the church's "adherence to the moral law of God as revealed in the Old and New Testament, that . . . the practice of homosexuality is sin."[27]

When progressives sought policies promoting LGBT interests, there was always a "yes, but" faction. This was especially true as the various policy statements were often watered down by convention delegates by adding a "yes, but" statement that reiterated traditional views.

Yet, it was not purely political, as even the progressives struggled with notions of sin. While the church promoted compassion and understanding, it was always against the assumption that homosexual behavior was sinful. As we are about to embark on our journey, there were few voices that dared disagree with this basic, traditional premise. Social statements often hesitantly stepped up to the door, peered in, but never quite dared to enter, and convention delegates routinely slammed the door shut.

Later, we will hear the story of lesbian Episcopal priest Ellen Marie Barrett and the bishop who ordained her, Paul Moore Jr. For now, one crystalline moment in that story needs retelling. Bishop Moore wrote of this exchange that occurred during a session when he faced hard questioning from the priests and parishioners of his diocese. After a tense hour, a critical priest finally raised *the* question that the bishop knew would come, and the room fell silent:

"Bishop Moore," he asked, "do you think homosexual activity is a sin?"[28]

Bishop Moore was right, that would be *the ultimate question* the church would wrestle with for the next forty years.

NOTES

1. Michael Fader, quoted in David Carter, *Stonewall: The Riots That Sparked the Gay Revolution* (New York: St. Martin's Press, 2004), 160.

2. R. S. Umoja [pen name, UMC clergywoman], "My Cup Runneth Over," *Open Hands* (Spring 1991), 17. She is also cited in Gary David Comstock, *Unrepentant, Self-Affirming, Practicing: Lesbian/Bisexual/Gay People within Organized Religion* (New York: Continuum Publishing, 1996), 183.

3. An oft-quoted phrase dating to the late nineteenth century and associated with gay lovers Lord Alfred Douglas and Oscar Wilde.

4. Comstock, *Unrepentant*, 3.

5. Edsall, *Toward Stonewall*, 278.

6. Ibid., 279.

7. Ibid., 244.

8. B. S. Robbins, "Psychological Implications of the Male Homosexual 'Marriage,'" *Psychoanalytic Review* 30 (1943): 428–37. Also cited in Edsall, *Toward Stonewall*, 245.

9. Edsall, *Toward Stonewall*, 247.

10. Comstock, *Unrepentant*, 4.

11. Harry Emerson Fosdick, "The Ministry and Psychotherapy," *Pastoral Psychology* 11:101 (1960): 13, cited in Heather Rachelle White, "Homosexuality, Gay Communities, and American Churches: A History of a Changing Religious Ethic, 1946–1977" (PhD diss., Princeton University Department of Religion, September 2007), 28.

12. As early as 1973, the American Psychiatric Association removed homosexuality from its list of pathological disorders. Since 1975, the American Psychological Association has urged its members to work to remove the stigma of mental illness associated with sexual orientation. More recently, the American Psychological Association has debunked the notion of reparative or conversion therapy. See Gregory M. Herek, PhD, "Facts about Homosexuality and Mental Health," on the website of the University of California, Davis, Psychology Department, http://psychology.ucdavis.edu/rainbow/html/facts _mental_health.html, © 2012. The article relates the history of policies of the American Psychiatric Association and the American Psychological Association toward homosexuality and also contains an exhaustive bibliography.

13. White, "Homosexuality, Gay Communities," 44.

14. Heather Rachelle White, Comments at the LGBT-RAN Annual Dinner, May 31, 2008, on the website of the Lesbian, Gay, Bisexual, and Transgender Religious Archive Network, accessed May 16, 2013, http://www.lgbtran.org /Papers/WhitePresentation.pdf.

15. White, "Homosexuality, Gay Communities," 40, 44.

16. The Roman Catholic Diocese opposed the repeal effort, and repeal failed. White, "Homosexuality, Gay Communities," 54.

17. White, "Homosexuality, Gay Communities," 58.

18. Ibid., 74.

19. Ibid., 74.

20. John D'Emilio, *Sexual Politics, Sexual Communities: The Making of Homosexual Minority in the United States 1940–1970* (Chicago: University of Chicago Press, 1983), 192-85, 202, 214-15.

21. White, "Homosexuality, Gay Communities," 96.

22. Ibid., 91.

23. Ibid., 91.

24. Ibid., 99.

25. George Dugan, "Lutherans Urge Open Mind on Sex," *New York Times*, July 3, 1970.

26. White, "Homosexuality, Gay Communities," 100.

27. From the *Minutes* of the 1970 General Assembly of the United Presbyterian Church in the U.S.A., cited in White, "Homosexuality, Gay Communities," 117.

28. Paul Moore Jr., *Take a Bishop Like Me* (New York: Harper and Row, 1979), 161.

* 2 *

THE BAPTIST, THE UNITARIAN, AND THE GAY ARCHBISHOP

Though the primary focus of this wayfarer's account of the journey toward full inclusion will be the ecumenical Protestant denominations, we have several preliminary stops before our principal journey begins.

At the outset we will travel to the West Coast to attend a small worship service convened by Baptist preacher Troy Perry. In October 1968, twelve persons gathered in Perry's Los Angeles home, taking the first halting steps toward a church that welcomed rather than judged gays and lesbians—a full eight months *before* Stonewall. Perry, a defrocked gay Baptist preacher, felt called to found a church for his gay community, and their tiny house church became the first of the Metropolitan Community Churches, a denomination that now numbers more than 250 congregations. Their forty thousand members and clergy are predominantly gay and lesbian.[1]

Then it is on to LaForet, Colorado, to listen to a speech by Unitarian Pastor James Stoll. Stoll had been a Unitarian minister for years when he publicly acknowledged his sexuality in a speech to college Unitarians on September 5, 1969, two months after Stonewall, and he repeated his story to multiple Unitarian audiences over the ensuing months. Though Stoll himself soon vanished from public view, his "coming out" speaking tour set the Unitarians on a speedy course toward full inclusion.

Finally, we arrive in New York City in time to watch independent (non-Roman) Catholic priest Robert M. Clement participate in the first gay pride march on the first anniversary of Stonewall, June 28, 1970.

Father Clement's Church of the Beloved Disciple would become a sanctuary for New York City gays and lesbians during the early years of the gay liberation movement, and Clement would later bear the title "Archbishop of North America of the original American Catholic Church."

———·—

First, we listen to Troy Perry's story.[2] Born in the rural south in 1940 to a family of bootleggers, Perry became a Baptist preacher at age fifteen, married a preacher's daughter at age nineteen with whom he fathered two children, and was assigned as pastor to a Pentecostal Church in Santa Ana, California, at age twenty-two. But then his life fell apart when he realized he was gay, believing he was the only person in the world who felt as he did. His bishop forced Perry to renounce himself from the pulpit and resign, and Perry duly complied. Half a dozen years later—divorced, defrocked, and demoralized—he slit his wrists and lost consciousness in his bathtub, but his neighbors found him, bandaged his wrists, and rushed him to the hospital. While he was sobbing in the emergency waiting room of Los Angeles General Hospital, a black woman leaned over and handed him a religious magazine and said, "Some of us care about you."

"I felt a weight go out of my life," Perry would later write. "My whole attitude toward God and death and life had shifted. I knew that God cared about me and that God was with me, all the way——wherever that would lead me."

Where would God lead? Perry would build a bridge between Christianity and his gay community. Now twenty-eight years old, Perry sensed a call to return to the ministry. He would start a new church, a radically different church, a church that ministered to his gay community with a message of God's inclusive love.

Gay friends were skeptical. "Helping queens get religion isn't anybody's bag," said one, but Perry persisted. He scheduled a worship service in the rented house he shared with friends and spread the word. "Situated between editorials about gay cruising sites and notices for local gay bars," Perry advertised the first service in the *Los Angeles Advocate*, a gay newspaper.[3] He was warned the police would come and bust everyone as the

San Francisco police had done three years earlier during the CRH benefit ball sponsored by clergy.

When the day arrived, October 6, 1968, twelve persons dared to show up. They sang. They read Scripture. They prayed. Perry preached. Listen to Perry's own account:

> I prayed again, and then I looked up and said, "We're going to have open communion," there wasn't a dry eye in the place. A hush fell over the place and everybody in that small living room was weeping silently. We all felt that we were a part of something great. God was preparing to move. We were to see God's handiwork, and that would be unbelievable. We gathered and we just couldn't quit crying. We all sat around and said we had felt the spirit of the Lord. One young man came up to me, and said, "Oh, Troy, God was here this morning! I haven't been in a church in eight years. And even when I left the church, the one I'd been in, I never felt anything like I felt here this morning, in this living room."[4]

Indeed, God's handiwork would prove to be unbelievable. The humble house church grew and multiplied. By the first anniversary of the initial service of twelve, the gay congregation had grown to three hundred members. Mission churches spread to gay communities in other cities. Within four years, the denomination numbered twenty-five congregations across the country.[5]

Perry's charismatic leadership was certainly a prime factor in the growth, but it was more than that. Though Perry himself brought a Pentecostal background and worship style to the fellowship, early members included men with ministerial backgrounds in Reformed, Presbyterian, and Catholic liturgies, and they offered various worship practices.[6] Thus, gays of varying Christian backgrounds would find something familiar in an MCC worship service.

But it was the most radical component of the MCC that was the most appealing, its message. Contrary to the ecumenical Protestant denominations that retained elements of sin and sickness in their policy statements—even as they advocated compassion, civil rights, and decriminalization—the MCC "emphasized homosexuality as an aspect of human identity that was acceptable to God and argued that homosexual orientation was as inconsequential to central matters of Christian faith as race, gender, ethnicity, or any human difference."[7]

Growth of the MCC was countered by homophobic reaction, including violence and murder. The New Orleans MCC congregation had customarily met in the UpStairs Lounge over the Jimani, a gay bar in the French Quarter. Although the location had changed weeks earlier, on the last Sunday in June, 1973, around sixty persons moved upstairs from the bar after a free beer celebration of Pride weekend. Pride events had not yet come to New Orleans, but the men—and one woman, a mother—celebrated what was going on in other cities that Sunday. They gathered around a piano and sang their anthem, a pop song by "The Brotherhood of Man."

"United we stand, divided we fall . . .
And if our backs should ever be against the wall,
We'll be together . . .
Together . . . you and I."

The congregation members repeated the verses again and again, swaying back and forth, arm in arm, happy to be together at their former place of worship on Pride Sunday, still feeling the effects of the free beer special.

At 7:56 PM a buzzer from downstairs sounded, the one that signaled a cab had arrived. No one had called a cab, but when someone opened the second floor steel door to the stairwell, flames rushed in. An arsonist had deliberately set the wooden stairs ablaze, and the oxygen-starved fire exploded. The still-crowded bar became an inferno within seconds.[8]

In sixteen minutes, twenty-nine died, and three more would die later, undoubtedly the largest mass murder of gays in the history of the United States. The deceased included the MCC pastor (Rev. William R. Larson), the mother and her two sons (Willie Inez Warren, Eddie Hosea Warren, and James Curtis Warren), and the assistant pastor—who initially escaped but returned to try to rescue his partner, and their bodies were found lying together (Duane George "Mitch" Mitchell and

Louis Horace Broussard). Altogether, a quarter of the MCC congregation perished in the fire.

Though no one was ever charged with the crime, it was widely assumed that it was the action of a single perpetrator, a man with psychiatric problems who had been kicked out of the bar earlier that day. He committed suicide a year later.

However, it was the aftermath of the horrific tragedy that revealed institutionalized homophobia on the part of New Orleans' churches, the press, and local government. Most churches refused to allow a memorial service on their premises, and a closeted gay Episcopal priest who held a small service in the sanctuary of St. George's Episcopal Church was immediately rebuked by his bishop, and his mailbox filled with hate mail. Later, a Unitarian congregation offered their building and so did a Methodist congregation, and it was there that a July 1 memorial service was attended by 250 persons, including a closeted gay Methodist bishop, Finis Crutchfield, as well as MCC founder Troy Perry. A few families refused to claim the remains of their dead kin, and four of the deceased were never identified and were buried in a common grave.

Press and radio reports included unnecessary jokes and hateful comments from the public: "I hope the fire burned their dress off." "What will they bury the ashes of the queers in? Fruit jars." "The Lord had something to do with this." Within a few days, the local press ignored the story altogether.

No elected officials offered condolences. The police dismissed the importance of identifying the bodies or investigating and prosecuting the perpetrator, because "you know this was a queer bar." One of the injured, who died two weeks after the fire, was a local school teacher who was notified in the hospital that he had been fired.

Earlier, in 1972, the home church in Los Angeles had been torched without any injuries. The third incident of arson occurred a month after the New Orleans fire. On July 27, 1973, the MCC church building in San Francisco was set afire early one Friday morning and heavily damaged. Undeterred, the congregation accepted the invitation of the Mission Presbyterian church to hold services that Sunday a few blocks away in the Mission facilities.

That evening the congregation—under tight security of police protection—marched from the burned-out church, singing hymns such as "We Shall Overcome," to what would become their new church sanctuary at 23rd and Capp streets.

Rev. Sandmire announced to the triumphant applause of nearly 600 people gathered for Sunday evening worship, "We are meeting again, AS USUAL!" In attendance were Rev. Perry and the pastors of several local MCCs, the religious leaders of several local straight congregations, members of the gay and lesbian community and various gay organizations, and several prominent local and state politicians . . . "a bridge for the straight and gay community, where we could meet on a common ground of our belief in God."

City Council Member Dianne Feinstein immediately pledged the first $100 towards [a building fund] and in the weeks and months that followed, benefits and fundraisers by the drag and leather communities were held and special collections were made at local bars, and telegrams offering financial support came from across the country.[9]

By the time of Perry's retirement in 2005 as head of the Metropolitan Community Churches, the denomination had grown to more than 250 congregations in 26 countries with 43,000 members. According to their website, their core value is inclusion: "Love is our greatest moral value and resisting exclusion is a primary focus of our ministry. We want to continue to be the conduits of a faith where everyone is included in the family of God, and where all parts of our being are welcomed at God's table."[10]

———

The setting belied the scene. A tall Ponderosa Pine sighed in the late afternoon breeze; to the west, purple smears of the sunset outlined the snowy crags atop Pike's Peak. Into this tranquil setting, the September students scurried into the hall, filled with the zest of a new year. Active and aware, this convention of Unitarian collegians—they called themselves the "Student Religious Liberals"—were veterans of antiwar and women's rights campaigns, and tonight they would be introduced to a new cause. Most had heard of the Stonewall riots a little more than two months earlier; tonight, September 5, 1969, the gay liberation movement would come to the forested slopes of the Rocky Mountains and the denomination known as Unitarians.

The Unitarian Universalist denomination (UU) is small (around a thousand congregations in 2011) with Jewish-Christian roots,[11] revering Jesus of Nazareth as a man chosen by God but not part of the Godhead. Dating to the Reformation era, Unitarians "put the *protest* in Protestant,"[12] but even their fellow reformers were uneasy with the Unitarian's denial of trinitarian dogma. For this reason, many Unitarians hesitate to call themselves Christian.

Throughout their history and into the 1960s the Unitarians, "Had the distinction of being the most liberal church in town. . . . Having been abolitionists and feminists when no one else was, Unitarians had a tradition of contorting tradition."[13] Thus, when the frumpy and overweight Unitarian pastor ambled to the podium at the Unitarian Student Convention in LaForet, Colorado, and announced "I am gay," his words resounded in friendly ears, and the Unitarians embraced the cause of gays and lesbians in the church. LaForet was merely the first stop on a speaking tour through the winter and into the spring of 1970 for the Rev. James L. Stoll, but he then largely left the cause, as well as the Unitarian ministry, and became involved in mental health and drug abuse treatment fields.

Others quickly picked up the gauntlet, notably the Rev. Richard Nash, another gay pastor, who offered his own "coming out" sermon in West Covina, California, in March 1971 to an overflowing assembly, "the largest crowd in the [fellowship's] history."[14] The summer before, Nash had presented a resolution to the UU General Assembly on July 4, 1970. The adopted resolution read: "[A] growing number of authorities on the subject now see homosexuality as an inevitable sociological phenomenon and not as a mental illness [and that] there are Unitarian Universalists, clergy and laity, who are homosexuals or bisexuals." The resolution urged that: "All peoples immediately bring to an end . . . all discrimination against homosexuals, homosexuality, bisexuals, and bisexuality."[15]

The next few years in the UU saw the distribution of a sex education program that affirmed that LGBT sex was natural and should not be criminalized, the utilization of UU meeting halls by new congregations of the spreading MCC, and the formation of an Office of Gay Concerns within the UU hierarchy.[16]

For our story of gays and lesbians in the pulpit, the Unitarians never debated the issue; it was simply a given assumption and entirely consistent with the Unitarian DNA.

The progressive stances, the liberal bent, the gay dances, and the organizing meetings—all these prodded Unitarians toward affirmation of sexual minorities. When the radicals, liberals, feminists, and, ultimately, homosexuals came knocking, all religions had to respond. . . . But the Unitarian character forced Unitarians to answer first, and they answered the ordination question simply; they never debated it. It was taken for granted that homosexuals could be ordained.[17]

Sunday sunrises were unknown in Greenwich Village, and not merely because the Manhattan skyline obscured the sun until midmorning. As gray shades of dawn seeped in, the streetlights flickered off, and the jazz clubs emptied. Late night revelers would pass by a few early churchgoers, but villagers mostly slept in on Sunday mornings. By the time the sun appeared, it was already high in the sky over the boroughs across the East River, and the sparse and laid-back Sunday morning crowd would pay no heed.

But this Sunday, June 28, 1970, would be different. A light beamed from the Oscar Wilde bookstore, and, as if drawn by a beacon, a few faceless strangers shuffled out of the shadows to gather in awkward silence. By the time the sun first peeked over Brooklyn, a crowd of hundreds milled about the bookstore that had become the de facto headquarters for the audacious planners of Christopher Street Liberation Day to celebrate the first anniversary of Stonewall, but this multitude was unaccustomed to the sun, at least, as gay persons. Gays belonged to the dark of night, but now they dared congregate in the light of day. Silently, the crowd moved to Sixth Avenue and joined the throng swelling along Waverly Place. There was apprehension in the air, even fear, but also a hopeful expectancy. As the sun rose high in the sky, so did the signs: "Gay Pride," "Gay is good," "Lesbians united," . . .

Father Robert Mary Clement had arisen before dawn that morning as he always did on Sundays.[18] Normally, he prepared for mass for his twenty or thirty parishioners, but this Sunday Father Clement and his life partner, John Darcy Noble, prepared a placard and organized leaflets printed on colored paper, mostly orange. Like every Sunday, Father Clement donned his priestly garb, and then they departed to join the mass of LGBT folks that stirred along Waverly Place.

The mass swelled to thousands as it moved north fifty-one blocks along Sixth Avenue to Central Park. Curious onlookers first assumed it was an antiwar march, but when the truth came out, mouths dropped; some jeered and offered a middle-finger salute. Although police honored the marcher's parade permit, they turned their backs toward the entourage that snaked its way through Manhattan.

Father Clement's presence garnered much attention, especially by the press and the picture-takers, second only to the drag queens; after all, he marched as an openly gay priest, in collar and cassock, carrying the banner, "Gay People, This Is Your Church." Meanwhile, Noble distributed their colored fliers inviting people to attend the Church of the Beloved Disciple, stating: "Gay people of New York, here at last is a traditional church which you can enter proudly and as yourself, without fear of censure or denunciation. . . . If you can accept your own homosexuality honestly within yourself, then here is a church where you can face your God openly, with the same honesty and self-respect."[19]

Father Clement had been born of Roman Catholic and Episcopal parents in 1925, and he had been raised as an "Anglo-Catholic" (high-church Episcopalian). When he responded to a call to the priesthood at university, he came into contact with "Old Catholicism," a loose grouping of churches that had split with Rome a hundred years earlier following Vatican I and the dispute over papal infallibility. As a dissident church, Old Catholicism had long attracted those dissatisfied with tradition, yet Old Catholic churches remained very liturgical and ceremonial in their worship practices. Father Clement had been ordained to the priesthood of several independent (non-Roman) Catholic churches beginning in 1948.

During the fifties, he had worked in both the secular and ecclesiastical world. He had learned the nuances of the burgeoning television industry that would later serve him well as a spokesperson for the gay community immediately after Stonewall. Around 1960, he had moved into New York City with John Darcy Noble, who would be his life partner. He worked with various congregations of independent Catholics, but in 1968 he formed his own, unaffiliated parish that he and Noble named "The Church of the Beloved Disciple," which ministered to a very small, poor, and ethnically mixed congregation.

And then Stonewall and its aftermath had exploded, literally in his neighborhood. Hear the story in Father Clement's own words:

> [T]he freedom that occurred at that point freed me from the falseness or the limitedness of what had gone before. But what had gone before, I hoped, prepared me for something great to come. And in the heart, if no other way, greatness did come. As they say, it's thrust upon you. I hope I'm not vain in saying that. There was a period of greatness in the world, and for GLBT people thrust on us, and I was happy to grab hold of it.
>
> [Y]ou must realize, before Stonewall, and I'm sure you do, which rankled almost worse than not being able to be honest at all times in the church, was in our society what rankled was that I was a criminal. We were all criminals. We were outside the law, and the law was specifically written against us, and we were unwelcome and unwanted in our society.
>
> I was the only real clergyman walking around. And people knew I was a priest. And so right away, "What are you going to do about us? Where do we fit in? And if we're the noisy ones and so on, do you accept us?"
>
> I had to put together a context of what it was about, what it meant, and how accepting we were of our brothers and sisters that something existed. Because at that time, they had nowhere to go. There was no such thing as an open affirming parish of any sort.[20]

Father Clement and his small parish heard the call. They would offer their congregation as sanctuary for gays and lesbians—hungry for God, thirsting for the divine—who had nowhere else to be nourished. In the months after Stonewall, they had planned and raised funds. They would use the Christopher Street Liberation march as their publicity opportunity to spread the word with a placard and their orange leaflets. Optimistically, they paid a healthy fee to rent a larger sanctuary from Holy Apostles Episcopal church in lower Manhattan. The first mass would take place on a sunny afternoon in July 1970, soon after the march.

[W]hat happened was that day we still worried about, especially the far right fundamentalists who could still be physically vicious or active, not just verbally. And we thought oh, boy, imagine if someone comes asking people to come to the church, and there's violence. So what we did is . . . We got a hold of some of our leather boy friends. And we asked a few of them in particular to stand outside in case, this is simple, anyone might come to offer violence. It never happened. But it was so nice. Because one or two of them showed up on motorcycles, and they were outside in their leathers.

It was about a quarter to two, and we looked into the church and we said, oh, it is going to be ourselves. Can you imagine, at a quarter to two, there was virtually no one there? One or two people. We thought, well, okay, the people didn't read or didn't respond to the fliers. And we'll have our lovely service that we planned. And we'll have our own people and a few more. That's nice. That will work. Well, that was at 1:45; it seemed like there was no great appeal.

Two o'clock, we opened the side sacristy door for our procession. We couldn't believe it. It wasn't just that every seat in the church was filled, the aisles were packed. That church, which would hold maybe six hundred plus in a squeeze, had over eight hundred people in it, and we don't know how many people were turned away that day who couldn't get in.

Because we had all the Protestants, the Orthodox, the Catholics. And on top of it all, you had, the most incredible thing, we had Jewish people, a lot of them. Because they wanted a home. Even though it was Christian, *people were seeking God, they were seeking a relationship to the divine, and they would come to us because everyone else had rejected or turned them away. They had nowhere to go.* [emphasis added][21]

Later that year, Father Clement and Noble coined the phrase "holy union," and their co-conspirator from the West Coast, Pastor Troy Perry, officiated at the holy union of Clement and Noble. During the early years of the 1970s, the Church of the Beloved Disciple would serve as the sanctuary and house of worship for the gay community of lower Manhattan, and Clement became well-known as a willing source for local media. Clement and Noble would eventually move to the West Coast; although his Church of the Beloved Disciple would not grow into a full-fledged gay denomination like Perry's MCC, Clement remained active in various gay, independent Catholic organizations, and he would become a bishop and then an archbishop.

———

We are now ready to embark on our primary journey, the journey toward full inclusion of the five denominations that comprise ecumenical Protestantism. We have seen how these denominations moved from the assumptions of the 1950s—sin, sickness, and criminality—to a more progressive posture by the late 1960s, encouraging compassion and care while advocating for elimination of criminal treatment but still a long road away from full inclusion, still burdened by their traditional understanding of LGBT sex as sinful.

We have seen how independent gay clergy, Pastor Troy Perry and Father Robert Mary Clement, used their autonomy and the fresh attitudes of pride and assertiveness of the late 1960s, exemplified and unleashed by Stonewall, to establish welcoming sanctuaries where gays and lesbians hungry for God could be fed. And finally, we have seen how the Unitarians—of course—were the first denomination (albeit it small and outside the Christian mainstream) to accept gays and lesbians into their pulpits.

The examples of the MCC, the Unitarians, and the Church of the Beloved Disciple challenged the halting steps of the ecumenical denominations and encouraged gays and lesbians within those denominations that full acceptance was possible. If the MCC could offer a worship home "where all parts of our being are welcomed at God's table" and the Church of the Beloved Disciple could provide sanctuary "where you can face your God openly, with honesty and self-respect" then why not the ecumenical denominations?

A 1971 article in the prestigious *Christian Century* magazine articulated the rising hopes of LGBT Christians and the continuing challenge for the ecumenical churches: "Homosexuals do not wish to be treated as lovable 'sinners' subjected to paternalistic good will or merely tolerated. In their eyes, compassion and theological abstraction are devices invented by heterosexual Christians for their own comfort."[22]

Let the journey begin.

NOTES

1. "Who We Are," *History of the MCC*, on the website of the Metropolitan Community Churches, accessed May 28, 2011, http://mccchurch.org/overview/; http://mccchurch.org/overview/history-of-mcc/.

2. Rev. Elder Troy Perry, *History of MCC*, accessed May 28, 2011, http://mccchurch.org/overview/history-of-mcc/.

3. White, "Homosexuality, Gay Communities," 133.

4. Rev. Elder Troy Perry, *History of MCC*, accessed May 28, 2011, http://mccchurch.org/overview/history-of-mcc/.

5. White, "Homosexuality, Gay Communities," 120–21.

6. Ibid., 134.

7. Ibid., 125.

8. This quotation and the details of the UpStairs Lounge fire are from the Jimani Bar website, accessed June 22, 2013, http://www.thejimani.com/the-historyof/theupstairslounge.html.

9. MCC historian Lynn Jordan, "MCC San Francisco, July 1973," on the website of the Lesbian, Gay, Bisexual, and Transgender Religious Archives

Network, accessed January 18, 2012, http://www.lgbtran.org/Exhibits/Sampler/mcc-video.aspx.

10. MCC, "Statement of Purpose," on the website of the Metropolitan Community of Churches, accessed May 28, 2011, http://mccchurch.org /overview/our-purpose/.

11. "Each of the 1,041 congregations in the United States, Canada, and overseas are democratic in polity and operation; they govern themselves. . . . Unitarian Universalism is a liberal religion with Jewish-Christian roots. It has no creed. It affirms the worth of human beings, advocates freedom of belief and the search for advancing truth, and tries to provide a warm, open, supportive community for people who believe that ethical living is the supreme witness of religion." See the website of Unitarian Universalist Association of Congregations, "About Our Unitarian Universalist Association of Congregations," accessed December 7, 2011, http://www.uua.org/association/index .shtml.

12. Mark Oppenheimer, *Knocking on Heaven's Door* (New Haven, Conn.: Yale University Press, 2003), 31.

13. Ibid., 34.

14. Ibid., 41.

15. Ibid., 39–40.

16. Ibid., 50–59.

17. Ibid., 59.

18. Based upon Father Robert Mary Clement's biographical notes, http://www.lgbtran.org/Profile.aspx?ID=97, and an interview by J. Gordon Melton, August 18, 2007, on the website of the Lesbian, Gay, Bisexual, and Transgender Religious Archives Network, accessed December 21, 2011, http: //www.lgbtran.org/Exhibits/OralHistory/Clement/RClement.pdf.

19. White, "Homosexuality, Gay Communities," 148.

20. Melton, interview with Robert Mary Clement.

21. Ibid.

22. Elliot Wright, "The Church and Gay Liberation," *The Christian Century* (March 3, 1971): 281–85.

✳ 3 ✳

ROADMAP

In order to keep the five parallel journeys cohesive, we will deal with each denomination *in toto*, from beginning to end, and then on to the next. To provide a map that highlights the common roads traveled, we shall begin here with an overview. Later, we will follow each separate journey more slowly, spending time with the pilgrims we meet along the way.

THE SEVENTIES

The 1950s had been characterized by the notions of "sin, sickness, and criminality," but real flesh and blood gays and lesbians were closeted and unknown. By the end of the 1960s, each of our ecumenical denominations had issued policy statements calling for care, compassion, and decriminalization; gays and lesbians began to be humanized even as they remained largely invisible in the life of the church.

It was easy for the denominations to call for nondiscriminatory governmental policies and decriminalization, but what would happen when confronted with the baby on the doorstep? How would the churches react when they realized there were gays and lesbians in their own pews, or, heaven forbid, in their pulpits? How would the churches respond when it was their own internal policies that were challenged?

Not well.

Until the first pilgrims began to "come out," gays and lesbians in the church were a nonissue. In one way or another, the seventies witnessed a collective coming-out of gays and lesbians in the pews and pulpits. When gays and lesbians first dared shed their cloak of invisibility to claim personhood by standing up and proclaiming, "Here I am," the responses of their congregations and denominations were essentially cases of first impression, and, with a few notable exceptions, uniformly negative.

We will start with the atypical experience of the United Church of Christ and Bill Johnson. Johnson came out during seminary in 1970 but continued on a path toward ordination. In 1972, he became the first openly gay candidate to be ordained by a major Christian denomination in modern history. To be sure, the local nature of UCC polity enabled his ordination in a northern California association while the rest of the UCC watched with great interest but without the authority to interfere.

The UCC national church soon joined the journey. By the late 1970s a human sexuality statement was adopted that stressed the positive relational aspects of human sexuality without distinguishing between heterosexuals and homosexuals. Clearly, the UCC was at least a full generation ahead of the other denominations.

The Episcopal Church also moved more quickly than the Lutherans, Presbyterians, and Methodists to accept LGBT clergy, but not without tremendous internal wrenching. For the Episcopalians, the struggle for female ordination and LGBT ordination were closely entwined. Our early journey will pass through Philadelphia on a sweltering summer's day in 1974 when eleven women broke down the doors of a patriarchal church to be ordained as Episcopal priests, despite nearly two millennia of tradition and the lack of denominational approval. Two years later, after the triennial General Convention voted to officially authorize female clergy, an open lesbian was among the first wave of female ordinands. The conservative outcry resounded through Episcopal pews and pulpits across the nation. The General Convention in 1979 was the height of Episcopal homophobia, passing a resolution stating: "it is not appropriate for this Church to ordain a practicing homosexual." Yet, the autonomy of diocesan bishops and a "conscience clause" created by conservatives to preserve their right to refuse to ordain a *woman* left the gate partially open.

The Lutheran path in the seventies was perhaps the smoothest, because the collective coming out of Lutheran gays and lesbians was the most passive. The formation of a gay caucus created a bit of a stir middecade, especially because the initial gathering was funded with a small allocation from the American Lutheran Church (ALC), but LGBT ordination was barely on the Lutheran horizon by the end of the decade. The Lutheran decade ended with a sexuality statement offered by the ALC that said "homosexual erotic behavior [was] contrary to God's intent for his children."

Pastor David Bailey Sindt, a gay Presbyterian, stood on a chair at the 1974 General Assembly of the United Presbyterian Church and held a sign high: *Is anybody else out there gay?* His assertive coming out serves as theme for the seventies. The next year, seminarian Bill Silver of the New York Presbytery sought to be the first openly gay Presbyterian to be ordained. When his presbytery sought "definitive guidance" from the national church body, a task force was commissioned which submitted a gay-friendly report to the 1978 General Assembly. Commissioners (delegates) rejected the report and overwhelmingly rendered definitive guidance that stated "homosexuality is not God's wish for humanity" and "unrepentant homosexual practice does not accord with the requirements for ordination." Subsequent decades would witness ecclesiastical trials that extended the scope and effect of this "definitive guidance."

The Methodist experience was even worse. With the first whiff of gay clergy in 1972, the delegates to the General Conference adopted a policy that would resist all attempts at repeal. "We do not condone the practice of homosexuality and consider this practice to be incompatible with Christian teaching," said the delegates, and this millstone would weigh heavily on future generations of gay and lesbian Methodists. LGBT clergy were outed and defrocked. LGBT applicants to seminary were denied, and gay seminarians were expelled. Loyal bureaucrats toiling within the offices of church ministries were fired.

Pastor Sindt's sign held high was no mere whim. It was part of a calculated strategy, a "ministry of presence," that Sindt and other LGBT activists within the ecumenical denominations would pursue. By their openness and their presence, they implicitly proclaimed, "We're here, we're queer, and we're Presbyterian (or Lutheran, or Episcopalian, or Methodist, or UCC), but we're not merely *the gay issue*; we're flesh and blood human beings."

That day at the Presbyterian General Assembly in the summer of 1974 is celebrated by More Light Presbyterians as their birthday; 1974 was the also the year of birth for the Lutheran Gay Caucus and the Episcopal advocacy group called Integrity. The UCC Gay Caucus, later the Coalition, dates from 1972, and the Gay Methodist Caucus from 1975. That all five ecclesial homophile[1] organizations appeared virtually simultaneously was not coincidental; they were networked through a gay task force that grew out of the Council on Religion and Homosexuality (CRH). With Pastor Bill Johnson serving as CRH executive director from 1973 to 1975, group leaders organized themselves into a task force and achieved recognition from the National Council of Churches (NCC). Presbyterian David Bailey Sindt would serve as a task force representative to the first national gathering of Integrity. Other task force members would serve as facilitators at the first meeting of Lutherans Concerned. Sindt also met with the organizers of the first gathering of the Methodist Gay Caucus. The overlapping linkages are striking.

Johnson warned against "allow[ing] ourselves to be rendered ineffective through an endless series of meetings setting up the 'machinery' for dialogue." Then, in a statement that would define the "ministry of presence," Johnson uttered these prophetic words: "The denominations will listen primarily to persons from within the respective structures, and essentially, only when the issues have been personified, personalized via the coming out of persons whose commitment to the church is recognized."[2] Sound strategy, to be sure, but it would not produce immediate results. The formation of gay caucuses and the collective coming out across the denominations initially resulted in a hardening of denominational policies. "No gays allowed," read the sign hanging from the pulpits by the end of the seventies, except for the UCC.

"We do not condone . . . ," said the Methodists; "homosexuality is not God's wish" and "unrepentant homosexual practice does not accord with the requirements for ordination" added the Presbyterians; homosexual behavior was "contrary to God's intent for his children" repeated the Lutherans, "it is not appropriate for this Church to ordain a practicing homosexual," concluded the Episcopalians, who had the last word as the 1970s ended.

Stonewall exemplified and encouraged an attitude of pride, assertiveness, and openness. Instead of remaining invisible, gays and lesbians came out, and suddenly they were discovered in the pews and the pulpits of the ecumenical Protestant denominations. Only the UCC reacted positively.

The decade had begun in a burst of hope in the aftermath of Stonewall. The MCC was exploding, and the Church of the Beloved Disciple ministered to the gay community in Manhattan. Liberal denominations such as the Unitarian Universalists and Quakers welcomed gays and lesbians. The UCC had ordained openly gay William Johnson, but by the end of the decade, the other ecumenical churches had rejected LGBT clergy in chilling resolutions.

THE EIGHTIES

The year 1980 would see the election of the most conservative U.S. president in modern history, "shop till you drop" consumerism (Madonna's "Material Girl" would appear this decade), and two hundred thousand evangelical Christians would descend upon the nation's capitol for a "Washington for Jesus" march, sprinkled with antigay speeches from emerging culture warriors Jerry Falwell and Pat Robertson. In 1986, the United States Supreme Court decided *Bowers v. Hardwick* (478 U.S. 186), a five to four decision that upheld the constitutionality of a Georgia sodomy law when applied to gays. The concurring opinion of Chief Justice Burger relied upon the historical legacy of homophobia from ancient times through nineteenth-century Victorian England to justify late-twentieth-century criminality:

> Condemnation of those practices is firmly rooted in Judeo-Christian moral and ethical standards. Homosexual sodomy was a capital crime under Roman law. . . . During the English Reformation, when powers of the ecclesiastical courts were transferred to the King's Courts, the first English statute criminalizing sodomy was passed. . . . Blackstone described "the infamous crime against nature" as an offense of "deeper malignity" than rape, a heinous act "the very mention of which is a disgrace to human nature," and "a crime not fit to be named."

Also in 1986, the Vatican would issue a "Letter to the Bishops of the Catholic Church on the Pastoral Care of Homosexual Persons," which stated: "Although the particular inclination of the homosexual person is not a sin, it is a more or less strong tendency ordered toward an intrinsic moral evil; thus the inclination itself must be seen as an objective disorder."[3] Gay and lesbian Catholics wondered what was happening to the progressive spirit of Vatican II. "An intrinsic moral evil?" "An objective disorder?" Dignity USA, the gay Catholic organization, had once been welcome but now was ostracized. This terminology of Cardinal Ratzinger, the future Pope Benedict, would control Catholic policy for decades.

How would the emerging LGBT movement in the church survive in the reactionary milieu of the eighties, much less move forward on the journey toward full inclusion? The decade would demonstrate that the journey toward full inclusion would be a slow slog.

Gay caucuses—the homophiles—had appeared in each denomination in the seventies but matured as well-organized advocacy groups in the eighties. For many gays and lesbians, local chapters of the homophile organizations served as their church where they found safe sanctuary. The eighties also witnessed the rise of the gatekeeper organizations: the UCC Biblical Witness Fellowship (BWF); the Episcopalians United for Revelation, Renewal and Reformation (EURRR); the Presbyterian Lay Committee and their magazine *The Layman*; and the Methodist Good News.

Not much changed with denominational polices except to build the barriers of LGBT exclusion higher. Presbyterian courts ossified "definitive guidance" into ecclesiastical law. Methodists reacted to an LGBT-friendly bishop from Colorado by writing the exclusion of LGBT clergy into their *Book of Discipline*. The UCC remained the exception. Open and affirming had become denominational policy in 1985, and a few years later Pastor Bill Johnson was hired by the national office to administer a gay ministry. Though most of the decade had been quiet, fires of controversy burned across denominations at decade's end.

In 1985, TEC elected a progressive presiding bishop to replace a conservative southerner, and momentum for Episcopal LGBT inclusion accelerated; when Newark Bishop John Shelby Spong ordained a gay man to the priesthood at the close of the decade, the national press was on hand to record the event, and the gatekeepers watched with keen interest.

LC/NA had been collegial and cautious as Lutheran eyes focused on the merger that produced the ELCA in 1988, but when the new church revoked the ordination approvals of three gay seminarians within weeks of the ELCA's birth, the scales fell from the eyes of Lutheran gays and lesbians, and they became confrontational. The decade ended with a pair of old San Francisco congregations threatening to ordain gays and lesbians in defiance of church policy.

For the Presbyterians, the explosive event was a youth convention and a progressive pamphlet that sought to address teen angst over emerging sexual identity issues. According to the gatekeepers, the pamphlet was solicitation to "the gay lifestyle." For the gatekeepers, talking about homosexuality was akin to encouraging youth to become gay. Fanning the issue also helped with fundraising for the Lay Committee.

In a prelude to the season of trials that would characterize the nineties, the Methodists placed a lesbian woman on trial when she sought to transfer her clergy credentials to the Unitarian Universalists. When she shared her reasons by coming out to her bishop, he suggested reparative therapy and instituted disciplinary proceedings to defrock her rather than allow a quiet transfer.

Except for the UCC, the decade ended with all denominations in turmoil, bubbling cauldrons ready to boil over.

THE NINETIES

The O. J. Simpson murder case, the "trial of the century," riveted the nation in 1995. The brutal murder of a young gay man in Wyoming, Matthew Shepherd, in 1998 shocked the complacency of middle America. President Bill Clinton would endure the indignity of an impeachment trial in 1999. Yet, the nineties would also witness the pardon of Nelson Mandela after twenty-seven years of incarceration in a South African prison and a notable Supreme Court decision that recognized the right of gays to equal protection under the fourteenth amendment (*Romer v. Evans*, 517 U.S. 620, 1996). Would the nineties also witness the breakthrough for gays and lesbians in the church?

Not without trials. Except for the UCC, each of the ecumenical denominations would litigate LGBT issues in ecclesiastical courts during this decade. Tense, dramatic, and emotional trials would serve as the decade's landmarks on the journey toward full inclusion.

For the Episcopalians, a heresy trial would be the breakthrough that legitimated gay clergy, at least as judicial precedent. Bishop Spong had become a lightning rod; his ordination of a gay man at the turn of the decade had resulted in a mild rebuke, but he would not be deterred. Spong and his assistant bishop, as well as others, continued to ordain gays and lesbians, and Spong became the floor leader for LGBT causes in the House of Bishops.

In 1996, a group of conservative bishops would make an Alamo-like last stand. They brought heresy charges against Bishop Walter Righter, Bishop Spong's assistant. They would force the church, through an ecclesiastical trial, to adjudicate whether the 1979 resolution against LGBT clergy was core doctrine of the church; if so, Bishop Righter would be convicted of heresy and further ordination of gays and lesbians would be stopped, once and for all; if not, the dam would burst and LGBT ordinations would become an unstoppable wave. Their gambit failed, Bishop Righter was exonerated, and TEC would join the UCC in regularly ordaining LGBT clergy, at least in friendly dioceses.

At decade's end, the Episcopal journey would be sidetracked by the worldwide Anglican Communion. At the 1998 decennial gathering of Anglican bishops at Lambeth (London), Anglicans from developing nations successfully pushed a harsh antigay resolution, and the Episcopalians were suddenly pariahs within their communion. Even the archbishop of Canterbury seemed against them.

In 1990, the two San Francisco Lutheran congregations followed through with their plans to ordain gays and lesbians despite the lack of official approval, and the local bishop commenced disciplinary proceedings again the congregations. The offending congregations were placed on probation and later expelled from the ELCA when they refused to comply with ministry policies that prohibited gays and lesbians.

Just a few years later, the same Bay Area bishop brought charges against one of his pastors, this one ordained many years earlier, who came out to his congregation in the midst of a sermon. That trial resulted in a defrocking of the pastor, but Lutheran public opinion in that region was swinging decidedly toward the LGBT pastors. The 1994 Assembly of the Sierra Pacific Synod adopted a resolution of support for the defrocked pastor and his congregation. A newly elected bishop refused to remove the pastor from the pulpit and allowed him to remain in place at his congregation with a procedural sleight-of-hand. Ecclesiastical disobedience in the ELCA was rising to include bishops.

Meanwhile, at the national level, the process of considering a Lutheran human sexuality statement spiraled out of control. Conservatives successfully prevented any revision of denominational ministry policies. National and regional assemblies were conflicted and chaotic. The newly elected presiding bishop masterfully understated the obvious, "We have not yet reached consensus."

The Presbyterians also witnessed the demise of a task force study on human sexuality. The trial and subsequent appeal of the case of Rev. Janie Spahr tightened the legal straightjacket of the earlier "definitive guidance" by using it to block her call to pastoral ministry, though she had been ordained for two decades. The case and its publicity lionized Rev. Spahr, and she became a highly visible advocate for LGBT inclusion.

At the 1996 General Assembly, a new standard was adopted to replace the "definitive guidance" of 1978 because the Presbyterian ecclesiastical courts had grown critical; "fidelity in marriage and chastity in singleness" became the policy to preclude LGBT ordination. Known as "Amendment B," this provision would be the field of Presbyterian battles for more than a decade. Several times, the General Assembly voted to replace Amendment B with affirming language, but Presbyterian polity intervened. The required approval by the regional presbyteries repeatedly failed.

The issue for the Methodists during the season of trials in the nineties was not LGBT clergy but "covenant ceremonies," the blessing of same-gender couples by Methodist clergy. In the second half of the decade, two Methodist pastors were charged and tried in ecclesiastical courts for performing covenant ceremonies. In fact, Pastor Jimmy Creech of Nebraska was tried twice.

Pastor Creech was acquitted in the first trial, but the decision was based on a narrow interpretation of church policy, which was then reversed by the Judicial Council and rewritten by the General Conference, and Creech was convicted and defrocked in his second trial. Pastor Greg Dell of Chicago was also convicted and punished with suspension but not defrocking. All the trials received substantial national attention.

Though the church rules led to convictions, the trials galvanized public opinion within the church.

At the end of the decade, the "Sacramento 68," a mass of Methodist clergy, came together to jointly perform a covenant ceremony. They were not prosecuted. And the presiding judge at the Dell trial in Chicago, Bishop Jack Tuell, had a change of heart and became a public advocate for gays and lesbians.

As the size and funding of the homophile organizations grew, so did their gatekeeping counterparts. The mostly LGBT More Light Presbyterians were joined by a well-heeled straight ally, the Covenant Network of Presbyterians, that was organized and funded by church and seminary leaders and "high steeple" pastors. On the gatekeeping side, the nineties witnessed the emergence of the Institute on Religion and Democracy (IRD), a neoconservative political organization that influenced the Episcopal, Presbyterian, and Methodist gatekeeping organizations. This book will have much to say about the IRD. The Lutherans witnessed the emergence of their own gatekeeping organization; arising out of conservative reaction to the formation of the ELCA in the early nineties, the "WordAlone" movement took off as the opposition to a full communion agreement with the Episcopal Church at the end of the decade, and they would stay around to contest LGBT inclusion after the turn of the century.

THE NEW MILLENNIUM

Within secular America, events began to move quickly, and the church kept pace. Undoubtedly, the brutal murder of Matthew Shepherd in the fall of 1998 had galvanized public awareness of the abuse of gays. "Matthew Shepard's murder was a defining moment in our history—in our history as Americans, in our history as gay people, in our history as people who are in the middle of a social justice fight and, some would say, in the middle of a social justice war."[4]

In June of 2003, the Supreme Court reversed itself and the case of *Bowers v. Hardwick* decided merely seventeen years earlier. *Lawrence v. Texas* (539 U.S. 558) overturned a Texas law that had criminalized gay sodomy. Writing for the court, Justice Kennedy eviscerated the court's earlier rationale: "The Supreme Court in *Bowers*," Justice Kennedy ruled, "had been mistaken from the moment it opened its mouth. The gay claim . . . was not, as Justice Byron White suggested in *Bowers*, laughable. It was in fact indisputable."[5] Marriage equality became the secular battleground. In 2003, the Massachusetts Supreme Court ruled in favor of marriage equality, and other jurisdictions soon followed, by judicial decree or legislation. President George W. Bush's 2004 inaugural address declared the nation must "defend the sanctity of marriage." Three weeks later, Gavin Newsom, the mayor of San Francisco, ordered the city clerk to grant marriage licenses to same-gender couples. When the California Supreme Court ruled in favor of marriage equality, Proposition 8 soon followed to prevent gay marriages and began a meandering journey through the federal court system.

With the election of President Barack Obama in 2008, gays and lesbians had a friend in the White House; "Don't Ask, Don't Tell" disappeared from the military, and the president and his party openly supported marriage equality. A groundswell in the states led to one victory after another as jurisdictions rushed to adopt marriage equality by judicial decree or legislative enactment.

Against this secular background, progressive ecclesial LGBT policies advanced, slowly at first, but with a rush at decade's end. The big news in the first half of the decade was the Episcopal consecration of out gay priest Gene Robinson to be bishop of the Diocese of New Hampshire. Lutheran extraordinary ordinations accelerated, and the ELCA punishment became mere wrist-slaps. Presbyterian courts found excuses around denominational policies against LGBT clergy. A few Lutheran, Presbyterian, and Methodist clergy were defrocked, although jury nullification, or at least sympathetic statements by jurors, contributed to evolving attitudes.

Then in rapid succession the Episcopalians allowed gays and lesbians to be ordained to all levels of clergy in July 2009, the Lutherans followed suit just weeks later in August 2009, and the presbyteries of the PC(USA) finally ratified General Assembly approval of LGBT clergy on the fourth attempt in 2011.

As momentum for full inclusion was building across denominations, the gatekeepers beat the drums of schism. An alternative Episcopal church body, the Anglican Church in North America, roughly 5 percent the size of TEC, competed for recognition by the archbishop of Canterbury and the Worldwide Anglican Communion. Similarly, the ELCA lost 5 percent of its congregations, and the WordAlone movement spawned a pair of alternative denominations—Lutheran Congregations in Mission for Christ early in the decade and the North American Lutheran Church following the churchwide actions of 2009. The Presbyterian journey was two years behind, but there has been early schismatic rabble-rousing.

Then there is the journey of the Methodists. At each bend in the road, the Methodists have lagged behind the other ecumenical denominations. They are by far the largest, and inertia matters. In the end, the broadly democratic polity of the UMC that invites international Methodists to come to these shores and fully participate in UMC quadrennial General Conferences would prevent the Methodists from joining ecumenical partners in breaching the barriers to full LGBT inclusion. The incompatibility clause remained the policy of the UMC forty years after its enactment.

Yet, within many Methodist conferences and congregations, gays and lesbians thrive and calls for ecclesiastical disobedience grow ever louder. The end of the Methodist story is yet to be told.

Allow this brief introduction to provide a "big picture" overview of the parallel tracks toward full inclusion traveled by each denomination. Next, we will consider the journey of each denomination separately and in greater detail. We will begin with the UCC and the ordination of Bill Johnson in 1972. We will continue in the order in which each denomination moved toward full inclusion.

NOTES

1. The term "homophile" is a bit archaic. It was originally an alternative to "homosexual" because it denoted love rather than sex (from the Greek *philia*), and then it was used for the "movement"—the organizations of the 1950s and 1960s that promoted gay interests. These secular gay-friendly groups, the most notable being the Mattachine Society and the Daughters of

Bilitis, were collectively known as the "homophile movement." Though essentially secular, the Mattachine Society was started with the help of a Unitarian minister, and two original founders of the Daughters of Bilitis later helped organize the Council on Religion and the Homosexual (CRH) in San Francisco. (Comstock, *Unrepentant*, 6.) This book will deal with "the ecclesial wing" of the movement that first appeared in the 1970s. This book will extend the term "homophile" to refer to the groups affiliated with the denominations that have historically promoted LGBT interests and continue to do so, but there is a degree of anachronism in this usage.

Each of the organizations has undergone name changes along the way. Indeed, Lutherans Concerned/North America became ReconcilingWorks in the summer of 2012, but this book will continue to use the prior name because "ReconcilingWorks" would be anachronistic. To be consistent and current, this book will refer to them simply as the Coalition (UCC), More Light Presbyterians (MLP), Lutherans Concerned/North America (LC/NA), Integrity (Episcopal), and Reconciling Congregations Project (RCP), later Reconciling Ministries Network (RMN) of the UMC, a split off of what was originally Affirmation, which remains as a smaller UMC advocacy group.

2. White, "Homosexuality, Gay Communities," 169–70.

3. The Congregation for the Doctrine of the Faith and its Prefect, Joseph Cardinal Ratzinger (who would become Pope Benedict XVI in 2005), "Letter to the Bishops of the Catholic Church on the Pastoral Care of Homosexual Persons," on the website of the Vatican, accessed February 11, 2012, http://www.vatican.va/roman_curia/congregations/cfaith/documents/rc_con_cfaith_doc_19861001_homosexual-persons_en.html.

4. Moises Kaufman, playwright of *The Laramie Project*; quoted in Linda Hirshman, *Victory: The Triumphant Gay Revolution* (New York: Harper, 2012), 280.

5. Hirshman, *Victory*, 267.

PART I

~

The United Church of Christ

any streams have flowed into the United Church of Christ (UCC). Two major branches merged in 1957 to form the UCC, but each of these—the Evangelical and Reformed Church and the Congregational Christian Church—were themselves the confluences of multiple currents that streamed through the earliest American colonies and then the eighteenth-century American frontier. With headwaters in Europe, influences of Luther, Calvin, and English nonconformists (Puritans and Pilgrims) had spilled in and swirled about, and the Great Awakening and American revivalism had muddied the waters. Later, a wellspring of congregational Afro-Christians bubbled up from the South and poured into the pool.

Today, the UCC consists of approximately one million members spread over five thousand congregations. Predominantly liberal, mostly low-church (but celebrating the sacraments of baptism and holy communion), and locally autonomous, the UCC has historically been the most progressive of the ecumenical denominations, with an impressive list of "firsts": first religious publishing house (Pilgrim Press—the publisher of this book), early abolitionists, first published African American poet, first ordained African American pastor, first female pastor, and the first African American denominational leader. UCC predecessors founded leading institutions of higher education, including a first wave in New England (Harvard, Yale, and my own alma mater, Dartmouth College) and a second wave mostly in the Midwest (Oberlin, Ripon, Carleton, Grinnell, and numerous others). UCC predecessors, through the American Missionary Association, founded most of the historically black colleges in the south (Fisk, LaMoyne-Owen, Dillard, Talladega, Tougaloo, and others). Elmhurst College of Illinois produced theologians Reinhold and H. Richard Niebuhr and Walter Brueggemann and served as 1960s' rearing ground for a future seminarian named William R. Johnson.

The local congregation is the core unit of the denomination. Congregations are autonomous bodies with disparate practices and policies.

The autonomy of the Local Church is inherent and modifiable only by its own action. Nothing in this Constitution and the Bylaws of the United Church of Christ shall destroy or limit the right of each Local Church to continue to operate in the way customary to it, nor shall be construed as giving to the General Synod, or to any Conference or Association now, or at any future time, the power to abridge or impair the autonomy of any Local Church in the management of its own affairs, which affairs include, but are not limited to, the right to retain or adopt its own methods of organization, worship and education; to retain or secure its own charter and name; to adopt its own constitution and bylaws; to formulate its own covenants and confessions of faith; to admit members in its own way and to provide for their discipline or dismissal, to call or dismiss its pastor or pastors by such procedure as it shall determine; to acquire, own, manage and dispose of property and funds; to control its own benevolences; and to withdraw by its own decision from the United Church of Christ at any time without forfeiture of ownership or control of any real or personal property owned by it. (Constitution, Article V, paragraph 18)

The bodies within the UCC are held together in "covenant," which are mutual promises but not binding contracts. Phrases that characterize this relationship include: "consultation and collaboration"; "honor and respect"; "listens, hears, and carefully considers" (Constitution, Article III).

The next level up from the local congregation is the association. Episcopal oversight is provided collectively by congregations and ministers of an association rather than a bishop. *Ordination of ministers is a function of the association, and their decisions are not subject to review by higher authorities.*

> An Association or Conference acting as an Association is that body within a Conference of the United Church of Christ that is composed of all local churches in a geographical area, as well as all ordained ministers with standing or ministerial partnership standing, commissioned ministers with standing, and those licensed ministers who have been granted voting membership in the Association. An Association determines, confers, and certifies to the standing of the local churches of the United Church of Christ within its area. An Association grants, certifies to, transfers and terminates ordained ministerial standing or ordained ministerial partner standing in the United Church of Christ. (Manual on Church)

In some conferences, there are no associations, in which case the conference provides oversight. Conferences are larger regional bodies that usually include several associations. There are thirty-eight conferences in the UCC, and their primary function is to provide congregational support: resources, search and call process, and mission. Conferences usually have permanent, paid staff, but associations do not.

The General Synod is the primary deliberative body and meets every two years. Actions of General Synod are expected to be held in "highest regard," but they are merely influential and not binding. General Synod resolutions "speak 'to' but not 'for' the local church" (Manual on Church). The General Synod formulates policies that guide but do not control (Constitution, Article V, paragraph 19).

Delegates to General Synod come from Conferences and the Boards of the four covenanted ministries of the church that operate out of the national offices in Cleveland (General Ministries, Local Church Ministries, Wider Church Ministries, and Justice and Witness Ministries).

Deacons and elders are terms sometimes used to denote local, lay leaders. Associations are led by elected officers, including a moderator, conferences are led by conference ministers, and the chief officer of the denomination is the General Minister and President. Approximately ninety persons serve on the Executive Council, which functions precisely as the name implies; it is the executive arm of the UCC. With its officers and committees, the Council conducts the business of the national church:

> The Executive Council shall act for the General Synod ad interim, and . . . shall provide coordination and evaluation of the work of the Church and shall carry out such other responsibilities as may be from time to time delegated to it by the General Synod. . . . It shall facilitate the business of General Synod and assume such other tasks as may be assigned to it by the General Synod. It shall be a focal point for decision-making, overall planning and evaluation, and budgeting in the national setting. (Constitution, Article III, 229)

Late in 1968, Rev. Troy Perry had conducted a worship service for his gay community of Los Angeles. The following summer, the Stonewall riots blistered through the streets of Greenwich Village. By September, the gay rights movement had come to the Unitarian Universalists. In the midst of the watershed year of 1969, a ministry of the UCC issued a forward-looking report that set the course for the decade of the seventies. Under the leadership of Dr. Lewis Maddox, an ad hoc committee on homosexuality under the auspices of the UCC Council for Christian Social Action had issued a statement on April 12, 1969 (two months before Stonewall). The 1969 *Resolution on Homosexuals and the Law* addressed legal discrimination in housing, employment, military service, and law enforcement, but the underlying rationale was far-reaching and remarkably progressive for its time. Here is a pertinent portion with emphasis added:

> Such a Christian ideal [marriage], worthy as it is, should not blind us to variations and limitations which may preclude that ideal for many. Nor should it lead Christians to a rigid and graceless moralism which proscribes and persecutes those unable by constitution

or circumstance to fulfill their Christian hope. We believe that the Church, which has long honored both chastity and marriage as vocations, *must also learn to cherish, and not merely to condemn,* those whose sexual need and loneliness may prove importunate— though unmarried, unmarriageable, widowed, or homosexual.

Among these conditions, homosexuality has proved by far the most difficult for most of us to accept and to accord respect and freedom either in the church or in public life. Fortunately, new insights is [sic] available . . . .

The Council for Christian Social Action believes that *the time is long overdue for our churches to be enlisted in the cause of justice and compassion for homosexual persons* as well as for other socially rejected minorities. Clearly there are profound pastoral responsibilities unmet by most churches for homosexual persons in their own midst. Yet our particular concern as a Council is for the legal establishment of civil liberties—for whose denial *we in the church bear substantial blame.*[1]

The prophet Amos prayed, "let justice roll down like waters, and righteousness like an ever-flowing stream." Carried along by progressive currents, the UCC moved quickly toward full inclusion, and the unique local polity of the UCC was the vessel that allowed a swift journey.

NOTES

1. United Church of Christ, *Resolution on Homosexuals and the Law,* adopted by the Council for Christian Social Action, April 12, 1969.

* 4 *

COURAGE BORN OF RASHNESS

Sitting atop "Holy Hill," the neo-Gothic structures of the Pacific School of Religion (PSR) stand in stately vigil over San Francisco Bay across from the Golden Gate Bridge. Long before the neighboring Berkeley campus of the University of California became the icon of the sixties' counterculture, the stone and timber halls of PSR had witnessed Christian activism. Founded by Yankee congregationalists from the east in 1866, the seminary soon exhibited a "courage born of rashness."[1]

On November 11, 1970 seminarian William Reagan Johnson rose to speak to four hundred of his peers in the dining hall during a seminary symposium called "Homosexuality and the Church." The symposium was sponsored by a new group of "Gay Seminarians," and Johnson had cautiously attended their organizational meeting after coming out to himself months earlier. He hadn't planned to say what he did, but he couldn't allow a harsh comment to stand unchallenged.

"I am not a faggot, I am not a queer, I am not a fairy—but I am a practicing homosexual. And I can say that with joy—it is an affirmation which I make with pride."[2]

The young seminarian's spontaneity would change church history. In another setting, his statement would have been controversial, even shocking, but inside these comfortable walls, accustomed to rash and courageous behavior, Johnson's coming out speech seemed entirely congruent. In the back of the room, a UMC bishop leaned over to his friend, the UCC Conference Minister; "Better you than me," he joked.

Born in Houston in 1946, Bill Johnson and his two brothers had actively participated in the life of their church. Johnson served as president of his local youth fellowship and also the wider Christian Youth Council of Houston. His first jobs were as student pastor and youth minister in UCC congregations in Iowa, Washington, and California and as a chaplain's intern in Chicago and Oakland, and he attended UCC affiliated Elmhurst College in the western Chicago suburbs. "He is a moderately tall, gentle person, yet the firmness of his blue eyes behind rimless glasses belies the soft roundness of his face. He is a man who knows what he is about, and who decided while in seminary to be 'up front' with the church about his sexual identity."[3]

No openly gay person had ever been ordained to any traditional church in modern times, and Johnson's coming out statement jeopardized his chances.[4] The seminary president proposed to the faculty that Johnson be expelled, but the faculty thwarted the president. The president then urged that Johnson's transcript be stamped "homosexual," but again, the faculty refused. Johnson continued in seminary, and he received his Master of Divinity degree in 1971. Following graduation, he was hired to a specialized ministry in Southern California among unchurched individuals while he pursued ordination within the Northern California Conference. His persistence would overcome ecclesial resistance.

The deacons of his own congregation, Community United Church of Christ in San Carlos, California, unanimously supported his ordination. Johnson appeared twice before the Conference Church and Ministry Committee. Though his credentials were in order, and the committee determined him to be "well qualified in all aspects of training, theology, experience, etc.," the committee voted four to three in May 1971 against a recommendation for ordination. Undeterred, Johnson would pursue ordination by appealing directly to the thirty-one congregations of the Golden Gate Association, one of a handful of associations within the Northern California Conference.

As we have seen, the UCC functions with decentralized authority. From the early days of the Pilgrims and New England congregationalism, the autonomy of local bodies to manage their own affairs, including the selection of their ministers, had been an essential hallmark of the predecessor bodies to the UCC. The rejection by the committee of the Northern California Conference would not bind the local association.

To put it simply, it was the prerogative of local associations to make ordination decisions, which were not subject to review or control by higher authorities.

> Questions about who may be ordained are, finally, in the domain of association committees on the ministry. An ordination is approved and conducted by that committee in cooperation with a local church, often the church of the candidate's nurture and discernment, or sometimes in the church to which the candidate is called. This discernment process is guided by a Manual on Ministry (affectionately known as MoM). This manual is not a book of rules or laws, though it does include national UCC constitutional and bylaw statements on the ministry. We've used the phrase "practices common among us," as a way of describing the authority of the Manual—substantial, but not legal.[5]

The rest of the UCC across the country watched the proceedings in the Golden Gate Association of the Northern California Conference with "substantial" interest but without "legal" authority to interfere with the local ordination process. The initial response of the officers of the association was to create a task force to provide information and resources to the clergy and laity who would later vote on Johnson's ordination request. The task force chair was Pastor Bill Eichhorn, who would prove to be Johnson's ally. A pair of all-day sessions and several evening dialogues with small groups played out over the next several months.

Fifty persons attended the first meeting in October 1971. The task force arranged for two speakers—both gay-friendly. UCC pastor Tom Mauer came out twenty-six years after his ordination, and he worked for the Sex and Drug forum of the Bay Area. In his work, he had interviewed three thousand gays and lesbians, and the audience listened intently as he listed and dispelled popular myths about homosexuality. Pastor Henry Hayden of San Carlos Community Church, the sponsoring congregation where Johnson had served as youth minister, addressed biblical issues.

Sixty-five persons attended the second meeting in February 1972, which was more tense and conflicted. Once again, the task force had arranged for a speakers' panel: a psychiatrist, a seminary professor, a parish minister, and a gay attorney. The parish minister was negative, the others positive. During the free-flowing give and take, Johnson sat quietly in the back; speakers addressed the "issue," oblivious to the flesh and blood human being in their midst.

In the final days of the process, prospective delegates from the churches of the association were lobbied with letters, phone calls, and copies of magazine reprints. A committee of the association listened to Johnson's presentation and then voted three to two to recommend *against* his ordination, but, again, the recommendation was not binding.

Finally, the day of decision arrived: April 30th, 1972. The final hearing and vote would take place at San Carlos Community Church. Nineteen congregations of the Golden Gate Association sent delegations; altogether, there would be fifty-six lay voters and forty clergy voters, and the sanctuary also swelled with visitors. Association Moderator Bonnie Ploeger presided; earlier, at one of the prior gatherings, she had predicted their decision "will have an impact in churches all across the country, not just in this Association or this denomination but in all churches."

After Johnson read his ordination paper, an "open examination" began. Johnson diplomatically responded to each questioner as he had at prior meetings, despite some borderline personal attacks. During this examination and earlier, a few clergy, laity, and congregations within the Association opposed him, raising arguments that would become the boilerplate talking points of the traditionalist opposition of the ensuing generation.

Some congregations threatened withdrawal from the association if "that kind of person" or "that caliber of people" who "flaunted their homosexuality" would be allowed ordination. Some raised scientific arguments based on outdated psychiatric understanding; homosexuals exhibited an "abnormal sexual adjustment." Dismissing the idea of sexual orientation, one person suggested, "you're either oriented or you're disoriented." A pastor warned that Johnson would contaminate youth and unduly influence young men to become homosexuals. A neighboring congregation urged him to withdraw his candidacy in order to prevent a "collision course" that threatened church unity. A nearby church council member wrote, "If the Scriptures are not to be accepted as standards . . . then what is our authority in such matters?" Another congregation warned that the ordination would be "a deplorable act that . . . constitutes a defilement of the church." Another church leader predicted the ordination would contribute "to the further undermining of the whole fabric of marriage and the family."[6] These soon-to-be familiar arguments would be endlessly recycled over the next generation as sister denominations confronted the issue first addressed by the UCC.

With the hint that "Coffee is ready for the non-voting delegates and visitors," the moment of truth arrived. Visitors exited, the doors swung shut, and the secret debate and voting began. Small groups gathered on the lawn, reporters moved toward telephones to report, "No story yet"; motorcycles roared past the tense church. Finally, 55 minutes after the doors had been shut, they swung open as a crowd burst out.

Walking alone outside the church, candidate Johnson was immediately confronted by a hostile delegate. "You make me sick," he said, looking Johnson straight in the eye. "You're a disgrace, not a man. If this is what the church wants, I won't be a part of it." Behind him came another angry man. "I hope you're happy, you pervert," he shouted. "This is going to destroy the church." Then he spat in Bill's face.

One friendly young minister, spotting some of Johnson's supporters, flashed a quick thumbs-up sign. "Two to one," he grinned. "It's all over." Told the news, Johnson was quiet, his face blanched from the confrontation outside. "Not till I hear it from the Council itself," he said.

Minutes later, at exactly 7:00, that announcement came from Moderator Ploeger: "Number of possible voters in the Association—151. Number of eligible voters present—96. Number of ballots cast—96. Number of votes, 'Yes'—62. Number of . . .." But the cheering drowned out the rest.

The Council ended with exuberant singing of "Forward through the Ages" to the tune of "Onward Christian Soldiers."[7]

On June 25, 1972, two days before the third anniversary of Stonewall, Johnson was ordained a minister at the Community United Church of Christ where he had served as youth pastor. The crowd of three hundred included his mother and twin brother. A seminary class-mate presented a homemade robe, and the whole assembly laid on hands. Pastor Bill Eichorn, who had headed the task force, offered the "charge" to the new minister, encouraging him to remain authentic and to remember who he was.

The polity of the UCC had allowed Johnson's ordination; it was purely a local decision, and the national church body had no policy, much less the power, to restrain or overturn the actions of the Golden Gate Association of the Northern California Conference. Though the Johnson ordination did not reflect denominational policy, the reality was that if it could happen in Northern California, it could happen anywhere.

Pastor Bill Johnson would play a major prophetic role in the ongoing journey toward full inclusion, not only in his own UCC, but across denominations. Johnson organized the UCC Gay Caucus, the forerunner to the Coalition, and served as its national coordinator from '72 to '77 and later as editor of the group'snewsletter, *WAVES*.[8] His first organizing activity was to mail an invitation to twenty-five gays and allies within the UCC community to come out and to "openly work for gay rights in the UCC." He titled his letter, "The People That Walked in Darkness Have Seen a Great Light."[9]

Once ordained, Bill Johnson had hoped to enter the parish ministry, but that never happened because no congregation dared to issue a call. Thus, in January 1973, his first employment after ordination was as exec-utive director of the Council on Religion and the Homosexual (CRH) in San Francisco.[10] We have previously discussed this organization that arranged the benefit ball raided by police back in 1964 and that became emblematic for clergy providing moral cover for LGBT rights—"the cloak of the cloth." In this capacity, Johnson was a godsend to the overall homophile movement by serving as a contact person and inspiration for aspiring denominational startup homophile organizations. For instance, his speech at United Theological Seminary in New York inspired sem-inarian Bill Silver to seek Presbyterian ordination and to work with David Bailey Sindt in organizing the Presbyterian Gay Caucus (see "Part Four: The Presbyterians"). Johnson would serve on a task force on homosex-uality created by the CRH and recognized by the National Council of Churches, which would play an important advisory role to the development of LGBT organizations within the denominations. In his travels, he met many exceptional gays and lesbians, and he arranged the first national gathering of the Coalition at Buffalo, New York, in 1981 so that the network of UCC gays and lesbians could meet each other.

He also became the de facto pastor to the LGBT community, a listening ear to a host of gays and lesbians within the church, especially closeted clergy, according to Pastor Loey Powell, who became his associate within the UCC Coalition half a dozen years later.[11]

The journey toward full inclusion passed through a seminary that demonstrated "courage born of rashness"; here, a prophet arose who ministered to the LGBT community while advocating across denominations and within his own UCC. In the forty-plus years since his ordination, Pastor Bill Johnson has served as *the* icon for gay ordination, the UCC has established an endowed scholarship in his name for gay seminarians, and his undergraduate alma mater, Elmhurst College in the western Chicago suburbs, has instituted an annual William R. Johnson LGBT lecture series.

His early ordination was rendered possible by a policy of local autonomy that had allowed the Golden Gate Association to ordain him while the rest of the UCC watched. But what of the denomination as a whole? What effect did Johnson's ordination have on national policy? Where would we encounter the UCC along the road, as a builder of barricades or of bridges?

NOTES

1. *History of Pacific School of Religion*, on the website of the Pacific School of Religion, accessed April 12, 2012, http://www.psr.edu/history-pacific-school-religion.

2. This retelling of the ordination of Bill Johnson is based on six sources:
W. Evan Colder was an eyewitness to the events, and he has written two accounts. W. Evan Colder, "Faith Not Fear, Ordaining a Homosexual Person," William Reagan Johnson, *And So We Speak*, quoted in a booklet compiled by the UCC Coalition for Lesbian, Gay, Bisexual, and Transgender

Concerns, 1998; and W. Evan Colder, "The Ordination of Bill Johnson," *San Francisco Sunday Examiner & Chronicle* (June 25, 1972).

Other biographical details are obtained from the Profile of Rev. Dr. William R. Johnson, on the website of the Lesbian, Gay, Bisexual and Transgender Religious Archives Network, accessed May 28, 2011, http://www.lgbtran.org/Profile.aspx?ID=3.

A documentary movie, "A Position of Faith," contains film of actual events. United Church of Christ YouTube Channel, accessed May 28, 2011, http://www.youtube.com/watch?v=8gorrOIo8Wg.

Bill Johnson, Loey Powell, and others presented a panel discussion review of UCC Coalition history during the fortieth anniversary celebration of Johnson's ordination at Elmhurst College on June 26, 2012, and the author was present.

Finally, Bill Johnson has fact-checked the manuscript for this book and added personal details in direct correspondence with the author (September 12, 2012).

3. Colder, "The Ordination of Bill Johnson."

4. Except for the fledgling Metropolitan Community of Churches.

5. Clyde Steckel, professor emeritus of United Theological Seminary of the Twin Cities, private e-mail to the author, November 8, 2011.

6. White, "Homosexuality, Gay Communities," 163–64.

7. Colder, "Faith Not Fear."

8. Profile of Rev. Dr. William R. Johnson.

9. White, "Homosexuality, Gay Communities," 173.

10. Ibid., 165.

11. Rev. Lois Powell, private interview with the author, April 11, 2012.

✳ 5 ✳

THE CHURCH RESPONDS

In 1620, a group of dissidents departed Europe aboard the Mayflower seeking religious liberty in the wilderness that would become Massachusetts. The Pilgrims had been irritants who incurred the wrath of King James before they left England. Their pastor encouraged them to keep their hearts and their minds open to new ways in the new world because God "hath yet more truth and light to break forth out of his holy Word."

The UCC and her predecessor church bodies going back to the Pilgrims boast many progressive milestones, including a stand against slavery a century and a half *before* the Civil War, the first African American ordained minister, and the first female pastor. It was not by accident that the first openly gay person to be ordained would be in the United Church of Christ.

The next General Synod of the UCC following Pastor Bill Johnson's ordination convened in 1973. Johnson's straight ally, Rachel Barnsley, an officer of their Golden Gate Association, accompanied him to General Synod, and they set up a booth that garnered strange glances as well as several folks who hovered nearby before cautiously stepping forward. They posted signs in the elevators, "Take a lesbian to lunch," and several accepted the challenge, including one elderly female couple.

Johnson had penned a gay-affirming resolution that called for dialogue and education that was submitted through the Golden Gate Association, but it didn't make it to the floor. Such untreated resolutions automatically rolled over to the Executive Council for later consideration, but Johnson wanted to ensure that the church and the Council afforded the resolution a high priority; thus, he devised a visibility strategy. During the closing worship service, Johnson and another gay man, Darryl Notter, walked hand in hand to the stage and presented a letter to the UCC's shocked secretary, Joseph Evans. The letter expressed disappointment that the resolution had not been considered and insisted that an openly gay person be present whenever LGBT concerns were to be discussed, but the real message was conveyed by the dramatic delivery. Leaving the stunned assembly, the two gay men retreated to a nearby gay bar because they felt safer there.

Secretary Evans duly forwarded the letter to the Executive Council, the ninety-member panel that conducted the business of the church. In response, the Executive Council adopted a "recommendation" in October 1973 consistent with the national church's limited authority to prescribe ordination standards and consistent with the tradition that the national church speaks "to" and not "for" its constituent bodies; yet, the recommendation was a stunning victory for Johnson and the cause of LGBT ordination:

> The Executive Council, recognizing that Associations have final responsibility for ordination and standing and acknowledging that such responsibility must be exercised within the context of a clear understanding of the theology of ordination,
>
> A. Recommends that congregations, Associations and Conferences initiate programs of study and dialogue with regard to the implications (meanings) of human sexuality, in all its mystery, at its broadest and deepest levels in the theological context.
>
> B. Directs the Council for Church and Ministry, and its successor body, to continue its study of the relationship between ordination and human sexuality in consultation with congregations, Associations and Conferences for the purpose of developing resources for the study of human sexuality and developing a process for decision making that may be utilized by Associations in the matter of ordaining affirmed homosexuals.
>
> C. Recommends to Associations that as they continue to clarify their understanding of the theology of ordination they give serious consideration to the position of the Council for Church and

Ministry in the matter of human sexuality: "In the instance of considering a stated homosexual's candidacy for ordination, the issue should not be his/her homosexuality as such, but rather, the candidate's total view of human sexuality and his/her understanding of the morality of its use (expression)."[1]

As we shall see later, the Presbyterians also had a longstanding tradition of local autonomy regarding ordinations, but that wouldn't prevent the highest Presbyterian ecclesiastical courts from intervening to prevent gay ordinations. To their credit, the UCC Executive Council refused to bend to traditional fear of gays. What is more, they affirmatively stated that homosexuality per se shouldn't be a bar to ordination. Similar proposals in sister, ecumenical denominations would be rejected. Though Bill Johnson's ordination had been a local issue, the national church—at least the Executive Council—had essentially affirmed his ordination when first presented with the issue.

Meanwhile, the Gay Caucus surged forward with favorable tail winds. Sixty-four persons had signed up for the mailing list at General Synod 1973, and Johnson added the names of all regional and national church leaders. When the first Gay Caucus Newsletter was sent out in January 1974, Johnson received a polite letter of thanks from the UCC president, Robert V. Moss. The gay community had a place at the UCC table.

Yet, the church had not spoken through its elected delegates, and until the matter would be put to a vote, it would remain unsettled; there was persistent grumbling in the pews and rumbling in certain associations. The issue would arise at the Tenth General Synod in 1975 in response to a "pronouncement"—a UCC statement on a significant justice issue—on civil liberties without discrimination based on affectional or sexual orientation. It was accompanied by a resolution calling on the church to respond to the special needs of gay and lesbian clergy, who were the victims of such discrimination. Both were submitted by the gay caucus, now called the UCC Lesbian and Gay Caucus. As soon as the pronouncement reached the floor, a carefully choreographed strategy designed by Bill Johnson unfolded. Twenty-five supporters—gays, lesbians, and allies—immediately lined up behind the "yes" microphone, each with a complementary message. The intention was not only to elevate the debate but to visibly show the breadth of support among lay and clergy leaders.

The two-part measure passed overwhelmingly. First calling for resource development for counseling LGBT clergy and lay leadership (appropriately and not reparatively), the resolution concluded with a call for a sexuality study that would include recommendations for church policy:

> The United Church of Christ has not faced in depth the issue of human sexuality. Changing morality and ethics within American society present both problems and challenges to the church.
>
> Therefore, the Tenth Synod requests the Executive Council to commission a study concerning the dynamics of human sexuality and the theological basis for a Christian ethic concerning human sexuality, and to recommend postures for the church, to be presented to the Eleventh General Synod.[2]

UCC eyes around the country looked to the 1977 General Synod, but first the focus was on the study team and the diverse group of consultants who considered biblical interpretation, psychology, and ethics. The task force included lesbian campus minister Jan Greisinger (later to serve as Coalition Coordinator) and Pastor Bill Eichorn from the Golden Gate Association, who had shepherded the Bill Johnson ordination process. Leading consultants included:

- the head of the Religious Studies Department at Penn State

- an associate professor of Christian ethics from Union Theological Seminary

- a faculty member from the Department of Community Medicine at Michigan State

- a professor of Christian ethics from Union Theological Seminary

- a professor of New Testament from Eden Theological Seminary

- an associate professor and chair of the graduate program in sociology at the University of California Medical School

- a professor of Hebrew language and literature from Andover Newton Theological School

Pastor Bill Johnson and others from the Lesbian and Gay Caucus were invited to share their experiences. Staff persons from the UCC Office for Church Life and Leadership, the Office for Church in Society, and the United Church Board for Homeland Ministries administered the study and wrote the study report—a voluminous paperback book consisting of 258 pages.[3]

The study affirmed the goodness of created humanity of which sexuality is an integral part; it discussed biblical, societal, psychological, and educational perspectives. In all this, no distinctions were drawn between heterosexual and homosexual behaviors; implicitly the commentary, conclusions, and ethical insights applied to all sexual relationships regardless of the genders of the partners.

The core of the study report was a two-page definition of human sexuality that included these statements:

One's sexuality involves the total sense of self as male and female, man and woman, as well as perceptions of what it is for others to be female and male. It includes attitudes about one's body and others' bodies. It expresses one's definition of gender identity. Sexuality is emotional, physical, cognitive, value-laden, and spiritual. Its dimensions are both personal and social. . . . Sexuality, is, then, an integrated, individualized, unique expression of self.

For Christians, sexuality is understood as the gift of God and as a dimension through which the love of God and neighbor is expressed.

Our sexuality belongs first and foremost to us. It is pleasure we want to give and get. It is physical expression of attachments to other human beings.

One's values determine approaches to honesty, fidelity, promise-keeping, truth-telling, and the purposes of sexual expression.

Sexuality is a central dimension of each person's selfhood, but it is not the whole of the selfhood. It is a critical component of each person's self-understanding and of how each relates to the world.[4]

A few pages were devoted specifically to LGBT relationships, and the following statement aptly characterized the affirming tone of the study: "The gay rights movement has called attention to the concerns for the dignity of all persons. The word gay, signifying joyfulness, delight, buoyancy, and aliveness, has been reclaimed as a word of positive self-affirmation for a significant number of Americans."[5]

The preliminary study and a discussion guide were widely disseminated with the understanding that the study would be considered by the 1977 General Synod. General Synod XI convened in Washington D.C. in June 1977. The contingent from the UCC Lesbian and Gay Caucus was there on their typical shoestring budget. Loey Powell laughingly remembers two gay men and two lesbians sharing a hotel room, sleeping boy-girl, boy-girl.[6]

Upon a resolution "to receive the study and commend it to the church," the matter came to the floor; after a contentious and often emotional debate, the resolution passed by a margin of 66 percent to 34 percent (409 for and 210 against). The resolution consisted of three pages, with provisions encouraging national, regional, and local units of the church to develop educational resources and plans for ministry in the area of human sexuality, to consider ceremonial rites of blessing of relationships, family planning, abortion rights, countering sexual violence and abuse, and the use of feminine metaphors for God in liturgies.[7]

Though the report was "preliminary" and not intended to be *the* definitive statement regarding LGBT issues, it would become precisely that. This was not a judicial decision, nor a decree from the Executive Council, nor a committee report; a decisive majority of elected representatives had spoken for the whole church. A waypoint had been established that would guide the further journey toward full inclusion. The reception of the report would serve as the de facto stamp of approval of William Johnson's ordination five years earlier and would open the door for future ordinations.

The 1983 General Synod would adopt four interrelated resolutions expanding LGBT inclusive policies, all flowing from the Human Sexuality Statement.[8] In 1977, the preliminary draft of that statement had become the bedrock for subsequent gay-friendly policies, and now the preliminary approval became final. The first of the four adopted resolutions was the receipt of the final draft of the Human Sexuality Statement, which included these provisions:

- Programs would be developed to end violence against men, women, and children regardless of sexual orientation.

- Differences of opinion within the denomination were acknowledged.

- Educational and resource material would be developed for congregations to facilitate ministry with and to gays and lesbians.

- While recognizing the prerogative of local associations to make ordination decisions, the Statement recommended that sexual orientation should not be grounds for denying ordination or a factor in choosing lay staff and volunteers.

A second resolution recognizing "Institutionalized Homophobia within the United Church of Christ" passed with a 95 percent majority. A third resolution "Recommending Inclusiveness on Association, Church, and Ministry Committees" also passed with a 95 percent majority. Among other things, the resolution recognized that gays and lesbians had always been serving in church ministries and recommended that congregations include gays and lesbians on their important committees. The fourth resolution to pass with a 95 percent majority pertained to nontraditional families, recommending that "all families be ministered to creatively and that persons, regardless of their family patterns, be affirmed and supported in the life of the church, manifesting our unity as a family in Christ."

The UCC was a full generation ahead of its sister ecumenical denominations. Not only had an openly gay man been ordained, delegates from far and wide had gathered together in General Synod and adopted a progressive sexuality statement. As we shall see, the other denominations would each attempt comprehensive study by blue-ribbon panels, but their reports would be roundly criticized by gatekeeper organizations and soundly rejected by voting delegates at national conventions. For decades, the UCC would stand alone; while its journey toward full inclusion would be short, for the others, it would be long.

NOTES

1. United Church of Christ, *Human Sexuality and Ordination*, adopted by the Executive Council, Omaha, Nebraska, October 28–31, 1973.

2. United Church of Christ, *Resolution on Human Sexuality and the Needs of Gay and Bisexual Persons*, adopted by the Tenth General Synod, Minneapolis, Minnesota, June 27–July 2, 1975.

3. The United Church of Christ, *Human Sexuality: A Preliminary Study* (New York: United Church Press, 1977).

4. Ibid., 12–13.

5. Ibid., 30.

6. Rev. Lois Powell, private interview.

7. United Church of Christ, *Recommendations in Regard to the Human Sexuality Study*, adopted by the Eleventh General Synod, Washington, D.C. (July 1–5, 1977).

8. United Church of Christ, *Resolutions*, Fourteenth General Synod, United Church of Christ, Pittsburgh, Pennsylvania, June 24–28, 1983, on the website of the Lesbian, Gay, Bisexual and Transgender Religious Archives Network, accessed July 12, 2012, http://www.ucc.org/LGBT/statements.html.

✳ 6 ✳

MODERN DAY PILGRIMS IN A PILGRIM CHURCH

As we have seen, Pastor Bill Johnson was a major prophet for the cause of gay inclusion, not only within the UCC but across denominations. Of course, he was not alone, and it is time to meet other UCC pilgrims on the journey.

Although Bill Johnson was the first openly gay person to be ordained, he was not the first out gay clergyman in the UCC; as early as 1956, UCC Pastor Robert Wood's photo appeared in a gay magazine to which he had submitted an article. In 1960, he wrote the first book to ever mix homosexuality and Christianity in a positive way, and his picture, name, and the identity of his congregation appeared on the dust cover. *Christ and the Homosexual* received the following review: "Sparkling, intimate, compassionate and well-informed—this book is among other things probably the best and most readable description of gay life currently in print. . . . This is the first book written by a responsible clergyman to welcome homosexuals into the Church without demanding that they give up the practice of homosexuality."[1] Until his retirement in the late 1980s, Pastor Wood had lived openly with his partner during twenty-seven years of parish ministry.

Roy Birchard was another gay UCC clergyman who came out in 1970, a year *after* his ordination.[2] Birchard had been ordained in 1969 by the Addison Association of the Vermont Conference of the UCC, but he immediately returned to school to pursue a doctorate in English at the University of Wisconsin–Madison. While there in 1970, he came out as a gay man, and he quickly joined the Madison chapter of the Gay Activists Alliance, but that was a secular group, and Birchard believed the church should play a positive role in advancing the cause of gays and lesbians. When he read an article to the same effect, he drove to New York City to meet the author, John Rash, a librarian at Union Theological Seminary. Rash had written: "A ministry to the gay community and the recognition of that community as having a legitimate, good, and valuable part to play in the Church is not an isolated project, an end to itself. It is only another part of Christian reconciliation and witness. But the time is late and the cause urgent."[3] Birchard's advocacy moved with him to New York City, and he sought funding and institutional support from UCC national headquarters, directing his appeal to Dr. Lewis Maddox, whom he identified as a likely straight ally. Dr. Maddox had directed the UCC ad hoc committee on homosexuality that had authored an LGBT-friendly policy statement adopted by the UCC Council for Christian Social Action on April 12, 1969 (see above).

Due to the inertia of the institution, by the time a funding offer was extended, Birchard had moved on. He had become involved in the fledgling Metropolitan Community Churches, serving as assistant pastor at a newly organized MCC congregation in New York City. Though Birchard's subsequent journey tracked within the MCC, the UCC honored him and recognized his ministry by retaining his UCC clergy credentials intact.[4] Just a few years later, his journey would intersect with Bill Johnson's when both served on the National Council of Churches Task Force on Gay People in the Church.

In 1975, the Rev. Oliver G. Powell penned a piece for the UCC's national publication, *A. D. Magazine.* Rev. Powell served a Boston congregation in the Massachusetts Conference. His article was entitled, "What a beautiful, heady, exasperating, hopeful mix!" and he wrote affectionately of his UCC as "a people of risky adventure."

In describing us, Powell not only detailed our headier traits, but brought life to our fun-loving ones as well. Not surprisingly, he lifted up images of sauerbraten and potatoes, long draughts of dark beer, romantic poetry and Bach chorales. He talked of New England boiled dinners and baked beans, Ralph Waldo Emerson, and skylight filtering through clear, freshly-washed, church-window panes.[5]

Later, Rev. Powell and wife Eleonore would be "people of risky adventure" who would "exemplify courageous leadership in Open and Affirming Ministry" as supporters of their daughter Lois (Loey) Powell, a lesbian ordained in 1978. Parents and daughter would each serve as highly visible leaders along the UCC journey toward full inclusion.

Loey Powell graduated from Pacific School of Religion in 1977, the same "rash and courageous" institution that had witnessed Bill Johnson's dining-hall speech seven years earlier. Echoing her father's "heady, exasperating, and hopeful" sentiment, Powell remembers her seminary days as filled with the exhilaration of movement politics.[6] She had come out early in her seminary life, and fondly remembers the Bay Area UCC gay caucus that gathered for monthly potlucks and nationally at UCC General Synods: "incredibly spirit-filled worship, doing the justice-making work of advocacy, being there for those who were wondering about their sexuality."[7] Like the sun piercing the fog over San Francisco Bay, feminism, liberation theology, and gay rights burned through the timbered halls of the seminary. And it wasn't just the seminary. The Northern California Conference of the UCC was in the vanguard of hope, alive with possibilities.

Though Powell was out to her friends and the PSR community, when she and two other women sought to be ordained together, they were not officially out to their Golden Gate Association and Northern California Conference. It probably wouldn't have mattered, and many within the Association probably knew but chose to ignore the sexuality of the candidates, a "don't ask, don't tell" situation. Thus, though their ordinations occurred in 1978, the distinction of being the first out and acknowledged lesbian to be ordained would fall to Ann Holmes, who was out when she was ordained in 1982 (see below).

As the daughter of an esteemed elder of the church, Powell was free to be a "poster lesbian." While serving with Bill Johnson as co-coordinator of the Gay Caucus, soon to be renamed the UCC Coalition, Powell accepted an interim position with the Northern California Conference Staff in 1980. She also served as associate pastor at a San Francisco congregation until 1982.

That's when reality bit. Though available for call, Pastor Powell went seven years from 1982 to 1989 without a full-time church job, and

Powell supported herself with various secular jobs, including a women's moving business, receptionist, office manager of Redwood Records, and a technical assistant at the Oakland Museum. She was *too* out for a congregation to take a chance on her. Not yet.

Bill Johnson had experienced the same lack of openness to a call to a traditional UCC ministry. Pastor Bill Eichhorn, who had served as chair of the Bill Johnson association task force, was Powell's mentor and confidant, and he encouraged her to remain hopeful. Pastor Powell remained active in the UCC at all levels: congregation, association, conference, and general synod. She founded a congregation in Oakland, chaired the Committee of Ministry for the Northern California Conference, and served on the board of directors for the UCC Coordinating Center for Women and on the UCC Executive Council in 1987, an elected position.[8]

Then a breakthrough in 1989. For the first time in any ecumenical denomination, an openly gay clergyperson was called as sole pastor to a traditional ministry through the normal call process. Although she had been leery of the Florida Conference Minister's antigay reputation, she submitted her resume to the United Church of Tallahassee. She would be the first of three persons to interview; later, a member of the call committee said, "We were willing to extend a call to you right then and there, and we struggled through the two remaining interviews, knowing that we wanted you." Pastor Powell would remain at United Church for seven fruitful years of ministry before accepting a position in the UCC home office in Cleveland, where she has continued to serve, most recently on the Justice and Witness Ministry Team as Executive for Administration.[9]

In April 1982, Anne Holmes would become the first open and acknowledged lesbian ordained within the UCC. Rev. Loey Powell and two other lesbians had been ordained four years earlier, but their sexual orientation had not been acknowledged to their association. Though Ann Holmes was closeted at the outset, the ordination process outed her. "I didn't want this [her sexual orientation] to become the issue, but I was too honest to hide it."[10] After graduation from Vanderbilt Divinity School, Holmes spent two years as a supervisor-in-training as a clinical pastoral counselor at St. Elizabeth Hospital in Washington, D.C., but then she pursued ordination. During candidacy interviews when she responded honestly to the question "are you a homosexual?" her sexuality was out and the ordination process was suddenly colored by her candor.[11]

The first step in the candidacy process was to obtain approval from her home congregation, Emmaus United Church of Christ of Vienna, Virginia. Though a strong majority of the congregation would ultimately support her candidacy, the process was painful, and nearly 20 percent of the membership would depart the congregation following several contentious open meetings.[12]

After congregational approval, the next step was the Potomac Association of the Central Atlantic Conference. In her personal and spiritual biography presented to the Association, she wrote candidly about discovery of her sexual orientation as an undergraduate and the self-hatred that followed.[13]

Over the next few months, Holmes visited the twenty-six congregations of the association. The largest gathering was an association workshop on November 14, 1981. Holmes offered these comments: "I do not intend to hide this part of me, but I do not intend nor desire to become a *cause célèbre*. I have never sought, nor do I seek, ordination for any other purpose but to answer the call of God to ministry. Ordination, I feel, is not an issue of politics or cause; it is response and commitment to God."[14]

The Potomac Association voted ninety-four to thirty-six to ordain her, and she was ordained on April 25, 1982. Though she was by nature apolitical, and her journey to ordination unintended to be anything other than a response to a call to ministry, Pastor Holmes would participate in the Coalition, and she became an icon as the first acknowledged lesbian to be ordained by the UCC.

———•———

As early as 1956, Pastor Robert Wood, a UCC gay clergyman, had been open about his sexuality. Pastor Roy Birchard came out as a gay man in 1970, a year after his ordination. Openly gay William Johnson was ordained in 1972. In 1977, Loey Powell and two other lesbians were ordained. Though they were not officially out, many in their association were aware of their sexuality. In 1982, Ann Holmes came out during her candidacy process, but that didn't prevent her ordination later that year. Gay and lesbian clergy had become a fact of life for the UCC.

NOTES

1. Profile of Rev. Robert W. Wood, on the website of the Lesbian, Gay, Bisexual, Transgender Religious Archives Network, accessed April 19, 2012, http://www.lgbtran.org/Profile.aspx?ID=28.

2. White, "Homosexuality, Gay Communities," 158–60.

3. John Nash, "Reforming Pastoral Attitudes Towards Homosexuality," *Union Seminary Quarterly Review* 15:4, reprinted by the Minnesota Council for Church and the Homophile (Summer 1970): 439–55. Also quoted in White, "Homosexuality, Gay Communities," 158.

4. White, "Homosexuality, Gay Communities," 159–60.

5. Rev. J. Bennett Guess, "A 'Heady, Exasperating Mix'?—Don't Forget 'Beautiful,' 'Hopeful,' Too," *United Church News* (June–July 2007).

6. Rev. Lois Powell, private interview with the author, April 11, 2012.

7. Rev. Lois Powell, address to National Gathering of UCC Coalition, June 27, 2011, personal copy given to the author by Powell.

8. Profile of Rev. Loey Powell, on the website of the Lesbian, Gay, Bisexual, Transgender Religious Archives Network, accessed April 13, 2012, http://www.lgbtran.org/Profile.aspx?ID=75.

9. Rev. Lois Powell, private interview.

10. Marjorie Hyer, "United Church of Christ Will Ordain a Lesbian to Ministry on Sunday," *Washington Post*, April 24, 1982.

11. "Anne Holmes to be Ordained," *Waves*, (March 1982). *Waves* is the newsletter of the United Church Coalition for Lesbian/Gay Concerns.

12. Hyer, "United Church of Christ Will Ordain."

13. Ibid.

14. "Anne Holmes," *Waves*.

* 7 *

DUELING INTEREST GROUPS

As noted, a 258-page study and discussion guide regarding human sexuality was written by a blue ribbon task force and presented to General Synod 1977, which voted "to receive the study and commend it to the church." This action served as bedrock for the inclusive attitude of the UCC from that point forward, but not without dissenters.

The conservative opposition during the plenary discussions of General Synod 1977 galvanized into a special-interest group that called itself "The United Church People for Biblical Witness" (later the Biblical Witness Fellowship or BWF). Here is the "birth announcement" from the group.

> On October 25th, 1978 the renewal movement known as Biblical Witness Fellowship was incorporated as United Church People for Biblical Witness. We were birthed out of the Synod of 1977 at which the first sexuality report was accepted which opened the door to all the many resolutions sanctioning sexual perversity which have followed. At that Synod a young pastor's wife from Pennsylvania named Barbara Weller made an impassioned call for a return to Biblical faith and several hundred responded to that call.[1]

This statement highlights two characteristics of the gatekeeper organizations that would arise within each denomination to oppose LGBT inclusivity. The first is a rhetorical tone that betrays the lack of rational discourse; indeed, the hyperbole evinces a gut-level response to LGBT issues. In this example, reference to "sexual perversity" is a telling expression of the BWF's fear and loathing of gay persons and LGBT issues. Second, the statement calls for "a return to Biblical faith"; similar refrains will echo from the gatekeepers across denominations. Such statements are code language for a literalistic, proof-texting, sin-and-damnation oriented biblicism. Wielded by the gatekeepers, a few out-of-context and misconstrued Bible verses would become "clobber passages." Visceral aversion to gays comes first; biblical justification follows.

A few months after General Synod 1983, the BWF gathered in Dubuque, Iowa, at the University of Dubuque Theological Seminary. In response to the overwhelming adoption of LGBT-friendly policies at the General Synod, the BWF participants issued a declaration written by local professor Donald Bloesch, and it came to be known as the "Dubuque Declaration." The one-page statement is hardly a radical document, merely restating allegiance to orthodoxy, creeds, and confessions, and with special emphasis on biblical authority, but for the BWF, the declaration was necessary because "We perceive an erosion and denial of these truths in our church."[2] The declaration became an outlet for conservative congregations to sign, thereby giving voice to those who disagreed with church policy regarding gays and lesbians. Perhaps this document served as a pressure release valve that allowed conservatives to have their say without leaving the denomination. In any case, the BWF settled into "a grassroots renewal organization"; thirty years later, it was still around, still chafing at UCC policies, still calling for reform.[3]

There would be a notable difference between BWF and the corresponding gatekeeper organizations in other denominations. BWF would be a singular failure in resisting the UCC journey to inclusivity, but gatekeepers in other denominations would successfully construct roadblocks that slowed the journey. Although the BWF would maintain a highly visible presence at General Synods immediately following their organizational birth, their lobbying efforts directed at resolutions to change the course of the UCC routinely failed.

Another difference between BWF and other gatekeeper organizations, a positive distinction, is that BWF did not foment schism in response to gay-inclusive breakthroughs. Perhaps the same congregational polity that had allowed William Johnson's ordination in the first place granted sufficient space between national church policy and local practice. Conservative local congregations were secure in the knowledge that they retained control over their own affairs notwithstanding the progressive trend of the national church.

Furthermore, the BWF may not be as conservative as other gate-keeper organizations. The theologian/author of the Dubuque Declaration, Donald G. Bloesch—though critical of the liberalizing trend of the UCC—was "dissatisfied with the theological right (fundamentalism and certain strands of evangelicalism)" and his critique of the UCC "was tempered by his warnings of conservative orthodoxy's missteps."[4] To the same effect is the BWF policy of supporting women in the ministry and racial minorities.[5] Other gatekeeper organizations will reflect sexist and antidiversity attitudes.

Or maybe BWF continues to believe, or hope, that their views will eventually prevail based on an apocalyptic view of the future of the UCC. Consider this recent statement from the BWF executive director: "It is my conviction that when the UCC and the other mainline denominations fragment . . . those who have had the clearest witness will have a role to play much as we saw happen in the sudden fragmentation of the Soviet Union."[6]

In any case, BWF has not championed schism from the church body to the extent that other gatekeeper organizations would do.

———·———

With his travels, Pastor Bill Johnson had established a national network of gay and lesbian leaders, but the UCC Gay Caucus existed initially as a mailing and telephone list. By the end of the decade of the seventies, it was time for the network to gather face to face for the first time.

A handful of persons arrived in Rochester, New York, in 1981 for the first national gathering of the Coalition,[7] and fifteen gathered from around the country for a second national gathering a year later. They planned a "ministry of presence" at General Synods. Singing to the delegates in the hallways would become a tradition, and the singing actually became quite polished. "Singing For Our Lives," aka "We Are a Gentle, Angry People," the Holly Near song written in response to the assassinations of Harvey Milk and George Moscone in 1978, would become the gay anthem; eventually, the Coalition singers would be invited to sing inside the plenary hall for the assembled delegates and visitors in General Assembly worship.[8]

The birth and development of the Coalition would parallel similar homophile groups within sister denominations during the same time frame of the late seventies and early eighties: Integrity (Episcopal), Lutherans Concerned, More Light Presbyterians, and Methodist Affirmation/Reconciling Congregations. Each of these would serve two essential purposes: as an advocacy group and as a community where gays and lesbians found sanctuary.

As to this latter characteristic, UCC Pastor Barbara Lohrbach offers a lifesaving example. In 2003, her sixteen-year-old daughter confided to her that she was a lesbian contemplating suicide. What should a mother do? Who to turn to for help and support? Pastor Lohrbach delivered her daughter to the annual gathering of the Coalition and into the care of fellow gays and lesbians. The daughter discovered a safe and nurturing community that changed her life and impelled her forward; in 2012, the daughter was finishing seminary.[9]

UCC Pastor John MacIver Gage of Connecticut offered his own experience of the Coalition. "We come to find people who are like ourselves, to find sanctuary with like hearts and minds, with people who know the experience of our own flesh. That is an incredibly powerful gift the Coalition has offered since the beginning." He also noted learning from others unlike himself whose experience he could not know; lesbians, transgendered folk, and persons of color.[10]

Similar stories and sentiments would be echoed over and over again in each of the homophile organizations.

NOTES

1. "Short History of BWF!" on the website of Biblical Witness, accessed April 16, 2012, http://www.biblicalwitness.org/short_history_of_bwf.htm.

2. Biblical Witness Fellowship, "The Dubuque Declaration," Dubuque, Iowa (November 17, 1983), on the website of the United Church of Christ, http://www.ucc.org/education/polity/pdf-folder/the-dubuque-declaration.pdf.

3. *The Living Theological Heritage of the United Church of Christ*, Frederick R. Trost and Barbara Brown Zikmund, eds., vol. 7, *United and Uniting* (Cleveland: Pilgrim Press 2005), 342–43.

4. John Dart, "Theologian Bloesch, 82, Sought Renewal in UCC while Resisting Literalists," *The Christian Century* (October 5, 2010): 15.

5. "Fact vs. Fiction," on the website of Biblical Witness, accessed April 17, 2012, http://www.biblicalwitness.org/fact_vs.htm.

6. "Why We Stay," on the website of Biblical Witness, accessed April 16, 2012, http://www.biblicalwitness.org/BWFStay.htm.

7. According to a private e-mail to the author from Andy Lang, Executive Director of the UCC Coalition (April 18, 2012), the "UCC Gay Caucus" became "The United Church Coalition for Gay Concerns" in 1979. At the First National Gathering held in Rochester in June 1981, that name was revised slightly to "United Church Coalition for Lesbian/Gay Concerns," and later to the "UCC Coalition for Lesbian/Gay/Bisexual/Transgender Concerns" around 2000.

8. Rev. Lois Powell, private interview.

9. Rev. Barbara Lohrbach, statement of gratitude spoken to the 2012 Coalition gathering at Elmhurst College, June 25, 2012. The author was present for this gathering and heard the statement, which was later confirmed in private e-mails from Lohrbach to the author August 1, 2012.

10. Rev. John MacIver Gage, statement spoken to the 2012 Coalition gathering at Elmhurst College, June 25, 2012. The author was present for this gathering and heard the statement, which was later confirmed in private e-mails from Gage to the author July 12, 2012.

* 8 *

OPEN AND AFFIRMING

Our journey now brings us to 490 Riverside Drive in the upper west side of Manhattan, an address sandwiched between Broadway Avenue and the Henry Hudson Parkway along the Hudson River. Here we find the high steeples of the famous Riverside Church. A national park dedicated to President Ulysses S. Grant is across the street (yes, he's there in his tomb), and the campus of Columbia University is all around.

Previously, we encountered Pastor Harry Emerson Fosdick, an early advocate for clergy to take on the role of counselors. Fosdick was the founding pastor of Riverside Church. With Pastor Fosdick's leadership and his friend John D. Rockefeller's money, Riverside Church was constructed at this address during the late twenties, and Fosdick became the first pastor in 1930. The interdenominational church has ties to American Baptists and the UCC and has been the scene of famous speeches and famous persons making the speeches—King, Clinton, Mandela, and many more.

Pastor Bill Johnson moved from San Francisco to New York City in June 1977. In the fall, he met with the senior pastor of the Riverside Church, William Sloane Coffin, whom he had known since college, and Johnson proposed the creation of a parish-based ministry for lesbians and gays at Riverside. At first, Coffin was uncertain, asserting that there were not many such folks at Riverside.

"There are enough gays and lesbians, just in the chancel choir," Johnson replied.

Coffin was persuaded that he needed to educate himself more on the needs of America's "newest" minority. By spring of 1978, Coffin and Johnson agreed that Riverside would host two after-worship forums on homosexuality and the church. Johnson invited Carter Heyward, a Union Seminary doctoral student and Episcopal priest, recently of the Philadelphia Eleven (see "Part Two: The Episcopalians"), and other movement leaders on the NCC Task Force on Gay People in the Church, to be presenters. More than thirty persons attended, and at the end of the second session the assembled group agreed there was a need for a new organization at Riverside. The result was "Maranatha, Riversiders for LGBT Concerns," the first parish-based LGBT ministry within the UCC. Maranatha participated in the gay pride march that year and would develop into a significant New York City LGBT-Christian ministry. Coffin would soon emerge as one of the nation's strongest allied voices for the rights of LGBT people.

As we shall see, congregationally based LGBT ministries would spring up across the ecumenical denominations in the late seventies and early eighties. Later known as the "welcoming church movement," the congregational gay ministry of Riverside Church in upper Manhattan would have parallels in sister denominations, starting with the Presbyterian "More Light " program in 1978—which also originated in the upper west side of Manhattan. From this example, the Methodist "Reconciling Congregations Program" followed in 1982 and the Lutheran "Reconciled in Christ" program in 1983 (later renamed to "Reconciling in Christ"). A UCC "More Light" resolution at General Synod 1983 was pulled back and taken off the table by its supporters rather than face defeat, but that temporary setback proved to be the genesis of the Open and Affirming UCC movement.

Somerset, Massachusetts, is a working-class community south of Boston. A neighborhood women's softball team with "E R A" emblazoned across their T-shirts would prove to be far more powerful than mere athletic exploits on the field would indicate. They were not sponsored by a laundry detergent as many assumed; instead, they were feminists and supporters of the Equal Rights Amendment. The team included several women who would become major players in the LGBT movement for full inclusion: Carter Heyward, irregularly ordained as an Episcopal priest and later a leading lesbian theologian; Mary Glasspool, the first lesbian to be consecrated as an Episcopal bishop in 2010; and UCC pastor rosi olmstead (she prefers no capitals) and her partner Marnie Warner, the team manager, would pioneer the UCC Open and Affirming movement.[1]

Marnie Warner had served on the Massachusetts delegation to the 1983 UCC General Synod. Warner was out to her friends, but she was not out publicly for fear of losing her job with the Massachusetts court system. Though she supported the "More Light" sentiment, she was not then a member of the Coalition, and she had been among those who disagreed with linking the UCC closely to the Presbyterian More Light movement. She had spoken against the 1983 More Light resolution before it was withdrawn from consideration. And then she went to work.

Along with her partner, clergywoman rosi olmstead, and Harvard Divinity School students Susan Harlow and Margarita Suarez, Marnie drafted a resolution on her dining room table that would be entitled "Calling on United Church Congregations to Declare Themselves Open and Affirming." At the 1984 Massachusetts Conference Annual Meeting, rosi presented the resolution. Standing on a theater stage, she fielded questions and biblical challenges for an hour; though she hadn't prepared for a scriptural debate, her answers were inspired, and the Conference adopted the resolution by two to one.[2]

A Massachusetts Task Force was convened, to be chaired by Rev. Ann B. Day. In January 1985, Rev. Day called a conference center to schedule the first meeting, and she referred to the "O and A" task force, which then appeared on the conference calendar as "O 'n A," and the popular name ONA was born. The task force arranged a Massachusetts "Day of Conversation" in May 1985, and then it was on to General Synod.[3]

Ames is not a regular stop on the national convention circuit, but this central Iowa city of fifty thousand hosted the 1985 UCC General Synod. Episcopal Archbishop Desmond Tutu managed to find his way from South Africa to offer the keynote address, and Rev. Jesse Jackson added to a spirited convention.

Marnie Warner and Pastor Ann B. Day were the delegates who would shepherd the Massachusetts resolution through the snares of General Synod. Assisted by allies from the Rocky Mountain Conference, who carried a similar resolution in their back pocket, the first struggle was in committee. At first, the committee wouldn't let the Massachusetts matter go forward because it was too similar to the withdrawn resolution from the previous General Synod, but when the Rocky Mountain Conference delegates pulled out their own resolution—"well then, how about this one?"—the committee relented. The Massachusetts Conference minister, who had been quiet in his support till then, offered a spirited affirmation of the resolution on the Synod floor. On the last day of General Synod, 98 percent of the delegates voted for the resolution. The Open and Affirming movement (ONA) within the UCC was born.

The resolution essentially did two things: a) it established that the UCC as a denomination was open and affirming and b) it encouraged regional conferences, subregional associations, and local congregations, as well as "related organizations" to issue similar pronouncements of welcome to the LGBT community. The resolution affirmed that:

- we believe that lesbian, gay and bisexual people share with all others the worth that comes from being unique individuals;

- we welcome lesbian, gay and bisexual people to join our congregation in the same spirit and manner used in the acceptance of any new members;

- we recognize the presence of ignorance, fear and hatred in the church and in our culture, and covenant not to discriminate on the basis of sexual orientation, nor any other irrelevant factor, and we seek to include and support those who, because of this fear and prejudice, find themselves in exile from a spiritual community;

- we seek to address the needs and advocate the concerns of lesbian, gay and bisexual people in our church and in society by actively encouraging church instrumentalities and secular governmental bodies to adopt and implement policies of non-discrimination; and

- we join together as a covenantal community, to celebrate and share our common communion and the reassurance that we are indeed

created by God, reconciled by Christ and empowered by the grace
of the Holy Spirit. . . .

- We do not discriminate against any person, group or organization
  in hiring, promotion, membership appointment, use of facility,
  provision of services or funding on the basis of race, gender age,
  sexual orientation, faith nationality, ethnicity, marital status, or
  physical disability.[4]

After this statement of the whole church, the resolution then encouraged the various subentities of the church to issue similar policy statements and used the terminology of a "Covenant of Openness and Affirmation."

Therefore, the Fifteenth General Synod of the United Church
of Christ encourages a policy on nondiscrimination in employment, volunteer service and membership policies with regard to
sexual orientation; encourages Associations, Conferences and all
related organizations to adopt a similar policy; and encourages
the congregations of the United Church of Christ to adopt a
nondiscrimination policy and a Covenant of Openness and Affirmation of persons of lesbian, gay and bisexual orientation within
the community of faith.[5]

———•———

ONA was off and running. After the Presbyterians in 1978, the
Methodists in 1982, and the Lutherans in 1983, the UCC would join
the welcoming church movement in 1985. In this case, it was not the
UCC that took the lead . . . or was it? The movement in the sister
denominations was always an outsider program promoted by the various
homophile organizations in critical tension with denominational policies.
For the UCC, ONA would not be an extrinsic program of the Coalition—it would be an intrinsic policy of the UCC itself—though once
established, it would be administered by the Coalition beginning in 1987.

Fittingly, Riverside Church of Manhattan became the first UCC congregation to issue an "Open and Affirming" statement, reflecting the

reality of their first congregation-based gay ministry instituted seven years earlier.

Although General Synod 1985 had adopted the ONA resolution and posture, it had not envisioned an ongoing administrative, organizational structure nor had it allocated any funds for the purpose. The UCC Coalition stepped in and provided the operational framework for the work and expansion of ONA.

Raised as a Southern Presbyterian and with Methodist and Lutheran family members from the Shenandoah Valley, Ann B. Day was ordained following graduation from Vanderbilt Divinity School in 1978.[6] For the next three years, she served as associate pastor at First Congregational Church UCC of Holden, a small city located in the center of Massachusetts between Boston and the Springfield/Hartford area. In 1980, her partner, Donna Engberg, entered her life, and they would later be married after Massachusetts law changed decades later.

In 1981, Rev. Day became active in the Coalition and within the Massachusetts Conference of the UCC. In 1984, after the Conference adopted the Open and Affirming resolution, Rev. Day became the task force leader and then worked with Marnie Warner for passage at General Synod 1985.

In 1987 when the Coalition assumed responsibility for funding and administering the ONA project, Day and Engberg took over and would serve as staff and inspiration for the next twenty years; they would be much more than merely the "keepers of the list." Under their leadership, the movement established a structure, a network of ONA churches, and a method of joining. Along the way, Day and Engberg developed resource materials, including sample resolutions, films, study packets, books, and articles.

Mostly, Day and Engberg encouraged intentionality and articulated the rationale for joining the movement. To the oft-heard refrain, "our congregation already welcomes everybody," Pastor Day responded that the actual experience of gays and lesbians had often been rejection, even when a congregation claimed "all are welcome," and thus an intentional statement of affirmation was necessary to counter low expectations.

Pastor Day balanced reasoned argument with tongue-in-cheek humor. Here are samples of each from her writings:

WELCOME means affirmation of personhood . . . such an affirmation conveys the good news that we are ALL children of God and brothers and sisters to one another . . . we are entitled to dignity, justice, and care . . .

WELCOME means recognizing fear and discrimination . . . it is essential for the Church to face the fear and prejudice which has surrounded gay, lesbian, and bisexual people for centuries and continues to cause untold pain and hardship . . .

WELCOME means advocating for justice . . . if we are to truly embrace gay, lesbian, and bisexual people in our churches, their needs and quest for justice must be incorporated into the life of our church's fellowship and ministries. . . .[7]

PRESS RELEASE from a long, long, long, long time ago . . .

HEAVEN—A news conference was held yesterday just outside the Ruby Gates. (The Pearly Gates are closed off due to repairs necessitated by deferred maintenance). Spokesangel, Gabriel, announced that, in an unprecedented initiative, God will offer self-revelation in the human community on the planet Earth (see map of the Milky Way). The Holy One will do this through a baby soon to arrive in a town called Bethlehem. Gabriel indicated that arrangements for the child's birth were complete; a woman named Mary will be the mother. No further details were offered.

According to Gabriel, the child, to be named "Jesus," will be "God with" the people. It is hoped that Jesus will clearly convey to all the depth and breadth of God's love and passion for justice, especially as they relate to the poor and outcast. The Holy One is reportedly determined to make the divine invitation to abundant life unmistakably clear and "will allow nothing to prevail against it, not even death."

Some in the "Communion of Saints Lobby" (COSL) objected to this initiative, contending that it should go without saying that "God so loves the world," and that means everyone. Citing previous covenants, a burning bush, manna in the wilderness, messages from the prophets, and other actions, members of COSL said it should be perfectly clear that God is compassionate and committed to the salvation of all the created order. Sending Jesus to proclaim the "good news" and to make explicit its application to particular folks (namely those lowly and marginalized), they respectfully deemed "unnecessary."[8]

By the late nineties, Pastor Day and the ONA movement had become important leaders in the broader welcoming church movement across denominations. In leadership gatherings, Day would share strategies with a veritable "Who's Who of LGBT" leaders within the ecumenical denominations. Two whom we will mention, in particular, were Mark Bowman, the founder and longtime leader of the Methodist Reconciling Congregations Program, and Chris Glaser, an early Presbyterian pioneer and later the editor of *Open Hands*, which had become the publication of several of the welcoming church organizations. We will encounter both these pilgrims along our journey.

In 2003, transgender persons were added to the ONA policy. ONA would become the largest of the various welcoming church movements, both in terms of actual congregations to join and especially in terms of percentage of congregations. By 2012, more than one thousand congregations had joined plus eleven (of thirty-eight) Conferences, and numerous other organizations such as seminaries.

NOTES

1. Marnie Warner, private conversation with the author, June 25, 2012.
2. Ibid.
3. Letter to the author, received from Ann B. Day, dated June 28, 2012.
4. United Church of Christ, *Calling on United Church of Christ Congregations to Declare Themselves Open and Affirming*, adopted by General Synod XV, UCC, Ames, Iowa, July 2, 1985. See http://www.ucccoalition.org/programs/ona/background/1985/.
5. Ibid.

6. Profile of Ann B. Day, on the website of the Lesbian, Gay, Bisexual, and Transgender Religious Archives Network, accessed April 19, 2012, http://www.lgbtran.org/Profile.aspx?ID=69. Additional details from private e-mail to the author from Rev. Day, April 19, 2012.

7. Ann B. Day, "What Is an 'Open and Affirming' Church?" mass mailing sent December 22, 1988.

8. "News and Views of the ONA Program in the UCC," *ONA Communiqué* 24 (Fall 1998).

✳ 9 ✳

BE PRACTICAL, BE PASTORAL, BE PROPHETIC

During the decades of the nineties and into the new millennium, the vessels carrying the Episcopal, Lutheran, Presbyterian, and Methodist gay community nearly capsized in stormy waters. Meanwhile, gays and lesbians in the UCC enjoyed fair winds and following seas. Conflict, marked by ecclesiastical trials and pitched battles during national conventions, dominated the sister ecumenical denominations during this period, but the UCC gay community was comfortably ensconced as full participants in the life of their church.

In 1985, the church had established open and affirming as church policy. In 1987, that policy became an organization when the Coalition agreed to administer the ONA program. The year 1987 also witnessed another development that would serve as both symbol of the UCC commitment to gay ministry as well as to accomplish practical results of that commitment.

In that year, three principal ministries within the UCC came together in a collaborative effort to deal with the developing HIV/AIDS epidemic. Their loose network would grow and evolve over the years; the collaborative effort would come to be known as UCAN (United Church of Christ AIDS/HIV Network).[1] Once again, Pastor Bill Johnson was instrumental in the creation and administration of UCAN and its various programs and offshoots.

In 1990, Bill was elected to the UCC national staff as a Program Minister of the United Church Board for Homeland Ministries, Division of the American Missionary Association, and served as

Minister for HIV/AIDS Ministries and Lesbian, Gay, Bisexual and Transgender Concerns for 11 years. In that position he helped establish the AIDS National Interfaith Network, which he served as Program Officer and as Interim Executive Director, established the United Church HIV/AIDS Network, co-authored (with Cindy Bowman) the UCC AIDS prevention curriculum, "Affirming Persons—Saving Lives," the first such curriculum for use in Christian education settings (1993). In 1999, he hosted "Called Out for Good," a consultation with openly gay, lesbian and bisexual UCC pastors focused on the special challenges and concerns of being out in parish ministry. With the Rev. Loey Powell, he advocated for domestic partner benefits for GLBT employees of the UCC national setting, which were put into place by the UCC Pension Boards in 1996.[2]

The practical benefits of these collaborative ministries are self-evident; what is striking, symbolically, is that the UCC since the late eighties and continuing has employed gay persons to administer a variety of programs and ministries of special interest to the gay community—openly and proudly. Though closeted gays would serve in the bureaucracies of other denominations, perhaps with a wink and a nod from their peers, the openness and intentionality of the UCC offered a "city on a hill" example that implicitly critiqued the institutionalized homophobia of sister denominations while simultaneously affording encouragement and hope to LGBT Christians everywhere.

After eleven years of service to UCC LGBT ministries, Pastor Bill Johnson stepped down in 2001. His successor (following a short-term temporary interim) was Rev. Michael Schuenemeyer. When U.S. presidents succeed one another, there is a tradition of a personal and private note left in the Oval Office desk. When Pastor Schuenemeyer arrived for work in his new position, he found a similar message from Pastor Bill Johnson, in the form of a sticky note. It stated, "Be practical, be pastoral, be prophetic."[3]

In 2003, the General Synod authorized a publicity campaign called "God is still speaking" with the slogan, "Never put a period where God has put a comma." Using print, broadcast, and social media, the campaign sought to "brand" the UCC as a progressive, inclusive community. That is, it was an attempt to tell the world what it had done. Though not organized around the ONA program specifically, the ONA theme of extravagant welcome was the central message of the campaign.

One TV ad in particular parodied gatekeepers as "bouncers" at the door of the church, deciding who would be allowed to enter. The acceptables were white and affluent, but the unacceptables were dark-skinned, the disabled, and—look quickly for the three-second cutaway—two men holding hands. The premise of the ad, extravagant welcome, distinguished the openness and inclusivity of the UCC from churches that gave mere lip service to welcome. When the ad was rejected by CBS and NBC, the UCC benefited from closer inspection, including favorable *New York Times* editorial opinion.[4]

The BWF was still around, and their publication, *The Witness*, offered a sarcastic response: "The rejection of the UCC ad would indicate that God is certainly still speaking and the message is clear. The commercial has been rejected because it sends an arrogant and negative message that the UCC stands apart from the rest of the Christian church who are portrayed as rejecting people based on how they look."[5] Years later, the Rev. Otis Moss would capture the spirit of the UCC identity expressed in the Still Speaking campaign. "God says I am the Alpha and the Omega, COMMA, who is, COMMA, and who was, COMMA, and who is to come, COMMA!"[6]

In 2005, the UCC stepped forward again. On July 4, 2005 (Independence Day), the Twenty-fifth General Synod adopted a resolution entitled "Equal Marriage Rights for All," which acknowledged that UCC clergy had been performing commitment services for some time and resolved that "The United Church of Christ affirms equal marriage rights for couples regardless of gender and declares that the government should not interfere with couples regardless of gender who choose to marry and share fully and equally in the rights, responsibilities and commitment of legally recognized marriage."[7]

Of course, like a Newtonian law of physics, for every action there is a reaction, and the marriage equality resolution would trigger an immediate, apocalyptic response from the executive director of BWF:

We are in the vortex of political and social forces that would sweep marriage and family into the confusion of a sexually licentious culture. Sadly, many leaders and congregations in the United Church of Christ have publicly sided with this culture against marriage between one man and one woman as the foundation of human order. The Synod of July 2005, tragically, gave a false and idolatrous religious encouragement to the spiritual forces that are in revolt against the sanctity of marriage.[8]

But that wasn't enough; immediately after General Synod, UCC conservatives arranged a hastily assembled gathering in Lexington, North Carolina. The Lexington gathering spawned another gatekeeper organization. Their "Lexington Confession" stressed adherence to orthodoxy, creeds, and Scripture precisely as the "Dubuque Declaration" of the BWF had done more than two decades earlier—and acknowledged that God was still speaking, but they claimed they heard God differently than the rest of the UCC.[9] Following the meeting in Lexington, an organization called "Faithful and Welcoming Churches of the United Church of Christ (FWC)" was born during a follow-up gathering in January 2006. Shall we call it irony when an organization whose very existence is predicated on gatekeeping calls itself "welcoming," or is it something else? Their website states: welcome to "all" (tied to repentance), welcome to "fresh" scriptural insight (consistent with prior understandings) and "new" ideas. As we shall see, gatekeeper organizations consistently misused words like "fresh," "new," and "reform" to encourage a return to old ways. "Those of us who dissent with the current direction of the denomination were simply trying to identify the common denominator that was drawing us together as "the loyal opposition" within the UCC . . . "Evangelical, Conservative, Orthodox and/or Traditional."[10]

As of April 2012, the FWC listed fewer than eighty member congregations on its website.[11] The FWC documents do not indicate why a separate "confessional" organization was necessary or why the BWF—which had been around for three decades—failed to satisfy their need for an outlet to express dissent from UCC policies.

In June 2012, Elmhurst College hosted a four-day Coalition conference that celebrated the fortieth anniversary of Bill Johnson's historic ordination. Pastor Johnson, of course, was the honored guest. The high esteem of the UCC LGBT community is exceeded only by its love of this once blond but graying teddy bear with dimples. On several occasions during the four-day conference, Pastor Johnson received long and warm standing ovations. At the conclusion of a panel discussion about Coalition history, Loey Powell tearfully paid homage to Johnson, not merely as an *iconic* historical figure and not merely as the *prophetic* voice that echoed through the decades, but as the *pastor* to an entire generation of LGBT Christians. Powell credited Johnson with thousands of hours spent counseling through dark nights. Though Bill Johnson is certainly aware of his role, not only in the UCC but across denominations, he retains a boyish, self-effacing humility.

"Be practical, be pastoral, be prophetic": these are signposts that guided the UCC road toward full inclusion. Along the way, we saw an out pastor in the early sixties, ordination of a gay man in 1972, a progressive sexuality statement in 1977, the development of an institutional open and affirming program in 1985, gays and lesbians serving openly and proudly in the church hierarchy beginning in 1987, and a statement of support for marriage equality in 2005.

To lead on socially progressive issues is simply part of the DNA of the United Church of Christ. We will now follow along as the other denominations set out on the trail blazed by the UCC, but the paths of the others will prove to be twisted, steep, and often impassable. Their journeys will be much longer than that of the UCC with ambushes, skirmishes, and conflict at every turn.

NOTES

1. The network originally consisted of the Church Board for Homeland Ministries, the Office for Church in Society, and the Council for Health and Human Service Ministries. "A History of UCAN," from the website of the United Church of Christ, accessed April 18, 2012, http://www.ucc.org/ucan/history-of-ucan.html.

2. Profile of Rev. Dr. William R Johnson.

3. Private conversation between Rev. Michael Schuenemeyer and the author, April 11, 2012.

4. Peter Steinfels, "Religion and Advertising," *The New York Times*, December 18, 2004.

5. Rev. David Runnion-Bareford, executive director, "BWF Responds to Ad Controversy," *The Witness* vol. XXVI, no. 1 (Winter 2005): 7.

6. Micki Carter with Rebecca Bowman Woods, "Electrifying Preaching Punctuates UCC Friday Night Worship," *United Church of Christ News* (June 27, 2009).

7. United Church of Christ, *Equal Marriage Rights for All*, Twenty-fifth General Synod (July 4, 2005), 2.

8. David Runnion-Bareford, *BWF Executive Director's Pastoral Letter on Marriage* (Summer 2005).

9. Hedrick's Grove UCC, "Lexington Confession," Lexington, North Carolina (July 7, 2005).

10. Rev. David B. Roberts, *What Is ECOT?* (October 10, 2006).

11. "A List of the Faithful and Welcoming Churches," on the website of Faithful and Welcoming Churches, accessed April 19, 2012, http://faithful andwelcoming.org/find.htm.

PART II

~

The Episcopalians

Samuel Seabury was a priest of the Church of England: born, bred, and ordained to ministry in the British colony of Connecticut. During the Revolutionary War, he remained loyal to the Crown and was briefly imprisoned by revolutionary troops before taking refuge with the King's army in New York City. Following the war, he understood that his world had changed, and he adapted; he remained in America with loyalties to the new nation. When he was elected to be a bishop by fellow Connecticut clergy in 1783, there were no Anglican bishops to consecrate him, and he sailed to London, but then another problem arose. Bishops within the Church of England were required to pledge allegiance to the Crown. He turned to other Anglicans wary of the King, the Scottish Episcopal Church, and he was consecrated in Aberdeen in 1784. This caused British Parliament to eliminate the requirement that international bishops swear allegiance to the Crown. Bishop Seabury returned to Connecticut and became a leader in the emerging Episcopal Church, with historical ties to the Church of England but not subject to her control.

The Anglican Communion was born, and the Episcopal Church became the first Anglican Province outside the British Isles.

The Episcopal Church (TEC) continues to participate in the world-wide Anglican Communion as an autonomous province, now one of thirty-eight such provinces internationally. The Communion consists of the heirs of the Church of England, an ecclesiastical remnant of the British Empire. With a common heritage, the autonomous national and regional churches of the communion come together to consult and to collaborate, but the communion is not a governing body. The various churches of the communion have traditionally held the mother church in high esteem and especially the archbishop of Canterbury.

Recent growth in the Communion has primarily been in developing nations, and especially Africa. In 1951, there were two Anglican dioceses in Nigeria: by 1977, sixteen; by 2000, seventy-six; by 2007, one-hundred-twenty-one.[1] The African Church has developed in patriarchal societies in which polygamy is still practiced, female genital circumcision is wide-spread, and morally stringent Islam has competed for new converts side by side with Christianity. In particular, societal attitudes toward homo-sexuality are draconian and unenlightened.[2]

With technological advances in communications and travel, the African Anglicans had a window into America. They didn't like what they saw. Perhaps it was merely the clash of cultures, perhaps it was anti-Americanism, perhaps it was the pride and independence of coming of age, or perhaps it was the perceived threat to their own patriarchal values, but the African Anglicans exploded with righteous condemnation in response to the advances in the Episcopal Church regarding women priests, women bishops, and LGBT clergy. As we shall see, the Episcopal path toward full inclusion would pass through minefields placed by for-eign provocateurs associated with international conspiracies. The bonds of affection that held the Anglican Communion together would be severely tested.

TEC is divided into one-hundred-plus regional dioceses (a few are outside the United States), which vary considerably in geographical and membership size. Each diocese is led by a bishop elected without term by a diocesan convention (bishops elsewhere in the Communion are appointed). A bishop's election by a diocese is subject to national church consent, which is usually a mere rubber stamp approval following a tradition of diocesan autonomy and prerogative.

In addition to the diocesan bishop (called the "ordinary"), larger dioceses sometimes elect bishops suffragan, who assist the ordinary and have tenure until death or retirement. Other dioceses hire, on a year-to-year basis, assistant bishops, who serve at the pleasure of the ordinary. This practice eliminates the necessity for the search process, and the assistants are frequently retired bishops from other jurisdictions. Successors to diocesan bishops are often elected to serve concurrently until the death or retirement of the diocesan bishops, and these successor bishops are known as bishops coadjutor. All bishops diocesan, bishops suffragan, and bishops coadjutor, active and retired, are eligible to participate in the House of Bishops, but only bishops ordinary can vote on certain matters designated by the constitution (such as the election of a presiding bishop).

The governing authority of TEC is vested in the General Convention, which meets once every three years, but there is great diocesan autonomy, and Episcopal polity could rightly be characterized as a confederation. The General Convention enacts resolutions and canons (church law), and we will see later disagreements over the effect of noncanonical resolutions and the extent to which they bound the actions of diocesan bishops. The House of Bishops serves as the "upper chamber" of the bicameral legislative structure at General Convention and also functions during the triennium in an advisory capacity. The House of Deputies consists of laity and clergy elected by their respective dioceses. Legislative actions may arise in either house but require the concurrence of both houses to be adopted.

The House of Bishops elects a presiding bishop, who must receive the consent of the House of Deputies, who presides over the House of Bishops and many other church ministries and boards, and who serves as the chief ecumenical officer of the church, including as one of thirty-eight "primates" within the Anglican Communion. Each diocese and the national church elects a standing committee that functions much like a bishop's privy council.

TEC is the most "Catholic" of the ecumenical protestant churches: bishops are considered to be within the "apostolic succession" and are chosen for life; worship frequently consists of a "high church" liturgy (especially congregations within the "Anglo-Catholic" tradition); and the denomination has a strong patriarchal tradition, which is where our Episcopal journey begins.

NOTES

1. The Church of Nigeria, accessed June 15, 2012, http://www.anglican-nig.org/main.php?k_j=24.

2. There are exceptions, of course. The Anglican Church of Southern Africa, the church of Archbishop Desmond Tutu, has a very progressive history.

✳ IO ✳

THE DENIAL OF ME AS A CHILD OF GOD

The struggle for LGBT ordination is first cousin to the slightly earlier skirmishes over female ordination. In TEC, the issues were contemporaneous, intertwined, and demonstrate the close connectedness of the movements.

As points of reference, the 1956 General Conference of the UMC approved full clergy rights for women,[1] the first woman ordained in the PCUSA was also in 1956[2] (female ordination later contributed to a conservative Presbyterian schism in 1973), and both of the primary Lutheran bodies, the LCA and ALC, first ordained women in 1970.[3] Once again, the example of the UCC was ahead of the others—in this case a full century. The first woman to be ordained in the predecessor bodies of the UCC occurred in 1853[4]; yet, UCC female clergy remained rare until the women's rights movement of the sixties and seventies.[5] Compared to these, the Episcopalians languished well behind—women were not even privileged to serve as deputies (delegates) to General Convention until 1970.

In the other four denominations considered by this book, women's ordination was not as contentious as it would be in TEC, which in style and substance remained more Catholic, and thus more patriarchal, than its ecumenical Protestant sisters. The story of the "Philadelphia Eleven" is told as follows, which in many ways broke ground for the journey toward LGBT clergy, and not only in TEC.

Seventy-nine-year-old Jeannette Picard awoke early. She hadn't slept well during a steamy night in Philadelphia. Forty years earlier, in 1934, she had made history as a high-flying balloonist; with her husband, she had piloted a balloon to the stratosphere nearly eleven miles above Lake Erie, which seemed small from her vantage. Today, July 29, 1974, she would make history again.

For the first time in the history of TEC, women had been allowed to serve as deputies (voting delegates) at the 1970 General Convention. That convention also voted to allow women to be ordained as vocational deacons, a nonsacerdotal role but often a stepping stone to the priesthood. But, at the 1973 General Convention, a resolution to allow female ordination to the priesthood had failed; what was worse, John Maury Allin, a conservative Southerner and opponent of female ordination, had been elected to serve as presiding bishop.[6] The next General Convention would not meet until 1976, where the outcome remained uncertain—at best—and some grew impatient and chose to forge ahead despite the lack of legislative approval from General Convention.

Piccard's bishop at the time wrote: "Jeannette Piccard is a woman of causes. She loves a fight. She feels strongly called to the priesthood. I understand that those who are 79 years old have to be in a hurry."[7]

Alla Bozarth was another impatient woman who had completed seminary. Bozarth later wrote:

> I began to question the inconsistencies between the Church's teaching and practice with regard to women. I perceived that the Church which had taught me to believe in my human dignity had itself denied me that dignity. . . . I began to understand that I was unacceptable as a woman by the very Church that had taught me to celebrate my womanhood. . . . Eventually, anger subsided into heartache and deep loneliness. The denial of my calling to the priesthood was *the denial of me as a child of God* (emphasis added).[8]

Defying nearly two thousand years of catholic convention and the lack of General Convention approval, eleven women, aided and abetted by a few brave men, would force the issue. The women would become ordained "irregularly," but the Episcopal rite of ordination required a bishop to lay on hands. Dr. Charles Willie, a black professor from Harvard, issued a rousing call on June 14, 1974:

And so it is meet and right that a bishop who believes that in Christ there is neither Greek nor Jew, male nor female, ought to ordain any . . . person who is qualified for the Holy Orders. A bishop who, on his own authority, ordains a woman deacon to the priesthood will be vilified, and talked about, but probably not crucified. Such a bishop would be following the path of the Suffering Servant, which is the path Jesus followed. It requires both courage and humility to disobey an unjust law.

The church is in need of such a bishop today.[9]

After that, events moved fast. Not one, but four bishops answered Dr. Willie's call, and a rite of ordination was scheduled for Philadelphia a month later. Eleven women, including Piccard and Bozarth, would be ordained by the defiant bishops.[10]

On a blistering-hot summer's evening in Philadelphia, July 29, 1974, the feast day of Saint Martha (her sister Mary's feast day is a week later), the "Philadelphia Eleven" challenged the patriarchal traditions of Christianity. As the eleven ordinands vested in an anteroom in white albs and red stoles, spontaneous laughter and applause erupted in the sanctuary that swelled with supporters.

Carter Heyward, one of the eleven, remembered the scene:

We began to move slowly in toward the nave. Smiling, we nodded in salutation to several scores of our brother and sister clergy, vested and ready to fall in with us. . . . Approaching the door to the nave, my eyes began to pop. There was no aisle, no room to walk. Well over a thousand, maybe two thousand people were pressed in close to participate. The path to the chancel cleared itself as we moved steadily, if timidly, on through jubilant hellos, waves, hugs, flash bulbs and television cameras moving with us. When Bishops Corrigan, DeWitt, Ramos, and Welles stepped through the door, applause burst forth so resoundingly as to fill the space around and within us. The foundations of the Church seemed to tremble. I myself began to tremble. Tears ran down my cheeks.[11]

Fittingly, Dr. Willie delivered the sermon in the finest tradition of civil rights oratory, and then the historic deed was done. The bishops laid on hands, and eleven women became Episcopal priests.

The defiant actions of the eleven women and four bishops shocked the Episcopal Church. Even supporters of female ordination questioned the irregular process, fearing it would damage the legitimacy of the push for female priests. The next regular meeting of the House of Bishops was scheduled for early fall, but the recently elected Presiding Bishop John Allin, a Southerner elected by a coalition of Episcopal conservatives, called for an unprecedented special meeting during the dog days of August at a hotel near O'Hare airport in Chicago.

August is usually a down time, reserved for family and vacation, for the hundred-plus Episcopal bishops, so the emergency meeting pulled the bishops from Montana ranches, Martha's Vineyard, and Florida beaches; one came from a boat, another from a mountaintop. No one was happy to be there.[12] The hotel air conditioners, operating at full capacity, barely cooled the temperatures, much less the bishops' temperament.

The offending bishops were present, seated by themselves on one side with the appearance of defendants in a trial. The eleven women were also invited, but a preliminary procedural decision left them without voice, denied the right to speak on their own behalf, and they sat with the press and observers who squeezed into the too small gallery.

What would the bishops do? Order an ecclesiastical trial? Impose censure? A mild rebuke? Upon the bishops? The eleven women? Eventually, the bishops were censured, and a motion to simply declare the ordinations invalid passed overwhelmingly. Dr. Charles Willie, the Harvard professor who had played an important role in the ordinations, spoke to the assembled press and TV crews and angrily resigned his position as vice-president of the House of Deputies for the upcoming General Convention. The crowd cheered.

The next two years were tense and fractious, as each side mustered its forces in anticipation of General Convention in 1976 in Minneapolis. A second, less publicized, "irregular ordination" took place in Washington. The newly ordained female priests were widely invited to celebrate the eucharist in churches around the country. Attempts by conservatives to punish the offending congregations and their rectors were soon abandoned. Diocesan conventions passed conflicting resolutions.

In the meantime, something surprising happened; when the bishops gathered for their regular meeting a few months after the steamy O'Hare hotel gathering, emotions had cooled, and the bishops voted two to one to support female ordination, but it was merely a statement of intent; only the General Convention could enact such a change in the church canons.

The Philadelphia Eleven had the church's attention. Had they created the momentum for change?

The constitution of the Episcopal Church was written by many of the same men who had written the U.S. Constitution, and there are many parallels, especially the bicameral legislative bodies: the House of Deputies consisting of laity and clergy, akin to the U.S. House of Representatives, and the House of Bishops, akin to the Senate. As with the U.S. government, a measure must pass both houses. The resolution was worded as follows: "The provision of these canons for the admission of Candidates, and for the Ordination to the three Orders, Bishops, Priests, and Deacons, shall be equally applicable to men and women."[13] The House of Bishops was predictably favorable based on their earlier vote, and barely twenty bishops voted against the resolution.

The bishops and all interested parties moved to observe the proceedings in the House of Deputies where similar resolutions in the preceding General Conventions of 1970 and 1973 had been summarily defeated. The deputies' hall was a huge amphitheater; at one end was a raised platform that served as the dais in front of nearly a thousand seats for the deputies. Twenty rows of bleacher seats were filled along each side, and standing observers massed in the open spaces near the doors. The murmurs of excited conversation filled the hall until the chairman called for silence, and then it seemed that not even a single person was breathing.[14]

Routine matters are usually handled by voice vote, but on matters of grave importance such as this, a more deliberate process is employed called a "vote by orders." Each diocese is entitled to one clergy vote and one laity vote, even though they may have more deputies present. Thus, the dioceses vote internally to determine how the diocesan single clergy and single laity votes are to be recorded. Often, a diocese has four clergy deputies who vote separately from the four laity deputies, and the chair of each deputation has each person sign a written form signifying their vote. If the result is a tie (two for and two against), the divided vote is recorded as a "no," a further burden against passage.

After the arduous process of voting by orders, the chair called for a recess in order to count the ballots, and the murmurs swelled for the next twenty minutes but ebbed suddenly as the vote was to be announced.

The clergy voted sixty yes and thirty-nine no with fifteen divided votes (counted as no). Sixty to fifty-four—the motion passed the clergy.

The laity voted sixty-four yes and thirty-six no with thirteen divided votes. Sixty-four to forty-nine—the motion passed the laity.

"There was no cheering and no groaning . . . instead, I saw deputies on opposite sides . . . rush over to one another to shake hands, to embrace. Nearly everyone's eyes were filled with tears."[15]

The story has a pair of postscripts. First, the convention decided to receive the irregularly ordained women through a service of recognition without being re-ordained. Second, a year later in 1977 at the regular gathering of the House of Bishops, Presiding Bishop Allin, the conservative Mississippian, dropped a bombshell in his opening remarks, "I cannot accept women in the priesthood," he said, and he offered to resign if it was the will of the bishops.[16]

His conservative supporters argued that the church should honor his conscience, and theirs as well. Thus, the 1977 House of Bishops session adopted a "conscience clause" that served the immediate purpose of retaining the presiding bishop and also allowed other conservative bishops to refrain from ordaining women in their dioceses; later, the precedent of conscience would play an ironic role when the question became LGBT ordination.

Allow New York Diocese Bishop Paul Moore Jr. to have the last word. Moore was a leading progressive who supported women's ordination but who had disagreed with the "irregular" ordinations, believing that the church needed more time and that the regularity of official process was important. After the smoke had cleared, he mused that perhaps he had been wrong, perhaps the ecclesiastical disobedience had been necessary, perhaps history had been accelerated by the actions of the Philadelphia Eleven: "In retrospect, however, it seems doubtful that the convention would have acted positively had it not been for the Philadelphia ordination and the vigorous discussion it aroused."[17]

———

In the decades following the historic but "irregular" ordinations, the proponents of LGBT clergy applied lessons learned from the experience of the Philadelphia Eleven. Some traditionalist opponents of LGBT clergy suggest that the women's movement within the church created a slippery slope, and the church plummeted toward LGBT clergy. While I would disagree with the characterization, I agree with the central premise.

- Activists learned that aggressively pushing beyond barriers and moving past accepted standards can be effective (ecclesiastical disobedience).

- The same critical biblical scholarship that provided warrant for female clergy could be utilized to support full LGBT inclusion.

- With the ascendancy of women to leadership roles, the churches became more progressive.

The second half of this chapter will consider each of these in order, and we will conclude with an evaluation of the fears that feed misogyny and homophobia.

The road toward full inclusion of gays and lesbians would have many waypoints in which brave pilgrims pushed back against recalcitrant institutions and entrenched policies. Ecclesiastical disobedience, in the sense of an intentional disregard of policy, would often be an effective strategy along the journey toward full inclusion. The experience of the eleven Episcopal women served as precedent for presenting the church with a fait accompli and soon a de facto status became de jure.[18]

Thirty years after her ordination as one of the Philadelphia Eleven, Dr. Carter Heyward applied lessons learned. She defied her bishop in the Diocese of Massachusetts over instructions to his priests to refrain from performing same-gender marriages after they became legal in that state. Among her reasons for doing so, she stated,

I believe (as do many others) that, *for the Church to change, the Church must act its way into new ways of thinking.* The Episcopal Church will not be able to think its way successfully toward an inclusive gay-affirming reimaging of Christian marriage until there are gay and lesbian Episcopalians who are married. People act—only then do laws change. The canons and liturgies catch up with people's lives over time. That's how laws get changed inside and outside the church.[19]

Wayfarers on the journey toward full inclusion would frequently bump up against church leaders for whom unity and the good order of the church were higher priorities than justice for the gay community. When faced with paradigmatic challenges, institutions instinctively recoil into self-preservation mode. Central authority always prefers continuity rather than change. The words of Martin Luther King Jr. that challenged timid church leaders over black civil rights apply also to LGBT inclusion:

> I must confess that over the last few years I have been gravely disappointed with the white moderate. I have almost reached the regrettable conclusion that the Negro's great stumbling block in the stride toward freedom is not the White Citizen's Councillor or the Ku Klux Klanner, but the white moderate who is more devoted to "order" than to justice; who prefers a negative peace which is the absence of tension to a positive peace which is the presence of justice; who constantly says, "I agree with you in the goal you seek, but I can't agree with your methods of direct action" . . . who lives by the myth of time and who constantly advised the Negro to wait until a "more convenient season." Shallow understanding from people of good will is more frustrating than absolute misunderstanding from people of ill will. Lukewarm acceptance is much more bewildering than outright rejection.[20]

Just as Dr. King and others engaged in "sit-ins" in Birmingham, and just as the Philadelphia Eleven challenged two thousand years of patriarchy, LGBT activists would use ecclesiastical disobedience—"persistent annoyance"[21]—to prod a stubborn church into action.

Historian John Boswell offers appropriate context:

> Finding oneself in conflict with the church is a hallowed Christian tradition. Suffragettes, abolitionists, pilgrims, Protestant reformers, St. Joan of Arc, St. Francis, early monastics—almost every major reformer in Christian history was condemned and opposed by other Christians for beliefs or lifestyles or both. This might have been anticipated: the founder of the religion also encountered opposition and hostility from the authorities of his day, and he explicitly warned his followers that they would not endear themselves to the establishment—religious or secular—by pursuing his teachings.[22]

A second lesson learned from the ecclesiastical controversies over female ordination was scriptural. In a recent statement, Bishop Gene Robinson stated the matter succinctly,

> Religious institutions of all stripes are asking this big question: Could the church have gotten it wrong in using a few verses of scripture to condemn homosexual people, just as it got it wrong about using isolated verses to justify slavery and the denigration/ subjugation of women? More and more religious people and institutions are moving toward a "yes" in response to that question. The church has misunderstood God's will before, but over time, we get it right. I believe that this is one of those moments.[23]

Biblical authors, especially the apostle Paul, should be understood in their own cultural context. If the church could reexamine traditional perceptions of Pauline patriarchy, then why not his harsh rhetoric regarding same-gender sexual relationships? The basic analogy is simple; if Paul's letters may be contextualized regarding the role of women in church, why not apply the same hermeneutic to his writings regarding same-gender sexual behavior? When traditionalists argue that the church is setting aside two millennia of tradition, they may be right,[24] but the same may be said of the reevaluation of the role of women in the church just a generation or two ago.

Pauline attitudes toward slavery, the role of women in the church, and same-gender sexual relationships all require contextual understanding, and Paul's own inclusive, boundary-breaking egalitarianism is the best lens for interpreting his writings. It was no accident that Dr. Willie couched his ringing sermon in the language of Paul's letter to the Galatians—*no longer Jew nor Greek, slave or free, male or female*—and the same passage would be oft cited a generation later as the skirmishes over LGBT clergy heated up.

Presbyterian seminary President Jack Stotts, in a 1998 speech to the Covenant Network of Presbyterians, suggested that this same Galatians passage has become the functional canon within the canon of the last half century: "It is this oneness in Christ that makes all of us brothers and sisters. It is that oneness in Christ that opens places of shelter to those who have none. It is that oneness in Christ that elevates the virtues of solidarity and mutuality. This struggle for inclusiveness in the Church is the institutional incarnational consequence of unity in Christ."[25]

Here is a critical point.

In church discussions, conservatives will not be influenced by abstract reference to justice and equal rights; they need to be convinced by Scripture. A couple of slogans, often associated with evangelicals, provide a convenient entry point into discussions: "Keep the main thing, the main thing" and "What would Jesus do?"

Rev. Jack Rogers, former moderator of the Presbyterian General Assembly and Professor of Theology Emeritus, suggests a Christocentric hermeneutic with which Martin Luther and his "canon within the canon" would agree:

It seems to me that the church and every person within the church is faced with a choice: to witness to an ancient Near Eastern cultural bias of male gender superiority, or to witness to Jesus Christ and his redemptive life and ministry. The best methods of biblical interpretation, from the Reformation on down through today, urge us to reject narrow historical and cultural bias and instead to follow Jesus' example . . . Those who choose to witness to an ancient cultural bias will always be able to find certain passages, take them out of context, and turn them into church laws that benefit them and discriminate against those whom they dislike. Those who choose to follow Jesus will see Jesus as the center of the biblical story and interpret each passage in light of his ministry. Using this Christ-centered approach enriches our understanding of the gospel and brings us into a closer relationship with God and our fellow human beings.[26]

This is indeed the course the church followed in reevaluating the role of women, and the journey toward full LGBT inclusion would follow a similar scriptural path, avoiding the pitfalls of "proof-texting" the so-called "clobber passages." By reevaluating traditional scriptural interpretation regarding the role of women, the church dared to move beyond biblical literalism in forming policy. In many ways, this was the coming of age of critical biblical scholarship; though long accepted in academia, critical scholarship now moved into the realm of policy formation. The precedent of allowing critical biblical scholarship to inform policy regarding women's ordination, thereby overturning centuries of tradition, would offer warrant for the church to do the same in the debates over LGBT ordination.

In a moment, we will discuss the multilayered and complex problem of homophobia. As we shall see, one level of fear relates to the loss of a simple Sunday school faith where critical biblical scholarship is seen as a threat.

Third, there is statistical evidence that females, especially female clergy, tend to be more progressive than their male counterparts, which suggests that the increased role of women in church leadership positions would tilt their individual congregations and the church as a whole in a more progressive direction.

One need look no further than national voting trends and the "gender gap" in which women tend to be more supportive of Democrats than men. "A recent Gallup analysis [2009] confirmed the existence of a fundamental gender gap in American political party identification today . . . 41% of women identify as Democrats, some nine points higher than the 32% of men who identify as Democrats."[27] For even stronger results in a survey in a specifically religious sphere, consider the 2008 Presbyterian Religious and Demographic Profile: "Male and female pastors differ, on average, in their theological beliefs. While 51% of female pastors label themselves theologically as "very liberal" or "liberal," only 23% of male pastors do so. Similarly, while 62% of female specialized clergy see themselves as theologically "very liberal" or "liberal," that compares with 45% of male specialized clergy."[28]

On this issue, we agree with the conservatives who link an increase in female representation with a shift toward progressive policies. Here's an example, written soon after the ELCA voted to allow LGBT clergy in 2009: "The ELCA has a particular history that has compounded these problems. . . . Among them was a quota system [mandating equal female participation] that skews every committee, council, task force, synod assembly, and national assembly toward the 'progressive' side. . . . The losers, of course, are white male pastors."[29]

With this tacit appeal to sexism, we segue to the fourth, and perhaps most important point. Some suggest that misogyny (antifemale) and homophobia (antigay) are two sides of the same sociological coin.[30] In a patriarchal system such as traditional Christianity, the two are yoked as a paired tandem. Listen to Catholic priest Father John McNeill:

At the heart of all homophobia is feminaphobia and the repression of the feminine. Gay men are seen as a threat to patriarchy because they are frequently in touch with and act in accord with the feminine dimension of themselves. It is clear that feminine and gay liberation are so intimately linked that gays should give full support to women's liberation and vice versa.[31]

Once more, Dr. Carter Heyward speaks:

Fear is the primary spiritual energy of fundamentalism . . . fear of terrorists, fear of feminists, fear of lesbians and gay men, fear of immigrants, fear of "the other" . . . fear of a merciless God who smites his enemies.

It is not that this [fear-based] god is "unreal" or doesn't "exist." To the contrary, he is a powerful global force, based largely in men's fear and their need to control forces that seem, and often are, beyond their control—plagues of locusts and tsunamis, hurricanes and disease, planes that fly into skyscrapers and gun-wielding teenage assailants at Columbine, the simple teachings of an itinerant preacher named Jesus, and . . . the real power of women's sexuality and child-bearing capacities, and the ubiquitous presence of gay kids, gay parents and gay families. *Patriarchal religion is always born and sustained in the fear of dynamic social forces* [emphasis added].[32]

"Homophobia" and "homophobe" are loaded terms. They are often used in a pejorative manner to stigmatize opponents of LGBT inclusion, and the terms are abused when used in name-calling. Though gatekeepers will vehemently deny any element of "phobia" in their attitudes, it is true that fear, often deeper than self-awareness perceives, is invariably present in one form or another for those who resist full inclusion.

First, there is the level of *aversion*. This is what is commonly implied when the term "homophobia" is used. It is often expressed in terms of *loathing, disgust,* or simply a *discomfort.*

I am not gay; I am a straight ally. Yet, at the ELCA Churchwide Assembly of 2009, I experienced a homophobic reaction from a pastor from a rural Pennsylvania congregation. I was wearing a prayer shawl that identified me as an advocate from Goodsoil, the lobbying presence of a coalition of LGBT organizations. The pastor assumed I was gay, and when we sat next to each other during lunch, his body language spoke eloquently of his *discomfort*. He squirmed, he didn't look me in the eye, his conversation was guarded, he shrunk away from any possibility of an accidental touching. He was uncomfortable sitting next to me, and this was homophobia in the classic sense.

The McNeill and Heyward quotes above identified other levels of anxiety: fear of the feminine, fear over one's own issues of sexuality or masculinity, fear of the other, fear of uncontrollable forces, fear of a wrathful God.

The gatekeepers, by their own definition, are confessionalists. In this sense, a confession is a creed, a statement of beliefs or foundational assumptions, accompanied by an implicit dogmatic warning . . . *this ye must believe lest ye be condemned.* If one's salvation is tied to the truth of one's confessional principles, then defense of those beliefs will be a pitched life or death struggle. Fears arising out of the challenge to literalist beliefs are often behind the gatekeeper's impassioned defense of *their* orthodoxy.

For the confessionalists, the Bible—or at least their understanding of it—is the core confession, and they argue that the current debate is not about homosexuality per se but about biblical authority. The battle over Scripture may indeed be the crux of the matter, as the traditionalists insist, but for different reasons than they would acknowledge, and it still comes down to fear. Not aversion to gays or lesbians, but fear that their literalism may be a house built on sand. *This ye must believe lest ye be condemned.*

Dare not question; dare not wonder; dare not test preconceptions; dare not consider experience or allow for reason. It is Galileo versus the Pope; it is evolution versus creationism; it is fear of rationalism and the "historical-critical" method of biblical study. The theology of the *Word* is abused, and the Bible becomes the *words* of God (watch a biblicist cringe at the suggestion that God didn't write the Bible). Though far more erudite than the unthinking literalism of a Jerry Falwell, it is nevertheless a strain of fundamentalism that the gatekeepers defend. "Soft literalism" is what theologian Marcus Borg calls it, and he suggests all the impediments to a "paradigm shift" are in play. Borg adds that the defenders of the old paradigm maintain that "believing is the central requirement; it is *believing* that will save you."[33] Thus, if their literalist beliefs fail, their salvation is jeopardized. If the tides wash away the house built on sand, what is left? Frightening, indeed.

Noted clergyman William Sloane Coffin Jr. of Riverside Church in Manhattan stated the matter forthrightly, suggesting that the misuse of Scripture reveals that homophobia not homosexuality is the root problem:

> Clearly, it is not Scripture that creates hostility to homosexuality, but rather hostility to homosexuality that prompts certain Christians to retain a few passages from an otherwise discarded law code. The problem is not how to reconcile homosexuality with scriptural passages that appear to condemn it, but rather how to reconcile the rejection and punishment of homosexuals with the love of Christ. I do not think it can be done.[34]

Bishop Gene Robinson, whose story we will soon consider, suggests it is the fear of being wrong that paralyzes those who refuse to dialogue: "My speech in a conservative diocese can be scary to conservatives only because my witness might be compelling. . . . Maybe the real fear in allowing people to listen to me is that I *might not* appear crazy, immoral, illogical, or faithless."[35]

Why have gays and lesbians in the church been subjected to unrelenting spiritual abuse? Because the struggle for LGBT inclusion has become a proxy battle in which LGBT Christians and their allies have become the scapegoat for modernity, for historical-critical exegesis, for the purveyors of rationalism who would question the literalism of the gatekeepers—all complex influences that threaten a simple faith.

The resistance to LGBT inclusion is merely the latest instance of a cultural/religious struggle that dates to the Renaissance and Reformation. It is supremely ironic that supposed heirs of Luther, Calvin, Knox, Hooker, and Wesley now retreat behind hoary old tradition to fend off the reforms of this era and to allay their fears of modernity; they would have the reformed church cease reforming.

First the women and then the LGBT community would use critical biblical exegesis that focused on the life and teachings of the man from Nazareth rather than culturally conditioned passages that reflected an ancient, patriarchal worldview. This has shaken the gatekeepers to their confessional core and provoked an apocalyptic response. The gatekeepers are right; their gay-bashing is not about gays—instead, it is a visceral, frightened reaction to the march of time.

Even the fearmongers, who manipulate the fears of others to drive an agenda, may be motivated by their own fears of liberal elites—the media, the government, church leaders, Hollywood—who are leading the nation off the cliff of modernity.

So, yes, homophobia is an apt term, even though fear is a complex, multivalent, and subtle phenomenon seldom recognized in self. Telltale clues are intemperate speech, an unwillingness to dialogue, and disproportionate attention to gay sex. Proof-texting the Bible and reliance on outdated or junk science becomes a justification for irrational motivations. And there's the rub; deep-seated emotions will not yield to rational argument. You can't rationalize with the irrational. That's why the journey will be long and arduous.

The spirit of reform and egalitarian, inclusive impulses—once freed from the shackles of tradition—will blow where the spirit blows. Women have blazed the trail to an inclusive priesthood of all believers—not just male and not just straight. Alla Bozarth's lament—*the denial of me as a child of God*—would resonate in a religious culture that made gays and lesbians lesser citizens of God's church on earth, and a woman's cry for human dignity makes common cause with others burdened with the weight of oppressive institutions and policies.

> For so many centuries, we have looked at the world through straight, white, male eyes. Even those of us who are neither straight, white, nor male have done so, confusing that viewpoint with reality, dismissing other points of view as irregular. There is nothing wrong with a straight white male perspective, but it is very limited and one dimensional.
>
> We diminish ourselves and render the world drab and lifeless if we do not, like Jesus, display a wild and extravagant embrace of all creation; if we do not allow our spheres of sight to converge and bring us a vision that is multi-dimensional.[36]

The march toward women's ordination provides path, precedent, and permission. Traditionalist opponents of LGBT clergy are correct in this much: the women's movement in the 1960s and 1970s foreshadowed and provided impetus for the crusade to allow gays and lesbians into the pulpit a generation later.

NOTES

1. Vicki Brown, "Women Clergy: Church Marks 50th Anniversary of Full Clergy Rights for Women," United Methodist News Service, accessed December 9, 2011, http://archives.umc.org/interior.asp?mid=1021.

2. "Quiet Pioneer," from the website of the PC(USA), accessed December 9, 2011, http://oga.pcusa.org/ga217/newsandphotos/ga06066.htm.

3. ELCA website, accessed December 9, 2011, https://www.elca.org/Who-We-Are/History/ELCA-Archives/Exhibits/It-Did-Not-All-Begin-with-Ordi-

nation/Ordination.aspx. Also the biography "Pastor Barbara Andrews—ALC, 1970," accessed December 11, 2011, http://elcacoach.org/Bios/Andrews%20 Bio.htm. Each denomination had considered the issue in convention, and female ordination was approved by approximately 55 percent to 45 percent margins. ELCA Churchwide Assembly, "25th Anniversary of the Ordination of Lutheran Women," *Minutes* (1995), 77.

4. United Church of Christ, "UCC Celebrates an Anniversary: 150 Years of Women Clergy," accessed December 9, 2011, http://www.ucc.org/ucnews /sep03/ucc-celebrates-an.html.

5. Clyde Steckel, private e-mail to the author, dated December 11, 2011.

6. Bishop John Shelby Spong, *Here I Stand: My Struggle for a Christianity of Integrity, Love, and Equality* (San Francisco: HarperCollins, 2000), 7. In this autobiography, Bishop Spong writes of John Maury Allin, the Mississippi conservative who was elected presiding bishop in 1973: "a deeply partisan person with little or no capacity to embrace reality beyond his conception of it. He also had tremendous control needs."

7. "Religion: Celebration of Defiance," *Time* (November 11): 1974.

8. Alla Renee Bozarth, *Womanpriest: A Personal Odyssey*, (San Diego: Lura-Media, 1979), 79.

9. Ibid., 93.

10. The eleven women were Merrill Bittner, Alla Bozarth-Campbell, Alison Cheek, Emily Hewitt, Carter Heyward, Suzanne Hiatt, Marie Moorefield Fleisher, Jeannette Piccard, Betty Bone Schiess, Katrina Martha Swanson, and Nancy Hatch Wittig. The bishops were Daniel Corrigan, Robert L DeWitt, Jose Antonio Ramos, and Edward R Welles. This list was published in Ann Fontaine, "Happy Anniversary: Ordination of Women in the Episcopal Church," Episcopal Café's website, accessed July 29, 2011, http://www.epis-copalcafe.com/lead/women/happy_anniversary_ordination_o_1.html.

11. Carter Heyward, *A Priest Forever* (New York: Harper & Row, 1979), quoted in Adams, *Going to Heaven*, 40.

12. Bishop Paul Moore Jr. of the Diocese of New York was both observer to and participant in the events of female and gay ordination in the late 1970s, and his memoir, *Take a Bishop Like Me* (New York: Harper & Row, 1979), serves as a primary resource for reporting these events.

13. Episcopal News Service, "History-making 65th Convention Ends," September 23, 1976.

14. Moore, *Take a Bishop Like Me*, 88.

15. Ibid., 90.

16. Ibid., 167.

17. Ibid., 191.

18. The ecclesiastical disobedience of the Philadelphia Eleven was itself learned from the earlier example of California Bishop James Pike, who had ordained a woman to the diaconate in 1967 despite church policy. In response, the 1970 General Convention of the Episcopal Church changed its canons to allow the ordination of women to the diaconal ministry. David Hein and Gardiner H Shattuck Jr., *The Episcopalians* (Westport: Praeger, 2004), 139–40.

19. Dr. Carter Heyward, *Keep Your Courage: A Radical Christian Feminist Speaks* (New York: Seabury Books, 2010), 23–24.

20. Martin Luther King Jr., *Letter from Birmingham Jail*, April 16, 1963.

21. Heyward, *Keep Your Courage*, 130.

22. John Boswell, Introduction to *Uncommon Calling: A Gay Christian's Struggle to Serve the Church*, by Chris Glaser (Louisville: Westminster John Knox Press, 1988), xiii.

23. Rt. Rev. Gene Robinson, "On gay bishops, what a difference a decade makes," *Washington Post*, June 7, 2013.

24. Boswell would disagree. His central premise in *Christianity, Social Tolerance, and Homosexuality*, 8th ed. (Chicago: University of Chicago Press, 2005) is that institutionalized Christian homophobia is a relatively modern development and that during various times and in various places the ancient church quietly accepted homosexuality.

25. Jack Stotts, "Unity and Diversity: An Enduring Agenda," Covenant Network of Presbyterians Luncheon Presentation, 210th General Assembly, Charlotte, North Carolina, June 15, 1998, accessed March 30, 2012, http://covnet pres.org/1998/06/unity-and-diversity-an-enduring-agenda/.

26. Rogers, *Jesus, the Bible and Homosexuality*, 109.

27. From the website of the Gallup Poll, accessed December 15, 2011, http://www.gallup.com/poll/120839/women-likely-democrats-regardless-age .aspx.

28. Presbyterian Religious and Demographic Profile 2008, on the website of the PC(USA), accessed December 15, 2011, http://www.pcusa.org/media /uploads/research/pdfs/fall08panel.pdf, 11.

29. Dr. Robert Benne, "How the ELCA Left the Great Tradition for Liberal Protestantism," *Christianity Today*, September 2009, (Web only), accessed May 23, 2013, http://www.christianitytoday.com/ct/2009/septemberweb-only /135-31.0.html. By constitution, ELCA voting members must be fifty percent

male and fifty percent female, sixty percent laity and forty percent clergy, and ten percent persons of color or whose primary language is not English. Dr. Benne was the director of the Center for Religion and Society at Roanoke College. During CWA09, he was a principal conservative voice during plenary session floor debates. The Center for Religion and Society headed by Dr. Benne resembles the Institute for Religion and Democracy (IRD), the neoconservative think tank that attempted to influence the Episcopal, Presbyterian, and Methodist churches. Though no formal relationship exists between these two entities, Dr. Benne has ties to Father Richard John Neuhaus, the former Lutheran cleric turned Roman Catholic priest and IRD founder, and Benne certainly shares the same neoconservative political views. See Benne, *The Ethic of Democratic Capitalism* (Fortress Press, 1981). See also the lengthy critique of Benne's politically motivated theology by Lutheran Pastor Ed Knudson, *Against His Church: The Sad Career of Robert Benne*, accessed June 27, 2012, http://www.pubtheo.com/page.asp?pid=1538. "Knudson does a remarkable job of documenting Benne's transformation, and the degree to which Benne has opposed his own church from its very foundation in the late 1980s. Even more usefully, he puts a finger upon the problems with Benne's theological method, which will surely be apparent to anybody familiar with other 'theocons' of the same generation. It boils down to a preference for economics to Scripture, and for ideology to compassion." Father Anonymous, Magdalene's Egg (blog), June 4, 2010, accessed June 27, 2012, http://magdalenesegg.blogspot.com/2010/06/bennes-sad-career.html.

30. Beverly Wildung Harrison, *Misogyny and Homophobia: The Unexplored Connections, Making the Connections* (Boston: Beacon Press, 1975), 135; G. Rattrey Taylor, *Sex in History* (New York: Vanguard Press, 1954), 72; John J. McNeill, *Freedom, Glorious Freedom: The Spiritual Journey to the Fullness of Life for Gays, Lesbians, and Everyone Else*, repr. ed. (Lethe Press, 2010).

31. John J. McNeill, "Misogyny and Homophobia," on the website of Dignity USA, accessed January 11, 2012, http://www.dignityusa.org/content/misogyny-and-homophobia.

32. Heyward, *Keep Your Courage*, 48–53.

33. Marcus J. Borg, *The Heart of Christianity: Rediscovering a Life of Faith* (San Francisco: HarperSanFrancisco, 2003), 11. Borg's entire book is an explication of the "two quite different answers to the question [what does it mean to be Christian?]. The first is an earlier version of Christianity; the second, an emerging vision. Both are present in the churches of North America today,

deeply dividing Christians. We live in a time of conflict and change in the church," xi.

34. William Sloane Coffin Jr., "The Prophetic Fire of William Sloane Coffin," Vanderbilt University Divinity School, *The Spire*, (Summer/Fall 1992).

35. Robinson, *In the Eye of the Storm: Swept to the Center by God* (New York: Seabury Books, 2008), 141–42.

36. UCC pastor Mary Susan Gast, Preface to *And So We Speak*, by the UCC Coalition for Lesbian, Gay, Bisexual, and Transgender Concerns, 1998, 9.

A LESBIAN PRIEST

While the Episcopal drama over female ordination took center stage, a subplot was largely unnoticed, but in the aftermath of General Convention 1976, it would rock the church. When General Convention opened the doors to women in the priesthood and female ordinands lined up to receive the blessing of their bishops and their church, the spotlight fell on a solitary figure, and murmurs swelled to a roar. Minor characters in earlier scenes now appeared as the protagonists in the unfolding drama. The female lead would be a shy and quiet woman born in the South; the male lead would be the bishop of the New York Diocese, a well-known leader of Episcopal progressives, whose insights as an observer informed our last chapter, but whose own actions would now become the storyline.

First, the prologue, a flashback to Father Robert Mary Clement, the independent Catholic priest who had marched in the first gay pride parade and who opened his Church of the Beloved Disciple to gays of New York City. When Father Clement had rented the Holy Apostles Episcopal Church building for his Sunday afternoon services, he dealt with parish priest Robert Weeks. Their relationship resulted in Father Weeks' own mingling in LGBT religious circles, though he was straight. In 1972, Father Weeks met Ellen Marie Barrett. Barrett was an out lesbian with a recent master's degree from New York University in Medieval History. She had a reputation as an advocate for gay causes, and she had authored several gay-friendly articles.

Barrett confided in Father Weeks; she wished to be ordained to the diaconate. The 1970 Episcopal General Convention had approved female vocational deacons, one of three levels of ordained ministry after bishops and priests. Vocational deacons were limited to administrative, clerical, or assistant roles and could not perform sacramental functions. Father Weeks arranged an appointment with Bishop Paul Moore Jr., who was skeptical because she was open about her sexuality, but he offered an interview.

I asked her to sit down on the sofa across from the wing chair where I usually sit when someone comes to see me. Ellen is tall, with dark brown hair conservatively styled. She, like many tall people, stoops a little as she walks. Her most arresting feature is her eyes, which appear honest, deep, and welcoming. . . . In conversation, she seems rather soft, until the discussion finds its way into an area of faith or conviction. Then you strike rock.[1]

Bishop Moore did not recommend Barrett, and the standing committee did not accept her for the diaconate in 1972, but the bishop's heart had been conflicted; he knew that there were many closeted gays in the ministry; why should Ellen Barrett be excluded because she was honest?[2] Meanwhile, Barrett would be persistent. She enrolled in seminary and also sought diaconal ordination through the Philadelphia Diocese, but that standing committee also turned her down. While Barrett attended seminary, homophile organizations were bubbling up across denominations, and she became involved with the Episcopal group called Integrity, serving as its first co-president.

Our journey now jogs briefly to Fort Valley, Georgia, to meet the founder of Integrity: Professor Louie Crew. Crew would be a bit player in the Barrett drama, and he would become a well-known character actor in Episcopal road shows for the next four decades.

The power of the post was preeminent for the early homophiles. Bill Johnson's mailing had inspired the formation of the UCC gay caucus. The first newsletters of Lutherans Concerned would go out "with an impact way out of proportion." *More Light* would be a newsletter before it lent its name to More Light Presbyterians. *Open Hands*, the quarterly journal of the Methodist Reconciling Congregations Project, would achieve awards for editorial excellence. So, too, with Integrity, the Episcopal homophile group. The Integrity newsletter actually predated and inspired the first meeting of organizers.

In October 1974, a few select Episcopalians around the country dis-covered a newsletter in their mailboxes bearing a postmark from Fort Valley, the county seat of Peach County, Georgia. The newsletter was called *Integrity: Gay Episcopal Forum*, and was circulated solely by Louie Crew, a young gay man just beginning his career as an English professor. Almost immediately, Crew received two calls from interested persons; coincidentally, they were both from Chicago, although they were strangers to each other, one a priest and the other a layperson. With Crew's encouragement from afar, those two and other gays from Chicago organized the first chapter of Integrity during a meeting at the apartment of James Wycliff in December 1974.

Only six months later, Integrity held its first national gathering at the Cathedral of the Chicago Diocese, boosted by the presence of noted theologian Norman Pittenger as keynoter. Pastor David Bailey Sindt of the Presbyterian Gay Caucus and the National Council of Churches Task Force attended as a resource person. Ellen Marie Barrett was elected to serve as co-president along with Wycliff. Crew noted that she was chosen to convey the message of gay men and lesbians uniting in this organization. Gays and lesbians working together in a common cause was characteristic of the Christian homophile organizations, a sharp departure from their secular forbearers. For instance, the Mattachine society had been strictly male and the Daughters of Bilitis strictly female.

In 1975, after compiling an exemplary record in seminary, Barrett returned to Bishop Moore and again requested ordination as a deacon. This time the bishop and the standing committee said yes. In December 1975, Bishop Moore ordained Barrett as a deacon at St. Peter's Episcopal Church, Chelsea, Manhattan. No one seemed to take notice of the momentous event. Less than sixty persons attended the ordination cer-emony, including a handful of church-lady regulars, a few neighborhood kids, faculty from a nearby seminary, and Barrett's mother, who sat proudly in the front pew with all the dignity of a southern lady. No one raised any objections.[3]

Nor was there any hue or cry from the press, the public, or the church. This ordination of a lesbian woman as a deacon simply did not seem to be noticed. Not yet. Meanwhile, Crew and Wycliff traveled, networked, and organized on behalf of Integrity. Crew stressed connections with the powers that be: "Every one of our leaders knows who's who in the Church in her diocese, in her parish, and in the Episcopal Church Center."[4]

Crew's salary as a young English professor at a small state college was minimal, but he had the benefit of paid airfare to attend seminars and conferences. He would pocket the airfare and travel to the conferences by Greyhound, stopping frequently along the way to network with bishops and others. The road toward full inclusion included bumpy bus rides.

As church officials prepared for the upcoming 1976 General Convention, Bishop George Murray and his commission were charged with drafting resolutions for consideration. Crew's networking and relationship building paid off. Bishop Murray willingly sat down with Crew and accepted Crew's input regarding several resolutions that recognized that LGBT folk had "a full and equal claim" as well as calling for equal protection under the law and the commissioning of a study report on LGBT ordination.

Seven months after Barrett's ordination to the diaconate, the scene shifted to the Minneapolis 1976 General Convention, filled with tension over the "Philadelphia Eleven" and the pending resolution to allow female clergy. Bishop Moore was onstage as a bishop and a recognized leader of the progressives. Ellen Barrett was offstage, asked by Bishop Moore to refrain from visible advocacy efforts, but Integrity was there. Integrity had exploded across the country with chapters in many cities; representatives of Integrity had been well received by official church spokesmen; and church leaders were accommodating to Integrity during the convention.[5]

In addition to the momentous actions regarding women's ordination, the 1976 General Convention also acted favorably on three LGBT measures, due in no small part to the efforts of Integrity:

- Resolution B-101: "That this 65th General Convention direct the Joint Commission on the Church in Human Affairs to study in depth the matter of the ordination of homosexual persons and report its findings, along with recommendations, to the Church at large for study."[6]

- Resolution A-71: "That this General Convention expresses its conviction that homosexual persons are entitled to equal protection of the laws with all other citizens, and calls upon our society to see that such protection is provided in actuality."[7]

- Resolution A-69: "That it is the sense of this General Convention that homosexual persons are children of God who have a full and equal claim with all other persons upon the love, acceptance, and pastoral concern and care of the Church."[8]

The 1976 resolutions offered a heaping plate for Episcopal gays and lesbians: authorization of a study report on LGBT ordination, equal legal protection of the laws, and "a full and equal claim . . . [for] love, acceptance, and pastoral concern."

Heady words, indeed, that lingered as the curtain fell on Act I, but as the curtain rose on Act II, the timpani in the orchestra sounded distant thunder. Enter, stage left, Deacon Ellen Marie Barrett and Bishop Paul Moore Jr.

Who could have known? Her ordination as a deacon just a year earlier had barely disturbed the church mice. The national convention had just closed with strong progressive momentum and powerful statements of LGBT affirmation. Ordination of females to the priesthood had been approved. Thus, when Deacon Barrett requested ordination to the priesthood soon after General Convention in the fall of 1976, Bishop Moore quickly agreed, but he was shocked at his clanging phone and his stuffed mailbox in the days before the scheduled ordination; what came before paled compared to what would come after.

Certainly, media attention was different this time. The New York press passed the story onto the nation. Three television networks asked to televise the ordination live, and a pool television camera was allowed into the sanctuary of the Church of the Holy Apostles in the Chelsea neighborhood of Manhattan. During the ordination service on January 10, 1977, a conservative clergy opponent, with hands shaking, read a statement that homosexuality was against Scripture and called the ordination a "travesty and a scandal." Afterwards, the bishop and the newly ordained priest addressed a gaggle of reporters. *Time* magazine ran a feature story.

"Why did you seek ordination?" Barrett was later asked.

"I remember Mrs. Rosa Parks' answer," Barrett replied, "about why she sat down that day on that bus: 'I don't know, just tired, I guess.' Yes, tired. . . . Tired of being second-class, good girl, virgin-whore, defective by nature. Tired of being told that the omnipotent God can't call me to the priesthood."[9]

After the ordination, the bishop received letters, hundreds of letters, from strangers and from friends. The occasional supportive, positive remarks barely offset the nastiness. Bishops from around the country reported unease in the ranks. Congregations threatened to withhold their financial assessments. His own priests in his own diocese disparaged Bishop Moore from the pulpit. Bishop Moore would later write,

> I had been through many crises both during the civil rights days and in the peace movement. I was used to criticism and knew that it was part of being a bishop. I had no idea, however, that the reaction to the ordination of a quiet young woman in a little downtown church would be more violent and last longer than all the rest of such experiences put together.[10]

In the midst of the tempest, Bishop Moore also experienced a moment of calm. On the night after the ordination, Integrity celebrated with a worship service.

> I could feel it come alive in the faces looking up at me. They knew what it was like to have to hide their love, their longings, their holiest feelings. They knew how it felt to be treated as less than human, as less than Christian, by the very church of their beloved Saviour.
>
> "Until now," one person said to me, "the church has only offered to 'help' us. That is the worst insult of all. We don't want that kind of condescending help."
>
> When I thought that perhaps I had let down the morality of the Church as so many said, I remembered those faces receiving communion and filled with love for their Lord. When I was told I had hurt the feelings of righteous Episcopalians, I thought of the faces hurt by years of prejudice and anger, and how those faces had been filled, that night, with joy.[11]

As winter turned into spring and then summer, all eyes turned toward the annual gathering of the House of Bishops scheduled for September

1977. What would the bishops do about the lesbian priest? Presiding Bishop Allin invited Bishop Moore to an advance meeting, and they agreed on procedures that would minimize confrontation and conflict. Then, as previously noted, the opening remarks of Bishop Allin, "I cannot accept women in the priesthood," shocked the bishops and momentarily diverted the attention away from Bishop Moore and Ellen Marie Barrett.

Eventually, a pair of resolutions were offered (a) strongly disapproving of the actions of Bishop Moore and (b) discouraging the bishop of California (where Ellen Barrett then resided) from issuing a license for Barrett to officiate as an ordained minister. First, an amendment to strengthen the resolution against Bishop Moore, to elevate it to censure, failed. Ultimately, both resolutions failed as well. Instead, a "pastoral letter" was composed to be circulated in the church. The letter contained the "conscience clause" discussed previously, which allowed the presiding bishop to remain in office in spite of his attitude toward female clergy and which allowed individual bishops and their dioceses to refrain from ordaining women. As to gays and lesbians, the letter stated, "Our present understanding of the Bible and Christian theology makes it inadmissible for this Church to authorize the ordination of anyone who advocates and/or willfully and habitually practices homosexuality."[12] The bishops had suggested a limited exception; homosexual orientation would not preclude ordination but only if the priest remained celibate . . . "anyone who advocates and/or willfully and habitually practices homosexuality" would be excluded. Whether or not Barrett was celibate was unclear, and some bishops protested when others questioned her private life, and that discussion ended.

Author Gary Comstock blasted this convenient but dubious distinction that the various denominations embraced as a foundation for church policy.

Such terms as "unrepentant," "self-affirming," and "practicing" have been written into formal positions of some religious bodies to describe the kind of homosexually oriented person who is not accepted. To be accepted one must be self-reproaching, self-denying, and celibate. One is not to declare frankly and openly love for or sexual intimacy with a person of one's own gender.[13]

This halfway measure would characterize the attitudes and pan-denominational policies of the churches for the next thirty years; homosexual orientation would not preclude ordination but homosexual behavior would. Perhaps it was not a sin to be a gay or lesbian, but it certainly was sinful to live one's orientation. Out of this false distinction between being and behavior comes the oft-repeated phrase, "love the sinner but hate the sin," that allows the church to comfortably ignore its institutionalized homophobia. This phrase and the banner on the church lawn that proclaims "all are welcome" are more about soothing the sensibilities of the self-satisfied than genuine concern for gays and lesbians. Despite the claim of love, gays and lesbians felt no embrace; despite the proclamation of welcome, gays and lesbians felt no hospitality.

Ironically, it is the unwelcome of the church that is the true sin of Sodom. Most Old Testament exegetes concur that the Genesis account of Sodom and Gomorrah is about ancient Semitic mores of hospitality. The words of Jesus and Old Testament references to the Genesis passage clearly identify the sin of Sodom as inhospitality. Rejection and mistreatment of outsiders is precisely the wickedness of Sodom.[14]

There is a further problem with the purported focus on behavior rather than orientation. The church's perceived need to control the bedroom left no room for consideration of the full depth and breadth of a loving human relationship, in which sexual intimacy is an important but limited aspect. Gays and lesbians were once invisible, and when they came out, all that some could see was sex, and other dimensions of their relationships remained unseen: tears and laughter; mutual support, encouragement, and nurture; subtle glances and stolen kisses; shared victories and defeats; squabbles and reconciliations; anniversaries; taking out the garbage and doing the dishes; helping the kids with homework; and falling asleep watching the ten o'clock news. The broad range of attributes of a committed relationship, including the positive benefits to the couple and to society, were simply nonfactors, squeezed out by a prurient interest in the "gay lifestyle."

One final scene remained, the 1979 General Convention, which received and acted upon the study report on ordination of LGBT persons commissioned in 1976. The study report positively suggested, "no human condition be made an absolute barrier to ordination." If a candidate was otherwise qualified, homosexuality should not preclude ordination.

But, it was not to be. The delegates to General Convention would reject the commission recommendation, and this would become a recurring theme across the ecumenical denominations. A convention would call for a sexuality study, a blue ribbon panel would be convened, and an exhaustive report would be issued, only to be rejected by convention and assembly delegates. Instead of accepting the recommendation of the committee, resolution A053 was adopted.

> Resolution A053: "That this General Convention recommend to Bishops, Pastors, Vestries, Commissions on Ministry and Standing Committees, the following considerations as they continue to exercise their proper canonical functions in the selection and approval of persons for ordination. . . . We re-affirm the traditional teaching of the Church on marriage, marital fidelity and sexual chastity as the standard of Christian sexual morality. Candidates for ordination are expected to conform to this standard. Therefore, we believe it is not appropriate for this Church to ordain a practicing homosexual, or any person who is engaged in heterosexual relations outside of marriage."[15]

If the progressives held sway in 1976, the conservatives had regained the upper hand at General Convention 1979. "It is not appropriate for this Church to ordain a practicing homosexual." These words were a stinging rebuke to Bishop Moore and lesbian priest Barrett and harsh rejection of the hope for full inclusion of the LGBT community.

But conservative bishops who had successfully sought an exception for conscience at the bishop's meeting in 1977 that allowed them to refuse to ordain women had unwittingly created an opening for progressive bishops to step in. Ironically, the progressives claimed a similar right to ordain whom they chose, contrary to the 1979 resolution, based on a similar right of conscience.

Twenty-one bishops signed a "Statement of Conscience," disagreeing with Resolution A053. According to Episcopal polity, the resolution was recommendatory but not prescriptive, and the statement of dissent from the bishops essentially said, "We'll ordain whom we choose to ordain." The dissent stated, *inter alia*: "We have no intention of ordaining irresponsible persons, or persons whose manner of life is such as to cause grave scandal or hurt to other Christians; but we do not believe that either homosexual orientation as such, nor the responsible and self-giving use of such a mode of sexuality, constitutes such a scandal in and of itself."[16] The official Episcopal News Service report following General Convention 1979 summarized the debate over adoption of A053:

What came out of long hours of often intense and passionate debate was adoption by both Houses of a resolution which carried with it the clear sense that the Church is still not prepared to welcome practicing homosexual men and women into the ordained ministry.

The key language of the resolution, which is not legally binding upon individual dioceses and local congregations but which, in the opinion of most delegates, will nevertheless be regarded as morally controlling, was the final paragraph in the report of the Bishops' Committee on Ministry:

"We re-affirm the traditional teaching of the Church on marriage, marital fidelity and sexual chastity as the standard of Christian sexual morality. Candidates are expected to conform to this standard. Therefore, we believe it isn't appropriate for this Church to ordain a practicing homosexual, or any person who is engaged in heterosexual relations outside of marriage."

The bishops had adopted this report as a policy resolution on Monday, overriding the recommendation of the Church's Joint Commission on Health and Human Affairs that "no human condition be made an absolute barrier to ordination."

Within hours, 21 bishops, whose number later rose to 23, had issued a "statement of conscience" affirming their intention not to abide by the recommendatory action but rather to deal with ordinands on an individual basis according to qualification.

Shortly after the vote [in the House of Deputies] an Eastern Oregon clergyman, the Rev. Jeffrey E. Sells, announced that he was associating himself with the dissenting bishops and asked other rectors and vicars to join him. More than 150 clergy and lay persons signed the statement.

There was substantial disagreement among many delegates as to the lasting effect of the split over the ordination issue, with most voicing the belief that it probably would not materially change the attitude or course of local bishops since those favoring ordination of homosexual persons could properly cite the recommendatory nature of the action.[17]

The backlash against women's ordination and Bishop Moore's ordination of a lesbian culminated in General Convention 1979, "the high water mark of homophobia," according to Louie Crew.[18] Ordained but ostracized, Ellen Marie Barrett would face a harsh journey.

As the curtain fell on the drama of the seventies, bad reviews suggested that LGBT ordination would have a short run.

NOTES

1. Moore, *Take a Bishop Like Me*, 40–45.

2. Ironically, Bishop Moore may have been one of those closeted gays that he wrote about. After his death in 2003, revelations came from family members that he may have been a hidden bisexual. A daughter, Honor Moore, wrote about her father's secret life in the New Yorker magazine and in *The Bishop's Daughter: A Memoir* (New York: W.W. Norton, 2008).

3. Moore, *Take a Bishop Like Me*, 3–4.

4. Crew, private e-mail.

5. Dr. Louie Crew, "A Brief History of Integrity," *Integrity Forum* 4.2 (December 1977–January 1978), accessed December 15, 2011, http://www.rci .rutgers.edu/~lcrew/pubd/briefhist.html. Dr. Crew is the original editor of Integrity publications.

6. General Convention, *Journal of the General Convention of The Episcopal Church, Minneapolis, 1976* (New York: General Convention, 1977), C-110.

7. General Convention, *Journal of the General Convention of The Episcopal Church, Minneapolis, 1976* (New York: General Convention, 1977), C-109.

8. Ibid.

9. Oppenheimer, *Knocking on Heaven's Door*, 159.

10. Moore, *Take a Bishop Like Me*, 100–105.

11. Ibid., 108–9.

12. Episcopal News Service, "Pastoral Letter Calls For Unity in Christ," October 7, 1977.

13. Comstock, *Unrepentant*, xiii.

14. Daniel A. Helminiak, *What the Bible Really Says about Homosexuality*, Millennium ed. (Tajique, N.Mex.: Alamo Square Press, 2000), 43–50. This book also contains a lengthy list of other publications addressing the Sodom and Gomorrah story.

15. General Convention, *Journal of the General Convention of The Episcopal Church, Denver, 1979* (New York: General Convention, 1980), C-93.

16. *Integrity Forum* vol. 6, no. 1, Advent 1979, accessed December 28, 2011, http://www.integrityusa.org/voice/1979/Advent1979.htm.

17. Episcopal News Service, "General Convention Summary 1979," September 27, 1979.

18. Louie Crew, "Changing the Church: Lessons Learned in the Struggle to Reduce Institutional Heterosexism in the Episcopal Church," in *Overcoming Heterosexism and Homophobia*, eds. James T. Sears and Walter L. Williams (New York: Columbia University Press, 1997), 347.

THE TIDE TURNS

In 1982, Ronald Reagan was in the White House, and Jerry Falwell's "Moral Majority" had helped to put him there. General Convention 1982 would be held in New Orleans and the Diocese of Louisiana, locales with well-earned reputations for jazz and jambalaya but not for progressive politics.

The bishop of Louisiana mandated that no Episcopal Church facilities would be available to Integrity and allies for eucharist during the convention. The two points of contention of General Convention 1982 were the efforts of Presiding Bishop Allin and his supporters to elevate Allin to the status of archbishop and to reverse the modernization of the liturgy that had occurred at General Convention 1976.[1] Allin was supported by the Prayer Book Society, which argued that the Episcopal prayer book of 1928 is "the last genuine Book of Common Prayer in America," with roots in the sixteenth century.[2] No inclusive language for thee. The Prayer Book Society would later expand its efforts beyond the liturgy and would hound progressive bishops with formal ecclesiastical charges.

It was not the best of times for progressives, and Integrity struggled to swim against the tide. The number of Integrity members in 1984 was the same as it had been in 1976.[3] The only good news was that Presiding Bishop Allin was rebuffed; he would not be named archbishop nor would the liturgy revert to "olde tyme religion." Better yet, his term would end in 1985.

Though the churchwide political ebb and flow was against LGBT inclusion in the first years of the decade, there were local, positive achievements at the level of the parish and in certain friendly dioceses. For instance, the Diocese of California founded the Parsonage in 1981, a peer counseling center in the Castro district of San Francisco, one of the nation's primary gay communities. California Bishop the Rt. Rev. William Swing was instrumental in creating and supporting the Parsonage. Much like the Council on Religion and the Homosexual (CRH) of the late sixties and early seventies, also based in San Francisco, the Parsonage sought reconciliation between the church and the gay community. Through the 1980s, the Parsonage provided spiritual support to a community wracked by the AIDS epidemic.

Eventually, the ministry of the Parsonage was taken up by Oasis California. Oasis communities formed in several dioceses in the mid- to late 1980s, with a similar goal of providing a welcoming, spiritual sanctuary for gays and lesbians who felt rejected in traditional church settings. Notably, the various Oases were not merely formed within a geographical diocese but were actually gay-outreach ministries sponsored by their dioceses.

General Convention 1985 would be convened in Anaheim, and the principal issue would be the election of a new presiding bishop. The term of Presiding Bishop John Allin would end; one of Bishop Allin's primary adversaries had been bishop of the Diocese of Newark, John Shelby Spong, who would later comment, "When Jack Allin finally lifted his dead weight off the life of the church by his retirement, new possibilities began to emerge."[4]

One of the four 1985 candidates to replace Allin would be bishop of the Colorado Diocese, William Frey, who had been an early and outspoken opponent of LGBT ordination. Back in 1977 when the bishop of New York, William Moore, Jr. was about to ordain lesbian Ellen Marie Barrett to the priesthood, Bishop Frey sent an urgent telegram to Bishop Moore:

Please, please do not go through with the ordination on Monday. Ordination of practicing homosexuals does not, underline not, represent the mind of the church, and it is plainly contrary to the teachings of Scripture which we have all been sworn to uphold. There are far more constructive ways to show pastoral concern for homosexuals than by attempting to bless that which God offers to redeem. Paul, you cannot imagine the tremendous harm you are doing to the rest of the Church. . . . Your proposed action appears to be totally irresponsible.[5]

Bishop Frey's phrase, "bless that which God offers to redeem," states the core issue exquisitely, even if his underlying premise is false. In church-speak, Frey merely restated the assumption that homosexuality was sinful, and that homosexuals must be contrite and repentant in order to receive God's forgiveness. Bishop Frey understood that Barrett's ordination would challenge the premise of sinfulness, and the gay activists promoted a radical notion—that their sexuality was part of their essential humanity, a blessing within God's good creation.

Traditional assumptions were under assault by the Bishop Moores and Ellen Barretts and Louie Crews, and the conservatives would fight fiercely. For Frey and his constituency, the very Bible and the very nature of church were threatened. In 1984 and 1985 Bishop Frey would mount a major offensive. First, he would found a conservative opposition group, with Integrity as his favorite scapegoat for the ills of the church, and, second, he would himself run for the office of presiding bishop to replace the retiring Bishop Allin.

Frey's group used pretentious alliteration in their name: "Episcopalians United for Revelation, Renewal and Reformation" (EURRR). Later, the group would become simply, "Anglicans United." Formed by Bishop Frey and a transplanted British Anglican bishop, the Rt. Rev. Michael Marshall, EURRR was after more than the LGBT community; they continued to contest women's ordination and fought tenaciously against the consecration of a female bishop in 1989 (Rt. Rev. Barbara C. Harris—see below).

There were four nominees for the office of presiding bishop: a pair of progressives (Bishops Browning of Hawaii and Walker of Washington, D.C.) and a pair of conservatives (Bishops Stough of Alabama and Frey of Colorado). Bishops Browning and Walker had been among the twenty-three progressive bishops who signed the "statement of conscience," opposing resolution A053 at General Convention 1979.

Episcopal elections of presiding bishop don't quite match the secrecy or ritual of the Roman Catholic College of Cardinals when electing a pope (no smoke signals), but the elections are private within a sequestered House of Bishops. On a beautiful California day in a church in Anaheim, Bishop Walker had a sizeable lead on the first ballot, and Bishop Frey finished last by a wide margin. By the third ballot, Bishop Browning had nudged ahead, and he was elected on the fourth ballot.[6] Clearly, the church was anxious to move away from the stagnation and repression of Bishop Allin, and his conservative heir, Bishop Frey, was not seriously considered by the House of Bishops. His candidacy had failed, and so, too, his agenda, at least for the moment, but he would become the lightning rod for the opposition to the emerging progressive direction of the denomination.

At a crowded press conference—"I've never been in this situation before," Browning said—the Presiding Bishop-elect was questioned on a variety of issues.

On women's ordination, he said, "I am tremendously committed to enhancing the ministry of women." He said he would begin with the National Church staff as a place for "incorporating women's talents."

On homosexuality, Browning said he differed from a 1979 House of Bishops statement that questioned the ordination of avowed and practicing homosexuals.

"I don't believe we should put anyone down," he said. "I don't believe that you legislate against people. In the Diocese of Hawaii, we have had a chapter of Integrity (the organization supporting homosexuals). I have tried to be as supportive as I possibly can be on gay rights at every level." He said he agreed with a resolution at this Convention to explicitly state that homosexuality can't be an obstacle to ordination.[7]

Integrity had successfully treaded water during the conservative administration of Bishop Allin. Bishop Browning quickly threw a lifeline. At his installation, he boldly proclaimed, "This church of ours is open to all. There will be no outcasts."[8]

Integrity took a deep breath and surged forward again on a changing tide. The period of stagnant growth was over, and Integrity doubled in size over the next decade, reaching seventy-five chapters and twenty-five hundred members.[9] By 1988, Integrity had become the most well-organized network at the triennial General Conventions.

Integrity spends about forty thousand dollars, which goes to housing for the [forty] volunteers (transportation and food are not paid), a booth, a nerve center, a hospitality suite, publications and other expenses. We divide the volunteers into a variety of task forces. Legislative volunteers, for example, monitor sessions of each house. Committee meetings begin at 7 AM.

The election of Browning and his support of "gay rights at every level" signaled a sea change that would quickly ripple through the denomination as Browning's leadership appointments replaced Allin's entrenched appointees. One progressive upgrade was the Standing Commission on Human Affairs and Health headed by Bishop George Hunt of Rhode Island. We'll return to this commission in a moment, but first we'll jump ahead to 1989 and the controversial, contested consecration of Barbara C. Harris, a black executive who entered seminary at the age of fifty and an outspoken liberal.

The 1976 enabling resolution for ordaining women clearly applied to all three orders of ordained ministry: bishops, priests, and deacons. Thus, there was nothing further required for the election and consecration of a woman bishop except to do it.

Some Anglicans within the worldwide Communion attempted to ambush the Episcopalians before it happened. Later, we will consider the decennial Lambeth Conferences in greater depth (an England gathering of all bishops of the Communion at the invitation of the archbishop of Canterbury). For now, we simply note that the bishops from developing nations at Lambeth 1988 were extremely uncomfortable at the possibility of the consecration of a female bishop. Lambeth 1988 overwhelmingly passed a resolution that focused upon the offended consciences of the bishops from developing nations. In Anglican parlance, the twenty-five provinces from developing nations are often referred to as the "Global South." This resolution presaged the later battle over LGBT ordinations to the priesthood and the episcopate, which also emphasized the wounded sensibilities of Global South Anglicans rather than issues of justice. The seeds of animosity between Global South Anglicans, especially Africans, and the Episcopalians over patriarchal, cultural issues that were sown in 1988 would ripen into full-blown religious warfare in later years.[10]

After playing minor roles in two earlier historic moments, Barbara C. Harris made history in 1989 as the first female consecrated as a bishop in the entire Anglican Communion. In 1965, Harris had participated in Martin Luther King's Selma march, and in 1974, she had interrupted a business trip in order to serve as the crucifer (cross-bearer) during the 1974 irregular ordination rite for the Philadelphia Eleven. In 1980 at age fifty, Harris left the private business world and became ordained, first as a deacon and then a priest. During the 1980s, she served as executive director of the Episcopal Church Publishing Company, which promoted peace and justice issues through *The Witness*, and Harris contributed her own column, *A Luta Continua* (the struggle continues).[11]

Though she was not a lesbian and gay issues not her primary concern, she was always an ally, and she shared common adversaries within TEC, notably the EURRR. Opponents mounted an intense lobbying effort and many claimed they would not recognize Harris as a bishop nor accept the validity of her sacramental acts.[12]

Support for LGBT causes was one of many peace and justice issues that she highlighted in her column, and this undoubtedly formed part of the reason for EURRR's advocacy against her. Integrity's founder, Dr. Louie Crew, noted her ties to Integrity, "Harris had directed the Consultation, an umbrella progressive group of which Integrity was a founding member."[13] In 1992, Integrity acknowledged her financial support as a member of their President's Club.[14]

The Episcopal Diocese of Massachusetts had elected Harris to be their bishop suffragan at their diocesan convention in the fall of 1988. The House of Bishops consented, and she was consecrated on February 11, 1989. Protesters picketed, and Harris was protected by a contingent of Boston police. She declined to wear a bullet-proof vest.[15]

But, the sky didn't fall. By the time of Lambeth 1998, eleven female bishops were included among those invited by the archbishop of Canterbury, including eight from the Episcopal Church of the United States.

The concretion of Harris early in the year provoked plenty of gatekeeping backlash, but it would be nothing compared to what happened at the end of 1989. For that story, we return to the Standing Commission on Human Affairs and Health, headed by Bishop Hunt.

When the Commission convened in the spring of 1986, it became clear that a recent appointee, Bishop Spong of Newark, would become the progressive point guard as the Commission wrestled with human sexuality issues. Though Bishop Hunt sought to be impartial, he soon allied with Spong and the other progressives on the commission.[16]

Rev. John Shelby Spong had been consecrated as the bishop of the Diocese of Newark in 1976, the same year that the Episcopal General Convention voted to ordain women, and he carried a reputation as a progressive; he was already gaining a national following as an edgy author. Following his election, he received the *pro forma* congratulatory call from the conservative presiding bishop, John Maury Allin, whose limp attempt at small talk would prove prophetic and humorous for any with an appreciation of irony.

With false laughter designed to cover his negativity, he said, "When I heard the news, I said, 'Dear God, the church does not need this!'"[17]

The Hunt Commission sought to engage all levels of the church in an ongoing discussion regarding human sexuality, and *The Episcopalian*, the official denominational magazine, would be the forum for a series of articles, with pro and con positions written by Commission members from each side of the issue. The articles would begin with the February 1987 edition of *The Episcopalian*. When the secular press plastered the nation with exaggerated, sensationalist, and often misleading storylines, the organizers of the series found themselves enmeshed in pitched discussions far beyond their hopes for a reasoned discussion, but they certainly had captured the church's attention.

During that summer of 1987, Bishop Spong received a letter from a seminary graduate from Texas, Robert Williams, a partnered gay man. "If you really mean what you say," Williams wrote (referring to Spong's articles in the denominational magazine), "why don't you test it and act on it by considering me for ordination within your diocese?"[18]

Spong accepted the challenge and invited Williams to his Newark office. The tall and tan Texan was articulate and bright, and he hoped to open a diocesan ministry for gay and lesbian people who had only experienced abuse and rejection by the institutional church. Williams suggested the Oasis concept, a sanctuary, where gays and lesbians would be welcomed and safe to discuss their unique issues.

Bishop Spong was convinced, and a two-year process began that would conclude with the ordination of Williams and the establishment of the Oasis of Hoboken. In June 1989 Bishop Spong ordained Williams as a deacon.

Much like the ordination of lesbian Ellen Marie Barrett to the diaconate nearly fourteen years earlier, no one noticed, but the *New York Times* soon did a feature story about the startup of the Oasis, which Deacon Williams was organizing. The story appeared on the front page of the Metro section with a picture of the deacon in clerical collar standing in front of an altar and noted that he was a partnered gay man. The article concluded with the note that Williams would be ordained to the priesthood in December.[19]

The unique aspect of the pending Williams' ordination was that it had gone public. There had been occasional, quiet ordinations of out LGBT persons by progressive bishops in certain dioceses, but they had been handled in a "don't ask, don't tell" manner—at least insofar as the whole church was concerned. Once the Williams story was out, Bishop Spong embraced the notoriety and boldly defended the ordination in a letter to his fellow bishops, noting the statement of conscience from the 1979 General Convention, which had been signed by the current presiding bishop, Edmond Browning.

The brazenness of Bishop Spong and the celebratory attitude toward the pending Williams ordination especially galled the gatekeepers. A conservative bishop from Dallas was particularly upset and called his own press conference to denounce Bishop Spong. The allure of sex and religious controversy only heightened the interest of the secular press, and Bishop Spong did not shy away. Just prior to the December ordination, the diocese issued a press release, announcing that it would celebrate the ordination of a noncelibate gay man to the Episcopal priesthood.[20]

Two protesters picketed outside the church; a third was ejected when he attempted to interrupt the service. A pair of Episcopalians offered opposing statements at the point in the service when given an opportunity to do so. One called homosexuality a "degenerate activity." On the brighter side, Williams' partner of four years served as presenter and litanist during the ordination ceremony.[21]

Bishop Spong had to worry about tripping over television cables during the ordination service. The networks were there, the New York City local stations were there, CNN was there and looped the story as their lead every half hour.[22]

Spong estimated that a third of the congregation that day were gay or lesbian persons who shed many tears during the rite of ordination. "I remember the emotions of the moment quite vividly to this day. This was one of the exquisite times of gospel proclamation in my life. The love of God broke into circles and crevices of life where it had generally not been thought of as present before."[23]

Bishop Spong, a widower, remarried weeks later on January 1, 1990, but he wouldn't have a quiet honeymoon.[24]

NOTES

1. Spong, *Here I Stand*, 293–97.

2. "About Us," on the website of the Prayer Book Society USA, accessed June 15, 2012, http://pbsusa.org/about-us.html.

3. Louie Crew, "Changing the Church," 345–46.

4. Spong, *Here I Stand*, 310.

5. Moore, *Take a Bishop Like Me*, 101–2.

6. Spong, *Here I Stand*, 312.

7. Episcopal News Service, "Browning Elected 24th Presiding Bishop," September 19, 1985.

8. Crew, "Changing the Church," 347.

9. Ibid., 345.

10. Lambeth Conference, 1988, *Resolution One: The Ordination or Consecration of Women to the Episcopate*, http://www.lambethconference.org/resolutions/1988/1988-1.cfm.

11. Episcopal News Service, "Profile, Barbara Clementine Harris," September 29, 1988.

12. Peter Steinfels, "Many in Church Oppose Naming Woman Bishop," *New York Times*, November 26, 1988.

13. Crew, "Changing the Church," 349.

14. Bruce Garner, "President's Club," *The Voice of Integrity* vol. 2, no. 4 (Fall 1992), accessed December 30, 2011, http://www.integrityusa.org/voice/1992/Fall1992.htm.

15. Lynn Rosellini, "The First of the 'Mitered Mamas,'" *U.S. News & World Report* (June 19, 1989).

16. Spong, *Here I Stand*, 313–17.

17. Ibid., 7.

18. Ibid., 337–38.

19. Ibid., 357–59. Supplementary information was provided by Bishop Spong in a private conversation with the author on April 3, 2012.

20. Mireya Navarro, "Openly Gay Priest Ordained in New Jersey," *New York Times*, December 17, 1989.

21. Spong, *Here I Stand.*

22. Spong, private conversation, April 3, 2012.

23. Spong, *Here I Stand*, 370–71.

24. Spong, private conversation, April 3, 2012.

✳ 13 ✳

MAVERICK BISHOPS

Normally frigid January was unseasonably mild in the New York/New Jersey area; 1990 would prove to be the warmest year on record. Perhaps it was the incendiary response to actions of the bishop of the Diocese of Newark that warmed the local climate. Bishop John Shelby Spong had not only ordained an openly gay man, but he had done so in a highly public manner, inviting fiery rebukes from many of his fellow bishops.

"The seeds of anarchy are sown," charged eight bishops in the Midwest. An "open and deliberate violation . . . a blatant disregard of the teaching of the Church Catholic," cried a Texas bishop. A Florida bishop accused Spong of "an act of arrogance," and the bishop of Northern Indiana suggested Bishop Spong was motivated by "publicity and little else."[1]

As to the press coverage of the ordination, Spong argued that the business of the church should always be conducted openly and honestly. Working closely together, Bishop Spong and the president of Integrity pointed out that many bishops had been quietly ordaining openly gay candidates for years.[2] "Since 1977 on average at least five open, noncelibate lesbians or gays have been ordained every year in dioceses from coast to coast," said Integrity president Kim Byham. "Other ordinations may not have received such widespread press and television coverage, but they nevertheless involved priests who were open about their sexuality with their bishops, standing committees, and commissions on ministry."[3] And then the temperature spiked higher.

The newly ordained priest didn't handle the pressure of press scrutiny well. No, that's an understatement. He self-destructed. When badgered by a reporter in Detroit, his own temperature rose to feverish levels, and his intemperate remarks smacked of delirium. Though he was partnered, he criticized gay monogamy. The reporter pressed further.

"Are you saying that sex is good for everyone?"

"Yes, that is what I am saying."

"Are you saying that Mother Teresa would be better off if she had sex?"

"Yes. Mother Teresa would be better off if she got laid."[4]

Williams' call to be the chief missioner at the Oasis was doomed. Bishop Spong, his ardent supporter, couldn't help him; the Oasis board, mostly gays and lesbians, fired a defiant Father Williams in January 1990.

The gatekeepers wanted more; they saw their chance to correct the liberal drift in their denomination. Here was the issue to promote their antigay agenda; here was the scandal that would rally the troops (and loosen their purse strings) for their holy crusade; here was proof of the inherent promiscuity of gays and their lack of sexual ethics or boundaries; here was the demonstration that the LGBT community and their supporters were leading the church into sin and apostasy. Gay-bashing, cloaked in churchly niceties, would be their *cause célèbre* to wrench control of the denomination away from the progressives, who had elected one of their own, Presiding Bishop Edmond Browning, in 1985; who had successfully advanced progressive policies at General Convention 1988; and who had promoted the consecration of a woman, and a well-known progressive voice, to be a bishop in 1989 (Rt. Rev. Barbara Harris).

Bishop Spong became their fund-raising foil amidst calls for censure, at least, or defrocking, preferably. Long a thorn in the side of progressive Episcopalians, the Prayer Book Society called for an end to Bishop Spong's "dominion and authority," language usually reserved for satanic activity.[5]

It was a hot and contentious summer. The gatekeepers had pounced with glee, Presiding Bishop Browning and other progressive bishops had not been as supportive as Bishop Spong and the LGBT community expected, and Louie Crew, the Integrity founder now resident in Spong's diocese, together with other gays, lesbians, and allies, proclaimed a fast from the communion table.[6]

At the urging of the Prayer Book Society, formal charges, known as a "presentment," were filed against Bishop Spong. Their power play backfired, due largely to their own deception by claiming the signature of a retired bishop who later denied any involvement. Not only were the charges dismissed, but the instigators were publicly rebuked by Presiding Bishop Browning: "it must be concluded that these ineffectual attempts to expose him to ecclesiastical discipline constitute harassment of the bishop of Newark."[7]

By overplaying their hand, the gatekeepers had moved the presiding bishop and others back toward supporting Bishop Spong. Later, at the regular fall gathering of the House of Bishops in September, Bishop Wantland, the self-educated bishop of Eau Claire, Wisconsin, pressed to have the House of Bishops "disassociate" from the ordination of Williams. Though the motion was successful, Spong's critics were stunned by the close margin (eighty to seventy-six). "From one supporter in February to [seventy-six] in September was a remarkable transformation. My critics could not believe the closeness of the vote. Since they had talked only to people with whom they agreed, they thought they would win this vote hands down."[8]

Presiding Bishop Browning had promised Bishop Spong the privilege to speak following the vote. Never a shrinking violet, Bishop Spong delivered a stinging indictment of the hypocrisy of his detractors, "forty-five minutes of what surely must be described as passionate purple oratory."[9] He reminded his peers of their own endorsement of a conscience clause only a decade earlier that allowed conservative bishops to refuse to ordain women in defiance of denominational policy.

"I wonder if this House can embrace the fact that other bishops besides [the conservatives] have a conscience that cannot and will not be compromised?" Spong asked. "The way the church treats its gay and lesbian members so deeply violates my conscience that it strains my life by tearing it between my loyalty to Jesus Christ, who made a habit of embracing the outcast, and my loyalty to a church that I dearly love. But it nonetheless is a church that has historically rejected blacks, women, and gays, in succession."

Spong concluded that the last year, despite all the controversy, was "the most exhilarating, growing, eventful year of my life. And the primary reason for that is that I have experienced firsthand the prejudice and the negativity and the pain and the fear that is the daily bread of gay and lesbian people. Their ability to forge relationships of durability, commitment, and faithfulness—living under that kind of hostile, negative rejection—is, in my opinion, almost a miracle."

"It is not the bishop of Newark who is violated by this process. It is the gay and lesbian members of this church," Spong added.[10]

Following his speech, Spong noted a definite mood swing in his favor. He estimated that a dozen or more bishops clustered around his desk and said they wished they had heard his speech before they voted. Spong believed that a majority of the House of Bishops now supported his position.

Late that night, two bishops separately came to Spong's room and tearfully confessed they were closeted gay men, one of whom had actually voted against Spong. "I am so afraid," he said, "that I will be exposed. I cover that fear by being negative and harsh on this issue on every public occasion."[11]

Bishop Spong had survived the most tumultuous year of his life, and so had the momentum toward full inclusion.

———

The upcoming General Convention in 1991 would become the next battleground. Though the temperatures returned to normal in New Jersey at year's end in 1990, the withering heat of Phoenix in July would greet thousands of arriving delegates and visitors to General Convention 1991.

Not that the fire of controversy needed stoking, but Bishop Ronald Haines of Washington, D.C., did precisely that; on June 5, 1991, just days before the convention, he ordained an open lesbian, Elizabeth Carl. Bishop Haines admitted his own discomfort over his decision. Yet he proceeded with the ordination because candidate Carl had exhibited all the requisite attributes of priesthood, and he didn't believe the mere fact of her sexuality should be an absolute bar to ordination.[12]

For the first time in General Conference history, openly gay and lesbian delegates served in the House of Deputies; for the first time, a female was elected to serve as president of the House of Deputies; but, not for the first time and not the last, the progressives faced stiff and organized opposition. The initial quandary facing the progressives was that Arizona had refused to adopt the Martin Luther King holiday. The Los Angeles Diocese was the leading voice, among several, that demanded that the Convention be moved; others threatened a boycott. However, the coalition of progressive organizations known as the "Consultation" encouraged attendance lest the conservatives would dominate the Convention.[13]

The second problem was that the conservatives were energized. EURRR would later report that they had maintained "an effective presence at General Convention (Phoenix) 1991 by means of a widely circulated daily newspaper . . . distributed to Deputies to the Convention; a large display booth; one hundred volunteers staffing a legislative task force and luncheon briefings for Deputies."[14]

The 1991 General Convention agenda included possible action on the report of the Hunt Commission, formally known as the Standing Commission on Human Affairs and Health. For years, Bishop George Hunt of Rhode Island had chaired a committee that studied LGBT issues. This was the Commission in which Bishop Spong played the role of chief progressive voice and which had engaged in public discussions through a pro and con forum in the denominational magazine *The Episcopalian* in 1987. Spong's tenure on the committee had ended in 1988. In January 1991 the Hunt Commission report had been released, and the conservatives howled. The report recommended that individual dioceses and their bishops should be the sole arbiters to determine the fitness of candidates for ordination. Openly LGBT persons could be considered at the discretion of individual bishops. The report also called for further study on blessing same-gender relationships. In many ways, the report recognized and sought to regularize the de facto situation and to make it de jure. Individual bishops were already ordaining gays and lesbians, and many priests were blessing LGBT relationships.[15]

During the Phoenix convention, *three thousand persons* attended a hearing to discuss the Hunt report. Spokespersons from both sides presented their case. Speakers for Integrity and in favor of gay and lesbian causes included the leading theologian in the House of Bishops, Bishop Frederick Borsch of the Diocese of Los Angeles (and a member of the Hunt Commission), an openly gay priest, and an openly lesbian priest.[16]

Speaking against the adoption of the report's recommendation was the former Colorado bishop, the same William Frey who had been the co-founder of EURRR and a failed candidate for the office of presiding bishop in 1985. Frey had shocked his Colorado constituency by resigning in 1989 in order to become dean of Trinity Episcopal School for Ministry in Ambridge, Pennsylvania, a financially strapped evangelical school of about seventy students where one of his sons was a freshman. This seminary was the locus for gatekeeper sentiment, later for schism. The successive seminary deans were the leading spokesmen for antigay sentiment.[17]

"We've sinned as a church, and I believe we are under God's judgment," Frey warned, "the love of God is 'a severe mercy,' for the Lord 'disciplines those whom he loves.'"[18]

The gatekeepers would also offer a seemingly innocuous canon (church law), put forth by Frey: "All members of the clergy of this church . . . shall be under the obligation to abstain from genital sexual relations outside of Holy Matrimony."[19]

Although the proposed canon made no reference to gays or lesbians, neither the House of Bishops nor the House of Deputies was deceived; the resolution was aimed directly at LGBT clergy, who could obviously not be legally married at that time. If the canon passed, the accelerating process of ordaining LGBT clergy would be stopped. In Episcopal polity, a canon is a binding law as opposed to a less binding, instructive resolution, which is what was on the books from the 1979 General Convention and which many bishops were ignoring.

The proposed canon failed!

"I didn't really expect that it would pass," Frey said. "I wasn't overly optimistic . . . I don't think we've lost any ground." Other conservatives didn't mask their disappointment. John Rodgers, Bishop Frey's predecessor as dean of the Trinity Episcopal School for Ministry, criticized "this House's unwillingness to affirm biblical and classical Anglican sexual morality"; the director of Frey's own EURRR admitted, "we're distressed"; an issue of the *United Voice* claimed its followers were "disappointed but unbroken"; and a retired bishop from South Carolina warned that the "stymied discussion of sexuality may be evidence of God's wrath."[20]

Although they had averted defeat, Integrity and their allies could not claim complete victory, either. The recommendation of the Hunt Commission to leave ordinations to the discretion of individual bishops and their dioceses was rejected. The de facto situation was not rendered de jure, but neither had it been reversed by canon law. An adopted resolution "affirmed" (rejecting the term "acknowledged") the church's traditional view of marriage while noting the "discontinuity" between the traditional view and the experience of some members, confessing the failure of the church to agree, and promising continuing study.[21] To be sure, convention actions were a compromise and mixed result, but subsequent events would demonstrate that progressive momentum had not been stemmed and continued to accelerate.

During the triennium following General Convention 1991, the striking symbolism of events augured well for General Convention 1994.

- On September 14th, 1991, Bishop Spong ordained another openly gay man, but this one didn't attract the glare of publicity; the ordination of Barry Stopfel was a low-key family affair. Dr. Carter Heywood, one of the irregularly ordained Philadelphia Eleven in 1974, offered the sermon.[22] A year earlier, Stopfel had first been ordained a deacon by Bishop Spong's assistant bishop, Walter Righter; unknown to the participants, they would later become the litigants in an unprecedented heresy trial based upon this diaconal ordination that would serve as a landmark on the road toward full inclusion.

- By the time of the 1994 General Convention, at least a dozen bishops had quietly ordained openly LGBT persons.[23]

- Bishop Shimpfky of El Camino Real walked in the June 1992 gay pride march in San Jose. "The appalling silence of decent people in positions of leadership and the demonization of gay people by right-wing officials and 'traditional values' groups is largely responsible for this violence [against LGBT persons]," Shimpfky said. "It is important to me to be in the parade as a way of challenging a morality that accuses people for what they are, not who they are as children of God. It is wrong to do that. Gay and lesbian people are being scapegoated and abused."[24]

- The keynote speaker at the 1992 national convention of Integrity was none other than the presiding bishop, Edmond L. Browning, who made a "dramatic pastoral visit," urging lesbian and gay Episcopalians to "keep the faith" and continue to "tell their stories" in a church that sometimes does not want to listen.[25]

- In response to the call for a study on human sexuality at General Convention 1991, a parish study/dialogue process was initiated in August 1992, designed to "develop an understanding and, perhaps, appreciation of each other." According to formal feedback questionnaires received by the committee, the parish participation in the dialogue was significant.[26]

- The keynote speaker at the 1993 national convention of Integrity was President Pamela Chins of the House of Deputies, who came out as the mother of a gay son and who promised to appoint gays and lesbians to General Convention 1994 committees.[27]

- In the fall of 1993, the Rt. Rev. Otis Charles, former bishop of Idaho and former dean of the Episcopal Divinity School, came out to the House of Bishops, thereby becoming the first openly gay bishop of the Episcopal Church or of any ecumenical denomination. Following his coming out, Bishop Charles became a leading advocate for LGBT causes through the 1990s and the first decade of the new millennium—within the House of Bishops and elsewhere. "I have promised myself that I will not remain silent, invisible, unknown. After all is said and done, the choice for me is not whether or not I am a gay, but whether or not I am honest about who I am with myself and others. It is a choice to take down the wall of silence I have built around an important and vital part of my life, to end the separation and isolation I have imposed on myself all these years."[28]

As General Convention 1994 approached, the focus was on the bishops' attempt to lower the temperature by treating LGBT issues pastorally rather than legislatively. The bishops had been meeting privately for three years to hammer out a document that came to be known simply as the "Pastoral." The Pastoral was a dialogical, teaching, study document that was intended to carry the church forward in "continuing dialogue." Anglicans United (the new name for EURRR) criticized the secrecy surrounding the contents of the document, a problem they solved by leaking it ahead of General Convention, incurring a rebuke from Presiding Bishop Browning.[29]

The bishops' approach was largely successful in cooling down overheated floor battles. Dr. Louie Crew noted that there was a radical difference in mood compared to GC 1991, and he attributed that to the momentum swinging toward inclusivity.[30] The official Episcopal News Service also noted, "In a surprisingly congenial debate in the convention's opening day, the bishops agreed to commend the document to the wider church."[31]

Of course, no one truly expected that General Convention 1994 would be without controversy, and it began with a statement of "Affirmation" circulated by conservative bishops from the southwest. This document "claimed the Pastoral was a substantial departure from traditional biblical Christianity and reaffirmed that the only appropriate context for sexual intimacy is within lifelong, monogamous, heterosexual marriage."[32]

What was contained in the Pastoral that incensed the conservatives? A section of the Pastoral entitled "Guidelines While We Continue the Dialogue" seemingly allowed for a "local option," a recognition of the de facto situation in which some local bishops were ordaining LGBT candidates. The pertinent language stated that bishops would ordain "only persons [they] believe to be a wholesome example to their people."[33] If a bishop believed a gay candidate was a "wholesome example" to the people of that diocese or parish, the policy would seemingly allow the ordination. Yet, ambiguity persisted; conservatives argued that no "local option" existed, and dialogue—or debate—would continue.

During the convention, the conservatives succeeded in significantly watering down the bishops' Pastoral—to the point that the LGBT allies who initially supported it ending up voting against it, but it passed anyway. Bishop Spong blamed a failure of leadership. His gay friends from New Jersey, Louie Crew and Kim Byham, the current president of Integrity, were devastated when they encountered Spong in the hallway. "[T]hey felt beaten up and abandoned by the church they were just beginning to trust. They expressed grief and anger, and their tears revealed enormous hurt. Their pain registered on me deeply, but I did not know what to do about it. We had just seen a total liberal leadership collapse."[34]

The bishops had presented their "Pastoral" document. The gatekeepers had responded with their own statement, which they called

"Affirmation" (certainly not affirmation of LGBT but affirmation of the law), and they succeeded in amending the original Pastoral beyond recognition. In a convention of dueling documents, Bishop Spong then countered with his own "Statement of Koinonia" after a sleepless night following his gay friends' tearful confrontation.

In the middle of the night, Bishop Spong began to write in longhand on a legal sized tablet. Before 5:00 AM, he awoke his sleeping wife and asked if she could type it up at the hotel copy center. She agreed, and soon they had a copy to be edited and printed for distribution.[35]

During the plenary session the next day, Bishop Spong asked to read a personal statement. The presiding officer recognized him, and Spong strode past the floor microphones straight to the podium.

> We believe that both homosexuality and heterosexuality are morally neutral. We believe that marriage is to be held in honor . . . but we also believe that those who know themselves to be gay or lesbian persons, who do not choose to live alone, but forge relationships with partners of their choice that are faithful, monogamous, committed, lifegiving, and holy are to be honored.[36]

When the presiding officer tried to cut him off after eight minutes, Bishop Spong held up his hand like a traffic cop and continued reading.[37]

> We also believe that the ordained ranks of this church are open to all baptized Christians. . . . We pledge ourselves to ordain only those persons whom the testing and screening process reveals to be wholesome examples to the flock of Christ. But let there be no misunderstanding, both our lives and our experiences as bishops have convinced us that a wholesome example to the flock of Christ does not exclude a person of homosexual orientation nor does it exclude those homosexual persons who choose to live out their sexual orientation in a partnership that is marked by faithfulness and life-giving holiness.[38]

When he finished, wife Christine distributed copies, including to the press, and Bishop Mary Adelia McLeod of Vermont stepped forward saying she wanted to sign the document. Other bishops did the same, disrupting the business of the day. Eventually eighty-five bishops signed the document, representing the largest dioceses in the nation and the greatest number of church members.[39]

Led by Bishop Spong, defeat had been turned to victory, but he was not the only maverick bishop in the nineties—Bishop Hunt and Bishop Borsch led the way on the commission report of 1991, Bishops Righter and Haines had publicly ordained gays, Bishop Shimpfky walked in a pride parade, Presiding Bishop Browning encouraged the Integrity community at their convention, Bishop Otis Charles came out and became a gay voice within the House of Bishops, and Bishop Mary Adelia McLeod led eighty-five bishops to the podium to sign the statement of Koinonia.

But the gatekeepers would seek their revenge.

NOTES

1. Episcopal News Service, "Ordination of Gay Priest Stirring Nation-Wide Reaction," January 10, 1990.

2. Episcopal News Service, "Ordination".

3. Spong, *Here I Stand*, 365.

4. Ibid., 374.

5. Episcopal News Service, "Ordination".

6. Spong, Here I Stand, 378.

7. Episcopal News Service, "Panel Rules against Attempted 'Presentment' of Spong: Presiding Bishop Calls the Attempt 'Harassment,'" August 23, 1990.

8. Spong, *Here I Stand*, 380.

9. Ibid., 380.

10. Episcopal News Service, "Bishops Narrowly Vote to 'Disassociate' from Homosexual Ordination in Newark," September 26, 1990.

11. Spong, *Here I Stand*, 375.

12. Peter Steinfels, "Lesbian Ordained Episcopal Priest," *New York Times*, June 6, 1991.

13. "2 Episcopal Groups Will Skip Phoenix Convention," *Los Angeles Times*, March 16, 1991, 17. Louie Crew lauded the networking effectiveness of the umbrella progressive group the Consultation during that time period. Barbara

Harris, the female bishop elected in 1989, had been director of the Consultation. Crew, "Changing the Church," 349.

14. "About Us," on the website of Anglicans United, accessed February 23, 2012, http://www.anglicansunited.com/?page_id=72.

15. Episcopal News Service, "How the General Convention Reached a Compromise on the Sexuality Issue," July 25, 1991.

16. Crew, "Changing the Church," 350.

17. *Los Angeles Times*, "Bishop Quits Colorado for Eastern Seminary," October 28, 1989.

18. Episcopal News Service, "How the General Convention Reached a Compromise."

19. Ibid.

20. Ibid.

21. Ibid.

22. Episcopal News Service, "Spong Ordains Homosexual Priest in Suburban New Jersey Parish," September 17, 1991. Rev. Dr. Heyward had also offered the sermon at the *extra ordinem* ordinations of Lutheran lesbians and gays in January 1990 (see below).

23. Crew, "Changing the Church," 351.

24. Episcopal News Service, "Bishop Marches in Gay Pride Parade to Promote Tolerance," June 26, 1992.

25. Episcopal News Service, "Browning Tells Lesbian and Gay Episcopalians to 'Hang in' Despite Church's Ambiguity," July 30, 1992.

26. Crew, "Changing the Church," 350–51.

27. Ibid., 350.

28. Profile of Right Rev. Otis Charles, DD, STD, on the website of the Lesbian, Gay, Bisexual, and Transgender Religious Archives Network, accessed February 23, 2012, http://www.lgbtran.org/Profile.aspx?ID=129.

29. Episcopal News Service, "Sexuality Issues Continue to Provoke Debate," September 7, 1994.

30. Crew, "Changing the Church," 351.

31. The full title of the "Pastoral" was "Continuing the Dialogue: A Pastoral Study Document of the House of Bishops to the Church as the Church Considers Issues of Human Sexuality." Episcopal News Service, "Sexuality Issues Continue to Provoke."

32. Episcopal News Service, "Sexuality Issues Continue to Provoke."

33. Ibid.

34. Spong, *Here I Stand*, 403.

35. Ibid., 405.

36. Excerpts from Statement of Koinonia from the Website of Integrity USA, http://integrityusa.org/archive/samesexblessings/a_statement_in_koinonia .htm, accessed May 20, 2013.

37. Spong, private interview.

38. Excerpts from Statement of Koinonia from the Website of Integrity USA, http://integrityusa.org/archive/samesexblessings/a_statement_in_koinonia .htm, accessed May 20, 2013.

39. Spong, *Here I Stand*, 450.

* 14 *

A HERESY TRAIL

As 1995 began, a mood of Armageddon stirred the camp of the gate-keepers. It was time for a D-Day assault, a beachhead that would turn the tides of war and wipe out further LGBT ordinations. Although the gatekeepers hoped for Normandy, their attack turned into Pickett's charge at Gettysburg.

The final confrontation would be waged in the ecclesiastical courts. To hell with collegiality. For the first time in seventy-five years and only the second time in the entire history of the Episcopal Church in America, ten bishops would file charges of heresy against a fellow bishop.

The prosecuting bishops intended a series of trials against offending bishops, the likes of Bishop Spong of Newark and Bishop Haines of Washington, D.C., but the first trial, for reasons of the statute of limitations, would be against Bishop Walter Righter, Bishop Spong's assistant, who had ordained Barry Stopfel as deacon a year before Bishop Spong ordained him a priest.

Of the ten bishops who signed the presentment against Bishop Righter, five were from Texas, but the document was drafted by Bishop William Wantland of Eau Claire, Wisconsin.[1] We encountered Bishop Wantland earlier when he led the 1990 effort to have the House of Bish-ops "disassociate" with Bishop Spong's ordination of Robert Williams. Bishop Wantland was a staunch conservative who vigorously opposed any accommodation of church tradition to the cultural conditions of the twentieth century—such as women's ordination. As late as 2009 when he departed TEC to join the schismatic Anglican Church in North

America (ACNA), he continued to rail against female priests, suggesting a female could not be an icon of Christ.[2]

At the time, Bishop Righter was seventy-one years old and retired. He had previously served sixteen years as bishop of Iowa before assisting Bishop Spong in Newark. His ordination of Stopfel to the diaconate had followed on the heels of the September 1990 House of Bishops meeting in which Bishop Spong had castigated his opponents, and Spong and Righter had judiciously decided it best if Righter rather than Spong officiate at the diaconal ordination.[3] Bishop Spong would officiate at Stopfel's ordination to the priesthood a year later, but it was the first ordination to the diaconate that was the subject of the heresy trial.

"This is ridiculous . . . It is harassment . . . not of me, but of the church," Bishop Richter said when informed of the presentment. Way back in 1991, the General Convention had already refused to censure Bishop Righter for the 1990 ordination of Deacon Stopfel.[4]

Others also questioned the presentment in light of the collegial atmosphere of the General Convention the previous summer; an ecclesiastical trial was decidedly not a continuation in dialogue. It was an interruption of a reasoned process; right here, right now, the conservatives would have the ecclesiastical court decide the policy of the church. Was the aggressiveness of the ten signatory bishops bold strategy or a desperate last stand? They had to know that four of the nine sitting judges had signed Bishop Spong's Statement of Koinonia the year before.

On May 18, 1995, Bishop Righter filed his answer, and his supporting brief framed the issue in the broadest possible terms: that the core doctrines of the church did not preclude LGBT ordination. If the conservatives wanted a test case to determine once and for all whether the church could or would ordain LGBT clergy, Bishop Righter and his allies would meet them head on. Bishop Righter's brief would deny that he had been:

Holding and teaching publicly or privately, and advisedly, any doctrine contrary to that held by this church. . . . There is no doctrine in this church pertaining to the qualifications of ordinands to the diaconate or limitations on a bishop's right to ordain a canonically qualified candidate . . . it is not contrary to the doctrine of this church to ordain to the diaconate a noncelibate homosexual man or woman.

But what of the 1979 resolution that included the language, "it is not appropriate for this Church to ordain a practicing homosexual"? That clause had resisted all efforts at rescission or modification at every General Convention since 1979. Should it not control the court's deliberations? Not so, said Bishop Righter's brief, which argued that the core doctrine of the church is based solely on Holy Scripture, canons, and creeds but not on mere resolutions, which are no more than teachings and subject to change and disagreement. Heresy charges should apply solely to core doctrines of the church.

"The moral and social teaching of the church, unlike its fundamental doctrine, is open to modification, development and even repudiation, in light of changing perceptions and understandings of the human condition," the brief added. "It is continuously under review and the subject of regular legislation by General Convention, but it is not the doctrine of the Episcopal Church."

"This attempt to use the church's judicial process to resolve an issue on which there is no agreement must fail," the brief concluded in asking the bishops to dismiss the presentment.[5]

Much like its civil counterpart, the ecclesiastical trial would involve precise, formal procedures. Much like the chronology of a civil trial, the heresy proceedings against Bishop Righter would be drawn out. More than a year would elapse after the filing of charges, and still Bishop Righter had not had his day in court.

On February 27, 1996, the latest in a series of pretrial hearings took place at the Wilmington Cathedral of Hartford, Connecticut. At issue was the central defense argument that mere resolutions were not equivalent to the core doctrines of the church. Local and national press swarmed about the cathedral, but when the parties and the judges began to meander through the thicket of Episcopal canon law, the mood turned quiet and solemn, with occasional snatches of humor, as often is the case in the verbal jousting of skilled lawyers.

Michael Rehill, Chancellor of the Diocese of Newark, served as counsel for the accused Bishop Righter. He argued:

The 1979 resolution of General Convention is "unenforceable because it doesn't say anything about enforcement, because it is not a law, it is not prescriptive, it is advisory." He contended that, if the church intended to prohibit the ordinations of non-celibate gays and lesbians, it could "do so easily by changing some of the canons, if that were the will of the Episcopal Church." He pointed out that efforts to change the canons "have failed again, and again, and again." And he said that the church had confessed that it was "not of a single mind" in its understanding on the issue.[6]

Sitting in the overflow crowd, Barry Stopfel and Will Leckie, partners for eleven years, watched with greater interest than the others. It was Stopfel's ordination nearly six years earlier and his relationship with Leckie that had triggered the charges against Bishop Righter. Stopfel willingly addressed the press, noting that he and Leckie had decided to sacrifice privacy in order to put their faces on the case, to remove it from abstraction to the personal: "At first I was hesitant to make myself . . . so visible. But more and more I thought: I want to put a face on this abstract concept. So Will and I just decided the price we were going to pay was to do that."[7]

As in a civil trial, the court adjourned and took the matter under advisement. Both sides were to present further written argument, and a decision was not expected soon.

Nearly three months later, on May 16, 1996, the court announced its decision based upon a seven-to-one vote of the sitting judges. Bishop Cabell Tennis of Delaware, a lawyer and member of the court, read a summary of the decision to a breathless crowd. Behind him, a stained glass depiction of the last supper seemed to suggest that Jesus was looking over his shoulder. When Bishop Tennis read that there was "no core doctrine prohibiting the ordination of a non-celibate, homosexual person living in a faithful and committed sexual relationship with a person of the same sex," the case was over and ordination of LGBT candidates had been countenanced by the highest Episcopal court.[8]

Even before the decision had been announced, several of the ten bishops who commenced the proceedings against Bishop Righter had expressed regrets. Their bold gamble had backfired, and they knew it. There would be no appeal of the dismissal of charges, and the plans to prosecute other bishops were abandoned. The instigators had been bluffing, hoping the church would issue a moratorium against further LGBT ordinations in exchange for dropping the charges. Presiding Bishop Browning called their bluff, the matter proceeded to trial, and the opinion of the court became official policy.[9]

The scorched earth policy of the ten conservative bishops had failed miserably. Ironically, the judicial process resolved the issue, but not in the manner the conservatives hoped or Bishop Righter and his allies feared. When the sitting judges, bishops all, who had each been elected during preceding General Conventions, issued their decision, the de facto practice in which individual bishops ordained openly gay persons to the priesthood was suddenly rendered de jure. The highest court of the church had just ruled that the core doctrine of the Episcopal Church did not preclude gay ordination; unless and until a General Convention would adopt canon law to the contrary, the law of the Episcopal landscape was now settled.

Although new battles lay ahead, often consisting of rear-guard actions, TEC had emerged from conflict; though battered and bruised, there would be no retreat. To continue the metaphor of warfare, the trial had been a Gettysburg moment, and, after General Lee's ill-fated command for Pickett's charge, the Confederacy was finished; only mop-up actions remained. Dr. Louie Crew, who had been on the frontlines from the beginning, offered this summation:

> After twenty years of struggle, with many tears and prayers, a great moral victory had been won . . . lesbigays are driven by the Gospel imperative, the profound faith that God loves absolutely everybody. . . . God is present in the world with a marvelous sense of humor, using gays and lesbians to evangelize the Church and bring it back to its first principle, namely, the boundless love of God and its absolute inclusiveness.[10]

In a symbolic sign of the times, the closing session of General Convention 1997 offered "a highly unusual apology to lesbians and gay men inside and outside the church for 'years of rejection and maltreatment by the church.'"[11] A resolution to create liturgical forms for same gender blessing ceremonies failed by a mere vote. Another resolution was adopted that would provide benefits for partners of homosexual employees of the church. Bishop Walter Righter was honored by the convention for his service to the church. Bishop Frank Griswold of Chicago, a signatory to the Statement of Koinonia, was elected to be the new presiding bishop.[12]

Just when it appeared that final victory was at hand, international intrigue intervened. The domestic gatekeepers would call in foreign reinforcements.

NOTES

1. Episcopal News Service, "Presentments Brought against Five Bishops Who Ordained Homosexuals," February 9, 1995.

Bishop Spong wrote of Wantland, "a self-educated former lawyer and family court judge in Oklahoma who had been ordained to the priesthood without attending an accredited seminary . . . who seemed to believe that Christianity was to be identified with the ancient formulations of the church fathers. . . . If one did not ascribe to the dogma of the church as the fathers articulated it, one simply was not a Christian in his mind." Spong, *Here I Stand*, 261–62.

2. Judith Duin, "New Anglicans Split on Women," *Washington Times*, July 2, 2009.

3. Spong, *Here I Stand*, 382.

4. Episcopal News Service, "Presentments Brought."

5. Episcopal News Service, "Bishop Responds to Charges He Ordained Gay Man Contrary to Church Doctrine," May 18, 1995.

6. Episcopal News Service, "Court Holds Hearing to Determine Church Doctrine on Ordination of Gays," March 7, 1996.

7. Jerry Hames, Episcopal News Service, "Stopfel, Partner Put Human Faces on 'Impersonal' Walter Righter Case," March 27, 1996. Hames was editor of *Episcopal Life*.

8. Episcopal News Service, "Court Dismisses Charges Against Bishop Walter Righter over Ordination of Homosexual," May 23, 1996.

9. Jerry Hames, Episcopal News Service, "Presenters in Walter Righter Case Did Not Want a Trial, Bishop Claims," March 27, 1996.

10. Crew, "Changing the Church," 352–53.

11. Episcopal News Service, "Convention Says 'Now, No, and Not Yet' on Sexuality Issues," August 6, 1997.

12. Spong, *Here I Stand*, 412.

* 15 *

LAMBASTING AT LAMBETH

As the decade wound down, Episcopal wayfarers on the journey toward full inclusion suddenly encountered a significant detour that would carry them across the sea to their ancestral homeland and a confrontation with their Anglican cousins. Lambeth, a district of central London and the location of Lambeth Palace, the London residence of the archbishop of Canterbury, had served as host for decennial gatherings of Anglican bishops from around the world since the first Lambeth Conference of 1867. Although recent conferences had been moved out of London to the university campus in nearby Canterbury, the Lambeth name endured. A U.S. bishop had suggested the first conference, and the Episcopalians from the United States had always been influential participants, but at the Lambeth Conference of 1998, the Episcopalians were suddenly on the defensive. At a time when Episcopal gays and lesbians had stepped forward on the journey toward full inclusion in the United States, the worldwide Anglican Communion stepped back at the Lambeth Conference.

Provinces from the developing nations considerably outnumber those from the Western democracies, and that is an advancing trend. The twenty-five provinces from developing nations are referred to as the "Global South." The Episcopal Church is one of thirty-eight autonomous regional provinces that can vary significantly in geography and population. For instance, one of the prickly thorns in the side of TEC would be the Province of the Southern Cone, consisting of the five southernmost countries of South America but having only twenty-two thousand members or approximately 1 percent the membership of TEC and smaller than many Episcopal dioceses.

The leader of each of the thirty-eight international provinces is referred to as a "primate," usually an archbishop or a presiding bishop. The four so-called "instruments of communion" have no juridical authority and are not so identified in any of the foundational documents of the Communion but have developed as Anglican custom. Three of the four are relatively recent; only the role of the archbishop of Canterbury as titular head of the Communion has been a part of the full history of the Communion, which dates to the consecration of Samuel Seabury in 1784. The next to develop was the Lambeth Conference in 1867. The third and fourth instruments of communion, the Primates Meetings and the Anglican Consultative Council, developed late in the twentieth century.

The archbishop of Canterbury is both the primate of the Church of England and the titular leader of the worldwide Anglican Communion. Once every ten years, the archbishop invites the active bishops of the world to a gathering in England known as the Lambeth Conference (retired bishops not included). Traditionally, only bishop ordinaries were invited until 1988, when bishops suffragan were added to the invitees. Since attendance is by invitation, the archbishop wields implicit authority in determining who is recognized as a bishop within the communion, which would become important later as rival bishops popped up on American soil sponsored by Global South dioceses. Resolutions passed at Lambeth carry influence but no legal authority over individual provinces.

The third instrument of communion is the Primates Meeting. The thirty-eight primates have gathered regularly since 1978 for leisurely paced consultations. The fourth, the Consultative Council, consists of several representatives of each province, including laity, and gathers in various provinces around the world once every two to three years. Each of these four instruments has developed over time as a matter of custom and practice but without any formal, legislative enactments, and they have historically been consultative gatherings without authority over the autonomous provinces. The archbishop of Canterbury functions as leader of the Lambeth Conference, the Primates Meeting, and the Consultative

Council. The archbishop has the power to invite, convene, moderate, appoint, and persuade but cannot formulate policy directly.

Two gatherings in 1997 set the stage for Lambeth the following year, and both involved bishops from the burgeoning Global South provinces of the Anglican Communion. Fully 80–90 percent of all Anglicans in the world reside in the nations included in the "Anglican Church of the South." In February 1997, eighty bishops gathered in Kuala Lumpur, the Malaysian capitol, and later, fifty African bishops were flown to Dallas in September for a meeting organized by English and American conservatives. The statement issued out of Kuala Lumpur was virulently homophobic, and the coordination arranged at Dallas would prove to be Machiavellian. The progressives from the United States and elsewhere expected that Lambeth 1998 would be difficult, but they were not prepared for the clobbering that would take place.

The Kuala Lumpur statement began with a litany of complaints against the domination of the West—ethnic hatred, political destabilization and neocolonialism, social injustice and marginalization, international debt, pollution and environmental damage, unbridled materialism and pervasive corruption. The document then made a bizarre pivot to attack sexual promiscuity and homosexuality as if sexual ills accounted for the world's troubles.[1] Not only was the Kuala Lumpur document starkly homophobic, it also included the hallmark fallacy of most confessional worldviews . . . *this ye must believe lest ye be condemned*. The Kuala Lumpur statement suggested that any who disagreed with its pronouncements must either be silenced or expelled from the church.[2] With such an absolutist attitude, the Global South delegates to Lambeth would be emboldened to attack the Americans or other Anglicans who disagreed with their unenlightened LGBT attitudes.

The Dallas Diocese (remember, five of the ten bishops who had pressed heresy charges against Bishop Righter were from Texas) hosted and largely financed the September conference. The meeting had been arranged ostensibly to discuss debt of developing nations, but it was a ruse. Conservative Episcopal bishops turned the focus of the conference away from debt and into another public condemnation of homosexuality. The true purpose of the conference was to fashion a coalition of Western conservatives with Global South bishops in order to control the upcoming Lambeth Conference and, especially, to smooth the way for adoption of the Kuala Lumpur statement by Lambeth.[3]

It is time to introduce the American Anglican Council (AAC) that would soon eclipse the EURRR as the principal opposition group within TEC, with some overlapping membership and leadership. The AAC dated to a pair of "Briarwood Conferences" in 1995 (twenty persons, including five bishops) and 1996 (seventy-five persons and nine bishops).[4]

But, to really understand the AAC, we must look to another organization, a political, neoconservative "think tank," called the Institute for Religion and Democracy (IRD).[5] The IRD meant to infiltrate and influence the Episcopal Church—and also the Presbyterian Church and the United Methodist Church—though the IRD per se was not Episcopal, Presbyterian, or Methodist. Even the progressive UCC was touched by IRD influences through the Biblical Witness Fellowship, the UCC gatekeeping organization.

Neoconservative Roman Catholics served as founding board members of the IRD in 1981, including Michael Novak, a prolific writer whose best known work is *The Spirit of Democratic Capitalism*, and Richard John Niehaus, a Lutheran minister who converted to Catholicism and became a Catholic priest in 1990. Other well-known Catholics have served on the board from time to time. The second Bush administration appointed an IRD advisory board member and influential Roman Catholic, Mary Ann Glendon, to be ambassador to the Vatican. Methodist Pastor Andrew Weaver has been a watchdog on the activities of the IRD, and he criticized the IRD attempt to destabilize the ecumenical denominations as "the most grievous breach in ecumenical good will between Roman Catholics and Protestants since the changes initiated by Vatican II."[6]

For present purposes, neoconservatism consists of a robust defense of a supply-side, market economy and a corresponding critique of social welfare programs; a nationalistic and dualistic worldview (good versus evil) that resulted in staunch anti-Communism during the Cold War era and anti-Saddamist bellicosity, tinged with a pro-Israeli bias, during the Bush presidencies; and a moral/religious view defending the virtue of American capitalism, especially against perceived socialism in justice movements borne of liberation theology. In this context, the well-worn quote from a South American cleric is apt: "When I feed the hungry, they call me a saint; when I ask why people are hungry, they call me a communist."[7] Neoconservatives disparage the labor movement, feminism, and gay liberation with the suggestion that progressive elites—liberal media, liberal government workers, and liberal church leaders—are eroding traditional American values of capitalism and dogmatic Christianity.

The IRD provided the nexus between neoconservative politics and religion with a purpose to blunt the progressive influence of the ecumenical churches. The IRD propped up and encouraged the gatekeepers with organizational and financial backing. The IRD openly supported Episcopal, Presbyterian, and Methodist gatekeeper organizations. Even the Lutheran gatekeepers were touched by neoconservative influence, though there is no evidence of IRD connections.

One of the early successes of the IRD in the eighties was a smear campaign that suggested monies raised in the collection plates of the ecumenical denominations funded Marxist guerrillas in Africa. That falsity was promoted in a mass mailing from the IRD and even *60 Minutes* picked up the lie. You don't get on *60 Minutes* without influence in high places.

> While showing horrific footage of a slain missionary, the program implied that the NCC [National Council of Churches] was responsible for the brutal murder. It was a lie that the top rated show in television told to tens of millions. The broadcast was highly damaging to mainline Protestants and the NCC.
>
> At the same time the program gave momentum to a fledging Washington "think tank," The Institute on Religion and Democracy (IRD), nearly 90% funded by right-wing benefactors like Richard Mellon Scaife and the Smith-Richardson Foundation. The IRD was a primary source of the false and reckless claims made by the *60 Minutes* segments.[8]

Two decades later, the long-time producer of *60 Minutes*, Don Hewitt, referred to this 1983 episode as the one he regretted most in his thirty-six years as a TV producer.

In a retrospective speech in 2005, Niehaus proudly acknowledged the insurrectionist history of the IRD within ecumenical churches:

How, if at all and in what ways, do we distinguish IRD from this remarkable insurgency that has rewritten the map of American culture and politics over the last 20 years, of evangelical, Catholic, generally conservative, religiously inspired political activism, dismissively called by our opponents the "Religious Right"? How did it happen, one might ask, that IRD became in many ways an ancillary, supportive, coordinating agency for insurgencies within these three denominations—the United Methodist Church, the Presbyterian Church-USA, and the Episcopal Church?[9]

A principal source of funds behind the organization was Richard Mellon Scaife (through foundations), one of the richest men in America and a well-known financier of conservative political causes, many of them secretive and nefarious; Scaife was the money-man behind the effort to impeach President Clinton in 1998–99.[10]

Another extremely wealthy name behind the IRD was Howard Fieldstead Ahmanson Jr., whose wife has served on the IRD board of directors. Ahmanson is known for his flirtation with the Christian Reconstructionist Movement that promoted a worldwide Christian theocracy. In 2005, *Time* magazine included the Ahmansons on their list of the most influential evangelicals in America, referring to the Ahmansons as "the financiers."[11] The Rev. David C. Anderson, pastor of the Ahmanson's California congregation, would serve as the AAC chair and spokesperson during the 2003 Episcopal General Convention. We will encounter Pastor Anderson again.

The Lynde and Harry Bradley foundation was a third major funding source. With ties to the John Birch Society, the Bradley foundation was antilabor and a proponent of unfettered capitalism and added $1.3 million to the IRD coffers up to 2001.[12]

By its own acknowledgement, the IRD meant to influence ecumenical church policy on issues such as LGBT inclusivity, but their core agenda may run deeper: "[T]he Institute on Religion and Democracy is funded chiefly by people whose interests are primarily political and economic. For them, changing the leadership and public voice of the mainline denominations is part of a broader undertaking to silence all effective forms of progressive opposition to the rightist turn in national policy."[13]

Listen again to Dr. Andrew J. Weaver, in an article posted on the University of Chicago Divinity School website:

> The political right-wing, operating in the guise of a gaggle of so-called "renewal groups," particularly one named the Institute on Religion and Democracy (IRD), has acquired the money and political will to target three mainline American denominations: The United Methodist Church, the Presbyterian Church USA, and the Episcopal Church. The IRD was created and is sustained by money from right-wing foundations and has spent millions of dollars over 20 years attacking mainline denominations. The IRD's conservative social-policy goals include increasing military spending and foreign interventions, opposing environmental protection efforts, and eliminating social welfare programs.
>
> In a document entitled "Reforming America's Churches Project 2001–2004," the IRD states that its aim is to change the "permanent governing structure" of mainline churches "so they can help renew the wider culture of our nation." In other words, its goal extends beyond the spiritual and includes a political takeover financed by the likes of Richard Mellon Scaife, Adolph Coors, the John M. Olin Foundation, and the Lynde and Harry Bradley Foundation of Milwaukee.
>
> These groups employ the propaganda method of "wedge issues" like abortion and homosexuality to cause confusion, dissension, and division.[14]

How did the IRD infiltrate the Episcopal Church? Through the American Anglican Council (AAC). Until her death in 2005, Diane Knippers served as president of IRD. She had cut her teeth as a staffer for the Methodist gatekeeper magazine, *Good News*, and she joined the IRD in the early eighties. She personified the IRD influence in the AAC. Together with a pair of former Reagan Justice Department officials, Knippers was an original incorporator of AAC in 1996, she served on the original AAC board, she was the AAC's first treasurer, and she served as AAC's legislative strategist at Episcopal General Conventions. She belonged to the same D.C. Episcopal congregation as Oliver North and Clarence Thomas, and their rector served on the AAC board of directors. The AAC offices were set up just down the hall from the IRD offices in D.C.[15]

Later, we will encounter an Episcopal schismatic leader named John Rodgers. He had served on the EURRR board of directors and later the IRD board of directors, and in 2000 he would be a chief organizer of a schismatic splinter group set up to rival TEC. Here is his 2005 eulogy for the recently deceased Knippers:

> It was my honor to serve on the Board of the IRD before and during Diane's service as its Director. She came to that position at a time when the IRD was in need of a fresh focus since the Iron Curtain had fallen and the anti-godly forces were no longer led by the Communist threat. It was Diane that helped us see that the Culture wars were even more dangerous and that we needed to assist the Churches to become conscious of their need to speak up and out concerning what was happening in the mainline Churches. Her leadership in this was superb. In addition she was a leader within the Episcopal Church in its attempts to stem the secularist tide. She was instrumental in forming the AAC, and a superb tactician for the forces of light at General Convention. She continued in giving leadership to the AAC right up until the end of her far too brief life.[16]

Knippers of the IRD was "instrumental in forming the AAC." Knippers of the IRD encouraged the AAC to focus on "Culture wars." Knippers of the IRD offered leadership to the AAC as a "superb" tactician. Rodger's comments provide a frightening insight into Knipper's worldview and tactics as the leader of an organization that sought to impose its neoconservative political will upon TEC through the AAC. With the loss of the Cold War Communist bogeyman, the IRD shifted its focus to the "anti-godly forces" within ecumenical Christianity, which were even more dangerous from the IRD's paranoid perspective.

Or was the IRD a Machiavellian puppet master that manipulated the paranoid elements within the churches for its own political purposes? To be sure, gatekeeping organizations were filled with many fearful persons—uncomfortable with gays and lesbians, anxious over their own sexual issues, challenged by modernity, frightened by the loss of a black-

and-white Bible, and afraid of the collapse of a simple faith—but there were also gatekeeping leaders who were fearmongers, willing to prey upon the fears of others in order to manipulate and control.

With this introduction to the IRD and the AAC, we return to Lambeth 1998. The gatekeepers arrived early at Lambeth to set up a command center and staging ground in a nearby Catholic facility. Here is an interim report emanating from the AAC camp:

> The AAC headquarters at the Franciscan Centre has become a hub of activity this week. There have been major receptions and meetings almost every night as well as daily meetings. We have offered bishops access to e-mail, FAX and phone facilities, and word seems to have gotten out that the Centre is a place for tired bishops to come get a break from the heavy schedule of the Conference.
>
> In addition, several of our staff are specifically working with bishops in the four sections, helping them write up proposals and hosting meetings of bishops who need a place to come together.
>
> Friday was Celebrate Nigeria night. Nearly 200 Nigerian bishops and wives came decked out in their traditional attire. There was worship, singing, and words of encouragement. One sensed corporately their confidence that their moment of leadership in the Communion has come. May it be so, Lord!
>
> On Saturday, the Franciscan Centre was quiet, but it is a calm before the storm. We are tracking the section reports and the proposed resolutions as they come in. We hope to be ready to help bishops respond to whatever comes out of the Resolutions Committee.
>
> Bishop Alex Dickson, the AAC Vice President, is retired and thus is not an invited member of the Conference. However, he is a presence. Alex took the initiative to lead the American bishops in an act of repentance before the Africans at the pre-Lambeth conference of the Evangelical Fellowship in the Anglican Communion (EFAC) [This refers to the furor over a Bishop Spong interview. See below.] Many believe that moment forged a bond of sympathy that has continued throughout the Conference.

Please pray that the Lord will give us and the bishops grace to make a strong finish. We enter into the decisive week of the Lambeth Conference. We have helped consolidate a massive bloc of support from around the Communion, particularly from the Third World, to speak for a biblical agenda.[17]

And here is the report from observer Stephen Bates:

The Evangelicals had cultivated the African bishops, stroked their egos and shared their pain and they would do so assiduously throughout the Conference. The strategy was highly effective in coordinating policy. The American Anglican Council, made up of conservative Episcopalians, set up headquarters in a Franciscan study centre on another part of the campus—"The Catholics were only too happy to rent it to us," said one who was involved—and offered open house. It was all most un-Anglican and organized like an American political campaign. Developing-world bishops, some with very little money or experience of life outside their own countries, who were ignored or patronized by first-world bishops, found their every need assiduously met by a team of helpful young American, British, and Australian graduates. "We gave them food, we ran errands, if they wanted a cup of tea or coffee they just had to raise their hand, we provided them with mobile phones and free telephone links home and we cast their speeches into good English."[18]

Bishop Spong's natural inclination was to be militant, aggressive, and outspoken, and those traits had served him well back in the United States but utterly failed him at Lambeth. It didn't help that his edgy theological writings were proving to be too provocative even for many moderates, and his latest release before Lambeth, *Twelve Theses*, was too controversial and too hot. Prior to the conference, the archbishop of Canterbury had accused Spong of a "hectoring and intemperate tone" in defense of his book and his views.

It would get worse; Spong became toxic as a result of an interview that became a twisted caricature of his views. In the interview, he suggested that emergent African Christianity and their leaders had not been educated in modern biblical scholarship, with the result that their views tended toward fundamentalism. Spong's characteristic outspoken honesty was insufficient for a delicate dilemma: how to criticize the unsophisticated views of the Anglicans from developing nations regarding homosexuality without appearing condescending or even racist. On the eve of the conference, the interview appeared under the title "Bishop says Africans one step away from witch doctors." The article had been written by the son of the archbishop of Canterbury; it was not journalism, it was propaganda, and it succeeded.[19]

Word of Spong's remarks spread rapidly through a pre-Lambeth charismatic leadership retreat in Canterbury, hosted by several Anglican charismatic renewal groups sympathetic to the American conservative cause. Photocopies of the offending Spong article were circulated among the approximately 450 Anglican bishops, priests, and lay leaders present. The Americans at retreat, including many conservative Episcopal activists, decided to make a public apology, which was welcomed by their Southern colleagues with embraces and tears. Todd Wetzel of Episcopalians United described the moment as "one of the American church's finest moments in decades."[20]

We can be sure that the North American gatekeepers shed huge crocodile tears as they consoled the Africans. Bishop Spong and other progressive leadership had been effectively neutralized. The progressives were castigated—catcalls and derisive whistles would greet any attempt to speak on the floor of the conference.

Bishop Chukwuma of Nigeria was perhaps the most virulent and outspoken of the African bishops. His confrontation with the Rev. Richard Kirker, the long-time leader of England's homophile organization, the "Lesbian and Gay Christian Movement," was caught by the BBC cameras and beamed around the world.

"Leviticus ordained the death penalty for homosexuals," Chukwuma declared.

"Would you be prepared to stone us to death?" Kirker responded.

Chukwuma attempted to place his hands atop Kirker's head. "In the name of Jesus, I deliver him out of homosexuality. I pray for God to forgive you, for God to deliver you out of your sinful act, out of your carnality."

Kirker ducked and said. "May God bless you, sir, and deliver you from your prejudice against homosexuality."

"You have no inheritance in the kingdom of God," the bishop said with voice rising. "You are going to hell. You have made yourself homosexual because of your carnality.

Nearby, the bishop's wife murmured, "Alleluia."

By now, the bishop was shouting. "We have overcome carnality just as the light will overcome darkness. . . . God did not create you as a homosexual. . . . This is the voice of God talking. Yes, I am violent against sin."[21]

The Nigerian bishop didn't confine his badgering to gay men. Lesbian activist Clare Garner reported her personal experience.

Perhaps it is a little unwise to tell a bishop that his use of Bible quotations is selective. Without warning, the chubby finger complete with huge square-cut purple amethyst came jabbing towards my face.

"Do you know the wording of Corinthians?" the Right Rev Emmanuel Chukwuma, bishop of Enugu, Nigeria, shouted accusingly. When his question happened to be answered in the affirmative, he was momentarily wrong-footed. And changed tack. "Are you a lesbian?"

Perhaps I should have turned the other cheek, but I'm not in the business of being a martyr. When he persisted in pushing his finger in my face, I physically attempted to lower it myself. The more I tried to remove the bishop's thrusting hand, the harder it came pushing back.

The farcical scene came to an end when, with a cry of "You're a devilish woman," he turned on his tail and stormed off in a flush of episcopal purple.[22]

Spiritual abuse wasn't confined to the hallways. Civil discourse was entirely absent from plenary sessions, and the archbishop of Canterbury,

George Carey, bore much of the blame: ineffectual at best, homophobic and partisan at worst.[23] As the key resolution became increasingly negative following amendment after amendment, Carey spoke in favor. Later, the bishop of Edinburgh, the leader of Scotland's Anglicans, the Most Reverend Richard Holloway, said he felt "gutted, shafted, and depressed" by the "pathetic" speech of Archbishop Carey.[24]

The Global South delegations, principally the Africans, were like coming-of-age adolescents, reveling in their self-discovery, experimenting with new-found independence, expressing their individuality and separation from their parents. And the older, seasoned gatekeepers were there to encourage misbehavior: *go ahead, take a sip of the heady brew of self-assertion and defiance.*

In the end, Lambeth 1998 overwhelmingly adopted a version of the Kuala Lumpur statement (526 voted in favor, 70 opposed and 45 abstained). The Africans jubilantly shouted, "Victory."[25] Homosexual practice was deemed incompatible with Scripture; same sex unions should not be blessed or legitimated; gays and lesbians in relationships should not be ordained.[26] The recent developments and current practices within TEC had been repudiated, and progressive Episcopal leadership had been rebuked. So abused were the progressives that many actually voted *for* this resolution, fearing a worse alternative—or just fearful—but then soon issued an apology to the international LGBT community for the actions of the Conference. Only seventy bishops voted against the resolution and one-hundred-eighty issued the apology.

Even in the midst of all the nastiness, a touch of grace appeared. Bishop Spong and his wife began to receive bouquets of flowers, dozens and dozens, which they shared with friends. Back in the United States, Dr. Louie Crew and Integrity had arranged for the flower deliveries.[27]

Earlier we suggested that critical biblical scholarship, which has been accepted by religious scholars for nearly two centuries, may have come of age in the debates over female and gay ordination; for the first time, contemporary biblical scholarship informed policy as the church dared move beyond the literalist interpretations of the past. To the same point, Bishop Spong lamented Lambeth's failure to appreciate "the last 150 years of biblical scholarship. . . . A literalized Bible claiming inerrancy for its words has historically been a source of death far more than it has been a source of life. Yet, this kind of fundamentalism was clearly once again live and well in this Communion, making it all but impossible to build in our time a modern and relevant Christianity."[28]

Later, Christine Spong, the bishop's wife, reported to a national gathering of Integrity that the conservative rout at Lambeth may hold a silver lining by encouraging many in the United States to get off the fence and move toward a fully inclusive church.[29] Bishop Clark Grew of Ohio echoed that sentiment. Following plenary sessions punctuated with derisive laughter, hisses, and derogatory slurs toward LGBT supporters, Grew said, "For the first time, I could really understand the fear with which some gay and lesbian people live every day, and I return to Ohio more deeply committed to having our church be truly inclusive, a church where no person is excluded or oppressed because of a particular biblical interpretation."[30]

A conservative bishop from Ft. Worth (Texas, again), on the other hand, was elated. One night when he was out celebrating the unfolding events at Lambeth, he realized that "this is the way liberals must feel every night at our General Convention. And so now the shoe is on the other foot."[31]

In addition to the internal bickering emanating from the right side of TEC within the United States, Episcopalians would now endure the slings and arrows cast from afar. How would Lambeth impact the momentum for full inclusion within TEC? Would centrists be nudged off the fence as Christine Spong hoped or would the church be called back to the traditional biblical interpretations of most of the worldwide Anglican Communion as the conservatives hoped?

During the nineties, the Episcopal journey toward full inclusion approached the mountaintop. Though General Convention had not yet granted legislative approval for LGBT clergy, the ecclesiastical court had filled the breach. There would be future skirmishes on the horizon to include the threat of schism; gains needed to be consolidated; and strained relationships with Anglican cousins required attention. Yet, the decade had been very good for Episcopal gays and lesbians, and the promise of the new millennium appeared bright.

NOTES

1. Stephen Bates, *A Church at War: Anglicans and Homosexuality* (London: I. B. Tauris, 2004), 128.

2. Spong, *Here I Stand*, 420.

3. Ibid., 421.

4. "About Us: Our History," on the website of the American Anglican Council, accessed May 25, 2012, http://www.americananglican.org/our-history/.

5. For background information on the Institute for Religion and Democracy, see Adams, *Going to Heaven*, 122–23, and Swecker, ed., *Hardball on Holy Ground*.

6. Frederick Clarkson, "IRD Advisor to Be Nominated as U.S. Ambassador to the Vatican," on the website of Talk to Action, accessed August 23, 2012, http://www.talk2action.org/story/2007/11/6/235512/911, November 06, 2007.

7. Attributed to Brazilian Archbishop Dom Helder Camara by Zildo Rocha "Helder, o dom: uma vida que marcou os rumos da Igreja no Brasil," 53 (Petrópolis, RJ, Brasil: Editora Vozes, 2000).

8. Andrew J. Weaver and Fred W. Kandeler, "Being *60 Minutes* Means You Never Have to Say You are Sorry—Except Once," January 5, 2006, on the website of Talk to Action, accessed August 23, 2012, http://www.talk2action.org/story/2006/1/5/14192/68149.

9. Richard John Neuhaus, "Reflections on IRD," address to the IRD board, October, 2005, accessed May 28, 2012, http://www.theird.org/Page.aspx?pid=1128.

10. Dr. Andrew J. Weaver, *The Fighting Methodists*, July 10, 2003, on the website of the University of Chicago Divinity School, accessed May 28, 2012, http://divinity.uchicago.edu/martycenter/publications/sightings/archive_2003/0710.shtml.

11. "The 25 most influential Evangelicals in America." *Time* (February 7, 2005). Others on the list included IRD founder Richard John Neuhaus and IRD president Diane Knippers.

12. Weaver, *The Fighting Methodists*.

13. Methodist theologian John B. Cobb Jr., quoted in Swecker, *Hardball on Holy Ground*, vii.

14. Weaver, *The Fighting Methodists*.

15. Lewis C. Daly, "A Church at Risk: The Episcopal 'Renewal Movement,'" Institute for Democracy Studies, *Insights* vol. 2, issue 2 (December 2001).

16. Adams, *Going to Heaven*, 123.

17. American Anglican Council, "Diary from the Second Week of the Lambeth Conference of Anglican Bishops, July 26–August 1, 1998," from the website of American Anglicans, accessed May 28, 2012, http://www.americananglican.org/diary-from-the-second-week-of-the-lambeth-conference-of-anglican-bishops-july-26-august-1-199.

18. Bates, *A Church at War*, 131.

19. Spong, *Here I Stand*, 418–40; and Bates, *A Church at War*, 125–41.

20. Miranda Katherine Hassett, *Anglican Communion in Crisis: How Episcopal Dissidents and Their African Allies Are Reshaping Anglicanism* (Princeton: Princeton University Press, 2007), 73.

21. Bates, *A Church at War*, 137.

22. Clare Garner, "How I Felt the Wrath of a Bishop . . . Fury as the Church Votes for Gay Ban," *The Independent*, August 6, 1998.

23. Bates suggests Carey was picked by Prime Minister Margaret Thatcher in 1991 as "revenge on a Church of England that had made little secret of its distaste for her social policies . . . such trouble as Carey created was because of his inability to provide inspiring and decisive spiritual leadership . . . this may have been because of a lack of an intellectual self-confidence: Carey, gap-toothed and bespectacled, smiling as though he was somehow vaguely missing the joke, was the first archbishop for many generations, perhaps since the Middle Ages, who had not been university educated or raised among the landed gentry or middle classes." Bates, *A Church at War*, 102.

24. Alex Kirby, "Lambeth 1998: Unity at a Price," BBC News, August 8, 1998.

25. Bates, *A Church at War*, 139.

26. Lambeth Conference, *Resolution 1.10 (d)* ". . . homosexual practice as incompatible with Scripture . . . ," and (e) "cannot advise the legitimising or blessing of same sex unions nor ordaining those involved in same gender unions," from the website of the Lambeth Conference, accessed March 1, 2012, http://www.lambethconference.org/resolutions/1998/1998-1-10.cfm.

27. Bishop Spong, private conversation with the author, April 3, 2012.

28. John Shelby Spong, *The Bishop's Voice: Selected Essays*, compiled by Christine Spong, (New York: Crossroads, 2000) 111.

29. James E. Solheim, *Diversity or Disunity* (New York: Church Publishing, 1999), 198.

30. Ibid., 203–4.

31. Ibid., 207.

✳ 16 ✳

JUMPING OFF

Like wild-west stagecoach passengers, Episcopalians at the turn of the century had come a far piece through harsh terrain, and it was time to regroup at a way station before sallying forth with a fresh team hitched up for the last leg of the journey. Passengers had been cramped together, knees dovetailed, elbows and shoulders jostling, and some were mighty uneasy sharing buffalo robes with their neighbor. Some wished to turn the coach around altogether to leave the frontier and return to the land of law and order. Now it was time to stretch out for a spell, fill bellies with venison steaks, beans, and sourdough biscuits, and catch some shut-eye before the final dash through hostile territory.

As the road toward full inclusion rounded the bend at the end of the twentieth century, the Episcopalians paused to catch their breath, still sorting out the consequences of the heresy trial of Bishop Righter and the lambasting at Lambeth. General Convention 2000 would be a lull after the breakneck pace of the nineties but before new controversies would spring from the bushes.

Who would lead the way into unknown territory? Presiding Bishop Frank Griswold would preside over his first General Convention in 2000. Bishop Spong of the Diocese of Newark had retired months before General Convention, bound for the professor's chair at Harvard; LGBT clergy were now commonplace in his diocese and elsewhere—the bishop estimated there were thirty to thirty-five LGBT priests in his diocese by then, most of them partnered—but who would pick up his legacy of lone-wolf leadership?[1] The third and final term of Dr. Pamela Chinnis, the first woman to serve as president of the House of Deputies and a strong ally of gays and lesbians, would end that year. When Archbishop Carey announced his retirement in 2002 ahead of schedule, the progressives hoped to replace him with one of their own. They would, but he would turn out to be a balky, bucky member of the new team.

As the stage left the station, distant drumbeats sounded trouble ahead.

First, a January report from an unofficial grouping of Anglican bishops singled out American progressives for jeopardizing the unity of the Anglican Communion. The general sense of the report was that "universal responsibility must over-ride local preference. Anglicanism is indeed in favor of local contextualization but not in contradiction to universal norms." While implicitly recognizing that the Anglican Communion had no legal authority over the policies of TEC, the international bishops did their best to exert their power of persuasion, always threatening to play the unity card.[2]

Just three months later, primates from the thirty-eight provinces of the Anglican Communion issued a joint communiqué following a Portugal gathering. The communiqué continued to blame LGBT-friendly dioceses for threatening the unity of the Communion:

> [T]he communiqué expressed deep concern with dioceses that repudiate the 1998 Lambeth Conference . . . [which] "have come to threaten the unity of the communion in a profound way. We strongly urge such dioceses to weigh the effects of their actions, and to listen to the expressions of pain, anger and perplexity from other parts of the Communion."[3]

The cruel irony of the statement was mind-boggling. There was no accounting for the "pain, anger, and perplexity" experienced by *gays and lesbians*; instead, gay-friendly dioceses were held accountable for the harsh heterosexism of others—a perverse, collective example of blaming the victim. Inclusion of gays and lesbians in the life of the American church remained a greater sin and impediment to unity than the atrocious treatment of gays and lesbians in the continent of Africa. The statement was an unwitting confession, clear proof that homophobia and not homosexuality was the root issue.

Meanwhile, Presiding Bishop Griswold and Episcopal leadership kept the home fires burning. At the January meeting of the executive council,

Griswold reported that a New York retreat had been "an extremely rich and positive exchange" as participants shared views on LGBT issues. House of Deputies President Chinnes reported that reconciliation was a major part of planning for General Convention later that summer and also that South African Anglican bishop Desmond Tutu had encouraged reconciliation in a recent World Council of Churches speech from the pulpit of Martin Luther King Jr. at Ebeneezer Baptist in Atlanta.[4]

Under the inspiration of Dr. Louie Crew, the original founder of Integrity in 1974 and a continuing leader in the decades that followed, an independent task force was organized that spring to promote unity. The "New Commandment Task Force" included liberals, moderates, and conservatives who sought common ground while "Searching for Solutions to Potential Schism."[5] Meanwhile, a similar impulse toward unity spurred a widely attended forum in Texas that offered speakers with differing points of view.

In July, Episcopal deputies and bishops gathered near the eastern slopes of the Rocky Mountains in Denver, but General Convention 2000 would not confront any major policy issues. Bishop Griswold hailed the spirit of "gracefulness and graciousness" in debate, which was easier without major disputes on the plenary floor. The biggest issue was whether a formal rite of blessing of LGBT relationships would be written into the church liturgies; of course, such blessing ceremonies were already widespread, but officially sanctioned liturgical language would be an important symbol of inclusion and affirmation. Ultimately, the deputies and the bishops agreed with the advance report of the Commission on Liturgy and Music. More dialogue, said the report. There is no consensus, the report added. An absolutist policy that binds all dioceses to uniformity risks schism, the report warned. For now, leave policies about blessing LGBT relationships to the dioceses, the report concluded.[6]

The AAC as an international lobbying force had debuted at Lambeth 1998; in 2000, the AAC would make its first formal appearance at the TEC General Convention. The 150-member AAC contingent included legislative committee advisors and prayer warriors, led by chief strategist Diane Knippers, the president of the Institute for Religion and Democracy (IRD), the right-wing think-tank that sought to penetrate TEC through the AAC.[7]

Although the LGBT Episcopalians and their allies were disappointed at the failure of the rite-of-blessing issue, especially since a similar measure had failed by a mere vote at the prior General Convention (1997, before Lambeth), the gatekeepers had once again failed to reverse the course of the church. Indeed, the adopted language about LGBT relationships affirmed "other life-long committed relationships" which were "characterized by fidelity, monogamy, mutual affection and respect, careful, honest communication, and the holy love which enables those in such relationships to see in each other the image of God."[8]

As our metaphorical stagecoach careened out of Denver following the General Convention, there were passengers who ignored the Wells Fargo "rules of the road" painted ominously inside the coach. *In the event of runaway horses, remain calm. Leaping from the coach in panic will leave you injured, at the mercy of the elements, hostile Indians, and hungry coyotes.* Some folks perceived TEC to be a runaway denomination, and they jumped.

Earlier that year, a few Global South bishops and former Episcopal bishops from South Carolina and West Virginia had brazenly consecrated rival American bishops (not part of TEC) in a ceremony in Singapore in order to "actively seek to plant Anglican missions in areas [in the United States] where there are receptive communities." Even the archbishop of Canterbury expressed disappointment in the provocative proceedings, and Archbishop Carey refused to recognize the new bishops— Charles H. Murphy III, rector of All Saints Episcopal Church in Pawley's Island, South Carolina, and Dr. John H. Rodgers Jr., dean emeritus of Trinity Episcopal School for Ministry in Ambridge, Pennsylvania, the rearing ground for schismatics.[9]

Rodgers had a lengthy history as an Episcopal gatekeeper; he had served on the board of directors for EURRR, then the board of IRD, and finally as a founding board member of the AAC. Following the General Convention, the two schismatic bishops who weren't really bishops predicted that numerous congregations would join their rival group; by then they audaciously called themselves the "Anglican Mission in America" (AMiA) and claimed recognition by several foreign provinces, including those that had ordained them in Singapore, but they would not be recognized by Archbishop Carey.[10] The first schismatic jumpers had jumped, abetted by a few foreigners who undoubtedly delighted in their reverse colonialism *into* the United States. A year later, the Singapore consecrations would be repeated in Denver and four more dissident Episcopal priests would be consecrated as AMiA bishops.

Long before schismatic John Rodgers was consecrated in Singapore as a largely self-appointed bishop, he had wedged himself as a prickly thorn in the side of TEC. We earlier quoted his 2005 eulogy for Diane Knippers regarding her dual leadership role within IRD and AAC, but it bears repeating here to define Rodgers himself:

> It was my honor to serve on the Board of the IRD before and during Diane's service as its Director. She came to that position at a time when the IRD was in need of a fresh focus since the Iron Curtain had fallen and the anti-godly forces were no longer led by the Communist threat. It was Diane that helped us see that the Culture wars were even more dangerous and that we needed to assist the Churches to become conscious of their need to speak up and out concerning what was happening in the mainline Churches. Her leadership in this was superb. In addition she was a leader within the Episcopal Church in its attempts to stem the secularist tide. She was instrumental in forming the AAC, and a superb tactician for the forces of light at General Convention. She continued in giving leadership to the AAC right up until the end of her far too brief life.[11]

The worldview of Rodgers, and presumably his IRD cronies, was astonishing. He considered progressive elements within the ecumenical churches (often *the* denominational leaders) to be an "anti-godly force" more dangerous than the Communist threat during the Cold War era. That the current IRD president is a former CIA analyst only enhances the appearance, if not the reality, of a right-wing political conspiracy that uses wedge issues, especially feminism and LGBT inclusion, to blunt progressive impulses within the ecumenical churches.

To conclude this chapter with our wild-west metaphor, we repeat the warning posted inside the Wells Fargo stagecoach: *In the event of runaway horses, remain calm. Leaping from the coach in panic will leave you injured, at the mercy of the elements, hostile Indians, and hungry coyotes. The*

IRD and its monied backers would prove to be *hungry coyotes*. Despite the warning, the AMiA bishops were the first few jumpers to abandon the Episcopal stagecoach. The AAC was in cahoots, and they wanted to bail out also:

> It is doubtful that this coalition of conservative Episcopalians ever really believed that the Episcopal Church would change and conform to the theology and political direction espoused by the AAC. Although not stated overtly at the time of its founding, the AAC had [a goal of] schism that would result in the formation of an alternative Anglican province in the United States, recognized by the archbishop of Canterbury—a province, which, they believed, would maintain an "orthodox" form of Anglicism, free of the tainting influence of progressives, whom they called "revisionists."[12]

The AAC fretted that no one would leap with them. They needed to frighten the passengers. Not to worry, there would be a dangerous desperado 'round the bend.

<hr/>

NOTES

1. Bishop Spong, private conversation with the author, April 3, 2012.

2. Episcopal News Service, "Delegation of Bishops Issues Critical Report after Visit to the Episcopal Church," January 13, 2000.

3. Episcopal News Service, "Anglican Primates Struggle for Unity in the Face of Sharp Differences on Sexuality," April 13, 2000.

4. Episcopal News Service "Executive Council Sifts through Variety of Concerns, Votes against Using Denver Hotel," January 31, 2000.

5. Episcopal News Service, "New Task Force Promotes Reconciliation," April 13, 2000.

6. Episcopal News Service, "Commission on Liturgy and Music Says Sexuality Decisions Belong on Diocesan Level," February 18, 2000.

7. Daly, *A Church at Risk*, 5.

8. Episcopal News Service, "Convention Recognizes Faithful Relationships Other Than Marriage," July 13, 2000.

9. Episcopal News Service, "Two Consecrated in Singapore to Minister to 'Divided' American Church," January 31, 2000.

10. Episcopal News Service, "Murphy and Rodgers Launch Traditionalist Anglican Mission in America," August 22, 2000.

11. Adams, *Going to Heaven*, 123.

12. Ibid., 122.

* 17 *

THE DEVIL IS LOOSE IN THE CHURCH

The small, liberal arts college known as Sewanee sits atop the Cumberland Plateau just west of the Appalachians in middle Tennessee. It is said that Sewanee students "look beyond the mountain," but history major and class of 1969 graduate Gene Robinson didn't recognize that the outbreak of the Stonewall riots in Greenwich Village just days after his commencement held much significance for him. Indeed, at that time in his life, Robinson's gay sexuality was merely an uneasy gnawing at the edges of his self-awareness.[1]

Sewanee, aka the University of the South, is affiliated with the Episcopal Church. In addition to providing Robinson with a quality education, Sewanee also influenced Robinson's move from the fundamentalist church of his youth to the Episcopal Church, and he was confirmed as an Episcopalian his senior year. His thirteen unbroken years of perfect Sunday school attendance as a youngster demonstrated that he had always been serious about his religion, but it was a fearful, hell-fire-damnation theology that had gripped him then but which he rejected at Sewanee. "One screw-up, one screw-up in timing, and you are a goner," he said. "When you compare what life must be like, lived in that atmosphere, versus, 'Oh my God, what a beautiful day—what can I do with it?'— well, one seems like death to me and the other one seems like life."[2]

During Robinson's seminary days of the early seventies at General Theological Seminary of New York City, he served an internship at the University of Vermont, and the Kentucky-born son of the South was introduced to upper New England and to his future wife, Isabella "Boo"

McDaniel. As their relationship turned serious, Robinson worried about his sexuality. They continued to date and eventually married in 1972 even though Robinson remained fearful that "this thing would raise its ugly head some day, and cause her and me great pain."[3] Two daughters would be born of their marriage.

In 1975, after ordination to the diaconate, and then the priesthood, and then a year of parish ministry in New Jersey, Gene and Boo would return to upper New England and the rustic life of the farm. New Hampshire—the home of the White Mountains, the Granite State, the "Live Free or Die" state, the refuge of flinty Yankee conservatism—would become Robinson's adopted homeland. Husband and wife would pursue an entrepreneurial adventure; they would build a retreat center to be named, "The Sign of the Dove." In the winter months, Robinson would lead weekend retreats, often for youth, and Boo would run "The Pony Farm"—a camp for kids centered around horseback riding—during the summers. A nearby pastor spoke of the retreats led by Robinson: "The retreats were fun and appropriate for youth with some serious talking about faith and what it means in your life, and Gene was very skilled as a facilitator of these things. It was a wonderful addition to the diocese, and many, many congregations utilized it."[4]

By the late seventies, Robinson had begun to read about LGBT issues and spirituality, but it was for professional and not personal reasons, but that all changed in the early eighties when a book by John Fortunato became a mirror into his own soul; what had long been suspected, now became accepted. The following passage "unlocked the rest of my life. Pure and simple. Literally, my life changed upon finishing that book."[5] Fortunato wrote, and the words transformed Robinson:

> Now I knew. Now I understood. And it was as though large chunks of who I had been began falling away, tumbling through time and space and eternity. I just let them fall. No fear now, no resistance, no sense of loss. All that was dropping away. It was unnecessary now, extraneous.
>
> I began to feel light and warm. Energy began to surge through my whole being, and widen me as though I were a rusty old turbine that had been charged up and was starting to hum.

Then two strong, motherly arms reached out and drew me close to the bosom of all that is, and I was just there, just being, enveloped in being.

And we wept.

For joy.

Gene and Boo pursued counseling, but they soon realized they each deserved space to find a mate to be fully loved with all aspects of their being. Gene sold his interest in the retreat center to Boo; they separated and eventually divorced in 1985. After the divorce hearing, the couple retired to their church for a ceremony in which they returned their wedding rings, celebrated communion together, and asked each other for forgiveness for their brokenness.

We had taken those vows in front of God, and we didn't want to sneak away as if they had just melted or something. So, . . . we celebrated the Eucharist together. In the context of that we asked forgiveness for whatever ways in which we had hurt one another, and we pledged ourselves to the joint raising of our children. We gave each other our wedding rings back, that symbol of the wedding vows that we no longer held each other to, and we cried a lot, and then we had Communion. It was just an—astounding moment.[6]

Within a few years, Boo had remarried and Gene had found his future partner, Mark Andrew. By 1990, Gene and Mark were living together openly. Gene and Boo would remain close, and his former wife would be one of his laity presenters during his consecration to the episcopate in 2003.

During their separation process, Gene and Boo visited the recently consecrated New Hampshire bishop, the Rt. Rev. Doug Theuner. Robinson came out to his bishop, and by the way, he mentioned, he would soon need a job. The bishop helped Robinson retain his part-time position as secretary to the New England province, and he also created a *per diem* consultancy for Robinson; thus began a relationship that would continue for seventeen years until the protégé would replace his mentor. Officially, Robinson would become the "canon to the ordinary" (the bishop's assistant). Bishop Theuner didn't know much about

LGBT issues, but hiring Robinson just seemed the right thing to do, and his accidental advocacy soon mushroomed into a role as leading spokesman for LGBT parents to adopt and AIDS advocacy, and ten years later Bishop Theuner would serve as one of the judges that heard the heresy trial of Bishop Walter Righter that changed the course of Episcopal history.[7]

In the mid- to late nineties, others recognized that Robinson had bishop potential; those who worked with him in New Hampshire and beyond attested to Robinson's organizational skills and pastoral leadership, and his reputation opened doors. Robinson was seriously considered for several bishoprics, including as replacement for the retiring Bishop Spong in the Diocese of Newark.

Soon after the dawn of the new millennium, Bishop Theuner informed the Diocesan Standing Committee, his privy council, that he intended to retire by his sixty-fifth birthday, and a two-year process was set in motion to nominate and elect his successor. His protégé, Gene Robinson, became a candidate.

Rev. David Jones was picked to co-chair the Search and Nominating Committee. Rev. Jones described himself as a conservative from the evangelical wing of the church with evangelist Billy Graham as a major influence in his faith formation. He had also served in the Pittsburgh Diocesan office that would soon become the principal base of opposition to Robinson's election. But perhaps he had acquired a bit of granite himself, a gritty streak of Yankee independence, and Jones would vigorously defend the process by which Robinson was nominated because of his fervent belief that it was a Spirit-filled, Pentecostal experience.

This whole adventure, the search process and its outcome, has really been an interesting spiritual journey for me. It's not that I've changed my basic theological position at all, but it's forced me to think about how, if you consistently and accurately apply what you say you believe, you might come out in a place you didn't expect . . . the hand of God and the power of the Spirit is so clearly in charge. . . . Well, it was sort of like *wind*, it was sort of like *fire*, it was sort of like *jabberwocky*. . . . I don't know how to tell you. But nobody doubted it.[8]

Robinson was one of five candidates selected by the nominating committee; one withdrew upon election to another diocese, leaving four choices for the New Hampshire election. Mike Barwell, a layperson and media consultant, volunteered to be the press contact for the circus that he knew would soon descend upon New Hampshire. Barwell had prior experience as a writer for the Episcopal News Service, and he had covered four General Conventions as well as the consecration of Bishop Barbara Harris in 1989. As he expected, the national media arrived in force for the June 7, 2003, election.

Just as David Jones had felt the Spirit during the nomination process, many more sensed the Spirit's presence for the election. Listen to the remembrance of one in attendance, Paula Bibber, Bishop Theuner's executive secretary:

> In the very beginning, everything was pretty normal: it was a full house; there was excitement, because we were there for a very special reason; but when the final vote was announced the feeling in that church was just amazing. I think everybody felt it; the place was charged. I know that it stayed with people; it stayed with me. Later, I could not unwind, I felt so energized by all that had happened that day. I think everybody felt it a little differently, and of course we had a ton of reporters there with cameras and everything, but even that didn't take away from the feeling in the room. Even they must have felt what was going on, it was so powerful.[9]

So, too, the bishop's own recollection of the moment his life changed, and that of the church as well:

> The atmosphere at St. Paul's Church, Concord, on that summer morning was electric. The Holy Spirit seemed so palpably present that people spoke of the hair standing up on their necks. While the first ballots were being counted, you could have heard a pin drop, as people sat silently or knelt humbly in prayer. When the final result was read, announcing my election as the ninth bishop of New Hampshire, a rush of wind swept through the congregation as people rose to their feet to applaud, cheer, laugh, cry, and

rejoice. People who were there still refer to it as one of the most moving and powerful experiences of God in their lifetimes.[10]

Gene Robinson's own Diocese of New Hampshire had elected him to succeed his mentor as bishop coadjutor on the second ballot by healthy majorities of laity and clergy (a coadjutor is a successor bishop who serves jointly with the diocesan bishop for a temporary period until the diocesan bishop retires or dies). Those who knew him best, who had worked with him for more than two decades, had affirmed his leadership skills, but more than that, his calling, and by simply following the will of God, as they understood it, history was made. Of course, they all knew that Gene must still be approved by the national church, and preparations for General Convention 2003 began immediately.

The New Hampshire Diocese elected Robinson on June 7, 2003; across the sea at Lambeth palace, the news was not received well by the recently enthroned archbishop of Canterbury.

When the name of Rowan Williams had first been mentioned as the probable successor to George Carey as the archbishop of Canterbury, the wide grin of the progressives had been matched by the grimace of the conservatives. Then serving as the archbishop of Wales, the scholarly Williams had earned a reputation as a "bit of a lefty," who had "written and spoken tolerantly on the gay issue."[11] In February, 2003, Williams had become the 104th archbishop of Canterbury:

> [In a] scene rich in reds, purples, blues and greens with Williams himself resplendent in yellow, [and] to the sound of African drums and a Welsh harpist, Rowan Williams was enthroned as archbishop of Canterbury, reflecting his homeland and the importance of Africa within the world-wide Anglican Communion.
>
> Almost all the primates of the 38 provinces of the Anglican Communion were present at the service to mandate Williams, aged 52, as the 104th Archbishop of Canterbury and spiritual head of the Church of England.

Also in the congregation in the majestic medieval cathedral in south-east England was the church's full company of bishops, representatives of world faiths, the heir to the British throne, Prince Charles, and Prime Minister Tony Blair.[12]

After kissing and swearing an oath upon the Canterbury Gospels, a manuscript presented to the see of Canterbury by Pope Gregory the Great (CE 590–604), the new archbishop ascended the marble throne of St. Augustine that dates to the thirteenth century and assumed his place as head of the Church of England and spiritual leader of millions of Anglicans around the world.

Just a few months later, when he faced his first obstacle, Archbishop Williams stumbled. Confronted with the recurring leadership task of balancing justice for some against the resistance of others, Williams chose expediency. Like so many church leaders before him, Williams surrendered to fears that the good order of the church would be impaired if he allowed the march of history to proceed forward.

But it was not the election of Gene Robinson that tested the archbishop's leadership; it was the virtually simultaneous appointment of a gay priest to be a bishop suffragan in the Diocese of Oxford, in the archbishop's backyard (a suffragan is an assistant bishop without the right of succession). In July 2003, barely a month after Robinson's election in New Hampshire and only days before the scheduled consecration of the Rev. Jeffrey John, Archbishop Williams confounded his liberal supporters by intervening in Rev. John's appointment. (In the United States, bishops are elected by a diocese, subject to consent of the national church; in the rest of the Anglican Communion, they are appointed.) Rev. John had been living openly with another English priest for many years, but that hadn't stopped his appointment by the bishop of Oxford nor had it lessened the broad support from a distinguished group of English clerics.

"Unity! Unity!" howled the Global South Anglicans as John's consecration approached. "Schism! Schism!" The threats echoed through the ancient halls of Lambeth Palace, haunting and frightening the novice archbishop. On July 6, 2003, the Most Reverend Rowan Williams, the 104th archbishop of Canterbury in a line that dated to the fifteenth century, sacrificed Rev. Jeffrey John on the altar of church unity. What is more, he coerced Rev. John into stating withdrawal was his own idea, but John soon set the record straight after the deed was done; in fact, he attempted to rescind his withdrawal and fight, but it was too late.[13]

Conservative Anglicans around the world exhaled with relief, but they barely had time to draw another breath before the Episcopalians loosed the devil in the church. Just a few weeks after Archbishop Williams chopped the knees off of the Rev. Jeffrey John, TEC gathered in Minneapolis for their 2003 General Convention. Robinson's election by his own diocese wasn't final; Episcopal polity required national approval, and since his election had been less than 120 days before the scheduled General Convention, it would be the deputies and bishops who gathered in Minneapolis at the end of July who would have the last word.

———————

Minneapolis is the city of lakes, located in Minnesota, the land of ten thousand lakes. July in Minnesota is splendid, and the freezing blizzards of January are merely a test of character for the thousands of Minnesotans whose reward is to wet a fish line or take a dip in the sky-blue waters of midsummer. Yah, sure, you betcha.

The Episcopalians had been there before. In 1976, they had come to Minneapolis for their General Convention. Before they would leave, they had voted to reform their canons to allow women to be ordained to the priesthood. Six years into the future in 2009, the ELCA Churchwide Assembly would gather in the Minneapolis Convention Center, and they would adopt historic measures embracing LGBT clergy. A year after that in 2010, the Presbyterian General Assembly would also convene in the same Minneapolis Convention Center, and they too would reverse long-standing policies and vote to allow LGBT ordinations.

There must be something about the Minnesota water.

Just three weeks after the archbishop of Canterbury's weak-kneed failure to stand up to the bullies of the worldwide Anglican Communion, the Episcopal General Convention deputies and bishops would spend a fortnight in Minnesota in the Minneapolis Convention Center. The Episcopalians, too, would take a dip in the water.

If Lambeth 1998 had been the scene of a U.S.-style political convention on the part of the conservatives, it was the Episcopal progressives who had learned their lessons well. Gene Robinson was a candidate running for office with a well-oiled campaign. His supporters roamed the hallways sporting buttons that said "Ask Me about Gene." Robinson himself wore one that said, "I AM Gene" as he chatted and greeted all comers with a friendly grin and firm handshake. Partner Mark followed closely, appearing a bit self-conscious, and a burly security man with a crewcut kept a close watch.[14]

A standing-room-only audience followed Robinson's speech before a committee considering the consecration of bishops. Many more clustered around the closed-circuit TV monitors in adjacent rooms. Part of Robinson's task, now and continuing throughout the convention, would be a rebuttal of lies put out by his adversaries. He had not abandoned his wife and children, and they said so in highly supportive terms (his relationship with Mark Andrews began a couple of years *after* the divorce). Robinson's twenty-one-year-old daughter appeared in person and read aloud a statement prepared by her mother, which demonstrated her continuing high regard for the man who had once been her husband: "Our lives together both married and divorced have been examples of how to deal with difficult decisions with grace, love, integrity, and honour. He is worthy of your affirmation. His charisma will draw in many more people to the church than will leave due to his sexuality. He will be a truly great bishop."[15]

The House of Deputies would vote first, and Robinson needed to receive a majority of both the laity and the clergy and also overcome the convoluted rules that voting was by order. Tie votes within an order counted as a no vote. Nevertheless, Robinson was easily approved by roughly two-to-one majorities.

Before the House of Bishops' vote the following day, which was likely to be dicey anyway, the scent of scandal wafted out of the AAC headquarters with an allegation that placed Robinson's ordination in serious jeopardy. A different allegation that arrived by e-mail had to be dealt with first. Bishop Gordon Scruton of the Diocese of Western Massachusetts was assigned to investigate.

The first allegation developed from an e-mail sent by a TV viewer back in New England who had been watching a news report of the proceedings. Mr. David Lewis claimed he had been touched inappropriately by Bishop-elect Robinson at a regional church gathering years earlier. Even the normally reliable Episcopal News Service was swept up in the emotion of the moment, falsely reporting that "a Vermont man sent an e-mail to bishops accusing Robinson of *fondling* him" [emphasis added].[16] The unfortunate word choice was a sensationalist misstatement—Lewis' e-mail made no such claim.

When the investigating Bishop Scruton contacted Mr. Lewis, he backed off and asked that the matter be dropped. The alleged "touching" of years earlier turned out to be entirely innocuous. In a crowded conference room, Robinson had passed Lewis and stopped briefly to exchange a greeting. In doing so, Robinson had grasped Lewis' upper arm and patted him on the back.[17]

Shocking. Objection overruled.

The second allegation was even more titillating. Robinson was connected to pornographic websites, according to a "portly, red-faced pseudojournalist addicted to conspiracy theories and running his own raucously partisan conservative website." During his fifteen minutes of fame, the man strutted around the convention media center, gleefully sputtering, "I have found the smoking gun. We got him!"[18] The accuser's last name was Virtue. You can't make this stuff up.

Mr. David Virtue was part of the gatekeeping organization the American Anglican Council (AAC). It had been the AAC chairman, David C. Anderson, who first alerted church authorities to the allegations of Mr. Virtue. "I think the bishops in considering his worthiness would want to weigh that,"[19] Anderson said as he bounced around the convention press center, hoping that substance would back up the flimsy allegation, even while sanctimoniously claiming otherwise.

Supporters were stunned. Bishop Samuel G. Candler of the Diocese of Atlanta had spoken passionately on behalf of Rev. Robinson, but he admitted that he was shaken by the allegation.[20]

Detractors smugly asserted, "We told you so." Rev. Donald Armstrong of Colorado Springs, an opponent of Robinson, claimed that the allegation about pornography was entirely predictable because of Robinson's disordered sexuality, and he suggested that Robinson ought to withdraw his candidacy.[21]

Robinson seemingly went into hiding. After a private meeting with church leaders, he sought privacy while the storm whirled around him. Robinson himself would later use the metaphor of the storm's eye to describe that day:

> I received a photograph from a fellow priest of the diocese—a weather satellite photo taken miles above a huge hurricane in the Atlantic. In the center of that terrible and fierce storm was a tiny pinpoint of calm. That is where I have tried to put myself ever since my life changed.
>
> But the fact of the matter is that I cannot live in the eye of the storm on my own. Only God can calm and soothe me when hatred and vitriol come my way. Only God can persuade me not to step into the powerful winds swirling about me; when I do, only God can keep me from being swept away by their destructive power.[22]

A Fox News commentator, Fred Barnes, repeated the allegations on the blog of the Rupert Murdoch–supported neocon magazine *The Weekly Standard*. It would turn out that Mr. Barnes had connections to IRD, the politically motivated "think tank" that sought to influence TEC, the UMC, and the PC(USA).[23]

The investigation into the pornographic website complaint revealed no connection to Robinson whatsoever. It was a "six degrees of separation" claim run amok. The questionable link had been placed on an organization's website long after Robinson was no longer involved with the organization. The guilt-by-association smear tactic of unvirtuous Mr. Virtue failed. The investigator, Bishop Scruton, reported to his fellow bishops that there was "no necessity to pursue" either complaint further.[24] Objection overruled.

When the bishops finally conducted their own vote a day late, Robinson's ordination to the episcopate was approved by nearly 60 percent. Perhaps a vote or two swung in favor of Bishop-elect Robinson due to the underhanded tactics of the gatekeepers. Presiding Bishop Griswold voted in favor. "There was nothing to stop his consecration now, no archbishop to apply the thumbscrews as Rowan Williams had done to Jeffrey John a month earlier."[25]

General Convention 2003 witnessed the emergence of a gatekeeping leader, Bishop Robert Duncan of the Pittsburgh Diocese, soon to become the preeminent schismatic. Duncan had been Robinson's seminary mate twenty-five years earlier. Bishop Jack Iker of the Fort Worth Diocese was another conservative who had been in seminary with Robinson and Duncan. Even then, Robinson remembered there were two groups with differing worldviews, a telling foretaste of their ideological differences two and a half decades later: "There was this great divide at the seminary," Gene said. "There was one group who were always fighting about—or talking about—what kind of vestments should be worn and how many candles should be at the altar, and all this kind of froufrou, churchy stuff. And then there were others of us who were trying to figure out what it meant to be a priest in those turbulent times [of the early seventies]."[26]

Following General Convention's endorsement of Rev. Robinson's episcopacy, Duncan and his cronies announced a Texas meeting in October to promote schism. Their announcement blustered: "This decision has denied the plain teaching of Scripture and the moral consensus of the church. . . . With grief we bishops must reject this action. May God have mercy on his church."[27] *Lord have mercy. Christ have mercy. Lord have mercy.* It never occurred to the gatekeepers that perhaps God was, indeed, being merciful. *Kyrie Eleison.*

Meanwhile, across the Atlantic, the archbishop of Canterbury also scheduled an October emergency meeting for primates of the world. With Bishop-elect Robinson's consecration set for November, it would be a busy fall.

———

By November 2003, the leaf-peeping tourists had long since departed upper New England. The once brilliant shades of orange, red, and yellow now lay in a patchwork quilt on the forest floor of the granite mountains. A fresh crowd—an eclectic mix of church people, law enforcement, news media, LGBT folk, and students—descended on the campus of the University of New Hampshire in Durham on the first weekend of the month. The dozens of armed and uniformed policemen, some on horseback and some posted on rooftops as snipers, said this was more than a fall football weekend. So did the array of dozens of satellite dishes mounted on news trucks.[28]

Saturday, November 1, was a day of anticipation and preparation as the hockey arena was transformed into a cathedral. Cranes hoisted banks of theater lights into place, bishop's chairs and altar were set as centerpieces, and miles of electrical cords were stretched and nestled around the edges. In the middle of the afternoon, "Gene and his partner Mark arrived, beaming, with a large entourage of security. Unlike the affable bodyguards who had been accompanying Gene during the past few weeks, these were stone-faced Secret Service types from a Boston agency, with curly cords fastened behind their ears. Immediately they started scanning the arena for potential security loopholes."[29] A fence had been constructed to encircle the small area away from the arena where the clown show from Westboro Baptist Church would perform (this is the Fred Phelps family that haunts military funerals and other events to spew antigay venom). When Gene and Presiding Bishop Griswold robed the next day, they would don bulletproof vests under their outer garments, as would partner Mark. Death threats from crackpots were treated seriously. Airport security devices guarded the arena entrances.

Late on Saturday evening, a haggard Mike Barwell, the media coordinator, drained his final cup of coffee and mumbled to no one in particular, "Everything will be fine. Everything will be fine."[30]

The consecration service was scheduled to begin at 4:00 o'clock on Sunday afternoon. By 10:00 that morning, the committee members and volunteers began to assemble. They would assist the bishops and dignitaries who would arrive for an 11:00 AM rehearsal. After the rehearsal, the lights were turned low, and the staff that had been working and planning for months enjoyed a last meal together: box lunches and caffeinated sodas.

The first arrivals were the musicians: the orchestra and the two-hundred-member choir from around the diocese. The church delegations of clergy, wardens, and banner-bearers began to mill around the arena floor. High above the arena in the outer ring behind the seats, bishops in purple shirts with gold crosses dangling from heavy chains stepped off the elevator into their gathering space, the Sky Lounge. The festive mood spilled down from the Sky Lounge and also seeped up from the arena floor to the slowly filling seats and a murmuring crowd. By 3:45 PM, thousands packed the arena.

And then it began, and history unfolded before the eyes of those present and a multitude huddled around distant televisions.

A hush fell over the assembly as a youth bell choir filed onto the floor to take their places around a white-draped table. When the soft peals of the hand bells died out, the organ and the brass stirred the crowd with a fanfare, and the procession began with the first hymn: "The Church's One Foundation." First came acolytes bearing crosses and torches, then came the clergy and banners of each parish in the New Hampshire Diocese, then more acolytes escorting the huge contingent of nondiocesan clergy and interfaith guests—the Jewish yarmulkes and the black crown of an Orthodox priest stood out—then the first hymn was over and the second began. A roar went up as the third wave of acolytes preceded the procession of bishops arrayed in white albs under red cassocks and individualized stoles. A second roar sounded as the six co-consecrating bishops entered in resplendent floor-length, cape-like copes and tall mitres, except for diminutive Bishop Barbara Harris, consecrated fourteen years earlier as the first female bishop in Christendom. Other co-consecrators included former Presiding Bishop Edmond Browning and Bishop Emeritus of the Lutheran Church of Sweden Krister Stendahl.[31]

Some folks continued to sing, but most were crying. "The sight of so many clergy in courageous partnership with so many lay people, and the gravity and joy of the historic moment, were intensely moving, and no one, even the most seasoned Anglican groupies, had ever seen anything like this."[32] Finally, Gene Robinson entered in a simple white monk's cassock with hood, accompanied by his partner, his former wife and their daughters, his parents and other family members, Dr. Louie Crew of Integrity, and other friends, followed by the presiding bishop. With a soprano descant, the procession ended, and the liturgy began.

Prayers were offered, scriptures were read, hymns were sung, objectors raised objections and embarrassed themselves, and then Gene's mentor and predecessor, Bishop Doug Theuner, offered a "prophetic, moving, often funny, and inspiring" sermon. After a formal questioning of the prospective bishop, recitation of the Nicene Creed, and the singing of the ancient hymn, *"Veni Creator Spiritus"* ("Come, Holy Spirit"), the moment of laying on hands arrived. Gene knelt in front of the presiding bishop and all the other bishops assembled behind, the first layer touching Gene and the outer layers touching those in front.

After consecrating prayers, the Rt. Rev. Gene Robinson was now the bishop coadjutor of the Diocese of New Hampshire. A gold satin stole was placed over his shoulders by his parents and his sister; a bishop's mitre, a gift from his partner Mark and Mark's family, was placed on his head; Bishop Theuner placed a shepherd's crook in his hand; and an earlier bishop from New Hampshire placed his own ring on Mark's finger. Up in the press box, even the reporters exchanged handshakes with moist eyes.

As the news traveled instantly through the array of satellite dishes into cyberspace, the response of some was decidedly other-worldly. "The devil has clearly entered the church," said the archbishop of Kenya, even before the maintenance crew had finished cleaning up.[33]

NOTES

1. For full treatment of the Gene Robinson story, see Bates, *A Church at War*; the excellent authorized biography by Adams, *Going to Heaven*; and Bishop Gene Robinson's own reflections, *In the Eye of the Storm*.

2. Adams, *Going to Heaven*, 26.

3. Ibid., 31.

4. Ibid., 48.

5. John Fortunato, *Embracing the Exile: Healing Journeys for Gay Christians* (New York: Seabury Press, 1982), 18. Also cited in Adams, *Going to Heaven*, 54.

6. Adams, *Going to Heaven*, 56.

7. Ibid., 59–71.

8. Ibid., 88, 90.

9. Ibid., 98.

10. Bishop Gene Robinson, *In the Eye of the Storm*, 1.

11. Bates, *A Church at War*, 144.

12. Cedric Pulford, Episcopal News Service, "Sounds of Africa and Wales Usher in New Leader of Anglican Communion," February 28, 2003.

13. See Bates, *A Church at War*, 155–79, for an excellent, in-depth review of the Jeffrey John story. Of course, the Anglican Communion had countless gay bishops in the past, but they were closeted. Retired Utah Bishop Otis Charles had come out after his retirement a decade earlier. Rev. John was appointed to the prestigious deanship of St. Albans as a consolation prize a year later by Prime Minister Tony Blair. It is sometimes supposed that Rev. John's withdrawal meant that Gene Robinson would become the first openly gay person ordained an Anglican bishop. Though Robinson would be the first openly gay *Episcopal* bishop, there is clear evidence that other openly gay persons had been ordained bishops elsewhere in the Anglican Communion. One example, of many, is Mervyn Castle, an openly gay priest from South Africa, who was consecrated as the bishop of False Bay by Archbishop Desmond Tutu in 1994 (Castle claimed to be celibate) without controversy.

14. Bates, *A Church at War*, 181.

15. Ibid., 183.

16. Episcopal News Service, "Allegations Stall Robinson Vote," August 4, 2003.

17. Monica Davey and Al Baker, "Gay Bishop Wins in Episcopal Vote; Split Threatened," *New York Times*, August 6, 2003.

18. Bates, *A Church at War*, 185.

19. Monica Davey, "Sexual Accusations Delay Vote by Episcopalians on Gay Bishop," *New York Times*, August 5, 2003.

20. Davey and Baker, "Gay Bishop Wins."

21. Davey, "Sexual Accusations."

22. Robinson, *In the Eye of the Storm*, 2.

23. Fred Barnes, "The Gay Bishop's Links: Episcopalian Bishop-Elect Gene Robinson Has some Curious Affiliations," *The Weekly Standard*, August 4, 2003, http://www.weeklystandard.com/Content/Public/Articles/000/000/002/954kbxkw.asp. Mr. Barnes later served on the Board of Directors of the Institute for Religion and Democracy.

24. Davey and Baker, "Gay Bishop Wins."

25. Bates, *A Church at War*, 187.

26. Adams, *Going to Heaven*, 27.

27. Bates, *A Church at War*, 188.

28. The description of the consecration of Bishop Gene Robinson is a summary derived from the excellent, in-depth, eyewitness account of biographer Elizabeth Adams, "Consecration," in *Going to Heaven*, 181.

29. Ibid., 183.

30. Ibid., 184.

31. Three years earlier, Stendahl had participated in the *extra ordinem* ordination of Lutheran Anita C. Hill in St. Paul, Minnesota (see "Part Three: The Lutherans"). Curiously, the Roman Catholic Church does not acknowledge the "apostolic succession" of Anglican bishops, but it does accept the succession of Swedish bishops within the Lutheran Church of Sweden. The Rt. Rev. Herbert Donovan Jr., the retired bishop of Arkansas; the Rt. Rev. Thomas Eastman, the retired bishop of Maryland; and the Rt. Rev. Chilton Knudsen, the bishop of Maine and president of the New England province, filled out the group of six co-consecrators. Adams, *Going to Heaven*, 200.

32. Adams, *Going to Heaven*, 194.

33. Bates, *A Church at War*, 4.

* 18 *

THE WINDSOR REPORT

At Archbishop Williams' emergency October 2003, meeting at Lambeth, the Global South Anglicans huffed and puffed and threatened to blow the house down; minus a few shutters and shingles, the house still stands. That same month in Texas, the Episcopal gatekeepers, amidst grand promises for their own future and doomsday forecasts for the Episcopalians, would indeed wrench open the floodgates of schism . . . and a trickle dribbled through. While offering a grand gesture to the Anglican Communion, TEC would not retreat from prior gains and continued to march boldly toward full inclusion.

These will be the triple threads woven into this chapter, together with a note about the retirement of Archbishop Williams and the enthronement of his successor.

First, we visit the Lambeth Summit, the emergency meeting called by Archbishop Williams in October 2003 just a few weeks before the New Hampshire consecration of Gene Robinson. Williams had invited the thirty-eight primates from the worldwide provinces to Lambeth Palace to consider the Anglican Communion's response to Rev. Robinson's pending consecration as well as pro-LGBT actions of the Canadian church.

The Anglican Church of Canada was in much the same place as the Episcopal Church. Both North American provinces had been moving steadily toward full inclusion of LGBT persons and were thus castigated by many Anglicans from developing nations. For the Canadians, the principal issue had been rites celebrating same-gender relationships, especially after the Diocese of New Westminster, British Columbia, authorized such a rite in 2002 and the national church quietly acquiesced. In 2004, by action of their General Synod, all Canadian dioceses would be authorized to follow the lead of New Westminster.[1] These actions presaged the changes in the civil law in Canada; following judicial decisions in 2003 that opened many jurisdictions to marriage equality, the Canadian Parliament passed the Civil Marriage Act, effective July 20, 2005, which authorized same-sex marriage across the entire nation.

Initially, a few Africans threatened to boycott the opening Eucharist that included Episcopal Presiding Bishop Griswold and the Canadian delegation, but Archbishop Williams persuaded the dissenters, and eventually all the primates participated. The North Americans would not back down, and the African bullies would not get their way; there would be no ham-handed attempt to intervene in the Robinson consecration. Archbishop Williams gingerly handled the lid atop a bubbling cauldron by appointing a study commission.

Specifically, Archbishop Eames of Ireland was appointed head of a commission to solicit input and suggest a path that would preserve peace and harmony. Eames had performed a similar service for the Communion regarding the ordination of women a decade earlier.

A year later, the Eames Commission would issue the so-called "Windsor Report." The Windsor Report of October 2004 concluded that unity could only be restored if the Episcopalians accepted harsh recommendations. The pertinent section suggested that TEC should "be invited to" express regret for allowing the consecration of Robinson, the co-consecrators should "be invited to" temporarily withdraw from participation in the Anglican Communion, and the Episcopalians should "be invited to" effect a moratorium on future LGBT episcopal ordinations.[2] Windsor treated TEC as a misbehaving child, forced into a time out.

On the other hand, those who had sponsored rival bishops in the United States were also displeased that the report called for a moratorium on their incursions onto U.S. soil. From Archbishop Akinola of Nigeria: "How patronizing! We will not be intimidated. In the absence of any signs of repentance and reform from those who have torn the fabric of our Communion, and while there is continuing oppression of those who uphold the Faith, we cannot forsake our duty to provide care and protection for those who cry out for our help."[3]

Although the LGBT inclusion policies of the North American Anglicans provided the impetus for the Windsor Report, the report said little about human sexuality but plenty about Anglican Communion polity. The report proposed the concept of a formalized "covenant" (contract) that would define the institutional Communion and create mutual rights and responsibilities between the signatory parties. Local and regional autonomy of dioceses and provinces would be diminished. Institutional authority would move to the collective body of primates. Since change rarely occurs in a top-down fashion (Vatican II is the exception that proves the rule), the diminution in the voices of the church swelling up from below would render the Communion institutionally conservative and slow to move. Critics charged that the Windsor Report proposed a papal Curia and Magisterium model.

> Windsor was supposed to define a way through a "crisis," whose presenting issue was human sexuality, especially the acceptability of non-celibate homosexual lifestyles among the clergy and leaders of the church. Its approach is to forward a new polity for the Anglican Communion, one that translates the poetry of mutual affection and nostalgia for Canterbury into institutional structures that move in the direction of international canon law. What was formerly a loose federation of legally independent churches would now be bound together by a covenant, which would be given legal status by each of the member churches passing a canon to observe it.[4]

The overriding Episcopal sentiment was to encourage continuing communion internationally but without sacrificing the inclusive gains that had been attained domestically. A delicate balance, indeed, and TEC sought that balance up to and including General Convention 2006, when the church would offer a *beau geste*.

First, the Episcopal House of Bishops would issue a "Covenant Statement" in March 2005 that affirmed a fervent commitment to the Anglican

Communion, expressed regret for "any failure to consult" (but not for consecrating Gene Robinson), and promised to encourage Episcopal dioceses to delay any episcopal elections (not just for LGBT candidates but all elections) until after General Convention 2006. The statement was meant as an in-kind, good faith response to the recommendations of Windsor.[5]

Neither the domestic nor foreign gatekeepers were satisfied. Nothing less than confession, repentance, and complete prohibition of LGBT clergy would suffice. The gatekeepers sought neither dialogue nor compromise, only capitulation, and failing to achieve surrender, then schism.

From the American Anglican Council (AAC):

Behind all the momentous meetings and breathless statements of the past year, the spiritual truth remains: the Episcopal Church and Anglican Church of Canada have erred and will not repent. Anyone who thinks the Windsor Report can wash away this fact is a Pollyanna. Anyone who lives inside these churches knows the truth: homosexuality is acculturated in these churches beyond return. They will not back down under any circumstances. They would rather die than change.

The Global South leaders—a substantial majority of them at any rate—consider the actions of the Episcopal Church and the Anglican Communion to be heretical and church-dividing. They are not willing to coexist with churches that teach heresy and practice immorality. They are not interested in clever compromises.[6]

———

Next, we visit the Texas meeting in October 2003, called by Pittsburgh bishop Robert Duncan, that resulted in more meetings and another splinter group. Duncan was emerging as a bomb-thrower, willing to do great damage to the Episcopal Church on these shores and the Anglican Communion abroad. We will witness his destructive tendencies in a moment. Following the preliminary meeting, an "organizing convocation" on January 19–21, 2004, adopted a charter and elected Duncan as moderator. This organization eventually settled on the name the "Anglican Communion Network" (ACN).[7]

Even as the ACN organized, it was forced to issue sputtering denials of its schismatic, confrontational, and litigious plans as revealed in a confidential document announcing the new organization. Recipients of the document had been warned to share it "in hard copy (printed format) only with people you fully trust, and do not pass it on electronically to anyone under any circumstances."[8]

On December 28, 2003, Geoff Chapman had sent the confidential document to inform interested parties about the upcoming convocation and outlining strategy and goals. To the great embarrassment of movement leaders, the *Washington Post* obtained a copy and published a report on the eve of the convocation, January 14, 2004. The document encouraged widespread disobedience and challenge to the authority of Episcopal bishops. "Our ultimate goal," the document stated, is a "replacement jurisdiction" to supplant the Episcopal Church within the Anglican Communion. The document, and Chapman the author in a subsequent phone interview, encouraged resort to the civil courts and the Episcopal ecclesiastical courts to fight over church property.[9]

Despite their denials, the gatekeepers clearly had auspicious goals and were prepared to pursue audacious means to achieve them. Six years later, the AAC's CEO and chaplain J. Philip Ashey reportedly stated, "We do not believe that Canterbury will recognize us, at least while the current archbishop is still in office." But, he added, "Like Special Forces, we go behind the scenes and we blow up things."[10] Duncan and the insurrectionists would perform as promised.

For those keeping score at home, the remnants of EURRR continued as Anglicans United, and the American Anglican Council (AAC) still had a head of steam, although its vice-president (Duncan) now sought salvation elsewhere. These organizations were now joined by Duncan's ACN. For the time being, these various gatekeeping factions remained *within* TEC. Meanwhile, the Anglican Mission in America (AMiA), of the Singapore consecrations and foreign oversight of a few American bishops and congregations, continued to sputter along as a schismatic organization *outside* TEC. Be forewarned, there will be more fiefdoms and self-appointed bishops to come.

At General Convention 2006, gales from across the Atlantic—the oner-ous Windsor recommendations—and a brewing storm at home—the auspicious and audacious "replacement jurisdiction" of the AAC/ACN—inspired the Episcopalians to choose a leader who understood navigating difficult wind currents. Once again, the Episcopalians would make his-tory. For the first time ever, the leader of a major denomination would be a woman; Rev. Katharine Jefferts Schori, a licensed airplane pilot and bishop of the Diocese of Nevada, was elected to be the 26th presiding bishop of TEC on June 18, 2006.

The Episcopalians would not ignore their detractors, foreign and domestic, and wrestled mightily with an action that would placate mother England and Canterbury, the Anglicans of the Global South, and those who had one foot out the Episcopal door. But neither would they offer appeasement, and the election of the female bishop from Nevada to be presiding bishop signaled their continuing willingness to lead, but in a progressive, inclusive, twenty-first-century direction, and they would not delay long to wait for the privileged protectors of patriarchy to catch up.

After much debate and the suspension of parliamentary rules, the General Convention offered a *beau geste*, "a fine gesture with unwelcome or futile consequences." On the last day of the legislative sessions, reso-lution B033 was adopted during an extraordinary joint session of the Houses of Bishops and Deputies, with the support of outgoing Presiding Bishop Griswold and incoming Presiding Bishop Jefforts Schori. The resolution committed the church to "exercise restraint by not consenting to the consecration of any candidate to the episcopate whose manner of life presents a challenge to the wider church and will lead to further strains on communion."[11]

Even Bishop Robinson offered tepid support if it would strengthen Presiding Bishop Jefferts Schori, as she would be the first female primate within the Anglican Communion:

[T]o give her everything that she can have in her pocket to go to the primates meeting, to go to the rest of the Communion," he said. "In some sense, having given the Anglican Communion what it asked for regarding gay and lesbian members of this church, we'll be looking to them to see if they were serious about wanting to be in conversation about this, or whether they wanted this to end the conversation."[12]

For his part, the archbishop of Canterbury, Rowan Williams, expressed guarded optimism in a meandering "reflection" that concluded, "My hope is that the period ahead—of detailed response to the work of General Convention, exploration of new structures, and further refinement of the covenant model—will renew our positive appreciation of the possibilities of our heritage so that we can pursue our mission with deeper confidence and harmony." But, for the archbishop, unity still trumped justice; he maintained that fair treatment for LGBT persons in civil society was appropriate but that the status of gays and lesbians in the church remained a murky, unresolved issue. The archbishop still argued that the consecration of Robinson ignored the "mutual respect" of the disparate elements of the Anglican Communion, a unilateral action that had "costly consequences" for the Communion. In effect, he urged the Episcopalians to cease and desist as the Communion sought consensus.[13]

At General Convention 2006, TEC did indeed push the "pause" button. Would that satisfy either the domestic or the foreign gatekeepers? Or, would they insist on "stop" or even "rewind?" Bishop Robinson correctly identified the response to resolution B033 as a test of the intentions of the gatekeepers, "we'll be looking to them to see if they were serious about wanting to be in conversation about this, or whether they wanted this to end the conversation." Would they see this Episcopal gesture as the way forward to further discussions or would it be rejected as insufficiently penitent and short on prescriptive measures toward gays? Was "dialogue" in their vocabulary?

The gatekeepers would soon give their answer. The leader of the international conspiracy, Robert Duncan, declared the See of Canterbury and the Lambeth Conference to be "lost."

The grand premise of ACN, according to the confidential letter quoted above, was to be a "replacement jurisdiction" that would supplant TEC as the North American expression of Anglicism. Failing that, the schismatics at least expected to be a parallel province to TEC, but Archbishop Williams had refused to recognize the schismatic bishops, ordained through international dioceses. Robert Duncan, the bomb-throwing moderator of the ACN, blamed the archbishop of Canterbury for the failure of the schismatics to achieve the lofty goals promised earlier, and now the very institution of the See of Canterbury became the object of Duncan's wrath.[14] Duncan had broken with the Episcopal Church and now he had broken with the archbishop of Canterbury. Soon, he would organize a rival gathering of Anglican bishops to challenge the institution of the Lambeth Conference.

Even some of his allies believed Duncan had gone too far. ACN co-founder Rev. Ephraim Radner stepped away from Duncan and the ACN, stating,

> It is with sorrow and deep disappointment that I tender my resignation from the Anglican Communion Network. Since the time I assisted in its founding, its leaders, members, and mission have been dear to me, even when I have disagreed with some of its corporate actions. The recent statements by the Moderator of the Network, Robert Duncan, however, so contradict my sense of calling within this part of Christ's Body, the Anglican Communion, that I have no choice but to disassociate myself from this group, whom I had once hoped might prove an instrument of renewal, not of destruction, of building up, not of tearing down.
>
> Bishop Duncan has now declared the See of Canterbury and the Lambeth Conference—two of the four Instruments of Communion within our tradition—to be "lost." He has said that God is "doing a new thing" in allowing these elements to founder and be let go. . . . Bp. Duncan has, in the end, decided to start a new church. He may call it "Anglican" if he wishes, though I do not recognize the name in these kinds of actions that break communion rather than build it up—for such building is what I have long perceived to be the "thing" God was "doing" with the earthen vessel of our tradition.[15]

In June 2008, less than a month before Lambeth, the Global Anglican Future Conference (GAFCON) was a poorly arranged gathering of conservative Anglican bishops and leaders held in Jerusalem. Intended to last two weeks, it was shortened to one because neighboring Jordan raised diplomatic issues. Once again, Duncan would be at the epicenter of the cabal, surrounded by the usual Global South suspects: Archbishops Peter Akinola of Nigeria, Benjamin Nzimbi of Kenya, Donald Mtetemela of Tanzania, Peter Jensen of Sydney, Australia, and Presiding Bishop Greg Venables of the Southern Cone. In a press release, the local bishop of Jerusalem harshly criticized the gathering, though he shared conservative views of sexuality:

> "Regrettably, I have not been consulted about this planned conference," said Bishop Suheil. "The first I learned of it was through a press release."
>
> "I am deeply troubled that this meeting, of which we had no prior knowledge, will import inter-Anglican conflict into our diocese, which seeks to be a place of welcome for all Anglicans."
>
> "It could also have serious consequences for our ongoing ministry of reconciliation in this divided land. Indeed, it could further inflame tensions here. We who minister here know only too well what happens when two sides cease talking to each other. We do not want to see any further dividing walls!"[16]

Duncan and the ACN forged ahead despite foreign and domestic criticism from all sides, and Duncan and his international allies ripped the fabric of worldwide Anglicism. Key actions at GAFCON included a call to create the Anglican Church in North America (ACNA), establishment of a "Primates Council" in direct opposition to its counterpart, the Anglican Communion's Primate Meeting, and a declaration that recognition by the archbishop of Canterbury was unnecessary. All of this was based on the premise that the Anglican Communion promoted a "false gospel."[17] Not only would Duncan foment domestic schism in TEC, he and his co-conspirators would trash their relationship with the archbishop of Canterbury, with Lambeth, and with the rest of the worldwide Anglican Communion.

Although more than 800 bishops were invited to Lambeth 2008, only around 650 attended compared to 749 in 1998. Bishop Robinson was notably not invited, and the dissidents from GAFCON were absent. One observer suggested 200 of the missing bishops were from Africa, including 137 from Nigeria alone.[18] Despite the lack of an invitation, Bishop Robinson traveled to London and stayed close by, hoping for interaction with his fellow bishops, but that never materialized to the extent hoped.

Missing the principal provocateurs, Lambeth 2008 was notably sub-dued compared to the contentiousness of 1998, with the emphasis on dialogue rather than legislation. What would a future Anglican Communion look like? What if provinces failed to sign on to a proposed covenant? How could a covenant be fashioned that would satisfy all sides? How would independence and autonomy be respected in the face of proscribed uniformity? Does unity require uniformity?

Nothing was decided by Lambeth 2008 except to continue discussion and discernment over the concept of covenant. The existing Covenant Design Group continued to fine tune draft documents after the close of Lambeth.

Had the GAFCON dissidents overplayed their hand? Had they alienated those who remained uncomfortable with the North American LGBT policies but who were willing to continue dialogue? Perhaps. Though consensus on LGBT issues remained elusive, the mood of Lambeth 2008 was to muck through and find a way to hang together as a Communion. "The bleaker its prospects have looked, the keener its bishops have appeared to preserve it."[19]

Meanwhile, the Windsor process of formulating an Anglican Covenant continued. The Covenant went through a number of drafts based on communion-wide feedback, and the final text was issued in December 2009. Each of the thirty-eight provinces would be asked to consider and to sign on. The Province of Mexico was the first to do so in June 2010. By the time this book was published, most provinces had not yet taken action, but preliminary responses suggest this Covenant, and perhaps the very idea of covenant, are in serious jeopardy. The initial approvals came from conservative provinces and the initial rejections from progressive provinces. The principal objection remained the creation of centralized authority that would stifle the autonomy of dioceses and provinces. "The proposed Covenant establishes mechanisms which would have the effect of forcing member churches to conform to the demands and expectations of other churches or risk exclusion from the Communion."[20]

Archbishop Williams' own Church of England rejected the Covenant—twenty-six dioceses against and eighteen in favor—in April 2012.[21] On June 8, 2012, the Church of Scotland General Synod overwhelmingly rejected the Covenant—112 against and 6 for with 13 abstentions—but adopted a resolution affirming commitment to the Communion. Here are excerpts of the speech the Primus of the Scottish Episcopal Church, the Most Rev. David Chillingworth, presented to his Scottish church:

This resolution invites us to affirm the life of the Anglican Communion. We have decided not to adopt the Anglican Covenant. Some thought it was un-Anglican. Others that it would not achieve its purpose. Others were troubled by the fact that its genesis was in a single complex of issues.

I believe that the movement to develop the Anglican Covenant has been a genuine and honourable attempt to heal the life of the Communion. Across the Communion, it has focused attention and thinking on what it means to be a Communion and what is special about the Anglican Communion.

The Anglican Communion matters deeply to us in the Scottish Episcopal Church. In this Motion we invoke the history of Samuel Seabury, consecrated in 1784 by the Scottish bishops as the first bishop of the church in the United States of America. We believe that we were part of the founding of the Anglican Communion. We want to be part of the re-founding—the bringing to birth of a new phase of Communion life. The Anglican Communion also matters to us because we are a small church and are enriched by being part of a bigger whole. And I am convinced that we discern that our particular attitude to authority—rooted in the collegiality of a College of Bishops—is echoed in the aspiration to a dispersed rather than centralised authority which is the vision of the Anglican Communion.

So our decision not to adopt the Anglican Covenant is not a decision to reject the Anglican Communion. Nor are we indifferent to deeply held differences of view which are held across the Communion. For those differences are also present in this church and they are part of our daily life and relationships. We hold a range of views. They are expressed with integrity, listened to with care and we are committed to living creatively with our diversity.

Our Communion is a gift to the world. A global institution which is determined to exist largely without centralised authority and which prizes unity in diversity—such a Communion models things which are very important for the world community. Such a Communion is attractive in mission because it has learned to transcend conflict. I believe that we now have a historic opportunity to reshape the Anglican Communion so that it may become an instrument of God's mission to the world. We as a church—a small church with a part in the founding history—are by God's grace called to play our part in that rebirth.[22]

Meeting in Indianapolis, Indiana, for General Convention in July 2012, TEC decided to neither accept nor reject the Covenant, postponing consideration until General Convention 2015, implicitly affirming commitment to the Anglican Communion but rejecting the premise of centralized authority.

The lack of acceptance by Western provinces–England, Scotland, the United States, and probably Canada (to be considered in 2013)—will likely be the death knell of the impetus toward regularizing the informal status of the Anglican Communion, which will remain a de facto fellowship of autonomous churches bound neither by formal agreements nor confessional statements. Bishop Chillingworth's speech to the Scottish Episcopal Church may well serve as the Covenant's eulogy.

The Windsor Report and the covenant movement it birthed were based on a false premise.

Windsor failed to understand that the problem was prejudice, not disunity. Responsibility for the threat to unity was not attributed to those who made the threat. The report implicitly asked the silly question whether the Episcopalians desired to be in the Communion; of course they did, the issue was with those who would expel them! The commission would have been better served by starting with the toxicity of Lambeth 1998 rather than a consecration in New Hampshire or a covenant ceremony in western Canada. The poisonous homophobia spewed at Lambeth 1998 was the problem—not Durham, New Hampshire, or New Westminster, British Columbia. With a faulty starting point, the solution proposed would impose unity by allowing, nay encouraging, continued discrimination against the LGBT community.

Finally, we offer a footnote to our discussion of the Windsor Report, the archbishop of Canterbury, and the Anglican Communion. In March 2012, Archbishop Williams announced his resignation effective at year's end. Thus, continued wrestling with the problems of unity amidst diversity would fall to his successor, who would need "the constitution of an ox and the skin of a rhinoceros"[23] Williams conceded the likelihood that the most conservative elements would continue to separate themselves from the body.

On March 21, 2013, Prince Charles and the Duchess of Cornwall, United Kingdom Prime Minister David Cameron, archbishops and bishops from around the world, and other religious dignitaries attended the enthronement of Justin Welby, Rowan Williams' successor as the archbishop of Canterbury. Amidst great pomp and circumstance, the new archbishop was plopped down in the muddle of local controversy, as the British Parliament wrestled with marriage equality.

Strongly backed by conservative Prime Minister Cameron, a bill authorizing full marriage equality for British gays and lesbians was adopted by Parliament in the summer of 2013. Earlier, the new archbishop had voiced opposition to the bill. While indicating support for a civil partnership law that would include LGBT couples, Archbishop Welby said he endorsed the traditional view and the official understanding of the Church of England "of marriage as being between one man and one woman."[24]

Peter Tatchell is an outspoken LGBT activist in England, and he called the new archbishop a homophobe in a open letter to the archbishop on March 20, 2013. To his surprise, the archbishop responded by inviting him to a private meeting on April 18. After the meeting, Tatchell was encouraged by the openness of the archbishop. Though the archbishop did not express a change in views, Tatchell said, "He struck me as a genuine, sincere, open-minded person, willing to listen and rethink his position." Then, in a comment reminiscent of President Barack Obama, Archbishop Welby said, "Marriage may evolve."[25]

We conclude this chapter by returning to U.S. soil and the founding of the Anglican Church in North America (ACNA), the progeny of ACN, and the long-threatened and much-hyped "replacement jurisdiction" to supplant the Episcopal Church. Robert Duncan, the Episcopal bishop of the Diocese of Pittsburgh, former vice-president of the American Anglican Council (AAC) and the moderator of the Anglican Communion Network (ACN), would become the archbishop of the Anglican Church in North America (ACNA). As his former colleague in the ACN accused, he "decided to start a new church."[26] Before considering the constituting convention of the ACNA in the summer of 2009, we will review the rapid-fire events involving Duncan and four schismatic dioceses following Lambeth 2008.

- As of September 20, 2008, Duncan was deposed (removed) from his role as Pittsburgh bishop by Presiding Bishop Jefferts Schori with the consent of the House of Bishops (eighty-eight to thirty-five in favor) "based on Robert Duncan's actions and statements to facilitate the departure of congregations out of the Episcopal Church." Two days earlier, Duncan had been recognized as a bishop within the Province of the Southern Cone (South America).[27]

- On October 4, 2008, Duncan's Diocese of Pittsburgh voted at its diocesan convention (204 to 102) to disassociate with TEC and associate with the Province of the Southern Cone, joining the Anglican Diocese of San Joaquin (Texas), which had switched late in 2007. Provisions for a successor TEC diocese were immediately instituted by Jefferts Schori together with loyal Episcopalians from the diocese.[28]

- On November 7, 2008, the Diocese of Quincy (Illinois) at its diocesan convention voted to depart TEC and align with the Southern Cone. In the absence of a sitting bishop, a vicar was appointed by the Southern Cone.[29]

- On November 14, 2008, the Diocese of Fort Worth at its diocesan convention voted to depart TEC and align with the Southern Cone.[30] On November 21, Presiding Bishop Jefferts Schori "inhibited" Bishop Jack Iker of the Diocese of Fort Worth, ordering that "he cease from exercising the gifts of the ordained ministry of this

Church" for abandoning Communion with the Episcopal Church.[31] A year later, the reconstituted TEC Diocese of Fort Worth ordained its first female priest. The former diocese had been a long-standing patriarchal bastion. When the conservatives left, the fresh breeze of reform blew in behind them.[32]

With these initial four splashes, the schismatics believed they had burst the dam. "We are part of something big," Duncan boasted.[33] However, the anticipated reservoir of support for schism would turn out to be drier than the schismatics hoped.

In June 2009, less than a month before the TEC General Convention, the Anglican Church in North America (ACNA) held its own constituting convention, and Duncan was installed as archbishop. Many of the previously mentioned schismatic organizations would gather under the ACNA umbrella: AMiA, AAC, ACN, and others. In addition to the four defecting dioceses from TEC, ACNA would soon authorize additional dioceses. As of midsummer 2013, the ACNA website claimed twenty-five dioceses, one hundred thousand members, and one thousand North American congregations. It also claimed to be a "an emerging Province in the global Anglican Communion," recognized by many conservative international provinces—usually the same that professed to be in "impaired communion" with TEC.[34] The ACNA has *not* been recognized by the archbishop of Canterbury or the other institutions of the Anglican Communion. Then Archbishop Williams noted in 2009 "some of the enormous difficulties around parallel jurisdictions" and underscored that the entity is "not a new province—it's a coalition that has drafted a constitution. What its institutional relationship is with the communion is very unclear."[35]

When individual members, congregations, and even the leadership of four dioceses departed TEC, there was plenty of hand-wringing, and the pain of separation and brokenness, akin to that of a divorce or an estrangement in a family, should not be understated. The emotional anguish and the financial hardship caused by the departure of fellow Episcopalians was, and continues to be, acute.

On the other hand, the leakage has not been as predicted. While the ACNA boasts of one hundred thousand members, that compares with over two million Episcopalians still in TEC. Certainly litigation that has successfully retained church properties for TEC has stemmed the flow. ACNA is neither the "big thing" promised by Duncan nor the "replacement jurisdiction" planned years earlier following the consecration of Bishop Robinson.

Though bruised a bit, the Episcopalians moved forward. Correspondingly, the "thorn in the side" effect on TEC had greatly diminished with the departures of the irritants. At the 2006 General Convention, TEC had agreed to "pause." Subsequently, ACNA had broken away and the conservative provinces internationally had created GAFCON as a rival to Lambeth. As General Convention 2009 neared, the Episcopalians were ready to hit the "play" button to finally realize full inclusion.

NOTES

1. Ibid., 157–59, 214.

2. *The Windsor Report* 2004, Section D "On elections to the episcopate," paragraph 134 excerpt, on the website of the Anglican Communion, http://www.anglicancommunion.org/windsor2004/section_d/p2.cfm:

- the Episcopal Church (USA) be invited to express its regret that the proper constraints of the bonds of affection were breached in the events surrounding the election and consecration of a bishop for the See of New Hampshire, and for the consequences which followed, and that such an expression of regret would represent the desire of the Episcopal Church (USA) to remain within the Communion.

- pending such expression of regret, those who took part as consecrators of Gene Robinson should be invited to consider in all conscience whether they should withdraw themselves from representative functions in the Anglican Communion. We urge this in order to create the space necessary to enable the healing of the Communion. We advise that in the formation of their consciences, those involved consider the common good of the Anglican Communion, and seek advice through their primate and the

Archbishop of Canterbury. We urge all members of the Communion to accord appropriate respect to such conscientious decisions.

- the Episcopal Church (USA) be invited to effect a moratorium on the election and consent to the consecration of any candidate to the episcopate who is living in a same gender union until some new consensus in the Anglican Communion emerges.

3. Episcopal News Service, "From Nigeria's Primate, Archbishop Peter Akinola: Statement on *Windsor Report*," October 19, 2004.

4. Marilyn McCord Adams, in Andrew Linzey, *Gays and the Future of Anglicism: Responses to the Windsor Report*, eds. Andrew Linzey and Richard Kirker (New York: O Books, 2005), 70.

5. Episcopal News Service, "House of Bishops Adopts 'Covenant Statement,'" March 15, 2005.

6. Stephen Noll, *Put Not Your Trust in Windsor*, October 24, 2005, on the website of the AAC, accessed May 31, 2012, http://www.americananglican .org/put-not-your-trust-in-windsor.

7. Episcopal News Service, "New Anglican Network Signs Charter, Elects Duncan Moderator," January 21, 2004.

8. Jonathan Clatworthy, *The Windsor Report, a Liberal Response*, eds. Jonathan Clatworthy and David Taylor (New York: O Books, 2005), 5.

9. Alan Cooperman, "Plan to Supplant Episcopal Church USA Is Revealed," *The Washington Post*, January 14, 2003.

10. Susan Russell, "Ants at the Anaheim Picnic, An Inch at a Time" (blog), July 3, 2009, http://inchatatime.blogspot.com/search?q=ants+at+anaheim, accessed May 22, 2013.

11. Pat McCaughan, Melodie Woerman, Jim DeLa, and Nicole Seiferth, Episcopal News and Service, "UPDATE: From Columbus: Convention Responds to Windsor Report's Call for Moratorium," June 21, 2006. At the time, Woerman was director of communication for the Diocese of Kansas; DeLa was director of communications for the Diocese of Southwest Florida; and Seiferth was editor of *The Episcopal New Yorker*.

12. Matthew Davies, Episcopal News Service, "From Columbus: Major Windsor action draws mixed reactions," June 21, 2006.

13. Archbishop Rowan Williams, *The Challenge and Hope of Being an Anglican Today: A Reflection for the Bishops, Clergy and Faithful of the Anglican Communion*, on the website of the archbishop of Canterbury, http://www.arch-bishopofcanterbury.org/articles.php/1478/the-challenge-and-hope-of-being-an-anglican-today-a-reflection-for-the-bishops-clergy-and-faithful-o.

14. John B. Chilton, "Radner: 'Duncan Starting a New Church,'" Episcopal Café's website, August 1, 2007, accessed June 6, 2012, http://www.episcopal-cafe.com/lead/episcopal_church/radner_duncan_starting_a_new_c.html.

15. Rev. Ephraim Radner, "Resignation from ACN," on the website of The Anglican Communion Institute, July 31, 2007, accessed June 6, 2012, http://www.anglicancommunioninstitute.com/2007/07/resignation-from-acn/.

16. Bishop Suheil Dawani, "Jerusalem Speaks on GAFCON," Thinking Anglicans (blog), January 2, 2008, accessed June 7, 2012, http://www.thinking anglicans.org.uk/archives/002831.html.

17. GAFCON, Final Statement issued June 28, 2008, on the website of GAFCON, http://gafcon.org/news/gafcon_final_statement/.

18. George Conger, The Religious, Political and Cultural Journalism of George Conger, "Boycott of Lambeth 2008 is most serious challenge yet," accessed June 7, 2012, http://geoconger.wordpress.com/2008/08/28/boycott-of-lambeth-2008-is-most-serious-challenge-yet-cen-82908-p-6/.

19. Robert Pigott, "Lambeth Diary: Anglicans in Turmoil," BBC News, August 4, 2008.

20. "International Campaign Seeks to Stop Anglican Covenant," press release November 3, 2010, on the website of No Anglican Covenant: Anglicans for Comprehensive Unity, http://noanglicancovenant.org/index.html, accessed June 10, 2012. The press release indicated the four national leaders of this organization were Reverend Dr. Lesley Fellows (England), Dr. Lionel Deimel (USA), Reverend Malcolm French (Canada), and Reverend Lawrence Kimberley (New Zealand).

21. A chart entitled "C of E Diocesan Synod Debates on the Anglican Covenant," on the website for Modern Church, accessed June 10, 2012, http://www.modernchurch.org.uk/resources/mc/cofe/2012-1.htm.

22. Primus of the Scottish Episcopal Church, the Most Rev. David Chillingworth, Bishop of St Andrews, Dunkeld and Dunblane, on the website of the Scottish Episcopal Church, "General Synod votes against adoption of the Anglican Covenant," updated June 8, 2012, accessed June 10, 2012, http://www.scotland.anglican.org/index.php/news/entry/general_synod_votes_agains t_adoption_of_the_anglican_covenant/.

23. Robert Pigott, "Archbishop of Canterbury Rowan Williams to Stand Down," BBC News, March 16, 2012.

24. Alan Cowell, "New Archbishop of Canterbury Takes Office," *The New York Times*, February 4, 2.

25. Peter Tatchell, on the website of the Peter Tatchell Foundation, "Archbishop Welby struggles to support gay equality," April 18, 2013, http://www

.petertatchell.net/religion/Archbishop-Welby-is-struggling-to-support-equality
.htm, accessed May 22, 2013.

26. Rev. Ephraim Radner, "Resignation."

27. The Province of the Southern Cone consists of the five southernmost countries of South America but with only twenty-two thousand members or approximately 1 percent the membership of TEC and smaller than many dioceses. Presiding Bishop Venables had long been a principal schismatic figure in the Anglican Communion.

28. Mary Francis Schonjberg, Episcopal News Service, "Pittsburgh Votes to Leave Episcopal Church, Align with Southern Cone," October 4, 2008.

29. Joe Bjordal, Episcopal News Service, "Bulletin: Quincy Members Vote to Leave Episcopal Church, Align with Southern Cone," November 7, 2008.

30. Pat McCaughan, Episcopal News Service, "Fort Worth Delegates Vote to Leave Episcopal Church, Realign with Southern Cone," November 15, 2008.

31. Mary Francis Schonjberg, Episcopal News Service, "Presiding Bishop Inhibits Fort Worth Bishop," November 24, 2008.

32. Pat McCaughan, Episcopal News Service, "Fort Worth Diocese Ordains its First Woman Priest," November 9, 2009.

33. Pat McCaughan, Episcopal News Service, "North American Anglican Group Holds Inaugural Gathering," June 25, 2009.

34. "About the Anglican Church in North America," on the website of the Anglican Church in North America, accessed June 8, 2013, http://anglican church.net/?/main/page/about-acna.

35. Matthew Davies, Episcopal News Service, "Conservative Anglican Primates Recognize Proposed North American Entity," April 16, 2009.

* 19 *

ALL THE SACRAMENTS FOR ALL THE BAPTIZED

By General Convention 2009, the Episcopal Church had fully embraced cyberspace with an online media hub that offered Twitter feeds using the hashtag "#ecgc," live streaming plenary sessions, live chat, a blog roll, Flickr photos, links to news releases, etc. Blogger Rev. Elizabeth Keaton sets the scene:

> So, fast forward to General Convention, July 5–18, 2009, in Anaheim, CA. The baptismal water is already starting to bubble, pop and hiss, and the steam is starting to rise.
>
> But, there's a wee problem: The threat that 'the Anglican Sky is falling' and we're all doomed to schism, well, just hasn't happened. Yes, I know. Some have left and others have left but they really don't want to so they make up interesting names and titles and claim to be THE Anglican presence in the dioceses they've left.[1]

Of course, Integrity was there, with their slogan "All the sacraments for all the baptized,"[2] and President Susan Russell provided daily "IntegriTV" YouTube updates as well as her own daily blog reflections. Thus, participants in the historic convention included many more than the thousands who were physically present in Anaheim, California, July 8–17, 2009.

Rev. Kaeton of the Diocese of Newark witnessed the doings of General Convention and reported in daily blog posts:

> On any given day, there were 5–7,000 people here, including over 800 deputies, more than 200 bishops and, as Jonah once

said of the people of Tarshish, "Many who do not know their right hand from their left."

The days are long—beginning at 5:30 AM to start with the first legislative team meeting at 6:30, to be at legislative committee sessions or hearings at 7:30 AM, to be at the media briefings at 8:45, to be at the legislative sessions at 9:30, to be at the daily Eucharist at 11:30, followed by various presentations and caucuses, before the legislative sessions begin again at 2 PM and end at 6 PM.

But wait—there's more!

The evenings were often filled with more hearings, more programs, more caucuses, lots of lobbying and activism and various debriefings.[3]

The American Anglican Council (AAC) would be there but with diminished influence since many of the gatekeepers now resided elsewhere than TEC. Yet, their newsletter encouraged the "orthodox" and promised to be there with support. "Pray for the orthodox bishops, clergy and laity who will be deputies to General Convention. The AAC will be there to assist the orthodox in their witness."[4]

Archbishop Williams dropped by, and he received a very warm welcome. Once again, he offered a mixed message to LGBT Episcopalians. During a Eucharist meditation, he called a gay man, William Stringfellow, "the greatest Episcopalian theologian and perhaps the greatest American theologian of the twentieth century . . . not the least of the gifts which the Episcopal Church has given the rest of us." But he also pleaded, "Of course I am coming here with hopes and anxieties—you know that and I shan't deny it. Along with many in the Communion, I hope and pray that there won't be decisions in the coming days that could push us further apart."[5]

His plea would be refused.

Resolution B033 from General Convention 2006 was the self-imposed moratorium enacted in response to the Windsor Report in which the church agreed to "exercise restraint by not consenting to the consecration of any candidate to the episcopate whose manner of life presents a challenge to the wider church and will lead to further strains on communion." Repeal of B033 would be the starting point for discussions at General Convention 2009.

First would come committee testimony followed by votes in the House of Deputies and the House of Bishops. On July 9, a thousand spectators watched the proceedings before the World Mission Committee. Fifty-one persons testified late into the evening; ten were in favor of retaining B033 but forty-one spoke against it. The Diocese of Fort Worth had long been a patriarchal protectorate until the leaders had bolted for the ACNA. Victoria Prescott, a lay deputy from the reconstituted TEC Diocese of Fort Worth spoke of the change:

> Before the Diocese of Fort Worth disaffiliated from the Episcopal Church, the only choice "was to be silent toward full inclusion of gays and lesbians in the church." Because she advocated for that inclusion she was unable to move forward in discernment. She urged the gathering to offer "radical hospitality to those we disagree with and join together in moving beyond B033."[6]

Next stop, House of Deputies for more debate. In a departure from parliamentary procedure, the twenty-seven speakers were determined by random selection on July 9, as deputies drew numbered slips of paper. Those holding the lowest numbers were entitled to speak. Of those who spoke, nineteen advocated some form of rejection of B033, while eight asked that it be preserved. Speakers for retention of B033 parroted the usual arguments about unity within the Anglican Communion. A speaker opposed replied, "Will we continue to sacrifice a portion of God's people for a false sense of security with those who don't want to be with us?"[7]

Meanwhile, a resolution had percolated to the top as a replacement for and rejection of B033. Resolution D025 provided, *inter alia*,[8]

> That the 76th General Convention reaffirm the continued participation of The Episcopal Church as a constituent member of the Anglican Communion . . .
>
> That the 76th General Convention affirm the value of "listening to the experience of homosexual persons," as called for by the Lambeth Conferences of 1978, 1988 and 1998, and acknowledge that through our own listening the General Con-

vention has come to recognize that the baptized membership of
The Episcopal Church includes same-sex couples living in lifelong committed relationships "characterized by fidelity,
monogamy, mutual affection and respect, careful, honest communication and the holy love which enables those in such relationships to see in each other the image of God . . ."

That the 76th General Convention recognize that gay and
lesbian persons who are part of such relationships have responded
to God's call and have exercised various ministries in and on
behalf of God's One, Holy, Catholic and Apostolic Church and
are currently doing so in our midst . . .

That the 76th General Convention affirm that *God has called
and may call such individuals to any ordained ministry in The Episcopal
Church* [emphasis added].

Two days later, Resolution D025 came to the floor of the House of
Deputies. The debate sounded familiar themes. Again, the conservatives
attempted to play the unity card. Amendments were offered and defeated.
Finally the vote: seventy-seven to thirty-one laity; seventy-four to twenty-
five clergy. Motion adopted.

But the House of Bishops stood in the path. The House of Lords.
The ones who had to face the hoots and catcalls of their fellow bishops
at Lambeth. The leaders of the church, charged with preserving the
church. For more than forty years LGBT hopefuls had come to General
Convention, only to be rejected time and time again for the good order
of the church. Dr. Louie Crew and Integrity had been there since 1976,
always hoping but always disappointed, always waiting. Next year in
Jerusalem.

A new generation of leaders had picked up the gauntlet. Susan Russell, the current president of Integrity, expressed optimism:

I know, I know . . . the bishops aren't going to do anything.
They've already decided to block anything that comes through
on any of "these issues." They've drunk the Lambeth Kool Aid.
We should just give up and go home. In fact, it was a waste of
time to bother to come in the first place. Nothing is going to
happen. The bishops aren't going to let it.

I appreciate the emails. Really I do. And the blog comments. They help me know that someone out there is actually reading all this stuff.

But here's the deal: I think you're wrong. And it's not because Integrity and our allies have some secret plan, strategy, agenda or weapon.

It's because I have more faith in our bishops than that. I have more faith in the church than that. And I certainly have more faith in the Holy Spirit than that (emphasis added).[9]

Ninety-nine bishops for, forty-five against with two abstentions. Motion carried. And the bishops weren't finished. On July 15, the bishops overwhelmingly called for rites of same-gender liturgical blessings.

And just to show that the church meant it, LGBT candidates soon appeared on diocesan ballots for election to the episcopate. In December 2009, lesbian Mary Glasspool was elected to be a bishop suffragan in the Diocese of Los Angeles. Years earlier, she had played softball on the same women's team with the ERA T-shirts that included Marnie Warner and rev. rosi olmstead, founders of the UCC ONA program, and Carter Heyward of the Philadelphia Eleven and a noted feminist theologian.

Bishop Glasspool was consecrated in May 2010 before three thousand persons in attendance and surrounded by a cloud of witnesses that burst open the doors and led her down her pathway, including the Philadelphia Eleven, Dr. Louie Crew, Rev. Ellen Marie Barrett, Bishop Paul Moore Jr., Bishop Edmond Browning, Bishop Barbara Harris, Bishop John Shelby Spong, Bishop Walter Righter, Dean Jeffrey John, and Bishop Gene Robinson.

NOTES

1. Rev. Elizabeth Kaeton, "A Little Inspiration from Mark Twain," May 21, 2009, Telling Secrets (blog), accessed June 11, 2012, http://telling-secrets .blogspot.com/2009/05/little-inspiration-from-mark-twain.html.

2. Within Anglican sacramental theology, ordination and holy matrimony are "commonly called sacraments" while baptism and eucharist are "sacraments ordained of Christ."

3. Rev. Elizabeth Kaeton, "And He Had Compassion on Them," Telling Secrets (blog), July 19, 2009, http://telling-secrets.blogspot.com/2009/07/and-he-had-compassion-on-them.html.

4. "A Message from Bishop David Anderson," American Anglican Council weekly update March 20, 2009, on the website of the American Anglican Council, http://archive.constantcontact.com/fs096/1102375357573/archive/1102515394767.html.

5. Episcopal News Service, "Archbishop of Canterbury Offers Meditation, Expresses Gratitude to Convention," July 9, 2009.

6. Pat McCaughan and Melodie Woerman, Episcopal News Service, "Testimony Is Overwhelmingly in Favor of Moving Beyond B033," July 9, 2009.

7. Melodie Woerman, Episcopal News Service, "Resolution B033 continues to spark passionate debate," July 10, 2009.

8. *Commitment and Witness to Anglican Communion*, adopted by General Convention 2009, http://www.episcopalarchives.org/cgi-bin/acts/acts_resolution-complete.pl?resolution=2009-D025.

Resolved, That the 76th General Convention reaffirm the continued participation of The Episcopal Church as a constituent member of the Anglican Communion; give thanks for the work of the bishops at the Lambeth Conference of 2008; reaffirm the abiding commitment of The Episcopal Church to the fellowship of churches that constitute the Anglican Communion and seek to live into the highest degree of communion possible; and be it further

Resolved, That the 76th General Convention encourage dioceses, congregations and members of The Episcopal Church to participate to the fullest extent possible in the many instruments, networks and relationships of the Anglican Communion; and be it further

Resolved, That the 76th General Convention reaffirm its financial commitment to the Anglican Communion and pledge to participate fully in the Inter-Anglican Budget; and be it further

Resolved, That the 76th General Convention affirm the value of "listening to the experience of homosexual persons," as called for by the Lambeth Conferences of 1978, 1988, and 1998, and acknowledge that through our own listening the General Convention has come to recognize that the baptized membership of The Episcopal Church includes same-gender couples living in lifelong committed relationships "characterized by fidelity, monogamy, mutual affection and respect, careful, honest communication and the holy love which enables those in such relationships to see in each other the image of God" (2000-D039); and be it further

Resolved, That the 76th General Convention recognize that gay and lesbian persons who are part of such relationships have responded to God's call and have exercised various ministries in and on behalf of God's One, Holy, Catholic and Apostolic Church and are currently doing so in our midst; and be it further

Resolved, That the 76th General Convention affirm that God has called and may call such individuals to any ordained ministry in The Episcopal Church, and that God's call to the ordained ministry in The Episcopal Church is a mystery which the Church attempts to discern for all people through our discernment processes acting in accordance with the Constitution and Canons of The Episcopal Church; and be it further

Resolved, That the 76th General Convention acknowledge that members of The Episcopal Church as of the Anglican Communion, based on careful study of the Holy Scriptures, and in light of tradition and reason, are not of one mind, and Christians of good conscience disagree about some of these matters.

9. Susan Russell, "But What about the Bishops?" Inch at a Time (blog), accessed June 11, 2012, http://inchatatime.blogspot.com/2009/07/but-what-about-bishops.html.

✳ 20 ✳

THOU ART A PRIEST FOREVER

Ordination liturgies often quote the Letter to the Hebrews. *thou art a priest forever*. Ordination is both a public call to ministry and a deeply personal understanding of self, an identity bestowed that parallels the sacrament of baptism in being claimed and called.

Ellen Marie Barrett, ordained as the first openly lesbian Episcopal priest in 1977, whose story we related earlier, now resides in New Jersey, living a quiet monastic life as Sister Bernadette, Order of Saint Benedict. In a private e-mail, she shared reflections on her ordination and her personal journey of conflict and celebration, which shall serve as the coda to this section on the Episcopal Church:[1]

> First of all, if it hadn't been me it would have been someone else, and probably someone stronger and more worthy. The Spirit was moving, and once She gets going there's no stopping Her. In fact, choosing me probably indicates a cosmic sense of humour, since a lot of what carried me through was more than conviction of the justice of including open gays in the discernment process for ordination. Whatever virtues I may have had were balanced, and perhaps in a strange way bolstered, by their defects. Courage and fortitude? More like heedlessness of consequences and not really understanding that there would be all these long years after. . . . Maybe that's what it took—that combination of altruism and the willful blindness of the young.

The joy—that first time I could bestow rather than simply ask a blessing. The first time I gave absolution. Above all, to hold in my hands the body of my Lord as a priest. The pain—commitment to the priesthood and Bishop Myers refusing to license me to officiate for some six months, even though he had given me license to officiate during the 13 months of my diaconate. I hated being turned from a person into a problem to be discussed without my input by people who did not know me. It was almost as difficult being turned into some sort of heroic figure, equally as unreal as the villainess who was accused of causing everything from tornadoes to the death of a Bishop!

I have always been very vulnerable when it comes to a desire/need to be wanted, to be included, and neither the hatred nor the adulation hit anything but the raw nerves. I'm fairly shy and awkward, and for several years I could hardly bear to pick up the phone or open the mail.

Would I do it again? Knowing what I know now? That's not a question that can possibly have an answer. Today is a very different time. I have no idea whether God would have moulded my combination of weakness, pig-headedness, and some talent into what another time would need. I was what I was, and I did what I did, in the context of a particular time and socio-political climate.

Am I still convinced it was the right thing to do? Yes. Done the right way by the right person? Who knows? It is what it is. And priesthood is as much a part of me as green eyes and once black hair turning white. I am a priest forever. That's all.

I am terribly sorry for all the people who were damaged by my actions, for family and friends lost. I regret the decades that I was unable to follow my first vocation (to monastic life). I regret the weakness that left me emotionally rolled up like a hedgehog for so many years that it took a traumatic shock to open me up to begin to become the priest and religious I was meant to be.

Of the unimportant things, I rather regret the career path that leaves me with a risible pension, but prudence and prophecy rarely go well together, even for a reluctant prophet!

I am glad to see the generations of fine gay clergy who have followed me and who have been able to be honest about the person God called. Even bishops now! God knew whom (S)he called, and now they are more able to respond with honesty and integrity. So many of them, some of whom I taught, are so much better than I could ever be. I'm proud to have been a tiny part of what set their gifts free in the world and in the Church.

When I became a Benedictine I took the name Bernadette—not because of her visions of Our Lady, but because of the humility and peasant honesty of her life at Lourdes and later in the convent. She once remarked that the Virgin had used her as one might a broom, and what do you do with a broom when you've finished sweeping up? You put it away. I'm not sure I'm anything so useful as a broom, but perhaps I served to wedge the door open so that others could come through upright. That's enough. I can't go back into the closet, but I am content in my "broom cupboard" (insert grin), if you see what I mean, as an ordinary Religious among my Brothers and Sisters. Simply that—nothing special.

Nobody special except as each one of us is special to the God who loves every one of us as if there were only one of us.

NOTES

1. Sister Bernadette Barrett (formerly Ellen Marie Barrett), private e-mail to the author January 23, 2012. Quoted with permission.

PART III

~

The Lutherans

The roots of the Evangelical Lutheran Church in America (ELCA) are buried deep in the northern European churches that followed Martin Luther's break with Roman Catholicism in the sixteenth century. Luther was a Roman Catholic monk, priest, and university professor whose ninety-five theses critical of the Catholic Church served as a catalyst for the Reformation in 1517. Luther's famous 1521 trial at the Diet of Worms in which he refused to recant, even in the presence of the Emperor and papal legates, also serves as a notable moment in Reformation history (he survived by being spirited away by German princes). The recently invented printing press allowed widespread dissemination of Luther's writings, as well as his translation of the Latin Bible into the German language, and the reform movement ignited by Luther sparked across northern Europe like wildfire.

Lutherans of all stripes continue to express adherence to the theology of Luther developed in his voluminous writings as well as those of his associates, most notably the Augsburg Confession and the works included in the Book of Concord, but with widely disparate opinions of the implications for policy. While the ELCA is decidedly ecumenical in its religious worldview, the insularity and exclusivity of the Lutheran Church Missouri Synod, the Wisconsin Synod, and a handful of lesser Lutheran bodies are polar opposites. Compared to these smaller, conservative Lutheran denominations, the ELCA is notably more progressive. While the ELCA is in full communion with the other four denominations treated in this book, the relationship with other Lutheran bodies is strained, and official ties are tenuous and diminishing.

There never was a "Lutheran" church as such in northern Europe but a variety of local and national churches that all claimed a Lutheran heritage (Germany, Norway, Sweden, Denmark, Iceland and Finland). Thus, the churches did not develop uniformly in the succeeding centuries: some exhibited a pietistic strain, some were sacramental and ecclesiastical, but others were "low church." Revivalist movements touched many regions. In particular, the influence of the itinerant, revivalist lay preacher from Norway, Hans Hauge, left a decidedly anticlerical, antiecclesiastical, antisacramental strain within the Norwegian Church at the beginning of the nineteenth century. Hauge's influence also touched neighboring Sweden, but the Swedish followers of the lay revival movement eventually split from the Lutheran Church to form the Swedish Covenant Church, with U.S. heirs today in the Evangelical Covenant Church.

Although there were Lutherans in the American colonies as early as 1620, they remained a tiny sliver of U.S. Christianity until the waves of German and Scandinavian immigration in the second half of the nineteenth century. Thus, compared to the other ecumenical churches of the United States, the Lutherans were the last to arrive, and they settled into small ethnic pockets with little or no relationship to each other. For instance, from the years 1840 to 1875, fifty-eight separate Lutheran Synods had organized in the United States,with clergy supplied from the "old country" and services conducted in mother tongues into the twentieth century. The ELCA still reflects the geographical pattern of immigrant settlements, with few congregations in the South but a heavy concentration in the Midwest where many Germans and Scandinavians settled.

This is also my personal legacy, as my great-grandparents arrived from Sweden in the 1880s (one set from Denmark) and settled near a Swedish enclave named after Uppsala, Sweden. In Upsala, Minnesota, my maternal ancestors were early pioneers in the formation of the Sand-vikens Swedish Evangelical Lutheran Congregation, now Gethsemane Lutheran of the ELCA. My maternal grandmother and her siblings were confirmed a century ago following lessons taught in Swedish. Meanwhile, my paternal ancestors were early leaders in the smaller Swedish Covenant Church, which thrives today as Community Covenant Church of Upsala.

By the twentieth century, the small church bodies had begun to band together, and the first unions were ethnically based; Norwegian synods merged into the Norwegian Lutheran Church in America, German synods into the United Lutheran Church in America, the Swedes joined the Augustana Synod, the Fins the Suomi Synod, and so on. The continuing process of merger would characterize the twentieth century. In 1960, the American Lutheran Church (ALC) was formed by merger of several smaller bodies, and two years later, the Lutheran Church in America (LCA) came into being in the same manner. These two, along with the Lutheran Church Missouri Synod (LCMS) were by then the three principal Lutheran bodies, dwarfing several smaller bodies that had little interest in unity with the others. About that time, the LCMS began a steady theological drift to the right, and its relationship with the ALC and LCA slowly deteriorated even as the ALC and LCA discussed their own merger, which finally came to fruition with the creation of the Evangelical Lutheran Church in America (ELCA), effective January 1, 1988; the merger also included the Association of Evangelical Lutheran Churches (AELC) a small, moderate splinter from the LCMS.

The ELCA is strictly a U.S. church (with some Caribbean congregations) that has international ties to other Lutherans through the Lutheran World Federation, a consultative, collaborative body that has no governing functions. Thus, in the ELCA journey toward full inclusion, international Lutherans exerted scant influence, contrary to the example of the Episcopalians within the Anglican Communion, much less the experience of the UMC, which allows international Methodists voice and vote at UMC General Conventions. It is interesting to note that the Scandinavian Lutheran churches, especially the Swedish church, are very progressive. A partnered lesbian was elected to serve as bishop of the Diocese of Stockholm in 2009. On the other hand, Lutheran churches in Africa are uncomfortable with the progressive policies of the ELCA.

The term "evangelical" has several meanings in current parlance. The origin of the term is the Greek word found in the New Testament that is translated as "gospel" or "good news," and this root is common to all current usages, together with the implication of spreading the good news (evangelizing).

Labeling conservative Christians as "evangelical" is a twentieth-century etymological development. Historian David Hollinger cites the 1942 formation of the National Association of Evangelicals as the origin of the usage of "evangelical" to denote "conservative Christian."[1] Such modern-day "evangelicals" are to be found across denominations and emphasize personal conversion, biblical inerrancy, Jesus as the exclusive access to God, and missionary efforts focused on converting the world. However, an older understanding that dates to Luther and the Reformation is simply "Protestant," that is, not Roman Catholic. Thus, the term "evangelical" within the ELCA's name is a historical vestige that connotes this earlier meaning, and the ELCA as an institution has little in common with evangelicals of the religious right, a fact that is often confusing and misunderstood by many, including the press.

Prior to January 1, 1988, the effective date of merger that created the ELCA, the LCA had been the largest U.S. Lutheran body, and the ALC had been the second largest. Thus, when these two merged (along with the much smaller LCMS splinter, the AELC), the new ELCA dwarfed all other American Lutheran church bodies with more than five million members. This was also a merger of the moderate, ecumenical Lutherans, and all the other Lutheran denominations were considerably more conservative and insular.

The ELCA is structured on three levels called "three expressions of church": the local congregation, the regional synod, and churchwide (national). Maps for sixty-five synods were drawn according to population, which meant that some synods were very large geographically and others very small, but each would have roughly equivalent numbers of parishioners. While Minnesota and Wisconsin each boast six synods, the entire region of Alabama, Mississippi, and Tennessee comprises only one synod.

Each synod is led by an elected bishop. Synodical bishops serve as the chief executive of the synod with several full-time clergy assistants and a clerical staff. The sixty-five synodical bishops collectively serve on a Conference of Bishops with advisory but not legislative authority. Retired bishops have no official standing and often return to other ministries of the church when their term is completed. Annual synod assemblies serve as the legislative arm of the synod. Every congregation is entitled to send its clergy and two or more lay members, often a husband and wife, as voting members to synod assemblies. Larger congregations are entitled to additional voting members. Synod assemblies, in turn, elect the voting members to the biennial Churchwide Assembly (after 2013, the Churchwide Assembly will move to a three-year, triennial cycle).

The churchwide presiding bishop is elected by the biennial Churchwide Assembly for six-year terms and may be reelected. The presiding bishop presides over Churchwide Assemblies and also serves as the chief executive officer and chief ecumenical officer of the ELCA. Since the ELCA's inception in 1988, there have been three presiding bishops (the Rev. Dr. Herbert Chilstrom 1988–1995, the Rev. H. George Anderson 1995–2001, and the Rev. Mark Hanson 2001–2013).

The biennial Churchwide Assembly is the ultimate legislative authority of the church, and the elected Church Council the penultimate authority that functions during the two-year biennium. The Conference of Bishops is advisory only. Voting members to annual synod assemblies and to the biennial Churchwide Assembly are elected according to a quota system: 50 percent male and 50 percent female; 40 percent clergy and 60 percent laity; 10 percent persons of color or with English as a second language. Polity influences policy, as we have seen, and the egalitarian structure of the ELCA would draw the ire of conservative Lutherans who correctly understood that the mandated participation of women, minorities, and laity would have a moderating influence on the ELCA.

The monk and priest Martin Luther was celibate, as all good monks and priests should be, according to the wisdom then prevailing. But the brisk breeze of the Reformation blew away this custom along with the rest, and Luther married his love, the nun Katharina von Bora, when he was forty-two years old. Suddenly, he awoke with "a pair of pigtails on the pillow that were not there before." They parented six of their own children and adopted four more; Katie managed the household, a farm, a brewery, and the students who clustered around the reformer and freed Martin for his theological work; he spent money, she saved it; when he fell ill, she nursed him; they prayed and studied together, and she joined in the "table talk" with the students. The once celibate cleric would later exclaim, "There is no bond on earth so sweet, nor any separation so bitter, as that which occurs in a good marriage."[2]

Nearly five centuries later, the heirs of Luther rediscovered this truth.

NOTES

1. Hollinger, *After Cloven Tongues of Fire*: "with the founding in 1942 of the National Association of Evangelicals (NAE), this term came to be more narrowly associated with all the groups who opposed the Federal Council of Churches (FCC, which after 1950 became the National Council of Churches, or NCC). . . . What united this new, highly organized evangelical alliance was what its leaders saw as an orthodox alternative to the liberalizers who had effective control of all the major, standard denominations and the principle cross-denominational organizations," xiii.

2. Martin Luther, quoted by Dr. Ken Curtis, Christian History Institute, and published on the website of Reformation Tours, accessed June 19, 2013, http://www.reformationtours.com/site/490868/page/204052.

* 2 I *

Dollars for Disobedience

In the aftermath of Stonewall, gays and lesbians began to come out to their churches. The uncloaking of Lutheran gays and lesbians in the seventies was subtle, and it did not involve an individual but an appropriation. In the early 1970s, ALC Pastor Jim Siefkes, a straight man, served as Western Region Stewardship Director with offices in Palo Alto, California, where he developed a program called "Matrix," which explored social ministry opportunities for the church. "In brief, the plan was to bring together a group of clergy (and their spouses or "significant others") for a several-day experience and reflection on the issues of the day. Participants experientially had exposure to issues such as race, the environment, sexuality, drugs, campus riots, poverty, Vietnam, a night on the town with runaway youth, communes, etc."[1]

Matrix came to the attention of the ALC home office in Minneapolis, and Pastor Siefkes was offered a position to develop something similar; he was to establish and lead a new ALC department to be called "Congregational Social Concerns." So far, so good, but when he invited approximately sixty persons from the Twin Cities (Lutheran and Catholic Social Services, ALC executives, an ALC bishop, the YMCA, the University of Minnesota Medical School, and more) to a seminar to evaluate the potential for ministry in the area of human sexuality, "the milieu heated up," according to Siefkes.

Following the event, the University Medical School participants "were so impressed that they ended up making a near duplicate of the ALC seminar a required course for students," but the Director of Catholic Social Services was scandalized by the frank treatment of human sexuality, and he "outed" the program in an unfriendly article published in the national Catholic journal *Commonweal* entitled "Sex, Sex, Sex." Suddenly, Siefkes and his program became scrutinized by the self-appointed watchdogs of Lutheran morality.[2]

Later, Siefkes and his social ministry program successfully sought small ALC appropriations of a few thousand dollars:

> To enable at least one national meeting of up to twenty ALC homosexual persons plus five resource persons to discuss their sexual orientation and their relationship because of it, to society and their church; to the end that they may address the church and the church might respond to them and become less a source of oppression to ALC and other persons with homosexual orientation."[3]

On Sunday afternoon, June 16, 1974, Pastor Siefkes settled into his plush easy chair and turned on the TV to watch the Minnesota Twins game against his childhood favorites, the Cleveland Indians. His heroes had been Lou Boudreau, Bob Feller, and Satchel Paige, but now the Indians had fallen on hard times, and the big ballpark in Cleveland was nearly empty. Earlier, Siefkes, his wife Sally, and their three teenagers had attended Sunday services at their suburban Twin Cities Lutheran congregation.[4]

He couldn't get interested in the ballgame. He pestered Sally. He muddled with a few chores, but he had mowed the lawn and finished most that needed doing on Saturday. He considered but rejected a jog down their street, across a walking bridge, over a creek, and on to the jogging track in the park just beyond. He returned to the ballgame in time to see Rod Carew slap a single to left field, his fourth hit of the day. He checked his watch again.

When he had left work on Friday, he had been satisfied that all arrangements were in order, but now he worried. His lack of control over the way the weekend would unfold left him uneasy. He stared out the window toward the Minneapolis skyline as if he could see the university campus just beyond the southeast corner of downtown, high on the banks of the Mississippi that streamed through the heart of the Twin Cities. He had arranged a weekend gathering on the east bank in a medical school building they called the "battery factory," but he chose to stay away to let the five gay Lutherans decide their own future, or, at least, to decide if their group had a future. Would this meeting be the first of many or merely the first and last? Second thoughts crept in. Perhaps he should have met with the group Friday evening as they embarked on their weekend of exploration. Perhaps he should have been present throughout.

He turned from the window and checked his watch against the clock on the wall. It was only late afternoon, but he would fire up the grill for burgers. He wanted to leave plenty of time to get ready; he and Sally would join the five, along with three facilitators, for a concluding social event and report that evening at a professor's house near campus.

To arrange the meeting, Siefkes had tapped into the homophile network. He had previously worked with Pastor Chuck Lewis from San Francisco. Pastor Lewis was one of the mainstay clergy members of the Council on Religion and Homosexuality (CRH), the early pan-denominational homophile organization of the 1960s and '70s. Pastor Lewis had been there as witness to the police harassment at the 1964 ball, and he was a clergy participant at the press conference the next morning that galvanized local, regional, and national outrage over the legal abuses suffered by the LGBT community. He served on the CRH board and for a term as its president through the early 1970s, a period that would overlap with Pastor Bill Johnson's service as executive director. Lewis' own ministry was to the North Beach community, and later to a crisis "Night Ministry."[5] Pastor Siefkes solicited Lewis' counsel from afar even though Lewis could not be in attendance at the Minneapolis meeting in June 1974.

Siefkes had arranged for three facilitators. Baptist Louise Rose and Episcopalian John Preston both served on the NCC task force with Bill Johnson and David Bailey Sindt, and the third was a local Quaker, Ron Mattson. Siefkes had mailed invitations to around twenty potential participants. About half sent thanks but could not attend. Five didn't respond at all, but six accepted the invitation. One person came for the first day only. The key part of the weekend would come on Sunday when five LGBT Lutherans would meet alone to decide their future course.

As Pastor Siefkes and Sally drove toward campus Sunday evening, the sun was still high in the western sky as the summer solstice neared, *midsommer* in Scandinavia where the ancestors of many U.S. Lutherans had celebrated new life and fertility. *Midsommer* lore also warned of the gathering of a witch's coven. A wry grin spread across Siefkes' face.

When they arrived, the sweet voice of Louise Rose, accompanied by piano, spilled onto the professor's front lawn. Lutherans Concerned for Gay People had been born that afternoon. Five LGBT Lutherans and three facilitators would have "an impact way out of proportion to their numbers."[6] Sort of like five fishes and two loaves.

The original five persons included Marie Kent (instructor to the mentally challenged, Minneapolis), Allen Blaich (student at the University of Utah), Diane Fraser (professor, Gustavus Adolphus College in nearby St. Peter, Minnesota, an LCA institution), Howard Erickson (reporter, *Minneapolis Star Tribune*), and the Rev. Jim Lokken (American Bible Society headquarters, New York City). Decisions made that day would have far reaching implications:

- The organization would be pan-Lutheran to include the ALC, LCA, and even the LCMS, although that was also the time of the Missouri Synod's sharp turn to the right, with a purge of moderates resulting in Seminex (seminary in exile).

- They would seek to be a national organization with local chapters.

- Bare-bones bylaws were drafted.

- Erickson would be the editor of their newsletter, to be called *The Gay Lutheran*.

- The name of the organization would be Lutherans Concerned for Gay People.

- The only point of disagreement was over their public statement and the public face of the participants (none were out at that time), and Rev. Lokken protested that he could not safely come out.[7]

The first newsletter was distributed just a month later, dateline July–August, 1974, with bold headlines proclaiming:

- *We confront church*: "As gay Lutherans, we affirm with joy the goodness of human sexuality which God has given us. We are to be found in the pulpits and pews, the schools and offices of Lutheran churches and organizations throughout the land. We have received the sacraments, listened to the preaching of God's word, taught in the schools and worked in the committees and organizations of Lutheran churches."

- *How we'll do it*: simple and flexible committees and caucuses led by a steering committee

- *Members needed*: gay or straight, willing to be active, financial benefactors

- *Help wanted*: a call for volunteers and funds to staff a booth at the upcoming ALC convention in Detroit

- *Our leaders*: only Fraser and Blaich were identified at that time

- *News & notes*: a gay rights antidiscrimination bill in Colorado and the UCC endorsement of the ordination of Bill Johnson[8]

The newsletter was distributed to religious news media; clergy; congregations; local, regional, and national church offices; and college libraries. The conservative Lutheran press criticized the fledgling group, even reprinting the newsletter (including the subscription form!) and unwittingly helped to spread the word.

Pastor Chuck Lewis established a San Francisco chapter of Lutherans Concerned that fall and Chicago also started a chapter. Pastor Lewis was invited to the monthly meeting of the Minnesota chapter in the spring of 1975, and his comments were preserved in the notes of Marie Kent.

"How do we get past being ignored or put off by the church hierarchy," asked a listener.

"Keep pushing those new frontiers forward," Lewis replied. "Keep the pressure going."

"Lovingly, of course," added another.[9]

Thirty-five years later at the momentous 2009 ELCA Churchwide Assembly, volunteer advocates for the cause of LGBT clergy were trained in "graceful engagement," an approach first adopted in 2007 but a legacy of these early suggestions to apply pressure lovingly.[10]

In 1975, the nation was attempting to get over the Watergate scandal and the resignation of President Nixon the previous August. Within Lutheran circles, conservatives successfully whipped up the folks in the pews by hyping their own sense of scandal. "Dollars for Disobedience" was the headline and the response to Pastor Siefkes' successful advocacy for a small appropriation for start-up of the tiny, fledgling group of Lutheran gays and lesbians. Conservative Lutheran publications were ablaze with criticism of the group and the ALC: "For a major board of one of the country's major denominations to identify through its budget an organization promoting the blatant transgression of the revealed word of God is a sign of sinking back to the level of official immorality that prevailed when Christianity emerged. Concerned members of the ALC will know how to express their outrage . . ."[11]

Indeed, at the October 1974 National Conference of the ALC in Detroit, some had expressed themselves by repeatedly tearing down the banner directing delegates to "Gay Headquarters," the small booth staffed by a few LGBT Lutherans. Others were sympathetic to those staffers, including several who received emotional support for their own conflicts of sexual identity.

By 1978, the organization had grown to twenty-two chapters nationwide and convened its first national assembly July 7–9 in Milwaukee. The name became "Lutherans Concerned" and by 1980, it would become "Lutherans Concerned/North America" or "LC/NA" for short. The Milwaukee gathering proved to be a smashing success and the first of regular assemblies that would follow in two-year cycles thereafter. The keynote speaker that first year was Dr. Elizabeth Ann Bettenhausen, a Secretary for Social Concerns at LCA national headquarters, and Rev. Chuck Lewis was the worship preacher. About sixty persons participated, representing various Lutheran denominations and synods, including the LCA, ALC, LCMS, AELC and the ultraconservative Wisconsin Synod.

> Coordinators Diane Fraser and Howard Erickson reported to the Assembly on their activities—taking part in the ALC's consultation on sexuality in April, speaking before church audiences and preparing for our presence at national conventions. Erickson reported that membership rose 36% in the preceding 12 months—due largely, he said, to a developing gay and non-gay backlash to Anita Bryant. "She has made a lot of people angry enough to get out of their chairs and do something," he said.[12]

One of the original five founders and newsletter editor Howard Erickson would later reminisce, "We five had our differences, all right, but it started to look like this nestling we'd hatched just might be around for awhile."[13]

The decade began with the LCA issuing a document entitled "Sex, Marriage, and Family," and it would end with its sister denomination, the ALC, issuing its own document entitled "Human Sexuality and Sexual Behavior" in 1980. As the two denominations entered upon serious discussions for merger in the 1980s, these statements of the "predecessor bodies" would become the policies of the ELCA until such time as the ELCA adopted its own.

Each document offered a general statement affirming the good gift of human sexuality:

> (LCA 1970 statement) Human sexuality is a gift of God for the expression of love and the generation of life. As with every good gift, it is subject to abuses which cause suffering and debasement. In the experience of human sexuality, it is the integrity of our relationships which determines the meanings of our actions. We do not merely have sexual relations; we demonstrate our true humanity in personal relationships, the most intimate of which are sexual.[14]

> (ALC 1980 statement) Human sexuality includes all that we are as human beings. . . . Sexual behavior includes what we do with our sexuality. In general it is the way male and female relate to God, to neighbor, to nature, to the structures of society, and to self. Sexual behavior acts out the special qualities and abilities male and female uniquely bring toward wholeness in the human community. Most specifically sexual behavior acts out the pleasure-producing, self-fulfilling sensations of sexual arousal and release. God created all human beings. Each is unique, each has a special identity; each receives individual abilities and opportunities to use them; each is called to use the gift of life in service to God, to neighbor, and to self. Sexual human life is a gracious gift, a sacred trust, from God.[15]

Standing alone, these general statements would logically include same-gender couples: unique individuals created by God; whose sexuality is gifted by God; whose true humanity is demonstrated in personal relationships, the most intimate of which are sexual; and who are called to use God's gifts in service to God, neighbor, and self.

But logical consistency would be negated by visceral fears. Traditional taboos would be carved out and placed in a separate section entitled "Considering Homosexuality."

(LCA 1970 statement) Scientific research has not been able to provide conclusive evidence regarding the causes of homosexuality. Nevertheless, homosexuality is viewed biblically as a departure from the heterosexual structure of God's creation.

(ALC 1980 statement) We note the current consensus in the scientific community that one's preferred sexual behavior exists on a continuum from exclusively heterosexual to exclusively homosexual and that homosexual behavior takes a variety of forms. We believe it appropriate to distinguish between homosexual behavior and orientation. Persons who do not practice their homosexual erotic preference do not violate our understanding of Christian sexual behavior.

This church regards the practice of homosexual erotic behavior as contrary to God's intent for his children. It rejects the contention that homosexual behavior is simply another form of sexual behavior equally valid with the dominant male/female pattern.

The possibility of LGBT ordination was not even a consideration of the policy statements. The only reference to clergy in either document was contained in the last paragraph of the 1970 LCA statement under the heading "A Call," which stated, "The Lutheran Church in America calls upon its pastors to reinforce the covenant of fidelity . . . a dynamic, lifelong commitment of one man and one woman in a personal and sexual union . . . a mutual commitment to lifelong faithfulness." As we shall see, when the question of LGBT clergy burst on the Lutheran scene a decade later, the newly merged church, the ELCA, would generate a hurry-up policy to justify its rejection of LGBT clergy candidacies.

For the Lutherans, not much had changed in the decade of the seventies. Though out gays had begun to appear, their presence had not been as assertive as in other denominations, and the Lutherans had not witnessed the conservative backlash—apart from the rants against the small appropriation that funded the startup meeting of Lutherans Concerned for Gay People—that would characterize the Episcopal, Presbyterian, and Methodist experience in the seventies . . . not yet, at least.

NOTES

1. Jim Siefkes personal correspondence contained in an unpublished booklet prepared by Jeannine Janson, "Lutherans Concerned for Gay People, the Beginning," compiled in 2008. In addition to Siefkes' correspondence, the booklet includes other materials from the formative years of Lutherans Concerned, such as recollections and notes of the founders and early newsletters.

2. Janson, "Lutherans Concerned for Gay People."

3. Ibid.

4. The retelling of the events of June 16, 1974, is based on e-mail correspondence from Pastor Siefkes to the author dated December 28, 2011.

5. Profile of Rev. Chuck Lewis, on the website of the Lesbian, Gay, Bisexual, and Transgender Religious Archives Network, accessed December 23, 2011, http://www.lgbtran.org/Profile.aspx?ID=126.

6. Janson, "Lutherans Concerned for Gay People."

7. Ibid.

8. Ibid.

9. Ibid.

10. The author participated in such training as a volunteer for Goodsoil, the umbrella organization that included Lutherans Concerned, Wingspan Ministries, and Extraordinary Lutheran Ministries.

11. Editorial "Dollars for Disobedience," *Christianity Today* (May, 1975): 47. Also quoted in Janson, "Lutherans Concerned for Gay People," 377.

12. Janson, "Lutherans Concerned for Gay People."

13. Ibid.

14. The Lutheran Church in America, *Sex, Marriage, and Family*, adopted by the Fifth Biennial Convention, Minneapolis, Minnesota, June 25–July 2, 1970.

15. American Lutheran Church, *Human Sexuality and Sexual Behavior*, adopted by the Tenth General Convention of the ALC, October, 1980.

* 22 *

EARLY OPTIMISM

In this decade of Ronald Reagan, culture warriors Pat Robertson and Jerry Falwell, and the "objective disorder" statement of Cardinal Ratzinger, as the UCC General Synod encouraged congregations to become open and affirming and Episcopal politics turned in a progressive direction, the Lutherans in the 1980s were about the business of merger.

Amidst high expectations, the LCA and ALC, the two largest Lutheran denominations, and the AELC, a smaller moderate spinoff from the LCMS, would come together in a grand union to form a church body nearly as large as the Presbyterians and Episcopalians combined. After years of discussion and negotiation, national conventions of the three Lutheran bodies held simultaneous votes on September 8, 1986, and each assented overwhelmingly to the merger: LCA 611 yes, 11 no; ALC 897 yes, 87 no; and AELC 136 yes, 0 no. The merger would become official on January 1, 1988.[1]

The early LC/NA relationship with predecessor bodies had been more collegial than adversarial. With proper information and education, the LGBT leaders assumed that the church would grow increasingly friendly and welcoming. The egalitarianism of the new church structure—inclusive policies for women, persons of color, and laity—carried an implied promise to all minorities, including LGBT Lutherans. At LC/NA gatherings, influential friends appeared, giving the impression of support from high places. Bishops, seminary presidents, even the future presiding bishop of the ELCA offered friendly encouragement.

Around eighty participants had attended the 1980 LC/NA biennial assembly in San Francisco. Local LCA Bishop Stanley Olson presented the keynote address; Walter Stuhr, President of Pacific Lutheran Theological Seminary, presided over eucharist; and Anita Hill and Leo Treadway were elected co-chairs. Hill and Treadway would each play major roles in the early years, and Hill would become a national figure twenty years later when she would be ordained as an out lesbian.[2] At that time, Hill was from Ann Arbor, but she would soon join Treadway in St. Paul, Minnesota, as members of St. Paul-Reformation Lutheran Church, and St. Paul-Ref would become the home of Wingspan Ministry and the de facto flagship LGBT-friendly congregation in the ELCA.

In 1982, Houston hosted the biennial assembly, and noted Catholic priest/theologian/advocate Father John McNeill offered the keynote. Representatives of the Chicago chapter reported on their positive experience hosting a hospitality suite at the recent national convention in their city. Advocacy regarding denominational policies had not yet attained primacy for LC/NA; the early emphasis was on chapter development, membership, and mutual support—a gay fellowship within the larger church. National membership was noted to be 462 members, and the annual budget was around five or six thousand dollars.[3]

The 1984 LC/NA gathering convened at St. Paul-Reformation Lutheran and celebrated the tenth anniversary of the group's formation at the nearby University of Minnesota campus. Bishop Lowell Erdahl from the Southeastern Minnesota District (ALC) offered a worship service sermon, and Bishop Herbert Chilstrom of the Minnesota Conference (LCA) sent a written welcome. Chilstrom would soon be elected the first presiding bishop of the newly formed ELCA, and Erdahl would later become the bishop of the St. Paul Area Synod of the ELCA. After their retirements, Chilstrom and Erdahl would become major supporters of LGBT causes, including jointly authoring a book about sexuality.[4]

The 1984 LC/NA assembly had witnessed a major step forward in the formal procedures of the group that had been incorporated as a nonprofit two years earlier. The 1984 assembly documents include numerous written resolutions and a packet of regional reports, several task forces were formed or offered reports, and the organization chose to make decisions by "consensus," a tradition that would become a permanent fixture of LC/NA.[5]

Noted biblical scholar Robin Scroggs offered the keynote, Emily Eastwood, who served as the worship planner for the assembly, was elected co-chair (she would become the dynamic executive director of the organization in 2003), and the Reconciled in Christ Program was up and running (later to be renamed Reconciling in Christ). Similar to More Light Presbyterians, which had been formed in the late 1970s, and the Methodist Reconciling Congregation Project (1984) and the UCC Open and Affirming program (1985), the LC/NA Reconciled in Christ (RIC) Program was premised upon local congregations proclaiming themselves to be LGBT friendly.

The 1984 LC/NA assembly considered a draft of a "Manifesto to Lutheran Churches." This document would later be retitled "A Call for Dialog," and tens of thousands of copies would be distributed. Containing biblical, theological, and pastoral warrant for full inclusion of LGBT, the six-page document concluded: "In the Spirit of Christ, whose frequent words to his followers were, 'Do not be afraid,' we invite our churches to join us in a new journey of mutual understanding, respect, and love."[6] Two years later at the 1986 LC/NA assembly in Los Angeles, the president reported:

> The central event of the past two years has been publication of "A Call to Dialog." No longer are we in an essentially reactive position in our relationship with the church. We have taken the initiative. The reception of the document has been extremely warm and has had the intended effect of engaging the church in dialog. It has been gratifying to have a number of non-gay people around the church seek me out to tell me how lucid, well-reasoned and useful this document has been.[7]

"A Study of Issues Concerning Homosexuality," released by the Lutheran Church in America (LCA) in 1986, drew little attention, dwarfed by issues of merger. Perhaps the context of its preparation and issuance also contributed to the relative lack of scrutiny the statement received: "It is important for the reader to understand that this material is the report of a committee. It is not intended to become a social statement or even a resolution of the church. As such, the report does not and will not represent any official stance of the Lutheran Church of America on issues of sexuality."[8] Nor did the LCA advisory committee have an end game beyond a concluding *recommendation* that various ministries, agencies, constituencies, and other groups within the LCA *consider* the report. Undoubtedly, some did, but without a built-in-trigger for action by assembly, council, bishops, and the like, the report grew cold as more pressing issues of the rapidly approaching merger heated up. As we shall see, half a dozen years later, development of a human sexuality statement by the merged church would set off a nuclear explosion compared to the muted firecracker of the 1986 report.

This inattention to the 1986 LCA report was unfortunate because it offered excellent starting points for discussion.

Regarding biblical and theological considerations, the LCA report concluded: "Rather than base our understanding of our relationship with God on an arbitrary list of sins—some more heinous than others—we argue that sin is that rebellion against God in which we all share equally. Likewise, God's gift of justification is one in which we all share undeservedly, no one more justified than another."[9]

Regarding psychological and biological considerations, the report concluded that "the emerging consensus is that homosexual orientation is a given rather than a choice. Even to admit the *possibility* of this tendency makes it inappropriate to isolate homosexual orientation as a sin."[10]

Regarding ethical considerations, the report concluded:

What is unambiguous about this approach to ethics is the gospel, the message that God accepts us in spite of our selves and that in becoming God's children we are sisters and brothers to one another. This certainty enables us to live with the ambiguities of life and to risk making ethical decisions even without conclusive answers.

Surely there is no comfort in the ambiguities of these situations. It would be easier to work with strict rules and regulations than to wrestle with what is appropriate to our relationships with God and with others. Yet there is also little comfort in arriving at simple answers when the questions involve people who were created in God's image and for whom Christ died.[11]

LC/NA contributed to the LCA study and offered warm but qualified endorsement of the report's conclusions, but the LGBT community, too, was swept up in merger anticipation. Lutheran gays and lesbians optimistically believed that their time would come, and this report encouraged their hopes. The LC/NA president commented in 1986:

> Parts of it are quite good, even innovative. Other parts show the collision of scholarship and sensitivity with political realities of a conservative church in which people often remain ill-informed and fearful. To view the product as the final word is to see only the flaws, not the progress that has been made in clarifying and articulating issues of importance to us.[12]

Six years earlier, at the 1980 assembly, "Goals and Strategies for the '80s" had been adopted. Divided into six categories, the document had listed workshops at denominational conventions, development of position papers, gay parents networking, fund raising, and dozens of other stated goals. Under the heading "For the Church," the first item was "ordination of gays," but it wasn't until the 1986 LC/NA assembly that this goal attained concrete status in the form of a resolution. After a number of "whereas" clauses, the resolution concluded:

> Be it therefore resolved that LC/NA reaffirm its commitment to work toward the day when being lesbian or gay will no longer be a barrier to ordination or certification as a lay professional, and,
> Be it further resolved that LC/NA affirm those openly lesbian and gay seminarians, clergy, and lay professionals who seek to work in the church, and
> Be it further resolved that LC/NA dialog with the Lutheran churches of North America regarding the ordination and call of openly gay and lesbian clergy and lay professionals, and
> Be it further resolved that the LC/NA board consider preparing a study report on the ordination and call of openly lesbian and gay clergy and the certification and hiring of openly lesbian and gay lay professionals, for dissemination to the Lutheran churches of North America.[13]

In December of 1987, on the eve of the ELCA merger that would become official on January 1, 1988, it appeared that the goal of ordination was on the horizon. Three openly gay senior seminarians from Pacific Lutheran Theological Seminary embodied the hopes of all gay Lutherans.

On December 9, 1987, the seminary faculty, on behalf of the ALC, voted unanimously to approve Joel Workin for certification, along with a full slate of other seniors who were members of the ALC. Two days later, on December 11, 1987, the Professional Preparation Commission of the Pacific Southwest Synod of the LCA also voted unanimously to approve a full slate of LCA candidates that included Jeff Johnson and James Lancaster. In due course, pursuant to merger policy, all such candidates approved for ordination in the LCA and ALC would be commended for ordination in the new ELCA.

At least, that's what the gay seminarians assumed.

NOTES

1. These voting results are from Edgar R. Trexler, *High Expectations: Understanding the ELCA's Early Years, 1988–2002* (Minneapolis: Augsburg Fortress, 2003), 9. Trexler served as editor of *The Lutheran Magazine*, the official publication of the ELCA, for the first eleven years of the ELCA.

2. LC/NA archives, typed notes and worship bulletin, 1980, Gerber-Hart Library, Chicago, Illinois.

3. LC/NA archives, typed notes, 1982.

4. Herbert W. Chilstrom and Lowell Erdahl, *Sexual Fulfillment: For Single and Married, Straight and Gay, Young and Old* (Minneapolis: Augsburg Books, 2001).

5. LC/NA archives, miscellaneous 1984 assembly documents.

6. LC/NA archives, typed notes, letter from Bishop Chilstrom, proposed rough draft and working document, "A Manifesto to the Lutheran Churches, 1984."

7. LC/NA archives, President's Report 1986.

8. Lutheran Church in America, "A Study of Issues Concerning Homosexuality," Report of the Advisory Committee of Issues Relating to Homosexuality (1986), 1.

9. Ibid., 19.

10. Ibid., 27.

11. Ibid., 37.

12. LC/NA archives, President's Report, 1986.

13. LC/NA archives, Task Force Report: Goals and Strategies for the '80s, "A Resolution Regarding Lesbian/Gay Church Professionals," President's Report, 1986.

✳ 23 ✳

BROKEN PROMISES

In the first dozen years of LC/NA, their relationship with the Lutheran denominations had been characterized by a collegial, get-to-know-us posture. Lutheran LGBT leaders had not been as assertive as their peers in the other denominations, and the rancorous conflicts that characterized the Episcopal, Presbyterian, and Methodist journeys in the seventies and eighties were absent in the Lutheran church bodies. The optimism and high expectations associated with the birth of a new church extended to LGBT Lutherans. By constitutional mandate, women would have equal representation as voting members and on committees and councils, persons of color would have allotted representation, laity would have a greater voice than clergy in the legislative assemblies of the church, and the Conference of Bishops would be advisors and not legislators—no House of Lords in the egalitarian ELCA. There was a widespread sense that the new church would be all things to all people.

It was 8:35 AM, five minutes after the usual time of opening for business. But on Monday, January 4, 1988, the tardiness could be forgiven. Amid excitement and crowding, the headquarters staff of the new church squeezed around the fountain in the lobby of the Lutheran Center at 8765 West Higgins Road, Chicago. It was the first official workday of the Evangelical Lutheran Church in America.

Secretary Lowell G. Almen presided over the "service of entrance" . . . after a brief liturgy, Almen's homily, and [singing],

... the crucifer led a half-dozen staffers with scissors toward a gold ribbon stretched across the corridor to the elevators. The staffers snipped, and the workday began.[1]

Almost immediately, the high expectations began to unravel. When the delegates from the three denominations had voted simultaneously for merger on September 8, 1986, there was a seemingly innocuous hint in the vote totals; the delegates from the smaller AELC had voted 100 percent for merger, the LCA voted 98.2 percent favorable, but the ALC only 91.1 percent.[2] The ALC was largely Norwegian and Midwestern while the LCA was mostly Swedish and Eastern. These are broad generalizations, of course, but those who would soon rail against the ELCA tended to come from the old ALC. Were there residual sibling grudges between Scandinavian sisters? Or a prairie populism that resented the Eastern establishment? This latter consideration could also apply to the later disagreements over full communion with the Episcopal Church.

Or were the latent rifts deeper still? For the leading ELCA antagonists, the course of the new church was ill-chosen, and they believed the egalitarian impulses written into constitutional quota requirements were symptomatic of the malaise of ecumenical Protestantism generally. Twenty years later, there were still those who lamented the loss of influence for "white male pastors," according to an article by Lutheran neoconservative Robert Benne. Even the article title was revealing: "How the ELCA Left the Great Tradition for Liberal Protestantism."[3] And there was truth in the charge; the new denomination would indeed move in step with the ecumenical denominations and the legacy of liberal theologians Wellhausen, Schleiermacher, Von Harnack, Bultmann, and Tillich—more recently, Borg and Crossan—and away from the pietistic orthodoxy of the increasingly conservative Lutheran Church Missouri Synod and the Wisconsin Synod. Some would say, with justification, that the fissures in Lutheranism didn't begin recently following the creation of the ELCA but centuries ago and the dawn of the Enlightenment.

For these "confessionalists," a "Call to Faithfulness" Conference quickly became an ELCA-bashing forum.

Approximately 900 people gathered in June 1990 on the campus of St. Olaf College in Northfield, Minnesota, for an independent theological conference in which critics hurled barbs at the ELCA. For three days during the "Call to Faithfulness" conference, prominent theologians chastised the ELCA for its ecumenical policies, its approach to social involvement, its mission philosophy, the content of its periodicals, its encouragement of inclusive God language and its alleged lack of theological direction. The ELCA's problems, they said, were caused by the church's failure to be faithful to biblical theology and Lutheran confessions.

Carl E. Braaten, professor of systematic theology at the Lutheran School of Theology at Chicago, was interrupted nine times by applause when he described the church as struggling between traditional concepts of evangelization and a new mission philosophy whose proponents contend that words like *humanization, development, liberation, wholeness,* and *justice* are simply different words for salvation.[4]

Seeds of disunity were planted in the Call to Faithfulness Conference that would later blossom into the WordAlone movement of the late nineties, initially to oppose an ecumenical agreement with the Episcopal Church, and then ripening into a full-fledged schismatic movement in the aftermath of the historic 2009 Churchwide Assembly. In 2009, WordAlone Vice President Mark Chavez wrote an article that traced the lineage:

In June 1990, more than a thousand ELCA members—bishops, pastors, theologians and lay leaders—from all parts of the ELCA attended a conference. . . . The title of the conference was "Call to Faithfulness."

All of the prominent ELCA biblical and confessional Lutheran theologians participated as speakers and workshop leaders. . . . It was a who's who in confessional Lutheranism in the ELCA.

[A]lmost every speaker, workshop leader and participant agreed in June 1990 that the Word of God was being silenced in the ELCA. The symptoms for the diagnosis included universalism, liberation theology, radical feminism, avoiding the use of God's revealed name and approval of sex outside of marriage. A second Call to Faithfulness conference was held in 1992. I left the first conference expecting an organized reform effort to emerge to serve the ELCA by helping it remain a faithful confessional Lutheran church.

The next organized effort by confessional Lutherans began in December 1996 . . . by using an e-mail discussion list. Eventually the e-mail list became known as WordAlone . . . the WordAlone Network was formally organized in March of 2000 to work for reform and renewal within the ELCA.[5]

The circle would be completed in August 2010 at the Lutheran CORE Convocation in Fishers, Indiana. Lutheran CORE was the latest incarnation of WordAlone. At the Fishers Convocation, Lutheran CORE formally decided to spawn a schismatic church body that would split from the ELCA. The speakers at the Fishers conference? "It is important to note that some of these theologians were presenters at Call to Faithfulness in June 1990 at St. Olaf College," Chavez wrote, and the person who called for the Fishers conference was the same Carl Braaten who had been the mainstay of the confessionalist conference twenty years earlier.[6]

———

For LGBT Lutherans, high expectations were dashed in a heap of broken promises within months of the ELCA startup. The collegial relationship evaporated in an instant, soon replaced by a confrontational militancy.

The road to broken promises began in the final months before the merger in Berkeley, California. In October 1987, four seminarians from Pacific Lutheran Theological Seminary in Berkeley drove across country to participate, along with half a million others, in the "National March on Washington for Lesbian and Gay Rights," which inspired the first "National Coming Out Day" on October 11. The four gay men were Joel Workin, Jim Lancaster, Greg Egertson, and Jeff Johnson.[7] Egertson was a junior in seminary, and he had been the first to come out, well before the trip to D.C. The other three came out after their trip to Washington. Egertson was a pastor's kid; in fact, his father, Paul, would later become a bishop with a distinguished record of support for gay rights.[8] The other three were seniors who had been approved for ordination by ALC and LCA committees in December 1987, just prior to the merger, with the expectation that they would be commended for ordination within the new church body.

Concord, the newsletter of LC/NA, reported the pending ordinations with great optimism:

> Three openly gay Lutheran seminarians have been certified for call and ordination in two separate but related actions by Lutheran church authorities. The students were certified by their respective synodical bodies prior to the merger of those bodies into the Evangelical Lutheran Church in America.
>
> On December 9, 1987, the faculty of Pacific Lutheran Theological Seminary, on behalf of the American Lutheran Church (ALC), voted to approve Joel Workin for certification, the first step in the ordination process. Workin was a member of the ALC and is openly gay. He was approved unanimously by the faculty, without comment, along with a slate of other ALC candidates.
>
> On December 11, 1987, the Professional Preparation Commission of the Pacific Southwest Synod of the Lutheran Church in America (LCA) also voted unanimously to approve openly gay candidates Jeff Johnson and James Lancaster, both LCA members.
>
> Since the ALC and LCA were part of the merger which formed the Evangelical Lutheran Church in America (ELCA) on January 1, 1988, these three candidates were commended for ordination in the new church upon satisfactory completion of seminary work and the receipt and acceptance of a valid call from a congregation or agency of the church.
>
> "The real difficulty," observed Lancaster, "will be locating parishes willing to accept openly gay ministers." A call from a parish or church agency is a prerequisite to ordination in the ELCA.[9]

If it had only been true, and the optimism rewarded. The drama played out in the pages of the *Los Angeles Times*.

On February 24, 1988, the *Times* reported on the "unprecedented event" of three openly gay seminarians receiving certification for the ministry. Pressed for a comment, a spokeswoman for the churchwide office in Chicago could only state that the church was studying the issue, but that ordination was usually a matter left to local congregations and synods.[10]

On February 27, 1988, the *Times* quoted Jeff Johnson stating that public attention "turned out to be a little bigger deal than I thought it would be." Statements out of Bishop Lyle Miller's office indicated the ordination approvals were being reconsidered.[11] Adding to the personal drama, Johnson's pastor when he had been confirmed had been this same Lyle Miller, who now served as the bishop of the Sierra Pacific Synod as controversy engulfed the bishop and his former confirmand.

At the March meeting of the Conference of Bishops, the newly elected bishops from the sixty-five synods wrestled with an appropriate response to the developments in California. Eventually they settled on this statement: "Persons of homosexual orientation who seek to be ordained or who are already ordained will be expected to refrain from homosexual practice."[12] While the church and others assumed this statement to be the definitive and controlling policy of the church, the reality was that the statement carried no authority. According to the brand new ELCA constitution, the Conference of Bishops was advisory only and legislative authority rested solely in the biennial Churchwide Assembly and in the Church Council during the biennium between Assemblies. No one at the time picked up on this important limitation on the authority of the bishops.

On April 8, 1988, the *Los Angeles Times* quoted Presiding Bishop Herbert Chilstrom of the churchwide office in Chicago, who stated that the pending ordinations "set off an avalanche of letters and phone calls to parish pastors, synodical bishops and our church-wide office here in Chicago."[13]

The heat was on, and even a straight ally such as Bishop Chilstrom, charged with shepherding a fragile new church body without a deposit of accrued legitimacy, felt the pressure to preserve the institution. The ELCA constituency was inherited from its predecessors, not earned, and all eyes watched with suspicion as the first crisis of the new church unfolded. The confluence of high expectations of gay Lutherans with a new church start-up proved to be ill-timed.

Chilstrom's 1990 journal entry offered rare insight into the anguish of leadership faced with the conflicting demands of unity versus justice:

I continue to wonder how I got into all of this and how I can carry such a load. . . . I feel so divided. I wish so very much that the church was ready to accept such persons. But it isn't, by any stretch of the imagination. So I must do my duty. I must support denial of ordination for them. I feel very torn apart by it. At times I even wonder if I should resign because of the conflict between my conscience and the stance I must take as the bishop.[14]

The gay seminarians were grilled. Were they presently celibate, and would they promise to remain so? Johnson's response was typical. Though he assured church officials that he was celibate, he left open the possibility that he might one day fall in love. Even for the sake of his ordination candidacy, Johnson would not make a promise he might not be able to keep.[15]

The fledgling ELCA, just months into its new existence, caved under pressure of the public hue and cry. Yes, the gay seminarians would be acceptable but only if they promised to remain celibate in the future. On the fly, a new criterion had been added to the candidacy process, which now sounded McCarthy-like. "Are you now or will you ever?" The candidates eventually replied honestly; they could not promise to never fall in love.

The church would have accepted the candidates if they had lied. The courage of the candidates stood in stark contrast to the timidity of the church. The integrity of the candidates embarrassed the church that reneged on its agreement. The approvals for ordination were withdrawn.

Like a foul wind, the rejections chilled the July 1988 LC/NA assembly in Toronto.[16] The written report of one of the co-chairs stated:

We are all aware of the great sacrifice made by the seminarians Jeff Johnson, Joel Workin, and Jim Lancaster, who declared their gay orientation, were certified as openly gay candidates for ordination, and then saw their chances to receive a call denied to them in a firestorm of negative criticism of their God-given capacity for love. . . . What Jeff, Joel, and Jim accomplished at the highest personal cost was to publicize the double standard applied to lesbian/gay people . . . our living in the closet lends consent to the damaging notion that we are rare and freakish . . . that our lives and our loves are too shameful to be revealed . . . we wake up each day to an emotional and spiritual apartheid.[17]

The September, 1988 issue of *The Lutheran Magazine* (the official publication of the ELCA) quoted LC/NA President Ralph Wushke:

"The spirit of the assembly was much more radical than in the past," Wushke said in an interview. "We must begin to call the church to account for its discrimination against gay and lesbian people."

But that radicalism, he added, "has been translated into a time of taking stock. We are not prepared to act immediately out of anger. We want to channel our anger into a measured and intentional response."[18]

As the decade closed, Lutheran gays and their allies fumed and contemplated "a measured and intentional response" to the jarring rejection of the already approved seminarians. Meanwhile, a coalition of congregations, clergy, and lay individuals in the San Francisco Bay Area plotted an extraordinary journey that would usher in a tumultuous decade in the ELCA. As the East Coast blazed with the controversy surrounding Episcopal Bishop Spong and the ordination of an openly gay man in Newark, the extraordinary Lutheran ordinations of a gay man and a lesbian couple would ignite a conflagration on the West Coast.

NOTES

1. Trexler, *High Expectations*, 14.
2. Ibid.
3. Benne, "How the ELCA Left," *Christianity Today*.
4. Trexler, *High Expectations*, 19–20.
5. Mark C. Chavez, WordAlone vice president and Lutheran CORE director, "A Reconfiguration of North American Lutheranism," on the website of

WordAlone, http://www.wordalone.org/docs/chavez2010.shtml, November 2009.

6. Ibid.

7. Michael Wilker, "Honoring Joel Workin's Impact on LVC," on the website of the Lutheran Volunteer Corps, updated October 21, 2010, accessed January 3, 2012, http://www.lutheranvolunteercorps.org/index.cfm/news_joel-workins-impact-on-lvc.

8. Bishop Paul Egertson would resign following his participation in the *extra ordinem* ordination of Anita Hill in 2001.

9. The newsletter was initially called *The Gay Lutheran* but was renamed in the mideighties. "Concord," *Newsletter of Lutherans Concerned/North America*, 1988, Number 2.

10. "First Step Toward Ordination 3 Gays Certified for Lutheran Ministry," *Los Angeles Times*, February 24, 1988.

11. Mathis Chazanov, "Openly Gay Seminarians Pose Dilemma for Lutheran Officials," *Los Angeles Times*, February 27, 1988.

12. Trexler, *High Expectations*, 72.

13. "2 Gay Seminarians Vow to Refrain From Sex; 3rd Student 'Unclear,'" *Los Angeles Times*, April 8, 1988.

14. Herbert W. Chilstrom, *A Journey of Grace: The Formation of a Leader and a Church, An Autobiography*, (Minneapolis: Lutheran University Press, 2011), 422–23.

15. John Dart, "Southern California File," *Los Angeles Times*, April 23, 1988.

16. A Canadian, Ralph Wushke, served as president that year, and there were several Canadian LC/NA chapters.

17. LC/NA archives, Kerry Bossin, LC/NA co-chair report to the 1988 LC/NA Assembly.

18. "Gays, Lesbians Avoid a Confrontation," *The Lutheran Magazine*, September 7, 1988, 29.

✳ 24 ✳

EXTRAORDINARY

Poet and Professor Gerhard Frost touched many with his teaching and meditative writings. Prior to his death in 1988, he had built a distinguished teaching career, first at Iowa's Luther College and then for twenty years at Luther Seminary in St. Paul. His writings, often reflections on suffering, have been reprinted and remain popular long after his death. Perhaps his most popular collection is entitled *Blessed Is the Ordinary*, but his daughter Ruth would follow an *extraordinary* path to ordained ministry.

In the few years prior to his death in 1988, Professor Frost knew his daughter's pain of rejection by the church, his church, the church to which he had dedicated his life. Ruth Frost had graduated from his own Luther Seminary in 1984 as a candidate for the ministry, but she found it an inhospitable place for one wrestling with doubts, and guilt, about her own sexuality.[1]

Following graduation, her interview with a Lutheran bishop in New York City went well, but, "feeling absolutely crazy," she had kept silent about her secret. Following the interview, she stumbled upon a gay pride march weaving its way up Fifth Avenue, and she was trapped on the sidewalk between the bishop's office and those on the street. Stepping in one direction would mean turning her back on the other.

She stepped sideways. She didn't step out but she didn't pursue the call process, either. She returned to Luther Seminary for more studies while she attempted to sort things through, but then she fell in love, and she followed her heart into a relationship with Phyllis Zillhart, a fellow seminary student at Luther. Later, Frost would say that Luther "was an expensive dating service, but it worked.[2]

Ruth Frost prepared a coming out speech for her parents, but she had barely uttered the words, "I am a homosexual," when her father knelt before her, grasped her hands, and comforted his beloved daughter. "You poor girl," he said. "The pain you have been secretly carrying must be overwhelming. You know we will always love you."[3]

Over her father's shoulder, her mother Ivern's shocked face nodded forcefully as her husband offered encouragement. From the very first moment, Professor Gerhard Frost and Ivern Frost became Ruth's ardent supporters and advocates.[4]

Suddenly, Zillhart's call to the ordained ministry was also in doubt. She interviewed in Southwest Minnesota where she had grown up, but when the bishop followed up on the interview, she lied. Zillhart denied rumors that she was a lesbian, but in that moment of deceit, she came out to herself. The guilt, not for her sexuality but for the deception, wrenched her insides, and she withdrew from consideration for that congregation. When she was later assigned to a new district and a new bishop—Lowell Erdahl in Southeast Minnesota—she would not repeat her lie, and she would confide in her bishop, accompanied by her new partner. She said, "I just can't live this fractured life that's cutting me off from the source of integrity, joy, and meaningfulness in this ministry, and it's sabotaging this relationship."[5]

The bishop was stunned. He knew Ruth Frost, whose family was part of the establishment of the ALC. Later, Bishop Erdahl would become an unabashed supporter of LGBT ordination, but at that moment, he insisted that Zillhart withdraw her candidacy. Frost and Zillhart were forced to choose between their love for each other and their call to the ministry, and they celebrated their love while grieving their loss, which lasted roughly five years until they heard God's call again, together.

Called by some the gay capitol of America, the Castro District of San Francisco was the neighborhood of Supervisor Harvey Milk's rise to prominence and then to martyrdom. In two traditional Lutheran congregations located nearby, the paths of Frost and Zillhart would intersect with recent seminary graduate Jeff Johnson.

In the summer and fall of 1988, a group of San Francisco/Bay Area lay individuals, clergy, congregations, and other communities of faith formed a coalition to do something about the rejection of seminarian Jeff Johnson earlier that year and establish a credible LGBT outreach ministry at the same time. The coalition came to be called Lutheran Lesbian and Gay Ministry (LLGM). As set forth in its newsletters at the time, LLGM was "committed to the Gospel, to lesbian/gay ordained pastoral leadership and to progressive ministry, with, by and for the lesbian/gay community."[6]

Among the congregations of LLGM were First United Lutheran, led by Pastor John Frykman, and St. Francis Lutheran, led by Pastor James DeLange. St. Francis Lutheran was a congregation located near the Castro, and First United Lutheran was four miles away in the Richmond District, a family-oriented residential neighborhood known for its quiet pace and the persistent fog that rolled in from the Pacific. Both congregations were Reconciled in Christ and saw participation with LLGM to be the significant next step in their witness toward the lesbian/gay community.

LLGM developed a bold plan to arrange for the call and ordination of openly gay and lesbian clergy, and First United and St. Francis would issue the calls. ELCA ordinations required approvals and recommendations at several levels, including from the local bishop, but the San Francisco congregations and their candidates would proceed outside the formal procedures, *extra ordinem* (extraordinary), relying on the precedent of Martin Luther and remembering the recent experience of the irregular ordinations of the Philadelphia Eleven.

In 1989, a joint call committee began to search for a gay candidate for First United and a lesbian candidate for St. Francis. LLGM would provide financial assistance to the two congregations to help with salaries. First United soon settled on Johnson and St. Francis on Frost and Zillhart as a clergy team that would split one full-time position. Pastor Frykman invited Johnson to lunch and asked him if he would be interested in serving as his associate pastor.

"I can't," Johnson replied, "because the bishop won't recommend me for call."

"We know that," Frykman said, "but both the congregation and myself personally are willing to take the consequences."[7]

We noted the Conference of Bishops statement in March of 1988 that led to the withdrawal of the ordination approvals of Jeff Johnson and his seminary mates. Yet, the Conference of Bishops had no legislative or judicatory authority; their function was advisory only. "The statement on ordination of practicing homosexuals [and other matters] . . . were adopted as advice to the church, but they were never challenged. . . . They took on the stature of policy even though they are not."[8]

Not to worry, the ELCA Church Council got wind of what was going on in California, and swooped in with an explicit policy. The Church Council did have legislative authority, second only to the Churchwide Assembly. As part of the routine of becoming a church, many written policies were formulated during the first years of the ELCA. One document, *Definitions and Guidelines for Discipline*, had been in process for six to nine months, but at the November 1989 meeting of the Council, the chair of the Legal and Constitutional Review Committee urged immediate passage of the current draft "because some synods have immediate need [for] such guidelines, in order to deal with issues already pending." The document lumped prohibited sexual behavior together: "adultery, promiscuity, the sexual abuse of another, the misuse of counseling relationships for sexual favors, and homosexual genital activity constitutes conduct that is incompatible with the character of the ministerial office."[9]

The Council adopted the proposed draft at that November 1989 Church Council meeting, but by then First United and St. Francis had already voted to call the candidates, and they didn't change their plans. Meanwhile, Sierra Pacific Synod Bishop Lyle G. Miller addressed letters to both congregations urging them not to proceed and warning of sanctions if they did.

The two congregations and their called candidates were undeterred, and the extraordinary ordinations of Johnson, Frost, and Zillhart were scheduled for January 20, 1990. Frost and Zillhart relocated to San Francisco from the Twin Cities on January 1, 1990, and immediately began to receive press and media requests. A television camera recorded the sentiment of one middle-aged parishioner who was asked about the prospect of discipline for her congregation.

"I think we'll probably be in a bit of trouble," she said with stoic understatement, "but I'm all in favor of it."

Anticipating a crowd larger than either the First United or the St. Francis sanctuaries could handle, the rite of ordination would be in historic St. Paulus Lutheran Church in the heart of San Francisco. Around the country, seven satellite services occurred simultaneously, arranged by Leo Treadway of St. Paul Reformation and former co-chair of LC/NA. The Sons of Orpheus, a drum corps attired in monkish robes, beat a welcoming cadence as guests ascended the steps into the sanctuary. A trumpet fanfare signaled the start, and the largest crowd ever to swell the old church arose in jubilation as fifty-three robed Lutheran clergy led the procession toward the altar. Fifty clergy from Presbyterian, Episcopal, and Methodist churches also participated. Incense and hymnody filled the hall. A liturgical dancer with a fire stick touched a flame to the foreheads of the three ordinands and to the lips of the preacher, Episcopal priest Rev. Dr. Carter Heyward, who had been one of the Philadelphia Eleven sixteen years earlier. After the clergy laid on hands, the three ordinands moved to the center of the assembly, and a thousand or more extended hands of blessing and affirmation.

"It was a sacred moment," Pastor Johnson would recall.

The event was covered by CBS newsman John Blackstone, whose report concluded with the words, "The months ahead will reveal whether these Lutherans are out of step with their church or a step ahead."

It didn't take long for Bishop Miller and the Sierra Pacific Synod Council to bring charges against the two congregations.[10] The formal charges were not specifically for calling gays or lesbians but for failing to follow constitutionally mandated call procedures, specifically that the candidates were not on the approved clergy roster: "[Congregations] agree to call pastoral leadership from the clergy roster of this church in accordance with the call procedures for this church" (ELCA Constitution 8.21.d).

The ad hoc ELCA Committee on Discipline that would function as judge and jury consisted of appointees by the synod and by ELCA churchwide offices. Though the parties essentially stipulated to the facts, nearly one hundred witnesses were called to the three-day ecclesiastical trial during July 7–9, 1990. The charges were sustained and both congregations were suspended for a five-year period, with the proviso that they would be expelled from the ELCA if they failed to conform to ordination requirements and procedures within the probationary period.

The written opinion of the committee also contained a tacit invitation to the ELCA to change its policies, which would also serve to remove the suspension.

As any good attorney knows, the importance of judicial decisions is often not the specific outcome but the written opinions, which cast the clear light of reason on difficult issues, and the reasoning later becomes the rationale behind policy change. Thus, we will consider the written opinions of the "Decision of the Discipline Committee" filed on July 18, 1990. The Decision consisted of twenty-four pages of opinion, including both a majority report and a minority report (which agreed with the suspensions but not the expulsion penalty), as well as statements from individual jurors.

The document evinces the high emotion and internal struggles of the prosecution, the jurors, and Bishop Miller, who had known Jeff Johnson since Jeff's childhood, but who felt compelled as bishop to uphold constitutional provisions and the good order of the church, as did the Discipline Committee. The document lauded the "spirit of cooperation, mutual respect, and Christian love" exhibited by all participants. The document expressly suggested, and implicitly hoped, that the ELCA would change its ordination policies during the probationary period, which would allow full reinstatement of the congregations.

The majority opinion concluded,

We have been moved by the testimony of the members of these congregations and their pastors as they have described their ministry to AIDS victims and members of both the homosexual and heterosexual communities. Like us, these are God's people doing his work. We can all learn from each other.

As the Lutheran Church, we cannot remain true to our own purpose and confession as an open, teaching, and inclusive church unless we are willing to engage in genuine dialogue with gay and lesbian persons.

Tony Tanke, laity from San Mateo, served as co-chair of the Discipline Committee; Mr. Tanke agreed with the decision and, yet, as he looked at Rev. Frykman and Rev. DeLange, pastors of the congregations accused of violating church policy, he said, "I could not help but believe that if Christ were with us now, in body as well as spirit, we would find him seated at their table. I regard myself fortunate to be part of a church that counts them as pastors."

The Discipline Committee, and then the regional body, the Sierra Pacific Synod, invited the rest of the ELCA into the discussion. Specifically, the 1990 Assembly of the Sierra Pacific Synod asked the ELCA Church Council and the Conference of Bishops to "authorize a study of the ordination of homosexual persons."[11]

The response of the ELCA Church Council was twofold. First, at its October 1990 meeting, a ministry policy entitled *Vision and Expectations* was debated and adopted, and, second, further study was referred to the Division for Ministry and to a task force that would study and report on a possible Social Statement on Human Sexuality.

Vision and Expectations was a conservative document; it did not move the discussion forward and merely reworded the hastily adopted *Definitions and Guidelines for Discipline* a year earlier. Once again, the false distinction between homosexual practice and homosexual orientation was used to justify discriminatory church policy.

The pertinent portion of *Vision and Expectations* stated: "Ordained and commissioned ministers who are homosexual in their self-understanding are expected to abstain from homosexual sexual relationships." The minutes of the October 1990 Council meeting reveal a robust discussion over this document. The document was adopted, but the minutes do not reflect an actual vote tally. Though *Vision and Expectations* would serve as denominational policy preventing LGBT ordination for the next nineteen years, that was not the stated understanding of the Council at the time of adoption. "[A member] inquired in what sense is the document to be considered policy. [Another member responded], 'it is not a juridical document that is to be used in an official sort of way. It is rather a document that describes the behavior of clergy. It is not a prescriptive document.' [Another member] termed the document 'a teaching resource.'"[12]

The document was published in booklet form and widely distributed. A derivative policy was instituted for seminarians, who were required to subscribe to a Sexual Conduct Statement. Both in writing and subsequent oral interviews, candidates would be grilled, "Do you intend to live in accord with . . . *Vision and Expectations?*"[13]

A student at Trinity Lutheran Seminary in Columbus, Ohio, lamented, "I could lie about who I am. I could deny who I am. I could say openly who I am. The first two options meant loss of my self. The third option meant loss of my calling."[14]

The second response of the Church Council was to refer the matter for study with reports, and possible action, at the 1993 Churchwide Assembly; with delays, consideration would be deferred to 1995.

In the meantime, Pastors Johnson, Frost, and Zillhart fulfilled their call, ministering to the San Francisco LGBT community at the height of the HIV/AIDS epidemic. It was often a death-bed ministry to the afflicted and their friends and families. In fact, Pastor Zillhart had to step out during the trial in order to conduct a funeral. Joel Workin, one of the three seminarians rejected for ordination along with Jeff Johnson, was one of those who died from AIDS in 1995. Surrounded by friends and family, he rose from his coma to proclaim, "We're all God's children! Can I get an amen to that?"[15] In the midst of devastation, the outlaw pastors and congregations were there to speak their amens to the dying, even if the church as a whole was not.[16]

The last bishop to serve the Pacific Southwest in the former Lutheran Church in America (LCA) before the 1988 merger had been Rev. Stan Olson. Bishop Olson had long been a straight ally, and he had preached at LC/NA biennial assemblies in 1980 and 1986. He participated in the extraordinary San Francisco ordinations of 1990, and he would participate in later extraordinary ordinations.

In 1993, Rev. Olson would join with Rev. Jeff Johnson and Greg Egertson, the fourth seminarian who had participated in the 1987 trip to Washington, D.C., in founding an organization they called Extraordinary Candidacy Committee, later the Extraordinary Candidacy Project (ECP). ECP would work closely with LLGM in the Bay Area and later nationally. ECP would screen and credential potential LGBT candidates for ministry, much as an official ELCA candidacy committee would do, and LLGM would help to identify ministry opportunities. In 1995 LLGM went national and became Lutheran Lesbian and Gay Ministries. ECP and LLGM worked together but as separate organizations until 2007, when they merged into Extraordinary Lutheran Ministries (ELM).

Neither First United nor St. Francis attempted to comply with the terms for reinstatement, and after five years, the congregations were expelled from the ELCA, effective January 1, 1996. Even then, they did not go quietly, and St. Francis invited the bishop to come to their congregation and formally expel them. By then, Bishop Miller had resigned, and Bishop Robert Mattheis had been elected as his successor. Bishop Mattheis was sympathetic, and he willingly participated in a ritual of expulsion. A cloth banner was ripped apart, and the bishop exited the sanctuary of St. Francis with shreds of the banner streaming from his crosier. Afterwards, he said, "I grieve [the expulsion], but I remain hopeful that God is a God of the future."[17]

Professor Gerhard Frost died in 1988, just before daughter Ruth embarked on her *extra ordinem* journey. He would have been with her along the way, and undoubtedly he was. Ruth's favorite of her father's poems is called "His Way for Me" from his collection *Blessed Is the Ordinary*, and we quote it here in honor of Professor Frost's extraordinary daughter and God's way for her:

The profoundest thing
one can say of a river
is that it's on its way to the sea.

The deepest thought
one can think of a person
is that he or she is a citizen of eternity.

Moments and years,
years and moments,
pass like sea-bent streams.
And I? I'm carried by the current
of an all-possessing Love.
I'm on my way, God's way for me,
so let it be.[18]

NOTES

1. Except where otherwise noted, the details of the story of Ruth Frost and Phyllis Zillhart are based on a private interview of Frost and Zillhart by the author on February 12, 2012.

2. Profile of Rev. Ruth Frost, on the website of the the Lesbian, Gay, Bisexual and Transgender Religious Archives Network, http://www.lgbtran.org /Profile.aspx?ID=291, accessed January 1, 2012.

3. This is a paraphrase of Professor Frost's words of encouragement, since Ruth remembers only the sentiment but not the actual words.

4. Mrs. Ivern Frost outlived her husband by fifteen years, and she became in many ways the "Grand Dame" of the Luther Seminary community. She invited key professors to her house for tea, one on one, and enlisted their support for gay causes. Later, when Bishop Lowell Erdahl was in his final term as bishop of the St. Paul Synod, she encouraged him to take a leading role in the struggle for gay inclusion, and he did.

Pastors Frost and Zillhart also shared another poignant vignette during their interview with the author. The Frost family was part of the Lutheran aristocracy that shared a corner of a lake in Northern Minnesota. The owners of the cabins of "Pastor's Point" included bishops, professors, theologians, and pastors of "high steeple" churches. In 1993, Frost and Zillhart were canoeing as the sun was setting. Zillhart was visibly pregnant with their soon-to-be daughter. In the distance, they spied a solitary figure standing at the end of a dock. As they came closer, they saw that it was Al Rogness, the patriarch of one of the influential Lutheran families, enjoying his favorite spot for smoking his pipe. When Rogness recognized them, he waved them closer. As they approached, the white hair of the elder statesman glowed in the aura of the setting sun. And then he blessed the couple and their unborn child.

5. Sasha Aslanian, "Lesbian Clergy Once Expelled, Now Embraced," Minnesota Public Radio News, accessed January 1, 2011, http://minnesota.publicradio.org/display/web/2010/09/16/elca-lesbian-clergy/.

6. Rev. James DeLange, private conversation with the author, July 7, 2012; Jeannine Janson, private correspondence with the author, November 18, 2102; and *The Newsletter of Lutheran Lesbian and Gay Ministry*, vol. 1: no. 5 (July 1989).

7. This conversation, other comments, and the description of the ordination that follow in this chapter are based upon a documentary video: "In the Beginning," on the website of Extraordinary Lutheran Ministries, accessed May 28, 2011, http://www.youtube.com/watch?v=PVOz3Z7t9L0.

8. Trexler, *High Expectations*, 73–74.

9. ELCA Church Council, November 18–19, *Minutes* (1989), 37, and *Agenda*, 6, 8. There is an unexplained inconsistency between the language quoted in the Council *Minutes*, "homosexual genital activity constitutes conduct that is incompatible with the character of the ministerial office," and later references to the document *Definitions and Guidelines for Discipline*, which states, "practicing homosexual persons are precluded from the ordained ministry of this church." The best explanation is that between the time the Council approved the document and the time it was actually printed and distributed, an unidentified editor sought to clarify the Council's intent.

10. "Decision of the Discipline Committee," filed July 18, 1990, contained on the website of Extraordinary Lutheran Ministries, accessed January 3, 2012, http://www.elm.org/wp-content/uploads/2010/08/SF-FU-ELCA-Decision 0001.pdf.

11. ELCA Churchwide Assembly, "Report of the Church Council," in *Minutes* (1991), 907.

12. ELCA Church Council, *Minutes* (Oct 20–22, 1990), 123–24. The *Minutes* of the 1997 Churchwide Assembly contain background information regarding the history and usage of the *Vision and Expectations* document and note that in March 1997 the Division for Ministry formally approved use of the document to screen potential ministry candidates, thus rendering de jure what had been de facto from its inception. ELCA Churchwide Assembly, *Minutes* (1997), 394–98. That the policy issued originally as a majority action of the Church Council would become a critical factor later when CWA09 adopted a procedural rule that revisions to the policy merely required a majority vote and not a supramajority.

13. Division for Ministry, "Candidacy Manual," Evangelical Lutheran Church in America, 6.

14. Comstock, *Unrepentant*, 137.

15. "Honoring Joel Workin's Impact on LVC," on the website of the Lutheran Volunteer Corps, October 21, 2010, accessed January 3, 2012, http://www.lutheranvolunteercorps.org/index.cfm/news_joel-workins-impact-on-lvc.

16. In February 2012, when Pastors Frost and Zillhart met with the author and retold the story of their San Francisco ministry, Pastor Frost spoke passionately of those days—not for the way she was treated, but for the lack of a churchwide outreach to the gay community dying of AIDS—as a striking modern version of the familiar Lucan parable in which the priests and the

Levites moved to the other side of the road, but the outcast Samaritan offered assistance. Pastor Frost spoke of Jesus' call to Lazarus, "Come out," and to the bystanders, "Unbind him" (John 11:43–44). After many years of service in San Francisco, Pastors Frost and Zillhart have chosen to continue their careers as hospice chaplains in Minneapolis.

17. *San Francisco Chronicle*, "Lutherans Expel Two S.F. Groups," January 1, 1996.

18. Gerhard E. Frost, "His Way for Me," *Blessed Is the Ordinary* (Minneapolis: Winston Press, 1980), 9. Reprinted with permission of Ruth Frost.

✳ 25 ✳

A SECOND BAY AREA TRIAL

In the aftermath of the *extra ordinem* ordinations of Johnson, Frost, and
Zillhart, Bishop Lyle Miller of the Sierra Pacific Synod was confronted
with a fresh act of ecclesiastical disobedience; another gay man would
come out and challenge the church's ordination policy. This time, the
gay man was already ordained and called to St. Paul Lutheran Church of
Oakland, California. Pastor Ross Merkel came out to his congregation
in June 1993 on the fifteenth anniversary of his ordination.[1] Pastor Merkel
and his congregation had been LLGM supporters from the outset.

St. Paul Lutheran Church of Oakland had an interesting history of
gay ministry. When they called Pastor Merkel in the early 1980s, they did
not have a noticeable gay population nor a particular outreach to the
LGBT community, and Merkel characterized the congregation as "staid,
conservative, and traditional." However, there was an evangelism group
that called itself the "Communicating Faith Committee" that was open
and wanted the church to grow. In 1983, LC/NA began the Reconciled
in Christ project, fashioned after More Light Presbyterians. St. Paul of
Oakland was one of the first two congregations to join,[2] and suddenly they
had a very intentional ministry to the LGBT community that included:

- hosting a PFLAG chapter (Parents and Friends of Lesbians and
  Gays).

- advertising a word of welcome in a gay newspaper.

- creating an AIDS task force and inviting persons with HIV/AIDS
  and their families and caregivers.

Our task force—and I have to tell you this because this is part of who this church is—this task force would do everything from shopping and taking people to doctor's appointments to going and cleaning their houses and doing their laundry, to the doctors and nurses in the parish would help people with their transfusions. We would bathe them. We did everything in our power to keep them in their home as long as possible and to keep a quality of life that worked. It was really a very powerful ministry for those who received it and those who gave it.[3]

When Pastor Merkel overtly came out to his congregation in 1993—introducing his partner, his partner's parents, and his partner's adult children (his own parents were deceased)—there was neither surprise nor shock: "Everybody in the parish knew it. I mean, anybody who didn't know it was because they didn't want to know it." The Church Council of St. Paul immediately called a meeting and affirmed his pastorate.

Bishop Miller happened to be on sabbatical when word filtered to the synod office. A representative of the synod made an impromptu visit to Pastor Merkel.

"You know, if you would just say it's not true, this'll go away," the official said. "Just say that they misunderstood or something."

"I'm not doing that," replied Pastor Merkel.

"Well, if you resign, we'll do everything we can for the congregation."

"I'm not resigning."

Later, the Synod office again encouraged him to resign so the congregation wouldn't have to endure any trauma.

"It's no trauma for us. This is your trauma, not ours," Pastor Merkel said. "I'm not resigning. I've done nothing wrong. I refuse to resign and just disappear."[4]

Back from sabbatical, Bishop Miller ordered a disciplinary hearing scheduled for February 1994; this time, the case would be directly against the pastor rather than the congregation. On Annunciation Day, March 25, 1994, the decision was announced; Pastor Merkel was defrocked, and he was removed from the clergy roster of the ELCA. Bishop Miller then resigned.[5]

Just two weeks later, the annual assembly of the Sierra Pacific Synod commenced in Fresno on April 8, 1994. Friends and colleagues of Pastor Merkel moved a resolution entitled "In Support of St. Paul Lutheran Church and Rev. Ross D Merkel."

> Resolved, that we, the Sierra Pacific Synod in Assembly, lament the ELCA's loss of Pastor Merkel as a rostered clergy person and pledge our continuing partnership in ministry with St. Paul Lutheran Church, Oakland, California, and its pastor, the Rev. Ross D. Merkel, for in our understanding and experience of God's love and grace in our own lives we can do no other.[6]

The motion carried.

Newly elected Bishop Robert Mattheis respected the sentiment of his synod, and he treated the St. Paul pulpit as between calls and open, and he resisted those who would have placed the congregation on trial. The congregation would not be punished by the ELCA even when they persisted in their continuing call to their now nonrostered pastor, precisely the offense committed by the two San Francisco congregations in 1990. St. Paul Lutheran would remain an ELCA congregation, and Pastor Merkel would remain their minister. His local conference (a synod subgrouping of ELCA congregations) soon elected him dean. Similarly, Pastor Jeff Johnson of the earlier trial would serve two terms as dean of his conference.[7]

Though Pastor Merkel remained in place, he had been wounded by the institutional church, which seemed more interested in self-preservation than justice.

> I do want to emphasize that it was incredibly painful to be removed from the roster. When I was ordained, my ordination was probably the most significant day in my life in terms of my whole life because it was such a spiritual moment, and I wanted to be a pastor. I felt called. I still feel called to be a pastor. So that was very painful, the reality of it, although I knew that would happen.[8]

Around the turn of the century, a Lutheran pastor pursuing graduate theological studies, Diane Bowers, would join Pastor Merkel's congregation at St Paul Lutheran. "The ELCA does not recognize Ross Merkel as a pastor," Bowers wrote. "He was removed from the roster in 1994. Yet he leads the largest, growing urban ELCA congregation in the East Bay. When new members are asked why they joined the congregation, Ross' preaching and the inclusive community are the number one reasons given."[9] Bowers commented on Pastor Merkel's provocative sermon, "If I were not gay, I wouldn't be a pastor in the Lutheran church."

[This] is a Christian statement. What is more, it is profoundly Lutheran. Lutheran Christians are blessed to be the bearers of a grace-filled tradition of paradox, of holy simultaneity. Lutheran theology lifts up Jesus' paradoxical message that the Reign of God is truly and completely both now and not yet. Deep in our bones, we affirm Paul's teaching that we are simultaneously sinners and saints. Our daily experience of life in the world confirms that it is in weakness, when we are most dependent, that we find strength and are made strong.

The paradox of Ross' experience is that the grace of Jesus Christ was mediated by its earthly vessel, the church, to a man whom the church rejected. The power of the church's message that all are loved and valued by God was stronger than the church's power to counteract its own message.

Ross' statement "if I were not gay, I would not have become a pastor" reveals the heart of the Christian faith: the rejected one is become elect; the despised one is called and empowered to bear God's gift of grace to many. The one who was a stumbling block for many is become the shepherd of many, a strong building block in the family of faith. Surely you see it—is this not an image of Jesus Christ? Ross Merkel's journey, and the journey of many like him, follows in the footsteps of the cross. Why does the church persist in opposing their resurrection? For they are rising and have already risen. The church must run to the tomb and see.[10]

NOTES

1. In anticipation of the 2012 twenty-fifth anniversary of the formation of the ELCA, the ELCA has commenced an oral history project entitled *Voices of Vision: The ELCA at 25*, now available in the ELCA Archives. As a part of this project, Pastor Merkel was interviewed by Rev. Karen Bockelman (former assistant to the bishop, Northeastern Minnesota Synod) on May 10, 2010, and the transcription of the interview is now available at the ELCA archives in Chicago. Much of the information here is based on that interview.

2. St. Paul-Reformation Lutheran Church of St. Paul, Minnesota, was the other. St. Paul-Reformation Lutheran Church would play a significant role in the history of the Lutheran journey toward full inclusion, including its *extra ordinem* call to lesbian Anita Hill in 2001.

3. Merkel, interview by Bockelman, May 10, 2010, 11.

4. Ibid., 14.

5. Bishop Lyle Miller's reasons for resignation are unknown. Presumably, he had his fill of overseeing trials, but it does not appear that his attitude changed, since he spoke against the Synod Assembly's resolution of support for Pastor Merkel a short time after his resignation. Many years later, he did show a change of heart and only ill health prevented him from attending the worship service that welcomed St. Francis back into the ELCA.

6. Sierra Pacific Synod Assembly, *Minutes* (1994), 61–63. The concluding phrase, "we can do no other," would ring in the ears of Lutheran listeners as an allusion to Martin Luther's famous "Here I Stand" speech before a court of papal inquisitors and Emperor Charles V. At the 1521 Diet of Worms, Luther refused to recant his opposition to the church's teachings. Though scholars question the actual words of Luther, a popular version depicts Luther concluding his self-defense with these words:

> Unless I am convinced by the testimony of the Scriptures or by clear reason (for I do not trust either in the pope or in councils alone, since it is well known that they have often erred and contradicted themselves), I am bound by the Scriptures I have quoted and my conscience is captive to the Word of God. I cannot and will not recant anything, since it is neither safe nor right to go against conscience. Here I stand. I can do no other. May God help me. Amen.

Luther was declared an outlaw, but he survived due to protection from German princes. This would be one of the key moments marking the start of the Protestant Reformation. Martin Brecht, "Luther, Martin," in *Oxford Encyclopedia of the Reformation*, ed. Hans J. Hillerbrand, trans. Wolfgang Katenz (New York: Oxford University Press, 1996), 1:460.

    7. Profile of Rev. Jeff R. Johnson, on the website of the Lesbian, Gay, Bisexual, and Transgender Religious Archives Network, http://www.lgbtran.org /Profile.aspx?ID=112.

    8. Merkel, interview by Bockelman, May 10, 2010, 24.

    9. Diane V. Bowers, "Reflections on Experiencing the Leadership of Gay Clergy," *Let's Talk: Living Theology in the Metropolitan Chicago Synod* vol. 8, no. 2 (summer 2003), accessed January 21, 2012, http://www.mcsletstalk.org /vol8no23.htm.

    10. Bowers, "Reflections."

* 26 *

WE HAVE NOT YET REACHED CONSENSUS

As the Lutherans wandered in the wilderness in the nineties, they were not alone.

As we shall see, much like the Lutherans, both the Presbyterians and the Methodists would endure a season of trials that only entrenched restrictive policies toward LGBT persons, even as they contributed to shifting opinion. To the contrary, the Episcopal heresy trial of Bishop Walter Righter resulted in a stamp of judicial approval for LGBT ordinations.

Another commonality was that each denomination developed studies on human sexuality. The UCC had considered and adopted its own statement in the late seventies, but the other four denominations would simultaneously consider their own version in the early nineties. In each case, a blue-ribbon panel would be convened and would offer gay-friendly recommendations, but the national conventions of the denominations would reject the reports.

At the 1991 General Convention of the Episcopal Church, the report of the Hunt Commission, following three years of study of LGBT issues, recommended that individual bishops and dioceses should be allowed leeway to ordain qualified gays and lesbians to the priesthood. Three thousand persons attended a meeting to debate the report. Delegates voted the recommendation down. For the Presbyterians, extremely bad press would contribute to nearly 95 percent of the delegates voting to reject their study report, and the gay caucus would respond with an emotional floor demonstration. Similarly, when the Methodist study report was released recommending a reversal in restrictive gay policies, the conservative Methodist press would rally their forces, and the 1992 General

Conference rejected the recommendation. The Methodist gay leadership would also object with a floor demonstration.

The Lutherans had also been conducting a study of human sexuality in the early nineties; after several delays, the report landed on the doorstep of the 1995 ELCA Churchwide Assembly, and that is where we now turn our attention, but the first order of business for the Lutherans would be the election of a new presiding bishop.

More than a thousand voting members gathered in Minneapolis in August 1995 for the fourth biennial Churchwide Assembly of the ELCA. The term of Presiding Bishop Herbert Chilstrom was ending, and the major agenda item for the assembly would be the election of a replacement. Chilstrom had been the only presiding bishop to serve since the formation of the ELCA eight years earlier, and he had been bishop of the Minnesota Conference of the LCA before that. He had a reputation as progressive and pro-gay. In later years, during their retirement, Chilstrom and his wife, Corinne, would be unabashed advocates for LGBT interests.

The ELCA uses an "ecclesiastical ballot" process to elect bishops, which means the first ballot is essentially a nominating ballot and anyone and everyone may receive votes. Through a winnowing process, those receiving the fewest votes drop off subsequent ballots to narrow the field. At the 1995 Assembly, when only seven remained, they each addressed the assembly, and when only three remained, they participated in a question and answer session.

The three final candidates were H. George Anderson, the president of Luther College in Iowa, Bishop April Ullring Larson of the LaCrosse, Wisconsin, Area Synod (the first female bishop in the ELCA), and Bishop Richard Foss of the Eastern North Dakota Synod. Based upon their respective answers to a question about the church and LGBT persons, it appeared that Foss was dubious about LGBT ordination, Ullring sounded the most progressive, and Anderson's comment "we have not yet reached consensus" aptly described the mood of the assembly and the church; Anderson was elected and Ullring finished second.[1]

Unquestionably, the most contentious portion of the assembly pertained to the anticipated report and possible action on the Social Statement on Human Sexuality and related studies that had been underway for several years. After several drafts, countless public hearings, congregational studies, and endless delays, the church appeared to be hopelessly split. Many individual synods had submitted conflicting memorials (proposals). The Human Sexuality Statement had faced a perfect storm of negativity.

First, the confessionalist theologians and clergy of the "Called to Faithfulness" conferences were generally critical of the church's involvement in social justice issues, and the sexuality statement played directly into their narrative.

Second, the events in San Francisco frightened many in the pews.

Third, the feminist Re-Imagining Conference in Minneapolis in 1993 featured a pair of Lutheran speakers, though the ELCA had no formal role. ELCA feminists and progressives were forced onto the defensive by sensationalist media coverage of the conference. Rituals and images celebrated the birthing, mothering, and sexual roles of women, and the conference used feminine pronouns for God. But it was "Sophia" that really unnerved the conservatives. "Sophia," a biblical metaphor for divine wisdom, served as a re-imagined feminine image of the divine during the conference; for the conservatives, "Sophia" became a twisted caricature of a pagan goddess worshiped by heretical, radical feminists.[2] The Re-Imagining Conference also played directly into the narrative of the confessionalists.

Fourth, the rollout of a draft of the ELCA Statement on Sexuality was woefully mismanaged, with the result that negative press defined the statement in the public's eye before ELCA bishops, clergy, and laity had even read the document. In particular, the damage caused by a sensationalist Associated Press account was impossible to overcome. A banner headline on the front page of AP newspapers across the country proclaimed, "LUTHERAN GROUP CHALLENGES TRADITIONAL VIEWS ON SEXUALITY," and the first paragraph of the AP article referred to masturbation, homosexual unions, and condom use as a "moral imperative."[3] Of course, the sensationalist AP news report failed to capture the real gist of the study; the words "masturbation" and "condom" each appeared only once in the entire multipage document.

Nearly twenty-five thousand callers tried to reach ELCA headquarters. Two sitting ELCA synodical bishops in particular attacked the document, Ken Sauer and Paul Spring.[4] Fifteen years later, they would become leaders of the Lutheran schismatics who departed the ELCA.

Here is the conclusion of the draft regarding the church and LGBT persons:

> Throughout Scripture, heterosexual assumptions clearly are present. It follows that no passage specifically addresses the question facing the church today: the morality of a just, loving, committed relationship between persons of the same sex.
>
> Among members of our church, three responses are common: 1) To love our neighbor means to love the sinner but hate the sin. 2) To love our neighbor means to be compassionate toward gay and lesbian persons and understanding of the dilemma facing those who do not have the gift of celibacy. 3) To love our neighbor means open affirmation of gay and lesbian persons and their mutually loving, just, committed relationships of fidelity.
>
> Response 1 needs to be questioned on biblical and theological grounds, indeed, challenged because of the harmful effect on gay and lesbian people and their families. Responses 2 and 3 are strongly supported by responsible biblical interpretation within a Christ-centered Lutheran theological framework.[5]

To the conservatives who actually took the time to read the draft, the suggestion that their pet aphorism to "love the sinner but hate the sin" might actually be harmful was jarring. The statement unmasked the comfortable slogan for what it was—justification for antigay attitudes that conditioned welcome on denial of self. This phrase is more about soothing the sensibilities of the self-satisfied than genuine concern for gays and lesbians. Suddenly on the defensive, conservatives would lash out by attacking the document, those who prepared it, and the ELCA that sanctioned it (though the ELCA as a body had not approved the statement).

At the 1995 Churchwide Assembly, ELCA Vice-President Kathy Magnus offered this summary of the mood of the Church Council:

> During this biennium, the Church Council has struggled and debated and discussed the study of human sexuality. We have

been profoundly disappointed in the tone of the discussion across this church. We have listened carefully to the advice of the Conference of Bishops, to the board of the Division for Church in Society, the responses from the church, and the consulting panel, which we put in place in December 1993. In our opinion, we do not believe that we have enough consensus to move ahead . . . and took action at our pre-assembly meeting [to remove the Social Statement from consideration].[6]

Ultimately, it would be up to the assembly itself to decide whether to proceed and under what conditions. Thus, the floor debate was supposedly not over the substance of the latest draft of the proposed social statement, but how to proceed forward, if at all. Consideration was scheduled for the afternoon plenary session on the next to last day of the assembly. Debate spilled into the evening, and the session was extended several times and finally adjourned without action. The next day, during the final plenary session, a resolution was finally adopted, in a split vote, that deferred consideration of the Social Statement on Human Sexuality to the 1997 Assembly but only after removing from consideration that portion of the statement that dealt with homosexuality, yet urging that "work continue unabated on resolving the church's position on homosexuality."[7] It was a confused muddle that reflected a deeply divided church.

The 1990s' version of a Social Statement on Human Sexuality never did come up for action and essentially disappeared. In its place, a ten-person advisory committee drafted an innocuous statement recognizing "the number of things we can say with a significant amount of agreement," which meant, of course, that it said nothing about gays and lesbians.[8]

The 1990 San Francisco *extra ordinem* ordinations, the 1994 defrocking of Pastor Merkel, and the 1995 Human Sexuality Statement had certainly stirred conversation, but consensus was elusive. At the final two Churchwide Assemblies of the decade, in 1997 and 1999, little action was taken by the voting members.

At the 1997 Churchwide Assembly, the Sierra Pacific Synod (and other synods) submitted memorials (proposed resolutions) to excise the language pertaining to homosexuals from the *Definitions and Guidelines for Discipline of Ordained Ministers* and *Vision and Expectations*. Of course, such action would have the effect of opening the door to LGBT clergy. By the time the resolution reached the floor, the Memorials Committee had offered a substitute motion that declined action at this assembly and merely referred the question of LGBT ordination to the Division for Ministry with the expectation of a report in 1999. The "kick the can down the road" resolution passed overwhelmingly.[9]

However, when 1999 rolled around, the resolution that reached the floor again called for further study and deferred action. Supporters of LGBT ordination offered two amendments: first, to set a date certain for the end of deliberations and a time for action, and second, to suspend the prohibition against noncelibate LGBT clergy in the meantime. Both amendments failed by wide margins.[10] As we shall see in a moment, a proposed ecumenical agreement with the Episcopal Church sucked the air out of the convention hall during the 1997 and 1999 Churchwide Assemblies.

Although there would be no breakthrough developments in denominational policies and positive momentum was difficult to discern, the journey toward full inclusion moved forward in small steps, often in the background and often led by youth. The Lutheran Youth Organization designated 1998 as a "Year of Prayer" for gay and bisexual youth and would have offered a gay youth event if they could have figured out how to create a safe environment.

College campuses provided safe havens for rational discourse devoid of the visceral fears of other arenas. Roanoke College in Virginia hosted a conference. The University of Michigan hosted a conference called "The Gifts We Offer, the Burdens We Bear: The Vocation and Ministry of Gay and Lesbian Persons in Church in Society" sponsored by Lutheran Campus Ministries, the Gay and Lesbian task force of the SE Michigan Synod, and the Great Lakes Chapter of LC/NA. The centerpiece of the conference was a report entitled *Pulpit Fiction*, a compilation of the personal stories of thirty-five closeted gay or lesbian ELCA pastors, twenty-one in committed relationships and six actually living with a partner in the church parsonage.

"While our pastors were often anxious about coming out to other persons, they generally had no such problems with God," said Dr. Carolyn J. Riehl, project director and assistant professor of education at

U.M. "They are steeped in the theology of justification by grace through faith"—a central doctrine of the Lutheran church.[11]

Recently retired Presiding Bishop Herbert Chilstrom addressed the conference: "More and more people are saying a committed relationship would be appropriate," that is, gays in committed relationships should be eligible for ordination.[12]

There was also plenty of churchwide activity behind the scenes, organized by the ELCA headquarters at Higgins Road in Chicago. When the voting members at Churchwide Assemblies had called for study and discussion, the Division for Ministry and others within the ELCA hierarchy accepted this call seriously; opportunities for discussion were arranged in various venues and forums, and representatives of LC/NA and LLGM were often invited to participate—as were those known to be opposed to LGBT ordination. Various ELCA units attempted to referee an orderly process and serve as "bridge-builders" between those of differing views and between past and future.

At the end of the decade, many congregations took advantage of a resource entitled *Talking Together as Christians about Homosexuality*, prepared by the Division for Church in Society. The guide encouraged respectful discussion, emphasized a Christ-centered approach to Scripture, included around a dozen first-person stories from LGBT individuals or their families, and allowed room for reason and intuition. The guide was full of open-ended discussion questions without suggested answers; nevertheless, critics charged it was overly gay-friendly.[13]

A second impulse toward study came from the Division for Outreach. What factors make for a truly welcoming church? A report suggested:

- gays look for clergy and laity who model hospitality in word and deed
- strong leadership prepared to minister pastorally amid potentially painful conversations
- congregations must be prepared to discuss ceremonies of blessing and gay ordination
- congregations must have a strong history of conflict resolution[14]

At the 1999 Churchwide Assembly, various ELCA internal units submitted a joint report (called an "Inter-unit Response") that contained results and reports from these studies and activities. However, their recommendation was merely for further study and discernment.

The decade had opened with *extra ordinem* ordinations, two San Francisco trials resulting in expulsion of congregations and a pastoral defrocking, and a call by the Sierra Pacific Synod to "authorize a study of the ordination of homosexual persons." The decade ended with essentially the same call. Anger and frustration flowed freely from all sides.

We have not yet reached consensus. Bishop Anderson's comment during his pre-election screening understated the turmoil of the ELCA in the 1990s.

By the end of the decade, another issue had clouded the horizon, an issue that had nothing to do with sexuality. To the surprise of many, a proposed full communion agreement with the Episcopal Church exploded into controversy (first called "The Concordat" and then revised as "Called to Common Mission [CCM]"). The last two Churchwide Assemblies of the decade were consumed in rancorous debate over this issue. Opponents exhibited visceral animosity toward the ELCA and spawned an opposition group known as the "WordAlone Network," which would have later consequences as the journey toward full inclusion continued in the new millennium. As we have seen, the WordAlone movement had its genesis in the ELCA-bashing "Call to Faithfulness" Conferences earlier in the decade.

In simple parlance, an ELCA full communion agreement means interchangeable clergy and full table fellowship based on mutual recognition of the validity of the other's sacraments of baptism and the eucharist. The ELCA had earlier consummated full communion agreements with three denominations with reformed backgrounds (the UCC, the PC[USA]), and the Reformed Church in America) and would later adopt agreements with the Moravian Church and the UMC. None of these had been or would be controversial and all were adopted with broad majorities.

With the Episcopalians, the hang-up was the "historic episcopate,"[15] and like a snowball rolling downhill, many Lutheran clergy became wrapped up in status issues. Since Lutheran clergy had not been ordained by a bishop in the "historic episcopate," many inferred that the implementation of the historic episcopate for future Lutheran ordinations signified an inferior status for their own ordinations. "The Episcopal refusal to accept us 'as we are' is at the heart of our disagreement," said a former presiding bishop of the ALC.[16]

The opposition became organized, vocal, and increasingly strident—even nasty. The Concordat barely failed to pass by the required two-thirds (achieving only 66.1 percent) at the 1997 Churchwide Assembly, and the renamed and marginally revised Called to Common Mission agreement squeaked through at the 1999 assembly (with approximately 69 percent favorable).[17]

> The soaring arches of the National Cathedral in Washington, D.C., thundered with the singing of 3,500 voices as the ELCA and the Episcopal Church celebrated. Processions into the cathedral included representatives from all 65 ELCA synods and nearly three-quarters of the 100 U.S. Episcopal dioceses. . . . Before the service, the St. Olaf College Choir from Northfield, Minnesota, presented a prelude concert.[18]

While church leadership celebrated, the dissidents plotted. The establishment of the WordAlone Network as a perpetual thorn in the side of the ELCA would prove to be the significant consequence of the furor. Luther Seminary in St. Paul would become a tense hotbed of dissent with open animosity and mistrust between professors. With many of the same ELCA critics who had appeared at the beginning of the decade in the "Called to Faithfulness" conferences, the WordAlone Network would propagate dissident and schismatic organizations in the new millennium, including Lutheran Congregations in Mission for Christ (LCMC), Lutheran CORE, and the North American Lutheran Church (NALC).

As the decade ended, the WordAlone president offered a defiant battle cry: "We aren't going to go away . . . this is our church and it was stolen from us . . . we're going to work to defeat bishops . . . and draft synod resolutions."[19]

When the clamor over full communion with the Episcopalians eventually died down, the LGBT community and their allies would become the focus of WordAlone vitriol. LGBT issues would become the foil the confessionalist conservatives would use to frighten folks in the pews and rally support for their anti-ELCA attitudes.

NOTES

1. ELCA Churchwide Assembly, *Minutes* (1995), 130.

2. The book of Proverbs (chapters 1, 8, and 9, NRSV) presents a personification of divine "Wisdom" as a woman preaching to youth. Scholars often refer to this woman as Lady Wisdom. Christian feminists point to this personification of divine wisdom as a feminine image of God. What is more, many scholars point to Proverbs 8:23–24 as forerunner or inspiration for the first verse of the Gospel of John: "In the beginning was the Word, and the Word was with God, and the Word was God." The Proverbs verses read: "The Lord created me [Wisdom] at the beginning of his work, the first of his acts of long ago. Ages ago I was set up, at the first, before the beginning of the earth." In other words, biblical scholarship reveals that this Proverbs imagery of divine wisdom also has connections to the Johannine treatment of Jesus. The Greek word for wisdom is *sophia*. Thus, the "Sophia" referenced by the Christian feminists at the Re-Imagining Conference has a solid biblical basis—hardly a "pagan goddess" as portrayed by the conservative press. For Bible-touting critics, the irony was that they really didn't know the Bible well enough to recognize "Wisdom."

3. David Briggs, Associated Press, "Lutheran Group Challenges Traditional Views on Sexuality," October 20, 1993.

4. Trexler, *High Expectations*, 91–92.

5. Ibid., 89.

6. ELCA Churchwide Assembly, *Minutes* (1995), 430.

7. Ibid., 484.

8. Trexler, *High Expectations*, 96.

9. ELCA Churchwide Assembly, *Minutes* (1997), 394–403, 490–91, and 763–69.

10. ELCA Churchwide Assembly, *Minutes* (1999), 409–15, 509–16, 534–46, and 689–705.

11. ELCA News Service, "Vocations of Gay and Lesbian Lutherans," March 17, 1997.

12. Trexler, *High Expectations*, 97.

13. Evangelical Church in America, Division for Church in Society, *Talking Together as Christians about Homosexuality: A Guide for Congregations* (1999).

14. Trexler, *High Expectations*, 98.

15. The "historic episcopate" is a tradition that there is an unbroken succession back to the first apostles that has been passed from one bishop to the next through the ritual of laying on hands. Only a bishop in the historic episcopate may ordain clergy in some ecclesial traditions, including the Episcopal Church. The historic episcopate was not part of Lutheran ecclesiology (the succession had been broken at the time of Luther), and a full communion agreement would recognize existing Lutheran ordinations as valid. However, going forward, the ritual of laying on hands by a bishop in the historic episcopate would become part of Lutheran ordinations. For a full discussion of the controversy, see Trexler, *High Expectations*, 117–49.

16. Trexler, *High Expectations*, 135.

17. Ibid., 117–49.

18. Ibid., 142. The service took place on January 1, 2001.

19. Words of Roger Eigenfeld, the WordAlone Network president, in Trexler, *High Expectations*, 145–46.

* 27 *

SATAN HAS A HOLD OF YOU: HAPPY EASTER

Shreveport is tucked into the Northwestern corner of Louisiana near Texas and Arkansas. Legendary bluesman Lead Belly performed in Shreveport's red light district a century ago. Later, a popular Shreveport radio program called "The Louisiana Hayride" featured the broadcast debut of Elvis Presley. About the time of Presley's radio appearance, Anita C. Hill was born in the city and raised Roman Catholic. By her high school years of the sixties, the family had moved to Crystal Springs, Mississippi, located on the freeway between New Orleans and Jackson. There Hill joined a Methodist congregation, and later she attended Mississippi State, where she obtained a Bachelor of Science degree in general sciences.[1]

By then she was married and followed her husband to Ann Arbor, Michigan, but the marriage ended. Soon a series of influences would impact her life. Feminism focused her on career, professionalism, and self-realization, which in turn allowed personal sexuality introspection. She began dating a woman who happened to be Lutheran, and they became active in Lutheran Campus Ministry. Finally, by the end of a Sunday evening Bible study that explored human sexuality in light of Lutheran theology of a gracious God, Hill was committed to Lutheranism, ministry, and LGBT advocacy.

By 1980, Hill had joined LC/NA and attended the biennial assembly in San Francisco; in fact, she was elected to serve as co-chair. Three years later, she was hired by Wingspan Ministry, a developing LGBT outreach program of St. Paul-Reformation Lutheran Church in the Summit Hill neighborhood of St. Paul, Minnesota. That same year, St. Paul-Ref became one of the first two Lutheran congregations to sign on to the LC/NA Reconciling in Christ Program.

In the late eighties, Hill encouraged her friends Ruth Frost and Phyllis Zillhart to look into the San Francisco congregation that was seeking to call a lesbian pastor. Meanwhile, Hill had heard her own call to the ordained ministry, but the ELCA seminary just down the road (Luther) had built a roadblock in the form of the student sexuality statement derived from *Vision and Expectations*. Thus, she enrolled at United Theological Seminary of the Twin Cities, an ecumenical seminary affiliated with the UCC, even as she continued as Pastoral Minister at St. Paul-Ref. During her time at United, she received awards for her scholarship and her service. During this period she also met her life partner, Janelle Bussert, and they were blessed in a service at St. Paul-Ref in 1996, followed by a dance in the freshly painted church basement that lasted for hours, "there were a few elders who sat up past their bedtime watching people of the same gender dance."[2]

Hill graduated from United Seminary in 2000 and pursued ELCA ordination through regular synod channels. The St. Paul Area Synod bishop at the time was Mark Hanson, soon to be elected to be the ELCA presiding bishop. St. Paul-Ref asked the synod, which in turn asked the ELCA Church Council, for an exception to the current guidelines. Prior to Council action, St. Paul-Ref sent a letter to the Council.

"We focused the Council's attention on three ideas, evangelism, justice and Gospel," said St. Paul-Ref Pastor Tidemann. "We believe these to be compelling reasons to call qualified gay and lesbian persons to ministry. In the letter we stated that our request comes from our pastoral concern, our passion for justice and our theological conscience."[3]

When the ELCA Council denied the request in November 2000, it was time to follow the path of *extra ordinem* ordination once again, the same route pursued a decade earlier by the two San Francisco congregations that had resulted in their expulsion from the ELCA. St. Paul-Ref was willing to bear the consequences and passed a resolution (176-0) in December 2000 to proceed.

> In the resolution approved today, the congregation went on record saying we can no longer, in good conscience, comply with the ELCA's policy because it is unjust (and) at odds with the mes-

sage of the Gospel. We take this action with courage and conviction that it is Gospel-based and at the heart of what the Lutheran Church has stood for theologically.[4]

Biblical obedience mandated ecclesiastical disobedience.

But Anita Hill would not be the first to be ordained in a new round of irregular ordinations; that would be Donna Simon, who was called to Abiding Peace Lutheran Church of Kansas City and ordained in October 2000. Simon's extraordinary ordination did not capture the level of national attention focused on Anita Hill six months later.

When Donna appeared before her ELCA candidacy committee in 1999 for the final step before ordination, she told them that she would not pledge compliance with the church's Vision and Expectations Statement, which requires lifelong celibacy for gay and lesbian candidates. Though the candidacy panel recommended approval, the full committee postponed her approval pending change in denominational policy.

Donna was approved by the candidacy committee of the Extraordinary Candidacy Project later that year, and called to serve Abiding Peace Lutheran Church [of Kansas City, Missouri] in August of 2000.[5]

On Sunday, April 21, 2001, the regular worship service at St. Paul-Ref closed with a ritual. Pastor Paul Tidemann removed the deacon's stole from Anita Hill and laid it on the brass communion rail. It was an ending that signaled a new beginning. The congregation erupted in applause. It was the beginning of a festive week.

The ordination was moved to the nearby facilities of Lutheran Church of the Redeemer, which would be better able to handle the anticipated throng. A thousand or more swelled the old sanctuary on Saturday, April 27, including more than two hundred clergy—Lutherans, of course, but also Presbyterians, Roman Catholics, Baptists, a rabbi, and a Buddhist monk—and three Lutheran bishops, Krister Stendahl, Paul Egertson, and Lowell Erdahl.

Retired Swedish bishop and Harvard professor Krister Stendahl would also be a co-consecrator for Bishop Gene Robinson in 2003. We encountered Bishop Lowell Erdahl earlier as the bishop who urged Phyllis Zillhart to withdraw her candidacy. Erdahl had been encouraged by the mother of Ruth Frost to become a leader for LGBT advocacy during his final term as bishop. He heeded her plea. By the time of Hill's ordination, Erdahl was bishop emeritus of the St. Paul Area Synod, the predecessor to Mark Hanson. Bishop Paul Egertson was an active ELCA bishop, serving the Southern California (West) Synod. He was the father of Greg Egertson, the junior seminarian whose three senior friends were first approved for ordination, then rejected back in 1987–88. Following his participation in Anita Hill's ordination as an active bishop, he was forced to resign. When he resigned, he stated, "I went there because I wanted to protest this policy and ecclesiastical disobedience is a perfectly respectable form of protest speech. I knew punishment would go along with this, but one theory of passive resistance is to break the laws and take the consequences so that the law is reconsidered."[6] Biblical obedience mandates ecclesiastical disobedience.

After the clergy clustered six deep around the altar to lay on hands, Anita Hill was introduced to the assembled as Pastor Hill, and the congregation erupted in boisterous hand clapping and foot stomping, shaking the old stone church to its foundation—and the ELCA as well.

A decade earlier, the cost of discipleship had been expulsion from the ELCA for the disobedient San Francisco congregations. This time, Bishop Mark Hanson and the St. Paul Area Synod slapped St. Paul-Ref on the wrist. The congregation was merely admonished in a letter from Bishop Hanson, and their members were censured, which precluded them from synod participation.

Pastor Hill would soon become senior pastor, and she remained at St. Paul-Ref until May of 2012 when she accepted a position with LC/NA. As we shall see, she remained a highly visible advocate for LGBT inclusivity. Over the years, she has received plenty of hate mail, but one letter in particular still brings a smile. "You are leading people down the path to hell. Stop this madness. Satan has a hold of you. Happy Easter. Yours in Christ."[7]

The pace of *extra ordinem* ordinations would pick up through the decade. By the time of the 2009 Churchwide Assembly, eighteen persons had been ordained through ELM. "From 1990 to 2009, ELM (and its predecessor bodies) made it possible for these gifted leaders to serve as openly LGBT pastors in Lutheran congregations and ministries. These leaders served the Lutheran church faithfully and were a prophetic witness to a church that would one day welcome and recognize their gifts."[8]

Pastor Hill shall have the last word, looking back at her long ministry at St. Paul-Ref, which became a haven for those once abused by church yet who yearned for spiritual nourishment. Here was a place to find sanctuary in a congregation led by one of their own.

"I've seen gay and lesbian people come here who have never heard the words "gay and lesbian" said out loud in a holy place. . . . I've seen people come here and sit and cry their way through their first service. Many times."[9]

NOTES

1. The story of Anita C. Hill is based on a private interview by the author, July 18, 2012, and on her biographical profile on the website of The Lesbian, Gay, Bisexual and Transgender Religious Archives Network, accessed October 21, 2012, http://www.lgbtran.org/Profile.aspx?ID=36

2. Private interview of Anita Hill by the author, July 18, 2012.

3. St. Paul-Reformation Church, St. Paul, Minnesota, Press Release, "St. Paul-Reformation Lutheran Church Votes to Call Anita C. Hill as a Pastor," December 3, 2000.

4. Ibid.

5. "The Rev. Donna Simon," on the website of Extraordinary Lutheran Ministries, accessed June 19, 2012, http://www.elm.org/2011/01/04/donna-simon/.

6. Paul Egertson quoted by Carl Matthes, "The American Family", on the blog of LA Progressive, accessed October 20, 2012, http://www.laprogressive.com/american-family/#sthash.pvVCJc1N.dpbs.

7. Private interview of Anita Hill by the author, July 18, 2012.

8. "Historic ELM Roster," on the website of Extraordinary Lutheran Ministries, accessed June 19, 2012, http://www.elm.org/historic-elm-roster/.

9. Private interview of Anita Hill by the author, July 18, 2012.

✳ 28 ✳

THIS WIDOW KEEPS BOTHERING ME

"Why do thousands of people gather to watch the same old regulars go round and round in circles?"

The congregation hooted at the preacher's Indy 500 racetrack metaphor, which fit the LC/NA Eucharist Service in the midst of the 2001 Churchwide Assembly (CWA01) in Indianapolis. But there was anticipation, too; justice was coming; and persistence would be rewarded, the preacher promised. "I feel like I'm standing on the edge of something, about to jump! Something's going on that matters, and you've been invited into the fray. My preacher's heart has the inclination not just to go, but to go and go and go."[1] Even the St. Paul-Ref letter of admonition had hinted at the inevitability of change. Censure would be imposed unless or until the ELCA Churchwide Assembly "would remove the necessity for such censure."[2]

Luke the evangelist relates the parable of the persistent widow. She sought justice, but the judge refused her plea. She appealed to the judge, over and over again. Persistent annoyance. "This widow keeps bothering me," the judge said, and eventually he relented (Luke 18:5).

The Lutheran LGBT community would persist. If not this Church-wide Assembly, then the next. Or the next. They would keep-a-knockin'. Two years later at the 2003 Churchwide Assembly, retired Presiding Bishop Herb Chilstrom offered the LC/NA eucharist sermon, and he joined those knocking on the door. "Yes, the time has come," he said. "In fact, it is long, long overdue."[3]

Although ministry policies would not be changed at CWA01 in Indianapolis, there were two significant actions that would have future consequences. Processes were set in motion.

First, Mark Hanson was elected to be the third presiding bishop of the ELCA, succeeding H. George Anderson, who chose not to seek a second term. Hanson would prove to be a steady and unflappable shepherd of the ELCA flock, though the gatekeepers would have a different view. Jaynan Clark, president of WordAlone, would later rant: "Congregations and members have become like sheep without a shepherd, scattered and led astray. That is not the work of the Good Shepherd but of His temporal adversary, the Wolf in sheep's clothing and his hirelings."[4] Although the full communion agreement with the Episcopal Church was now in place, and the furor over its adoption had largely passed, the WordAlone Network remained as the loyal opposition, but they would become increasingly disloyal as the years passed.

By CWA01, a Luther Seminary professor had become a principal WordAlone spokesman. Professor of church history and storyteller James Nestingen spoke with a folksy country drawl befitting his North Dakota upbringing as a Norwegian Lutheran pastor's kid. He had offered the keynote address at the WordAlone constituting convention in 2000, and at the 2001 Churchwide Assembly he became a gatekeeping candidate for presiding bishop.

As mentioned earlier, the ELCA uses an "ecclesiastical ballot" process for electing its presiding bishop; the first ballot serves as a nominating ballot, and those at the bottom of the vote totals are dropped from succeeding ballots, and the field is winnowed. By the third ballot, Mark Hanson was the clear leader with 53 percent (60 percent% required until only two candidates remained), and Nestingen was a distant third with 22 percent. He was removed from the fourth and final ballot, and Hanson was elected. Nestingen graciously urged unity. "Fraction is terrible," he said, but he would soon forget.[5]

The second major action of CWA01 was the adoption of three separate but related resolutions calling for a social statement on human sexuality, a study of homosexuality, and development of a plan and timeline for reconsideration of ministry policies regarding LGBT ordination. The resolutions resulted in a two-stream process: the development of a social statement and consideration of a revision in ministry policy regarding LGBT ordinations.[6] As we shall see, over the course of the next eight years, these two streams would merge; after multiple delays, the river of change would overflow the Churchwide Assembly of 2009. But we are getting ahead of the story.

ELCA social statements are teaching documents that assist members in their thinking about social issues. They are meant to aid in communal and individual moral formation and deliberation. Social statements also set policy for this church and guide its advocacy and work in the public arena. They result from an extensive process of participation and deliberation and are adopted by a two-thirds vote of a Churchwide Assembly.[7]

Ten years earlier, a similar call for a social statement on human sexuality had ended in chaos and controversy: "We have been profoundly disappointed in the tone of the discussion across this church. . . . In our opinion, we do not believe that we have enough consensus to move ahead," said the vice-president at the 1995 Churchwide Assembly. Now, the process would begin anew.

In 2002 during the biennium between Churchwide Assemblies, LC/NA reported two major news items. First, for the first time since its inception in 1974, LC/NA would be officially recognized by the ELCA. Formal recognition would permit exhibits at synod assemblies, and LC/NA would be eligible to seek grants from independent foundations that required a formal denominational relationship as a prerequisite.[8] Second, LC/NA hired Emily Eastwood as the full-time director of the Reconciling in Christ program (RIC). Two decades earlier, she had served as co-chair of LC/NA. She had also been a victim of *Vision and Expectations* when her seminary journey had been cut short. Emily, along with several other LC/NA leaders, was a member of St. Paul-Ref. Two years later, Emily's great success would lead to an expanded role as the executive director of LC/NA, and she would provide inspired and able leadership for the last miles with the journey's end in sight. In her statement of acceptance as RIC director, Emily said,

God's call is clear. God says yes. The church has said no, only because I love a woman.

I wrestle with the church as Jacob wrestled with God at Peniel. I will not let the church go, until it blesses me, even though that means I've been wounded many times in the fight. I am not alone in this struggle. It is my sense of call, my undying love of my church, and my care for GLBT Lutherans and their families, that have brought me to this moment.[9]

The big news at the August 2003 Churchwide Assembly in Milwaukee (CWA03) was not Lutheran; the Episcopal Diocese of New Hampshire had elected Gene Robinson as a bishop in May, and the Episcopal General Convention had approved the election just days before the ELCA Churchwide Assembly opened. A few panicked Lutherans urged that the full communion agreement with the Episcopal Church be suspended, but their resolution failed. There were also assurances from the chair of the Task Force for ELCA Studies on Sexuality, Bishop Margaret G. Payne of the New England Synod, that Robinson's election would not affect her Task Force's ongoing process.

The most controversial issue at CWA03 was the timing of the ongoing development of a social statement on human sexuality and the concurrent development of a study of ministry policies regarding partnered gays and lesbians. These processes had been set in motion at CWA01, but which study should come first and which should inform the other? Many, including church leadership, wanted to push back the ministry proposal until 2007 when the Sexuality Statement would be considered.

By the 2003 Churchwide Assembly, the Lutheran Alliance for Full Participation (a coalition including LC/NA, ECP, LLGM, the Network for Inclusive Vision, and Wingspan Ministry of St. Paul-Reformation) had a definite place at the table, and the Alliance strongly opposed the proposal to push back consideration of the task force report regarding ministry policy. Further delay would amount to another broken promise. Direct conversations with church leadership took place on August 13, 2003, in the midst of the Churchwide Assembly in Milwaukee. The issue was timing and the pace of the study process regarding human sexuality and LGBT ordination set in motion two years earlier at CWA01.

"We oppose delay," said Jeff Johnson, Berkeley, Calif., president of the Extraordinary Candidacy Project, an organization of The

Alliance. "It is safe to say that we are invested in the study process. We see it as the end of a policy of oppression."

Johnson said many have great hopes for the outcome(s) of the studies on sexuality, but while the four-year process unfolds, "this policy is still an active, intimidating animal." The policy "destroys and intimidates" people, he said.

While the study process unfolds, the ELCA policy continues to damage people, said Mari Irvin, co-chair of Lutheran Lesbian and Gay Ministries (LLGM), San Francisco. "It is a tremendous violation to the integrity of a person," she said.

Emily Eastwood, Minneapolis, representing the organization Reconciled in Christ, said she is concerned that during the study process, people "on the other side" are becoming agitated with the issues and in some cases have begun "outing" pastors who may be in homosexual relationships.

Greg Egertson, LLGM co-chair, said it is odd for him to seek pastoral care from the church whose institutional policy is creating problems for gay and lesbian people. "The pastoral care that needs to happen is the policy needs to be changed," he said.

Jeannine Janson, co-chair of Lutherans Concerned/North America, Chicago, asked the ELCA leaders if they understood that the ELCA policy forces people into deception.

Johnson summarized the conversation, saying that many in the gay and lesbian community fear that the study is prolonging a period of "endless study."[10]

The voting members adopted a resolution confirming the timeline favored by the Alliance and rejected other resolutions that would have moved the social statement ahead of any consideration of ministry policy. Thus, revised ministry policies contained within *Vision and Expectations* would be first in line for consideration in 2005.[11]

The persistent widow kept pleading for justice, and the Lutheran LGBT community and allies kept knocking on the door.

NOTES

1. ELCA News Service, "ELCA Assembly Prompts Gay and Lesbian Meetings," August 10, 2001. The preacher was Rev. Deborah D. Conrad of the local Indiana-Kentucky Synod.

2. ELCA News Service, "ELCA Synod to Censure Congregation in Saint Paul, Minnesota," June 14, 2001.

3. ELCA News Service, "Former Presiding Bishop Says Time Has Arrived For Policy Change," August 16, 2003.

4. Jaynan Clark, letter to Presiding Bishop Mark Hanson, June, 2010, on the website of WordAlone, accessed June 23, 2012, http://www.wordalone.org/docs/jaynan-excerpts.shtml.

5. ELCA Churchwide Assembly, *Minutes* (2001), 138.

6. ELCA News Service, "ELCA Assembly Elects Bishop, Adopts Bylaw, Authorizes Study," August 17, 2001.

7. "ELCA Social Statements," on the website of the ELCA, accessed June 20, 2012, http://www.elca.org/What-We-Believe/Social-Issues/Social-Statements.aspx.

8. News Release, "ELCA establishes formal relationship with LC/NA," October 31, 2002, on the website of Reconciling Works, accessed June 20, 2012, http://www.reconcilingworks.org/news/news-archive?staticfile=archive%2F2002-10-31.htm.

9. News Release, on the website of Reconciling Works, "LC/NA votes to call Emily Eastwood to RIC position," updated June 16, 2002, accessed June 20, 2012, http://www.reconcilingworks.org/news/news-archive?staticfile=archive%2F2002-06-16.htm.

10. ELCA News Service, "ELCA Leaders and Lutheran Alliance for Full Participation Leaders Meet," August 15, 2003.

11. ELCA News Service, "ELCA Assembly Declines to Alter Studies on Sexuality Time Line," August 16, 2003.

✳ 29 ✳

Knockin' on Heaven's Door

A Bob Dylan song title, "The Times, They Are a'Changin'," characterized the raucous sixties and the beginning of our journey. As we near the
end of the Lutheran journey, another Dylan masterpiece, "Knockin' on
Heaven's Door," will be the theme of this chapter.

The long-anticipated recommendations of the ELCA Sexuality Task
Force released on January 13, 2005, was intended as a compromise, but
neither the LGBT community nor the gatekeepers were pleased.[1] On
the one hand, the Task Force recommended that the policy of *Vision and
Expectations* remain in place. "Ordained and commissioned ministers who
are homosexual in their self-understanding are expected to abstain from
homosexual sexual relationships." But the Task Force recommendation
also recognized that a few congregations had called and would call gays
and lesbians to their ordained ministry and that the slight penalties
imposed on St. Paul-Reformation reflected the bound conscience of
those involved. Thus, the recommendation would change the ministry
policy to remove any penalties for those who "in good conscience . . .
call or approve" partnered gay or lesbian candidates.

Perhaps with Pastor Merkel of Oakland in mind, who had come out
years after his ordination and whose congregation retained him as their
pastor, the recommendation would also change the ministry policy to
refrain from disciplining those rostered people so approved and called.

The Task Force had attempted to hew a pastoral middle way.

The initial response of LC/NA was "dismay and deep sadness."[2] A
small contingent representing the Alliance sat respectfully during three

days of the April 2005 Church Council meeting until a council member requested that they be allowed to present a petition. Alliance leaders Jeff Johnson and Jeannine Janson spoke for the Alliance delegation and presented the Council with a petition with around fifteen hundred signatures, objecting to the task force recommendations and requesting that the church put forth resolutions at the upcoming Assembly that would "remove all policy obstacles" for the ordination of partnered LGBT persons.[3]

What the LGBT coalition understood, but the Task Force and the Church Council did not, was that any policy that maintained different standards for gays and lesbians was inherently discriminatory. The church hadn't learned the lesson from the civil rights movement and *Brown v. Board of Education*—there is no such thing as separate but equal. Full inclusion doesn't mean *almost* full inclusion. It was also not merely about the handful of potential LGBT clergy affected by the policy, it was about the whole host, the thousands upon thousands of LGBT Lutherans who were not fully embraced; the symbols of discrimination cut deep and wreak their pain at the level of heart and soul. Merely creating exceptions to an inherently discriminatory policy was the equivalent of separate but equal.

The Alliance objections extended beyond the substance of the recommendations to the process. At the ELCA Church Council meeting of November 2004 the Council had decreed that any changes to the ministry policy must receive a supramajority of two-thirds in order to be adopted at the upcoming 2005 Churchwide Assembly.[4] Remember this; we will return to this parliamentary, procedural issue later. For now, we will simply note that the ELCA constitution requires a two-thirds majority for only three things: constitutional amendments, social statements, and full communion agreements. We will also note that the ministry policy in question, expressed in *Vision and Expectations*, had been adopted initially by the Church Council, a lesser authority than the Assembly, and by a simple majority vote.

But, it was what it was. The recommendations would be what they would be, and by the time Assembly rolled around, it would be the LGBT activists and their allies who pushed for adoption. Small steps forward are better than no steps at all.

Mickey Mouse, Donald Duck, Goofy, and the rest frolic year-round at Disney World near Orlando, Florida. On August 23, 2005, Hurricane Katrina formed in the Bahamas and crossed over southern Florida on its way to death and destruction, the greatest natural disaster in the history of the United States. Somewhere between the banality of Disney and the malevolence of Katrina, the ELCA gathered in Orlando August 8–14, 2005, for their biennial Churchwide Assembly.

Back in 1993, the Rev. Dr. Mel White, speechwriter and ghost writer for Jerry Falwell, Billy Graham, and other well-known evangelicals, and his partner Gary Nixon, had begun a public advocacy of LGBT causes that would become known as Soulforce. Soulforce was at the height of its influence and public visibility in the late nineties and early years of the new millennium. As we shall see, Soulforce played a highly visible role leading demonstrations during Methodist ecclesiastical trials and General Conferences.

Soulforce also organized direct action at ELCA Churchwide Assemblies in 2001 and later. ELCA LGBT-advocacy groups, including LC/NA, ECP, LLGM, the Network for Inclusive Vision, and Wingspan Ministry of St. Paul-Reformation, participated in the direct action. With each succeeding Churchwide Assembly, the role of Soulforce diminished and the Lutheran Alliance for Full Participation (the Alliance), the name adopted by the Lutheran advocacy groups when acting in concert at assemblies, increased. By the time of the 2005 Churchwide Assembly, the Alliance had become Goodsoil, and Soulforce Central at the assembly became Goodsoil Central.

Soulforce was still around providing logistical and organizational support, but Goodsoil now led the way. The funding and organization had advanced. Training was provided in nonviolence. Arrival and setup was filled with giddy anticipation.

Goodsoil Central took on a life of its own on the 4th floor of the West Tower in the Marriott. Banners, rainbow stoles, goodsoil buttons, soda, and lots of food as well as warmth and camaraderie, prayer and meditation greeted goodsoil representatives and visitors.

Activities by goodsoil during the Assembly will include silent witnessing, vigils, leafleting, presentations, non-violent direct actions intended to make the Assembly aware of the injustice of the current situation. Midweek, goodsoil will sponsor a Festival Liturgy, co-celebrated and preached by ordained, openly GLBT clergy. During the worship service, vows of baptism, ordination, and covenanted relationships (including marriage) will be renewed. Current and former ELCA Bishops will help lead the renewal of these vows. More than 400 of those attending the Assembly are expected to be at the service.[5]

Although the Task Force recommendation regarding LGBT clergy would be the most contentious agenda item, the Task Force had also recommended a policy regarding clergy blessing of same-gender relationships. Except for a 1993 opinion of the Conference of Bishops, the church had no policy. Remember, in ELCA polity, the Conference of Bishops is advisory only and has no legislative authority. The Task Force essentially recommended that the church adopt the 1993 Conference of Bishops' statement as official policy. When the recommendation came to the floor, there was considerable debate, and conservatives offered several amendments that failed. The recommendation of the Task Force was adopted, with minor tweaking.

WHEREAS, this church holds that "marriage is a lifelong covenant of faithfulness between a man and a woman"; and WHEREAS, the Conference of Bishops in October 1993 stated, "We, as the Conference of Bishops of the ELCA, recognize that there is basis neither in Scripture nor tradition for the establishment of an official ceremony by this church for the blessing of a homosexual relationship. We, therefore, do not approve such a ceremony as an official action of this church's ministry. Nevertheless, we express trust in and will continue dialogue with those pastors and congregations who are in ministry with gay and lesbian persons, and affirm their desire to explore the best ways to provide pastoral care for all to whom they minister": therefore, be it RESOLVED, that the Evangelical Lutheran Church in America continue to respect the guidance of the 1993 statement of the Conference of Bishops; and be it further RESOLVED, that this church welcome gay and lesbian persons into its life (as stated in Churchwide Assembly resolutions from 1991, 1995, and 1999), and trust pastors and congregations to discern ways to provide faithful pastoral care for all to whom they minister.[6]

Even though this was not marriage, and though there was no "official" ceremony, the church would trust clergy discretion to provide pastoral care to all, and the church would not stand in the way of those pastors and congregations who chose to bless LGBT relationships. That was already the situation on the ground, and the de facto situation would become de jure according to the recommendation of the Task Force.

This recommendation passed by a margin of 670 to 323 (67 percent to 33 percent). Knock, knock, knockin' on heaven's door.

Earlier that year, the United Church of Christ (UCC) had affirmed their own policy of same-gender blessings, and Goodsoil presented an award of appreciation to the UCC representative present during the Assembly. In turn, she presented Goodsoil with a letter from UCC President John H. Thomas:

> This gracious gift reminds us that we need each other in the body of Christ as we travel roads that at times appear blocked by insurmountable barriers. We in the United Church of Christ know how hard this path can be, and how easy it is to become discouraged or fear that the deep divisions will lead us to abandon our struggle to hear God's word clearly. Our prayer for our beloved sisters and brothers in the ELCA is that you experience this week what we did in our own recent deliberations: a dialogue that, while not without conflict, retained a posture of civility toward and care for the other; a deliberation that did not take the form of debate but rather an exchange of deeply held conviction; and a discussion in which, by the grace of God, the deeply held convictions were respected, and in which members worked hard not to impugn each other's integrity even in disagreement.
>
> And above all, we in the United Church of Christ will hold you and all of our sisters and brothers in the ELCA in prayer that you will hear God's word of comfort, courage, love, and support. We expect nothing less from the God who came to us in

human form, proclaiming that in each and every one of us, without exception or condition, is found God's extraordinary image.[7]

The debate over the blessing resolution had consumed the morning plenary session of Friday, August 12. That afternoon, the Task Force Recommendation on LGBT ordination came to the floor. The heart of the resolution read as follows:

1. Affirm and uphold the standards for rostered leaders as set forth in "Vision and Expectations";

2. Create a process for the sake of outreach, ministry, and the commitment to continuing dialogue, which may permit exceptions to the expectations regarding sexual conduct for gay or lesbian candidates and rostered leaders in lifelong, committed, and faithful same-sex relationships who otherwise are determined to be in compliance with "Vision and Expectations."[8]

As debate was about to commence, one hundred or so gays, lesbians, and allies moved from the visitors' section to the center of the plenary hall, directly in front of the dais. They stood silently and refused to leave, despite repeated requests from Presiding Bishop Hanson. Their presence reminded the voting members that they were discussing the lives of flesh and blood human beings, their sisters and brothers baptized into the family of God. If the plenary was to talk *about* them, even as they refused to talk *with* them, at least they would see the objects of their discussions. Pastor Paul Tidemann of St. Paul-Ref moved suspension of the rules to allow ECP-rostered pastor and visitor Anita Hill to speak, but his resolution failed. A motion to recess failed. Finally, the debate simply continued, as the protesters stood firm in their places.

Pastor Anita Hill would later retell the story in a sermon to her flock at St. Paul-Ref.

I saw 100 people wearing rainbows (including 15 St. Paul-Ref members) walking to the front of the plenary hall as the business ground to a halt. As Margaret Schuster said: "There was disapproval raining down on our heads." My heart beat fast and my hands shook. I heard the voice of our presiding bishop asking us

to return to the visitor section. I heard the tension in the murmurs and groans of many voting members. It was hard to stand
still. Bishop Mark Hanson was my bishop in St. Paul before his
election to churchwide office. He has been my shepherd. I know
his voice.

But we stood firm in our places.

We risked our reputations, risked losing the respect of the
church we've been nurtured in along with our families for generations. We studied non-violence, sought to let our love be genuine, especially toward those we perceived to be against us;
searched our hearts for ways to express God's love as we brought
our message to the church. Even without voice our message was
delivered: no longer can you make decisions about us as though
we are an "issue" to be handled by policy and procedure. We are
human beings beloved of God, marked with the cross of Christ
forever, just like you. As you make decisions, you'll have to look
into our eyes and faces, and see that we love God enough to suffer
and to persevere in prayer and action.

But we stood firm in our places.

I'm convinced that whether the change we seek comes sooner
or later, we must continue to be a congregation that embraces
"justice rooted in gospel." I'm ready for the day when I am a
pastor known not only for being lesbian, but known for teaching,
preaching, and leading in ways that move our community to care
for those who are hungry, homeless, or sick, those in need of love
and care, the "little ones" of the world. Let our community grow
in global awareness and response even as we care for this particular metropolitan area. Let us live well and share well and witness
well. Let us confound those who cannot fathom our faithful
enterprise.

But we stood firm in our places.[9]

From the left, amendments were offered that eliminated any special
provisions regarding LGBT candidates. Exceptions would be unnecessary. These amendments were rejected overwhelmingly. From the right,
amendments to keep *Vision and Expectations* entirely prescriptive and

exclusive without the possibility of any exceptions were also rejected by wide margins. The recommendation in its original form survived largely intact as the debate proceeded. Suppertime slipped by as the plenary session continued into the early evening, and the protesters stood firm in their places.

Finally, the members voted: 490 for the recommendation and 503 against. Because of the requirement of a two-thirds supramajority, the resolution failed by a large margin, but Goodsoil and their allies dared hope and wonder, "What if?" What if the next Assembly, or the next, adheres to a mere simple majority and what if just a few minds are changed? Knock, knock, knockin' on heaven's door.

The next Churchwide Assembly would be in Chicago in 2007, but there wouldn't be a major legislative focus similar to the Task Force Recommendations, and it wouldn't be the long-expected Social Statement on Human Sexuality, either. The Task Force had reported to the Church Council in April 2005 that it had been so focused on the ministry recommendations that their work on the Social Statement on Human Sexuality could not be completed in time for the 2007 Churchwide Assembly; accordingly, the Church Council postponed the final consideration of the social statement to the 2009 Assembly, and a reformed Task Force reconvened and began work anew in February 2006 under the leadership of the bishop of the Northeast Minnesota Synod, Rev. Peter Strommen.[10]

We will get to CWA07 soon enough, but first another ecclesiastical trial with a surprising twist reminiscent of the famous line of the Dickens' character, Mr. Bumble, "If the law says that, the law is an ass, an idiot."

Pastor Bradley Schmeling had been ordained in 1989; while pursuing a call with St. John's Lutheran Church of Atlanta in 2000, Pastor Schmeling told his bishop that he was a celibate, gay man, currently in conformity with *Vision and Expectations*, but that he could not promise that would always be true. He assured the bishop that he would advise any change in circumstances, and the bishop allowed the process to continue. Pastor Schmeling was called to St. John's in 2000. Of course, St. John's was always fully aware of Pastor Schmeling's sexuality as well.

In 2005, Pastor Schmeling's relationship status changed; he fell in love with another ELCA clergyman, Rev. Darin Easler, the pastor of a

Zumbrota, Minnesota, parish. In 2006, Easler joined Schmeling in Atlanta. Later, when Rev. Easler requested an extension of his "on leave from call" status, he was summarily removed from the clergy roster according to a form letter he received from the ELCA. Meanwhile, Pastor Schmeling fulfilled his earlier promise to his bishop and advised of his relationship change, and his bishop felt obligated to bring charges against him. Following a six-day trial in January 2007, a fourteen-page decision was issued in February. By a 7 to 5 vote, disciplinary committee members (jurors) held that Pastor Schmeling was precluded from the ordained ministry of the church by virtue of *Vision and Expectations* and *Definitions and Guidelines for Discipline*, and the majority stated that they felt compelled to so find according to the ministry policies. But the committee was nearly unanimous in declaring that the two documents were "at least bad policy, and may very well violate the constitution and bylaws of this church." "The law is a ass, an idiot," implied the committee, joining Mr. Bumble, and their written opinion called on synods to memorialize CWA07 seeking policy change.[11] Though Pastor Schmeling was removed from the ELCA clergy roster, he continued to serve at St. Johns; the congregation stood in solidarity with their pastor, and the bishop refused to pursue any action against the congregation.

At the end of June 2007, LC/NA Executive Director Emily Eastwood reported that twenty-three out of sixty-five synods had memorialized CWA07 for a change in the ministry policies. "Remember the ultimate outcome is assured. Only the time, the when it happens, is in question. Win or lose in 2007, we will make history and real progress toward full inclusion."[12]

During CWA07, eighty-two LGBT Lutheran clergy were listed in a devotional booklet prepared by LC/NA for distribution to voting members. Many of those listed were rostered by the ECP and already out, but many others were on the ELCA roster and, until then, officially in the closet, thus potentially subjecting themselves to the same process of ecclesiastical trial and removal from the clergy roster experienced by Pastor Schmeling months earlier. But there would be no more trials; CWA07 easily adopted a resolution (55 percent to 45 percent) that said the Assembly "prays, urges, and encourages synods, synodical bishops, and the presiding bishop to refrain from or demonstrate restraint in disciplining" pastors "who are in a mutual, chaste and faithful, committed, same-gender relationship." The resolution added that the same restraint should apply toward disciplining the congregations who called the pastors.[13]

Although Goodsoil objected to further delay, the numerous memorials urging ministry policy changes were bundled by CWA07 and passed on to the Task Force that was already working on the Social Statement on Human Sexuality to be considered at CWA09. Knock, knock, knockin' on heaven's door.

The two streams—A Social Statement on Human Sexuality and review of ministry policies regarding LGBT candidates—that had sprung from CWA01 had now merged into a rushing torrent that would flow into the lakes and rivers of Minnesota, the site of CWA09.

Remember, Minnesota is where they have that special water.

NOTES

1. ELCA News Service, "ELCA Task Force Issues Recommendations on Homosexuality," January 13, 2005.

2. LC/NA, Press Release, *Lutheran Alliance Remains Focused on the Full Participation of Gays and Lesbians in the Life of the Lutheran Church*, January 13, 2005.

3. LC/NA, Press Release, *Goodsoil Petitions ELCA Church Council to Rescind its Policy of Discrimination*, April 11, 2005.

4. ELCA News Service, "ELCA Council Sets Stage for Decisions on Sexuality," November 19, 2004.

5. LC/NA, Press Release, *Daily News Reports from the Evangelical Lutheran Church in America 2005 Churchwide Assembly in Orlando*, August 12, 2005.

6. ELCA Churchwide Assembly, *Minutes* (2005), 309–36.

7. LC/NA Press Release, *Daily News Reports from the Evangelical Lutheran Church in America 2005 Churchwide Assembly in Orlando*, August 11, 2005.

8. ELCA Churchwide Assembly *Minutes* (2005), 309–36. These pages of the *Minutes* include the debate and action on this resolution and also the interruption caused by the protesters.

9. From a sermon delivered by Pastor Anita Hill to her congregation at St. Paul-Reformation Church following the Assembly.

10. "ELCA Task Force on Human Sexuality Begins Anew," *ELCA News Service*, February 10, 2006.

11. ELCA, *In the Matter of the Disciplinary Proceedings against the Rev. Bradley E. Schmeling*, February 7, 2007. Appeals from the verdict affirmed the decision. Pastor Schmeling was surprised when his name appeared on the ecclesiastical ballot for the office of synod bishop in June, and he remained among the final seven candidates. A friend and staunch ally was elected. Following the ELCA ministry policy changes in 2009, Pastors Schmeling and Easler were the first to return to the clergy roster in May 2010, and in June 2012 Pastor Schmeling was called to be senior pastor to a "high steeple" church, Gloria Dei, the largest congregation in St. Paul, Minnesota.

12. LC/NA message to members, *Synod Assembly Season is Finished—On Now to Churchwide*, June 27, 2007.

13. ELCA News Service, "ELCA Assembly Encourages Restraint in Discipline of Congregations, Leaders," August 11, 2007.

* 30 *

THEY CALLED THE QUESTION

Red-vested volunteers with big smiles stood behind a bank of registration booths and greeted the arrivals to the 2009 Churchwide Assembly. The buzz of excitement concealed the tension. By ones and twos and clusters of threes and fours, the arrivals explored the long and wide corridors of the Minneapolis Convention Center to learn the lay of the land, aided by more folks in red vests who served as ushers and travel guides. Large screens strategically filled corners, ready to beam images from the plenary proceedings; those at home would watch via live feeds available on the ELCA website.

Two massive, adjacent conference halls, each the size of an aircraft hangar, would serve as the plenary chamber and the worship space. In a back corner of the makeshift cathedral, the four gospels from the hand of calligrapher Donald Jackson were on display, with their radiant gold leaf and illustrated art. Jackson had been commissioned by Saint John's Abbey and University of Collegeville, Minnesota, to produce a hand-written, hand-illuminated Bible; the Benedictine monks had gladly loaned the gospels for use during the daily worship services. Augsburg Fortress, the publishing house of the ELCA, occupied the principal meeting room outside the conference halls with thousands of books and teaching, music, and worship resources available for sale. Tucked around the corner were two press rooms, one for *The Lutheran Magazine* and one for the ELCA News Service, and an array of computers in a darkened room, free for all to check e-mails, browse the web, or post a blog or twitter feed updating the latest happenings.

One thousand and forty-five voting members, plus another thousand or more visitors, press, churchwide officials, and miscellaneous others filtered through the revolving doors of the Minneapolis Convention Center on August 17, 2009. One-time candidate for the office of presiding bishop, James Nestingen, who had urged unity following his third-place finish in 2001 but who now stood in open rebellion against the ELCA, offered this falsehood about those who gathered: "The hallways and the back of the assembly fill up with gay advocates bussed in to influence the voters using, commonly enough, intimidation up to and including physical threats."[1]

Yep, I was one of those thugs, threatening folks with my prayer shawl. In truth, the Goodsoil volunteers were trained in *graceful engagement.* "Just tell your own story, share your favorite Bible verses, express your love of the ELCA, but if you encounter an unfriendly person, politely disengage."

WordAlone had cloned itself into a new organization called Lutheran CORE with common office space and leadership. CORE had rented a hospitality suite, a prominently located meeting room just off the main lobby. There were looping videos, the opportunity to meet an "ex-gay" from Exodus International, plenty of handouts, and a vigilant cadre of CORE clergy, recognizable by their Luther Rose lapel pins, trim black suits, and clergy collars.

Meanwhile, Goodsoil Central was far down the hallway and up an escalator in a huge room the size of a double tennis court with throngs of volunteers, exhibits, and a lounge area. Emily Eastwood made limited appearances because she had been quite ill. Her young deputy, Ross Murray, filled in capably but with a harried frown that suggested he always had one more thing to do. Hand-knit prayer shawls were heaped high in the center of the room, and each volunteer and each visitor chose one to wear and to keep. As the week wore on, the numbers of volunteers, visitors, and voting members wearing prayer shawls around the Assembly grew and grew as a visible sign of the swelling momentum.

First day, first victory. Contrary to four years earlier when the Church Council had said a two-thirds supramajority would be necessary for adoption of revised ministry policies, the Council had decided in November 2008 and reaffirmed in March 2009 that a simple majority would be sufficient.[2] Since Assemblies set their own procedural rules, the Council action would serve as a nonbinding recommendation, and this question was debated extensively in the opening plenary session. Debate went on for more than an hour with speakers alternating between those favoring and those opposing the motion.

The conservatives argued that changes to long-standing policies and attitudes should only come about through strong consensus, such as a two-thirds majority, even if the constitution didn't require it. Not so, came the response. Since the ministry policy had been adopted by a simple majority of the Church Council in the first place, reversal of the policy should also require a mere simple majority. One speaker pointed out that when previous assemblies voted to allow female clergy, a mere simple majority had been required. When the debate ended and the voting members cast their ballots electronically, the results flashed on the two huge screens that flanked the podium. The procedural rule requiring a mere majority to revise the ministry policy had been adopted, 57 percent to 43 percent, a telling signal of the mood of the Assembly.[3] Of course, the social statement would require a two-thirds majority because that was mandated by constitution.

The Assembly settled into a rhythm of plenary sessions, worship, speakers, and Bible study. The two big items would be the Social Statement on Human Sexuality, scheduled for the Wednesday plenary, and a series of resolutions regarding ministry policy, which would be debated on Friday. The two actions were complementary but not interdependent. One could be passed without the other. One was a teaching document and a statement of understanding, which did not address specific church policies or procedures, and the other was purely policy. The social statement provided the rationale for gays and lesbians to be fully included in the life of the church while the ministerial policies provided the enabling mechanism for allowing gays and lesbians to become ordained clergy.

The social statement, entitled "Human Sexuality: Gift and Trust,"[4] consisted of thirty-two pages, most of them about sexuality in general with only a small section about homosexuality in particular. The essential theme was of relationship and trust. Here is a brief sample: "The sharing of love and sexual intimacy within the mutuality of a mature and trusting relationship can be a rich source of romance, delight, creativity, imagination, restraint, desire, pleasure, safety, and deep contentment that provide the context for individuals, family, and the community to thrive."

The document made no definitive statement regarding gay and lesbian relationships except to note the church was not of a single mind, and a continuum of four differing attitudes were identified; the statement concluded:

> Although at this time this church lacks consensus on this matter, it encourages all people to live out their faith in the local and global community of the baptized with profound respect for the conscience-bound belief of the neighbor. This church calls for mutual respect in relationships and for guidance that seeks the good of each individual and of the community. Regarding our life together as we live with disagreement, the people in this church will continue to accompany one another in study, prayer, discernment, pastoral care, and mutual respect.

In mid-afternoon on Wednesday, a tornado touched down in the neighborhood of the Convention Center. *Outside*, fully leafed branches broke away from tree trunks and crashed to the ground, and chairs, tent, and debris were strewn about from the outdoor pub set up at Central Lutheran Church across the street. Some chairs were found atop the four-story convention center. A traffic light stanchion was bent to a seventy-five-degree angle. The cross atop the steeple of Central Lutheran had been broken. *Inside*, debate raged over the proposed social statement.

By late afternoon, the sun peeked out, and the voting members picked up their electronic voting devices, ready to vote. Professor Guy Erwin of California Lutheran University was a lay voting member from the Southwest California Synod. He was returning from a bathroom break when he heard the call to vote. He hustled back into the plenary hall and settled into his seat just as the presiding bishop said, "push one for yes, two for no."

Out of 1,045 registered, 1,014 were present. To reach the constitutionally mandated two-thirds of voters present and voting, the statement would need 676 affirmative votes. The vote totals appeared first on the monitor of the presiding bishop. With a quizzical look on his face, he turned to his parliamentarian for guidance, and then he announced, "the social statement is adopted," as the totals flashed on the big screens. There were precisely 676 votes for the measure. Not a single vote to spare.

Every single aye voter could legitimately claim to have cast the deciding vote; for Dr. Erwin and his sprint from the men's room, that seemed especially true. Remember the name of Guy Erwin. God had more in store for him.

"God will not be mocked, especially when steeples fall!" screeched Jaynan Clark, the president of WordAlone in her written response to the vote and the tornado.[5]

Others interpreted the rush of wind more charitably. That evening soon after the vote, at the Goodsoil worship service at that same Central Lutheran Church across the street from the Convention Center, Rev. Barbara Lundblad, professor of homiletics at Union Theological Seminary of New York, preached from the Markan text about a dangerous windstorm, laughing that she had written the sermon before the swirling winds of afternoon.

"Let us go across to the other side," Jesus said to his disciples. The other side of Lake Galilee was the land of foreigners: unclean Gentiles, outsiders, those who didn't belong, according to the Hebrew Scriptures and centuries of tradition. When the wind whistled down the gullies of the Galilean hillsides, their small boat was tossed about, and Jesus' disciples were afraid. "Teacher, do you not care that we are perishing?" Jesus woke up and rebuked the wind, and said to the sea, "Peace! Be still!" Then the wind ceased, there was a dead calm, and they reached the far shores.

More than a thousand gathered in the stately old sanctuary of Central Lutheran that evening to hear Pastor Lundblad's words and to share bread and wine and tears.

Thursday was a day to unwind from the emotions of Wednesday and to rekindle energy for Friday. Hopes were high that it would be historic.

The resolutions regarding ministry policies came up soon after the plenary opened on Friday morning.[6] During discussion setting the order for deliberation, former Minnesota governor Albert Quie, who was a voting member, surprised with a substitute resolution that would have stymied further discussion and reform in its tracks. His substitute motion was merely a restatement of the existing policy of *Vision and Expectations*.

His motion was easily defeated. Another conservative motion would have eliminated the procedure of "calling the question," which would have allowed endless amendments and discussion without any procedure for ending debate and moving forward. The gatekeepers were attempting to filibuster, but this motion was also easily defeated. After the stalling and obstructionist tactics of the conservatives had been defeated, the Assembly set the order in which the three, principal resolutions would be considered. A fourth resolution would be a procedural, implementing resolution in the event the first three were adopted. Here is the first of the three.

> RESOLVED, that in the implementation of any resolutions on ministry policies, the ELCA commit itself to bear one another's burdens, love the neighbor, and respect the bound consciences of all.

This resolution had been moved to the fore in order to be "a helpful preliminary to any of the other votes." Another speaker suggested this "always should be the first step in anything that this church does." Perhaps not surprisingly, there were some conspiracy-minded folks who saw a nefarious hidden agenda suggesting that "the idea of 'bound conscience' was being used to look past Scripture and sin in order to accept and embrace unrepentant sin." The resolution was adopted 771 to 230.

At this point, a conservative motion revisited the simple majority versus supramajority issue, but the attempt to impose a supramajority requirement failed by a greater margin than when it had been originally considered during the opening plenary. On to the next recommendation of the Task Force.

> RESOLVED, that the ELCA commit itself to finding ways to allow congregations that choose to do so to recognize, support, and hold publicly accountable lifelong, monogamous, same-gender relationships.

This simple and straightforward statement of affirmation, at least for willing congregations, would elevate LGBT relationships to equality with heterosexual relationships. Speakers pro and con recognized the implicit permission for formal blessings, perhaps even marriage ceremonies in jurisdictions that recognized marriage equality. When this resolution was adopted 619 to 402, the way was clear for the climactic proposal to revise ministry policies.

> RESOLVED, that the ELCA commit itself to finding a way for people in such publicly accountable, lifelong, monogamous, same-gender relationships to serve as rostered leaders of this church.

The debate began midmorning. Hours later, the word spread: "They called the question!" When the facilitator in the darkened computer room made this announcement, many abandoned their computer screens and scrambled back to the floor of the assembly. Others, tweeters mostly, remained at the ready to release the news—what news?—into cyberspace.

Up in the Goodsoil Central room, LGBT folks who had made a pilgrimage to share in this moment clustered around a big screen TV monitor, clutching the prayer scrawls wrapped warmly around their shoulders. A horde of red-vested volunteers left their desks or their floor monitoring stations and swarmed around the big screens in the lobby.

Was this another false alarm? The question had been called at 11:00 AM, but the vote to end debate had failed. The plenary session was adjourned for the midday worship service and those with differing views shared bread and wine together. Then came the lunch break followed by other scheduled business. In mid-afternoon, the question was called a second time, but again the motion to end debate failed and emotional three-minutes speeches continued rapid fire, first from the red microphone, then the green, then red again, back and forth. Pro and con would get equal time.

The tone of some was harsh: "Are you willing to jeopardize your mortal soul?" asked one from a red microphone, but that was the exception; most expressed the angst of interior wrestling. A young woman, about to enter her senior year of high school, nervously approached a green microphone. "Give us honesty," she said. "My generation is turned off by what they see as hypocrisy in the church. 'Love your neighbor' is on the lips of the church, but a cold shoulder is what my generation sees."

The motion to end debate and call the question succeeded on the third try, and the hall hushed as Bishop Hanson invited a prearranged member to lead in prayer. And then came the electronic vote; "Push one for yes, two for no," intoned the bishop. Seen only by him, the tally appeared on the bishop's monitor; he hesitated for a moment, and then said, "When the results appear on the big screen, please do not respond with clapping or cheering but with prayer."

The result was 559 yes, 451 no.

No one was surprised, but the moment had arrived. Gays and lesbians would soon be allowed into the pulpits and altars of their church to serve as ordained, rostered ministers of word and sacrament. To be host as well as guest. Openly and honestly. Recognized and supported. The reaction among a thousand voting members and another thousand observers was muted. The plenary hall was suddenly sacred space, and the quiet interrupted only by weeping and the murmur of prayer. By twos and threes and fours and fives, the children of God huddled together in tears and prayer, some in joyous thanksgiving and others in grief.

Press Release from Emily Eastwood on behalf of Goodsoil:

Today I am proud to be a Lutheran. Supporters and advocates of full inclusion have longed for this day since the inception of the ELCA, and for many of us what seemed like a lifetime. The ELCA has always had gay ministers, now those and all ministers are free to claim who they are and to have the love and support of a lifelong partner, regardless of orientation or gender identity, which is all we ever asked. Policy change is a beginning, not the end. We need to change practice as well as policy. Discrimination will diminish over time now. We pledge to work with the church, including with those who would oppose us, for reconciliation to fulfill our collective mission to spread the love of Christ for the sake of the world.[7]

Superficially, the vote was about allowing LGBT clergy, but it was much deeper than that. LGBT ordination would be the visible sign of inclusivity that beamed a welcome to the entire gay and lesbian community. An anonymous Goodsoil participant said this the following day,

I woke up this morning with the thought that we start our journeys home from Churchwide today.

Then it struck me that we came home Friday night . . .
We came home Friday night . . .
There is a hotel chain that says they'll leave a light in the window
    for us . . .
We too have been following a light left in the window for us—
    by Christ Jesus.
We came home Friday night . . .
Welcome home, everybody . . .
Welcome home . . .[8]

NOTES

1. Dr. James A. Nestingen, *Joining the Unchurched*, September 21, 2009. This article originally appeared on the website of WordAlone in October 2009, and also on the website of the Lutheran CORE, but it has now been removed.

2. ELCA News Service, "LC/NA 'Pleased But Cautious' in Response to ELCA Council Actions," April 3, 2009.

3. ELCA Churchwide Assembly, *Minutes* (2009), 45.

4. ELCA, "A Social Statement on Human Sexuality: Gift and Trust," August 19, 2009.

5. Jaynan Clark, "God will not be mocked—especially when steeples fall." *Word Alone Network News* vol. 10, issue 5, September–October, 2009. The frightening thing about Clark's rant was that she believed it. Her article repeatedly referred to her relationship with Africans who saw the wrath of God as the cause of natural disasters, or alternately, as the hand of the devil. Clark said, "As a former missionary who served in Tanzania, East Africa, I prayed, watched and hoped that the visible nature of God as I had experienced Him there among the faithful Lutherans in Tanzania would be revealed that week. In East Africa they have not yet gotten sucked in by this post-modern era . . . [the East Africans] know that spiritual warfare is a reality and that Satan . . . targets those whose witness will damage his kingdom." One is left to wonder

whether it was God or Satan who knocked over the Central Lutheran Church steeple in Clark's worldview.

6. The following discussion is based on ELCA Churchwide Assembly *Minutes* (2009), 340–55, 363–73.

7. Goodsoil Press Release, *Goodsoil Celebrates the Elimination of the Ban against Ministers in Same-Gender Relationships*, August 21, 2009.

8. Goodsoil Message to Members, *ELCA Churchwide Assembly, A Postscript*, August 23, 2009.

* 31 *

WE DIDN'T LEAVE THE ELCA.
THE ELCA LEFT US

"We didn't leave the ELCA. It was the ELCA that left us," a few schismatics griped as they rushed out, slamming the door behind them. Even before the close of the 2009 Churchwide Assembly, Lutheran CORE announced that it was relinquishing its ties to the ELCA as an affiliated organization. Simultaneously, CORE encouraged ELCA members and congregations to withhold the funds that normally flowed from congregations to synods and ultimately churchwide.[1]

We have seen how the roots of dissension go back to the very beginning of the ELCA and the Call to Faithfulness Conferences of the early nineties, featuring many of the principals who would now become schismatic leaders. To be sure, the dissidents had their theologians. Theological critiques of the ELCA actions were usually directed at fundamental questions of leadership and the process of decision making with a pining toward the rigidity of the Papal Curia and Magisterium rather than the democratic egalitarianism of ELCA polity.

First, in arguably sexist, certainly elitist, overtones, the theological critics of the ELCA uniformly derided its democratic polity. Carl Braaten, who had led the ELCA bashing conferences of the early nineties, lamented the loss of "the magisterial authority of the Roman Catholic Church" in favor of a "quota-selected majority of lay members."[2] Robert Benne criticized the ELCA quota system that mandated 50 percent female representation in committees and assemblies. For Benne, 50 percent female representation was somehow equivalent to "militant feminism . . .

The losers, of course, are white male pastors."[3] James Nestingen, the WordAlone ringleader, wrote, "Positive aspects of quotas can still be argued. . . . Quotas [do not place] an equal priority on characteristics like wisdom, fidelity and zeal. . . . Those most likely to be included are the manageable, those eager to please, no matter what their race or gender, while those most likely to be eliminated are the gifted and challenging."[4]

Second, according to the gatekeepers, orthodoxy, especially the historic confessions of the sixteenth century, must control. Is the reformed church still reforming? Is God still speaking? Does the Spirit continue to guide and inspire? Only through the deposit of faith handed down from yesteryear, according to the schismatic theologians. Braaten, dismissing the suggestion that the Holy Spirit might be doing a new thing, said, "The Holy Spirit had already spoken volumes through the millennia of Scriptural interpretation, the councils of the church, and its creeds and confessions."[5] Benne said, "The ELCA became the first American confessional church to cross that line by passing statements and policies that depart from Christian orthodox teaching and practice [that is] the testimony of the whole Christian moral tradition, the wisdom of its predecessor bodies."[6] Nestingen said, "And this is the importance of the confessions . . . each of the confessions became a public document, summing up Catholic faith in terms suitable to ongoing confession, witness. . . . The confessions are like the Magna Charta or the Declaration of Independence."[7]

Third, if we are known by the company we keep, the preferred friends of these theologians says plenty. Braaten, as cofounder of the Center for Catholic and Evangelical Theology, remained steadfast in his view that the future of Lutheranism lay in the direction of Rome rather than with the ecumenical denominations of the United States.[8] The recurring theme in Braaten's open letter to the ELCA's first presiding bishop, Herbert Chilstrom, on the eve of CWA09, was a critique of the ELCA's affinity with the Protestantism of the ecumenical denominations: "Turning left, theologically speaking, means to affirm the theology and methodology of liberal Protestantism; turning right means to reclaim the Great Tradition of historic Christianity prior to the Reformation, including the ancient Church Fathers and Medieval Doctors of the Church."[9]

Benne agreed: "A church of the future should diminish its ecumenical interest in declining, sectarian liberal Protestant bodies and increase it among orthodox bodies—Roman Catholic, Missouri Synod Lutheran, Reformed, [and] evangelical denominations."[10] Nestingen appreciated papal authority to control new ideas: "Therefore, the office of the papacy acts as a check, controlling the range of interpretation. The bishops share in this authority."[11]

These confessionalist theologians would have the church go back, not forward and right, not left.

CORE announced a convocation to be held at Fishers, Indiana, on September 25, 2009, a month after CWA09, to plan a "reconfiguration of North American Lutheranism," initially proposing an ill-defined concept of a "free-standing synod" within the ELCA. Though some leaders and congregations were already contemplating departing the ELCA, the initial mood out of Fisher's was to stay and save the ELCA from heresy with a return to orthodoxy. Former synod bishop and the CORE chair Paull Spring said at Fishers, "We want to be part of the solution with the help of the Holy Spirit. . . . God is calling us to do something. The ELCA has fallen into heresy. It is time for confession and time to resist. It is a time for new life."[12]

But with each passing month, CORE moved closer to schism. For one thing, the ELCA showed no sign of retreating from CWA09. As ELCA leadership moved to implement full inclusion, reality set in for the gatekeepers. More importantly, individual congregations, invariably led by a rabble-rousing pastor, were taking the first steps to exit the ELCA,[13] but these congregations were going elsewhere. CORE had to act quickly or lose its chance at luring ELCA congregations.

In 2009, Lutheran Congregations in Mission for Christ (LCMC) was not much more than a mailing list, a website, and a paid staff of two persons. LCMC was an "association of congregations" that reflected the old Hauge strain of anticlerical, anti-authoritarian Lutheranism. It had been a spinoff of WordAlone beginning with a few ELCA congregations that had splintered away from the ELCA after the turn of the century. By the time of CWA09, approximately 220 congregations belonged to the LCMC association.

But thanks to a handful of aggressive LCMC pastors who immediately courted ELCA congregations, mostly rural, that were confused and upset by the actions taken at CWA09, LCMC seized on the opportunity for "sheep stealing" based on fearmongering. CORE had cried wolf, but LCMC plucked up many of the frightened congregations. The mission field for LCMC consisted of ELCA congregations in neighboring small towns. A number of urban "megachurches" preferred the congregational autonomy associated with LCMC that allowed the megachurch to be an entity unto itself and also joined LCMC. They preferred the independence to do their own thing rather than support the many missions and ministries of the ELCA (that is, keep their money).

It was soon clear that congregations that departed the ELCA would not become part of a single, unified dissident body; instead two separate and distinct organizations competed for allegiance. And then there was the third organization, the WordAlone Network, that was the midwife for both but later found itself caught between but with an apparent lean toward CORE (shared offices and staff, for instance).

Public pronouncements from the two organizations did not hint at any competition—"two rails of the same track" said their spokesmen. Yet there were subtle indicators of tension. In February 2010, a disclaimer appeared on the WordAlone blog (since removed): "This website is sponsored solely by the WordAlone Network and is not a publication of LCMC—Lutheran Congregations in Mission for Christ."

Then there was this. After CORE announced plans to form a new denomination to be called the North American Lutheran Church (NALC), Pastor Bradley Jensen of the LCMC posted an open letter to CORE on February 10, 2010, followed a day later with further comments, questioning the rationale for the formation of NALC:

> Most of what the NALC is proposing already exists in LCMC. Many congregations who . . . are seeking to leave the ELCA will have already done so by joining LCMC long before the NALC's August 2010 constituting convention. Furthermore, LCMC has proved itself as a viable on-going entity whereas NALC has not. . . . What, specifically, does the NALC offer that LCMC DOES not or CANNOT offer?
>
> I think that traditional Lutherans are too optimistic about how many congregations will leave the ELCA (it won't be that many). . . . Thus, LCMC and NALC will be splitting a small pie.

LCMC is up, running, and viable for the long haul, and receiving new congregations every week. NALC is not. . . . I think that the energy for . . . leaving the ELCA is rapidly dissipating.[14]

Nevertheless, CORE spawned their own denomination (NALC) during a constituting convention in Columbus, Ohio, on August 27, 2010, almost exactly a year after CWA09. The NALC website reported a total of 250 congregations as of August 2011 and 355 congregations as of May 2013.[15]

Meanwhile, as of June 2012, the LCMC website directory listed 694 LCMC congregations in the United States, an increase of approximately 475 since CWA09.[16] A year later in May 2013, the number of congregations on the LCMC directory was 702, indicating minimal recent growth.[17] Most of these were formerly ELCA congregations, some were startups formed by splinter groups that had failed to convince their entire congregation to leave the ELCA, and a few were purely mission starts. These numbers for LCMC and NALC overlapped, as some congregations claimed dual affiliation.

At the ELCA 2011 Churchwide Assembly, Secretary David Swartling reported ELCA statistics, including information about departures in the two years following CWA09.[18]

- 95 percent of more than ten thousand ELCA congregations remained

- 94 percent of more than four million ELCA members remained

- There had been 832 first votes to leave (51 congregations voted multiple times)

- 621 congregations had passed the first vote

- 517 congregations had passed the second vote

- The greatest number of defecting congregations were rural

- The greatest number of defecting members were from large, urban congregations (megachurches)

Dr. Swartling's report also cited Synodically Authorized Worshiping Communities (SAWC). A SAWC is an interim, first step toward creation of a new congregation. In many communities where the existing ELCA congregation voted to depart, there would often be a remnant of ELCA loyalists. If there were no other ELCA congregations nearby to absorb these progressive fragments, many sought SAWC status. Here are a few comments sent to me by "Saucy Lutherans" who followed this process.

Just wanted to let you know that our SAWC is chartering this weekend! We're dropping the SAWC and want to get everything in order so that we can be accepted as a full-blown congregation at the June 2011 Synod Assembly. Even starting to outgrow our rented space and we are actively looking for property to create a new sanctuary. Needless to say, VERY excited about this weekend. All things happen for a reason, and there will definitely be a sense of renewal in Tomah this weekend! [Peace Lutheran Church of Tomah, Wisconsin]

Here in Clintonville, we are happy that now, with some needed remodeling and some comfortable chairs, we are growing. Our first confirmation will be this month. A number of our newer members were dropouts from the LCMC church. Some had bad experiences years ago and are now joining us. We are getting some very talented people. Faith still needs prayer and money so keep us in mind. [Faith Lutheran of Clintonville, Wisconsin]

Have you been following what is taking place in Hutchinson regarding the two former ELCA churches leaving the ELCA? By next month, I am confident there will be a new ELCA church in town—River of Hope Lutheran Church. At our first gathering, over 100 folks were in attendance and nearly $4000 was collected in the offering. We are psyched! We are energized with the spirit of Christ! Keep an eye on us. [River of Hope Lutheran Church of Hutchinson, Minnesota]

The paths of the Episcopal Church and the ELCA tracked closely together as the first decade of the twenty-first century wound down. In July 2009, the Episcopalians had adopted full inclusion policies, joined by the Lutherans a month later. As we shall see, the Presbyterians would follow close behind. In both TEC and the ELCA, long-simmering struggles for power finally boiled over. With progressives firmly in control, the gatekeepers in each denomination bolted, but the defectors would not succeed in becoming a "replacement jurisdiction" that would supplant the Episcopal Church nor a "reconfiguration of North American Lutheranism." In both instances, the schismatic splinters would be roughly 5 percent the size of the ecumenical denomination.

Schism is painful, and the anguish should not be minimized; friends, family, and former associates were gone, and their departure was accompanied by hurt feelings and harsh words. Yet, without diminishing the loss, it is clear that neither TEC nor the ELCA suffered the cataclysmic consequences predicted by the gatekeeping doomsayers.

NOTES

1. "ELCA Assembly Actions Draw Criticism, Praise from Advocacy Groups," ELCA News Service, August 21, 2009.

2. Carl E. Braaten, "The Aroma of an Empty Bottle," Lutherans Persisting (blog), September 2009, accessed January 13, 2010, http://lutheranspersisting.wordpress.com/carl-braaten-the-aroma-of-an-empty-bottle/.

3. Benne, "How the ELCA Left," *Christianity Today*.

4. Nestingen, *Joining the Unchurched*.

5. Braaten, "The Aroma of an Empty Bottle."

6. Robert Benne, "Why There Must Be New Beginnings," *Lutheran Forum*, accessed May 23, 2013, http://www.lutheranforum.org/sexuality/why-there-must-be-new-beginnings/.

7. Dr. James A. Nestingen, "Speech to WordAlone," March, 2000. From the WordAlone website, accessed May 23, 2013. http://www.wordalone.org /docs/wa-nestingen-speech-2000.shtml.

8. Website of the Center for Catholic and Evangelical Theology, accessed May 25, 2013, http://www.e-ccet.org/.

9. Carl E. Braaten, "Open Letter from Carl Braaten to Herbert Chilstrom," *Lutheran Forum*, August 1, 2009, accessed May 25, 2013, http://www.lutheranforum.org/sexuality/open-letter-from-carl-braaten-to-herbert-chilstrom.

10. Benne, "Why There Must Be New Beginnings," *Lutheran Forum*.

11. Nestingen, "Joining the Unchurched."

12. ELCA News Service, "Lutheran Core Leaders, Members Map Organization's Future, September 27, 2009.

13. The ELCA has a prescribed constitutional procedure for a congregation that wishes to disassociate. Requirements are in place for notice and consultation with synod offices and for two congregational votes, separated by a cooling-off period. Two thirds of members present for both the first vote and the second vote must be in favor of disassociation or the attempt to disassociate fails. Usually, departing congregations retain ownership of congregational property. ELCA, *Model Constitution for Congregations of the Evangelical Lutheran Church in America*, ch. 6.

14. The author quoted this letter and other comments from the LCMC forum on his blog, Spirit of a Liberal, http://www.theliberalspirit.com/, and soon after, the LCMC forum was made private.

15. "History," on the website of NALC, accessed June 25, 2012, http://thenalc.org/the-nalc-history.htm and the homepage accessed May 23, 2013, http://thenalc.org/.

16. "Congregations—United States," on the website of LCMC, accessed June 25, 2012, http://www.lcmc.net/components/general/congregations-usa.php?filter_organization_name=&filter_primary_city=&filter_primary_regi on_name=.

17. Congregations—United States," on the website of LCMC, accessed May 23, 2013, http://www.lcmc.net/components/general/congregations-usa .php?filter_organization_name=&filter_primary_city=&filter_primary_region_a me=.

18. ELCA Churchwide Assembly, *Minutes* (2011).

✳ 32 ✳

FINDING A WAY

Following CWA09, the ELCA had unfinished business. The historic resolution committed the church to "finding a way" to allow gays and lesbians in "lifelong, monogamous, same-gender relationships" to serve as ordained clergy. After CWA09, the church leadership set about the task of "finding a way."

First, the documents that defined ministry policies required revision. Then, based on the modified policies, the church would revisit earlier actions. Some pastors, once ordained and listed on the ELCA clergy roster, had been removed from the roster, notably Ross Merkel and Bradley Schmeling. There were congregations that had been expelled or otherwise disciplined. And there were nearly two dozen pastors, not on the roster, who had been ordained *extra ordinem*, starting with Ruth Frost, Phyllis Zillhart, and Jeff Johnson in San Francisco and continuing with Anita Hill and others in the years leading up to CWA09. Thus, an important aspect of "finding a way" pertained to rectifying past actions.

First, we consider the matter of revising the documents that collectively defined ministry policies. The drafting task fell to the ELCA Vocation and Education Committee headed by executive director Stanley N. Olson. The committee worked with church leaders and various constituencies during the revision process. The Conference of Bishops, exercising their advisory function, reviewed and commented on the proposed documents at their March 2010 meeting. The Church Council then overwhelmingly adopted the revised ministry policy documents on April, 10, 2010.[1]

The new documents imposed standards on LGBT relationships identical to those imposed on married clergy. Here is typical language:[2]

> A married ordained minister is expected to live in fidelity to his or her spouse, giving expression to sexual intimacy within a marriage relationship that is mutual, chaste, and faithful.
>
> An ordained minister who is in a publicly accountable lifelong, monogamous same-gender relationship is expected to live in fidelity to his or her partner, giving expression to sexual intimacy within a publicly accountable relationship that is mutual, chaste, and faithful.

This pattern would persist throughout the documents. Every provision regarding expectations of married clergy would be followed by a mirror-image provision pertaining to a "publicly accountable lifelong, monogamous same-gender relationship."

A few remedial actions were accomplished with a stroke of the pen. Censure and other sanctions on congregations that had called LGBT clergy were lifted. Bradley Schmeling and his partner, Darin Easler, were reinstated on May 4, 2010, the first gay clergy to benefit from the revised policies growing out of CWA09. Rev. Mary Albing, of Minneapolis, was a special case.

> Today, seven years after she was called by the congregation, the Rev. Mary Albing has been officially recognized as the pastor of the Lutheran Church of Christ the Redeemer in Minneapolis, Minnesota.
>
> When Mary was called by the congregation in 2003, all parties knowing that she was a lesbian, the bishop of the synod, Bishop Craig Johnson, said he could not sign approving the call. The position of pastor has been listed by the ELCA as "vacant" the entire time. But there is no denying that Mary has ministered to this congregation effectively. The congregation has been growing since 2005.
>
> The bishop kept the original letter he was asked to sign in 2003, and today signed it, yet another sign of the wondrous results of the 2009 decisions by the Churchwide Assembly and

the implementing actions of the ELCA Church Council in consultation with the Conference of Bishops earlier this year.

Mary was never off the roster of the ELCA clergy. She was officially listed as On Leave from Call for the period. Today's signing officially "fills" the pulpit of the Lutheran Church of Christ the Redeemer as Mary is returned to On Call status, something that has been seven years in coming for the congregation.[3]

What about those two San Francisco congregations that were expelled in the mid-nineties? Both were invited back into the ELCA by Bishop Mark Holmerud of the Sierra Pacific Synod. Though there were still some hard feelings toward the ELCA, St. Francis accepted the invitation, and a festive celebration on February 27, 2011, marked their return. Ruth Frost and Phyllis Zillhart participated. Fifteen years earlier, a prior bishop had departed the church with tatters from a shredded banner streaming from his crosier, a visible sign of the expulsion. Now, Bishop Holmerud participated in a reverse ritual. Arriving at the St. Francis sanctuary, the doors were closed. With his crosier, he knocked and asked to be let in.[4]

First United returned later due to the necessity to completely redraft their constitution. Their formal return to the ELCA occurred on October 14, 2012, during a service of Reconciliation and Healing.

Finally, we come to Pastors Frost, Zillhart, Johnson, Hill, and others on the ELM roster but not on the ELCA roster. The church never seriously considered re-ordaining them; that would have disrespected their original *extra ordinem* ordinations. Neither did the church seriously consider merely signing a paper signifying their inclusion on the roster; that would have understated the significance of the action. In consultations with the pastors involved and leadership of LC/NA and ELM, an innovative "Rite of Reception" was created that would have the ceremonial and liturgical trappings of an ordination but which honored the participant's earlier extraordinary ordination.

The first Rite of Reception was a big one—six pastors on the ELM roster from California were received at St. Mark's Lutheran Church of San Francisco on July 25, 2010. Additionally, Pastor Ross Merkel was reinstated during the same Rite of Reception. The six included Pastor

Jeff Johnson, one of the original trio from the San Francisco ordinations of 1990 that set the whole process of extraordinary ordinations in motion. His two compatriots from 1990 would come on board two months later (see below). The others received in San Francisco were Megan Rohrer, Paul Brenner, Craig Minich, Dawn Roginski, and Sharon Stalkfleet.

Rev. Nadia Bolz-Weber, a tall, slender, dark-haired, "cyber-punk" pastor and a self-described "cranky, post-modern gal of the emerging church *a la* Luther," preached the sermon. Her clerical robes barely concealed her tattooed arms. Pastor Nadia, a straight woman, was the founder of the Church for All Saints and Sinners in Denver, which is a sanctuary for many gays and lesbians abused by the church. In her sermon, she described her own spiritual awakening in the church of Ross Merkel as one who bore scars inflicted by the church of her youth, a recovering alcoholic and drug addict, and one who wanted nothing to do with anything Christian. But she learned Lutheranism from her mentor, Ross Merkel:

> God had literally interrupted my life and plucked me off one path and put me on another, bringing life out of the death of this Sinner/Saint. So when Pastor Merkel taught me that God brings life out of death, that we are all simultaneously sinner and saint; when he said that no one is climbing the spiritual ladder up to God but that God always comes down to us; when he said that God's grace is a gift freely given which we don't earn but merely attempt to live in response to . . . well, when he said all of this, I already knew it was true.

She concluded her sermon with this word of grace:

> And so, Paul, Jeff, Craig, Dawn, Megan, Sharon and Ross... know this: The Kingdom of God is also like right here right now. The kingdom of God is like this very moment in which sinners are reconciled to God and to one another. The kingdom of God is like this very moment where God is making all things new... even this off brand denomination of the ELCA. Because in the end, your calling, and your value in the Kingdom of God comes not from the approval of the other workers but in your having

been come-and-gotten by God. It is the pure and unfathomable mercy of God which defines this thing. And nothing, nothing else gets to tell you who you are."[5]

Less than two months later, on Saturday, September 18th, 2010, the Rite of Reception for Ruth Frost, Phyllis Zillhart, and Anita Hill was celebrated at Lutheran Church of the Redeemer in St. Paul, the same venue that had witnessed the extraordinary ordination of Pastor Hill nearly a decade earlier.[6] The assembled crowd stirred and swelled as a woodwind quartet played variations on "Hymn of Gladness," the chancel choir sang "Al Shlosha D'Varim," and the chancel brass announced the beginning of the processional with "Fanfare and Chorus."

Those gathered struggled through tears to sing the processional hymn. Here is the first stanza:

Here in this place the new light is streaming, now is the darkness vanished away; see in this space our fears and our dreamings brought here to you in the light of this day. Gather us in, the lost and forsaken, gather us in, the blind and the lame, call to us now, and we shall awaken, we shall arise at the sound of our name.[7]

The entire procession of bishops, active and retired, and countless clergy filed in through four stanzas of the hymn and more before all had reached their place, and then the first presiding bishop of the ELCA, Herbert Chilstrom, led the congregation in halting voice and failing eyesight in a litany of confession, which included a confession of the sins of the church toward gays and lesbians. Bishop Herb concluded with words of encouragement from the prophet Isaiah: "Do not fear, for I have redeemed you; I have called you by name, you are mine. When you pass through the waters, I will be with you; and through the rivers, they will not overcome you. You are precious in my sight, and honored, and I love you."

Hymns and prayers and greetings and readings followed, and the Chancel Choir sang the gospel acclamation as a procession carried the Bible to the center of the gathering. The congregation joined the choir in the refrain: "My heart shall sing of the day you bring. Let the fires of your justice burn. Wipe away all tears, for the dawn draws near, and the world is about to turn."[8]

Preaching minister Pastor Barbara Lundblad, professor of homiletics at Union Theological Seminary, read the gospel according to Matthew, chapter 20, the parable of the laborers in the vineyard. She said that this Matthew text was suggested by Pastor Hill in an e-mail, which addressed those who question her ministry.

> We are doing you no wrong by being received to the ELCA roster. . . . So why must our reception be seen as sullying the ministry for everyone? Do you not see the pain of not having . . . [our work] acknowledged for all these years?
>
> Or, as the gracious master in the parable asks, "are you envious because I am generous?"

Then came the Rite of Reception. Pastors Frost, Zillhart, and Hill knelt before the altar. They exchanged promises with the congregation "to give faithful witness in the world, that God's love may be known." The ordained clergy clustered about and laid on hands. Then the three moved to the center aisle and heard the words of their bishop,

> Let it be recognized and acclaimed that Ruth, Phyllis, and Anita are called and ordained ministers in the church of Christ. They have Christ's authority to preach the word of God and administer the sacraments, serving God's people as together we bear God's creative and redeeming love to all the world.

NOTES

1. ELCA News Service, "ELCA Council Adopts Significant Revisions to Ministry Policies," April 11, 2010. There were no nay votes, but at least one abstention.

2. *Vision and Expectations: Ordained Ministers in the Evangelical Lutheran Church in America,* as amended April 10, 2010. A related document is *Definitions and Guidelines.*

3. Lutherans Concerned News Archives, "Rev. Mary Albing Officially Recognized as Called to Christ the Redeemer," May 23, 2010.

4. Private interview of Frost and Zillhart by the author, February 12, 2012.

5. Nadia Bolz-Weber, "Sermon from Sierra-Pacific Synod," on the website of Extraordinary Lutheran Ministries/, accessed June 28, 2012, http://www.elm.org/2010/07/26/sermon-from-sierra-pacific-synod-service.

6. This account is based on the author's own witness of the event. After serving in San Francisco for more than a decade, Frost and Zillhart had returned to Minnesota and the Twin Cities, accepting calls as hospice chaplains. Pastor Anita Hill had continued as pastor of St. Paul-Reformation. Other, less publicized Rites of Reception continue.

7. "Gather Us In" by Marty Haugen, Copyright 1982 by GIA Publications, Inc., 7404 S. Mason Ave., Chicago, IL 50538, 222.giamusic.com, 800.442.1358. All rights reserved. Used by Permission.

8. "Canticle of the Turning" by Rory Cooney, Copyright 1990 by GIA Publications, Inc., 7404 S. Mason Ave., Chicago, IL 50538, 222.giamusic.com, 800.442.1358. All rights reserved. Used by Permission.

✳ 33 ✳

LATE-BREAKING LUTHERAN NEWS

Guy Erwin was born in Oklahoma with roots in the Osage tribe of Native Americans. His life in the church would be that of a scholar and academic. While studying at Harvard, the history of Luther and the Reformation led him to the Lutheran Campus Ministry and the Lutheran Church. Later, while undertaking graduate studies at Yale, he considered ordination within the Lutheran Church of America shortly before its merger into the ELCA, but more studies intervened—at Tubingen and Leipzig in Germany. Upon his return from Europe, the ELCA had been formed, and the newly created *Vision and Expectations* stood as a barrier to his call to ordained ministry. In 1994, he met his life partner, Rob Flynn, and Dr. Erwin assumed that was the end of his prospects for ordination.[1]

Dr. Erwin continued his career as an academic, settling in at California Lutheran University (CLU) by 2000, where he has served as a faculty leader. Ironically, he is a Lutheran confessional historian, the same general circle as that of the theological spokesmen for the Lutheran gatekeepers. From his bio on the CLU website:

> Dr. Guy Erwin, who joined the CLU faculty in the summer of 2000, is the first full-time holder of CLU's first endowed chair, the Gerhard and Olga J. Belgum Chair of Lutheran Confessional Theology. He also serves as Director of the Segerhammar Center for Faith and Culture. In the 2004–05 and 2005–06 academic years he served as CLU faculty chair. As holder of the Belgum Chair, he serves as a member of the CLU Office of University

Ministries, coordinating the work of the Chair, the Segerhammar Center, Campus Ministry, and Church Relations.[2]

Dr. Erwin had been a lay voting member at the historic 2009 assembly (remember his dash from the restroom in time for the social statement vote). Following the ELCA actions of 2009, he finally answered his call to the ordained ministry. Though Dr. Erwin has recently served on the board of directors of Extraordinary Lutheran Ministries and has been quite open about his sexuality, he has not been an outspoken LGBT activist, and he was better known for his scholarship. On May 11, 2011, he was ordained by Bishop Dean W. Nelson of the Southwest California Synod, who said,

> We are humbled and thankful to God for the privilege of receiving Dr. R. Guy Erwin onto the roster of ordained pastors of the Southwest California Synod. We have been blessed by Guy's ministry for over a decade, for in addition to teaching at California Lutheran University, Guy has been the Bible study leader and/or presenter at our Bishop's Colloquy for rostered leaders, at our Synod Assembly, and at our Synod's Equipping Leaders for Mission School. During that same period, he has also been a preacher and teacher at several of our Synod's congregations.[3]

Two years later, on May 31, 2013, Rev. Dr. Erwin allowed his name to go forward during the Synod election of a new bishop to succeed Bishop Nelson. He made it past the first couple rounds in the ecclesiastical ballot process, and he was one of the seven remaining candidates called upon to address the plenary and then one of three to participate in a question and answer session.

> A little nervous before he gave his opening speech, once at the microphone and speaking, he relaxed and told a bit of his story. He talked about Rob. The assembly listened silently in rapt attention, no chatting, no coughing or shuffling of papers. He did what he needed to do. He was completely authentic. From that point forward he was in his element, the teacher and pastor. He seemed to have fun with every question in the Q&A session,

especially the one asking about how he would handle ministry to LGBT people. You should have seen his face. What a softball question. He responded with care for those who might be at different points in the conversation on LGBT inclusion. His answer was full of grace and the love of Christ. At that moment, he was the bishop, and most everyone knew it.[4]

As the final vote tally was announced, Erwin sat with head bowed with partner Rob leaning in close. The weight of the moment was upon each of them. The call was clear and so was his commitment.

The crowd went wild. There was hardly a dry eye in the house. The assembly had elected the best candidate, he happened to be gay and Native American and a PhD, one of the world's best known Luther scholars, and a very good pastor.[5]

Emily Eastwood is a battle-scarred warrior. She has been active in LC/NA for over thirty years, the last decade as its leader. As the assembly applauded, she sobbed. "I cried. I cried as I had not in a long time, surprised by how much pent up hope there was in me for this historic moment. I know how to lose, but even now winning takes me by surprise."[6]

Decades earlier, the homophile organizations had recognized the necessity of personal relationships, a ministry of presence, that would allow the church to become comfortable enough with gay brothers and lesbian sisters to become fully inclusive. Certainly Dr. Erwin's lengthy relationship with the clergy and leaders of his synod prepared the way for his episcopal election.

> I know that many will see my election as a significant milestone for both LGBT people and Native Americans, and I pray that I can be a positive representation [sic] for both communities. There was a time when I believed that I would not be able to serve as a pastor in the ELCA. Our church has now recognized the God-given gifts and abilities that LGBT people can bring to the denomination.[7]

Dr. Erwin joined Episcopal bishops Gene Robinson and Mary Glasspool as the only openly gay persons consecrated as bishops in American Protestantism. During his sermon at the Integrity Eucharist in July 2012, Bishop Robinson thanked Bishop Glasspool for coming on the scene because now he was not the only one. With Bishop Robinson's retirement, Bishop Glasspool could express the same thanks to Bishop-elect Erwin. Early plans for Bishop-elect Erwin's consecration include Bishop Glasspool's participation as a consecrator.

Obviously, Bishop Robinson brings a unique perspective to the election of Dr. Erwin, and he wrote soon after the election,

> The perhaps unexpected reward that Dr. Erwin and the Lutherans will gain is a closer relationship with God. When we do justice work, stand with the oppressed, and put our lives and our faith where our inclusive theology is, we meet God there. A favorite saying of mine, given to me a month after my election, says, "Sometimes God calms the storm. But sometimes, God lets the storm rage, and calms His child." That is my prayer for Dr. Erwin and the Lutherans. Let God calm your hearts and soothe your souls. You are walking with God. I, for one, consider it an honor to be on this journey with you.[8]

Soon after his election, Bishop-elect Erwin received a congratulatory call from ELCA Presiding Bishop Hanson, who was pleased and supportive, according to Erwin.[9] They spoke of the election as the logical culmination of the 2009 revisions to the ministry policies, and Erwin was quoted by CNN to the same effect: "Eventually what seems revolutionary now will seem normal and predictable."[10] Though his election can be seen as the beginning of a new chapter, it is even better understood as the conclusion of a long narrative.

NOTES

1. Press Release, "Guy Erwin, Partnered Teaching Theologian, Ordained at California Lutheran University," from Lutherans Concerned/North America, May 11, 2011.

2. From the website of California Lutheran University, accessed June 1, 2013, http://www.callutheran.edu/schools/cas/faculty_profile.php?minor_id=32&profile_id=37.

3. Press release "Guy Erwin, Partnered Teaching Theologian."

4. Emily Eastwood, "Executive Director Column," *Concord: Newsletter of Reconciling Works*, Spring/Summer 2013.

5. Ibid.

6. Ibid.

7. Ross Murray, "Evangelical Lutheran Church in America elects first openly gay bishop," from the website of GLAAD, accessed June 1, 2013, http://www.glaad.org/blog/evangelical-lutheran-church-america-elects-first-openly gay-bishop.

8. Rt. Rev. Gene Robinson, "On Gay Bishops, what a difference a decade makes," *The Washington Post* June 7, 2013.

9. Dr. R. Guy Erwin, private phone conference with the author, June 17, 2013.

10. Dan Merica and Daniel Burke, CNN, "Lutherans Elect First Gay Bishop," June 3, 2013, accessed June 17, 2013, http://religion.blogs.cnn.com/2013/06/03/lutherans-elect-first-openly gay-bishop/comment-page-8/.

PART IV

~

The Presbyterians

I n 1548, a French galley rolled in the swells of the North Sea. Chained to benches, Scottish prisoners manned the oars as the galley patrolled the east coast of Scotland between the Firth of Tay and the Firth of Forth. One emaciated and feverish galley slave, a man of the cloth, couldn't last much longer; it had been a year since he and other Scottish rebels had surrendered to their French captors. As the sun settled on the Scottish lowlands, the clergyman spotted a familiar landmark, the spire of the parish church in the Diocese of St. Andrews where he had preached his first sermon. So near and so far.

"I shall not die until I preach there again," John Knox muttered, and he would make good on his promise.[1]

History failed to record the circumstances of his escape from near death on the French prison ship, but Knox would soon find himself in exile during an idyllic sojourn in Geneva, Switzerland, where he had sought asylum in the 1550s during the reign of Catholic Mary Tudor (Queen Mary I of England, aka "Bloody Mary"), who was burning dissenters at the stake. In Geneva, Knox learned reformed theology at the feet of John Calvin:

> I neither fear nor eschame to say, [Calvin's Geneva] is the most perfect school of Christ that ever was in the earth since the days of the apostles. In other places I confess Christ to be truly preached; but manners and religion so sincerely reformed, I have not yet seen in any other place.[2]

During a lull in the political/religious intrigues following the death of "Bloody Mary," Knox returned to Scotland to lead a Scottish Reformation inspired by the upheaval loosed a generation earlier when Martin Luther defied both the emperor and the pope. Knox would import the teachings of the reformers, particularly John Calvin, into Scotland.

The Scottish Parliament appointed Knox (with others) to draft the Scots Confession, which Parliament approved in 1560. Simultaneous acts of Parliament outlawed papal religion in favor of reformed theology and ecclesiastical structures. Knox and his fellows then drafted the *Book of Discipline*, which provided the organizational apparatus of the reformed church, or *kirk*. The church would democratically elect their own councils to govern instead of bishops. Parishes would be self-supporting and would choose their own pastors. However, civil strife stalled implementation when Mary, Queen of Scots and a Catholic, returned to Scotland from France (not the same person as Mary I of England who had died a few years earlier). Until his death in 1572, Knox railed against unjust earthly rulers, especially the female monarchs of his own experience.[3] Though Knox is acknowledged to be the founder of presbyterianism, it would take nearly a century and a half before the presbyterian form of church organization would become official for the Church of Scotland.

During the long reign of Good Queen Bess of England (Elizabeth I, 1558–1603), Catholicism ceased to be a viable option for official sanction in either England or Scotland. The Elizabethan Religious Settlement of 1559 established the queen as the head of the Church of England, independent of Rome. What is more, the Religious Settlement adopted protestant theological premises at odds with Catholicism. After Elizabeth put down a Catholic rebellion intended to place Mary, Queen of Scots, on the throne, a papal bull of 1570 declared that "Elizabeth, the pretended Queen of England and the servant of crime" was a heretic.[4] With nearly a half century under this protestant queen, those hoping for a Catholic restoration would be disappointed, and by the time of her death at the dawn of the seventeenth century, England and Scotland were unalterably protestant.

But what kind of protestant?

The British fought civil wars in the mid-eighteenth century over the authority of Parliament versus the monarchy, with Oliver Cromwell the Puritan leading the Roundheads (the parliamentary party) against the Royalists. A corollary to the political battles was the question of the episcopacy. Ecclesiastical skirmishes mirrored the political. Scottish Presbyterians and English Puritans—fellow Calvinists—jointly challenged the hierarchy of bishops. Thus, for a brief period when Cromwell and the parliamentary party were ascendant mid-century, so too did the Puritan-Presbyterian alliance prevail; during this period, the Westminster Confession of Faith was drafted pursuant to a request from Parliament.

The Westminster Confession of Faith became the leading Presbyterian document (second only to Scripture), written by "learned, godly and judicious Divines" meeting at Westminster Abbey beginning in 1643 and completed four years later. With its emphasis on the sovereign will of God, who "freely and unchangeably ordained whatsoever comes to pass," the document expressed the Calvinistic doctrine of predestination.[5] The Larger and Shorter Catechisms of Westminster contained a lengthy list of sins, as did the related Heidelberg Catechism, which would later prove problematic when a 1990s General Assembly action attempted to block LGBT ordination by referring to that "which the confessions call sin." As we shall see, the confessions were actually silent about gay sex but freely mentioned sins such as the "undue delay of marriage," marriage to "infidels, papists, or other idolaters," "immodest apparel," and a host of other culturally conditioned puritanical prohibitions. "There are at least 250 sins mentioned in the *Book of Confessions*, and we all practice at least some of them in good conscience."[6]

With the restoration of the Monarchy in 1660 (albeit in a weakened mode, soon to be subservient to the consent of Parliament), so too was the episcopal structure of the Church of England reinstated, and Royalists reportedly "pranced around May poles as a way of taunting the

Presbyterians and Independents."[7] Presbyterians retreated to Scotland and Puritans became dissenting nonconformists in England or fled to places such as the American colonies.

Finally, in the Acts of Union of 1706 and 1707, which combined Scotland and England into Great Britain, with one crown and one Parliament, the presbyterian model was allowed to the Church of Scotland, a concession to the Scots during the negotiations.[8] Thereafter, England was formally Anglican and Scotland was formally Presbyterian. A century and a half after the Scottish Reformation, the *kirk* of John Knox was officially established in the Church of Scotland.

With Presbyterian pockets located in various European countries besides Scotland, the American colonies were touched by Presbyterians from England, Holland, and elsewhere. Though Presbyterian influence may date to the Puritans and Pilgrims of the Massachusetts Bay Colony, credit for forming the first American congregation on a presbyterian model goes to Francis Makemie, a Northern Ireland clergyman who felt the sting of English oppression of religious nonconformists and arrived on American shores late in the seventeenth century.

Makemie organized the first Presbyterian congregation in Snow Hill, Maryland, in 1684; others soon followed, and in 1706 Makemie was instrumental in the creation of the first regional council, known as a presbytery, in Philadelphia. Makemie also played an important role in the development of American freedom of religion when he was arrested in the New York colony, which officially sanctioned Anglicism, for preaching without a license. His acquittal and the subsequent action of the New York legislature mandating toleration is considered a landmark freedom-of-religion development in U.S. history.[9]

Jonathan Edwards was a Presbyterian clergyman, and his preaching touched off the "Great Awakening" that leapt from his Northampton, Massachusetts, parish in 1733 and again a handful of years later. In 1746, the Presbyterian "College of New Jersey" (later to be Princeton University) was established, and one of its university presidents, the Rev. John Witherspoon, was a signatory to the Declaration of Independence. The first General Assembly, reflecting a national church body, convened in 1789, the same year the Constitution of the United States was adopted.

Northern and southern Presbyterians split over slavery in the years leading up to the Civil War, only to be reunited more than a century later with the formation of the Presbyterian Church (USA) in 1983. Hear the words of Presbyterian theologian and seminary professor James Henley Thornwell, written more than a century and a half ago, and listen for their echoes still ringing in the present:

> I have no doubts but that the Assembly, by a very large majority, will declare slavery not to be sinful, will assert that it is sanctioned by the word of God, that it is purely a civil relation with which the Church, as such, has no right to interfere, and that abolitionism is essentially wicked, disorganizing, and ruinous. . . . The parties in this conflict are not merely Abolitionists and Slaveholders; they are Atheists, Socialists, Communists, Red Republicans, Jacobins on the one side, and the friends of order and regulated freedom on the other. In one word, the world is the battleground—Christianity and atheism the combatants and the progress of humanity the stake.[10]

Just as the name of the Episcopal Church is derived from New Testament Greek passages describing the structure of the early church (the transliterated "episkopos" is commonly translated as "bishop"), so too is the name "Presbyterian" based on the same passages (the transliterated "presbuteros" is commonly translated as "elder").

Congregations are governed by "sessions," a council of locally elected elders, sometimes referred to as "ruling elders," as distinct from the pastor or minister of word and sacrament, who is often referred to as a "teaching elder." A unique feature of presbyterianism is that the ruling elders of congregational sessions, and also local deacons in specialized ministries, are considered to be ordained. Though ruling elders and deacons do not have seminary training, their status as ordained would have significant consequences for the journey toward full inclusion, since the prohibition on ordination of gays and lesbians extended beyond the pulpit to include all local leaders.

Congregations elect elders to gather in regional councils known as "presbyteries," which in turn gather in larger bodies known as "synods," and the national church is governed by the "General Assembly," whose elected "commissioners" gathered annually until recently and now meet once every two years.

> The General Assembly consists of commissioners elected by presbyteries. Half of the commissioners will be Ministers of Word and Sacrament, half will be elders. Few will ever have been commissioners to the General Assembly before, but most will have served in one of the other governing bodies of our church: the session, which provides care and oversight of a local congregation; the presbytery, which provides care and oversight of a group of congregations; or the synod, which provides care and oversight of several presbyteries.
>
> It reviews the work of synods, resolves controversies in the church, is responsible for matters of common concern for the whole church, and serves as a symbol of unity for the church.[11]

Serving as a check on the authority of General Assemblies, certain actions of the commissioners are not effective unless ratified by a majority of presbyteries following General Assembly. As we shall see, the General Assembly approved gay-friendly legislation four times before the presbyteries finally ratified assembly action. Each General Assembly elects a moderator to preside over the plenary sessions of that assembly, and the "Stated Clerk," elected for a four-year term, serves as the chief ecclesiastical officer of the denomination.

Presbyterians on their journey toward full inclusion would be challenged by their bloodlines, which included Calvinistic predestinarianism, Scottish stoicism, and Irish fatalism. While exhibiting a stiff upper lip in the face of adversity is a particularly British trait, passive resignation would not be the lot of LGBT Presbyterian pilgrims. From his chains, a nearly broken John Knox gazed longingly upon a steeple rising from the lowlands of St. Andrews. As with Knox, the hopes of Presbyterian gays and lesbians seemed so near yet frustratingly unattainable. Nevertheless, Presbyterian wayfarers stepped out again, and again, despite recurring fits and stops—hopeful advances followed by gut-wrenching reversals. Following one crushing defeat, a young woman cried out to her fellow travelers and those who had journeyed before: "Sit with me, cry with me, wail with me. It is risky to begin to hope. It is anguishing to have hope stripped away . . . as I struggle to get back up, I wonder how did they do it? How do you continue to do it?"[12]

In a moment, we will hear their stories, but our journey begins with a visit to an ancient Presbyterian landmark.

―――――

NOTES

1. Jasper Ridley, *John Knox* (Oxford: Clarendon Press, 1968), 75.

2. W. Stanford Reid, *Trumpeter of God* (New York: Charles Scribner and Sons, 1974), 132.

3. Geddes MacGregor, *The Thundering Scot* (Philadelphia: Westminster Press, 1957), 131–52.

4. Patrick McGrath, *Papists and Puritans under Elizabeth I* (London: Blandford Press, 1967), 69; Patrick Collinson, *Elizabeth I* (Oxford: Oxford University Press, 2007), 67.

5. For a full treatment of the historical circumstances of the Westminster Confession, see a 1906 publication of the Presbyterian Church in the United States entitled "The Origin and Formation of the Westminster Confession of Faith," accessed July 24, 2012, http://www.pcanet.org/general/cof_preface .htm.

6. Rogers, *Jesus, the Bible, and Homosexuality*, 122–23.

7. Peter King, "The Episcopate during the Civil Wars, 1642–1649," *The English Historical Review* vol. 83, no. 328 (July 1968): 523–37; Tim Harris *Restoration: Charles II and His Kingdoms 1660–1685* (London: Allen Lane 2005), 52–53.

8. P. J. W. Riley, "The Union of 1707 as an Episode in English Politics." *The English Historical Review* vol. 84, no. 332 (1969): 498–527 [523–24].

9. Francis Makemie's website, accessed July 24, 2012, http://www.francis-makemie.com/Francis_Makemie.htm.

10. Rogers, *Jesus, the Bible, and Homosexuality*, 19–20.

11. "General Assembly of the PC(USA): What Is It and What Does It Do?" on the website of the PC(USA), accessed July 24, 2012, http://oga.pcusa .org/section/ga/ga/.

12. Kraemer, "Wanderings in Grief and Rage."

* 34 *

THE SCRUPLE

The two foremost documents of American history were drafted in Philadelphia: the Declaration of Independence in 1776 and the U.S. Constitution in 1787. The first stop on our Presbyterian journey will be to the city of brotherly love to revisit the earlier enactment of another hallmark historical document, the Presbyterian Adopting Act of 1729, which established the Presbyterian right of religious dissent. As we shall see, in the final twists and turns on the road toward full inclusion, this venerable Presbyterian right of "scruple" would help twenty-first century pilgrims navigate around the final barriers, thereby encouraging the church to smash them down altogether.

The General Synod of 1729 convened in Philadelphia and acted on business that had been debated for several years. The Adopting Act of 1729 mandated that clergy candidates subscribe to the Westminster Confession.

> [W] are undoubtedly obliged to take care that the faith once delivered to the saints be kept pure and uncorrupt among us, and so handed down to our posterity; and do therefore agree that all the ministers of this Synod, or that shall hereafter be admitted into this Synod, shall declare their agreement in, and approbation of, the Confession of Faith, with the Larger and Shorter Catechisms of the Assembly of Divines at Westminster, as being in all the essential and necessary articles, good forms of sound words and systems of Christian doctrine, and so also adopt the said

Confession and Catechisms as the confession of our faith. And we do also agree, that all the Presbyteries within our bounds shall always take care not to admit any candidate of the ministry into the exercise of the sacred function but what declares his agreement in opinion with all the essential and necessary articles of said Confession, either by subscribing the said Confession of Faith and Catechisms, or by a verbal declaration of their assent thereto, as such minister or candidate shall think best."

However, in a compromise, candidates would be allowed to declare a "scruple," which was an objection or disagreement with lesser articles of the Confession, but not to "Essential and Necessary" articles, and it would be up to the Presbyteries to decide whether a particular scruple applied to essentials or nonessentials.

And in Case any Minister of this Synod or any Candidate for the Ministry shall have any Scruple with respect to any Article or Articles of sd. Confession or Catechisms, he shall at the Time of making his sd. Declaration declare his Sentiments to the Presbytery or Synod, who shall notwithstanding admit him to ye Exercise of Ministry within our Bounds and to Ministerial Communion if the Synod or Presbytery shall judge his scruple or mistake to be only about articles not Essential and necessary in Doctrine, Worship, or Government.[1]

In the early decades of the twentieth century, the old premise of the scruple, the freedom of conscience, established in the Adopting Act of 1929, was relitigated in what became known as the "Fundamentalist-Modernist Controversy." Indeed, it was this Presbyterian battle that birthed the term "fundamentalism." The vast resources of nineteenth century oilman Lyman Stewart funded the fundamentalists, a harbinger of the neoconservative backing of the Episcopal, Presbyterian, and Methodist gatekeepers at the turn of this century.

Let us set the stage.

Around 1615, Italian scientist Galileo Galilei was convicted of heresy for contradicting the biblical accounts of creation. He had promoted the theory of Polish astronomer Nicolaus Copernicus that the earth rotated around the sun rather than vice versa. In response to the controversy that raged around him, Galileo made several statements that proved relevant during the Fundamentalist-Modernist debate and remain so today:

> I should have in your place added that, though Scripture cannot err, its expounders and interpreters are liable to err in many ways; and one error in particular would be most grave and most frequent, if we always stopped short at the literal signification of the words.[2]

> The passage of time has revealed to everyone the truths that I previously set forth; and, together with the truth of the facts, there has come to light the great difference in attitude between those who simply and dispassionately refused to admit the discoveries to be true, and those who combined with their incredulity some reckless passion of their own.[3]

> I do not feel obliged to believe that the same God who has endowed us with senses, reason, and intellect has intended us to forgo their use.[4]

A century after Galileo, Europe was swept by the spirit of enlightenment during the Age of Reason; American rationalists provided the intellectual underpinnings of the American Revolution; and science challenged traditional assumptions. In 1859, Charles Darwin published *On the Origin of Species*, and his theory of evolution sparked a religious reaction that continues to the present.

While many religious folk resisted Enlightenment thinking, there were also many Christian rationalists who sought to interpret Scripture and develop theology consistently with the best scientific insights rather than in opposition to them. The scientific and intellectual study of Scripture came to be known as "historical criticism" or "higher criticism." "Liberal protestantism" and "liberal Christianity" are terms often applied to those scholars, schools, seminaries, and churches that utilize historical criticism to interpret the Bible.

Historical criticism is a method of biblical interpretation that seeks to understand God through the use of Scripture by applying the same modern interpretive methods used to understand any ancient writings without any preconceived notion of inerrancy or the correctness of church dogma. "Historical," used here, refers to the evaluation of the Scriptures in the historical context or circumstances in which they were written, involving a series of "W" questions. Who wrote the text? When? Where? Why? For whom? For historical criticism, a proper understanding of Scripture requires dusting off and closely examining the Bible that biblicists place high on a pedestal: beyond reproach, beyond scrutiny, beyond question.

German scholars of the nineteenth century (Schleiermacher, Wellhausen, von Harnack), and of the early twentieth (Bultmann and Tillich), became the principal champions of historical criticism. Many Presbyterians, as well as leading academics in the other ecumenical denominations, accepted historical criticism as the best way to understand Scripture, but others did not, and this difference became the essence of the "Fundamentalist-Modernist Controversy." The literalist interpretations of the fundamentalists were a reaction—some would say an overreaction—to historical criticism because the ancient church had always understood the religious language of Scripture to be largely metaphorical. In other words, biblical literalism is as new a phenomenon as historical criticism, perhaps newer.

Presbyterian theologian and church historian Jack Rogers (moderator of the 2001 General Assembly) suggests that Darwin's publication was the genesis of the Fundamentalist-Modernist debate that dominated Presbyterian discussions and General Assemblies in the 1920s.

> [M]odernists felt obliged to embrace the new science. They believed that the human race was moving toward God, Scripture represented the evolving experience of humankind, and creeds were only a human attempt to express religious experience.
>
> In contrast, others, who came to be called fundamentalists, believed that God had created the world once and for all in a certain way, the Bible contained God's literal words as recorded by humans, and creeds represented a systematic presentation of doctrinal truths.
>
> Modernists and fundamentalists in these churches fought each other for decades over the meaning of Scripture. Modernists

denied the authenticity of certain parts of the Bible, while fundamentalists insisted that the entire Bible, in the original manuscripts, was inerrant. By this, fundamentalists meant that God was the author of Scripture, and therefore whatever the Bible said could be applied directly to present-day circumstances, overriding science if science conflicted with their own views of what was considered biblical. Modernists, in frustration, appealed to the scientific method of observation and experimentation as having greater authority for modern people.[5]

At the beginning of the twentieth century, it seemed the Presbyterian fundamentalists had the upper hand; the so-called "five fundamentals" were enshrined by legislative act of the General Assembly, and all clergy candidates had to subscribe to these five—an orthodox litmus test—in order to proceed forward on the path to ordination.[6]

Presbyterian liberals chafed, and a 1922 sermon from the pulpit of First Presbyterian Church in New York City entitled "Shall the Fundamentalists Win?" ignited a national firestorm. This was the introduction of Rev. Harry Emerson Fosdick to the national stage, and intense debate followed with the three-time Democratic nominee for President, William Jennings Bryan, leading the response to Fosdick while also attacking Darwin's theory of evolution. The fallout from Fosdick's sermon led him and one of the parishioners, John D. Rockefeller, to construct the upper-west side cathedral that would become Riverside Church of New York.

Two years later, in 1924, Auburn theological professor Robert Hastings Nichols promoted a moderate document that would become known as the Auburn Affirmation. The Affirmation encouraged liberty of conscience, guided by the Spirit, over and against inerrancy. While it didn't necessarily contradict the five fundamentals (except for inerrancy), it simply suggested there was room for disagreement.[7] The premise of confessionalism, *this ye must believe*, was rejected. When more than a thousand theologians and clergy signed on to the Affirmation, the fundamentalist choke-hold was broken. At the 1925 General Assembly, moderator Charles Erdman dramatically left the chair and moved to the floor to propose a special commission to deal with "the causes of unrest" in the church.

This special commission became known as the "Swearingen Commission," and their report affirmed freedom of conscience, recycling the "scruple" of the Adopting Act of 1729. Furthermore, the Commission held that it was not the business of General Assembly to legislate beforehand what was essential and what was not. Such decisions should be left to specific cases and the presbyteries that performed the examination of candidates.[8]

Of course, the Auburn Affirmation and the report of the Swearingen Commission didn't mean the fundamentalists suddenly changed their minds; some left for more conservative pastures, but the remnants simply became the (mostly) loyal opposition, biding their time. For the turn-of-the-twenty-first-century progeny of their fundamentalist forbearers, the struggle for LGBT inclusion became the latest instance of the recurring Fundamentalist-Modernist divide, often with apocalyptic overtones reminiscent of the rhetoric that slavery-apologist Professor Thornwell had expressed 150 years earlier.

The Presbyterian contest between fundamentalism and modernism, the battle over Scripture, reflected similar developments across the ecumenical denominations. Indeed, one of the significant commonalities between the five ecumenical denominations under consideration here is that the modernists and their progeny have largely held sway in their seminaries and universities over the last century. To be sure, tweaks and refinements labeled "neo-orthodoxy" and "biblical theology" reminded academics that historical criticism was a means, not an end, and refocused exegesis on the redemptive life, work, and teachings of the man from Nazareth.

Here's the bottom line: inerrancy remained off the menu of the ecumenical denominations, and their schools and seminaries served up heaping plates of critical exegesis in the latter half of the twentieth century, though literalist junk food would reappear from time to time.

Finally, we are ready to make our beginning. We have reviewed our roadmap of the Presbyterian landscape. We have visited the landmark of the scruple. The subtle but sweet fragrance of flowers floats on the breeze, and we soon wander through a garden filled with multicolored irises, and we meet the young horticulturist responsible for their cross-pollination.

NOTES

1. From the minutes of the Philadelphia General Synod, September 19, 1729, quoted by Rev. Dr. David T. Myers, "September 19: The Standards of the Presbyterian Church," *This Day in Presbyterian History*, accessed October 21, 2012http://www.thisday.pcahistory.org/2012/09/september-19-the-standards-of-the-presbyterian-church/.

2. Galileo Galilei, "Letter to Benedetto Castelli, 1613," reprinted in the Interdisciplinary Encyclopedia of Religion and Science, accessed June 21, 2013, http://inters.org/Galilei-Benedetto-Castelli

3. Galileo Galilei, "Letter to the Grand Duchess Christina of Tuscany, 1615," reprinted in the Fordham University Modern History Sourcebook, accessed June 21, 2013, http://www.fordham.edu/halsall/mod/galileo-tuscany.asp.

4. Ibid.

5. Rogers, *Jesus, the Bible, and Homosexuality*, 35–36.

6. The list of five "essential and necessary doctrines" that all candidates for ministry had to affirm: (1) the inerrancy of Scripture, (2) Jesus' virgin birth, (3) his vicarious substitutionary atonement on the cross, (4) his bodily resurrection, and (5) the power of Jesus' mighty miracles." Rogers, *Jesus, the Bible, and Homosexuality*, 36.

7. For full treatment of the Fundamentalist-Modernist debate and the "Auburn Affirmation," see Lefferts A. Loetscher, *The Broadening Church: A Study of Theological Issues in the Presbyterian Church since 1869* (Philadelphia: University of Pennsylvania Press, 1964), 117–20; 134–35; Bradley J. Longfield, *The Presbyterian Controversy: Fundamentalists, Modernists & Moderates*, Religion in America (New York: Oxford University Press, 1991), 77–103; and Gary North, *Crossed Fingers: How the Liberals Captured the Presbyterian Church* (Tyler, Tex.: Institute for Christian Economics, 1996), 534–81.

8. "Report of the Special Commission of 1925 (Excerpt), *Journal of Presbyterian History*, vol 79:1, Spring, 2001.

* 35 *

Is Anybody Else Out There Gay?

For Minnesota farm kids growing up in the 1950s, 4-H was a primary social outlet and rearing ground for responsible leaders. The four H's are Head, Heart, Hands, and Health, explained by the pledge: "I pledge my head to clearer thinking, my heart to greater loyalty, my hands to larger service and my health to better living, for my club, my community, my country, and my world.[1]

Rural kids gathered in monthly 4-H club meetings to discuss their projects and to socialize; meetings would often conclude with popcorn and a root beer float. Typical projects might include raising hogs, developing film in a darkroom, or planning a community service event. The best projects were awarded blue ribbons at county fairs and then on to the Minnesota State Fair in August.

Although he was a city kid from Minneapolis, born in 1940, David Bailey Sindt lived that 4-H life.[2] David raised flowers: award-winning irises. By age thirteen, he had twice been honored with state 4-H championships in gardening. Later he was off to earn a horticulture degree from Iowa State in 1962, where he retained his passion for the iris, and he attained an international reputation for his cross-bred hybrids.

After college, David's head, heart, hands, and health took a religious turn. A lifelong Presbyterian with an uncle, grandfather, and great-grandfather serving as ordained ministers, David followed their path. After he completed work on his Master of Divinity degree, he was ordained in St. Paul, Minnesota, in 1965. He served congregations in St. Paul and the Chicago area before returning to university studies to obtain a Master's degree in Social Work, and by 1970 he was employed by the Illinois Department of Children and Family Services.

In 1974, David attended the national gathering of Presbyterians, the General Assembly of the UPC. As he sat among a thousand delegates and visitors in the Louisville convention hall, he was anonymous. And then he came out. He had carefully prepared a sign in his hotel room, which he raised high. In fact, he stood on his chair to lift the sign even higher.

Is anyone else out there gay?

Some folks snickered. Others looked away. Still others took the long path around his solitary vigil on the convention floor. Most wished he would simply go away and return to his anonymity, to become invisible again, but he was out, and now the Presbyterians had to deal with him and other gays and lesbians in their midst, ready or not.

Pastor Sindt had already experienced rejection by his church, with more to come. In 1972, his Lincoln Park Presbyterian Church had issued a call to him to become a part-time associate pastor with a special ministry to the gay community, but the Presbytery of Chicago's Ministerial Relations Committee blocked the call. Later, after his appearance at the 1974 General Assembly, he sought to have his ministerial membership in the Twin Cities Area Presbytery transferred to the Presbytery of Chicago, but Chicago denied the transfer (on the grounds that a gay minister could not objectively serve gay people!),[3] and subsequent ecclesiastical court proceedings left the denial intact.

Even before Rev. Sindt stood on his chair at the UPC General Assembly in 1974, he had begun organizing a gay caucus. Prior to the convention, he had mailed invitations to potentially interested persons, and they became the Presbyterian Gay Caucus. As the years passed, their name would become "Presbyterians for Lesbian and Gay Concerns (PLGC)." Here is the text of his letter:

> I am inviting you to participate in a caucus within the United Presbyterian Church in the U.S.A. designed to raise the consciousness of our denomination on issues related to Gay people (homosexuals). Our denomination's only relevant utterance, that

received by the 182nd General Assembly (1970), declares con-
tradictorily that Gay people are both sinful and sick because of
our homosexuality. . . . I suggest that we focus our initial efforts
nationally on a "ministry of presence" at the 186th General
Assembly in Louisville, Kentucky, June 17 to 26, 1974. . . . Our
goal is to work for change *within* the denomination, not to attack
it, from either within or without.

In peace and love,

Rev. David Bailey Sindt[4]

Rev. Sindt had ignited a flash fire, and Bill Silver fanned the flames.
Silver was a seminarian when he first encountered Sindt. Silver was also
influenced by a speech by Rev. Bill Johnson, the UCC clergyman who
had recently become the first gay man to be ordained; with youthful exuberance, and perhaps some naiveté, Silver would attempt to become the
first openly gay Presbyterian to be ordained.

The City of New York Presbytery didn't know what to do with Bill
Silver's candidacy; thus, the Presbytery requested "definitive guidance"
whether an "avowed homosexual" could be ordained to church office.[5]
The question was pushed upstairs to the 1976 General Assembly of the
UPC in Baltimore. Chris Glaser was another out gay Presbyterian seminarian filled with brash optimism as a member of PLGC and first-time
observer to the 1976 General Assembly.

> When the nearly seven hundred delegates gathered in the con-
> vention hall, they resembled a smaller version of a national polit-
> ical convention. And it *was* a political convention of sorts, replete
> with issues, lobbyists, resource persons, and hundreds of
> observers, including the media. But the issue that seemed to dom-
> inate both the mind of this Assembly and my heart was homo-
> sexuality . . . fifty years before, when the Presbyterian Assembly
> had last met in Baltimore, the delegates hotly debated the ordi-
> nation of tobacco-using clergy![6]

A General Assembly committee wrestled with the request for "definitive guidance" and an appropriate resolution to be moved on the floor.

On one hand, the committee was not prepared to recommend that gays or lesbians be ordained, and the resolution suggested gay ordination would be "injudicious if not improper." On the other hand, the committee believed that LGBT ordination required further discussion and called for a task force to lead the church in study of the issue because "God hath yet more light to break forth from his word," quoting from an old hymn and advice once given to Pilgrims seeking religious liberty. Though a conservative spokesman attempted to scuttle the resolution on the floor, it was adopted by the commissioners.[7]

Even though Silver's pursuit of ordination had not been approved, the core group of gay advocates—including Silver, Glaser, and Sindt—came away from the 1976 Assembly optimistic that God would shed more light on the pathway toward full inclusion for the gay and lesbian community. Glaser edited a quarterly magazine he called *More Light*, and Rutgers University Professor James D. Anderson edited a regional PLGC newsletter for the Synod of the Northeast. In 1980, their efforts coalesced into a national newsletter called *More Light News*, which soon became *More Light Update*, and Professor Anderson would serve as editor for the next twenty-two years.

Hopes remained high as the task force was formed. Though the panel included known conservatives and likely opponents of LGBT clergy, a friendly elder from Rochester, New York, would serve as task force chair; Ginny Davidson had lost her bid to be elected moderator of the recent General Assembly because she forthrightly supported LGBT ordination, but now she was appointed to chair the task force. Others on the blue ribbon task force included sociologists, psychologists, and persons from the field of medicine; a black man and black woman who knew firsthand the circumstances of prejudice and discrimination; Christian scholars from the fields of biblical studies, church history, Christian ethics, and applied theology; and . . . a gay seminarian and mainstay of PLGC, Chris Glaser.

The task force would take its time and allow the voices of Presbyterians from across the country to be heard in a series of public hearings. Their report would not be considered until the 1978 General Assembly. Glaser reported that the process grew tedious, and he was shocked at the lack of knowledge of those who stepped to the microphones at the public hearings.

Yet many of us on the task force found the hearings frustrating: we had already learned so much that we found ourselves astounded and exasperated by the ignorance of the majority of those who testified. . . . Many attacked us for *being* on the task force, questioning our own morals, character, and judgment. . . . Our faith and our intelligence were offended as person after person used their time (and ours) to read from a dusty Bible its handful of verses presumed to be about homosexuality—as if we hadn't heard them before, as if we couldn't recite them verbatim![8]

Church historian John Boswell, who would soon receive acclaim for his historical analysis of gays and the ancient church, offered compelling testimony before the task force. Boswell and Glaser together came to the view that advocacy could only be successful by straight folks encountering gay folks, that experience would change hearts and minds when reason could not. You can't rationalize with the irrational, but perhaps rubbing elbows would slowly erode barriers.

After every biblical, theological, ecclesiastical, historical, psychological, and biological question has been answered, antigay feelings will still be present in church and society. "One can't use reason to argue someone out of a position not arrived at by reason." . . . Phobias, irrational fears, are not overcome by reason so much as experience. I believe the church and society's phobia regarding homosexuality and homosexual persons will be overcome by experiencing us.[9]

This would be a critical insight of LGBT advocates across the denominations, expressed as a "ministry of presence" in Rev. Sindt's initial letter. Glaser's own rocky road to ordination illustrates the point:

I observed a phenomenon that would repeat itself over and over in my relationship with the church: the committee had recommended in favor of me, but the larger body to which it reported rejected its recommendation. The committee had the opportunity to know me as a person, but the larger group knew me principally as an issue. . . . I believe personalizing the issue becomes the central factor in transforming opinions on homosexuality. Every advance in the gay movement has been preceded by someone's willingness to incarnate the issue.[10]

At the 1977 General Assembly in Philadelphia, an effort to quash the task force, or to change its focus toward reparative therapy, failed. Thus, in August 1977, the task force reconvened in Chicago to finish its work by developing a statement to be presented to the church with recommendations for General Assembly 1978. Each member shared his or her personal views. Glaser spoke emotionally of the rejections he was encountering in his own journey to ordination, which was now seriously in doubt. He concluded with the recognition that he spoke not merely for himself, and not merely for other gays called to ordained ministry, but for all gay Presbyterians: "I am one with all these, and we are one with all 300,000 gay Presbyterians. To reject any of us because of our sexual orientation is to reject all of us."[11]

Though Glaser doubts whether his testimony changed any votes, it did deeply affect one task force member; Willard Heckel had served as moderator to the General Assembly. After Glaser's compelling testimony, Heckel spontaneously chose that moment to come out. After a moment of stunned silence, chair Ginny Davidson called for a brief recess, and Heckel was mobbed with hugs from most but not all of the task force members.

And then they voted; the majority of fourteen did not view homosexuality to be a sin or a bar to ordination, but a minority of five said it was both. A lengthy report would be drafted reflecting where the task force agreed with separate majority and minority recommendations to be written by each faction.[12]

The majority view said there was nothing in current policies to prevent LGBT ordination and suggested that the decision whether to ordain LGBT clergy should be left to individual presbyteries or congregations—a local option, which squared precisely with Presbyterian constitutional polity. That is, the majority report affirmed the basic Presbyterian principle that presbyteries have the prerogative to ordain or not ordain according to their discretion.

This sentiment behind the majority viewpoint was expressed in a background paper to the actual report:

May a self-affirming, practicing homosexual Christian be ordained? We believe so, if the person manifests such gifts as are required for ordination. . . . Spiritual maturity or the absence thereof is an attribute pertaining not to any *class* of people but only to *individual* persons. Thus, it must be distinctively identified and separately evaluated in each individual candidate for ordination as the church, led by the Spirit and guided by God's Word, seeks to discern and verify that particular candidate's gifts for ministry.[13]

This view became formalized in the majority recommendation to the 1978 General Assembly:

[I]it is the traditional duty and prerogative of presbyteries to make individual judgment concerning the fitness of a candidate for ordination . . . [the General Assembly should defer] to the presbyteries and congregations for further discussion and for adjudications made by individual Christian consciences considering individual cases and circumstances.[14]

The minority view disagreed, recommending:

[T]hat no possibility for the ordination of a self-affirming, practicing homosexual person should be granted lest the purity, peace, and unity of the church be undermined, lest the ability of the church to deal with homophobia be impaired, and lest the will of the church to develop authentic Christian outreach to the homosexual community be weakened.[15]

Patronizing at best and contemptuous at worst, the minority view focused upon the effect on the church, not the individuals affected by the policy—"approaching things from the privileged perspective of the normative group."[16] "Peace and unity" was a recurring theme across denominations that elevated the good order of the church over justice for individuals. And what of the condescension that drips from the term "purity"? Is this not an implication that gays and lesbians are impure, unclean, and unholy—an echo of the "thou shall not mix" ritual purity system of the ancient Hebrews? The latter two phrases of the minority recommendation patronized the gay community, suggesting *the church knows what is best for you*. There should be no gays in the pulpit lest homophobia in the pews be riled up. Tread lightly on the tender sensibilities of folks who might be offended lest their will to do ministry to the gay community be impaired.

In January 1978, the task force report was made public, and conservative opposition immediately mobilized. A "Chicago plan" grew out of an impromptu Chicago meeting in February, just a few weeks after the task force report had been released. The Chicago plan was raw politics in action: "a political strategy to defeat the task force majority report by pressuring Presbyteries to take positions and elect General Assembly Commissioners [delegates] opposed to it." Such political lobbying was unprecedented in the Presbyterian church, but overt advocacy would become the norm, from both sides, in the ensuing years.

> This scene would be replayed in a number of presbyteries throughout the country, so embedded and widespread was the homophobia. Presbyterians usually take pride in their scholarship. Generally they trust God to work through a committee process to illumine truth. Usually Presbyterians do things "decently and in good order." What the Chicago plan illustrated again and again was how unnaturally homophobia made many Presbyterians behave. They feared current scholarship, distrusted our task force, and behaved indecently in their efforts to coerce defeat for the majority report's recommendation.[17]

In May 1978, the General Assembly convened in San Diego. It would not go well for Glaser, the task force, or the PLGC and their allies. The "definitive guidance" offered by the General Assembly soundly rejected the majority recommendation. There would be no local option and no consideration of candidates on an individual basis. In fact, the General Assembly dispensed with the minority report and drafted its own blunt and unequivocal rejection of homosexuality and of gay clergy. The resolution that was adopted, by an overwhelming majority of 90 percent, stated: "homosexuality is not God's wish for humanity" and "unrepentant homosexual practice does not accord with the requirements for ordination."[18] These ominous, crushing, suffocating words would dominate Presbyterian policy for a generation.

The one piece of good news came in an amendment by Pastor John Connor, the General Assembly moderator the preceding year, stating that the policy "shall not be used to affect negatively the ordination rights of any United Presbyterian deacon, elder, or minister who has been ordained prior to this date."[19] This grandparent clause would protect many for awhile, but even this safeguard would later be stripped away— but now we're getting ahead of the story.

Soon after the General Assembly closed, the LGBT advocates received another blow. The Stated Clerk (the chief officer of the denomination), William P. Thompson, claiming the commissioners didn't know what they were voting for, decreed that the "definitive guidance" would have the force of law throughout the church and that presbyteries and congregations would be powerless to act otherwise. Members of the Presbytery of Long Island met with Stated Clerk Thompson and attempted to dissuade him of this view. The delegation of six included Bill Silver. Their subsequent report to their presbytery reveals the Stated Clerk to have been intransigent and perhaps duplicitous, and they failed to change his mind.[20]

The principal argument of the Long Island delegation was based on comments made by the drafters of the resolution during floor debate on the resolution. The chair of the committee that drafted the resolution, the Rev. Thomas Gillespie, who later became president of Princeton Theological Seminary, stated:

> When your son or daughter comes to you and asks for guidance, you should not respond by laying down the law. We propose, therefore, that this General Assembly not exercise its right to render a constitutional interpretation. We propose, rather, that it offer the "definitive guidance" requested. . . . We believe this recommendation, if adopted, will provide this policy statement with more "staying power" throughout the church than one which unnecessarily calls into question the constitutional rights of the presbyteries in the ordination process.[21]

Rev. John A. Huffman Jr., a second member of the drafting committee, offered a similar comment from the floor of the Assembly: "We have endeavored to give the presbyteries that definitive guidance which they have requested without pre-empting their constitutional rights and responsibilities."[22]

According to these statements from the drafting committee, the delegates were not voting on church law, much less a constitutional provision, when they enacted the "definitive guidance" sought by the presbyteries. Thus, when the Stated Clerk ruled otherwise, many felt betrayed. As we shall see, the scope and effect of this "definitive guidance" resolution would be litigated in numerous ecclesiastical trials over the next fifteen years.

Chris Glaser's path to ordination had been blocked, but he went in a different direction. West Hollywood Presbyterian Church had been doing ministry in the gay community as early as the sixties. In 1977, Glaser became founding director of the Lazarus Project, which received funding from the Mission Development Committee of the national church as well as from the synod, presbytery, and especially the West Hollywood congregation. Along with Bill Johnson's Maranatha at Riverside in Manhattan, Glaser's Lazarus Project became a paradigm of a local gay ministry that others would later emulate. The Lazarus Project also served an educational function, inviting noted speakers such as John Boswell, Bernadette Brooten, and Virginia Mollenkott. Glaser served as executive director for ten years, and later, he was the editor of *Open Hands*, the award-winning, pan-denominational publication. He was finally ordained by the MCC in 2005.[23] He continues his advocacy as author and speaker.

Let us pause to see where we are on our roadmap. Pastor Bill Johnson had been ordained in the UCC in 1972, and by decade's end, the UCC had adopted a progressive sexuality statement that affirmed gays and lesbians. The Episcopal Church was mired in heavy homophobia in a reactionary response to the approval of female ordination in 1976 and the ordination of an out lesbian in 1977. The 1979 Episcopal General Convention rejected the recommendations of its own task force and opposed LGBT ordination, but many bishops had signed a "statement of conscience" that indicated they would ordain whom they chose to ordain. Except for a minor flap over funding the original gathering that resulted in the formation of Lutherans Concerned, the Lutherans were a full decade away from significant confrontation. Later, we will see how the Methodist reaction to the first out gays was especially oppressive, with purges of gays and lesbians in seminaries and in the bureaucracy of the church.

When Rev. David Bailey Sindt stood on a chair in 1974 and asked, "Is anyone else out there gay?" Presbyterian gays were out. At first, the church didn't know how to respond, but as the decade wound down, the gatekeepers were firmly in control. The initial Presbyterian skirmishes proved to be bitter defeats for the naively optimistic cadre of gays and lesbians and their supporters. The harsh judgment of the church, "homosexuality is not God's wish for humanity," darkened the dawn of the decade of the eighties. The church needed more light.[24]

NOTES

1. The traditional 4-H motto. From the website of the National 4-H History Preservation Program, accessed May 16, 2013, http://4-hhistorypreservation.com/History/M-C-P/.

2. The account of Pastor David Bailey Sindt is based on his biographical profile on the website of the Lesbian, Gay, Bisexual and Transgender Religious Archives Network, accessed December 9, 2011, http://www.lgbtran.org/Profile.aspx?ID=33.

3. White, "Homosexuality, Gay Communities," 162.

4. This was the first issue of the first volume of the newsletter that would become *More Light Update*. "Letter of David Bailey Sindt," *More Light Update* vol. 17, no. 3 (January–February 1997). In the first few years, the group went through several name changes before settling on Presbyterian Lesbian and Gay Caucus (PLGC). In the late nineties, it became More Light Presbyterians (MLP).

5. James D. Anderson, "The Lesbian and Gay Liberation Movement in the Presbyterian Church (USA), 1974–1996," *Journal of Homosexuality* vol. 34, issue 2, 41–42. Anderson was associate dean and professor in the School

of Communication, Information, and Library Studies at Rutgers University and served as editor of *More Light Update* from 1980 through 2003.

6. Glaser, *Uncommon Calling: A Gay Christian's Struggle to Serve the Church*, by Chris Glaser (Louisville: Westminster John Knox Press, 1988), 1.

7. Glaser, *Uncommon Calling*, 145–46.

8. Ibid., 152-53.

9. Glaser, *Uncommon Calling*, 160–61. John Boswell published half a dozen books on gay history. His first and most famous, originally published in 1980, was *Christianity, Social Tolerance, and Homosexuality* (Chicago: University of Chicago Press, 1980). This text was reprinted in 1987 and 2005.

10. Glaser, *Uncommon Calling*, 166–67.

11. Ibid., 170.

12. Ibid., 167–71.

13. United Presbyterian Church in the United States of America, 190th General Assembly (1978). *Blue Book I: Report on the Work of the Task Force to Study Homosexuality* (San Diego: United Presbyterian Church [U.S.A.], May 16–24, 1978), 201.

14. United Presbyterian Church in the United States of America, *The Church and Homosexuality*, (San Diego: United Presbyterian Church [U.S.A.], 1978), 47.

15. Ibid.

16. A phrase borrowed from Virginia Ramey Mollenkott, Foreword to *Uncommon Calling*, by Chris Glaser, x.

17. Glaser, *Uncommon Calling*, 175–77.

18. United Presbyterian Church in the United States of America (UPC[U.S.A.]). *Minutes* (1978), part I, 213–67 (quotation on p. 265).

19. Glaser, *Uncommon Calling*, 198.

20. "In an Overture to the General Assembly, Long Island Presbytery Challenges State Clerk William Thompson's Interpretation of Last Year's G.A. Action," *More Light Update* vol. 17, no. 6 (July–August 1997).

21. Quoted by James D. Anderson, "The Lesbian and Gay Liberation Movement," 47.

22. General Assembly Daily News, May 23, 1978, 4, quoted in *More Light Update* vol. 17, no. 6 (July–August 1997).

23. Christ Glaser, Private e-mail to the author, August 29, 2012.

24. Pastor Sindt continued his advocacy efforts until his life was cut short as an early victim of the AIDS epidemic in 1986. He was one of thirteen persons inducted into the Chicago Gay and Lesbian Hall of Fame at a ceremony

on Wednesday, October 25, 1995, at the Cultural Center in Chicago. The Rev. Jeff Doane, pastor of Lincoln Park Presbyterian Church (LPPC), a More Light church where David had been an active leader, accepted on David's behalf. Mayor Daley presented the award. David lived alone, but his friends at LPPC formed a team to care for him in his home during the last months of his life. Each evening, someone prepared dinner, and they shared the meal. LPPC continues this ministry by taking a Sunday evening meal to the residents of a Chicago House facility. David's own home became the first Chicago House residence owned by the agency. LPPC still has some irises from David out front. More Light Presbyterians have named their annual service award after him. Karen Muller, "PLGC Founder Named to Hall of Fame," *More Light Update* vol. 16, no. 7 (February 1996).

Bill Silver was also an active campaigner for a few years, but he eventually pursued a career in graphic design following his disappointment with the church in 1982. When he came out during seminary, he sent birth announcements to family and friends. He also died of complications of AIDS in 2007.

* 36 *

Judicial Roadblocks

In the late nineteenth century, the Romanesque bell tower of a brown and red sandstone church building became the dominant landmark of an upper-west side neighborhood of New York City. A century later, high-rise apartments dwarfed the still-proud structure, which had become an anomaly among its skyscraping neighbors. In 1978, within months of the oppressive "definitive guidance" of the General Assembly, it was not the architecture but a statement of dissent issued by the congregation of West-Park Presbyterian Church that made this congregation stand apart from its Presbyterian neighbors around the country.

Manhattan was a pan-denominational wellspring of gay and lesbian ministries in the seventies. Father Clement's Church of the Beloved Disciple thrived in mid-Manhattan in the early years of the decade. In 1977, at the Church of the Holy Apostles, Bishop Paul Moore had ordained lesbian Ellen Marie Barrett, triggering the "height of homophobia" in the Episcopal Church. The Methodist bishop of the New York Annual Conference was in the midst of an unsuccessful attempt to oust gay Pastor Paul Abels from Washington Square UMC in Greenwich Village after a 1977 article in the *New York Times* publicized the covenant services performed there. In 1978, UCC pastor Bill Johnson founded Maranatha, a gay outreach ministry of Riverside Church, another iconic congregation of the upper-west side along with West-Park. For eight years, gay pride marches along Fifth Avenue had celebrated the Stonewall anniversary.

Now, it had come to the Presbyterians, and West-Park announced in September 1978 that it was stepping out on the journey toward full inclusion despite the policy adopted at the Presbyterian General Assembly earlier that summer. Indeed, the West-Park statement was intended as a rejection of the denominational action.

> West-Park Church affirms the civil rights of all persons . . . this community of faith welcomes as members homosexual persons who both seek and have found Christ's love.
>
> This local congregation will not select one particular element from a person's total humanity as a basis for denying full participation and service in the body of Christ. Nor will this community of faith condemn or judge our brothers and sisters who declare their faith in Jesus Christ as Lord and Savior and promise discipleship to Him. We affirm that in meeting each other in Christian love, God's spirit frees us all to live and grow, liberated from the oppression invoked upon us by ourselves and others.
>
> Within this context, West-Park Presbyterian Church reaches out to Christian and non-Christian homosexual persons with a ministry of support, caring and openness—a ministry in which the creative, liberating power of the Holy Spirit rules and guides.[1]

This public affirmation of full inclusion became the first "More Light" statement. A few months later, at a February 1979 "first annual winter meeting," PLGC decided to spread the idea of More Light congregations.

> Saturday's discussion groups reported their recommendations. Highlights included the suggestion, greeted enthusiastically, that PGC try to identify MORE LIGHT congregations—congregations in which gay people will be welcomed as full participants in the Body of Christ without having to hide or deny their sexual orientation, congregations anxious and willing to receive more light on questions of life style, sexuality, feminism, and mission and ministry with all peoples.[2]

The More Light movement had been born, and similar programs would soon follow: the UMC Reconciling Congregations (RCP—1982),

the Lutheran Reconciling in Christ (RIC—1984), and the UCC Open
and Affirming (ONA—1985). Nearly twenty years later in the late
nineties, PLGC would merge with the network of welcoming congregations, and their organization would be called More Light Presbyterians.

Less than five years after West-Park Presbyterian had issued the first
More Light statement, a Presbyterian congregation on the opposite end
of New York state issued their own. On June 15, 1983, the session (church
council) of Westminster Presbyterian of Buffalo adopted a More Light
Statement that asserted:

> The Session therefore declares this congregation to be a More
> Light congregation, extending to all of its members the oppor-
> tunity for leadership. This includes the right of homosexual per-
> sons to be ordained as elder and deacon. It is our belief that sexual
> orientation has no bearing on one's ability to benefit from and
> to contribute to the life of the church. Rather, we are bound
> together by God's love in ways that transcend differences.

As we have seen, polity influences policy. The congregational polity
of the UCC allowed a local association to ordain William Johnson in
1972 while the rest of the UCC nationally could only watch. The autonomy of Episcopal bishops allowed progressive dioceses to ordain openly
gay and lesbian persons well before the denomination as a whole sanctioned LGBT clergy. For the Presbyterians, a different polity was at play,
a structure that deemed local leaders to be ordained. Thus, when the
national church decreed that "unrepentant homosexual practice does not
accord with the requirements for ordination," the chill penetrated to the
heart of congregational mission and ministry.

> [T]here is a big difference between the More Light Churches . . .
> and their counterparts in other denominations. In none of these
> other denominations is it illegal, under church law, to permit full
> participation by lesbian and gay Christians at the congregational
> level in such roles as a member of a governing council or in special
> ministries to those in need. But it is illegal under Presbyterian law,
> which prohibits the ordination of any open, self-affirming, "non-
> repentant" homosexual as deacon or elder by the session of a local

congregation. Unlike most other denominations, local leaders in the Presbyterian Church—our deacons and elders—are ordained under the same standards (apart from education and training) as our ministers. This makes the apartheid policies of the [Presbyterians] the most restrictive of any mainline denomination.[3]

Because Westminster asserted the right of gays and lesbians to be their local leaders—deacons and elders—their policy would be the subject of an ecclesiastical trial and appeals for the next several years. The case would become known by the name of one of the litigant congregations—*Blasdell* (Union Presbyterian Church of Blasdell)—and the 1985 decision would serve as bedrock to a decade of judicial activism to restrict gay and lesbian ordination.

According to the constitution and earlier cases construing the constitution, it was the prerogative of presbyteries to test the qualifications of ordination candidates. When the "Supreme Court" of the Presbyterian Church said that the General Assembly could restrict the authority of the presbyteries to ordain whom they chose, it was a significant overreaching, and dissenting opinions of the court over the next decade would criticize the majority decisions. With each succeeding case, the minority grew stronger, and their opinions grew more critical. Finally, after ten years, seven commissioners of the General Assembly Permanent Judicial Commission (GAPJC) bluntly challenged *Blasdell's* constitutionality, and the issue of gay ordination was thrown back to the Presbyterian legislators, the commissioners (delegates) to General Assembly. That's the overview, now let us look at the particulars.

Blasdell began when seven congregations of the Presbytery of Western New York submitted a resolution to the presbytery (the so-called "Atkinson Resolution") that urged the presbytery to order Westminster to rescind its More Light Statement.[4] Instead, the presbytery merely requested that Westminster submit an "overture" to General Assembly for "study, debate, and action" that would affirm the rights of presbyteries and congregations to determine ordination qualifications. The presbytery refused to step in.

Not satisfied, the seven complaining congregations grew to twelve, and they each issued complaints against their presbytery for refusing to overrule Westminster. Their twelve complaints were consolidated for a trial before the Permanent Judicial Commission of the Synod of the Northeast.[5]

On June 18, 1984, the Synod court dismissed the complaints, ruling that the resolution of General Assembly 1978 was merely guidance but not law—precisely what the chair of the drafting committee had said in open floor debate prior to passage of the resolution. Since that resolution was not controlling, the Synod Judicial Commission reasoned, there was nothing in the laws or constitution of the church that "precluded a local congregation from electing and ordaining self-affirming and practicing homosexuals." The Synod court was chaired by Willard Heckel, the dean of Rutgers University Law School and formerly the General Assembly moderator.[6] Heckel had also served on the task force leading up to General Assembly 1978, and he had come out privately to the task force in a burst of emotion following fellow task force member Chris Glaser's speech to the task force.

Westminster had won at the level of the presbytery and now at the level of synod, but the litigant congregations weren't finished; they appealed to the Permanent Judicial Commission of the General Assembly (GAPJC), the highest Presbyterian Court of the land, a virtual Presbyterian "Supreme Court." This court consisted of a majority of men, and all but one voted to reverse the Synod's decision. All but one of the women voted to affirm. We have previously suggested that misogyny and homophobia are closely related and have free rein in patriarchal church bodies, and the decision of the men compared to the women of the GAPJC offered compelling corroboration. The patriarchal traditions of the church held firm.

The GAPJC ruled against Westminster in February, 1985, in the case that would be referred to as *Blasdell* and that would serve as the foundation for later cases:

> Based upon the foregoing, it is our considered opinion, and we so find, that the "Definitive Guidance" of the 190th General Assembly (1978) . . . on the issues of ordination of self-affirming, practicing homosexuals were, in fact and in substance, authoritative interpretations of the Constitutions as they were then and

as the Constitution presently exists. Therefore, it is unconstitutional for the Church to ordain any self-affirming, practicing, and unrepentant homosexual as elder, deacon, or minister of the Word.[7]

Although the men on the PJC had outnumbered and outvoted the women, four women and one man would have the last word with their dissenting opinion. First, the dissent noted that the majority was breaking with the Judicial Commission's own precedent, established in a 1962 case, which the dissenters quoted:

> It seems to us basic in our system, therefore, that the responsibility of testing the theological qualifications of a minister rests primarily with each presbytery. This is inherent in our policy and the vesting of that authority and responsibility must be scrupulously observed. Were that power invaded by either the Synod or General Assembly violence would be done to one of the basic concepts of our constitutional form of Church government. The review of presbyteries' exercise of that power must be limited, as we think it constitutionally is limited, to the most extraordinary grounds.[8]

Apparently, for the male majority, keeping gays and lesbians out of the sessions and ministries of local congregations constituted "extraordinary grounds" that justified "invading" local power and "doing violence" to one of the basic concepts of Presbyterian polity.

The minority of the court raised a second constitutional argument in conflict with the majority decision. The dissent quoted from the Presbyterian constitution . . . "No persons shall be denied membership because of race, ethnic origins, worldly condition, or any other reason not related to profession of faith" . . . and concluded with a ringing indictment of the majority decision . . . "this is the kind of discriminatory treatment we have been taught to abhor."

In 1992, the Presbyterian "Supreme Court" issued a pair of companion decisions that affirmed and extended *Blasdell*. The first case interrupted the process of ordination of a lesbian woman, Lisa Larges, to be a minister of word and sacrament, and the companion case precluded a previously ordained lesbian, Rev. Janie Spahr, from accepting a call to pastoral ministry.

Following graduation from St. Olaf College in Northfield, Minnesota, in 1985, Larges came under the care of the Twin Cities Presbytery as a candidate for ordination to the office of minister of word and sacrament in 1986. She satisfied all requirements during seminary and the candidacy process. On February 28, 1991, in preparation for her final interview with the committee on preparation for ministry (COPM), she came out to the COPM by letter and advised them that she was a lesbian. Nevertheless, she was certified by the presbytery. Larges would later credit the COPM's continuing and enthusiastic confirmation of her calling for encouraging her forward on her journey.[9]

However, watchdogs intervened and brought judicial proceedings to overturn the certification of the presbytery. Eventually, the gatekeepers were successful, and the GAPJC affirmed the law late in the year in 1992, but, strikingly, several members of the judicial commission offered a strongly worded concurrence that challenged the law without overruling it.

> We believe that there are multiple and severe flaws in the policy statement, which weaken its status as "definitive guidance" or "authoritative interpretation" of the Constitution. We believe that in several respects the policy statement detrimentally, and perhaps unconstitutionally, limits or restricts other provisions of the Constitution, including but not limited to qualifications for membership and the church's commitment to openness and inclusiveness. We empathize with those who feel the pain of having their God-given call to ministry thwarted by the processes of the church. Nevertheless, we conclude that while the "law" is destructive of the peace, unity and purity of the church, it is the law. As commissioners of the General Assembly Permanent Judicial Commission, we believe we are obligated to apply it.[10]

The companion case involving Rev. Janie Spahr not only affirmed *Blasdell*, but actually extended it by gutting the so-called "grandparent" amendment that protected LGBT clergy ordained before the "definitive guidance" of the 1978 General Assembly resolution. The grandparent amendment stated that the 1978 resolution "shall not be used to affect negatively the ordination rights of any United Presbyterian deacon, elder, or minister who has been ordained prior to this date."

Rev. Janie Spahr had been ordained in 1974, well before she realized she was a lesbian and four years before the 1978 definitive guidance against LGBT clergy. She had served Presbyterian congregations in Pennsylvania and California. When she realized her sexual orientation in the late seventies, she and her husband amicably divorced and remained close friends (she refers to herself as "wife emerita"), but her Oakland congregation asked her to leave when she came out. For the next two years, because her own denomination didn't quite know what to do with this "lesbyterian," she worked with the Metropolitan Community Church in San Francisco's Castro district. In 1982, Pastor Spahr co-founded the Ministry of Light, which became the Spectrum Center, in Marin County, California (resourced by Chris Glaser's Lazarus Project). She would serve as executive director of this multidimensional gay outreach center until 1993.[11]

During this entire period, her clergy credentials had never been questioned, and she eagerly accepted a call to return to Presbyterian parish ministry in November 1991. She would serve as one of four co-pastors at the Downtown United Presbyterian Church of Rochester, New York. The church proudly proclaimed that it had been a "More Light Church since 1979, and was the first church in the Presbytery of Genesee Valley to offer full participation in all aspects of church life to lesbian, gay and bisexual persons. At present openly gay and lesbian elders and deacons serve on boards." The Presbytery of the Genesee Valley approved the call, but then a coalition of one elder, fourteen pastors, and the sessions of nine congregations of the presbytery brought charges before the Permanent Judicial Commission (PJC) of the Synod of the Northeast.[12]

Following a May 1992 trial, the Synod PJC dismissed the complaints, concluding that the grandparent clause meant what it said. Since Spahr had been ordained four years before the ban became effective, the grandparent clause protected her, reasoned the Synod PJC, but the Genesee Valley gatekeepers appealed to the General Assembly Permanent Judicial Commission (GAPJC), the Presbyterian "Supreme Court."

In a decision that shocked court observers and dismayed the Presbyterian LGBT community, the GAPJC voted twelve to one that the call of Downtown United Presbyterian Church to Rev. Janie Spahr would be set aside. Her ordination was not revoked but neither was she eligible to receive a call. But what about the grandparent clause? In a perverse twist of logic that defied the spirit of the amendment, the GAPJC said that only applied to *repentant* homosexuals, who would receive "amnesty for past acts but not license for present or future acts."

As with the companion case of Lisa Larges, a concurring opinion expressed disagreement with the law but nevertheless upheld it in precisely the same language used in the Larges case. One bold voice dared to say the emperor wore no clothes. Commissioner W. Clark Chamberlain was the only one to stand against the others, and his dissenting opinion included these sentiments: "We thus are in danger of ignoring God by acting upon our own prejudice. . . . The definitive guidance is at variance with our knowledge of the world as God made it, and hence is bad exegesis, bad theology, bad psychology, bad science."[13]

Susan Kraemer was a supporter of Pastor Spahr, and she went to the presbytery office on the day the GAPJC would issue its decision. She was optimistic like everyone, and she wanted to be with friends to celebrate when the decision was announced. She would later recall that November, 1992 day:

> I remember where I was when I heard, or should I say "saw," the PJC decision. I was in our Presbytery Office. I had planned it like that. Fool that I was I thought that I and the Presbytery staff who have been so supportive could share these hopeful moments together. So I stood watching our Presbytery Executive dial PresbyTel. We bantered while he waited for an operator. I saw his face change from excited anticipation to grief stricken shock while he slowly shook his head from side to side. In my initial denial, I thought he was merely indicating that no operator had come on the phone yet. Through my denial cut his words, "They voted against—12-1."
>
> I also remember what I did in my anguish. I lifted my arms above me and I slammed my hands down on to the nearest desk

and I bellowed, "NO!" And then as someone put her arms around me, I choked out, "Someone someday is going to have to answer for our pain." And I wept.

As I think about the remaining hours of that day and the following hours and days, I also remember how little surrounding stimuli I could manage. The only thing I wanted to do was to listen to classical or instrumental music. If it had been summer, I would have gone and sat in our garden. I did not want to hear any more words, any more devastating, demeaning, rapacious words.

Nor did I want to hear well meaning but empty sounding words. I needed people simply to sit with me, cry with me, wail with me.

It is risky to begin to hope. It is anguishing to have hope stripped away. Certainly I did not expect the flinging wide of the door to all of us in the Church, but such a significant step in the long process this PJC decision would be.

I have been thinking a lot these days of our lesbian, gay, and bisexual sisters and brothers and supporters who have gone before us to bring us to this time and place. I wish that I knew more of their names. I wish I knew more of their stories. In the midst of my dashed hope, in the midst of my grief, as I struggle to get back up, I wonder how did they do it? How do you continue to do it?[14]

For her own part, Pastor Janie Spahr was resilient and buoyed the spirits of others. Two weeks after the GAPJC decision, she traveled to Rochester to worship with the congregation on Thanksgiving Sunday. Five hundred or so gathered that Sunday morning. Two separate protesters were drowned out by rhythmic clapping. When the worship service resumed, all eyes followed Pastor Spahr as she moved to the front:

When Janie stood in the center of the chancel to speak to the congregation, she immediately deflated the tension with her wonderful humor. "It's Advent! Surprises! Did we have a few this morning, huh? Expectations, whoa! Thank you, God! Good morning, woke us up a little bit, didn't it?"

Janie seemed to catch the eye and ear of everyone in the room when she said, "We have been preparing for this moment for ten years. Justice is ready to be born, and we have been prepared by God to birth it."

The congregation rose to its feet and demonstrated its enthusiasm by loud applause.

Six weeks later, the congregation of Downtown United reconvened to contemplate their next step, and it wouldn't be surrender. For three hours, on January 10, 1993, in a hall filled to overflowing, the congregation considered alternatives. Though Pastor Spahr could not be called to the pastoral ministry, the congregation decided to commission her to be an evangelist to spread "more light" to the denomination, and thus she began her travels as spokesperson for the cause of full inclusion.[15]

Rev. Spahr would move to the forefront of the Presbyterian journey toward full inclusion, and Lisa Larges became her protégé. We will encounter both of them again farther down the road.

There were other judicial cases that were litigated during this time frame.

- St. Luke Presbyterian Church of the Twin Cities Area Presbytery was barred from ordaining a gay elder. In response, the church simply called him an "elder-elect," and he served on the session as a "non-elder."

- Mt. Auburn Presbyterian Church of Cincinnati was forced to "counsel" and "correct" its irregular ordination of a gay elder.

- Central Presbyterian of Eugene, Oregon, ordained both a gay and a lesbian as deacons. In a convoluted decision, the GAPJC said both that the ordinations were irregular but also that they could not be annulled.[16]

In the Larges and Spahr cases of 1992, concurring opinions suggested the law was wrong but that the commissioners felt obligated to uphold it. By 1995, seven of the commissioners on the GAPJC went much further; not only did they say the *Blasdell* decision was wrong, but they would overturn it.

Here's the background. In 1993, First Presbyterian Church of Sag Harbor, New York, ordained two gay persons to the office of elder and deacon. When other congregations in the Presbytery of Long Island objected, the presbytery chose to do nothing, citing ongoing churchwide discussions and anticipated action at GA 1996. On October 29, 1995, the GAPJC agreed with this exercise of discretion. They refused to oust the gay elder and deacon, but did so on the limited basis that the church was currently in dialogue.

While that result was noteworthy in light of prior overzealous judicial activism against gay ordinations, the real heft in the decision came in the concurring opinion of seven of the commissioners, which stated in uncompromising terms that the prior judicial interpretations of the "definitive guidance" of 1978 should be overturned. In particular, the opinion said the 1985 bedrock case of *Blasdell* against a Buffalo, New York, More Light congregation was unconstitutional.

> We believe that . . . "the 1978 Statement" . . . and subsequent reaffirmations and judicial decisions . . . were adopted in violation of the Constitution for the following reasons.

- The General Assembly may not substitute its judgment for that of the ordaining body and ought not to abridge the powers of ordaining bodies except in the most extraordinary situations and for the most extraordinary reasons.

- To the extent that the General Assembly, through the 1978 Statement, attempts to usurp this authority and substitute its judgment for that of individual sessions, such action is unconstitutional.

- By imposing an arbitrary standard, the 1978 Statement would preclude sessions from carrying out their responsibilities in applying constitutional standards for examination, ordination and installation of elders and deacons

- In that the conclusion reached in the 1978 Statement can in no way be considered to be an "essential" of the Reformed faith and polity but, rather, consists of a detail on which reasonable people within the Reformed tradition

may have honest differences of opinion, the 1978 Statement, if it constitutes an "authoritative interpretation,"
unconstitutionally hinders officers in legitimately exercising freedom of conscience in respect to the interpretation
of Scripture.

- Finally . . . the *Book of Order* cannot be amended by a
  "definitive guidance." Decisions by this court and statements issued or actions taken by the General Assembly
  have erred in treating the 1978 statement as an authoritative interpretation or properly enacted amendment of the
  Constitution. *Blasdell* was wrongly decided and, like a
  house built on a foundation of sand, what has followed in
  reliance on *Blasdell* and its progeny is equally flawed and
  cannot stand. If the General Assembly wishes to change or
  amend the constitutional law of the Church, it must do so
  in accordance with the *Book of Order* through established
  process for amendments.[17]

The concurring Presbyterian commissioners correctly remembered
their own history. The Adopting Act of 1729 and the Swearingen Commission of 1927 clearly stood for the proposition that presbyteries, not
General Assembly, were to consider the qualifications of candidates for
ordination, and that the General Assembly could not predetermine what
was "essential and necessary."

For a decade, the Presbyterian "Supreme Court" had kept gays and
lesbians out of congregational leadership and pulpits. With this October
1995 Sag Harbor decision, the GAPJC had called itself out by acknowledging its overreaching. Suddenly, the issue of gay and lesbian ordination
would be thrown into the laps of the commissioners (delegates) of General Assembly, and Presbyterian eyes turned toward Albuquerque, New
Mexico, the site of General Assembly 1996.

Before we head to the Land of Enchantment, we will spend some
time with the Presbyterian pilgrims we have encountered on this journey,
remembering the anguished cry of Susan Kraemer, "How do you continue to do it?"

Along the way, we'll bump into their adversaries.

NOTES

1. "After 33 years: Hallelujah, Amen," West-Park Presbyterian Church, New York, N.Y., West-Park Press (blog), updated May 13, 2011, accessed March 24, 2012, http://west-parkpress.blogspot.com/2011/05/after-33-years-hallelujah-amen.html.

2. Although this is believed to be the first More Light church statement, credit should also be given to West Hollywood Presbyterian Church in Los Angeles, which had previously offered a full-scale gay outreach; the 1979 welcoming statement of Munn Avenue Presbyterian Church of East Orange, New Jersey, was the first that included the self-designation of "More Light." "New York Church Acts on G.A. Recommendations," *More Light Update* vol. 17 no. 6 (July–August 1997).

3. Anderson, "The Lesbian and Gay Liberation Movement," 45

4. Except as noted, the account of the judicial case of Westminster Presbyterian Church of Buffalo, New York, is derived from the official opinion in Presbyterian Church (USA) General Assembly, Permanent Judicial Commission, Union Presbyterian Church of Blasdell, New York, et al. v. The Presbytery of Western New York, Remedial Case 197–9 (February 17, 1985).

5. The Presbyterian Church (USA) has more than 11,000 congregations, which are organized into 173 presbyteries (district governing bodies) and 16 synods (regional governing bodies). From the official website of the PC(USA), accessed March 26, 2012, http://oga.pcusa.org/section/departments/mid-councils/links/.

6. Anderson, "The Lesbian and Gay Liberation Movement," 46.

7. Union Presbyterian Church of Blasdell, New York, et al. v. The Presbytery of Western New York.

8. Dissenting opinion in Presbyterian Church (USA), General Assembly, Permanent Judicial Commission, Union Presbyterian Church of Blasdell, New York, et al. v. The Presbytery of Western New York, quoting from Anderson v. Synod of New Jersey (*Minutes*, UPC[U.S.A.], 1962, Part I, 316, 325).

9. *Lisa Larges, Ordination Candidate for over 20 Years, Tells Her Story*, accessed March 29, 2012, http://www.youtube.com/watch?v=k7rx0VwvZNk.

10. Permanent Judicial Commission, General Assembly, Gary J. LeTourneau et al. v. The Presbytery of the Twin Cities Area, Remedial Case 205-4 (1992).

11. Profile of Rev. Dr. Jane Adams Spahr, on the website of the Lesbian, Gay, Bisexual, and Transgender Religious Archives Network, accessed March 28, 2012, http://www.lgbtran.org/Profile.aspx?ID=1.

12. Except as noted, the account of the judicial case of Janie Spahr and Downtown United Presbyterian Church of Rochester is derived from the official opinion in Presbyterian Church (USA), General Assembly, Permanent Judicial Commission, Ronald P. Sallade et al. v. Presbytery of Genesee Valley, Remedial Case 205-5 (1992).

13. Ronald P. Sallade et al. v. Presbytery of Genesee Valley.

14. This is but a portion of Susan Kraemer's lament printed in "Wanderings in Grief and Rage," *More Light Update* (February 1993).

15. "Janie Spahr, Evangelist," *More Light Update* (March 1993).

16. Anderson, "The Lesbian and Gay Liberation Movement," 51.

17. Permanent Judicial Commission, General Assembly, Central Presbyterian Church v. Presbytery of Long Island, Remedial Case 208-4 (October 29, 1995)

* 37 *

How Do You Continue to Do It?

Rev. David Bailey Sindt had organized the first Presbyterian gay caucus by holding a sign high at the 1972 UPC General Assembly. Sindt had also served as resource person for other homophile organizations, but his advocacy would be cut short in the early eighties when he contracted the AIDS virus, and he died in 1986. Bill Silver joined in by attempting to become the first openly gay Presbyterian to be ordained, and his presbytery sought "definitive guidance." Chris Glaser served on the Task Force whose report was rejected by the 1978 commissioners, followed by a decree from Stated Clerk William Thompson that the "definitive guidance" of the Assembly was church law. Professor James D. Anderson had become the editor of *More Light Update* in 1980.

Prior to the 1982 UPC General Assembly, Glaser and Silver met with Stated Clerk William P. Thompson and shared their strategy (naive in light of his 1978 decree and follow-up behavior). They intended for friendly commissioners to argue to the General Assembly that the Southern Presbyterians, soon to merge with the UPC of the northern Presbyterians, allowed presbyteries and congregations to retain ordination discretion regarding gays and lesbians. Thompson betrayed their trust and arranged to have the stated clerk from the Southern Presbyterian church immediately refute that argument on the floor. After that betrayal, Silver left the Presbyterian Church and was no longer involved with PLGC.[1]

Glaser and Anderson pressed on and others joined the journey. PLGC had maintained a "ministry of presence" at annual General

Assemblies since 1975, and the scope of that presence increased during the eighties. By 1980, PLGC was allowed to rent space in the exhibit hall (previously, the group enjoyed the hospitality of the peace and justice organization known as the Witherspoon Society). PLGC hosted annual luncheons and rented a hospitality suite. Circulation of *More Light Update* increased. Each year, the candidates for moderator would be questioned regarding their attitudes toward homosexuality. PLGC also participated in congregational, presbytery, and synod events.[2]

At the 1987 General Assembly, PLGC and allies, especially the Presbytery of Cayuga-Syracuse in upstate New York, had proposed that the church undertake a current study of human sexuality. The Committee on Justice and Rights of Persons moved a floor resolution to that effect, and the commissioners agreed. Isabel Rogers, the moderator of that General Assembly, was a friend of PLGC; when she was assigned responsibility for creating the task force, she ensured that PLGC and allies would be well-represented. With good reason, PLGC eagerly looked forward to the process of study and discussion that would occupy the remaining years of the decade. The task force report would be submitted to the 1991 General Assembly.[3]

But just as the PLGC grew in size and status, so did their formal opposition.

The Presbyterian Lay Committee and their press organ, *The Layman* magazine, had entered the fray over LGBT issues in the late seventies. The Lay Committee had been around as a conservative irritant since 1965, railing against a perceived shift away from biblical ethics toward "cultural and social values." Much like the Institute for Religion and Democracy (introduced earlier in the Episcopal section), the self-described pillars of the Lay Committee were:

> People of means and action. Besides being leaders in their churches, they were leaders in corporate America.
>
> The Presbyterian Lay Committee began in 1965 with elders who loved the Lord Jesus Christ. They loved the Presbyterian Church. They loved the Bible. They loved the Reformed heritage. . . . Although the PCUSA has wavered, the Lay Committee has stood firm. In the midst of a rising tide of cultural accom-

modation in the PCUSA, the Lay Committee has maintained at every turn the veracity of God's Word, the authority of God's Son and the present power of God's Holy Spirit to transform sinners even today.[4]

From its inception, the Lay Committee existed in tension with denominational leadership; their *modus operandi* appealed to the fears, prejudices, and base instincts of the laity by claiming that church leadership was leading the denomination down a slippery slope to ruin. At the 1990 General Assembly, their tactics got them in trouble, resulting in rules revisions pertaining to outside organizations (which also spilled over to PLGC), and the moderator at GA 1995 unsuccessfully attempted to have *The Layman* censured: popular in the pews, not so at denomination headquarters.

In 1989, PLGC's distribution of educational materials really fired up the gatekeepers. *I think I might be a lesbian, now what do I do? I think I might be gay, now what do I do?* A pair of brochures that addressed these questions were distributed at the PLGC booth at the 1989 Presbyterian Youth Triennium. Written by gay and lesbian youth, the brochures frankly discussed sensitive issues: *What does it mean to be gay (or lesbian)? How do I know? Am I normal? Whom should I tell? AIDS? How do I like myself? Books? Hotlines?* Certainly, the most provocative section dealt with engaging in sex "when you're ready."[5]

The Youth Triennium and the brochures distributed by PLGC provided the Lay Committee with the opportunity to launch an attack. The September/October 1989 issue of *The Layman* included an article entitled, "Gay/Lesbian Caucus Promotes Lifestyle at Youth Triennium." Polluting the minds of the youth with gay propaganda—that's how *The Layman* characterized the brochures distributed at the Youth Triennium, and this became the issue to frighten the folks in the pews. They were successful, and several overtures rose in the presbyteries to rebuke PLGC and outlaw the brochures. *More Light Update* reprinted such an overture arising in the Presbytery of Detroit. The overture stated, *inter alia*:

Whereas . . . PLGC had a booth at the Presbyterian Youth Triennium in 1989 and handed out non-Christian, secularly produced and PLGC endorsed brochures promoting homosexual practices . . . the only people [PLGC] represents are the homosexuals and the feelings and concerns of the heterosexuals are ignored . . . [the brochures] were solely based on obtaining sexual satisfaction in an un-Christian manner and any ethics were sadly missing . . . [the brochures] state that being homosexual is "normal" and implies that God approves . . . .

Therefore, be it resolved . . . that the General Assembly rebuke PLGC, direct PLGC to refrain from distributing the brochures, [and] continue a dialogue on homosexuality without infringing on the rights and beliefs of heterosexual members of this denomination.[6]

Although this particular overture did not result in General Assembly action, it demonstrates the effect of the fearmongering emanating from the Lay Committee. The privileged perspective of the normative group needed protection.

In the late eighties, Bethany Presbyterian of Sacramento was a bustling, thriving congregation. Because of the congregation's strong, service-oriented presence in the community, Bethany would soon receive the Ecumenical Service Award presented by the General Assembly. Rev. Scott Anderson, their head pastor, was an integral part of their successful ministries.

But then he was outed.

He chose to resign to avoid the "scorn," "derision," and an "enormous backlash" that would split the congregation, and he assumed he would merely fight a losing battle that would end with his defrocking anyway.[7] Anderson would later reflect:

Getting outed at Bethany was both the best and worst moment of my life. On the one hand, it was so freeing and empowering to finally be honest about the truth of who I am. On the other hand, it forced me to step away from my passion. The gay issue had never been part of my ministry at Bethany; it hadn't played any role at all in our conversations there. When out of the blue it became the conversation, I thought it best if I voluntarily resigned from Bethany. I didn't want the tumult caused by my staying to ultimately prove disruptive to the life of the church.[8]

Pastor Anderson's outing and resignation serve as prelude to the tumultuous nineties. Anderson would later become one of the preeminent pilgrims on the last leg of the Presbyterian journey toward full inclusion two decades later. As he cast off on his own journey, Pastor Scott Anderson chose not to rock the boat; that would come later. It would be a matter of scruple.

Stated Clerk William Thompson was no friend of PLGC in the late seventies and early eighties, but by 1990 he had experienced a conversion. After Rev. Scott Anderson's outing in 1989, Rev. Anderson did plenty of public speaking, and he reported on Thompson's change of heart:

> [In 1990] he and his wife Mary had come to an adult education class at Nassau Church to hear me tell my story of leaving the Presbyterian ministry. Bill and Mary invited me for lunch at their home, with other members of the church, and then offered to drive me to the airport for my trip back to California. At the end of the hour drive, as he helped me unload my suitcase from the car, Bill Thompson turned to me and said, "I believe our church has made a mistake."[9]

———•———

Chink. Chink. Chink. Chink.
All was silent save the sound of metal on metal, hammer on nail.
Chink. Chink. Chink. Chink.
Four slow, rhythmic taps.
Chink. Chink. Chink. Chink.
Another stepped to the cross and nailed a nail.
Chink. Chink. Chink. Chink.
Six gay persons pounded the massive spikes.
Chink. Chink. Chink. Chink.
Nine others had carried the heavy wooden cross forward.
Chink. Chink. Chink. Chink.
Silence.
And then rising voices . . . . *"We are a gentle, angry people. We*

are a gay and lesbian people. We are gay and straight together. We are a land of many colors. We are a justice-loving people. We are a resurrection people."[10]

Slowly the cross was carried out as voices swelled, *we are singing, singing for our lives*; many in the assembly reached out to touch the cross-bearers.

The 1991 General Assembly had returned to Baltimore. It was here that eager and naive Chris Glaser had attended his first General Assembly fifteen years earlier, and it was fifty years before that when the Presbyterians had convened in Baltimore to debate whether tobacco-using men could be ordained. Still eager, but now quite savvy, Glaser would be one of those who carried the cross to the front of the plenary hall. James Anderson was there, too, and as editor of *More Light Update* he would write:

> Presbyterian Act-Up, which planned and orchestrated the Baltimore demonstration, was a new, informal organization fighting for lesbian, gay, and bisexual rights in the church. Founded by the Rev. Howard Warren, its leaders are members of PLGC, but there is a distinction. PLGC is the "decency and order" organization . . . while Presbyterian Act-Up is the "Holy Spirit" organization, and in indecent times, the Holy Spirit may not always have the time or patience for orderly procedures.[11]

The floor demonstration was in response to the overwhelming rejection of the report on the task force on human sexuality that originated from a General Assembly resolution in 1987. To his credit, General Assembly moderator Herbert Valentine understood the need for gays and lesbians to express their frustration with the Assembly's rejection of the task force report. He had invited the LGBT leadership to his suite around midnight the evening before to plan the demonstration. Then, after a day of floor debate and a resounding vote to reject the report, Moderator Valentine appealed to the Assembly, "There are persons who feel it is important to affirm the authority of Scripture in this. They have been listened to. There are also persons who have acknowledged themselves as gay and lesbian, bisexual, partners, family and supporters. They need to be pastored to and understood and need to have their voices heard."[12]

Chink. Chink. Chink. Chink. The gays and lesbians were heard.

From the day the report of the task force on human sexuality had been released, the firestorm of angry protest had foretold its rejection by the General Assembly. A week prior to the assembly, the *New York Times* had reported that indignation over the report resulted in requests for more than thirty thousand copies from the Louisville denominational headquarters. "If good reviews sell books, bad reviews sell church reports."[13]

And it wasn't just because the report encouraged ordination of LGBT clergy. And it wasn't just because the report encouraged blessings of same-gender relationships. And it wasn't just because the report suggested a wedding ring wasn't the ultimate criterion of ethical sexual relations, preferring instead a morality based on responsibility, mutuality, and joyful caring. By the time the reader reached the argument that a "massive, deep-seated crisis of sexuality" was due to a patriarchal model that defined sexual relations in terms of dominance and subordination and that the "logical extension of patriarchy," was "heterosexism," they longed for less. True, perhaps. Honest, perhaps. Forward thinking, perhaps. But it was all too much.

Once again, the parallel tracks toward full inclusion followed by the ecumenical denominations intersected. The Episcopalians, Lutherans, and Methodists would also wrestle, an understatement, with human sexuality statements during this period.

NOTES

1. Chris Glaser, "Dedication," *More Light Update* vol. 17 no. 6 (July–August 1997).

2. Anderson, "The Lesbian and Gay Liberation Movement," 44.

3. Ibid., 48–49.

4. "The History of the Presbyterian Lay Committee," on the website of *The Layman Online*, accessed March 27, 2012, http://www.layman.org/About Us/History.aspx.

5. "Youth Triennium," *More Light Update* (March 1990), 5–13.

6. "Overtures Want Lesbian & Gay Youth Back in the Closet," *More Light Updat* (March 1990), 14–15.

7. Comstock, U*nrepentant*, 129.

8. John Shore, "Meet Scott Anderson, Soon To Be the First (Openly) Gay Minister Ordained by Presbyterian USA," October 3, 2011, on the blog of John Shore, accessed March 27, 2012, http://johnshore.com/2011/10/03/meet-scott-anderson-presbyterian-usas-first-openly gay-ordained-minister/.

9. Scott Anderson, "The Conversion of William P. Thompson," *More Light Update* vol. 21, no. 4 (March–April 2001).

10. *Singing For Our Lives*, Words and music by Holly Near, ©1979 Hereford Music (ASCAP). Reprinted with permission.

11. Anderson, "The Lesbian and Gay Liberation Movement," 48–50.

12. Ibid.

13. Peter Steinfels, "Beliefs," *New York Times*, May 25, 1991.

* 38 *

SOPHIA AND A SHOWER OF STOLES

Events of 1993 set the stage for General Assembly 1996. We previously mentioned the late fall '92 ecclesiastical court cases of Rev. Janie Spahr and Lisa Larges that affirmed and extended *Blasdell* even as the opinions of a solid bloc of judges criticized it. It was in 1993 that First Presbyterian Church of Sag Harbor, New York, had ordained two gay persons to the office of elder and deacon, thus setting in motion the judicial case that effectively overturned *Blasdell* in 1995, throwing the issue of LGBT ordination back to the legislators of General Assembly 1996.

There's more.

Upon an overture from the Presbytery of Memphis, the 1993 General Assembly adopted a resolution that invited congregations and presbyteries to a three-year study and discussion of LGBT issues with possible action at General Assembly 1996. It was this pending discussion that the presbytery relied on when they refused to overturn the Sag Harbor ordinations and which the GAPJC had cited as well.

There's more.

In November 1993, a women's conference in Minneapolis had unexpected and unintended consequences. The principal organizer was Mary Ann Lundy, a high-ranking woman in the national office of the Presbyterian Church. The idea for a conference first occurred to her five years earlier in 1988. Lundy's idea coalesced with women at a retreat in Minnesota, and they settled on the name "re-imagining." A group of nearly 150 clergy and laity organized the Re-Imagining Conference, which drew twenty-two hundred people from around the world to Minneapolis in November 1993. The conference was sponsored by the Minnesota, Greater Minneapolis, and St. Paul Area Councils of Churches and supported partially with funds from the Presbyterian Church and other denominations. That many of the female speakers at the Re-Imagining Conference were known or suspected lesbians didn't help.

"Sophia," a biblical metaphor for divine wisdom, served as a re-imagined feminine image of the divine during the conference; for the conservative religious press, "Sophia" became a twisted caricature of a pagan goddess worshiped by heretical, radical feminists.[1] Rituals and images celebrated the birthing, mothering, and sexual roles of women, and the conference used feminine pronouns for God. Howling with glee masked as righteous indignation, *The Layman* (Presbyterian) and *Good News* (Methodist) magazines stoked the fears of the folks in the pews. Here was proof that church leadership was pushing the faithful down a slippery slope straight to the gates of hell.

At a meeting of the Presbyterian Health, Education, and Welfare Association that took place during the ensuing 1994 General Assembly, Conference organizer Mary Ann Lundy made it clear that she had been fired from her position within the church because of her role organizing the Conference, and that the well-heeled influence of the Lay Committee had successfully hounded her out of office.

"[S]he began by looking the editor of the Presbyterian *Layman* (who was sitting in the front row) right in the eye and commenting that she had been followed, photographed and harassed by this man for months, and here he is again, looking for more material to distort."[2]

Remember the Institute on Religion and Democracy (IRD) and their leader, Diane Knippers? In the Episcopal section, we considered the IRD as a Roman Catholic–founded, neoconservative "think tank" that attempted to influence the Episcopal Church early in the twenty-first century through its puppet organization, the American Anglican Council. Later, we will also consider the IRD in its similar attempt to influence the United Methodist Church. The PC(USA) was the third major denomination to feel the nefarious fingers of IRD interference. We will briefly consider the evidence here, but the reader should refer to the Episcopal and the Methodist sections for in-depth analysis of the IRD.

The Re-Imagining movement provided the opportunity for the IRD to assail "radical feminism" and to deny the patriarchal two-thousand-year history of the church. IRD leader Knippers attended a follow-up Re-Imagining conference in 1997 and was the principal author of a manifesto entitled *A Christian Women's Declaration*, published in November 1997, that stated, *inter alia*:

[W]e are troubled by the following developments within our churches:

- The movement to "re-imagine" two thousand years of Christian faith. We repudiate the assumption that Christian faith and teachings were first "Imagined" by men and now should be "re-imagined" by women.

- The substitution of orthodox liturgies, sacraments, and hymnody with radical feminist rituals and songs that focus on women's suffering and victimization and obsessively glorify women's bodies and sexuality.

- The demand for rigid quotas for identical participation of women in church life and work.

- We Will Work to Reverse Detrimental Cultural Trends. . . . We Will Expose the Assumptions at the Foundation of the Radical Feminists' Philosophy. . . . We Will Press for a Renewal of Biblical Orthodoxy in the Church.[3]

In a 2004 *New York Times* article, Parker Williamson, the current leader of the Lay Committee, acknowledged the support from the IRD. Furthermore, as the 2004 General Assembly approached, the IRD's Presbyterian point man, Alan Wisdom, said, "[R]epresentatives of the institute will be there in force, calling attention to any liberal positions coming out of the church, distributing position papers to delegates and lobbying them in a conservative direction."[4]

When erstwhile IRD leader Diane Knippers died, her replacement in 2006 was a Presbyterian from the schismatic Presbyterian Church in America, the splinter that had left the PCUSA in 1973.[5]

Finally, the IRD website notes that its Presbyterian arm, known as "Presbyterian Action," attended the PC(USA) General Assembly of 2008 with "a team of nine steering committee members, volunteers, and staff," and a similar contingent in 2010. There was no mention of General Assembly 2012.[6]

This is merely a quick peek at the IRD vis-a-vis the Presbyterians. For greater detail on this right-wing, "theocon" organization, refer to the preceding Episcopal section and the following Methodist section.

———

PLGC and other observers didn't anticipate any significant actions on LGBT issues at the 1994 General Assembly in Wichita because the church was in the midst of a three-year study and discussion instituted at the last General Assembly in 1993. The process pointed to General Assembly 1996 when LGBT issues would be at the forefront. But, through a quirk in the rules, an unexpected measure came to the floor. At GA 1993, three similar overtures that discouraged same-gender union ceremonies were postponed for discussion, along with other LGBT issues, due to the study process. One of these overtures had not been submitted in a timely fashion at GA 1993, and according to a technicality, such untimely overtures were automatically rolled over to the next GA. Thus, the untimely overture of GA 1993 came before a GA 1994 committee where most expected it would be routinely laid aside for consideration at GA 1996.

> To everyone's surprise, delegates to the General Assembly, many of them angry over the "blasphemy" of the women's re-imagining conference, decided to show the folks back home that they could be tough in stamping out heresy, so a General Assembly committee ignored the advice of church leaders and approved this leftover overture. No one had testified before the committee in favor of it; the committee ignored the pleas of PLGC to leave it alone. When the overture reached the floor of the General Assembly, an angry delegate moved to change the word "inappropriate" to "prohibited." This major change was adopted with little discussion, and the Assembly then approved the revised overture. So now, for the first time in the history of the church,

a proposed constitutional amendment would put lesbian and gay people into the constitution of the church. The proposed change would "prohibit" Presbyterian clergy from "participating" in the blessing of same-sex unions.[7]

But the General Assembly action didn't make it law—not yet. According to Presbyterian rules of procedure, constitutional amendments passed at General Assembly would go out to the presbyteries, which must also pass the amendment to make it effective. One by one, 171 presbyteries around the land considered the measure at their next assembly.

In a shocker, the measure failed! For the first time in history, Presbyterian gays and lesbians celebrated a positive churchwide vote in their favor. Could the tide be turning? Was this a switch in momentum?

Meanwhile, the three-year period of dialogue continued with Albuquerque and the 1996 General Assembly looming. Some discussions were as intended, others, not so much.

Pastor Martha Juillerat jeopardized her ordination when she and her partner, Pastor Tammy Lindahl, set out on a journey by agreeing to participate in the scheduled discussions: "As soon as I signed that witness list, I knew I'd never be able to work in this church again, but I firmly believed that a dialogue process would tell us all what kind of church we really are."[8]

Pastors Juillerat and Lindahl traveled over five states, mostly at their own expense, in order to give their testimony. Their journey began and ended in the Heartland Presbytery, headquartered in Kansas City. On September 16, 1995, Pastor Juillerat addressed her presbytery.

I'm here today because I've come to the end of a long journey.

A little over two years ago, the General Assembly called for a three year period of dialogue on the ordination of homosexuals. They specifically asked the church to listen to the voices of the aggrieved, and called upon any LGBT folk who were in a position to do so, to come out to the church and tell their stories. My partner, Tammy Lindahl, and I signed our names to a national witness list, agreeing to break the long silence that we've lived under as ordained ministers.

Our first experience of dialogue was right here in Heartland Presbytery. Those of you who attended that meeting may remember it as a rare moment of grace, a time when we could agree to disagree, when we could treat each other with respect while struggling to understand another's point of view. It was a decent, orderly experience; John Calvin would have been proud!

Unfortunately, I must say that that was also our *last* real dialogue at that level. Although we've had some wonderful conversations with a number of individual congregations here and elsewhere, on the presbytery and synod level our experiences have ranged from formal debates to public hangings.

Some of the response has bordered on the absurd. We've run across videos by a doctor who has lost his license to practice medicine, so-called change ministries that make outrageous claims but refuse to document them, and proponents of therapies that have been dismissed as quackery by every branch of science and medicine, all presented in the name of "balanced debate." Every attempt imaginable has been made to reduce us to ridiculous stereotypes and to dehumanize us; we've been compared repeatedly to alcoholics, child molesters, predatory perverts, and even people who have sex with animals.

I remain stunned at the viciousness of some of my colleagues in ministry across the church, including one of our own elders here who said at the very beginning of this process that he would rather take us out into a field and shoot us than to talk to us.

So after much soul-searching, I've finally decided that the time has come for me to set aside my ordination as a minister in the Presbyterian Church, and to find a new way to do ministry. I know that God is much bigger than this issue; God is bigger than even this church. Like Jacob, I simply need to go out into the night and wrestle alone with God for awhile. I ask for your prayers in this new journey, as I will continue to pray for you.

Friends, no matter what your opinion is about all this, you can choose to be indifferent or you can choose to make a difference. If the General Assembly is serious about continuing this conversation, then it *must* begin to take direct responsibility for those who are being torn apart by its own actions. And if this is to be true dialogue, then the church *must* dismiss all the outrageous lies and stereotypes. If this debate cannot stand on its own theological, hermeneutical, and scientific merits, then it does not deserve to be debated at all, from any viewpoint. You, as a presbytery, can hold the church accountable for treating *all* of its children with dignity, even in the midst of strong disagreement. I challenge you to do that much, and to commit yourselves to continuing the dialogue right here as well.[8]

Reluctantly, the presbytery accepted the surrender of her clergy credentials, and submitted a letter to General Assembly:

[T]he Committee on Ministry of Heartland Presbytery met with one of our long-standing and dedicated ministers to consider her request that we set aside her ordination. The reason for her request relates to the offensive, sometimes brutal, treatment she has received as she has voluntarily participated in the General Assembly recommended dialogue on the status and role of gays and lesbians in the church within the Synod of Mid-America. While we reluctantly granted her request, considerable pain was felt by all at the meeting. We are impoverished by the absence of the active, energetic, creative participation of this minister as a leader in Heartland Presbytery.[9]

As Martha and Tammy prepared for the appearance before the Heartland Presbytery, they had sought moral support from friends and a demonstration that they were not alone as LGBT ministers. "Send a stole," they had requested, and each stole hanging in the sanctuary would represent a gay person of faith. They hoped for a couple dozen stoles, but they received eighty within a few days, and they kept coming. By the following spring, they had two hundred. The Shower of Stoles was born, which would become a permanent, traveling display, debuting at General Assembly 1996.[10]

As we are about to depart for Albuquerque, let us again check our roadmap. Where are the other denominations at this moment in the mid-nineties? With openly LGBT pastors Bill Johnson and Loey Powell working in UCC headquarters, the UCC had been fully inclusive for years and waited patiently for her denominational partners to catch up. Many Episcopal bishops were exercising their independence and ordaining gays and lesbians to the priesthood. In a last ditch effort, gatekeepers would bring heresy charges against one such bishop; when the ecclesiastical court ruled against them, gay ordination had been given an Episcopal, judicial stamp of approval. Meanwhile, the Lutherans were hopelessly muddled. Their ecclesiastical trials had defrocked a gay minister or expelled congregations that willfully called LGBT clergy following *extra ordinem* ordinations. In 1995, their newly elected presiding bishop would comment with masterful understatement, "we have not yet reached consensus." The Methodists seemed to be going in reverse. Their 1996 General Conference would enact the most restrictive resolutions yet regarding LGBT inclusion, and the end of the decade would see the defrocking or suspension of Methodist clergy who performed covenant ceremonies. LGBT ordination was barely an afterthought for the Methodists.

All roads pointed toward Albuquerque. The Sag Harbor judicial decision of 1995 had removed the judicial impediment to LGBT ordination, dumping the issue in the laps of the commissioners. The three-year process of dialogue instituted in 1993 also called for action at General Assembly 1996.

The Land of Enchantment beckons.

NOTES

1. The book of Proverbs (chapters 1, 8, and 9) presents a personification of divine "Wisdom" as a woman preaching to youth. Oftentimes, this woman is referred to as Lady Wisdom. This personification of divine wisdom is interpreted by many as a feminine image of God. What is more, this Proverbs imagery of divine wisdom has connections to the Johannine treatment of Jesus. Many scholars point to 8:23–24 as forerunner or inspiration for the first verse of the gospel of John: "In the beginning was the Word, and the

Word was with God, and the Word was God." The Proverbs verses read: "The Lord created me at the beginning of his work, the first of his acts of long ago. Ages ago I was set up, at the first, before the beginning of the earth." The Greek word for wisdom is *sophia*, and this usage appears in the early Greek versions of Proverbs. Thus, the "Sophia" referenced by the Christian feminists at the Re-Imagining Conference has a solid biblical basis—hardly a "pagan goddess" as portrayed by the conservative press. For Bible-touting critics, the irony was that they really didn't know the Bible well enough to recognize "Wisdom."

2. Ned Edwards, "Why Mary Ann Lundy was fired," Network News. Summer 94, vol. 14, Issue 3, 9.

3. Ecumenical Coalition of Women and Society, *A Christian Women's Declaration*, September 16, 1997.

4 Laurie Goodstein and David D. Kirkpatrick, *New York Times*, "Conservative Group Amplifies Voice of Protestant Orthodoxy," May 22, 2204.

5. Frederick Clarkson, "New IRD President is a schismatic Presbyterian," *Talk to Action*, accessed May 25, 2013, http://www.talk2action.org/story /2006/3/17/215329/263.

6. From the website of the Institute on Religion and Democracy, accessed May 25, 2013, http://www.theird.org/page.aspx?pid=231.

7. Anderson, "The Lesbian and Gay Liberation Movement," 54.

8. Martha G. Juillerat, "Setting Aside Ordination for the Sake of Dignity and Justice," *More Light Update* vol. 16, no. 7 (February 1996).

9. Ibid.

10. Ibid.

11. "Shower of Stoles Project," on the website of the Institute for Welcoming Resources, accessed August 4, 2012, http://www.welcomingresources .org/sosphistory.htm.

39

FIDELITY AND CHASTITY

The Rio Grande pours out of the Colorado Rockies as a stream of melted snow. As the river crosses into New Mexico, it flows past the Sangre de Cristo (blood of Christ) mountain range before meandering through the high desert plains. Here, the Pueblo people once lived in adobe villages and baked bread in their *hornos* (outdoor ovens). In June 1996 a thousand Presbyterians would gather together to break bread and drink el Sangre de Cristo on the banks of the Rio Grande.

The city of Albuquerque straddles the river as it winds its way toward the Mexican border. As the rays of the setting sun stream across the city, the slopes of the Sandia (watermelon) Mountains provide a soft pink backdrop to the city's eastern edge. Late June temperatures are warm but comfortable in the high desert, but the Presbyterian commissioners and visitors to their 208th General Assembly paid little attention to the weather or the scenery.

The judicial decision of the prior October was a call to action, to be sure. So was the three-year period of discussion that culminated here.

A seminary professor from Princeton University pointed out the apocalyptic expectations of both sides:

> [T]here are those of us who believe that nothing less than the survival of the faith is at stake. . . . The failure to maintain the standards of conduct that the community of faith has long rec-ognized to be normative would compromise the church's unique identity as a covenant people. . . . We are called to obey a God

who commands the covenant community to rid itself of every unsavory influence that might lead it to apostasy and the dishonor of God. We worship a God whose name is Jealous, a God who brooks no compromise.

On the other hand, there are those of us who are equally convinced that the authenticity of the church is in question if it is unchanging and exclusivistic. Again, nothing less than the survival of the faith is at stake for us. . . . The church is unfaithful if it turns its back on those who are marginalized in various ways by society or if the church itself excludes people on the basis of their race, gender, or sexual orientation from full participation in its life and leadership. . . . The church is called to be a community that manifests the inclusive grace and love of God. . . . We worship a God whose name is Compassionate, a God who is sovereign and free to extend grace to any and all.[1]

As commissioners and visitors descended upon Albuquerque, they were aware of survey results that had been released four months earlier in February 1996. The survey indicated that strong majorities of members, elders, and pastors opposed LGBT ordination, but that the margins had decreased by 10–15 percent from a similar survey in 1990.[2]

The commissioners were also aware that numerous presbyteries had offered conflicting proposals. Twenty-four presbyteries had submitted overtures recommending an amendment to the *Book of Order* that would clearly restrict LGBT ordination. Twenty presbyteries suggested the matter be left to individual congregations, a local option. One presbytery wanted more study.[3]

Finally, the commissioners were aware of the attitudes of the three candidates for moderator based on pre-assembly interviews granted to *The Layman* magazine. The clear conservative was John Clark Poling, who said, "Homosexual practice is not within God's purpose for our lives." The clear progressive was Norman Pott who said, "[W]e are violating the ministry of Jesus by rejecting a whole class of people before ever meeting them as human beings." John Buchanan was a moderate who favored the local option; he said, "I wonder if God is not calling us to find a new way to express the church's traditional commitment to faithful marriage and the family as God's good gifts, while respecting our church's traditional commitment to its congregations and Presbyteries as the places where faithful decisions are made about ordination."[4]

Late on Saturday, the Assembly quickly dispensed with the first order of business. John Buchanan was elected to serve as moderator on the second ballot.

PLGC had arrived in Albuquerque in force. In addition to dorm rooms and local hosts opening their homes, PLGC had reserved a block of fifty hotel rooms. PLGC conducted a pre-assembly workshop on Friday before the official Assembly start on Saturday, June 29, and hosted a hospitality suite, exhibit booths, and a Celebration of Reconciliation featuring the Shower of Stoles given by gay or lesbian ministers, elders, deacons, and seminarians and those barred from ordination because of their sexual orientation. Martha Juillerat and Tammy Lindahl administered the Shower of Stoles. More than three hundred stoles were worn in the convention halls. Each stole bore a message from the maker, some named, some anonymous. One read, "You know me. I am your daughter, your pastor. You nurtured me, encouraged me, ordained me. For over 20 years I have served at every governing body level. Yet I cannot tell you my name. For me the risk is still too great. I work and pray for the day when I am free to say who I truly am."[5]

The stole ministry proved to be a powerful experience:

I felt their stares burning through me, trying to get the heart of my soul. Their looks were judging my very right to be there in the same room with them, maybe even in the same world with them. I could feel deep fear, verging on hatred of me and people like me. I was completely caught off guard by their reactions. I could see their emotions well up in their eyes. I felt like I was drinking out of the wrong fountain in the deep South in the 1960s or sitting in the wrong place on the bus. I really thought about running very fast, and very far away. I was very confused about these strong reactions from people. After all, I was only walking through the main hall of General Assembly and none of these people could be threatened by me. After all, I am not that threatening to look at, very late thirties, extra 15–20 pounds, thinning hair, 5' 6½", white guy (actually I look a lot like most of the other people there—except 15–20 years younger), so why were they so moved? Then I remembered I was wearing MY STOLE.

Then my faith soared again when someone smiled at me and said, "Beautiful stole, thank you for being here." Then I increased my field of vision, not to look only at those closest to me, but to include all people in the hall. Many people were smiling back and many were wearing stoles, their own, their friend's, their children's, or a stranger's.[6]

On Sunday evening, PLGC offered an Opening Worship Service. The annual PLGC membership meeting took place mid-week.[7] For the first time, the network of More Light Presbyterian congregations had their own booth. This organization would soon merge with PLGC under the name More Light Presbyterians (MLP).[8]

As the assembly unfolded, all eyes were on the Committee on Ordination and Human Sexuality. Here was the landing zone for the fifty-one conflicting overtures—some wanting an explicit constitutional provision rejecting LGBT clergy and some wanting ordination decisions left to the discretion of local congregations and presbyteries. A crowd of a thousand gathered to listen to the committee hearing; more than a hundred actually spoke.[9]

A clear majority of the committee of fifty favored the prohibition of gay clergy, and they set out to draft an appropriate amendment to the *Book of Discipline*, the Presbyterian constitution, and their recommendation came to be known as the "Fidelity and Chastity amendment" or simply, "Amendment B" (G 6.0106b). While amendment B made no explicit reference to gays or lesbians, it obviously was intended to keep them out of the pulpit. Here is the text of the amendment:

Those who are called to office in the church are to lead a life in obedience to Scripture and in conformity to the historic confessional standards of the church. Among these standards is the requirement to live either in fidelity within the covenant of marriage of a man and a woman, or chastity in singleness. Persons refusing to repent of any self-acknowledged practice which the confessions call sin shall not be ordained and/or installed as deacons, elders, or ministers of the Word and sacrament.

Nineteen of the fifty favored the local option and submitted a minority recommendation, which the floor of the assembly voted down by a margin of 59 percent to 41 percent. The majority recommendation passed by a slightly smaller margin, 57 percent to 43 percent.

The hopeful words of the seven judges in the Sag Harbor judicial case issued in the waning months of 1995 had been erased by the commissioners at General Assembly 1996 and overwritten with the phrase "fidelity and chastity." Without mentioning gays or lesbians explicitly, their exclusion from the pulpit had now been written into the *Book of Order*. Fidelity and chastity would become law.

Once again at the invitation of the moderator, a floor demonstration ensued, reminiscent of the solemn nails in the cross demonstration of GA 1991.

> Nearly a third of the visitors and commissioners marched silently through the hall for nearly a half an hour, breaking into the song, "We Are Marching in the Light of God." The anger was there but faith, hope and love transcended it. Later, a large crowd gathered for a two hour impromptu worship service with many individuals giving personal testimonies of faith and new hope. One was especially moving. An Elder who was in the last stages of AIDS said his first reaction when the Assembly voted was to say to himself, "I will not live long enough to see justice in the Presbyterian Church." After the demonstration, he said he had a second reaction. "I decided to live longer!"[10]

Victory or defeat? Was GA 1996 a step forward on the journey toward full inclusion or a step back? Eighteen years earlier, the infamous 1978 "definitive guidance" had passed with more than 90 percent of the delegates voting for it. Now, only 57 percent supported LGBT exclusion from the ordained ministry. Victory or defeat?

A contributor to *More Light Update* offered encouragement.

> I want us to keep remembering, to not forget what happened in Albuquerque. Because I think in many ways we won. We won

because so many of us came. We won because so many of us learned and had our eyes opened to what it is we need to do on the local level to get our people behind pulpits. We won because we came together, stronger and more unified than ever before. We won because we heard new voices speak out and new faith stories being shared. We won because we came together as a faith community and witnessed to the entire Assembly what it is to be gay and lesbian Christians. We won because we had heterosexual allies in larger numbers than ever before speaking out for us and joining us as members of our family. We won because we spoke the truth of our lives and we let love cast out our fears. We won because we never stopped singing and dancing and believing that justice will come.[11]

Christians are optimists and none more so than LGBT Christians. Amendment B had passed at General Assembly, but to become effective it would need to be adopted by a majority of the 171 regional presbyteries . . . a process that would slowly wind its way around the country, staggered over time as the presbyteries gathered for their assemblies.

Critics of the amendment pointed out that it did more than preclude LGBT clergy; it altered bedrock Presbyterian attitudes toward Scripture and confessions. Historically, the *Book of Discipline* required ordained persons to be "instructed, led, and guided" by confessions, not "conformed" to them. More importantly, the *Book of Discipline* required ordained persons to be obedient to Jesus Christ, not Scripture as Amendment B mandated—a significant distinction. There were many prohibitions of Scripture that the church had long since abandoned, but if rigid obedience to Scripture became the norm, then all sorts of mischief would ensue far beyond issues of LGBT clergy.[12]

The focus on the confessions of the church led to an interesting discussion regarding the Heidelberg Confession, a particularly Presbyterian/Reformed document. Amendment B referred to "practice which the confessions call sin"; however, when reviewing the various confessions recognized by the Presbyterian Church, none of them referenced same-gender sexual behavior—except the Heidelberg Confession, which stated in a question and answer format (emphasis added):

Question: Can those who do not turn to God from their ungrateful, impenitent life be saved?

Answer: Certainly not! Scripture says, "Surely you know that the unjust will never come into possession of the kingdom of God. Make no mistake: no fornicator, or idolater, none who are guilty either of adultery or of homosexual perversion, no thieves or grabbers or drunkards or slanderers or swindlers, will possess the kingdom of God."

Yet, scholars have long known that the term "homosexual" is relatively modern, dating to the nineteenth century. How could the word be in the Heidelberg Confession, which dates to the sixteenth century? What German term in the original had been interpreted to mean "homosexual"? Professor Jack Rogers played the sleuth's role, and he traced the problem to a 1962 interpretation, and he asked the question directly of the still-living interpreters: "[W]hen I asked again, why they chose to insert the phrase 'homosexual perversion' when in fact there was no corresponding phrase in the original, he replied: 'We just thought it was a good idea.'"[13] The insertion was a pure fabrication. The original made no reference whatsoever to any terms remotely connected to same-gender sexual behavior.[14]

So, for all the bluster about conforming to confessions and denouncing that which the confessions call sin, there really was nothing in any confessions that pertained to LGBT relationships. So, too, for biblical translations that include the terms "homosexual" or "sodomite"—modern terms that have no equivalent in the Greek language of the New Testament.

A side note to continuing debate over LGBT inclusion would be reformation of the translation of the Heidelberg Confession to conform to its original language without the insertion of a gratuitous antigay phrase. There appears to be strong momentum, and minimal conservative opposition, to adoption of a revised translation that excises "homosexual perversion" on purely academic grounds rather than LGBT politics. That is, the error is obvious, and intellectual integrity encourages an accurate translation. As of midsummer 2013, more than two-thirds of the presbyteries have adopted the "new ecumenical English translation of the

Heidelberg Catechism." Prospects appear strong for the entire church to adopt this updated translation at the 2014 General Assembly in Detroit.[15]

As the presbytery voting process unfolded regarding Amendment B, it became obvious the vote would be close. When it finally passed, it did so with less than 51 percent voting for it, revealing a deeply divided church. Neither side was pleased. The progressives were angry that discrimination against gays and lesbians had been written into the constitution. Many feared a witch hunt. Conservatives worried that they were losing control, their bare majorities were slipping away, and church leaders seemed to be against them.

Various congregations and two presbyteries—Milwaukee and the Twin Cities—issued statements of dissent. "Jerry Van Marter, a spokesman for the PCUSA, said June 2 that 'several congregations a week that I'm aware of' are voting to adopt covenants of dissent, several versions of which are circulating through the denomination."[16] The Presbytery of the Twin Cities issued two documents—a dissent and an apology to LGBT persons. First, we quote from their dissent.

> Amendment B moves us from the faith-based criteria of the Reformed tradition to behavior-based criteria that place us in judgment of one another. New dividing walls of hostility are built and reconciliation is abandoned.
>
> Therefore, the Presbytery of the Twin Cities Area reaffirms its Scriptural and confessional heritage as an inclusive, welcoming, affirming, liberating, repenting, and reconciling community, being transformed by the power of the Gospel of Jesus Christ. Furthermore, we reaffirm the presbyteries' and sessions' historic right both to determine suitability for ordination and to ordain.
>
> We, the Presbytery of the Twin Cities Area, covenant together to elect, ordain, and install as deacons, elders, and ministers of Word and Sacrament "persons of strong faith, dedicated discipleship, and love of Jesus Christ" whose manner of life is "a demonstration of the Christian gospel in the church and in the world" (G-6.0106), without regard to sexual orientation and without regard to the provisions of Amendment B.[17]

This was a striking act of ecclesiastical disobedience. And here is their apology:

> [The Presbytery of the Twin Cities (PCTA)], this 10th day of June, 1997, acknowledges its corporate participation in a denominational policy offensive to the gospel of Jesus Christ, namely the adoption of Amendment B, and offers this Statement of Apology to all persons whose Christian faith and relationship with the church, as well as their personal God-given dignity, have been assaulted or in any other way diminished by the inclusion of Amendment B in the Constitution of the PCUSA. To those of our Christian sisters and brothers so terribly betrayed by their church we say, "We are truly sorry." Furthermore, with this Statement of Apology the PTCA solemnly pledges to be faithful to Jesus Christ in exhausting all means possible for assuring the just and loving full inclusion of all persons called by God through Jesus Christ to serve and minister in any capacity in the PCUSA.[18]

With presbyteries and congregations in open defiance, church leaders feared for church unity. Moreover, scholars and leaders of the church were troubled by the overreaching amendment—not only because of the onerous effect upon gays and lesbians but because it seemed to write biblical literalism into the constitution; they heard echoes of the Modernist-Fundamentalist debate of seventy years earlier. Even before the presbytery voting process had been completed, moderate and progressive church leaders began to push for a substitute amendment that would retain what they considered to be the traditional and proper understanding of the authority of Scripture and confessions.

The river of melted snow that splashes out of the Rockies doesn't stop in Albuquerque; the Rio Grande merely flows through the city with many bends and dams ahead before journey's end. General Assembly 1996 had settled nothing, except to provide the framework and language for the controversies that would spill into the new millennium.

NOTES

1. Choon-Leong Seow, Preface to *Homosexuality and Christian Community* (Louisville, KY: Westminster John Knox Press, 1996), a new collection of essays by Princeton Seminary faculty members.

2. Presbyterian Panel, Congregational Ministries Division, Presbyterian Church (USA), February 1996.

3. The Presbyterian Church (USA), "Gay/Lesbian Ordination: 1978 to 1997 incl.," on the website of Religious Tolerance, accessed March 30, 2012, http://www.religioustolerance.org/hom_pru10.htm.

4. Referenced in *More Light Update* vol. 16, no. 9 (April 1996).

5. *More Light Update* vol. 17, no. 1 (September–October 1996).

6. James Nicholson, quoted in *More Light Update* vol. 17, no. 2 (November–December 1996).

7. *More Light Update* vol. 16, no. 9 (April 1996).

8. *More Light Update* vol. 17, no. 2 (November–December 1996).

9. Although 203 persons had signed up to speak, due to time constraints, only 103 actually did so. Rogers, *Jesus, the Bible, and Homosexuality*, 118.

10. Rev. Harold Porter, quoted in *More Light Update* vol. 17, no. 2 (November–December 1996).

11. Lainey Rathgeber, quoted in *More Light Update* vol. 17, no. 2 (November–December 1996).

12. The Rev. Charles L. Rassieur, PhD, *More Light Update* vol. 17, no. 2 (November–December 1996).

13. Rogers, *Jesus, the Bible, and Homosexuality*, 115.

14. Letter and article from Louisville Presbyterian Seminary professors Johanna W. Bos and Christopher Elwood on More Light Presbyterian's website, accessed April 3, 2012, http://www.mlp.org/resources/ordination/heidelberg.html.

15. Janet Edwards, "The Passing of the Heidelberg: Just Short of Singing Kumbaya," June 13, 2013, on the website of More Light Presbyterians, accessed June 15, 2013, http://www.mlp.org/2013/06/13/the-passing-of-the-heidelberg-just-short-of-singing-kumbaya/.

16. "Milwaukee Presbyterians Defy New Church Rule," *The Christian Century* vol. 114, issue 19 (June 18, 1997).

17. "Presbyterian (Twin Cities) Resolution of Witness to the Gospel," on the website of Religious Tolerance, accessed April 3, 2012, http://www.religioustolerance.org/hom_pru1.htm.

18. "Presbyterian (Twin Cities) Statement of Apology," on the website of Religious Tolerance, accessed April 3, 2012, http://www.religioustolerance.org /hom_pru2.htm.

* 40 *

AMENDMENT A OR AMENDMENT B?

If one thing was clear from General Assembly 1996 and its aftermath, it was that nothing was clear. Lutheran Presiding Bishop H. George Anderson had understated the Lutheran situation when he noted, "We have not yet reached consensus." So, too, the Presbyterians. The church seemed to be split evenly, and neither side had the upper hand. Though the conservatives had barely held their ground in 1996, the progressives would storm back in 1997 at the General Assembly in Syracuse, New York.

A substitute amendment for consideration at General Assembly 1997, soon known as "Amendment A" or the "fidelity and integrity amendment," (as opposed to "fidelity and chastity") came to life in the committee on the *Book of Order*, under the chairmanship of Laird Stewart.

> Those who are called to office in the church are to lead a life in obedience to Jesus Christ, under the authority of Scripture and instructed by the historic confessional standards of the church. Among these standards is the requirement to demonstrate fidelity and integrity in marriage or singleness, and in all relationships of life. Candidates for ordained office shall acknowledge their own sinfulness, their need for repentance, and their reliance on the grace and mercy of God to fulfill the duties of their office.

PLGC and their allies quickly jumped on board, but conservatives opposed Amendment A. Why? Was it a not a compromise? Conservatives feared the ambiguity. Certainly, a progressive congregation, presbytery, synod, or Judicial Commission might allow gays or lesbians to slip in. Consider the changes:

- Candidates were to be "in obedience to Jesus Christ under the authority of Scripture" rather than being "in obedience to Scripture." This was a return to the traditional Presbyterian framework: a reversal of the biblicism of Amendment B.

- Candidates were to be "instructed by" the historical confessional standards of the church rather than be in "conformity" with those standards. Again, a restatement of traditional understanding.

- Candidates were to "demonstrate fidelity and integrity" in *all* relationships, rather than to be faithful in marriage or celibate if single. LGBT relationships too? The conservatives feared that possibility.

A pair of early actions by General Assembly 1997 suggested that Amendment A might have a chance. First, two conservative supporters of Amendment B were defeated, by very narrow margins, in elections to the Permanent Judicial Commission. Second, a conservative motion to impose doctrinal purity on seminary professors failed overwhelmingly.[1]

And then 60 percent of the delegates to GA 1997 voted for Amendment A. At a joint press conference following the vote, spokespersons for both sides appeared.[2]

James Logan spoke for a newly formed conservative group called the Presbyterian Coalition. He expressed concern for the peace, unity, and the funding and membership levels of the denomination. Many congregations who were opposed to homosexual ordination had withheld funds until after the original Amendment B was ratified. With the passage of Amendment A, the withholding of funds would increase. He was also concerned that "A" would water down the historical standards of the church. It "sends a fuzzy message to young people" when clarity is needed.

Scott Anderson, co-moderator of PLGC, said, ". . . a midcourse correction, not a stunning reversal. It is a nuance, not so harsh, more gracious. . . . Is my sexual practice an essential tenet of the reformed faith? . . . I don't see it as a Christian fundamental, my sexuality. Our polity is set up to put us in conflict with each other. That's the way we are as Presbyterians. The Holy Spirit is always moving, always challenging us to grow."

Laurene LaFontaine, the other co-moderator of PLGC, said, ". . . a necessary small step toward justice and reconciliation . . . a note of grace."

Janie Spahr of PLGC said, "Jim (Logan) finds homosexuality a sin, we find it a gift. . . . How can we share our faith together? It's our very being you're saying no to."

In September 1997, a group of "high steeple" church leaders organized to support Amendment A as it would wind its way through the presbyteries. They called themselves the Covenant Network of Presbyterians (CNP), and these weren't gays or lesbians but deeply entrenched representatives of the establishment; their co-founders were heavyweights—Robert Bohl, moderator of General Assembly 1994 and John Buchanan, moderator of General Assembly 1996. Their principal motivation was church unity.

"John Calvin's great vision 'that we may dwell in perfect unity' seems more critical than ever for our beloved church," say Bohl and Buchanan. "We believe that Amendment A offers a real opportunity for unity and expresses the feeling of the broad middle of the church. The Covenant Network is pledged to seek the common ground that will allow us to move beyond differences on specific issues to the vital mission the Spirit has in store for us."

According to Buchanan and Bohl, Amendment A "clarifies that our obedience is to Jesus Christ. It restores the Reformed understanding of vocation by acknowledging that service in ordained office is possible only because of God's grace—not because of our human efforts. On the critical issue of standards for officers, it demands 'fidelity and integrity in marriage or in singleness, and in all relationships of life.' While requiring moral sexual behavior, it also demands integrity in, for example, our work and family relationships, our financial stewardship, and other areas."[3]

But proponents of Amendment A say the debate this time is not about sexual fidelity as much as it is about fidelity to a theological tradition that puts grace before judgment and about the unity of an increasingly fragmented church. Amendment B, they argue, skews Reformed understandings of sin, particularly sexual sin, scriptural authority and the role of the confessions. They also argue that it is divisive to legislate a solution now to a visceral debate that is so unresolved for many Presbyterians that succeeding General Assemblies have proposed virtually contradictory amendments.[4]

On the other hand, *The Layman* magazine disagreed in highly charged, confrontational editorials, such as the following.

Praising Amendment A for "requiring moral sexual behavior," as the co-moderators do, is an astounding exercise in ecclesiastical doublespeak. . . . In an abrupt about-face, Amendment A now proposes replacing that standard with an endorsement of "all relationships," irrespective of gender, number, or kinship or blood relations, bounded only by participants' subjective notions of "fidelity and integrity."

Perhaps the most egregious assertion comes as Bohl and Buchanan state their belief that "Amendment A offers a real opportunity for unity and expresses the feeling of the broad middle of the church." Reality contradicts this reverie. . . . By any measure, gay-ordination advocates occupy the radical fringe of the PCUSA. Bohl and Buchanan do no service to the denomination by openly encouraging the radical fringe that seeks to destroy our historic standards and irrevocably divide the church. . . . Those at the Presbyterian Church (USA)'s fringe may feel the need for more covenants and more light. But Presbyterians centered around Jesus Christ already have all that they need.[5]

LGBT supporters once again suffered rejection. Amendment A was voted down by the presbyteries. The gatekeepers would retain control, albeit by slight margins, as the nineties would wind down. Amendment B remained intact by slight majorities at the 1998 and 1999 General

Assemblies. Fidelity in marriage and chastity in singleness would be the rule as the decade ended.

In the long run, perhaps the most important development was not the "what" of Amendment A, but the "who." The Covenant Network of Presbyterians (CNP) became a significant "insider" ally of PLGC. At the second annual gathering of CNP in November 1998, the organization developed plans for lobbying campaigns at General Assemblies, luncheons at Assemblies, the creation of local chapters, "monitoring" of judicial cases, "moral, legal and financial support to officers and sessions," and for publication of theological papers.[6] The potential funds at their disposal dwarfed the meager budgets of PLGC, and the cadre of potential speakers and writers included seminary leaders and the esteemed scholars of the church. The ranks of pilgrims along the journey toward full inclusion were suddenly swelled by a mass infusion of straight and well-heeled church leaders.

General Assembly 1996 had marked the beginning of a confusing and chaotic period for the Presbyterians. We quoted the newly elected presiding bishop of the ELCA to characterize the Lutheran status at the end of the nineties, "We have not yet reached consensus." Rev. Douglas Oldenburg would be elected General Assembly moderator in 1999, and his similar statement is an equally apt signpost. Referring to the story of King Jehoshaphat in 2 Chronicles, Oldenburg suggested the church should simply admit, as did the king, "We don't know what to do."[7]

Clearly, the momentum had swung toward greater inclusion of gays and lesbians but there would not be consensus. There seemed to be an intractable split, very near the middle. Though the supporters of full inclusion remained in the minority, it was an ever-growing and strengthening minority that threatened to soon become the majority. But when?

NOTES

1. "News from the 1997 General Assembly," *More Light Update* vol. 17, no. 6 (July–August 1997).

2. The account of the press conference is from the website of Religious Tolerance, accessed April 1, 2012, http://www.religioustolerance.org/hom _pru10.htm.

3. *More Light Update* vol. 18, no. 1 (September–October 1997).

4. Alexa Smith, Presbyterian News Service, "'Fidelity and Integrity' Amendment Backers Gather," September 29, 1997.

5. Editorial, "Covenants," *The Layman*, posted October 1, 1997.

6. Jerry L. Van Marter, "Covenant Network of Presbyterians Vows to Carry On," *Network News* vol. 18, issue 4 (Fall 1998).

7. Ibid.

WOW!

We divert briefly from our purely Presbyterian journey to rest in a safe haven amidst the tall cornstalks of DeKalb, Illinois. Fellow pilgrims from many denominations have gathered here for the "Witness our Welcome" conference hosted by the welcoming church movement, an informal collaboration of the LGBT-advocacy groups we have encountered along our journey.

Pan-denominational collaboration began in 1990 when leaders of the various welcoming church organizations gathered to share ideas and resources, and they continued with annual meetings thereafter. In 1993, the group had decided to cooperatively publish the Methodist quarterly magazine *Open Hands* under the editorial leadership of Mark Bowman. In 2000 they would sponsor a big event, their first general convocation of a "diverse assembly of Christians." Dozens of volunteers had planned for more than a year for WOW 2000.[1]

As we wander the air-conditioned hallways of the Holmes Student Center at Northern Illinois University, we recognize familiar Presbyterian faces: Chris Glaser, Jim Anderson, Lisa Larges, Janie Spahr, and partners Martha Juillerat and Tammy Lindahl. Here too are others whose paths we have crossed or will cross: Methodists Mark Bowman (Conference Coordinator) and Morris Floyd, Ann B. Day of the UCC, and James Lokken of the ELCA (one of the five original founders of Lutherans Concerned). Dr. Carter Heyward, of the Philadelphia Eleven and the Episcopal Divinity School, dropped by to offer her words of wisdom.

Although the welcoming church movement and each of its constituent parts advocated for LGBT-friendly *denominational* policies, their special interest was to encourage individual *congregations* that were willing to buck denominational policy and fling open their doors to the LGBT community. It all started with the Presbyterians and the More Light Church statement of West-Park Presbyterian of upper Manhattan in 1978. Chris Glaser and Jim Anderson served as More Light volunteer leaders for many years, which included production and distribution of the *More Light Update* newsletter. In the nineties, volunteer leaders included Janie Spahr and Scott Anderson. At the end of the nineties, More Light Presbyterians hired Michael Adee as a staff person with the title "field organizer," and he would continue in that position for the ensuing thirteen years, with the title "executive director" added later.

In the early eighties, Mark Bowman encouraged the Methodist Gay Caucus to pursue a similar focus on local congregations, and the Reconciling Congregations Project (now Reconciling Ministries Network) was born. By the early nineties, Mark had been hired as executive director, and he was already the editor of *Open Hands* magazine, which would become the pan-denominational publication of the welcoming church organizations.[2] Presbyterian Chris Glaser would slide into the editor's chair when Mark stepped down after many fruitful years of service.

We have already visited extensively with Rev. Ann B. Day and the UCC Open and Affirming program. Ann would be instrumental in organizing early collaborations of welcoming church leaders.

These familiar wayfarers joined with a thousand others who sought sanctuary together in DeKalb, Illinois, and the campus of Northern Illinois University in August 2000 for the first conference of the welcoming church movement, called "Witness our Welcome" (WOW!).

Here are tidbits culled from the pages of *More Light Update*.[3] Michael Adee said,

History was made in DeKalb, Illinois, for the Welcoming Movement, and the Church, August 3–6, 2000, during the first-ever, historic ecumenical gathering of LGBT people and our allies at WOW 2000,

"Witness Our Welcome 2000—God's Promise Is for You." Over 1,000 people from a reported 27 denominational backgrounds, and over a dozen countries gathered for worship, prayer/meditation, fellowship/friendship, education, music, celebration and solidarity. . . . Over $40,000 was collected during the Saturday Night Banquet for the Welcoming Movement to use to plan for the next WOW Conference. Our Lisa Larges, who was key in the planning of WOW, was given recognition for creating the idea behind the "WOW" name.

Michael Kinnamon of the Disciples of Christ said,

GLBT people in the church are not a problem to be solved, an issue to be dealt with, or a crisis to be handled cautiously. The welcoming movement is an opportunity for the church to deepen its understanding of the Gospel, an opportunity for Gospel-faithfulness, and an opportunity for the renewal of the church.

Rev. Todd Freeman of Bethany Presbyterian Church of Dallas said,

There were also people in attendance from the Metropolitan Community Church, the Reorganized Church of Latter Day Saints, Roman Catholic, Quaker, and even a few Southern Baptists! "Welcoming Churches," like ours, are defined as "congregations or communities that have publicly declared that they welcome persons of all sexual orientations."

Chris Glaser alluded to the story of the Pentecost in the second chapter of Acts:

When the days of the WOW 2000 Conference were come, all the Welcoming Programs were together in one place. And suddenly from heaven there came a sound like the rush of non-violent wind, and it filled the entire Holmes Student Center of Northern Illinois University where they were meeting. Fired up with diverse perspectives, opinions, and strategies, God's glory rested on each of them.

Coming together for WOW moments such as these provided important respite for the Presbyterians, an "R&R" from the frustrations at the frontlines. General Assembly 2001 would revisit the pattern of advance followed quickly by retreat.

From the moment ally Jack Rogers was elected moderator of General Assembly 2001 on the first ballot, victory seemed close. With a 60 percent majority vote, the odious Amendment B was removed from the *Book of Order*; the "definitive guidance" dating to 1978 was repealed; and local presbyteries would again have full discretion over local ordination decisions: "[S]uitability to hold office is determined by the governing body where the examination for ordination or installation takes place, guided by scriptural and constitutional standards, under the authority and Lordship of Jesus Christ" [Amendment A].[4]

"The church has returned to its historic principles allowing local churches and presbyteries to make decisions about ordination," said Bill Moss, the MLP co-moderator. "This is the middle ground the church needed to move forward."[5]

Of course, Amendment B had been voted out before by commissioners at GA 1997 only to receive new life when the presbyteries failed to ratify the GA action. It happened again. In close votes across the nation, a solid majority of presbyteries rejected the actions of GA 2001. Amendment B, with all its baggage, remained the law of the Presbyterian landscape. Once again, the gays, lesbians, and their allies suffered a belly punch. Once again, they had to pick themselves up off the mat. Once again, they had to regroup.

Katie Morrison, field director for MLP, said, "[T]he question I am asked more than any other is, 'What's next?' My answer is always, 'We keep on doing what we have always been doing, for this work is urgent work.'"[6]

General Assembly 2001 moderator Jack Rogers suggested that the one LGBT-friendly action to survive was the creation of a Theological Task Force on the Peace, Unity, and Purity of the Church (the PUP Task Force). Twenty persons were appointed, and they toiled for four and a half years. Their "scrupulous" report was acted upon by General Assembly 2006, but now we're getting ahead of the story.[7]

In the fall of 2001, during the interregnum between the LGBT-friendly actions of GA 2001 and the unfriendly actions of the presbyteries that retained odious Amendment B, the Presbyterians took another step forward. Katie Morrison became the first out lesbian to be ordained in the Presbyterian Church. Morrison was a cradle Presbyterian, and both her parents had served as elders at the Pasadena Presbyterian Church. "When I was growing up, church was home. It was safe—like a second family."[8]

Soon after she came out to herself as a lesbian during her freshman year at college, Morrison attended her first General Assembly in 1992. She hung with other gays and lesbians at the PLGC booth, where a judgmental Southern clergyman condemned her.[9]

On September 21, 2001, the Redwoods Presbytery of California voted overwhelmingly to approve her ordination, and a month later, she was ordained in First Presbyterian Church of Anselmo, California. She had been called to serve as field organizer for MLP, and the presbytery recognized this call as sufficient for ordination.[10]

The gatekeepers wouldn't stand for it; even before the ordination ceremony, fellow ministers in the Redwoods Presbytery unsuccessfully sought a stay of enforcement of the presbytery's September 11 decision to ordain, and after the ordination, complaints were filed, and the matter ultimately wound its way to the Permanent Judicial Commission of the General Assembly (GAPJC).

Meanwhile, on Reformation Sunday, October 29, 2002, Pastor Morrison celebrated the eucharist at South Church in Dobbs Ferry, New York. With her court case still undecided, the congregation remembered Martin Luther's defiant "Here I stand" speech before the Diet of Worms that had been preceded by nailing ninety-five theses onto the Wittenberg Castle door, at least according to legend.

After processing in to "A Mighty Fortress Is Our God," and a call to worship that incorporated the voices of PC(USA) members stating why they cannot comply with [amendment "B"], we were invited to come forward and place pre-written statements of our vision of the reformation we would like to see the PC(USA) take on nails that protruded from a door at the front of the sanctuary. One by one, worship participants pushed their hopes onto the nails. This was followed by a "fanfare for organ and nails." Between waterfalls of booming organ scales came silence, and then hammering by host pastor Rev. Joe Gilmore of South Church from the balcony above.[11]

Following the sermon, LGBT elders reaffirmed their ordination vows. The wooden door with nails became the communion table, and Morrison celebrated the eucharist assisted by Lisa Larges as a gay men's chorus offered song.

The gatekeepers were vexed. *The Layman* Online headline proclaimed "Renegades have trashed the Lord's Supper," and the article stated:

> Not satisfied with open defiance that threatens to shred the Constitution of the PCUSA into so much confetti, an outlaw band of renegades, who have the arrogance to still claim to be Presbyterian though they have essentially said they have no use for Presbyterian polity or discipline, have now trashed the Lord's Supper!
>
> We've now had communion served from a "table" covered with prayers affirming that which God has declared sin is now holy. Maybe next time, there will be a pro–partial birth abortion group that will want to use the table from an abortionist's execution chamber.[12]

On March 3, 2003, the GAPJC announced its decision. Morrison's ordination stood!

The case had proceeded under the rules of Amendment B since the GA actions of that summer were not effective unless ratified by presbyteries (which didn't happen). Based on those restrictive policies, how was the ordination approved? It seems it slipped through under "don't ask, don't tell" circumstances. Though Morrison acknowledged her sexual orientation, no one on the committee asked whether she was celibate and Morrison didn't volunteer that she had been in a relationship for three years. On March 3, 2003, the GAPJC upheld her ordination, stating, "Therefore, if a person does not self-acknowledge a practice that the confessions call sin, then a governing body has a positive obligation to make further inquiry only if it has direct and specific knowledge that said person is in violation of the ordination and installation standards of the Constitution."[13]

Though it was a personal victory for Pastor Morrison and a symbolic victory for Presbyterian gays and lesbians, it had been possible only by navigating a narrow pathway around the rules rather than by overturning them. Pastor Morrison had been ordained in spite of the rules, and a few others were ordained during this period in similar fashion. Following *Blasdell* in 1985, an activist GAPJC had overreached to prevent LGBT ordination for a ten-year period. Now, in the first decade of the new millennium, the same court stretched and twisted in order to approve LGBT ordination, at least in individual cases.

MLP board member Elisabeth "Eily" Marlow was approved for ordination by the Milwaukee Presbytery on February 23, 2005, by an overwhelming vote of 104 to 20. She credited the strong educational and preparatory work of the presbytery staff, together with the tactic of avoiding discussion of sexuality issues during the candidacy interview that had been effectively countenanced by the Morrison court ruling. Later that fall, when she sought transfer of her ministry credentials to the Presbytery of the Twin Cities in order to accept a chaplaincy position at Macalester College in St. Paul, a conservative registered a protest, but no disciplinary action followed.[14]

Openly gay activist elder Ray Bagnuolo was even more confrontational, but a friendly presbytery, the Presbytery of the Hudson River, voted to approve his ordination eighty-eight to nine to one. According to Michael Adee's report posted on the MLP website,

> Bagnuolo stated that he could not and would not abide by the PCUSA's attempts to restrict the call of gays to serve the church, noting that "These restrictions are intentionally used to exclude lesbian, gay, bisexual, and transgender persons from serving, but more importantly, they add to the inherent violence in any policy of marginalization, in this case aimed at the gay population."[15]

On November 13, 2005, Bagnuolo was ordained as a minister of word and sacrament, and no disciplinary proceedings ensued.

Amendment B remained controlling. A small handful of friendly presbyteries had circled around the rules by avoiding discussions of sexuality issues during candidacy interviews. A significant step forward, to be sure, but Presbyterian pilgrims had not yet reached journey's end.

———

"You're a movement, why don't you act like one?"

With that challenge from activist and organizer Donna Redwing, the leaders of the welcoming church movement had an epiphany. In November 2002, during a retreat at Ghost Ranch Conference Center in Santa Fe, New Mexico, the Institute for Welcoming Resources (IWR) was born.[16] The IWR would be a permanent, staffed organization that would further the goals of the welcoming church organizations through the:

- Development, production, and distribution of resources to support the welcoming church movement;

- Development and planning of conferences and training events designed to inspire, empower, and equip members and leadership in the welcoming church movement;

- Expansion of networks and the creation of coalitions within and beyond the welcoming church movement.

In 2005, Rev. Rebecca Voelkel of the UCC became the executive director. "I believe that being an activist, a trouble-maker and a speaker of unwanted truths involves deeply spiritual work," she said.[17]

In 2006, the collaborative effort of the IWR was further enhanced by merger with the National Gay and Lesbian Task Force. That same year, Martha Juillerat of the Shower of Stoles (SOS) retired, and SOS became an adjunct of the IWR, and the number of stoles would grow to more than a thousand.[18]

Juillerat and Tammy Lindahl retired to Canada after their marriage there.

> After thirty years of fighting for equality and justice in the Presbyterian Church, Tammy and I have decided that it is time for us to rest. We leave this fight in the capable hands of a younger generation, with the heartfelt prayer that the hospitality, generosity of spirit, profound faith and affirmation we have come to

know in the United Church of Canada will one day become a reality in the Presbyterian Church (USA).[19]

The second Witness Our Welcome (WOW) gathering convened at the University of Pennsylvania on August 14, 2003. The arrivals buzzed with the news that the Episcopal General Convention in Minneapolis had approved the election of Bishop Gene Robinson just a week earlier. Once again, there was a decided ecumenical flavor, and once again there was plenty of star power. Presenters included two of the earliest icons in the march toward full inclusion, Pastor Bill Johnson of the UCC, ordained in 1972, and Rev. Troy Perry, founder of the MCC in the months before Stonewall in 1969.

MCC member Adam DeBaugh reported:

As if I wasn't giddy enough from all the emotional events of this year, last weekend I journeyed to Philadelphia for the WOW 2003 conference! WOW! Witness Our Welcome. Over 1,000 LGBT people and our straight allies were there, including some of the most amazing queer religious leaders in our history, all gathered in one place.

It was brilliant.

And throughout my entire experience at WOW last weekend, I couldn't help but think that all these people, Gay, Lesbian, Straight, Transgender, Bisexual, Queer, Intersexed, and Undecided; from a couple dozen different church traditions and liturgical habits; from all over the US and Canada; from different ethnic and racial backgrounds; from the very young to the very old, and from all kinds of economic and educational strata. All these people were here saying, "As for me and my house, we will serve God."

Because you see, this was my house, broader even than MCC, here was my Tribe, gloriously and radiantly arrayed, and we were affirming in the face of extreme prejudice and hate, that "As for me and my house, we will serve God."[20]

The Presbyterian contingent was easily the largest of any denomination; more than one hundred Presbyterians numbered among the eight hundred to one thousand attendees. With the repeated on-again, off-again, accept-then-reject actions and reversals of the triumvirate of the General Assembly, the presbyteries, and the Permanent Judicial Council, the jerked-around Presbyterian gay community needed a period of solace.

Three and a half centuries earlier, a church steeple rising from the mists of the Scottish lowlands had beckoned to John Knox, but in his chains, his hope seemed unattainable. In the first years of the new century, the goal of full inclusion for modern-day pilgrims seemed so close yet remained elusive.

NOTES

1. WOW 2000 document, "History of the Welcoming Church Movement," from the records of Ann B. Day, provided June 28, 2012.

2. The five principal ecumenical denominations plus others including the Unitarian Universalists, American Baptists, the Brethren/Mennonite Supportive Congregations, and even the UK Inclusive congregations.

3. *More Light Update* vol. 21, no. 2 (November–December 2000).

4. Jerry Van Marter, Presbyterian News Service, "Proposal to open the way for gay ordination passes with 60% approval," June 15, 2001.

5. *More Light Update* vol. 21, no. 6 (July–August 2001).

6. *More Light Update* vol. 22, no. 5 (Summer 2002).

7. Rogers, *Jesus, the Bible, and Homosexuality*, 124.

8. Don Lattin, "A First for the Presbyterian Church, a Lifelong Dream for Her," *San Francisco Chronicle*, November 11, 2001.

9. Ibid.

10. Press Release from More Light Presbyterians, October 22, 2001.

11. Katie Morrison, "Report to Allies," October 29, 2002. "A Mighty Fortress" is *the* anthem of the Reformation, composed by Luther. Popular legend suggests he borrowed a beer hall melody.

12. Ibid.

13. The Permanent Judicial Commission of the General Assembly of the Presbyterian Church (USA), Presbytery of San Joaquin v. Presbytery of the Redwoods, Remedial Case 215-8 (March 3, 2003).

14. Elisabeth Marlow, private conversation with the author, August 8, 2012.

15. Michael Adee, "The Adee Report," on the website of More Light Presbyterians, accessed August 8, 2012, http://www.mlp.org/article.php/2005 1119124040460.

16. *More Light Update* vol. 28, no. 2 (June 2008). Donna Redwing has served in various advocacy positions with the Interfaith Alliance, Human Rights Campaign, and more.

17. Ibid.

18. "Shower of Stoles Project," on the website of the Institute for Welcoming Resources, accessed August 4, 2012, http://www.welcomingresources.org /index.htm.

19. Martha Juillerat, "Part Wedding Story, and Part Goodbye," *More Light Update* vol. 27, no. 3 (August 2007). See Notes 637 and 761 for Juillerat's expanded comments regarding marriage equality.

20. Adam DeBaugh, "WOW! A Report from WOW 2003," on the website of Whosoever, accessed August 3, 2012, http://whosoever.org/v8i2/wow 2.shtml.

* 42 *

MARRIAGE EQUALITY ON TRIAL

After the turn of the century, marriage equality became the *cause célèbre* of the secular gay rights movement. On May 17, 2004, the Massachusetts Supreme Court had cracked open the door to marriage equality, ever so slightly; soon, other states burst through the gate, by judicial fiat or legislative enactment. In 2013, the U.S. Supreme Court struck down the Defense of Marriage Act, thus requiring the federal government to recognize same-sex marriages that are legal in their home states.

Churches were caught up in the rush.

Except for the Methodists, who put ministers on trial (see "Part Five: The Methodists"), "commitment ceremonies," "holy unions," "covenant ceremonies," or "rites of blessing" had long been practiced within the ecumenical denominations, openly or with a wink and a nod. Except for the Methodists, blessing of same-gender partners had never been a particularly contentious issue but always with the proviso that such blessings were not equal to marriage.

The semi-official policy of the ELCA was typical. In 1993, the Conference of Bishops issued an opinion (advisory only, since the Conference had no legislative authority) that stated,

> We, as the Conference of Bishops of the ELCA, recognize that there is basis neither in Scripture nor tradition for the establishment of an official ceremony by this church for the blessing of a

homosexual relationship. We, therefore, do not approve such a ceremony as an official action of this church's ministry. Nevertheless, we express trust in and will continue dialogue with those pastors and congregations who are in ministry with gay and lesbian persons, and affirm their desire to explore the best ways to provide pastoral care for all to whom they minister.[1]

In other words, use your discretion, bless your parishioners as you deem appropriate, but don't call it marriage. But as marriage equality became a reality in one jurisdiction after another, the churches had to revisit their policies.

In 2005, the UCC formally endorsed marriage equality.

Episcopal priest Dr. Carter Heyward reported that her bishop of the Diocese of Massachusetts initially said "don't do it" when marriage equality came to that state, a decree Dr. Heyward ignored.[2] By 2009, TEC General Convention had voted to allow "generous pastoral response to meet the needs of members of this church," and the bishop of Massachusetts not only authorized his parish priests to solemnize same-gender marriages, he was officiating himself—at the marriage of two of his leading priests, no less![3] At General Convention 2012, TEC adopted a provisional liturgy for same-gender blessings.

In the sweeping enactments of 2009, ELCA policy was changed to "allow congregations that choose to do so to recognize, support and hold publicly accountable life-long, monogamous, same gender relationships," which clearly implied rites of blessing, at a minimum, and probably marriage ceremonies in jurisdictions where permitted and in congregations that approved. For instance, when marriage equality became the law of Minnesota, effective in August 2013, Rev. Ann Svennungsen, bishop of the Minneapolis Area Synod, advised her congregations and clergy that congregations *may* allow their clergy to perform same-sex weddings but were not required to do so: "On August 6, 2013, ordained ELCA pastors in Minnesota will have legal authority to marry same-sex couples. However, it is the congregation's decision as to whether their pastor will preside at same-sex marriages."[4]

Numerous Minnesota Lutheran congregations and clergy performed same-sex weddings after August 6, 2013, when they became legal in the state.

For the Presbyterians on the final legs of the journey toward full inclusion, marriage equality shared the stage with LGBT ordination, and the message of judicial contortions was clear: clergy blessings of same-sex couples were entirely acceptable, but that was all. LGBT marriage was nonexistent in the eyes of the Presbyterian court. But, as one state after another legalized marriage for LGBT couples, the Presbyterian courts ran out of excuses to side-step the issue. Then, when the court finally upheld the conviction of Dr. Janie Spahr for performing marriages, her presbytery engaged in high-level ecclesiastical disobedience by refusing to censure her.

Let us begin at the beginning.

Marriage equality has been the national law of Canada since 2005 and in several provinces before that. On February 28, 2004, Rev. Dr. Janie Spahr had co-officiated in a legal same-gender marriage in Ontario. The marriage was recognized in that Canadian jurisdiction.

We first encountered Dr. Spahr during her first ecclesiastical trial in the early nineties when she had been the victim of judicial activism that gutted the "grandparent" clause of the definitive guidance policy and her call to parish ministry was blocked. The congregation, Downtown United Presbyterian of Rochester, New York, then called her to be a missionary to spread the hope of LGBT inclusion to the whole church, and her ministry became known as "That All May Freely Serve" (TAMFS). She became the Presbyterian lesbian evangelist *par excellence*. The couple she married in Ontario were her TAMFS board members.

The wedding came to the attention of the self-appointed watchers of Presbyterian morality, and an e-mail from an officer of a small gatekeeper organization called "Presbyterians for Renewal" launched an official inquiry, and a complaint was filed against Spahr.[5]

When the Presbytery of the Redwoods determined that her level of participation (co-officient) was insufficient to sustain the charges, the complaint was amended, based on two additional marriages performed by Spahr in October, 2004 and March, 2005. However, these two purported marriages were not recognized in the civil jurisdiction where they were performed, a critical factor for the court. The charges would eventually be dismissed by the Presbyterian "Supreme Court," the GAPJC. The court ruled on April 28, 2008, that same-gender marriage was impossible under Presbyterian policy; thus, in the eyes of this court, the purported weddings were merely a ceremony of blessing, nothing more, and thus Spahr had broken no rules. Since the marriages were not official in their civil jurisdictions, the rationale of the court that they must be merely blessing ceremonies jibed with their legal status.[6]

Spahr disagreed: "It was a denial of the ministry that I do, but most of all a denial of the relationships of the couples. That was unconscionable. Do anything to me, but don't say their relationships don't count!"[7]

Shower of Stoles director Martha Juillerat provided eloquent testimony of the importance of full marriage equality in a farewell to her friends in MLP written in an open letter published in *More Light Update*. In 2004, Juillerat, her partner Tammy Lindahl, and MLP director Michael Adee were together, and Juillerat was considering an invitation to speak at a Vancouver, British Columbia, conference of Affirm United (AU):[8]

"Early the next morning, I had another thought. Standing in the hall, I said to her, 'You know, while we're there, we could get married.' Michael, who was staying with us that week, popped right out of the bathroom with a face-full of shaving cream and declared, 'I want to be the flower girl!'"[9]

Juillerat and Lindahl had already been blessed in a commitment ceremony nineteen years earlier. Why take the further step of marriage, especially if it wouldn't be honored in their state of residence? "What we really wanted, I thought, was the impossible: a perfectly normal, legal, good old fashioned church wedding—in a church that would embrace us fully. Then came the promise that would change our lives forever." The Affirm United Conference organizer said, "We will be your church," and arrangements were made for the Saturday evening conference banquet to be transformed into a wedding and reception.

> It was the perfect wedding of our dreams. Afterward, we were given a wedding feast as a gift from Affirm United. In a room filled with balloons and decorations, three professional chefs

offered a fresh pacific salmon dinner with all the trimmings. A local jazz pianist played throughout the evening and gave us one of his CD's. A group of AU members from Quebec sang a French song. Finally, we were presented with an extraordinary framed print from a First Nation artist in British Columbia.[10]

The duration of their stay in Canada was equally glorious. They were respected as honeymooners by everyone they encountered.

This wedding–this marriage–was a transforming experience for Tammy and me that we weren't really anticipating after twenty years together. In the clear presence of God and in the affirmations of faith, in the offering of toasts and gifts, in the showering of prayers and blessings, we experienced the very depth and breadth of Christian hospitality. This is what it means to be the Church. . . . Very soon we came to realize the profound effect this was having on us: not only was our marriage possible here, it was normal.[11]

So normal, in fact, that Juillerat and Lindahl later relocated to Canada. Rev. Janet Edwards, a descendant of Jonathan Edwards of the Great Awakening, officiated at the wedding of Nancy McConn and Brenda Cole in June 2005. Rev. Edwards had earlier served as moderator of the Pittsburgh Presbytery, but in November 2008, the Presbytery would place her on trial for the 2005 wedding ceremony. Though Rev. Edwards and the wedding couple agreed that it was a marriage, the ecclesiastical court unanimously acquitted Edwards. Since marriage equality didn't exist in Pennsylvania, she couldn't have performed a wedding, and the court ruled that performing a mere service of blessing was not actionable. This was precisely the rationale of the GAPJC in the Spahr case decided earlier that year, and the Pittsburgh court merely followed that precedent. Rev. Edwards remained an outspoken and oft-published advocate for LGBT inclusion, and she later served as co-moderator of MLP.[12]

The case of Rev. Jean Southard of First Presbyterian Church of Waltham, Massachusetts, was more complicated and wound its way to the GAPJC. Rev. Southard and her MIT-geology-professor husband,

John, "live in eastern Massachusetts on a plot of land large enough to grow our own fruits and vegetables, and plenty of flowers."[13] On March 1, 2008, Rev. Southard presided at a "Christian Marriage" of a lesbian couple, long-time faithful members of her congregation. Same-gender marriage was then legal in Massachusetts and the marriage was duly registered with the town clerk. When Pastor Southard was charged by her presbytery's judicial commission with violating the PC(USA) constitution and her own ordination vows "to be governed by our church polity" and to "abide by its discipline," her case became one of first impression for officiating at a marriage deemed legal in the eyes of the civil law.[14] The presbytery dismissed the charges, but the synod reversed and found Rev. Southard guilty. She appealed to the GAPJC, and they reversed her conviction on February 6, 2011.

Unfortunately, it was another symbolic but limited victory. Essentially, the court ruled that Southard had violated the constitution, but she didn't know it since the definitive statement of Presbyterian policy regarding marriage equality wouldn't be handed down until the Spahr decision of April 28, nearly two months after Southard officiated at the Massachusetts wedding. The prospective effect was that in jurisdictions that allowed same-gender marriage, Presbyterian clergy would not be allowed to perform "Christian Marriage" of LGBT couples.

> In light of the change in the laws of some states, this Commission reiterates that officers of the PCUSA who are authorized to perform marriages, when performing a ceremony for a same-gender couple, shall not state, imply, or represent that the same-gender ceremony is an ecclesiastical marriage ceremony as defined by PCUSA polity, whether or not the civil jurisdiction allows same-gender civil marriages.[15]

The court deferred to the General Assembly. Unless and until the General Assembly would change the policy, marriage equality wouldn't exist within the PC(USA). To their credit, eleven of the fourteen members of the court called on the General Assembly to make the change.

Finally, we journey to Northern California during the summer and fall of 2008 and the four-month window when same-gender marriage was legal in that state. Of course, this was after the earlier Spahr decision of April of that year when the GAPJC had ruled that same-gender marriage did not exist in the church according to the previously adopted policies of the General Assembly.

From June to November of the year that Barack Obama was elected to the presidency, Rev. Dr. Janie Spahr officiated at the legal-in-California weddings of sixteen LGBT couples. At least four of the couples included a clergyperson such as pastor Katie Morrison. Again, someone complained, and the Presbytery of the Redwoods felt compelled to bring judicial proceedings, especially since Dr. Spahr had persisted in spite of warnings issued in the prior case against her.

By the time of the weddings, Spahr had retired from her full-time ministry with "That All May Freely Serve," but she continued to serve the Presbytery of the Redwoods in an outreach ministry to the LGBT community. The Presbytery of the Redwoods consisted of fifty-two congregations along the coast of California from the Golden Gate bridge north to Oregon.

The trial would not take place until late August in 2010, just weeks after a federal appeals court judge had ruled that Proposition 8, which had outlawed marriage equality in California, was unconstitutional. Even though the civil case had no effect on the Spahr proceedings, it boosted spirits, and so did the fine Napa Valley wine shared by the "cloud of witnesses" that had gathered in support of Janie. Eleven of the couples Janie had married stood with her during the trial and testified on her behalf.

After four days of testimony, a split decision of the court decreed that Rev. Spahr be censured (the least of all possible penalties) because of her persistent disobedience, but not without questioning the church policy that compelled their decision. "[W]e have in our own Book of Order conflicting and even contradictory rules and regulations that are against the Gospel." The decision praised Rev. Spahr's "faithful compassion" and her thirty-five-year ministry to gays and lesbians.[16]

"The PJC's written decision dedicated more ink to rebuking the Presbyterian Church (USA) than Spahr," scoffed *The Layman* magazine.[17]

Censure was not imposed pending appeal. On March 25, 2011, the synodical PJC affirmed, and Spahr appealed to the GAPJC. On February 20, 2012, the "Supreme Court" also affirmed, despite six dissenting judges, and then something remarkable happened. With appeals exhausted, the matter was remanded to the Presbytery of the Redwoods to finally exact the punishment of censure. The Presbytery meeting was scheduled for May 16, 2012. Ninety-two commissioners of the presbytery appeared.[18]

It would be a *kairos* moment. *Kairos* is an old Greek word, a biblical word that means the right moment, the supreme moment, God's moment.

The presbytery voted seventy-four to eighteen to defy the determination of the highest Presbyterian court. The presbytery would not censure the Rev. Dr. Jane Adams Spahr and instead voted to support her. It would be the most extreme act of ecclesiastical disobedience in the entire history of the PC(USA). Never before had a presbytery openly defied a ruling of the highest court.

Of course, this ecclesiastical disobedience didn't resolve the issue, and full Presbyterian marriage equality would require action by the General Assembly, but the ecclesiastical disobedience of the presbytery reflected the changing mood of the church.

Although the 2010 General Assembly would vote for change regarding LGBT ministry policy (see the next chapter), marriage equality issues were deferred, pending further dialogue and study.

Marriage equality was a contentious issue at the 2012 General Assembly. Moderator Cindy Bolbach discouraged change on the heels of the revision to LGBT ministry policy a year earlier. It was too soon, she suggested, and the church needed more time to let the ministry changes sink in. Then, three days after her election as vice-moderator of the 2012 General Assembly in Pittsburgh, Rev. Tara Spuhler McCabe suddenly resigned, citing the fact that she had presided over a same-gender marriage in Washington, D.C., where marriage equality is the law.

The Committee on Civil Union and Marriage Issues proposed an amendment to the *Book of Order* that would change the definition of marriage from "a man and a woman" to "two people." The Committee also proposed an authoritative interpretation that would have granted discretion to ministers to perform same-gender marriages in jurisdictions that recognized marriage equality. After lengthy floor debate, both measures failed by very close margins. However, it was clearly the mood of the Assembly that the matter was not settled but simply needed more time and study. Specifically, the commissioners voted 489 to 152 to "move the whole Presbyterian Church (USA) into a season of serious study and discernment concerning its meaning of Christian marriage." The Office of Theology and Worship was directed to prepare educational materials. Following the season of study, the church would take up the issue of marriage equality at the 2014 General Assembly.[19]

The process of discernment was advanced when the Office of Theology and Worship released a "study on marriage" on April 29, 2013. According to the Theology and Worship coordinator, Charles Wiley,

> The issues of same-gender marriage are moving more quickly in our culture than anything we've ever seen. To show the depth and consider deeply and broadly what all the issues are in the midst of these shifts is challenging.
>
> As we added questions about same-gender marriage, we tried to be very careful about how we used sources and approached traditions. We wanted to make sure the study didn't influence participants in one direction or the other.
>
> It's the strength of our Presbyterian tradition, to really think through the issues of the day and understand how theology and Scripture relate to them.[20]

Already, Presbyterian eyes are on the Detroit skyline and General Assembly 2014.

NOTES

1. Evangelical Lutheran Church in America, "Conference of Bishops, October 5–8, 1993, Voted: CB93.10.25," ELCA Churchwide Assembly, *Minutes* (2005).

2. Dr. Carter Heyward, *Keep Your Courage: A Radical Christian Feminist Speaks* (New York: Seabury Books, 2010), 23–24. Within a few years, the bishop revoked his ban following the decision of the national church to allow the blessing of same-gender unions.

3. Lane Lambert, "Marriage of 2 Lesbian Episcopal Priests Adds New Twist to Gay Issues," *Patriot Ledger* (Quincy, Mass.), January 4, 2011.

4. Rev. Ann M. Svennungsen, Bishop of the Minneapolis Area Synod (ELCA), e-mail broadcast to synod recipients, June 26, 2013.

5. *More Light Update* vol. 25, no. 1 (Winter 2005).

6. The Permanent Judicial Commission of the General Assembly of the Presbyterian Church (USA), Spahr v. PC(USA), Disciplinary Case 218-12 (April 28, 2008).

7. Richard A. Lindsey, "The Trials of Janie Spahr," *Religion Dispatches* (RD Magazine), August 24, 2010.

8. Affirm United is the LGBT advocacy group of the United Church of Canada, which is the largest Protestant church in Canada, with more than three million members. The United Church has a mixed Protestant background in Methodism, Congregationalism, and Presbyterianism and a history of social justice progressivism.

9. The story of this Canadian wedding was told by Juillerat in "Part Wedding Story, and Part Goodbye," *More Light Update* vol. 27, no. 3 (August 2007), 2.

10. Ibid.

11. Ibid.

12. See Chris Glaser, *As My Own Soul: The Blessing of Same-Gender Marriage* (New York: Seabury Books, 2009), 1–4; Ann Rodgers, "Pastor Welcomes Church Trial for Lesbian Marriage," *Pittsburgh Post-Gazette*, November 6, 2006, and MLP board member biographies on the website of MLP, accessed September 19, 2012, http://www.mlp.org/board/.

13. *More Light Update* vol. 30, no. 1 (June 2010).

14. The Permanent Judicial Commission of the General Assembly of the Presbyterian Church (USA), Southard v. PC(USA), Disciplinary Case GAPJC 220-02 (February 11, 2011).

15. Southard v. PC(USA).

16. Maria L. La Ganga, "Presbyterians Censure Minister for Same-Sex Marriages," *Los Angeles Times*, August 27, 2010.

17. Edward Terry, "PJC Rebukes Spahr, then the PC(USA)," *The Layman*, August 28, 2010.

18. Maria L. La Ganga, "California Presbytery Defies Church, Backs Minister in Gay Weddings," *Los Angeles Times*, May 16, 2012.

19. Jerry L Van Marter, "Same-Gender Marriage," *Assembly in Brief 2012*, Office of PC(USA) General Assembly, 3.

20. Presbyterian News Service, "Study on marriage ready for congregational and presbytery use," April 29, 2013.

* 43 *

Rivers of Living Water

Remember what we told you about the Minnesota water?

The Episcopal General Convention came to Minneapolis, the city of lakes, in 1976, and their constitution was changed to permit the ordination of women. The Episcopalians returned in 2003, and the election of Bishop Gene Robinson was approved. In 2009, the ELCA gathered in the Minneapolis Convention Center, and they adopted a progressive human sexuality statement and revised ministry policies to permit LGBT ordination. Perhaps if more would come to test the waters of this progressive home of Hubert Humphrey, Eugene McCarthy, Walter Mondale, Paul Wellstone, and Michelle Bachmann . . . whoops! She's really from Iowa.

The Presbyterians came to the Land of Ten Thousand Lakes in 2010 and washed away the "fidelity and chastity" language of Amendment B. Ten months later, more serendipity. When the Presbytery of the Twin Cities ratified the GA actions, the 87th of 173 presbyteries to do so, a majority was achieved, and favorable GA action was finally ratified by the presbyteries after four attempts over a dozen years; the Presbyterians would soon welcome gays and lesbians into their pulpits. Before we visit Minneapolis and the 218th General Assembly of 2010, we'll track the final streams leading up to this watershed moment.

We have crossed paths with Scott Anderson previously. He was in the midst of a successful parish ministry in California when he was outed, and he resigned in 1990. He became active in MLP, including terms as co-moderator and as a contributor to *More Light Update*.

He would also prove to be a scrupulous historian of the church.

At the Philadelphia General Synod of 1729, provisions were enacted that required candidates for ordination to subscribe to the Westminster Confession. However, the Adopting Act of 1729 also allowed dissent from nonessentials, called a "scruple." A candidate for ordination could register a scruple, declaring disagreement with a particular article of the confession, and the candidate's presbytery would then determine whether the scrupled article was "essential and necessary" or not. If not, the candidacy would proceed, but if the article was deemed essential, the disagreement with it would cause the candidacy to fail. In the Fundamentalist-Modernist controversy of the 1920s, the Auburn Affirmation and the report of the Swearingen Commission affirmed freedom of conscience, and the centuries' old notion of scruple lived on.

At the 2001 General Assembly, moderator Jack Rogers had appointed twenty persons to serve on the Theological Task Force on the Peace, Unity, and Purity of the Church (PUP). Scott Anderson was one of the appointees. At that time, Anderson was employed as executive director of the Wisconsin Council of Churches. He had previously served in the same capacity with the California Council of Churches.

After four and a half years of discernment, the report was submitted to the church and adopted by the General Assembly in 2006. A critical insight of the PUP report was the reaffirmation of the legacy of the scruple applicable to the fidelity and chastity requirement for ordination. The PUP Report used the term "departure" instead of "scruple," but the principle of freedom of conscience remained.[1] Though conservatives "wanted to paint this as a new and dangerous innovation," it was merely a restatement of Presbyterian principles dating to 1729 and reaffirmed by the Swearingen Commission in 1927.[2]

The PUP report linked the time-honored concept of scruple with LGBT ordination under Amendment B. It would be up to individual presbyteries to determine whether "fidelity and chastity" was essential or nonessential. There were LGBT-friendly presbyteries; the recent "don't ask, don't tell" ordinations of Katie Morrison, Eilie Marlow, and Ray Bagnuolo proved that, and there were others. A local option had effectively been created . . . or had it?

Not so fast, said the GAPJC.

Was the "fidelity and chastity" requirement of Amendment B subject to avoidance based upon a candidate's scruple? Several presbyteries assumed as much but wanted to go on the record that it wouldn't happen in their conservative jurisdictions. Preemptive resolutions were adopted in a few presbyteries that effectively said they would not permit a scruple to avoid the "fidelity and chastity" requirement of Amendment B.

Only a lawyer could love the twists and turns in the Presbyterian path toward full inclusion over the next few years. The actions of the conservative presbyteries wound their way to the GAPJC, which handed down a ruling that went further than the conservatives hoped. On February 11, 2008, the court issued a complementary series of decisions that held that the doctrine of scruple applied only to "disagreement" and not to "disobedience." According to the court, the "fidelity and chastity" standard mandated certain behavior that could not be disobeyed by ordination candidates.

> The freedom of conscience granted in G-6.0108 allows candidates to express disagreement with the wording or meaning of provisions of the constitution, but does not permit disobedience to those behavioral standards. The fidelity and chastity provision may only be changed by a constitutional amendment. Until that occurs, individual candidates, officers, examining and governing bodies must adhere to it.[3]

Once again, Amendment B and its "fidelity and chastity" requirement and reference to "that which the confessions call sin" remained as the gate through which LGBT candidates could not pass. The Presbyterian courts guarded the gate closely and would not allow any opening unless and until the General Assembly would tear the gate down.

Once again, the ball was in the court of the GA. Once again, the GA acted. Based on an overture from Scott Anderson's John Knox Presbytery of Wisconsin, General Assembly 2008 adopted an "authoritative interpretation" of Amendment B, which would be known as the "Knox AI."[4]

First, as if reminding the court that adoption of the Task Force recommendation at GA 2006 had already included its own authoritative interpretation, the Knox AI stated: "The 218th General Assembly (2008) affirms the authoritative interpretation of G-6.0108 approved by the

217th General Assembly (2006)." Second, the Knox AI reminded the court that it was the presbyteries (examining bodies) that had the final say-so, based upon independent discretion, exercised on a case-by-case basis. The Knox AI required:

> Examining bodies to give prayerful and careful consideration, on an individual, case-by-case basis, to any departure from an ordination standard in matters of belief or practice that a candidate may declare during examination. However, the examining body is not required to accept a departure from standards, and cannot excuse a candidate's inability to perform the constitutional functions unique to his or her office (such as administration of the sacraments).

By a close vote (375 to 325), the Knox AI was adopted by GA 2008. Scott Anderson would immediately test the waters himself, and he sought ordination and filed his scruple, labeled an Affirmation of Conscience.[5] He would soon be joined by another familiar pilgrim on the Presbyterian journey, Lisa Larges. Larges had first sought ordination twenty years earlier, and more recently she had assumed the role of executive director of That All May Freely Serve (TAMFS) following the retirement of Rev. Dr. Janie Spahr.

Lisa Larges' ordination request arose in the Presbytery of San Francisco. Her earlier attempt at ordination in the nineties had been in the Presbytery of the Twin Cities. In 2004, Larges had unsuccessfully sought ordination in San Francisco when she acknowledged she was in a same-gender relationship and noncompliant with Amendment B. The Committee for Preparation for the Ministry (CPM) simply dropped the matter at that time. In 2007, Larges picked up the process again, this time noting her scruple: "By my conscience, faith and theology, I cannot and will not accept the terms of this standard."[6]

This time the CPM reported to the presbytery (by a twelve to nine vote) that "the Candidate was ready for examination for ordination pending a call with a departure." Instead of scheduling an examination of the candidate, the presbytery scheduled a hearing in her absence to consider the report of the CPM. After lengthy debate, the presbytery voted 167 to 151 to "accept the recommendation of the CPM and certify the Candidate as ready for examination effective January 15, 2008, with a departure." The matter was appealed and found its way to the GAPJC on November 2, 2009.[7]

The court punted.

The court deferred any decision on the merits of whether Larges could be or should be ordained, holding instead that such a decision would not be ripe until after the presbytery conducted the requisite in-person examination of the candidate. Since the presbytery's action was based solely on the report of the CPM and not on an examination of the candidate, the matter was not ripe, and the presbytery must first conduct the examination. The court would not prejudge the outcome.[8]

Back on track, Larges appeared before the presbytery in November 10, 2009, and they approved her for ordination and accepted her scruple after a four-hour debate and a vote of 156 to 138. The gatekeeper's appeal to the synodical PJC failed, and the Synod PJC affirmed the action of the Presbytery on September 29, 2010, in a split vote of five to four.[9] A final decision by the GAPJC would come later . . . unless?

Meanwhile, we return to Scott Anderson's journey.

Although gatekeepers attempted several procedural roadblocks and stays resulting in delays, Anderson finally had his day before his gathered presbytery on February 20, 2010. There would be no "wink and a nod" or "don't ask, don't tell" circumvention of the rules. Anderson and the presbytery confronted Amendment B head on.

> [T]he Candidate was known to the Presbytery to be living in a committed partnership of many years' duration with another man and not within a covenant of marriage between a man and a woman. During his examination by the Presbytery, the Candidate stated that "in every respect" his relationship with his partner is exactly like a marriage except for procreation, and that he has never taken a vow of celibacy. The Candidate stated at his examination that he believes his manner of life is consistent with Scripture and the Confessions, as well as with the ordination standards in the Book of Order.[10]

Following examination of the candidate and discernment by the presbytery, Scott Anderson was approved for ordination by a vote of eighty-one to twenty-five. The decision was appealed to the synodical permanent judicial commission, which affirmed in a seven to one vote, and then the matter was appealed to the GAPJC, which would render final judgment . . . unless?

With both the Larges and Anderson cases pending before the Presbyterian "Supreme Court," the Presbyterians convened in Minneapolis for their 219th General Assembly on July 2, 2010. The assembly theme was from the seventh chapter of John, "Out of the believer's heart shall flow rivers of living water." Two hundred miles north of the Twin Cities, a small stream splashed out of Lake Itasca and began winding its way to the Gulf of Mexico. Churning over St. Anthony Falls, the birthplace of Minneapolis, the pristine waters of the Mississippi had not yet become the "Big Muddy." It would be in the Twin Cities that the Presbyterians finally crossed over the river.

Year after year after year, LGBT Presbyterians had hoped, only to be disappointed. "How do you continue to do it?" Susan Kraemer had wailed in the mid-nineties. "We keep on doing what we have always been doing, for this work is urgent work," Michael Adee had urged following a defeat a decade later. "I shall not die until I preach there again," John Knox had promised despite his unlikely circumstances. Why hope, why keep on, why chase the promise?

"Out of the believer's heart shall flow rivers of living water."

There was actually a sound basis for optimism. Just a year earlier in the very same convention halls, the Lutherans had broken through to the end of their journey. The Episcopalians, likewise, out in Orange County, California. And last time, in 2008, the Presbyterians had come within a whisker. Amendment B had been removed by General Assembly 2008, and the voters in presbyteries across the land had nearly ratified, failing by a mere 51–49 percent of voters and a handful of presbyteries. Even at that, fully thirty-four presbyteries that had previously voted nay in 2001 had become yeas in 2008. Also in 2008, the onerous definitive guidance of 1978 that said "homosexuality is not God's wish for humanity" and "unrepentant homosexual practice does not accord with the requirements for ordination" had been nullified; this repugnant indictment of all gays, and all subsequent affirmations, "shall have no force and effect," the commissioners had said. Had the tipping point been reached?

"Out of the believer's heart shall flow rivers of living water."

In 2010, when Amendment B was replaced on the plenary floor, the mood was subdued. For the fourth time the General Assembly had acted, but the uncertainty of the presbytery ratification process cast a pall. Three times previously, the presbyteries had rejected similar GA action. "The presbyteries have previously voted three times on proposed amendments to G-6.0106b. They retained the "fidelity and chastity" language by votes of 114–57 following the 1997 Assembly, 127–46 following the 2001 Assembly and 95–78 following the 2008 Assembly."[11]

In a discouraging sign, the plenary vote was by a weak margin of 53–47 percent, less than the 60 percent of two years earlier. In Lutheran polity, actions of the Churchwide Assembly do not require subsequent ratification by regional synods; thus, a year earlier, when the Lutherans had called the question and opened their pulpits to LGBT ministers, this same plenary hall had been filled with sobbing, hugging, barely believing clusters of gays, lesbians, and their allies. For the Presbyterians, it was simply on to the next order of business. *D.C. al fine?* Would the song recycle again to the beginning or was this truly the beginning of the end?

The revised Amendment B removed the controversial language that had existed since 1997. "Fidelity in marriage and chastity in singleness" was gone. So, too, the reference to that "which the confessions call sin." Here is the full replacement text.

> Standards for ordained service reflect the church's desire to submit joyfully to the Lordship of Jesus Christ in all aspects of life. The governing body responsible for ordination and/or installation shall examine each candidate's calling, gifts, preparation and suitability for the responsibilities of office. The examination shall include, but not be limited to, a determination of the candidate's ability and commitment to fulfill all the requirements as expressed in the constitutional questions for ordination and installation. Governing bodies shall be guided by Scripture and the confessions in applying standards to individual candidates.

The presbytery ratification process would play out over the next year, one by one, 173 presbyteries in all. A simple majority, eighty-seven yes votes, would be necessary to ratify. Only a handful of presbyteries would need to switch from no to yes from the vote two years earlier. When first one, then two, then three presbyteries switched their vote, expectations began to rise. Then four, then five, then . . . eventually a net of sixteen presbyteries would switch from no to yes, considerably more than necessary. Once again, Presbyterian eyes turned to Minnesota and the Presbytery of the Twin Cities in May 2011. Ratification was now a foregone conclusion; only one more positive vote was necessary to reach eighty-seven, and more than twenty presbyteries had not yet voted.[12]

It was fitting that the Twin Cities Presbytery should have the honor of casting the decisive vote. This was the presbytery that had ordained State Fair 4-H gardening champion David Bailey Sindt, the one who stood with his sign at General Assembly 1974 and asked, "Is anybody else out there gay?"; this was the presbytery that had championed the ordination of Lisa Larges back in the early nineties; and this was the presbytery that had issued a public apology to the LGBT community after the church adopted Amendment B in 1997.

Then, too, there's the Minnesota water.

On a late-spring weekday evening, 264 elders and ministers gathered at Peace Presbyterian Church in suburban St. Louis Park, Minnesota. Interested observers crammed the doorways and hallways. Ratification passed easily, 205 to 56. Reaction came swiftly.

Moderator Cindy Bolbach emphasized that ordination decisions would be locally made, a return to traditional presbyterian polity: "This amendment does not require any session or presbytery to ordain a gay and lesbian person. It leaves it up to the discretion of the local body, which knows the person best."[13]

The Layman magazine, the Presbyterian voice of the loyal opposition since 1965, sounded a decidedly disloyal chord, an apocalyptic call to arms:

In rejecting the concept that the Bible means what it says, the current ruling majority in the PC(USA) has departed from the founding principles of both the PC(USA) and historic Presbyterianism.

The passage of Amendment 10A permitting self-avowed unrepentant sinners to be ordained is not the point of departure, but is symptomatic of a departure which already occurred in the minds of the voters. Collectively, the majority of presbyteries are convinced that it is better to evolve with culture than stand on the faith delivered to them by the apostles and passed down through the ages. . . .

The question is what will you do? . . . How you respond to 10A will communicate a lot about where you stand in terms of the nature of God, sin, the authority of the Scriptures, the Lord-ship of Jesus Christ and the nature of Christian doctrine. . . . Do you likewise have the courage of your convictions? Are you willing to risk speaking up for the truth?[14]

In the next chapter, we will see how the Lay Committee's call to arms played out.

The pending GAPJC cases against the ordinations of Scott Anderson and Lisa Larges were eventually dismissed as moot in in light of the changed circumstances and the revised language of Amendment B. By the time of the dismissal of the court case against her ordination, Larges had decided to return to her roots in Minnesota to seek ordination there. Here are snippets cut from her written statement:

Time, as they say, is a river—not pausing, never waiting, and carrying us on . . .

My friend and mentor Janie Spahr has counseled many LGBT folks like me struggling with the questions of whether to stay in the church, whether to pursue a call in our church, or come out to their congregation. The question she will ask is, "Are you willing to be curriculum for the church?"

All of the ups-and-downs and ins-and-outs of this long judicial process have been part of what it means to be curriculum for the church. We have to learn together, and we don't seem to learn well in the abstract. And I can't say that it's been anything but a privilege to do this work. At the same time, even as I understand in a deep way that the whole of this journey, and the good work of being "curriculum" has been a part of my sense of calling, this judicial process has also been personally painful. The many delays, and the waiting, have exacted a cost. There's a kind of spiritual pain here that I'm still figuring out. Suffice it to say that our judicial process, as necessary as it may be, is hard on everyone, from the commissioners to the legal counsels on both sides, to the individuals whose lives are directly affected.

But we believe in a God who is the redeemer of time, and we strive for that equanimity of thanksgiving that Paul speaks of and practiced in his own life. "Gratitude in good times," Calvin said, "patience in adversity, and [most of all] a wonderful security respecting the future."[15]

NOTES

1. "It is necessary to the integrity and health of the church that the persons who serve in it as officers shall adhere to the essentials of the Reformed faith and polity as expressed in The Book of Confessions and the Form of Government. So far as may be possible without serious departure from these standards, without infringing on the rights and views of others, and without obstructing the constitutional governance of the church, freedom of conscience with respect to the interpretation of Scripture is to be maintained. . . . It is to be recognized, however, that in becoming a candidate or officer of the Presbyterian Church (USA) one chooses to exercise freedom of conscience within certain bounds. His or her conscience is captive to the Word of God as interpreted in the standards of the church so long as he or she continues to seek or hold office in that body. The decision as to whether a person has departed from essentials of Reformed faith and polity is made initially by the individual concerned but ultimately becomes the responsibility of the governing body in which he or she serves." "A Season of Discernment," the final report of the Theological Task Force on the Peace, Unity, and Purity of the Church as approved by the 217th (2006) General Assembly, PC(USA), 4, note 5.

2. Doug Nave, PUP Task Force member and attorney, e-mail to Chris Glaser, August 2012.

3. The Permanent Judicial Commission of the General Assembly of the Presbyterian Church (USA), Bush et al. v. Presbytery of Pittsburgh, Remedial Case 218-10 (February 11, 2008).

4. The language of the AI Resolution "On Adopting an Authoritative Interpretation of G-6.0108 to Ensure Proper Application of Ordination Standards" and the text of the "rationale" are available on the website of the Presbyterian Church, accessed August 9, 2012, http://www.pc-biz.org/IOBView.aspx?m=ro&id=1497.

5. One commentator praised Scott Anderson's argumentation: "as elegant, succinct and persuasive a document as you'll ever read. . . . I believe history will remember it as seminal in the evolution of gay rights." John Shore, "Meet Scott Anderson."

6. The Permanent Judicial Commission of the General Assembly of the Presbyterian Church (USA), Naegli et al. v. Presbytery of San Francisco, Remedial Case 219-11 (November 2, 2009).

7. Ibid.

8. Ibid.

9. Anitra Kitts Rasmussen, "Lisa Larges Moves Closer to Ordination," *Presbyterian News Service*, September 29, 2010.

10. The Permanent Judicial Commission of the General Assembly of the Presbyterian Church (USA), Caledonia Presbyterian Church et al. v. the Presbytery of John Knox, Remedial Case 220-04 (August 1, 2011).

11. Jerry Van Marter, Presbyterian News Service, *PC(USA) Relaxes Constitutional Prohibition of Gay and Lesbian Ordination*, May 11, 2011.

12. Ibid.

13. Matt Sepic, "Twin Cities Presbytery Approves Gay Clergy," *Minnesota Public Radio*, May 10, 2011.

14. Forrest A. Norman III, "Choose This Day Whom You Will Serve," *The Layman* vol. 44, no. 4, June, 2011.

15. Lisa Larges, "Dreaming of the Church That Can Be," accessed August 10, 2012, http://dreamingchurch.wordpress.com/2012/05/01/lisa-larges-real-party-in-interest/.

44

A Slight "ECO"

The Presbyterian world changed when the Twin Cities Presbytery ratified inclusive ordination standards. The gates had finally been pushed open, knocked down, and trampled underfoot. The gatekeeping magazine, *The Layman*, barked a challenge to its followers, "What will you do?"

In August 2011, before the ink was dry on the new Presbyterian ordination policy, a group of disaffected conservatives raised the question, "[I]s that which 'is broken' capable of self-renewal?"[1] They did more than ask rhetorical questions; they organized. "To date, more than 1,200 people have indicated their support of this fledgling movement now called The Fellowship of Presbyterians," they reported.[2] Schism was on their minds.

Of course, conservative Presbyterian denominations already existed.

The Orthodox Presbyterian Church (OPC) split from the mainstream in the twenties. With the Auburn Affirmation, the modernist view prevailed, and the OPC was formed by disaffected fundamentalists. This denomination currently has less than thirty thousand members nationwide.[3]

The Presbyterian Church in America (PCA) was formed in 1973 as a negative response to merger discussions between the Northern Presbyterians and the Southern Presbyterians. Female ordination and the continuing fallout of the Fundamentalist-Modernist debate contributed to the formation of this schismatic denomination. Next to the PC(USA) with more than two million members, the PCA is the second largest denomination with approximately three hundred fifty thousand members.[4]

The Evangelical Presbyterian Church (EPC) was formed in 1981, and currently claims a hundred fifteen thousand members.[5] This denomination also traces its lineage to the Fundamentalist-Modernist controversy of the twenties, and the EPC intentionally reclaimed the "Five Fundamentals" of the earlier debate, albeit under a different name in order to avoid the stigma of the term "fundamentalism." A triggering factor for this schismatic departure from the mainstream was the rejection of an ordination candidate who unsuccessfully claimed a scruple based upon his disagreement with female ordination.

Following the removal of the gates that had barred LGBT clergy, fleeing conservatives thus had several alternative landing zones, but, as with the Episcopal and Lutheran schismatics, the preference was to form something new. Creating one's own denomination must be pretty heady stuff.

In January 2012, two thousand gathered in Orlando to give birth to a new denomination in the presbyterian tradition consisting of PC(USA) defectors. The Fellowship of Presbyterians would be the midwife, and the newborn would be named the Evangelical Covenant Order of Presbyterians, or "ECO" for short. Within a few months, the name was changed to the Covenant Order of Evangelical Presbyterians, but "ECO" remained.

Rev. John Crosby of Christ Presbyterian Church of Edina, Minnesota, was named interim president.

> "This is an uncertain time," Crosby said, noting that 60 percent of respondents to a pre-gathering survey said they were in "a period of discernment" about denominational alignment. "We are not angry, we are determined . . . we are not 'after' or 'against' them we all need time, space and grace. . . . We want to flesh out the options and then let God lead so we have the sense that we're all working together."[6]

Once again, the century-old Fundamentalist-Modernist undercurrent bubbled to the surface. Everything old is new again. In May 2012, the president of the Fellowship of Presbyterians expressed a longing to return to the straight-and-narrow certainty of the Five Fundamentals. He wrote,

> As we learn from our history (1925–1927), in the midst of the Fundamentalist/Modernist controversy, it was decided we should not specify our "essential" tenets. For a season those beliefs could still be assumed but, over time, many doctrines of the church were subtly eroded. . . . We do not believe broad theological diversity and pluralism are helpful in building flourishing churches to make disciples of Jesus Christ.[7]

"Diversity" and "pluralism" had become bad words.

But, there were Presbyterian centrists who disagreed with the new LGBT ordination policies yet discouraged schism. Twenty-four leaders, many of whom had attended the Orlando gathering that spawned ECO, signed a letter urging restraint. The signatories included presbytery and synod execs, seminary presidents, directors of mission organizations, and members of boards of directors of several institutions. According to the Rev. Paul Watermulder, who drafted the letter, the letter was intended to urge the leadership of the PC(USA) to be "bridge builders," and also "[t]o urge all those who are talking about leaving or distancing themselves from the PCUSA to slow down and recognize that there are several viable signs of unity coming to the GA in Pittsburgh which are supported by a wide range of centrist leaders."[8]

On May 1, 2012, *The Layman* magazine reported that forty-seven PC(USA) congregations had begun the process of separation in order to join ECO.[9] As of June 1, 2013, the ECO website did not report any numbers, but a map revealed that less than half the states of the United States had an ECO congregation.[10] Episcopal and Lutheran defections following their 2009 enactment of LGBT inclusion policies amounted to roughly 5 percent of the denominational congregations and/or membership. For the Presbyterians, it has been far less to date; only a slight "ECO" would remain of early schismatic bluster.

NOTES

1. Richard Gibbons, "How Can the Church Be More Biblical, Missional, and Intentional?" on the website of Fellowship of Presbyterians, accessed August 10, 2012, http://www.fellowship-pres.org/documents-2/.

2. Paul Detterman, "What Is in a Name?" on the website of Fellowship of Presbyterians, accessed August 16, 2011, http://www.fellowship-pres.org/documents-2/.

3. 2010 General Assembly Report, Orthodox Presbyterian Church, accessed August 11, 2012, http://opc.org/GA/77th_GA_rpt.html.

4. Administrative Committee Statistics, on the website of the Presbyterian Church in America, accessed August 11, 2012, http://www.pcaac.org/Statistics .htm.

5. Evangelical Presbyterian Church, "About the EPC," accessed August 11, 2012, http://www.epc.org/about-the-epc/.

6. Jerry L. Van Meter, Presbyterian News Service, "Fellowship of Presbyterians Unveils Name for 'New Reformed Body,'" January 19, 2012.

7. Jim Singleton, "Is ECO a Reformed Body?" Fellowship of Presbyterians, accessed August 12, 2012, http://www.fellowship-pres.org/is-eco-a-reformed-body/.

8. Jerry L. Van Marter, Presbyterian News Service, "24 PC(USA) leaders issue 'Letter of Reconciliation,'" January 24, 2012.

9. "Forty-seven churches preparing to join ECO", *The Layman* vol. 45, no. 3, May 2012.

10. Website of ECO: A Covenant Order of Evangelical Presbyterians, accessed June 3, 2013, http://eco-pres.org/membership/eco-members/

45

A Stole Returned

When Pastor Scott Anderson was outed by two members of his congregation in 1990, he hastily called a meeting of the Session of Bethany Presbyterian Church of Sacramento and resigned rather than face a contentious aftermath. The Session was shocked and reluctantly accepted his resignation. They raised nearly $8,000 as a parting severance to pay for a return to graduate school, not a trivial sum for the middle-class congregation.

In 2010, an unexpected e-mail came from California. "Please forgive me," said the woman from the past who had outed him two decades earlier.[1]

As noted, Rev. Anderson had been part of the Peace, Unity, and Purity of the Church Task Force (PUP). Rev. Mark Achtemeier, theology professor from Dubuque, Iowa, and a self-described "out, self-affirming, practicing conservative evangelical" also served on the Task Force. He had been a gatekeeper, an outspoken foe of LGBT ordination, who had keynoted conservative conferences that helped entrench the opposition.

> "I started out very sure and very settled and very content with seeing exclusion (of gays and lesbians from marriage and ordained office) as God's will for the church," Achtemeier said. "Like many, I had succumbed to the temptations of an ecclesiastical tunnel vision: I read authors I agreed with. I talked with people I agreed with. I hung out with people I agreed with. I was exceedingly comfortable holding the position I did, I was

supported in it, I was popular. And I had absolutely no reason to question any of it.

"But God had other plans. Out of the blue, opportunity opened up for serious conversation and friendship with some quite remarkable gay Christians. This was new for me. When you are a firebrand exclusivist, hurling thunderbolts and belching fire against the opposition, gay people with any sense tend to avoid your company, or at least they avoid telling you they are gay."[2]

Service on the PUP Task Force, was a "God thing" that turned his thinking about gays and lesbians upside down. Getting to know Scott Anderson and other gays and lesbians challenged his assumptions. In particular, Professor Achtemeier *assumed* that LGBT advocates and allies held "a fairly casual attitude toward Scripture," but he came to realize that his assumption was false. LGBT Christians didn't ignore the Bible, or treat it casually, but they interpreted it differently, based upon their lived experience. For gay and lesbian Christians, experience didn't trump, veto, or override Scripture but informed Scriptural understanding, and this realization was an epiphany for Achtemeier. What is more, Achtemeier came to understand that the positive experience of committed gays in a relationship, in contrast with the "spiritually and psychologically crippling" consequences of self-denial "ought to make us ask whether we've correctly understood the Bible's teaching. . . . There is a vast difference between vetoing what the Bible says on the basis of experience, and looking for understandings of the Bible that make powerful sense of our experience."[3]

Then, like a proper student of the Reformation, Rev. Achtemeier turned to John Calvin's own criticism of enforced celibacy.

"Marriage is given to us, not just in a form that responds to our need, but also in a way that is positively sanctifying and life-giving and permeated by grace," Achtemeier said. "If, as Calvin insists, it is foolish and rash for individuals to turn their backs on this divine gift and calling, how much more so when an entire church acts to withhold this gift from a whole class of human beings?"[4]

On Saturday, October 8, 2011, Rev. Achtemeier delivered the sermon during Scott Anderson's reordination service at Covenant Presbyterian Church of Madison, Wisconsin. Listen to a portion:

From the very beginning of its existence, the church has borne witness to holy occasions when the Word of God blazed to life, judging the thoughts and intentions of many hearts, overturning established assumptions, bringing light and life where formerly only darkness reigned.

The Gospel runs its course. What a remarkable privilege to be living in a time when once again the Word of God has come to life as good news for the broken-hearted! The Holy Spirit is abroad, blowing across the landscape of our established convictions and setting many hearts ablaze.

This new treasure we have found in the Scripture seems so obvious to many of us, but we have to remember it is not obvious to all. . . . And so in our own time, Christ grants us an important opportunity to bear witness to his love which binds us together even in the midst of our disagreements. . . . For that reason we must all be very patient, and very respectful, and very gentle with our sisters and brothers who take a different view of this day than we do.

Scott has led the way with this, going out of his way time and again to forge bonds of respect and caring and understanding across the lines of separation and disagreement. Other people have responded in kind, so that with rare exceptions, the life of this presbytery has been marked by kindness, mutual respect and forbearance grounded in the love of Christ.[5]

Outside, a hundred or more LGBT supporters waved rainbow flags to counter the hateful clown show of the Westboro Baptist Church. Inside the sanctuary, a stole returned to its proper place. In 1995, Anderson had offered his ministerial stole, given to him as a gift after his first year of service at Bethany in Sacramento, to the Shower of Stoles project. It was one of more than a thousand that had toured the country and appeared at important gatherings.

"Today, for the first time in the life of this collection, a stole is being returned, and in so doing, it is transformed from a symbol of loss to a symbol of hope," said David Lohman, of the National Gay and Lesbian Task Force, the director of the Shower of Stoles.[6]

With the stole draped around his neck, Rev. Scott Anderson beamed as he was presented to the crowd of more than three hundred. The assembly rose to its feet and began sustained clapping that broke into cheers and shouts.

John Knox had hoped, prayed, and promised to return to preach in his pulpit, and he did. Twenty years after his church had put him in chains, Rev. Scott Anderson had his own homecoming to the ordained ministry. He was the first fruits, the first out gay to be ordained under the new Presbyterian policy. Others would soon follow him into the pulpit.

NOTES

1. Private correspondence with the author, October 7, 2012.

2. Leslie Scanlon, "Achtemeier's journey to accept homosexual marriage, ordination," *The Presbyterian Outlook*; www.pres-outlook.org, December 14, 2009; Scanlon's interview with Rev. Mark Achtemeier is quoted with permission.

3. Ibid.

4. Ibid.

5. Mark Achtemeier, "Springs in the Desert" ordination sermon for Scott Anderson, on the website of the Covenant Network of Presbyterians, accessed August 10, 2012, http://covnetpres.org/2011/10/ordination-sermon-for-scott-anderson/.

6. Doug Erickson, "Re-ordination Caps Long Journey," *Wisconsin State Journal*, October 9, 2011.

PART V

The Methodists

What Martin Luther was for the Lutherans and John Knox for the Presbyterians, John Wesley and his brother Charles were for the Methodists, only more so. While Luther and Knox were the long-ago and far-away inspirations for the Lutherans and Presbyterians of the United States, John Wesley himself sent the first Methodists to evangelize the American colonies. This followed his own boots-on-the-ground experience as itinerant preacher and missionary to the Georgia colony, followed by half a century of theological and ecclesiastical development back home in England. Quite simply, Wesley was not only the founder of Methodism but also the influence behind its exportation to American shores, where it assumed much greater importance than in Mother England.

Wesley accepted the pejorative term "methodist" that had been applied to his methodically spiritual "holy club" back at Oxford around 1730. They fasted, took communion weekly, and read and discussed the

Bible constantly. They also visited prisoners and others who were sick or poor. Late in life, Wesley would become an ardent abolitionist.

An Anglican cleric to his death in 1791, Wesley became frustrated with the Church of England over its reluctance to send clergy to the United States following the Revolution. So he did it himself. Wesley laid hands on Anglican priest Thomas Coke and sent him off to America in 1784 to join with another Wesley disciple, Francis Asbury, to serve as co-superintendents of a to-be-formed church body. Wesley had sent Asbury to the colonies in 1771, and Asbury had remained in America during the Revolutionary War.

By the time Coke arrived, Methodism as an informal movement had already experienced expanding influence. A 1787 document looked back at their effort "to reform the continent, and spread Scripture Holiness over these Lands. As a proof hereof, we have seen in the Course of fifteen Years a great and glorious Work of God, from New York through the Jersies, Pennsylvania, Delaware, Maryland, Virginia, North and South Carolina, even to Georgia."[1]

Soon after Asbury's arrival in 1784, a convention was arranged in Baltimore, which would become famously known as the "Christmas Conference." Out of this gathering, the movement became formalized as the Methodist Episcopal Church. Asbury said he would become superintendent only if the conference agreed, and the authority of conferences to select church leaders became a foundational principle. The two superintendents soon claimed the status of bishop (despite Wesley's opposition), and the itinerant bishops evangelized with great success, Asbury in particular. Methodism jibed well with the Second Great Awakening that stirred the country at the turn of the century. By the time of Asbury's death in 1816, the Methodist Episcopal Church numbered more than two hundred thousand members, ministered to by seven hundred ordained clergy.

The Methodist Church is the most distinctively American of the ecumenical denominations. Save for the first few missionaries sent by Wesley, first-generation American Methodists were not immigrant stock that brought their religion with them, but locally born and bred converts to an emerging denomination. Contrary to the experience of the Episcopal Church, also Anglican offspring born of the American Revolution, the Methodist Church did not retain close ties with the Anglicism of the Church of England, and the emotional, enthusiastic, revivalist, frontier-preacher style of the Methodists contrasted sharply with their roots in the liturgical and sacramental ecclesiology of Anglicism. Circuit-riding preachers on horseback, seldom with theological training—or any education—fit well with the American frontier at the turn of the nineteenth century.

Such itinerancy may be the most distinctive feature of early Methodism, and this legacy remains a structural cornerstone of the twenty-first century church. Asbury and Coke explained itinerancy in an early version of the *Book of Discipline*, which is the defining and controlling document of Methodism in the United States:

> *Our grand plan*, in all its parts, leads to an *itinerant* ministry. Our bishops are travelling bishops. All the different orders that compose our conferences are employed in the *travelling line*; and our local preachers are, *in some degree*, travelling preachers. Every thing is kept moving as far as possible; and we will be bold to say, that, next to the grace of God, there is nothing *like this* for keeping the whole body alive from the center to the circumference, and for the continual extension of that circumference on every hand.[2]

In May of 1767, at a revival meeting in a barn in Lancaster, Pennsylvania, Martin Boehm, a Mennonite preacher, offered a personal testimony of crying out to God while plowing in the field. "Wir sind Brüder (we are brethren)," said Reformed pastor Philip William Otterbein. In 1800, the loosely connected group of Germans, whose religious practices mirrored their English-speaking Methodist neighbors, formally created the United Brethren, and Boehm and Otterbein were elected bishops. Although separated by language and ethnic heritage, the Brethren and the Methodists shared their American religious experience; Bishop Asbury spoke at the memorial services for Boehm and Otterbein.

The United Brethren became staunchly antislavery. After 1837, slaveholders were not allowed membership. By the end of the nineteenth century, the United Brethren had grown to more than two hundred thousand members and six bishops. Two factions of the Brethren split in 1887 but reunited in 1946.

Meanwhile, the Northern and Southern branches of Methodists split over slavery. Some Methodists were very active in the Underground Railroad. In 1939, North and South reunited but a small splinter of segregationist southerners, dissatisfied with the merger, split away in 1940.

In 1968, the main grouping of United Brethren (the Evangelical United Brethren) and the main body of Methodists merged to form the United Methodist Church. The UMC is easily the largest of the five ecumenical denominations considered here with more than eight million members in the United States and another four million overseas. This size and this combination of the U.S. and international conferences would have major implications for the Methodist journey toward full inclusion, as we shall see. The UCC, TEC, the ELCA, and the PC(USA) all have significant relationships with sister churches overseas, but the UMC is unique in its connection with its international brothers and sisters who vote, with increasing numbers and influence, at UMC General Conferences.

We cannot mention Wesley without a brief look at the Wesleyan Quadrilateral: Scripture, tradition, experience, and reason. Later writers distilled Wesley's views of the complex interplay of reason and revelation, and these became known as the Quadrilateral. The UMC *Book of Discipline* sums up Wesley's teaching this way: "Wesley believed that the living core of the Christian faith was revealed in Scripture, illumined by tradition, vivified in personal experience, and confirmed by reason. Scripture [however] is primary, revealing the Word of God "so far as it is necessary for our salvation."[3]

For Wesley, as for most Christian theorists, Scripture comes first, and tradition, reason, and experience are tools to aid in scriptural interpretation, under the guidance of the Spirit. Those who currently shout the Reformation refrain *sola scriptura* (scripture alone) oversimplify the nuanced understanding of the reformers. Ultimately, Wesley was a pragmatist, and he apprehended truth in the experience of life. "What the Scriptures promise, I enjoy," Wesley stated.[4] Even tradition, for Wesley, included the influences of one's environment—family, friends, and ideas encountered.

The key concepts in Methodist polity are connectionalism and itinerancy. In Methodism's infancy, informal groups, often a local prayer meeting, would regularly receive visits from a circuit-riding preacher, and this circle of local groups would be his "connexion." The minister would belong to the connexion rather than a local congregation.

Although Methodists take pride in their organizational structures, the many layers and connections are decidedly "methodical" and confusing. I'll try to keep it simple.

In current polity,[5] the UMC has no national office or chief executive officer. The Council of Bishops serves as the Methodist executive. The General Conference serves as the ultimate legislative body, the only entity empowered to enact policy for the whole church, and it meets once every four years. Delegates are half clergy and half laity, and they are elected by their regional "annual conferences." Even the term "annual conference" is confusing; it sounds like an event, but it is a regional body that performs legislative and budgetary functions for a geographic region. The sessions of the annual conference are annual conventions of the clergy and laity within the conference.

In the United States, there are forty-nine elected bishops, assigned to administer sixty-six annual conferences that are roughly contiguous to state borders. Obviously, boundaries are not precise and some states have more than one annual conference and some bishops serve more than one annual conference. The bishops collectively, active and retired, serve on the Council of Bishops and provide executive and administrative oversight for the whole church as well as their individual episcopal areas. Bishops generally serve one episcopal area for eight years before moving on to a new area or retiring.

Nine persons are elected at General Conference to serve on the Judicial Council, which acts as the ultimate appellate court of the church and provides the definitive interpretations of the *Book of Discipline* and the constitution. The majority of five alternates between laity and clergy.

To summarize, the quadrennial General Conference provides legislative functions, the Council of Bishops is the executive, and the Judicial Council, obviously, is the judicial branch. There are other structures (jurisdictions, the connectional table, districts, and so on) but these are irrelevant for present purposes. The other four ecumenical denominations considered here are well-settled in their organization and structure, but that is less true with Methodism, and organizational restructuring is the subject of continuing debate. At General Conference 2012, a proposal for significant restructuring was defeated, but that is not likely to be the end of a continuing reevaluation of UMC administration and governance.

In 1939, long after the Civil War, Methodists in the North and South were reunited with the addition of a Central Conference organized along segregated lines; that is, the Central Conference was black, but the rest of the church was white. This arrangement had a gerrymandering effect; all black influence was concentrated in a single conference. In 1968, in the merger that produced the UMC, this racial slight was corrected and delegates to the quadrennial General Conferences would be strictly allocated by geographic membership in an Annual Conference. While the term "Central Conference" was dropped in the United States, it is still used in regard to bodies outside the United States. This progressive policy—of removing race in the context of the United States—would have ironic consequences later when membership swelled overseas, and a solid bloc of international delegates from the Central Conferences joined antigay conservative forces in the United States to block progressive reform of LGBT issues.

There are three levels of ordained ministry within the UMC: deacons, elders, and bishops. Deacons are ordained to a ministry of service but not to a ministry of word and sacrament. A minister of word and sacrament is called an elder, which is the equivalent of an Episcopal priest, a UCC or Lutheran pastor, and a Presbyterian teaching elder. Elders may be elected and consecrated to service as a bishop.

It is the prerogative of annual conferences to ordain and bishops to appoint elders to specific congregations. That is, local congregations do not choose their own clergy; this is a vestige of the circuit-riding preacher and his "connexion." Ordinations occur once a year in a single service for all new ordinands during sessions of the annual conferences. Clergy appointments to individual congregations are usually made once a year during the sessions. Certainly, appointments are made in consultation with local congregations, but it is the bishop and not the congregation who has the last word.

Delegates to General Conference are selected by annual conferences, and the proportion of clergy to laity is fixed at 50–50 percent.

The number of delegates to General Conference is a fixed number (maximum of one thousand), and each annual conference is allocated representation based upon population. The proportional allocation is modified with each quadrennial General Conference as membership population changes occur. In the last decade, there has been a stunning shift in delegate allocations to the Central Conferences (international). In 2004, international delegates comprised 19 percent of the total, in 2008, the portion jumped to 28 percent, and in 2012 it leaped again to 38 percent.[6] Contrary to the experience of the other ecumenical denominations, the journey toward full inclusion has slowed in the Methodist Church, and this changing demographic of General Conference delegates is a primary factor.

For this denomination of circuit-riding bishops and clergy, the journey toward full inclusion would prove to be treacherous. At each bend in the road, the Methodists would lag behind the other ecumenical denominations. To be sure, Methodist gays, lesbians, and their allies found safe sanctuary in many places, and their numbers swelled along the way, but for all the genuine affection for their connectional history, in the end Methodist polity would prevent passage across the river, and the Methodist gays, lesbians, and their straight allies could only wonder, "How long, O Lord?"

NOTES

1. Russell E. Richey, *Methodist Connectionalism: Historical Perspectives* (Nashville: UMC General Board of Higher Education and Ministry, 2009), 20.

2. Ibid., 65.

3. United Methodist Church, *The Book of Discipline of the United Methodist Church* (Nashville: Abingdon Press, 2004), 77.

4. T. Jackson, ed., *The Works of John Wesley* vol. 10 (1831; repr., Grand Rapids: Baker, 1979), 79.

5. "Our Church," on the website of the United Methodist Church, accessed August 18, 2012, http://www.umc.org/site/c.lwL4KnN1LtH/b.1355347/k.2F4F/Our_Church.htm.

6. "Visitor's Guide," United Methodist Church General Conference 2012, 15.

✳ 46 ✳

WE DO NOT CONDONE

Pastor Gene Leggett didn't seek confrontation with the Methodist hierarchy; it was forced upon him by his bishop in the Southwest Texas Annual Conference. When Pastor Leggett dared to resist his bishop, the Methodists had to deal with an out gay man in their midst for the first time and in a very public forum; the national press picked up the story, and the eyes of the nation watched the unfolding drama in Texas in 1971.[1]

On the surface, Pastor Leggett's life had seemed rather normal. He had been ordained in 1961, married with three children, and appointed to serve as a parish pastor, but his secret life as a closeted gay man began to unravel in 1965. When a parishioner of his Austin, Texas, parish outed him, his superiors in the parish offered him a deal: resign and the matter would go no further. Resign he did, and he spent the next six years in nonparish ministry and graduate studies. His wife amicably divorced him, and she and the children departed.

By the spring of 1971, Pastor Leggett was ready to come out to family and friends, and he wrote in a letter, "I am a homosexual. This is not some new and frightening facet in my personality. I am still the same Gene Leggett you have always known."

That's when his bishop and the UMC hierarchy began to bully him. The Board of Ministry and Bishop Eugene Slater concluded that he was "unacceptable in the work of the ministry," without citing any rationale. This time, however, Pastor Leggett did not go quietly into the night, and he chose to challenge his bishop and the Board at the June 1971 Annual Conference of the Southwest Texas UMC. Speaking to the Conference of around six hundred clergy and laity, Leggett stated his hope, "to continue the ministry as a Christian and hopefully as Methodist."

Pastor Leggett's appeal to the 1971 Southwest Texas Annual Conference of the UMC failed, and the clergy-only vote to suspend him from the ministry was 144 to 117. Equally telling, and hurtful, was the "body language," the response of the assembly to speakers on his behalf, which included derisive laughter.[2]

Pastor Leggett wasn't finished. He took his plight to the next national gathering of the UMC, the 1972 General Conference, but his presence and his lobbying only served to inflame conservative sentiment. In the waning hours of the conference, while Leggett's own Bishop Slater took a turn as presiding bishop and allowed some parliamentary errors, the infamous *incompatibility clause* was adopted . . . "We do not condone the practice of homosexuality and consider this practice to be incompatible with Christian teaching."[3] In 1974 and 1975, Leggett sought reinstatement through ecclesiastical courts to no avail. Never were any charges made against him, but he was simply deemed unacceptable for the ministry because he was gay.

Ordinations within the UMC are done collectively rather than individually. Once a year, at regional annual conferences, all candidates are ordained in one grand service. In the late 1970s, Leggett appeared at such ordination services within the Southwest Texas Annual Conference, and he confronted his former colleagues with their earlier exclusionary actions toward him by moving to the front of the hall, gagged with his liturgical stole bound and tied around his mouth and head. Pastor Gene Leggett was out, and so was the question of gays in the UMC.

St. Olaf College sprawls across a hilltop overlooking the Cannon River Valley and Northfield, Minnesota, a community that proudly boasts of the defeat of the Jesse James gang following a botched robbery of the Northfield bank in 1876: "Get your guns, boys, they're robbing the bank." Founded by Norwegian Lutherans just a year before the arrival of the James gang, St. Olaf is currently one of twenty-six ELCA affiliated colleges and universities and claims a proud heritage of Lutheran clergy and theologians—and at least one notable Methodist pastor.

Minnesotan Rick Huskey matriculated at St. Olaf as a freshman in 1968. Three years later, he graduated *cum laude* as a religion major with minors in classics, philosophy, and urban studies, but he also had time to help organize the Northfield Gay Liberation Front in 1971. From St. Olaf, Huskey was off to Garrett Theological Seminary in Evanston, Illinois, and it took him only two years to obtain his Master of Divinity degree and two more for his Doctor of Ministry Degree from Chicago Theological Seminary.[4]

While a seminarian attending the 1972 UMC General Conference, Huskey had first met Pastor Leggett, who was there as a lonely gay voice protesting his expulsion earlier in Texas. Undeterred by the harsh admonition of General Conference, Huskey and Leggett spent the spring of 1973 on the east coast, attempting to build a network of gay Methodists, traveling the road toward full inclusion in a Dodge Dart. In December 1974, they spotted a newspaper article with the headline, "Methodists Reject Homosexual's Ordination Bid" about Steve Webster, a student in Madison, Wisconsin.[5] They sent him a letter of encouragement.

Steve Webster received numerous letters of support. A recent graduate of the University of Wisconsin with a philosophy degree, Webster had been a lay leader at University United Methodist Church in Madison with plans to attend Garrett Theological Seminary of Chicago. He was also an out gay man. The first step in the process toward seminary and ordination was to request a recommendation from his home congregation. On December 8, 1974, the congregation had voted thirty-two to nineteen in favor of the recommendation, but the vote failed because it required two thirds.[6]

Webster had first felt called to the ministry during confirmation class as a teenager, and he remained hopeful despite this initial setback. "This is not the end of my ministry, but more of a beginning," he said at the time. Webster would fulfill his promise and pursue a life of ministry, but not in the manner he expected. Ordination would remain beyond his grasp, and Webster's ministry would be as a lifelong LGBT advocate within the Methodist Church. It started when a closeted gay Methodist pastor in Madison suggested Webster contact Richard Cash, then a senior at Northwestern University in Chicago, who was interested in gay activism and who had connections as a youth member of several United Methodist agency boards. Webster also met Rev. David Bailey Sindt in

1975, the Presbyterian and NCC organizer who served as resource person for the creation of denominational gay caucuses.

Webster and Cash organized the first national gathering of LGBT Methodists. For a mailing list, Webster used the return addresses from the numerous letters of support he had received.

"I got a hold of one of those old mimeograph stencils and rolled it into my Smith-Corona typewriter and carefully typed up a flyer about the meeting," Webster would later reminisce.

Their efforts bore fruit in the summer of 1975 when nearly twenty LGBT Methodists gathered at Wheadon UMC Church in Evanston, Illinois. Leggett and Huskey were among the attendees that also included Pastor Earnest Reaugh of upstate New York, Peggy Harmon of Dallas, and Keith Spare of Kansas City. That meeting was the birth of the "United Methodist Gay Caucus, (UMGC)" soon to be renamed "Affirmation," and the "Reconciling Congregation Project (RCP)" would be a later outgrowth in the 1980s. At a second meeting that year in Kansas City, Michael Collins and others joined the group. Their primary activities in 1975 were to prepare for a ministry of presence at the 1976 UMC General Conference in Portland. By 1976, UMGC had connected with other gay caucuses that had sprung up in Southern California and the Bay Area.[7]

There were positive developments at GC 1976, including networking with like-minded groups. Common worship services were conducted with the Women's Caucus, the Young Adult Caucus, and the Methodist Federation for Social Action (MFSA). An active bishop and other denominational executives spoke at a worship service arranged by the progressive caucuses, and one reported it to be "the single most uplifting experience of this General Conference." A gay man, Keith Spare, was allowed to address the convention, the first openly LGBT spokesperson to do so, but Albert Outler of Perkins School of Theology responded with vitriol, protesting against welcoming "all persons regardless of sexual orientation into the fellowship and membership of the UMC" because gays were promiscuous and morally decadent. Proposed welcoming language was defeated by a wide margin.[8]

The gay caucus was slapped down by other conference actions, especially a prohibition against the use of church funds for any gay caucus or group, or to otherwise use such funds to promote the acceptance of homosexuality. This latter, "no-funding," resolution would have long-term consequences. Ten years later, a commentator noted,

> By adding paragraph 906.12 without adequately discussing it and before conducting any serious study of human sexuality, that General Conference was, in effect, preferring ignorance to education and thus endorsing the continuation of public prejudice. The legislation was seen by many as a weapon not only to stop education about sexuality and gay/lesbian people but also to exclude gay/lesbian persons from various aspects of church life.[9]

Surveys demonstrate the generational gap in public attitudes toward LGBT issues. Youth have always been far more progressive toward gays and lesbians than their grandparents, and this phenomenon helps explain secular and ecclesiastical advances over time and bodes well for the future. Methodist youth in the sixties and the seventies exemplified the split between young and old. Indeed, the funding ban enacted in 1976 was directed in substantial part toward the adjunct Council on Youth Ministries because of their support of the gay caucus. Not only was their funding cut, but adults were put in charge of what had been an autonomous youth organization.[10]

Earlier the UMC had funded a student-edited magazine called *Motive* for three decades, 1941 to 1971.[11] When it promoted progressive causes in the late sixties, especially feminism and gay rights, the UMC defunded the magazine in 1971. In 1972, the last two issues were published; one was devoted to lesbian issues and the other to issues of gay men. Here are snippets from the editorials of the last two issues:[12]

From the "lesbian/feminist" issue:

> *Motive*, a monthly magazine published by the United Methodist Church for over twenty years, is no more. This is its final issue. Throughout *Motive's* history, radical dissension within limits was tolerated with a few slaps on the wrist, but the church fathers really squirmed when the special issue on women appeared in March-April 1969. In the aftermath of the controversy over the

women's issue, the church began to reduce its support of *Motive* and *Motive* decided it could no longer function under the church. *Motive* could not survive without church money so the staff and editorial board decided to close up shop—using the remaining resources of the magazine to put out one final gay issue.

From the "Gay men's liberation and last motive" issue: "We know we exist. We are gay and we are proud. *Motive*, even with its long history and affiliation with the United Methodist Church, has come out. And gay people have brought it out.

Following the rejection of Gene Leggett in 1972 with the adoption of the "incompatibility clause" and the "no-funding" resolution of GC 1976, it would seem that the status of gays and lesbians in the UMC couldn't get worse, but it did. Though one notable purge attempt failed, the witch hunt was on.

Following ordination in the Minnesota Annual Conference of the UMC, Pastor Rick Huskey boldly, or naively, informed his bishop that he was gay and interested in creating a specialized ministry to gays in Minnesota. The bishop promptly removed him from his appointment as an associate parish pastor and two years later in 1977 the Annual Conference completed the process of defrocking, despite the support of one hundred protesters, including Gene Leggett.[13]

Rev. Paul Abels had been pastor of Washington Square UMC since 1973, and the church had a vibrant ministry to the gay community of Greenwich Village. Abels "initiated a $1.5 million restoration campaign, planned the church's 125th anniversary, and worked with the many community groups housed in the building, including the Harvey Milk School, a parent-run day care center, and many lesbian/gay support and social groups." In a 1977 *New York Times* article featuring the "covenant services" Abels had performed, he acknowledged that he was gay, and his bishop attempted to remove him. After initially failing to persuade Abels to take a leave of absence, the bishop was rebuffed, first by his own annual conference, which upheld Abels' appointment, and then by the Judicial Council of the UMC, which ruled Abels to be "in good standing" and "effective relation."[14]

Other persecutions proved successful:

- Garrett Evangelical Theological Seminary of Evanston, Illinois, expelled two "self-avowed homosexuals" (language that would come to dominate UMC debates and policy).[15]

- Iliff School of Theology of Denver, Colorado, refused to admit a candidate from the gay denomination the Metropolitan Community of Churches (MCC).[16]

- St. Paul School of Theology of Kansas City, Missouri, placed five students on probation because they distributed a gay-friendly pamphlet.[17]

- The Women's Division of the Board of Global Ministries fired Deaconess Joan Clark, employed by the agency for seven years, for coming out as a lesbian.[18]

For Methodist gays and lesbians at the close of the 1970s, it seemed the rout was on. Pastors Leggett and Huskey had been defrocked; seminarians were expelled or forced deep into the closet; even trusted servants serving in the bureaucracy of the church were persecuted. Like a dark cloud, the resolution of 1972, "we do not condone the practice of homosexuality," hung ominously on the horizon of the eighties.

NOTES

1. The account is based on the Profile of Pastor Gene Leggett, on the website of the Lesbian, Gay, Bisexual and Transgender Religious Archives Network, accessed December 8, 2011, http://www.lgbtran.org/Profile.aspx?ID=236.

2. "Homosexual Minister Is Ousted by Southwest Texas Methodists," *New York Times*, June 3, 1971.

3. "A Ministry and Movement of Reconciliation," *Open Hands* vol. 15, no. 4, (Spring 2000), 8.

4. Profile of Dr. Rick Huskey, on the website of the Lesbian, Gay, Bisexual, and Transgender Religious Archives Network, accessed January 11, 2012, http://www.lgbtran.org/Profile.aspx?ID=39.

5. "Methodists Reject Homosexual's Ordination Bid," *New York Times*, December 14, 1974.

6. This account and the quotes of Steve Webster are based on a private interview with the author on February 11, 2012.

7. "A Ministry and Movement," 9.

8. Ibid.

9. Dr. Nancy Carter, "Ignorance vs. Education: The UM Funding Ban," *Open Hands* (Summer 1986), 8.

10. Mark Bowman, private e-mail to the author, August 11, 2012.

11. Roy Eddey had been the spirited editor for the last eight years, and his papers are on the website of the Lesbian, Gay, Bisexual, and Transgender Religious Archives Network, accessed August 20, 2012, http://www.lgbtran .org/Collection.aspx?ID=203.

12. "Motive," on the website of the Rainbow History Project, accessed August 20, 2012, http://www.rainbowhistory.org/html/motive.htm.

13. Profile of Dr. Rick Huskey, on the website of the Lesbian, Gay, Bisexual, and Transgender Religious Archives Network, accessed January 11, 2012, http://www.lgbtran.org/Profile.aspx?ID=39.

14. Profile of Paul Abels, on the website of the Lesbian, Gay, Bisexual, and Transgender Religious Archives Network, accessed January 24, 2012, http:// www.lgbtran.org/Profile.aspx?ID=2.

15. Dr. Nancy Carter, "Ignorance vs. Education," 9.

16. Ibid.

17. Ibid.

18. "A Ministry and Movement," 9.

✳ 47 ✳

Good News? Hardly

In 1985, the UCC General Synod encouraged congregations to become "open and affirming." That same year, the Episcopal General Convention elected a presiding bishop who offered a radically inclusive vision compared to the conservative Southerner he replaced, and Episcopal momentum toward full inclusion was jump-started. Meanwhile, for the Methodists in the eighties, the only "Good News" was a misnamed gatekeeper organization that lobbied against all things gay. Though the decade began with positive developments, GC 1984 once again disappointed gays, lesbians, and their allies. A step forward, two steps back.

The Methodist gay caucus had been born in a meeting of twenty or so persons at Wheadon Church near Northwestern University in 1975. Meeting again in Chicago in the spring of 1978, approximately one hundred attendees renamed the group "Affirmation: United Methodists for Lesbian/Gay Concerns." Two persons, Rev. Michael Collins, a pastor from Oregon then residing in New York City, and Peggy Harmon, a laywoman from Texas, were hired (for nominal compensation) to travel and network in preparation for General Conference 1980.[1]

Actions on LGBT issues at GC 1980 were disappointing. LGBT allies failed to remove the "no-funding" ban from the 1976 GC. Interestingly, LGBT issues were promoted through the Women's Division of the Board of Global Ministries (the same that had fired lesbian Deaconess Joan Clark); the firing came from the board of directors rather than senior staff at the Division who actually supported Clark. It was the senior staff who promoted LGBT-friendly policies at GC 1980, working with Clark, who became a principal spokesperson for Affirmation.[2]

A common characteristic of the early gay activists in all denominations was naive optimism, and a common problem was dealing with the crushing disappointment that followed legislative defeats. Affirmation nearly died in the early eighties, partly for that reason and partly because of a short-lived breakdown in the partnership of gays and lesbians, male and female, following a gender-based skirmish in the spring of 1981 that led stalwarts Joan Clark and Peggy Harmon to quit Affirmation. Out of the soul-searching that ensued, especially on the part of Affirmation leader Michael Collins, a local ministry emphasis developed. While attempts to change hearts and minds of the whole church at General Conference would continue, Collins stressed "a focus on what Affirmation would do *after* [General Conference 1984] so that what he saw as the inevitable legislative defeats would not once again be so devastating to the group."[3] Because of Collin's ill health and subsequent death in 1984, the implementation of a local ministry focus fell to others.

Mark Bowman was an Affirmation newcomer at GC 1980. Married with two daughters, Bowman became aware of his own sexuality while in seminary at Boston University School of Theology, and he came out with the exuberance of self-discovery and self-affirmation. He immediately became active in gay rights activities in Boston, and he returned to the Midwest to participate with Affirmation's efforts at GC in Indianapolis in May 1980; a month later, his East Ohio Annual Conference ordained him as a deacon, but it wouldn't last; his probationary membership in the Conference would be discontinued because of his public involvement with Affirmation.[4]

While serving on Affirmation's coordinating committee in 1981–82, Bowman headed a task force to launch a congregation-based project modeled on More Light Presbyterians . . . "developing a program in which local churches will declare their support for the concerns of lesbians and gay men." The Reconciling Congregation Project (RCP) was created in 1983, and Bowman, along with Beth Richardson, served as volunteer coordinators. The second choice for the name of the organization demonstrated a sense of humor: "Self-Avowed, Practicing Churches," parroting the disciplinary terminology of the church.[5]

During the four-year quadrennium between General Conferences in 1980 and 1984, LGBT interests leaped forward thanks to a gay-friendly bishop in Colorado and several rulings from the United Methodist Judicial Council.

A standing Judicial Council is elected at General Conference, and the primary purpose of the Council is to interpret and correlate church law. It is not the function of the Judicial Council to conduct ecclesiastical trials, which are administered by the bishops of annual conferences on an *ad hoc* basis.

> "Is that resolution by General Conference in accord with The United Methodist Constitution?" "Was due process followed in that clergy trial?" "Did the bishop rule correctly on a point of law?"
>
> Deciding questions like these is the work of nine men and women who sit on the United Methodist Judicial Council, sometimes referred to as our "Supreme Court." The Council is at the apex of a carefully detailed chapter on judicial administration in the Book of Discipline.[6]

On October 31, 1982, the court ruled that the onerous "no-funding" provision adopted at GC 1976 applied only to national church expenditures. The California/Nevada Annual Conference was free to fund their three-year study on the causes of homophobia.[7]

A second case involved the refusal of Bishop Jack Tuell of the California-Nevada Annual Conference to appoint gay pastor Morris Floyd to a special appointment at a Minneapolis counseling center, placing Pastor Floyd on involuntary leave of absence instead. Though the Judicial Council upheld the decision of Bishop Tuell, Pastor Floyd's persistence would ultimately persuade his bishop.[8]

Pastor Morris Floyd had attended the 1978 Affirmation meeting in Chicago. His pastoral appointment had been as Executive Director for Youth Serving Ministries, in the National Division of the General Board of Global Ministries, based in New York City, and he was well-known to many bishops. He came out in the early 1980s, and he asked his bishop to appoint him to a Twin Cities counseling center that served a largely gay clientele. Because Bishop Tuell refused to appoint him to the counseling center, when Pastor Floyd accepted the position, it was not an official appointment. The next year, the bishop and the annual conference again refused his request to recognize his position at the agency as an official appointment, but the vote was close. Finally, Bishop Tuell granted his request the following year, and Pastor Floyd's ministry at the counseling center was officially recognized as an appointment within the UMC.[9] Later, following Bishop Tuell's retirement in 1992, he would serve as presiding judge at the trial of Chicago pastor Greg Dell, who was suspended for performing a covenant ceremony for two of his parishioners. Later still, retired bishop Tuell became an advocate for LGBT issues.

A third judicial decision stunned the entire UMC. The Judicial Council ruled that there was nothing in General Conference standards that would prohibit LGBT ordinations, and the ordination of an open lesbian was allowed to stand. The question arose following the ordination of lesbian Joanne Carlson Brown by Colorado Bishop Melvin Wheatley.[10]

While attending Garrett Theological Seminary in 1978, Joanne Carlson Brown had witnessed the expulsion of two gay men, two "self-avowed homosexuals," and she joined other Garrett students in protest. Brown would belong to the early Chicago core of Affirmation. In 1982, she sought ordination in the Rocky Mountain Annual Conference. Despite her status as an out lesbian, Bishop Melvin Wheatley ordained her; thus, Pastor Brown holds the distinction of being the first openly gay or lesbian person to be ordained within the UMC. Bishop Wheatley's action was appealed to the UMC Judicial Council, and the Council rocked the UMC by upholding the ordination.[11] Dr. Brown would go on to a distinguished career as an academic and theologian.

The ordination of Joanne Carlson Brown wasn't the first controversial action of Bishop Wheatley, the father of a gay son. At each General Conference, the UMC bishops collectively present an "episcopal" address. At the 1980 GC in Indianapolis, Bishop Wheatley stood alone as a solitary figure when he objected to his name appearing on the episcopal statement that year because it contained the language "homosexuality is incompatible with Christian teaching."

> I will not accept [this statement]. It states as an absolute fact what is an insufficiently documented opinion: that gay persons can't be Christians. . . . I personally know not one, but at least 50 gay

men and lesbians who are Christians. . . . I take Jesus Christ very seriously in making judgments, and the more seriously I take him the stronger is my feeling that this statement is an inadequate representation of Christianity.[12]

The next controversial action of Bishop Wheatley occurred just before the ordination of Joanne Carlson Brown in 1982. Bishop Wheatley riled up conservative Methodists when he appointed Pastor Julian Rush to St. Paul's UMC in Denver. For seventeen years, Pastor Rush had served in youth ministries, and his special niche was writing and directing musical drama. His youth groups regularly staged his original musicals as fund-raisers and occasionally took the shows on the road. In 1981 when he was in his early forties and married with two children, Pastor Rush's long repressed sexuality finally burst through. Though he had no intention to make a big splash in coming out, rumors soon spread beyond his inner circle, and he was confronted by the staff-parish relations committee of First United Methodist Church in Boulder, Colorado, where he had served the previous five years. Controversy immediately split the congregation; there seemed to be only his strong supporters or his equally strong detractors. And then the press swooped in.

Bishop Wheatley and his cabinet attempted to support Pastor Rush and encouraged the congregation to preserve his position, but it was not to be. After First UMC discharged Pastor Rush, Bishop Wheatley appointed him to St. Paul's, an inner-city Denver congregation, which allowed him to maintain his clergy credentials, but there was little pay, and he experienced severe financial and creditor problems and depression. The only jobs he could find were minimum wage positions as a janitor or sales clerk at Montgomery Ward. Prospective employment melted away when his notoriety would catch up to him. Even with a supportive bishop and a foundation built on many years of successful ministry, Pastor Rush was effectively drummed out of pastoral ministry and his calling as a lyricist, composer, and director of religious musical drama.

Being down is like down on the ground
With nobody, no place to go;
When the big creatures push you around,
And they make you feel . . . Oh, I don't know,

It's a feeling that's more like a pain in your heart,
And you feel like . . . you feel like . . . a worm.

Now an ant is an ant
And a worm is a worm
But an ant has to crawl
And a worm has to squirm,
So an ant shouldn't bother
Befriending a worm
Since a worm cannot crawl
And an ant cannot squirm
We're different and different we'll stay,
It's just God's will.
It's just God's way.

—From *The Resurrection Thing* by Julian Rush

Bend toward the middle and don't disagree.
It's all for the good of the group.
Don't try to live individually.
It's all for the good of the group.
We're one happy family who sticks together,
So don't venture out all alone in the weather.
We're brotherly birds
Of a sisterly feather.
It's all for the good of the group.
Learn to be tactful and always discreet.
It's all for the good of the group.
Try hard to avoid being too commanding,
For those who conform, life is never demanding,
So donate your thoughts to a mass understanding,
It's all for the good of the group.

—From *The Rise and the Fall of the Girl* by Julian Rush

All over town the lights go out.
The shades are being drawn

as shelter for approaching night
before a trembling dawn.
The tensions mount and tempers flare,
and underneath, the fear
that after what we face ahead,
the skies may not be clear.

—From *Don't take it so hard, Mr. Johnson* by Julian Rush[13]

Bishop Wheatley faced his own consequences for his faithful support of Julian Rush. A UMC pastor from rural Georgia filed a charge of heresy against Bishop Wheatley, but the charges were dismissed by a disciplinary committee.[14]

To summarize, during the quadrennium between GC 1980 and GC 1984, Affirmation redefined its mission to emphasize local ministries; Bishop Melvin Wheatley, who had created a ruckus at GC 1980 with his public opposition to the episcopal address, ordained an out lesbian and supported an outed gay pastor; and the Methodist Supreme Court surprised the church with its gay-friendly decisions. It seemed to many Methodists that anarchy was imminent. A maverick bishop was performing all manner of evil, and the Judicial Council allowed him to get away with it. Order must be restored; if the Judicial Council wouldn't interpret ordination standards to preclude LGBT clergy, then the rules needed beefing up. The delegates to General Conference 1984 in Baltimore would rewrite the standards to make prohibition of LGBT clergy explicit.

First, on May 9, GC 1984 added this sentence to the pertinent portion of the *Book of Discipline*: "While such persons set apart by the church for the ministry of Word, Sacrament, and Order are subject to all the frailties of the human condition and pressures of society, they are required to maintain the highest standards represented by the practice of fidelity in marriage and celibacy in singleness." The Judicial Council was immediately summoned for an opinion whether that language would preclude LGBT clergy. On May 10, the Judicial Council said no, that language wasn't strong enough, and the delegates responded by adding a second sentence to the discipline. "Since the practice of homosexuality is incompatible with Christian teaching, self-avowed practicing homosexuals are not to be accepted as candidates, ordained as ministers, or appointed to serve in The United Methodist Church."[15]

With this language, even the Judicial Council would be forced to rule that the GC had effectively written a prohibition of LGBT clergy into the ordination standards.

After GC 1984 concluded, the California/Nevada Annual Conference challenged the constitutionality of the restrictive "self-avowed, practicing" policy. Briefs were submitted by several Conferences and testimony was offered at an open hearing in the fall of 1984, hosted by Garrett-Evangelical Seminary. One of the briefs came from "Good News, a Forum for Scriptural Christianity, Inc," a self-appointed watchdog of Methodist morality. This would be the introduction of Good News to the Methodist stage. This organization would be the principal Methodist gatekeepers who preserved the purity of the pulpit by preventing LGBT ordination. Two constitutional questions were raised: whether the GC could bind annual conferences to this strict ordination policy and whether gays were a protected "status." The Judicial Council ruled this provision constitutional and bound annual conferences to this standard. A concurring opinion suggested the provision was constitutional, despite the possibility that homosexuality might be a protected "status" under the UMC constitution, so long as the rule applied only to "self-avowed practicing homosexuals" and not the status of homosexuality.[16]

Once again, a denomination had grudgingly recognized that homosexuality was an orientation and not a choice, yet adopted strict conditions on LGBT candidates, imposing the unfair, if not impossible, burden of celibacy. This critical comment quoted earlier is worth repeating: "To be accepted one must be self-reproaching, self-denying, and celibate. One is not to declare frankly and openly love for or sexual intimacy with a person of one's own gender."[17]

An anonymous Methodist seminarian spoke to the chilling effect of GC 1984's overt rejection of LGBT clergy on his own career plan as well as others.

There were all kinds of possibilities until 1984 when the church said, "We don't want you." It was then when I began to reconsider whether I would seek appointment to a local church. . . . It also affected other people who had to decide to keep in the fight or to look in other directions; and it affected, I think, whether a lot of gay/lesbian folks considered going into ordained ministry or not and said, "It's just not worth the fight."[18]

The odious effect of the restrictive policy extended to gays and lesbians in the pews and not merely those who felt called to ordained ministry. A devoted churchman in his forties appeared in his pastor's study the morning after the action of GC 1984.

"I quit! I won't take it anymore. I'm leaving the church!" Adam cried as he entered my office.

He was in obvious agony, his body shaking with anger and grief. His eyes were red and swollen, and they moved nervously back and forth between mine and the floor. He leaned forward, elbows on his knees, hands clenched in front of them, fingers interlocked so tightly that his knuckles were white.

"I won't be a member of a church that thinks that I'm some kind of pervert, that doesn't want me. . . . I've been a Methodist since I was ten years old. I've given the church my time, my money—and what do I get? . . . I don't want to be ordained," said Adam. "But I don't want to be told that I can't because I'm gay. I'm just as moral as anybody, just as good a Christian."[19]

The brief window of inclusivity that allowed the ordination of Dr. Brown was slammed shut. Not only was Dr. Brown the first openly LGBT person ordained within the UMC, she would be the last, until . . . ?

Mark Bowman and his associates in the Reconciling Congregation Program were prepared; after the legislative defeats of GC 1984, they passed out endless flyers to conference attendees, encouraging local congregations to become reconciling congregations. After the Conference ended, two congregations signed up—Washington Square UMC in New York City and Wesley UMC in Fresno, California—and the movement that would become the Reconciling Congregation Project (RCP) was off and running. Washington Square UMC was no surprise; that was the largely gay congregation of Greenwich Village with Rev. Paul Abels as pastor, but Abels would resign and leave the ministry due to the actions of GC 1984.[20] By the end of 1984, nine congregations had become reconciling.[21]

Defeats at the national level encouraged local action, and RCP continued to grow. In 1985, the California/Nevada Annual Conference passed a resolution commending RCP to local congregations. In 1986, the Northern Illinois Annual Conference became the first Reconciling Conference, and the Wisconsin Annual Conference encouraged congregations to consider RCP membership. Three more Annual Conferences would become reconciling in 1987.[22]

Coordinators Bowman and Richardson put together a quarterly resource for congregations called *Manna for the Journey* that included worship aids and a newsletter. In 1986, the newsletter became *Open Hands* magazine, and it quickly grew into a resource used not only by Methodists but by More Light Presbyterians, Open and Affirming (UCC), and Reconciling in Christ (Lutheran), as well as a few other gay-friendly organizations in smaller denominations.

In 1987, RCP conducted its first national convocation in Chicago, focusing on workshops, training, networking, and celebration with 125 attendees from RCP congregations, which would grow to thirty by the end of the year. The UMC General Commission on the Status and Role of Women initially approved a $1,000 grant to help fund the convocation, but conservatives cited the 1976 "no-funding" rule, and the grant was rescinded. RCP extended invitations to attend the convocation to certain boards within the UMC, especially the UMC Board of Discipleship. After much internal debate, the board voted to decline the invitation officially, but a few friendly board members attended unofficially.[23]

Affirmation and RCP moved forward on separate tracks. While RCP attempted to work with congregations to become welcoming, Affirmation provided a separate and distinct alternative to local congregations. Affirmation chapters around the country provided sanctuary for gays and lesbians who felt unwelcomed elsewhere. For many LGBT Methodists, Affirmation was church, their primary faith community. Here's the example of one man: "At Affirmation . . . he enjoyed, planned, and was part of inspirational worship services, Bible study, educational programs, AIDS ministry, and outreach to retirement centers."[24]

Another commented,

I think for most people who find Affirmation a place of community and support—an assurance about who they are and where Christ is really found in a community of faithful, committed Christians—to have the general church say you're unacceptable really hurts. But it doesn't change the reality of what we've experienced with other people in Affirmation, which has told us, "Yes, God really loves you, and you're really a good person, and it really doesn't matter what these people say."[25]

By 1988, RCP had outgrown its Affirmation roots. During a joint meeting of the RCP Advisory Committee and the Affirmation Coordinating Committee, it was decided that the two organizations would split. Affirmation would continue with local chapters, providing a sanctuary for those who didn't have a welcoming church home and would collaborate with RCP during General Conferences. Meanwhile, RCP would fund a half-time national staff person, and Mark Bowman would fill that role. In 1992, the position became full time.[26]

Subtle cracks in the hard veneer of UMC policies appeared during the 1988 General Conference in St. Louis.

First, the offensive "we do not condone" language of the Social Principles, dating to GC 1972, softened slightly: "Although we do not condone the practice of homosexuality and consider this practice incompatible with Christian teaching, we affirm that God's grace is available to all. We commit ourselves to be in ministry for and with all persons."

Second, for the first time, the denomination dared to talk about homosexuality in a meaningful way by commissioning the General Council on Ministry to

Conduct a study of homosexuality as a subject for theological and ethical analysis, noting where there is consensus among biblical scholars, theologians, and ethicists, and where there is not; seek the best biological, psychological, and sociological information and opinion on the nature of homosexuality, noting points at which there is a consensus among informed scientists and where there is not; and explore the implication of its study for the Social Principles.

Initial criticism of the lack of LGBT representation on the committee was resolved at the first meeting when a gay man and a lesbian were added.

The decade ended with all sides anticipating the committee report to be submitted to GC 1992. For the gays, lesbians, and their supporters, there was reason for optimism.[27]

- In 1989, Bowman and other RCP representatives were invited to testify before the committee.

- *Open Hands* became an award-winning periodical.

- RCP was formally organized as a nonprofit, and in 1992 a full-time Chicago office was established with Bowman as full-time coordinator.

- For the first time, an official UMC unit, the General Commission on Christian Unity and Interreligious Concerns, voted to become reconciling, and their action withstood a challenge when the Judicial Council unanimously upheld their decision.

- Going into 1992, there were fifty-four reconciling congregations.

But there was also reason for pessimism.

- A survey of attitudes of the delegates to the 1988 General Conference and other church members suggested stiff headwinds—"over two-thirds . . . agreed with denominational positions that homosexuality is incompatible with Christian teaching, that it was a sin to be a practicing homosexual, that openly declared or practicing homosexuals should not be ordained, and that the denomination should ban the use of church funds by any group promoting the acceptance of homosexuality."[28]

- In January 1992, eighty UMC evangelicals gathered in Memphis, Tennessee, and issued their "Memphis Declaration," reaffirming "Christian sexual morality and the current provisions of the United Methodist Discipline" and urged "rejection of the report and the recommendations of the Committee to Study Homosexuality." In fact, the Memphis Declaration expressed opposition to *any* study of homosexuality.[29]

The decade of the eighties would end with rising contentiousness across denominations. Only the UCC witnessed relative peace; indeed, Pastor Bill Johnson was hired to the staff of the national church. Bishop Spong ended the decade by ordaining an openly gay priest to an Oasis ministry, and the Episcopal gatekeepers geared up for holy war. Lutheran gays and lesbians felt betrayed after ordination approvals of out gays had been rescinded by a timid, newly merged church, and gays, lesbians, and their allies planned extraordinary ordinations. The voice of Presbyterian gatekeepers, *The Layman* magazine, frightened the folks in the pews with reports that the Presbyterian Lesbian and Gay Caucus was perverting kids at a youth convention.

The Methodist decade would also end in strife that presaged the tumultuous nineties. In a country church, not far from the locales of the Salem witch hunts of three centuries earlier, the Methodists put a lesbian pastor on trial after she had confided in her bishop.

NOTES

1. Ibid.

2. Pastor Morris Floyd, private interview by the author, January 27, 2012.

3. "A Ministry and Movement," 10.

4. Profile of Mark Bowman, on the website of the Lesbian, Gay, Bisexual, and Transgender Religious Archives Network, accessed January 17, 2012, http://www.lgbtran.org/Profile.aspx?ID=25, supplemented with details from a personal interview with Bowman on January 11, 2012.

5. "About Us: History 1982–1983," on the website of Reconciling Ministries Network, accessed January 30, 2012, http://www.rmnetwork.org/about-us/history/1982-1985/.

6. The United Methodist Church, "About the Judicial Council," accessed January 17, 2012, http://www.umc.org/site/c.lwL4KnN1LtH/b.5197237/.

7. United Methodist Church, Judicial Council Decisions, "In Re: Right of an Annual Conference to Create a Task Force to Study Homophobia," Decision number 491, October 31, 1980.

8. United Methodist Church, Judicial Council Decisions, "In Re: A Ruling by Bishop Jack Tuell on Discipline Par. 444 Regarding Leave of Absence for a Minister without Consent of the Minister," Decision number 524, April 22, 1983.

9. Pastor Morris Floyd, private interview by the author, January 27, 2012.

10. Judicial Council Decisions, "In Re: Legality of Ordination of Probationer of Same Sex Preference," Decision number 513, October 31, 1982.

11. Profile of Joanne Carlson Brown, on the website of the Gay, Lesbian, Bisexual, and Transgender Religious Archives Network, accessed January 18, 2012, http://www.lgbtran.org/Profile.aspx?ID=22.

12. "Biography," on the website of Bishop Melvin E. Wheatley Jr., accessed March 1, 2012, http://www.melvinwheatley.com/biography.html.

13. Lee Hart Merrick, *Julian Rush—Facing the Music: A Gay Methodist Minister's Story* (Lincoln, Neb.: Writer's Club Press, 2001), 37–38. This poignant book is written in the first person by a fellow minister who served with Rush using the format "as told by" Julian Rush. Interspersed throughout Rush's actual story are the lyrics of his musicals, including the preceding selections, which are reprinted here with the permission of Julian Rush. The Rocky Mountain Conference eventually appointed Pastor Rush to the Colorado AIDS project, where he served for seventeen years as executive director, but he never had time to continue his writing. First United Methodist Church of Boulder became a Reconciling Congregation in 1997, and Rush returned there as a congregant in 1999.

14. Mel Wheatley oral history and biographical notes, on the website of the Lesbian, Gay, Bisexual, Transgender Religious Archives Network, accessed March 1, 2012, http://www.lgbtran.org/Interview.aspx?ID=15.

15. United Methodist Church, Judicial Council Decisions, "In Re: Constitutionality of Par. 402.2, 1984 Discipline which Prohibits the Ordination and Appointment of Self-avowed Practicing Homosexual Persons," Decision No. 544, October 26, 1984.

16. Ibid.

17. Comstock, *Unrepentant*, xiii.

18. Ibid., 136.

19. Jimmy Creech, *Adam's Gift: A Memoir of a Pastor's Calling to Defy the Church's Persecution of Lesbians and Gays* (Durham: Duke University Press, 2011), 1–2. Pastor Creech describes this scene as his own Damascus road experience that set him on the path toward advocacy for the LGBT community as a straight ally. Fifteen years later, Creech would become a national

figure as a result of ecclesiastical trials because he celebrated holy unions of gay couples.

20. Comstock, *Unrepentant*, 149.

21. Mark Bowman, personal interview by and private e-mails to the author, January, 2012.

22. "About Us: History 1986–1989," on the website of Reconciling Ministries Network, accessed January 30, 2012, http://www.rmnetwork.org/about-us/history/1986-1989/.

23. Ibid.

24. Comstock, *Unrepentant*, 97.

25. Ibid., 184.

26. "About Us: History 1986–1989," on the website of Reconciling Ministries Network.

27. Ibid. and "About Us: History 1990–1993," on the website of Reconciling Ministries Network, accessed January 30, 2012, http://www.rmnetwork.org/about-us/history/1990-1993/

28. Mearle L. Griffith and C. David Lundquist, *An Analysis of Major Issues Addressed by the 1988 General Conference and a Comparison of Beliefs and Attitudes of Local Church Members* (Dayton: Office of Research, General Conference of Ministries, United Methodist Church, 1990), in Comstock, *Unrepentant*, 100.

29. The Memphis Declaration is available on the website of the Unofficial Confessing Movement Page, accessed October 24, 2012, http://www.ucmpage.org/news/anti_evangelical_book3.html#The Memphis Declaration.

48

ALL TRUTH IS GOD'S TRUTH

In 1636, Roger Williams, an advocate for religious freedom, and a small band of followers were exiled from the Massachusetts Bay Colony, but thanks to "God's Merciful Providence," they found a safe haven at the mouth of a river at the head of Narragansett Bay. More than three centuries later in 1947, a child would be born to a Roman Catholic family of Portuguese heritage in Providence, the capitol and major city of Rhode Island, and she too would become a religious exile.[1]

As a young girl growing up in a working class neighborhood, Miss Rose Mary attended Catholic parochial school, and at an early age she announced that she would become a nun and join a convent. She didn't; after high school, she joined the Air force and served as a communications specialist at Travis Air Force Base in California, which served as transit terminal to and from Vietnam. On a weekend outing to a Franciscan monastery, she met Brother William, aka Robert Denman, who would forsake his monastic vows in order to marry her, and she became Rose Mary Denman, a wife and soon a mother, and the family-to-be would return to New England after military discharge. The marriage would be short-lived because of her husband's affair.

Rose Mary had been the first in the family to achieve a high school diploma, and her parents scoffed when she enrolled in college as a single mother with a young son. She majored in religion at Barrington College, a nearby evangelical Christian institution. During college, she relied on the GI bill but also worked in church-related jobs: youth director, chaplain at a Boy Scout camp, and administrative assistant to a Jewish rabbi. Later, when she entered Bangor Theological Seminary in Maine, an ecumenical UCC school, she served as the education director at a United Methodist Church. On June 14, 1981, she was ordained by Bishop George Bashore as a deacon in the Maine Annual Conference of the United Methodist Church, and in 1983, she was ordained as an elder, the Methodist equivalent of a priest or minister of word and sacrament.

During the first few years of her ministry, Pastor Denman was appointed to several small "two-point charges." Bishop Bashore, whose episcopal area included much of New England, including Maine and New Hampshire, proved to be a friend and mentor. In 1984, the UMC General Conference adopted the policy that "No self-avowed, practicing homosexual would be accepted as a candidate, ordained into ministry, or appointed by the United Methodist Church." During a social visit prior to the vote, Pastor Denman and her bishop agreed with this restrictive position, and she suggested that she would probably quit the United Methodist Church if the General Conference would vote to ordain homosexuals. She meant it.

Pastor Denman had become a close friend to Winnie Weir, a UMC pastor's wife who ran a small Christian bookstore. When the Weirs separated in 1984, Pastor Denman agreed to provide temporary housing for her friend in the parsonage at her new appointment in Conway, New Hampshire. When Weir confessed to Pastor Denman that she was a lesbian, Pastor Denman warned that she would stand in the way of Weir's plans to seek ordination. She meant it.

But then she fell in love. With Winnie Weir.

I began to weep.

"What's wrong?" Winnie asked.

"Nothing's wrong. Everything is right. I feel as if I'm having a birthday. Thirty-seven years old, and I'm being born."

She held me close as I shed tears of joy and relief for having finally discovered such a huge part of the puzzle of who I was, and through the tears we continued to hold each other and to reverence the gift that God had given us in each other. I felt like a giddy child as a whole new and wonderful world unfolded before me, and as it did, I sensed God smiling.

"Ah, you've finally figured out who I created you to be."[2]

Now what?

Pastor Denman felt increasingly uncomfortable in the pulpit, living a lie, and she decided to take a leave of absence when her appointment expired in June of 1985. Rose Mary and Winnie moved to Portland, Maine, and secular employment. They stayed away from UMC congregations and found a safe haven in a Unitarian Universalist (UU) congregation. As spring approached in 1986, Pastor Denman was wrestling with her clergy status and her future plans. She sent a letter to Bishop Bashore requesting more time, and she was honest about her reasons. She came out to her bishop. Another year's leave of absence was granted, but the bishop suggested reparative therapy.

As the second year passed, Rose Mary decided to transfer her clergy credentials to the Unitarian Universalists (UU), a small, progressive denomination that had long accepted LGBT clergy, but more time was needed. She requested further leave of absence while the transfer process proceeded. She was shocked when her request was denied, and Bishop Bashore encouraged her to "withdraw voluntarily by surrender of your ministerial office. This would include the deposit of your credentials," and he again encouraged reparative therapy with a Dutch psychiatrist who offered "a new approach in therapy in the context of hope for change."[3]

Even though the process of becoming UU clergy would be lengthened and complicated if she acceded to the bishop's demand (it would no longer be a transfer but a reordination), it would still be possible. Should she fight or move on? Which decision would nurture her sense of self-worth? She discovered unknown personal resources—a gift of inner strength.

Pastor Denman invoked her right to speak directly to her peers, the ordained elders of the Annual Conference, and she would announce her decision then. Since she didn't immediately quit, Bishop Bashore filed a complaint with the Board of Ordained Ministry. Institutional order, discipline, and the rule of law would be maintained, above all else.

The first step would be a meeting with the joint review committee that would decide if there were grounds to proceed on the bishop's complaint, sort of like a grand jury.

"There were coffee, tea, and doughnuts for everyone. I felt like Alice in Wonderland conversing with the Mad Hatter. . . . We were all behaving as though we had no loftier decision to make than what to wear to the next tea party."[4] Following the review, the committee voted unanimously to terminate the membership of Rose Mary Denman in the annual conference. The connection would be broken.

The next step would be the Executive Session of the Annual Conference where she would exercise her right to address her peers, the ordained elders of the New Hampshire Annual Conference. Part of her speech follows:

> Augustine once said: "All truth is God's truth." This one simple statement has served as a support and beacon for me during my time of searching and struggling to know the truth about myself. If, in fact, all truth is God's truth, then I did not need to be afraid to discover the truth about myself, about my sexual orientation. If to discover that part of the truth of who I am is to discover that I am a lesbian, then this truth, too, must be God's truth. If all truth is God's truth, then all truth must be celebrated. I am a lesbian. Could I honor God more than by rejoicing and celebrating this truth?[5]

When the last words were out of her mouth—"I choose to exercise my right to trial"—the room crackled with angry energy. The stunned bishop barely maintained order. One elderly pastor worried, and rightfully so. "But, Bishop," he said, "If we allow a church trial, it will not be she who is on trial but the church."[6]

Following much preparation with the assistance of fellow pastor John MacDougall, who would serve as her trial counsel, and endless interviews with local and national media, August 24, 1987, finally arrived. The pastoral setting in rolling green hills belied the scene. With the press and a mass of supporters sprawled across the expansive lawn of St. John's Methodist Church of Dover, New Hampshire, the trial began.

Only fifty spectators were allowed inside, and they had to provide Methodist credentials—a few national media outlets deliberately sent Methodist reporters for that reason. An unfriendly bishop, picked to be the judge and to do the church's bidding, would not allow testimony from a recognized New Testament scholar (Burton Throckmorton), or from the chairman of the ethics department at Bangor University (Marv Ellison), or a specialist in feminist theology (Virginia Ramey Mollenkott). The judge hoped to prevent a show trial that would present a biblical, ethical, or theological challenge to Methodist policy, but during the dinner recess, the silenced witnesses offered their views to the eager press. Dr. Throckmorton suggested the proceedings "were a very sad day for the church. The Bible was being cited to support a prejudice. This whole trial is about preserving the patriarchal structure of our society."[7] Sometimes the stilled voice sounds the loudest.

Pastor MacDougall bravely cross-examined Bishop Bashore—his bishop and superior—privately joking about the "downward mobility" his role would have on his career. Contrary to the bishop's public stance that his hands were tied, that he had no alternative but to refuse the request for a further leave of absence and to press charges, the bishop's testimony revealed the contrary. His chosen course had been arbitrary and unnecessary. He could have allowed Pastor Denman's transfer without fuss, if he had chosen to do so. His attempt to force Pastor Denman to resign had backfired, and now he and the church were caught in denials and falsified records. The clergy in the room were also stunned to learn that their bishop, their pastor to the pastors, did not consider their private conversations to be confidential. Young Pastor MacDougall offered an eloquent summation warning against a legalistic use of the Social Discipline.[8]

When the presiding judge charged the jury, thirteen clergypersons from the New Hampshire Annual Conference, he told them their only task was to determine whether Rose Mary had broken church law.

An hour later, the jurors filed back in, and the foreperson read their verdict. "We find the Reverend Mary Rose Denman in violation of the Discipline," pointedly avoiding use of the word "guilty."[9]

The presiding bishop then charged the jury again to decide upon a penalty. He gave them only three alternatives:

- Suspension of ordination
- Involuntary termination
- Expulsion from the church

The judge explained that Pastor Denman could not perform ministerial functions during a suspension, but that her credentials would remain intact. Though the judge didn't elaborate, a mere suspension would also allow time for Denman to transfer to the UU without the necessity of reordination.

The sun set on the crowd milling about on the church lawn. Here and there in the corners of the yard, cigarettes glowed in the dark. At 10:45 PM, the jurors returned to the makeshift courtroom, silent and still save for the whir of the overhead fan. The foreperson was visibly shaking as she stood to read the sentence. The other jurors surrounded her as a sign of solidarity. They faced not the judge nor the prosecutor nor their bishop but looked straight at Rose Mary, with Winnie seated behind her.

We affirm the social principles of the 1984 Book of Discipline, which states, "Homosexual persons, no less than heterosexual persons, are individuals of sacred worth, who need the ministry and guidance of the church in their struggles for human fulfillment, as well as the spiritual and emotional care of a fellowship which enables reconciling relationships with God, with others and with self." It is not clear to us that the Reverend Rose Mary Denman has received the adequate spiritual and emotional care of such a reconciling fellowship within the United Methodist Church.

We now seek the spirit of such a reconciling relation, by recommending that the Reverend Rose Mary Denman be suspended from the exercise of the ministerial office until the next regularly scheduled executive session of the New Hampshire Annual Conference, scheduled for June 1988. We wish to have it recorded that our vote was 12 to 1 abstention.[10]

Bishop Bashore slumped over the table with his head in his hands.

"With the guidance of a spirit more generous than that of the Church," the jury would allow Pastor Denman to retain her credentials while she sought transfer into the UU denomination. On November 12, 1987, Pastor Denman met with the Ministerial Fellowship Committee and was granted fellowship in the Unitarian Universalist Association.

NOTES

1. The story of Rose Mary Denman is retold here based upon her memoir: *Rose Mary Denman, Let My People In* (New York: William Morrow, 1990). See also Neil Miller, *In Search of Gay America: Women and Men in a Time of Change* (New York: Atlantic Monthly Press, 1989), 211–27. Miller was a free-lance writer who faked his Methodist credentials in order to get inside the church where the trial occurred.

2. Denman, *Rose Mary Denman*, 136–37.

3. Ibid., 168.

4. Ibid., 172.

5. Ibid., 182.

6. Ibid., 187.

7. Miller, *In Search*, 225.

8. Denman, *Rose Mary Denman*, 238.

9. Ibid., 240.

10. Ibid., 242.

* 49 *

OPEN OR SHUT?

On Saturday, May 2, 1992, a once unwanted bay colt shocked the racing world with a homestretch dash to victory in the Kentucky Derby at Churchill Downs, Louisville, Kentucky. Lil E Tee scored one of the greatest upsets in Derby history that day, encouraging underdogs everywhere. As the dust settled at Churchill Downs, another group of unwanted underdogs descended upon Louisville to set up shop for Affirmation and RCP and the 1992 UMC General Conference opening on Monday, May 4. For two decades, Methodist gays and lesbians had struggled to get out of the starting gate; would this be the conference when the doors would finally swing open?

General Conference 1988 had offered tantalizing bits of hope that the Methodist history of harsh policies toward gays and lesbians might be softening. "We affirm that God's grace is available to all," said the 1988 revision to the Social Principles, and "we commit ourselves to be in ministry for and with all persons." The delegates backed these words up with the establishment of a "Committee to Study Homosexuality" that would issue a report and a possible call to action at GC 1992.

Hopes were further buoyed as the Committee had been formed. Though no openly LGBT members were included on the Committee, it appeared to be a blue-ribbon panel with familiar, friendly faces—but also some known detractors. "[T]he committee included persons with various forms of theological, ethical, biblical, and scientific expertise . . . to include inclusiveness of gender, racial/ethnic groups, clergy and laity, and geography."[1] As the committee had commenced its work, it seemed to be open and serious, and the LGBT community continued to be optimistic.

> Over the quadrennium, the Committee held eight plenary meet-ings of three or four days each. Regional hearings, to which all United Methodists were invited, were held before smaller panels of Committee members in each of the Jurisdictions. In addition to its own survey on the literature on homosexuality, the Com-mittee benefited from extensive interaction with several distin-guished biblical, theological, ethical, sociological, psychological, and physiological authorities, as well as discussions with repre-sentatives of action organizations and church leaders.[2]

Mark Bowman and other representatives of RCP and Affirmation offered testimony and resources, but so did the conservative represen-tatives of Good News and Transforming Congregations, a reparative therapy coalition. Perhaps most importantly, the Committee listened to personal stories and encountered gays and lesbians face-to-face as human beings and not merely as a disembodied "issue."

> Above all else, the Committee has sought to remember that homosexuality is a human condition. The moral counsel of the church is always a word addressed to human beings struggling to find fullness of life as God intends. In exploring the human reality, the Committee met with many persons who identified themselves as gay, lesbian, ex-gay, ex-lesbian, parent and other relative, friend, church official, pastor, church member.[3]

When the Committee finally finished its work and released the much anticipated report late in 1991, interested persons anxiously jumped to the conclusions and recommendations. The Committee offered both a majority recommendation and a minority recommendation. The majority recommended a monumental reversal in the Social Principles of the church. Since 1972, the church had consistently stated, "We do not con-done the practice of homosexuality and consider this practice to be incompatible with Christian teaching." The majority recommended this policy be reversed by adopting the following language: "The present state of knowledge and insight in the biblical, theological, ethical, biological, psychological, and sociological fields does not provide a satisfactory basis upon which the church can responsibly maintain the condemnation of homosexual practice." On the other hand, the minority recommended that the status quo should be maintained.

When the task force report became public, the conservative opposition went ballistic. *Good News* magazine used charged language to criticize the task force members, their process, and their conclusions: not "fair or evenhanded," "desperate evasions of biblical mandates," "blatantly falsified," "arrogantly asserting," "morally relativistic, presumptuous, and inflammatory," and questioned the need for the church to study homosexuality at all.

The author of the article, Thomas Oden, played a major role in the Institute on Religion and Democracy (IRD), the behind the scenes, neoconservative political organization that infiltrated the Episcopal, Presbyterian, and Methodist churches. We have already examined this organization extensively in connection with Diane Knippers and her role in Episcopal gatekeeper organizations. In fact, Knippers had entered the fray initially as a *Good News* staffer. Thomas Oden was her counterpart within the Methodist Church, and we will take a closer look at him and the IRD in a moment.[4]

The UMC allowed no booths or exhibits for unaffiliated groups at General Conference, but Affirmation's hotel suite cranked out around two thousand newsletters daily and served as headquarters for a coalition of Affirmation and RCP, the women's caucus, and the Methodist Federation for Social Action (MFSA). Affirmation volunteers would participate in, or at least monitor, committee meetings. Worship services and a dinner sponsored by Affirmation were well attended, and a chorus serenaded the delegates in the hallways.

When the delegates descended on Louisville on the same May weekend as long shot Lil E Tee won the Kentucky Derby, Randy Miller, a savvy veteran of prior conferences and church politics, knew how to handicap the electoral race, and he warned his enthusiastic LGBT colleagues that the votes would not be there to change UMC policies.[5] Don't bet on the long shot, he cautioned.

Unfortunately, he would be right.

The first General Conference setback occurred when the representatives of Affirmation and RCP were not allowed to speak during the plenary session's consideration of the Committee's Report. Pastor Morris Floyd, who wrote Affirmation's daily newsletter distributed to the Conference participants, noted the irony: "Society and church discount our lives by acting as if we did not exist—even when we are the subject of the story!"[6]

In response, Affirmation conducted a well-orchestrated floor demonstration. Holding aloft a thirty foot banner that read "The Stones Will Cry Out," thirty or more LGBT supporters proceeded to the dais, singing and encouraging others to stand.[7] At that time, the visitors in the plenary hall probably outnumbered the delegates, and they nearly all rose to their feet in support. Whether any minds were changed is uncertain, but the participants in the demonstration felt empowered.[8]

By the time the Conference was ready to vote on the recommendations of the Committee, LGBT supporters were anticipating defeat, and there would be no come-from-behind miracle. As expected, the Conference accepted the minority recommendation of the Committee to leave the language of the Social Principles unchanged, and voted to retain the "incompatibility" language.

Conservative delegates got worked up over what to do with the report, fearing that the normal parliamentary procedure of "receiving" the report implied endorsement, even though the body had just voted against the majority recommendation and for the minority restatement of existing language. Thus, the report was "received" but not "accepted," according to the resolution that was adopted. Yet, it was not total defeat; the report produced by the Committee would be made available for distribution to congregations and others as a study document.

Randy Miller had cautioned against hoping for a stretch run victory, yet,

> It was still sort of devastating to have folks vote to not have a speaker from Affirmation or a gay/lesbian person speak and then to vote down in a very mean sort of way the best part of the Study Committee Report. . . . It was not an enlightened discussion. . . . It was this kind of a discussion, despite all the high talk beforehand

that we were going to discuss theology and ethics. It was people regurgitating homophobia at a very low level. And it was very painful. [When the vote was over, the organist began to play "Standing on the Promises."] . . . And, of course, the conservatives leapt on that with great joy and starting singing as if they had just saved the church. . . . Then I did a TV interview right after that. And, lo and behold, I sort of fell apart in the TV interview, which just shows me again that I was more affected by this than I wanted to be.[9]

Many of the mainstays had had enough and would retreat to their Reconciling Congregations or their Affirmation chapter. Some of those called to the ordained ministry would look to a different denomination, such as the UCC, MCC, or the UU, which each offered a path to ordination for out gays.

[T]he reasons for leaving were the same as those for leaving a harmful relationship: "It has become clear to me once again just how much my relationship to [my denomination] was an abusive relationship. I have never really understood why abused women (and men) stayed with their partners who abused them, but I think I now have some inkling. . . . I have reached my limit, and I know that I don't need to be beaten up one more time to feel justified in leaving."[10]

And, yet . . . Christians are hopeful optimists, and none more so than LGBT Christians. A new generation of leaders and activists would step forward. Affirmation was infused with fresh blood: "I don't think its going to cave in. I think there are some people who are burned out and they'll back off, but I don't think that'll hold or dominate. What I saw in Affirmation was that a new national council was elected, and those people are enthusiastic, committed, and determined."[11]

During the quadrennium between GC 1992 and GC 1996, the "Confessing Movement" appeared across denominational boundaries, including the UMC, with murky support from the Institute on Religion and Democracy (IRD). We have already commented extensively on the IRD and its infiltration of the Episcopal Church through Diane Knippers and also briefly mentioned Presbyterian links. The reader is encouraged to return to earlier chapters to review the formation and function of this pseudo-religious organization whose real goal was to blunt the church's social justice movements that did not accord with the economic agenda of neoconservative politicos and their financiers.

John Thomas, former President of the UCC, described the IRD in these words,

> "Groups like the Evangelical Association of Reformed, Christian and Congregational Churches and the Biblical Witness Fellowship," he said last year, "are increasingly being exposed even as they are increasingly aggressive. Their relationship to the right-wing Institute for Religion and Democracy and its long-term agenda of silencing a progressive religious voice while enlisting the church in an unholy alliance with right-wing politics is no longer deniable. United Church of Christ folk like to be 'nice,' to be hospitable. But, to play with a verse of Scripture just a bit, we doves innocently entertain these serpents in our midst at our own peril."[12]

Inflammatory articles penned by Dr. Thomas Oden frequently appeared in *Good News* magazine. Methodist Professor Oden played the role of Diane Knippers within the UMC. Knippers, the IRD director, was Episcopalian, and she led the gatekeeper organization within TEC. Oden had served on the IRD board of directors, and as a Methodist theologian, he exerted influence within conservative Methodist circles. IRD infiltration into the Methodist Church was at least as great as in the Episcopal Church, with tentacles extending through the Confessing Movement.

> "The IRD is affiliated with no denomination and is accountable only to its own, self-perpetuating board of directors," write Andrew Weaver and Nicole Seibert, "[and it] focuses its principal expenditures and most of its efforts on the United Methodist Church."

> The IRD Methodist affiliate, Good News, not only has organized for schism but its leaders Rev. Scott Field and Rev.

James Heidinger told *Christianity Today* "institutional separation is all but inevitable."

Weaver and Seibert note that in 2002, a foundation controlled by Richard Mellon Scaife gave $225,000 to the IRD for its "Reforming America's Churches Project"—among whose stated goals is the elimination of the Methodists' General Board of Church and Society, the church's voice for justice and peace, as well as discrediting United Methodist Church pastors and bishops with whom they disagree by instigating as many as a dozen church trials over the next few years.[13]

In a moment, we will witness their judicial activism in bringing ecclesiastical trials against gays, lesbians, and their allies.

Whether Good News and the Confessing Movement were spurred by grassroots fears or encouraged by outside political interests, or a combination, the reality is that the voices on the right grew louder and more shrill during this period. As the RCP, Affirmation, and MFSA achieved notable successes locally and regionally, the intertwined conservative organizations propped up the barricades to thwart any progressive momentum toward changing national policies.

During this quadrennium, the advocates in Affirmation, RCP, and MFSA proved to be "enthusiastic, committed, and determined." Advocacy activities grew exponentially.[14]

1993: 278 persons attended the Third National Convocation of RCP held in Washington, D.C.

1993: A Reconciling Pastors' Action Network (RPAN) was formed.

1993: The Angel Campaign (fundraising) began, and the goal of $40,000 was exceeded.

1994: The report of the Committee to Study Homosexuality was released as a study guide, and congregations were encouraged to conduct discussions.

1994: RCP, Affirmation, and MFSA participated in discussions regarding "witness" at the upcoming General Conference as a result of their lobbying against a local antigay ordinance.

1994: RPAN grew to one hundred clergy members.

1995: Planning began for GC 1996 under the theme "Open the Doors."

1995: 325 persons attended the Fourth National Convocation of RCP in Minneapolis.

1995: 160 activists from thirty-three annual conferences participated in six regional training sessions for local Open the Doors efforts.

1995: Local activists wrote letters and met with General Conference delegates, organized Open the Doors' rallies, and enrolled Reconciling United Methodists.

1996: More than seventy-five RCP members and allies participated at General Conference in Denver. Posters proclaiming Open the Doors were distributed to downtown businesses. Volunteers opened doors for delegates and visitors. The names of more than ten thousand Reconciling Methodists were unveiled.

On the eve of GC 1996, a group of fifteen bishops startled the UMC by issuing a statement of support for the Open the Doors movement:

> We the undersigned bishops wish to affirm the commitment made at our consecration to uphold the *Discipline* of the church. However, we must confess the pain we feel over our personal convictions that are contradicted by the proscriptions in the *Discipline* against gays and lesbians within our church and within our ordained and diaconal ministers. . . . We believe it is time to break the silence and state where we are on this issue that is hurting and silencing countless faithful Christians. We will continue our responsibility to the order and discipline of the church but urge our United Methodist churches to open the doors in gracious hospitality to all our brothers and sisters in the faith.[15]

At General Conference 1996, a proposal to remove or revise the "incompatibility" policy was again the issue; a substitute was offered that recognized that Methodists were not of one mind. The Church and Society legislative committee moved this statement to the convention floor:

"We acknowledge with humility that the church has been unable to arrive at a common mind on the compatibility of homosexual practice with Christian faith. Many consider the practice incompatible with Christian teaching. Others believe it acceptable when practiced in a context of human covenantal faithfulness."[16]

But the convention delegates were unwilling to go along with the recommendation of fifteen bishops to "open the doors in gracious hospitality to all our brothers and sisters in the faith" and unwilling to accept the substitute statement of the legislative committee. First, the fifteen bishops were admonished, following a closed session with the other 109 bishops, for releasing the statement without approval of the Council of Bishops; then, with a 60 percent majority, the delegates voted to retain the same incompatibility clause that had been on the books since 1972.

Sixty percent opposed seemed a steep hill to climb. Yet a subsequent survey of delegates to GC 1996 suggested hearts and minds were slowly opening, even if the doors remained shut. Fully 15 percent of polled delegates suggested their experience at the convention moved them toward greater acceptance of gays and lesbians. The daring statement of the fifteen bishops was cited by survey respondents as the primary factor, and others who were already supporters of LGBT issues reported that the bishops' statement energized them and encouraged them to return to their congregations more vocal.

The same survey suggested stark regional differences, with ten Southern states solidly in opposition to LGBT issues while Western delegates favored opening the doors.[17] Of the few survey respondents who reported their negative attitudes had hardened during the convention, contact and discussion with international delegates was cited as a prime factor, an ominous note for LGBT supporters.[18] Alone among the ecumenical denominations, the United Methodists have significant international representation, and these delegates would form a solidly antigay voting bloc.

First lady Hillary Rodham Clinton, reared in a suburban Chicago Methodist congregation, presented the convention keynote address, and many delegates, even conservatives, noted that her speech had been the highlight of the convention. Though she did not specifically speak to LGBT issues, her linkage of personal faith and a sense of obligation toward others —"Jesus loves the little children, all the children of the world"—resonated with the delegates and may have contributed to the softening of hearts.[19]

Yet 60 percent opposed was the stark reality. The gatekeepers closely guarded the keys to the kingdom. By the end of the decade, they offered an insolent solution to continuing conflict—kick out the gays, lesbians, and their allies. Perhaps it was a preemptive strike. Sensing a progressive leadership bias and evolving attitudes in the pulpits and the pews, the conservatives would lay claim to "true Methodism."[20] In a paid advertisement in the official UMC publication, *The United Methodist Reporter*, the Good News board of directors published an open letter to the Council of Bishops:

> Taking note of "a growing movement within our church to disobey 'for conscience' sake' the *Discipline* of the church," the letter calls on the bishops to "deal with this renunciation of Scripture, Tradition, and our covenant." They request the bishops both to enforce church standards and "to work on processes that would allow the orderly withdrawal of those who, for whatever reason, cannot submit to the order and discipline of The United Methodist Church."[21]

Of course, gays, lesbians, and their allies did not accept the ungracious invitation to "an orderly withdrawal," and the Council of Bishops did not encourage such an exodus.

Decades earlier, Pastors Gene Leggett and Rick Huskey had been snubbed when their entreaties to GC 1972 resulted in the harsh "incompatibility" language of the Social Principles. GC 1984 added an explicit policy to exclude "self-avowed, practicing homosexuals" from the pulpit. Repeated attempts to revise the policies had been rebuffed.

As the 1992 General Conference had neared, a blue ribbon task force had recommended LGBT-friendly policy changes. Convention delegates disagreed, and the Methodist door toward full inclusion remained bolted shut. Four years later in the buildup to the 1996 General Convention, an "Open Doors" movement had received much attention and widespread support, even from many bishops, but once again, convention delegates slammed the doors shut with a resounding clang.

NOTES

1. Dorothy Williams, *The Church Studies Homosexuality* (Nashville: Cokesbury, 1994), 13.

2. Ibid.

3. Ibid., 13–14.

4. Thomas Oden, "Taking the Task Force to Task," *Good News* (January–February, 1992).

5. Comstock, *Unrepentant*, 15.

6. Ibid., 16.

7. "You have devised shame for your house by cutting off many peoples; you have forfeited your life. The very stones will cry out from the wall, and the plaster will respond from the woodwork." Habakkuk 2:10–11.

8. Pastor Morris Floyd, private conversation with the author, January 20, 2012.

9. Comstock, *Unrepentant*, 117–18.

10. Comstock, *Unrepentant*, 222. This comment actually comes from a Presbyterian candidate for ordination, but the sentiment applied equally to Methodists who departed the UMC to seek ordination elsewhere.

11. A lesbian UMC church administrator, quoted in Comstock, *Unrepentant*, 227.

12. Frederick Clarkson, "The Battle for the Mainline Churches," *The Public Eye* (Spring 2006).

13. Ibid.

14. "About Us: History 1990–1993" and "1994–1997," on the website of Reconciling Ministries Network, accessed February 7, 2012, http://www.rmnetwork.org/about-us/history/.

15. Creech, *Adam's Gift*, 91.

16. James Rutland Wood, *Where the Spirit Leads: The Evolving Views of United Methodists on Homosexuality* (Nashville: Abingdon Press, 2000), 21.

17. Ibid., 36, 28, 85.

18. Ibid., 91.

19. Ibid., 43, 47.

20. Just a few years later, Thomas Oden of IRD and the Confessing Movement would encourage "True Methodists" to bring lawsuits against the United Methodist Church. So too, an editorial in the fall 2000 official newsletter of the Confessing Movement: "One day a judge in a Federal courtroom will read our history and that of our opponents, and the issue will be, Who are the true

Methodists? If and when that day comes, it will be important that we show ourselves to be the rightful heirs, which we are." Swecker, *Hardball on Holy Ground*, 25–26.

21. Wood, *Where the Spirit Leads*, 24.

✳ 50 ✳

Bishops and Clergy Speak Out

With a 60 percent majority, General Convention 1996 had retained the onerous incompatibility clause; with momentum on their side, the conservative factions successfully added further harsh policies on the final day of the Conference. This time, ceremonies of blessing of same-gender couples were the target.

Variously called "holy unions," "covenant ceremonies," "commitment services," or "rites of blessing," such blessings had been performed by many Methodist pastors upon LGBT couples over the years. On three occasions early in the decade, bishops had called upon local congregations to refrain from performing covenant ceremonies: Dumbarton UMC in Washington, D.C.; University UMC in Madison, Wisconsin; and Walker Community UMC in Minneapolis. Yet there were no sanctions, and many clergy continued to quietly perform covenant services. One private service in Indianapolis was invaded by an uninvited guest—a UMC pastor who surreptitiously videotaped the ceremony—leading to bishops again warning against covenant ceremonies but apparently not against stealth videotapes.[1]

The issue of religious blessings for same-gender relationships had received heightened attention in April 1993 at a D.C. event organized by the Metropolitan Community Churches (MCC). MCC leader Troy Perry called it simply, "The Wedding," and he reported "[A]t least 2,600 same-sex couples, complete with tuxedos and wedding gowns, made a public commitment in a mass ritual and then celebrated their unions in privately organized receptions around the city."[2]

The UMC *Book of Discipline* is a compendium of official Methodist documents that includes the constitution, doctrinal and theological statements, and a large section detailing Methodist polity and organization. A separate section is entitled "Social Principles" with a genesis in a 1908 "Social Creed." In many respects, the Social Principles have sounded the prophetic voice of the Methodists. The preface to the Social Principles section of the *Book of Discipline* states:

> The United Methodist Church has a long history of concern for social justice. . . . The Social Principles, while not to be considered church law, are a prayerful and thoughtful effort on the part of the General Conference to speak to the human issues in the contemporary world from a sound biblical and theological foundation as historically demonstrated in United Methodist traditions. They are a call to faithfulness and are intended to be instructive and persuasive in the best of the prophetic spirit. The Social Principles are a call to all members of The United Methodist Church to a prayerful, studied dialogue of faith and practice.[3]

Against this background, in the last hours of General Conference 1996, the following provision had been added to the Social Principles of the United Methodist Church: "Ceremonies that celebrate homosexual unions shall not be conducted by our ministers and shall not be conducted in our churches."[4]

Eight years earlier, Pastor John MacDougall, the trial counsel for Rose Mary Denman, had offered a bit of sarcastic irony by noting the absurdity: "In my not entirely inglorious career, so far, I have blessed motorcycles, packs of dogs, a time capsule, mobile homes, insulation and even a toilet, but were I to bless the union of two Christian people (who were gay or lesbian), it would be an offense, chargeable before a trial."[5]

At General Conference 1996, fifteen bishops had stepped out in support of opening the doors to gays and lesbians. Although they had been rebuffed by their peers, the second half of the nineties would be characterized by the increasing willingness of the episcopate and the clergy to speak against church policy, and some dared confrontational acts of ecclesiastical disobedience by performing the now outlawed covenant ceremonies.

A recurring issue had come to the Methodists: unity and the good order of the church versus justice. The mutuality and reciprocity of covenant is an essential tenet of Methodist connectionalism, and that includes ordained clergy who are bound in covenant to all ordained clergy, especially those within their conference. Additionally, the *Book of Discipline* requires clergy to: "Be accountable to The United Methodist Church, accept its Doctrinal Standards and Discipline and authority, accept the supervision of those appointed to this ministry, and be prepared to live in the covenant of its ordained ministers."[6] How then could clergy register dissent against policies written into the *Discipline*, increasingly perceived to be unfair, nay, not just unfair but wrongheaded and false, without violating their covenant?

A decade and a half earlier, Bishop Melvin Wheatley had been a lonely voice crying in the wilderness when he protested the inherent falsity of the premise on which Methodist policy was based—"homosexuality is incompatible with Christian teaching." Untrue, untrue, untrue he had said then, citing his own extensive experience of persons who were both gay and Christian; now, as the century wound down, others began to echo his prophetic words.

John Wesley, the founder of Methodism, was fond of saying, "In essentials unity, in non-essentials liberty, in all things charity." On New Year's Day 1997, fifteen UMC pastors issued a written challenge to the church's antigay policies entitled *In All Things Charity*; by April, nearly thirteen hundred UMC clergy had signed the manifesto. Here are excerpts:

> As United Methodist Clergy, we are bound in covenant to uphold the *Discipline* of our denomination. By ordination, we are also "committed to becoming conscious representatives of the whole Gospel and are responsible for transmission of that Gospel to the end that all the world may be saved." (¶330, #1, '96 Discipline) There are times in history when those two expectations are in tension with one another . . . we are moved to a statement of conscience and commitment:

> 1. Scripture, tradition, reason and experience convince us that "the practice of homosexuality" is not in itself "incompatible with Christian teaching . . ."

2. The distinction between "being" and "practice" in our Social Principals gives rise to confusion. The statement in paragraph 65 that homosexual persons are of "sacred worth" but that the "practice of homosexuality is incompatible with Christian teaching" is not acceptable. One does not "practice" one's sexual orientation, one lives it . . .

3. We affirm appropriate liturgical support for covenantal commitments between same-gendered couples. . . . To withhold rituals of support and accountability for committed relationships is unconscionable. The standards for preparation and celebration of such services with same-gendered couples should be the same as for weddings of heterosexual couples . . .

4. We will continue to initiate and respond to opportunities to enter into dialogue with those whose point of view on these matters is different from ours . . .

5. We will pray and work for the ordination of gay men and lesbians who are otherwise called to and qualified for ordained ministry.

6. In all other matters regarding homosexuality, we are committed to charity, grace and accountability of the same character as applies to heterosexuality.[7]

Others challenged the church and her policies, not only in word, but also in deed.

Pastor Jimmy Creech of Nebraska ignored the policy against covenant ceremonies by performing a ceremony for a lesbian couple in his congregation (something he had done dozens of times over the years), and the Nebraska Annual Conference charged him and brought him to trial. In fact, Pastor Creech faced a pair of trials for performing covenant ceremonies.

In September 1997, he performed a covenant service in the sanctuary of his church, First United Methodist of Omaha. At his trial in March 1998, his defense argued that because the prohibition was contained in the Social Principles of the *Book of Discipline*, it was merely instructive and not prescriptive. After all, the preface clearly stated that Social Principles are "not to be considered church law." No Methodist had ever been tried for any reason contained within the Social Principles.[8]

The jury would agree with Creech's defense, and he was acquitted in March 1998. Later, the Judicial Council, the "Supreme Court" of the UMC, would hold that the prohibition contained within the Social Principles "has the effect of church law, notwithstanding its placement in [the Social Principles] and, therefore, governs the conduct of the ministerial office."[9] That ruling came too late for the first Creech trial, and the jury acquittal was unaffected. But, when Pastor Creech officiated at another covenant ceremony in April of 1999, a second jury convicted him and defrocked him in November of that year.

At the first trial, expert witnesses were allowed to criticize denominational policy toward gays and lesbians. As in the Denman proceedings in New Hampshire a decade earlier, it was church policies that were on trial. At the second trial, Soulforce, an emerging nondenominational LGBT-affirming organization, engaged in ecclesiastical disobedience by blocking the entrance to the trial, and many of the nonviolent protesters were arrested. Evangelical Pastor Mel White, who had been a speechwriter for Jerry Falwell, Pat Robertson, and others before coming out, was the Soulforce founder, and he coined the term "spiritual violence" to refer to the church's treatment of gays and lesbians.[10] Both Creech trials were highly publicized by national media.

Although no longer a Methodist minister, Pastor Creech would remain active in LGBT causes as a speaker and advocate. He would serve on the board of Soulforce and other progressive organizations. In his 2011 memoir, he wrote:

> I realized then that, while my relationship with the United Methodist Church had changed, I hadn't. I remained the same person I was before the trial. The church had taken away from me only what it had given, my credentials of ordination. The clerical frock was truly an adornment, not an essential part of who I was. Being defrocked took from me a title I had worn, but not my identity or vocation, which were so much more than a covering, so much more essential than a title. I might no longer be called a "Reverend," but I would always be a pastor.[11]

The two Creech trials served as bookends around other clergy acts of ecclesiastical disobedience.

Pastor Gregory Dell of Broadway United Methodist Church of Chicago was also convicted of presiding at a covenant ceremony. The membership of Broadway UMC was 30 percent gay when Pastor Dell performed a covenant ceremony on September 19, 1998. Bishop Joseph Sprague reluctantly filed charges:

> [D]espite my high regard for the Reverend Dell, as a person of integrity, who possesses an enviable record of pastoral faithfulness and effectiveness, my evaluation of The Reverend Dell as an exceptional pastor, and my own theological and pastoral disagreement with this component of church law, I do hereby file a formal complaint.[12]

Dell was convicted in March 1999, and he was suspended from his appointment to Broadway UMC. Initially, the suspension was indefinite, unless Pastor Dell signed a written pledge to refrain from further covenant services, but on appeal, the suspension was limited to one year, and Pastor Dell was not forced to sign a pledge. During his suspension, Pastor Dell served as executive director of *In All Things Charity*, and his colleagues in the Northern Illinois Annual Conference showed support by electing him as a delegate to General Conference 2000. He was reappointed to Broadway UMC by Bishop Sprague after his suspension.[13]

Meanwhile, on the West Coast, a large group of clergy would jointly perform a covenant ceremony in a highly visible act of ecclesiastical disobedience. The "Sacramento 68," as the pastors came to be known, were organized by Pastor Don Fado of St. Mark's UMC of Sacramento. Two of his parishioners, a lesbian couple, approached him and said, "It's time." The pair were well-known, not only in the congregation but in the entire annual conference because of their involvement in the regional church. Jeanne Barnett had served as the Conference's lay leader and Ellen Charlton had served on the Conference's Board of Trustees. Pastor Fado sent a letter to his fellow clergy inviting others to participate.

> We ended up with 95 from our annual conference . . . and another 25 from outside our annual conference, people from other denominations. In fact, we had requests from all over the country, from people who wanted to come. . . . Some of them

said, "This is the Selma, Alabama, of the gay rights movement, and we want to be there and make a statement to the country."[14]

Following the January 16, 1999, covenant ceremony, attended by twelve hundred to fifteen hundred guests, a complaint was filed and an investigation ensued. Once again, a bishop was put in the awkward position of defending a policy with which he disagreed. For bishops, their obligation to uphold the good order of the church is especially acute. Bishop Melvin Talbert echoed the sentiment expressed by his colleague, Bishop Joseph Sprague of Chicago regarding Pastor Greg Dell: "I will uphold the law, but I will not be silenced. I will continue speaking out against the law and will continue working to change the position of the church to be more in keeping with the teachings and compassion of Jesus."[15]

It would turn out that Bishop Talbert and the investigating committee would do more than mechanistically apply church law. Their advocacy moved beyond mere words and tilted toward action. Following three days of testimony and three more days of deliberation, the investigating committee (much like a grand jury) announced on February 11, 2000, that charges would not be pursued.

> It was clear at the press conference that the same-sex marriage issue . . . has captured the attention of the world outside the United Methodist Church. As Bishop Talbert read the committee's decision, a bank of television cameras kept up a steady clicking, and the conference room at the United Methodist Center was filled with media representatives and observers.
>
> The question before them, the committee wrote, was whether or not there were reasonable grounds to certify that the charge was proper for a trial.
>
> In the Feb. 1–3 hearing at Community United Methodist Church in Fairfield, the committee heard testimony from expert witnesses on Scripture, ethics and tradition within the church and the history of the annual conference. In its statement, the committee said, "We concluded that the answer required a methodology consistent with our whole faith rather than one limited by narrow focus."

The committee affirmed in its statement that "we in the California-Nevada Annual Conference are not of one mind regarding our church's ministry to the gay/lesbian community." The committee acknowledged the conference's "need for God's grace and the guidance of the Holy Spirit."

Talbert stated that, while the committee's decision may appear to have broken covenant with the denomination's *Book of Discipline*, there is "another more basic and fundamental covenant that has precedence over this one narrow focus of law." Talbert said that the Annual Conference is the covenant into which clergy members are received, and that the committee's decision "does reflect the longstanding covenant commitments for inclusiveness and justice" of the California-Nevada Annual Conference.[16]

Our journey through the 1990s has spilled over into the next decade. Before ending this segment of our journey, we will allow Bishop Jack Tuell to have the last word.

Bishop Tuell was the bishop who had reluctantly acceded to the requests of gay pastor Morris Floyd to be appointed to a mental health counseling center in Minneapolis way back in the early 1980s. Bishop Tuell, a trained lawyer, had drafted the 1984 resolution that became the Methodist law of the land regarding LGBT clergy—the infamous "self-avowed, practicing" prohibition. Finally, Bishop Tuell had presided over the trial of Pastor Greg Dell of Chicago that had resulted in Dell's suspension in 1999, and he would have presided over the case of the Sacramento 68 had that matter proceeded to trial.

On February 20, 2000, Bishop Tuell delivered a sermon to his congregation:[17]

> God is ever ready to do a new thing . . . the God we worship is not a static God, capable only of speaking to us from two, three or four thousand years ago. Rather, God is living, alive in this moment, revealing new truth to us here, now. . . . I believe that God is about to do a new thing among us.
>
> [O]ur real tradition is ignorance. In another way, however, we have a long tradition of change. . . . In the long run, we have always been able to discern when God is doing a new thing

in our midst. This capacity to change is among the noblest of our traditions.

What is the role of experience in the issue we speak of today? It is the personal encounter with the anguish, the pain, the hurt, the suffering, the despair which harsh and judgmental attitudes can have on persons of homosexual orientation.

I was wrong. It was experience that showed me I was wrong. . . . A year ago, when Bishop Joseph Sprague of Illinois asked me to come and preside over a church trial [of Pastor Greg Dell], experience made its compelling points with me. Ecclesiastically speaking, the decision was correct. As I understand the Spirit of God, it was wrong. . . . I began to see the new thing God is doing.

It is impossible to predict what actions [future General Conferences] may take, because the Spirit moves at its own pace—"the wind bloweth where it listeth (John 3:8)." But I believe that if the delegates are listening carefully, above the competing pressures of this group and that, they will hear the still, small voice whisper, "I am doing a new thing," and they will respond faithfully.

Amen.

NOTES

1. "About Us: History 1990–1993," Reconciling Ministries Network, accessed February 8, 2012, http://www.rmnetwork.org/about-us/history/1990-1993/.

2. Troy Perry, *Open Hands* vol. 12, no. 4 (Spring 1997), 4.

3. United Methodist Church, 2008 Book of Discipline, Part IV, Social Principles, Preface.

4. United Methodist Church, *1996 Book of Discipline*, paragraph 65.C.

5. John MacDougall, summation to the jury in the Denman trial, quoted in Denman, *Let My People*, 232.

6. United Methodist Church, *2008 Book of Discipline*, Part V—Organization and Administration, Chapter Two, "The Ministry of the Ordained: The Meaning of Ordination and Conference Membership," ¶ 304, j.

7. Creech, *Adam's Gift*,100.

8. Ibid., 184.

9. United Methodist Church, Judicial Council Decisions, accessed February 8, 2012, http://archives.umc.org/interior_judicial.asp?mid=263&JDID=873&JDMOD=VWD.

10. Creech, *Adam's Gift*,311–19.

11. Ibid., 327.

12. Bishop C. Joseph Sprague of the Northern Illinois Annual Conference, October 12, 1998. On June 22, 2012, in a private conversation with the author, Sprague said that his one regret from his eight years as bishop was signing this complaint.

13. "Gregory R. Dell," on the website of Affirmation, accessed February 9, 2012, http://www.umaffirm.org/cornet/gregdell.html.

14. "Reverend Donald Fado," interview on the website for PBS Frontline, accessed February 9, 2012, http://www.pbs.org/wgbh/pages/frontline/shows/assault/interviews/fado.html.

15. Wood, *Where the Spirit Leads*, 105.

16. Erica Jeffrey, United Methodist News Service, "Cal-Nevada Ministers Won't Stand Trial, Committee Decides," February 11, 2000.

17. Bishop Jack M. Tuell, Sermon: "'Doing a New Thing': The United Methodist Church and Homosexuality," Des Moines, Washington, Sunday, February 20, 2000, on the website of Affirmation, accessed February 9, 2012, http://www.umaffirm.org/gcnews5.html.

✳ 51 ✳

JUST KILL THEM!

Legend tells the story of Absalom Jones, Richard Allen, and other black Methodists who were forcibly lifted from their knees while praying at a Methodist church in Philadelphia in 1787. It seems some of the white Methodists didn't believe that blacks belonged at the prayer rail, and the black men were thrown out.

At the 2000 General Conference in Cleveland, Ohio, the Methodists repented of this act of racial discrimination and many others.

> Putting on sackcloth and ashes, the United Methodist Church confronted more than 200 years of institutional racism and discrimination that split John Wesley's Methodist followers into two distinct camps—black and white.
>
> In a stirring three-hour ceremony Thursday night [May 4], delegates to the church's 2000 General Conference apologized to black churches that left the Methodist church because of pervasive racial discrimination. In addition, they apologized to black United Methodists who still face racial prejudice.[1]

How quickly the lessons of history are forgotten.

Just a few days later, the delegates refused to revise onerous UMC policies toward gays and lesbians. In fact, the votes were decisive and slipped backwards. But there's a whole lot more to the story than mere vote totals, including the forced removal of gays, lesbians, and their allies from the plenary floor.

On Wednesday morning, May 10, 2000, defrocked pastor Jimmy Creech, suspended pastor Greg Dell, and Dell's bishop, Joseph Sprague, joined with three hundred or more protesters outside the convention center. The coalition of Affirmation, MFSA, and RMN organized the protest. A persistent drizzle failed to dampen their spirits or dull their rainbow colored armbands. Among the gathered were Mel White and other members of Soulforce, Yolanda King (daughter of Martin Luther King Jr.), Arun Gandhi (the grandson of Mohandas Gandhi), and Methodist Pastor James Lawson, an elderly veteran of protest who had taught MLK Jr. lessons of nonviolence that Lawson had learned at the feet of Gandhi.

Rays of sunshine streamed through the overcast skies to greet the first arriving delegates, and the protest began in earnest. The entire contingent sang hymns and circled the convention center once. Then a group of twenty or so peeled off and blocked the main entrance. The protesters had informed the police beforehand, and the officers politely went about their business, first issuing a warning, but the protesters held their ground and were duly arrested, only to be replaced by orchestrated waves of another group of twenty, then another group, and another until nearly two hundred had been arrested.[2]

Inside the plenary hall, a group of gays and supporters announced that Methodist clergy and laity were being arrested outside, and they chanted in unison, "Wide is God's welcome; extend the table."

The next day, Thursday, May 11, clerical stoles from the Shower of Stoles project provided a splash of color to an otherwise dreary assembly. Many stoles were sprinkled in the balcony where LGBT advocates monitored the plenary session below. When they began to march single file around the balcony as debate began over *their* issue, others joined them until they completely encircled the convention floor. They stopped and held hands as the debate raged below. As the votes rolled in with recurring losing margins of two to one, twenty-seven protesters shocked the assembly by stalking to the front of the podium where they turned to face the delegates and refused to move.[3]

"We shall overcome" broke out from the balcony above as many conservatives scurried away from the floor. A recess was called. A gay man at the piano accompanied hymn singing that was "alternately raucous and spiritual." The circle holding hands above the plenary floor remained in place. A quarter of the delegates on the floor rose to their feet in solidarity and so did fifteen bishops.

Then, a bizarre and spontaneous incident interrupted the floor demonstration. Suddenly, a stranger appeared at the rail at the balcony. "I am not a Methodist, but I have been a lesbian all my life," she screamed, and the crowd recoiled as it appeared she might jump. She slumped backward into the arms of two folks who reached to grab her. Later, at a local hospital, she explained that she was not connected to any group, but had come to watch the proceedings and had been overcome by the drama of the moment. "I got kinda overemotional," she said.[4]

The presiding bishop of the day adjourned the plenary session for lunch, but the balcony circle remained unbroken, and the twenty-seven protesters refused to leave. After lunch, they blocked the podium. When police officers approached the protesters, cries of "No!" and "Shame!" rained down from the balcony. Two elderly, conservative delegates slapped "high fives" to the accompaniment of sobs and wailing from the balcony.[5] A floor delegate from Texas screeched, "Just kill them." The presiding bishop of the day, who had exhibited graciousness toward the gays and lesbians, buried his face in his hands and said he could not watch the church do this to its people.[6]

The parallelism with the forced removal of the black men more than two centuries earlier was lost on most, but not on delegate Nancy L. Cukler from nearby Akron.

"Thursday night we apologized for something we did many years ago," she said. "I'm afraid we're doing something today that we will need to apologize for later."[7]

Ann F. Price, in her poem *The Restless Ones*, recreated the moment:

we are the restless ghosts
the past
present
God forbid—future

some walk the balcony
some seize the floor

we wear the stoles
that tell the stories of
gifts postponed

we wear the stoles
of those now dead
or living and hidden
rejected
by the church
because of who they are
created

created gay
born lesbian
transgendered
bisexual

others stumble
over the words
as we walk
the balcony
pray and hold the floor

movement stops
as fingers push buttons
the screen declares
inclusion defeated
again

people beneath the stoles
sigh and sing

trade stoles of beauty
for torn ones
ripped from fabric

as we are torn
all of us
body of Christ

once more
separated
severed from
a gentle weaving
of hope

now
delayed

we are the restless ones
past
present[8]

Each of the twenty-seven prisoners, including two bishops—Joseph Sprague and Susan Morrison (Sprague had also been arrested the day before)—was brought before an African American judge, who reduced the penalties and released them one by one with a whispered "keep up the good work."[9]

Others were less sympathetic.

Prior to the Conference, the gatekeepers had distributed a glitzy, professionally produced video to each delegate entitled "Decision 2000." The video invited the gays, lesbians, and their supporters to leave the UMC.

It's time for gay-affirming congregations to accept the decisions of previous conferences, [the narrator] says; if they cannot, they should be permitted to leave the denomination, "amicably." Departing churches would be allowed to retain their property under the Decision 2000 proposal, but the message of the video is clear: Get with the program or get out.[10]

Afterwards, the leader of Good News, James V. Heidinger II (to whom we are indebted for the suggesting the term "gatekeeper"), proclaimed for all to hear, "We think this is a very significant moment in which the church has spoken once again in the midst of incredible pressure, including from outside the denomination, and chosen to maintain its commitment to its tested long-term teaching on the area of human sexuality."[11]

With unintended irony, the conference keynote had been offered by the archbishop of Canterbury, George Carey, who had overseen the rout of the Episcopal Church two years earlier at Lambeth 1998. It was at Lambeth '98 that conservative Anglicans from developing nations had seized control of the Anglican agenda and mercilessly hounded gays, lesbians, and their supporters.

The Methodists had their own delegations from developing nations who openly offered their own homophobic rants at this Methodist General Conference. Liberian Bishop the Rev. Dr. Arthur F. Kulah was privileged to offer the sermon during one of the daily worship services, and he abused the pulpit to spew hateful words:

> Kulah maligned us during worship on Wednesday. For those who did not hear him, Bishop Kulah argued that the church is called to make disciples who will obey the authority of the Bible, but that homosexuals, at Satan's behest, choose to disobey that authority, setting themselves outside of Christianity. When the Church pays attention to them [our] demands, it abuses the authority of the Bible, which speaks unequivocally against homosexuality. "To ordain homosexuals," Bishop Kulah proclaimed, "is to ruin the hearts and lives of the church and hence the world."[12]

In an ominous challenge, Bishop Kulah and other African speakers demanded that the Methodist goal to be a *global* connection required strict adherence to the incompatibility clause; as the ensuing general conferences of 2004, 2008, and 2012 would demonstrate, his chilling words proved true. As the relative influence of the developing nations Central Conferences increased, the chances for liberalizing denominational policies toward gays and lesbians lessened. Even as members, congregations, and entire annual conferences within the United States moved toward ever-greater inclusivity, the rigid bloc of delegates from developing nations allied with the gatekeepers to prevent general conference reforms.

The heart-wrenching frustrations of General Conference 2000 would be repeated.

NOTES

1. Kevin Eckstrom, Religious News Service, "Methodists Issue Sweeping Apology for Church's Racism," May 5, 2000.

2. Natalie Davis, "One Broken Body," *Baltimore City Paper*, June 28, 2000.

3. Martha Juillerat, "They Know Not What They Do," *Open Hands* vol. 16, no. 1, (Summer, 2000), 13.

4. Davis, "One Broken Body."

5. Ibid.

6. Martha Juillerat, "They Know Not."

7. David Briggs, Karen R. Long, and Karl Turner, "Praying for Change: 200 Arrested in Protest of Church Stand on Gays," *Cleveland Plain Dealer*, May 11, 2000.

8. Ann Freeman Price, "The Restless Church," reprinted with permission. See her website for information about her many poems, compositions, and books: http://annfreemanprice.com/.

9. Juillerat, "They Know Not."

10. Davis, "One Broken Body."

11. Kevin Eckstrom, "Methodists Look to Future after Rocky General Conference," on the website of Beliefnet, accessed August 27, 2012, http://www.beliefnet.com/News/2000/05/Methodists-Look-To-Future-After-Rocky-General-Conference.aspx?p=2.

12. Rev. Dr. Jeanne Knepper, Press Release, on the website of Affirmation, accessed August 27, 2008, http://www.umaffirm.org/tm0504.html#kulah.

* 52 *

Witch Hunts

Prior to General Conference 2000, all delegates had received a video distributed by Good News that encouraged progressives and their congregations to depart the UMC.

"No thanks," the congregations had said, "this is our church and we're staying," and Good News took a harder tack.

Enter Rev. Thomas Lambrecht of Wisconsin, with an angular face and a disarming cant of his head to the right, who would become inquisitor general on behalf of Good News. At first, he was mere foot soldier, but his zeal was rewarded, and he would become vice president and general manager of Good News after ten years of duty as henchman *par excellence*. Lambrecht's debut would be as accuser of Bishop Joseph Sprague of northern Illinois, who had been arrested not once but twice at General Conference 2000. Before Lambrecht became involved, Bishop Sprague had been the subject of a complaint by a layperson within his own Illinois Annual Conference. Among other charges, Bishop Sprague was accused of encouraging study of Marcus Borg's works![1]

That case was summarily dismissed, but two years later, Lambrecht brought his own ecclesiastical charges against Bishop Sprague. Following publication of Bishop Sprague's book *Affirmations of a Dissenter* and his lecture at Iliff Theological Seminary, a group led by Lambrecht charged Bishop Sprague with heresy for questioning the divinity of Jesus. In dismissing the charges, the North Central Jurisdiction College of Bishops severely criticized Lambrecht's group for breaking confidentiality, calling it "regrettable and unconscionable," and ordered the complainants to apologize to Bishop Sprague while also calling for further dialogue and discussion of the issues raised by Bishop Sprague.[2]

It was in the context of Bishop Sprague's case that *Good News* magazine editor James V. Heidinger II referred to the necessity for pastors and bishops to be "gatekeepers," and we have applied the metaphor liberally to all those who would guard the pulpit against gay and lesbian entry.

Although Lambrecht's witch hunt failed, Bishop Sprague continued to be a person of interest for the Institute for Religion and Democracy (IRD), the neoconservative puppet master behind the gatekeeping organizations. Mark Tooley had come on board the IRD staff back in 1994 after eight years as a CIA analyst. Along with theologian Thomas Oden, Tooley was the principal Methodist connection for the IRD. Years later, Tooley would become IRD president (2009). In 2004, Tooley's title was director of UMAction, the IRD focal point for Methodists. His young assistant, a spymaster wannabe, was John Lomperis.

When Bishop Sprague's second term as bishop of the Northern Illinois Annual Conference ended in 2004, more than four hundred persons attended his retirement party—including John Lomperis, who attempted to be incognito.

> In the midst of nearly 400 people at a retirement banquet celebrating the ministry of Bishop C. Joseph Sprague, a young man dressed in a white shirt and black suit began to attract attention. He photographed and tape recorded every speaker. He noted who was in attendance. He took in the whole event in silence—until Bishop Sprague blew his cover and recognized him as John Lomperis, a member of the staff of the Institute on Religion and Democracy (IRD).
>
> Lomperis works for Mark Tooley. . . . Tooley and his staff have criticized, defamed, and hounded Bishop Sprague in their UMAction newsletter and on the IRD website. So it shocked many of us attending Bishop Sprague's retirement dinner when this blatant enemy of everything Bishop Sprague has stood for throughout his ministry "crashed" this final farewell for the bishop's friends and family.[3]

The IRD failed to silence Bishop Sprague. Since his retirement, he has been a sought-after preacher, speaker, and teacher, and he has received numerous honors and awards, including honorary doctoral degrees from Kendall College, Ohio Wesleyan University, and the Chicago Theological Seminary. He was the recipient of the AFSC Courage of Conviction Award, the Rainbow Push Civil Rights/Peace Award, and the William Sloane Coffin Award for Justice and Peace.[4]

—·—

A decade and a half earlier, a New Hampshire jury had effectively rendered a nullifying verdict in the ecclesiastical trial of Rose Mary Denham. Jury nullification occurs when jurors refuse to convict for violation of an unjust law. It is juror civil disobedience. In seventeenth-century England, jurors acquitted dissenting Quakers who were in obvious breach of religious conformity laws. In the antebellum North, jury nullification often occurred when defendants were charged with harboring runaway slaves in violation of the Fugitive Slave Act. Jury nullification reflects community values in conflict with existing law.

In 2004, another Methodist trial would result in jury nullification.

In February 2001, Rev. Karen Dammann sent a letter to her bishop advising him that she was "living in a partnered, covenanted, homosexual relationship," and a month later she wrote to her clergy colleagues in the Pacific Northwest Annual Conference, stating "I have formally 'come out' to the Bishop, the Cabinet, and the Conference Relations Committee of the Board of Ordained Ministry. . . . I have found that I can no longer live the life of a closeted lesbian clergyperson."[5]

Thus began a meandering trial process through the thicket of Methodist jurisprudence. Although a jury of her clergy peers would eventually acquit her in an act of jury nullification, the heavy hand of top-down authority would ultimately prove to be suffocating. We'll cut through and summarize.

After three years of up-and-down yo-yo hearings and appeals over the preliminary question whether there should even be a trial, on March 17, 2004, Rev. Dammann finally had her day in court before a jury of her clergy peers. The trial would play out in the pages of the secular press and in daily, sometimes hourly, news releases from the UMC news service that were posted to the UMC website.

The issue before the court was whether Pastor Dammann was guilty of "practices declared by the United Methodist Church to be incompatible with Christian teachings." A few days before the trial, she had married Meredith Savage, her partner of nine years.[6]

As the jury pool of fifty-five clergy arrived at Bothell United Methodist Church near Seattle, they were greeted by protesters from Soulforce. About thirty or forty protesters were arrested that morning. After jury selection, thirteen jurors were seated, and the public squeezed into the makeshift courtroom, normally the church fellowship hall.[7]

An early witness required assistance to take the stand; blind and retired, Dr. Robert Walker had served in parish ministry and also had chaired the Board of Ordained Ministries when Karen Dammann went through the process years earlier. The crowd murmured when Dr. Walker testified that his own ministry was "incompatible with Christian teachings" because he was blind. He referred to Leviticus 21 that decreed that a blind man should not be a priest (not allowed to approach God). The onlookers snickered when he added that the Levitical law-code also prohibited clergy "broken-footedness" because defense counsel Rev. Robert Ward happened to be hobbled with a splint on his foot.[8]

So it went for three days. The prosecution essentially relied on Pastor Dammann's own acknowledgement of her sexuality and relationship status. On the third day, the jurors began deliberations; after an evening adjournment the deliberations continued the next day (Saturday). For hours the press and the public waited. Dammann, Savage, and their five-year-old son prayed in the sanctuary, and supporters milled about in quiet conversation.[9] Finally, at 3:45 PM on Saturday afternoon, the jury verdict was announced. Nine of the thirteen jurors were required to convict, but the prosecution didn't even get a single vote for conviction; instead, there were eleven votes for *acquittal* with two abstentions.[10]

Two hours later, a jury spokesperson, Rev. Karla Frederickson, read a statement. Portions are reprinted here:

> While sustaining the specification that Rev. Karen Dammann is a self-avowed practicing homosexual, we, the trial court, do not

find the evidence presented by church counsel to be clear and convincing that Karen Dammann has engaged in any "practices declared by the United Methodist Church to be incompatible with Christian teachings." We cannot sustain the charge.

We, the trial court, reached our decisions after many hours of painful and prayerful deliberation, and listening for and to the word of God. We depended on the prayers of the whole church, which undergirded our process. We depended on the leading of the Holy Spirit.

We did see in the Discipline many declarative statements. An example is: "Inclusiveness means openness, acceptance, and support that enables all persons to participate in the life of the Church, the community, and the world. Thus, inclusiveness denies every semblance of discrimination."[11]

The outcry was immediate. Many bishops harrumphed.[12]

"A clear sign of rebellion," said the statement of Georgia Bishops Lindsey Davis and Mike Watson.

"Incomprehensible that a clergy jury can place itself above the law," said North Carolina Bishop Marion Edwards.

"A serious challenge to the order of the church," said Central Pennsylvania Bishop Neil Irons.

But a brave few dared to speak to the fears that others had fanned. Here is the affirming statement from California-Pacific Bishop Mary Ann Swenson: "[W]e fear the loss of certainty, of clear gender roles; we fear different definitions of what it means to be faithful, to be called, to be married. In all of these, we reveal our fear of the future. In fear, we cling to our past—not the best of our heritage, but rather those things which justify our fear, not our growth."[13]

Emotions hadn't yet cooled when the 2004 General Conference convened in Pittsburgh a mere month after the Dammann jury nullification verdict. For the gatekeepers, the General Conference provided the means to circumvent the rule that jury acquittals were not appealable. They would ask the Judicial Council for a declaratory judgment to interpret the decision of the trial court.[14]

In a sleight of hand that would make an impartial jurist cringe, the "Supreme Court" accepted jurisdiction and rendered lip service to the principle that the "Judicial Council has no authority to review the findings of that trial court" before proceeding to gut the decision of any import. The Judicial Council stifled the jury verdict and suffocated Dammann under the weight of doublespeak: "[This decision does] not address the case of the Reverend Karen T. Dammann. This decision shall be applied only prospectively . . . [but] a bishop may not appoint one who has been found by a trial court to be a self-avowed, practicing homosexual."

Since clergy appointments are made annually, Pastor Dammann was effectively barred from future ministry. It was also a clear warning to the bishops of the church—a shot across the bow of the episcopate— to enforce the rules of good order and kowtow to the company line. As a dissenting opinion claimed, it was also a consolidation of authority in the national church at the expense of individual annual conferences. The traditional prerogative of annual conferences to ordain, appoint, and oversee clergy had been effectively usurped by the General Conference.

A dissenting opinion indicted the kangaroo-court nature of the Judicial Council decision:

> This is simply another attempt to find a way to overturn the trial court decision in the case of The Rev. Karen T. Dammann. Par. 2715.10 of the 2000 Discipline is very clear in its statement that the decision of the trial court is final and that the church has no appeal from that decision. Further, this attempt is in direct contravention of Par. 31 of the Constitution which gives only the annual conference the right to vote on matters of conference relations of clergy members. The General Conference may not erode those rights by continually adding requirements which take that right away from the annual conferences. The prevailing opinion erodes those rights of the annual conference even further than the General Conference has already done.

The Judicial Council decision that came at the request of and in the midst of General Conference was only one of several ominous developments.

At General Conference 2000, an African bishop had castigated gays and lesbians *during a worship sermon*. Once again in 2004, the most strident antigay voices during the conference were the Africans, and their rock-solid voting bloc against all things gay was growing. At this 2004 General Conference, delegates from the Central Conferences (international) comprised 19 percent of all voting delegates. By 2008, the percentage would jump to 28 percent, and by 2102, fully 38 percent of all voting delegates would be from nations other than the United States.[15] Thus, the reception of the one million member Protestant Methodist Church of Cote d'Ivoire (Ivory Coast) into full membership as United Methodists served as a visible sign of the growing influence of the Africans within the UMC, and, indirectly, to future impediments to General Conference full-inclusion legislation.

Following the Dammann Judicial Council decision, the General Conference was emboldened to affirm existing policies against LGBT clergy; indeed, the restrictions were tightened by amending a portion of the *Book of Discipline* to give bishops, pastors, and diaconal ministers a clear list of chargeable offenses that could result in a church trial, including being "a self-avowed practicing homosexual" or conducting ceremonies that "celebrate homosexual unions or performing same-sex wedding ceremonies" (paragraph 2702). The Conference also voted overwhelmingly to support civil laws that defined marriage as the union of one man and one woman.

But in the midst of the conservative rout, the gatekeepers mishandled an explosive issue, and it nearly blew up in their face. Rev. Bill Hinson was the president of the Confessing Movement and Rev. James Heidinger II the president of Good News. Much as the video circulated prior to General Conference 2000 had done, these two conservative leaders floated a proposal to split the denomination.

> Two key conservative church leaders openly talked May 6 about an "amicable" divorce over "irreconcilable differences."
>
> "'United Methodist' is an oxymoron," said the Rev. Bill Hinson, president of the Confessing Movement and former senior pastor at First United Methodist Church in Houston. "We haven't been united for a long time. Others ridicule us as the 'untied' Methodist Church."
>
> "We have no expectation that we can ever reach an agreement," said the Rev. James V. Heidinger II, president of the Good

News organization, "and the dialogue and debate have gone on for 30 years. This is a deep theological divide."

Heidinger said the possible resolution "may or may not" be offered at this General Conference. Copies of the document were distributed to the media.

The proposed resolution calls for the creation of a special task force to prepare a process by which the denomination would amicably separate. The body would comprise "seven members from the 'progressive/liberal' constituency . . . seven members from the 'moderate/centrist' constituency . . . and seven members from the 'evangelical/orthodox' constituency."

The proposal calls for the "Task Force on Amicable Separation" to report to a special session of General Conference in 2006. The legislative meeting of the church is normally held every four years.[16]

When rumors of the proposal swirled through the hallways, the back draft nearly blew the conservative leaders over as they struggled to put the pin back in the grenade. Conservative and liberal delegates alike roundly criticized the proposal, and an impromptu unity resolution was brought to the plenary floor. First, the entire plenary session delegates held hands, hugged, and swayed as they sang "Blest Be the Tie That Binds," then they overwhelmingly adopted this resolution: "As United Methodists, we remain in covenant with one another, even in the midst of disagreement, and affirm our commitment to work together for the common mission of making disciples throughout the world."[17]

Although the Dammann jury decision had reverberated through the church, the Judicial Council and General Conference had effectively negated any precedential value. As summer turned into fall, all eyes turned toward another ecclesiastical trial winding through the maze of Methodist jurisprudence.

Pastor Beth Stroud was a cradle Methodist, and church had always been a huge part of her life, but when she realized she was a lesbian during her college years, she assumed she would have to choose between being true to herself and being a Christian. She left the church for a time, but she was relentlessly pursued by a stubborn Christ who kept calling her back when she strayed, encouraging her on, and shining a light on the path toward ordained ministry.[18] But she needed to be honest, and in a sermon she titled "Walking in the Light," she came out publicly to her congregation on April 27, 2003, though many already knew privately:

> I want to take that experience of the risen Christ out of the locked room, out of the closet, and into the world where everyone can see it. I want to walk in the light so that Christ might be revealed in my life.
>
> I know that, by telling the truth about myself, I risk losing my credentials as an ordained United Methodist minister. And that would be a huge loss for me. But I have realized that not telling the whole truth about myself has been holding me back in my faith. I have come to a place where my discipleship, my walk with Christ, requires telling the whole truth, and paying whatever price truthfulness requires. I don't feel afraid. I feel that God is with me.

She then introduced Chris Paige, her partner, and the Germantown, Pennsylvania, congregation responded with a standing ovation.[19]

As Pastor Stroud expected, she was subjected to ecclesiastical disciplinary proceedings. Let us skip the labyrinthine Methodist preliminaries and jump right to the December 2004 trial, seven months after the tightened denominational stance decreed by the Judicial Council and legislated by General Conference in Pittsburgh. The Stroud trial would also be in Pennsylvania but at the opposite end of the state near Philadelphia.

On Sunday evening, November 28, 2004, Pastor Stroud celebrated the eucharist with her congregation on the eve of her trial. The mood was solemn. Many were aware that this would probably be the last time she would have authority as minister of word and sacrament. As she began the communion liturgy, she stumbled on the words, then regrouped, "This could potentially be the last time, and I do it wrong!" The congregation laughed, and she continued, "Rejoice . . ."[20]

The trial began three days later on December 1, 2004. Witness the trial through the eyes of Carolyn Paige, Pastor Beth's mother-in-law, from an article published in *Christian Feminism Today*:

I had been in Philadelphia when Beth preached her coming-out sermon in April 2003. No one could have adequately described that experience to me or really shared the emotional impact of being in the presence of such a supportive congregation as Beth's. I knew this trial would have an emotional impact that would be impossible to fully feel from a distance or experience from second-hand descriptions. I had to be there.

Beth's parents, Bill and Jamie, were there, too. We had met them while Chris and Beth were dating, and they have become dear friends, sharing our love and support for our daughters.

Wednesday morning, December 1, we four parents drove together to Camp Innabah, a United Methodist summer camp near Pottstown, PA, where the trial would be held. The camp provided breakfast, lunch, and dinner for the jury pool, the trial participants, and Chris and Beth's families. That location was ideal. Beth had attended camp there, worked there, and was on the board of directors. It was a familiar and comfortable place for her.

Camp staff shuttled jurors and family members up the hill to the camp gymnasium, which served as the courtroom. When it wasn't raining, we walked. Chris and Beth walked, too. Cameras clicked whenever they came up the hill because the press was out in force. Along with Alan and Susan Raymond, who were producing the PBS documentary "The Congregation," there were reporters from CNN, the Associated Press, United Methodist Church news, local newspapers and TV stations. Whenever we came out of the gym, there were likely to be six TV vans, that many video cameras, and a dozen microphones. The press seemed confounded by Beth's attitude; they could not understand her not being angry and belligerent.

The number of uniformed police officers showed that we were not the only ones concerned about demonstrations. Still, I was relieved to learn that only groups that were supportive were gathering. Beth's own congregation, FUMCOG (the acronym that members fondly used in speaking about the First United Methodist Church of Germantown) and Chris' congregation,

Tabernacle United, were out in force. I was happy to see PFLAG and Soulforce signs.

Chris' pastor, Patricia, officiated at one of the most meaningful communion services I've ever attended. A woman I met there, whose own Baptist congregation had been disenfranchised because they affirmed homosexuals, had driven to Philadelphia from Ohio. We sobbed together with grief that our denominations have not found a wholesome sexual ethic that includes both heterosexuals and homosexuals. It overwhelms me to know how deep is the support, to know how many will travel hundreds of miles to offer their love and to share the pain.

Testimony started Wednesday afternoon. Bishop Weaver, who brought the charges, testified that all procedures had been followed, counseling had been given, and opportunity to move to another denomination had been offered. He also testified that Beth is a good minister and that she is called of God. Beth joked later, "With 'enemies' like that, who needs friends?" Actually, Beth wants it known that the Bishop is not her enemy; nor is the United Methodist Church her enemy. Our disagreements over the role of gays and lesbians in our faith communities are disagreements within a family.

Throughout the trial, Beth remained pastoral with her congregation who were there showing support. She was pastoral with the jury after the penalty phase when she went up to each one and shook hands or gave a hug. She was pastoral with the whole denomination when she acknowledged that either verdict would be painful. Because of her loving attitude, even though this was a trial, it was respectful and even reverent.

For me, various emotions kept recurring during the trial. The first was tremendous parental pride. I was so impressed with how articulate both Chris and Beth were. They behaved with such grace and dignity, calmly and patiently answering reporters' questions. They lovingly supported those sharing their pain and were mutually supportive of one another.

Another emotion I repeatedly felt was sadness. Many in our church families shared the pain of this trial. I was honored to wear a rainbow stole that had been worn by an observer at Rev. Karen T. Dammann's trial earlier in the year. Many of the camp staff and other church staff, while upholding the required neutrality, were privately supportive. I was drawn to a woman who worked in the church. She could not show her support publicly. She could not express the pain she felt publicly either. I could. And so I cried for her.

I saw sadness, too, when I watched the jury as they listened to such positive testimony about Beth's ministry and listened to Beth herself. The trial instructions would not allow them to follow their own convictions. The 7–6 penalty decision to strip Beth of her ministerial credentials shows they were not of one mind. One juror called Beth the weekend after the trial to ask how he could help get the *Book of Discipline* changed.

And, of course, I was sad for Beth and Chris. Knowing the likely outcome of an action doesn't make that outcome less painful. The pain of exclusion and the discrimination known by homosexuals is also shared by their family members who watch. I feel deep sadness when the church rejects my daughter and her gifts for ministry.

An unexpected emotion, however, was and is happiness. I am happy to know that Beth and Chris are helping moderates reconsider their position on the role of gays and lesbians in our faith communities. The night of the verdict, both families and the legal defense team all went out for a late dinner. It really was a celebration and more than just celebrating because the trial was over. The evening was very spirited and joyful. One of the nonfamily guests said," If this is how you are when losing, what must winning be like?"

We need more congregations like Beth's, which became a United Methodist Reconciling Congregation in 1989 and thus its members were prepared to support Beth. We need to nurture and grow congregations like that. God's call to ministry is not only to heterosexuals. Others besides Beth have answered, and the church needs the talents and gifts that the Spirit of God has bestowed on them. Our churches need to know that our faith family already includes homosexuals, often worshiping and ministering in silent distress.

I regret the outcome of the trial but do not regret the witness. I know that the trial and the events surrounding it have made at least some people think about gays and lesbians in a new way and to recognize their importance as members of God's family, called to serve Christ. Perhaps some people will also come to view relationships like that of Chris and Beth in a new light as well. For these reasons, I refuse to give into despair and instead have hope that attitudes in our churches, regardless of denominational affiliation, will change. In many ways, it is the church that is on trial.[21]

As noted, the jury convicted Pastor Stroud and stripped her of her clergy credentials. Subsequent appeals did not change the result. The rigidity of the UMC's actions the previous summer had proved to be unyielding. Pastor Stroud's congregation immediately rehired her as a lay minister, and she continued as before but not as celebrant of the sacraments. She remained so employed for nearly four years before she returned to academia to seek a teaching career.

Less than a week after the conclusion of the Stroud trial, a shocking act of exclusion in a congregation in Virginia put the lie to the "all are welcome" mantra that appears on the signboards of thousands of congregations across the land. Some congregations mean it; for others, it is merely false advertising.

On December 8, 2004, Rev. Ed Johnson of South Hill United Methodist Church, deep in Virginia tobacco country, advised his district superintendent that he was reluctant to allow a noncelibate gay man to become a congregational member. The gay man had met with the pastor on at least five occasions and expressed a desire to transfer his membership to South Hill from another denomination. A month later, Bishop Charlene P. Kammerer ordered Pastor Johnson to accept the gay man into membership, but Johnson refused and was suspended.

A year later, the matter arrived at the doorstep of the Judicial Council. Just as shocking as the original act of exclusion, the Methodist Supreme Court ordered the reinstatement of Pastor Johnson, holding that the many statements of inclusion within the Methodist *Book of Dis-*

cipline and Social Principles were merely permissive and not mandatory. Local congregations and juries were not allowed to *open* their doors to LGBT clergy, but they could *shut* them to any LGBT person: "The pastor in charge of a United Methodist church or charge is solely responsible for making the determination of a person's readiness to receive the vows of membership. . . . The pastor-in-charge is entrusted with discretion in the exercise of this responsibility.[22] Pastor Johnson's counsel later commented to a *New York Times* reporter that LGBT membership applicants must "struggle against [homosexuality] and repent of it."[23]

It's OK to be left-handed, just don't write with your left hand. The recurring distinction between orientation and expression of orientation was trotted out again. Perhaps the comment of gatekeeper James V. Heidinger II was the most ominous, "Most evangelical pastors would have made the same decision as Ed Johnson made."[24]

As Methodist exclusion dominated the TV news cycle, the UCC advertisement depicting a springboard to eject the wrong people from the pews, part of their "God is still speaking" campaign, created a stark contrast. At least the hue and cry across the Methodist landscape was critical of the exclusionary act and its judicial imprimatur. Perhaps the self-righteous and unapologetic discriminatory attitude of the pastor rubbed a raw nerve. His action and its approval by the Judicial Council proved embarrassing for the church, and the Council of Bishops implicitly challenged the ruling in a pastoral letter issued within days.

> The ripple effect of the court's decision was felt immediately in Lake Junaluska, where the Council of Bishops is holding its week-long fall meeting. The council spent at least four hours in closed session working on a statement responding to the ruling.
>
> "With the Social Principles of the United Methodist Church, we affirm that God's grace is available to all, and we will seek to live together in Christian community," the bishops said, quoting from the Social Principles in the Book of Discipline. "We implore families and churches not to reject or condemn lesbian and gay members and friends. We commit ourselves to be in ministry for and with all persons."[25]

The chilling effect of the events of 2004–05 drove Methodist gays and lesbians deep into the closet. Six-and-a-half years would pass from the end of the Stroud trial until the trial of Rev. Amy DeLong, who would challenge the church's dual ban on LGBT clergy and "holy union" ceremonies. On our way to her trial in rural Wisconsin, we will pass through Fort Worth, the site of General Conference 2008.

NOTES

1. United Methodist News Service, "Layman Files Letters of Complaint against Bishop Sprague," July 10, 2000.

2. United Methodist News Service, "Complaints Dismissed against Bishop Joseph Sprague, "February 18, 2003.

3. Linda S. Rhodes, "'Crashing' the Farewell Party," Swecker, *Hardball on Holy Ground*, 76–79.

4. The biography of Bishop C. Joseph Sprague, "Council of Bishops Gallery," on the website of the United Methodist Church, accessed August 28, 2012, http://www.umc.org/site/apps/nlnet/content2.aspx?c=lwL4KnN1Lt H&b=6387671&ct=7274629.

5. "Regarding Rev. Karen T. Dammann in the Pacific Northwest," on the website of Beth Stroud .info, accessed October 25, 2012, http://trial.beth-stroud.info/damman.shtml.

5. United Methodist News Service, "Dammann Trial Update," 11:30 a.m. PT, Wednesday, March 17, 2004.

7. United Methodist News Service, "Dammann Trial Update," 9:30 a.m. PT, Wednesday, March 17, 2004.

8. United Methodist News Service, "Dammann Trial Update," 3:39 p.m. PT, Thursday, March 18, 2004.

9. United Methodist News Service, "Dammann Trial Update," 10:30 a.m. PT, Saturday, March 20, 2004.

10. United Methodist News Service, "Dammann Trial Update," 3:45 p.m. PT, Saturday, March 20, 2004.

11. United Methodist News Service, "Jury Issues Statement on Decision in Dammann Case," March 20, 2004.

12. Linda Green, United Methodist News Service, "Individual Bishops Voice Disappointment at Verdict," March 26, 2004.

13. Ibid.

14. Based upon United Methodist Church, Judicial Council Decisions, Decision No. 985, May 4, 2004.

15. "Visitor's Guide," United Methodist Church General Conference 2012, 15.

16. Neill Caldwell, United Methodist News Service, "Conservatives Consider 'Separation' of United Methodist Church," May 6, 2004.

17. Linda Bloom, United Methodist News Service, "Wrap-up: 2004 General Conference," May 7, 2004.

18. Irene Elizabeth Stroud, "Walking in the Light," sermon to First United Methodist Church of Germantown (Philadelphia), April 27, 2003.

19. Ibid.

20. Peggy R. Gaylord, "Continued Prayers for Beth Stroud Urged," Affirmation News Release, November 28, 2004.

21. Reprinted with permission of the author, Carolyn Paige, on the website of *Christian Feminism Today*, http://www.eewc.com/BookReviews/churchtrial/.

22. United Methodist Church, Judicial Council Decisions, Decision No. 1032, October 29, 2005.

23. Neela Banerjee, "Methodist Bishops Protest Ruling in Exclusion of a Gay Congregant," *New York Times*, November 5, 2005.

24. Neela Banerjee, "Methodist Court Removes Openly Lesbian Pastor," *New York Times*, November 1, 2005.

25. Tim Tanton, United Methodist News Service, "United Methodist bishops affirm church membership open to all," November 3, 2005.

* 53 *

How Long, O Lord?

Moses and the Israelites wandered in the wilderness for forty years. It was 1972 when the Methodists turned their face away from Pastor Gene Leggett and said, "We do not condone the practice of homosexuality and consider this practice to be incompatible with Christian teaching." This denial of the sacred worth of hundreds of thousands of LGBT Methodists would be repeated and strengthened in four-year cycles with each successive General Conference. General Conference 2008 would mark the thirty-sixth anniversary of church-sanctioned discrimination and General Conference 2012 would mark the fortieth.

> But at my stumbling they gathered in glee, they gathered together against me; ruffians whom I did not know tore at me without ceasing; they impiously mocked more and more, gnashing at me with their teeth.
>
> How long, O Lord, will you look on? Rescue me from their ravages, my life from the lions! (Psalm 35:15–17)

The first eyebrow-raising news out of Fort Worth and the 2008 General Conference had been the stark jump in international delegates, especially African. At General Conference 2004, the delegates from the Central Conferences (international) comprised 19 percent of the total. At General Conference 2008, that percentage had spiked to 28 percent. It would spike again to 38 percent four years later at General Conference 2012.[1]

The next news item was troubling; most of the international delegates had received the gift of a cell phone from a coalition of gatekeeping organizations. A United Methodist News Service article included expressions of concern from church leaders:[2]

> The provision of cell phones "crosses the boundaries of what is appropriate in this kind of community, and I hope that it would cease," said Bishop Kenneth Carder, a professor at Duke Divinity School, Durham, N.C. Everyone, he said, needs to trust the integrity and the autonomy of a democratic process. "This seems to be an undue influence and violates the very essence of what it means to be Christian community."
>
> A joint monitoring team from the Commission on the Status and Role of Women and the Commission on Religion and Race said the giveaway "is inappropriate behavior and it destroys community. We have gathered for Christian conferencing, which requires trust, honesty, openness and respect. Whenever there is an imbalance of power relationships with the expectation of reciprocity, this behavior gives the appearance of paternalism, manipulation, exploitation and of course, racism."
>
> Jim Winkler, top executive at the United Methodist Board of Church and Society, said some renewal groups [gatekeepers] have journeyed across Africa "providing deliberately distorted and inaccurate information to African United Methodists." He views the distribution of cell phones "in the context of a pattern of manipulation of the African delegates, and that is what really, really troubles me."

Winkler's suggestion that the gatekeepers had travelled overseas and cultivated influence with the Africans smacks of the Institute on Religion and Democracy (IRD). The IRD had learned well from its experience in wining and dining the African Anglicans at Lambeth 1998, stirring up anti-American, anti-Episcopalian, and antigay sentiment that threatened the entire Anglican Communion. At Lambeth 2008, the Anglican gatekeepers had also gifted cell phones to the developing nations delegations. The gatekeepers had hit upon a successful strategy of divide and conquer that they now employed in the Methodist church.

Of course, the gatekeepers feigned indignation at the suggestion of impropriety. Tom Lambrecht, the accuser of Bishop Joseph Sprague earlier and soon to be the prosecutor in the Amy DeLong trial, served as the chairman of the gatekeeping coalition, and he said the coalition was "deeply disturbed by the charges that are leveled by the various church leaders. . . . We find the charges to be totally outrageous, and we lament the fact that no one who is making these charges contacted us to share their concerns or to ask for an explanation. We find this to be a violation of the covenant of holy conferencing.[3]

As they had done at General Conferences 2000 and 2004, the gatekeepers pressed for an end to debate on LGBT issues. It is settled, they claimed. Let's get on with the work of the church, they argued. Further debate is pointless and threatens unity, they urged. On the eve of the 2008 Conference, Rev. Dr. Jeanne Knepper wrote an article rebutting their arguments, and she offered a historical analogy.

In 1836, the Methodist Episcopal Church contained within it profound disagreement concerning the role of the church in the national controversy over slavery. That year, the bishops of the Church took up the topic of abolitionism in their Pastoral Address. They advised,

[W]e have been very much agitated in some portions of our work, with the very excitable subject of what has been called abolitionism. . . . From every view of the subject which we have been able to take, and from the most calm and dispassionate survey of the whole ground, we have come to the solemn conviction, that the only safe, Scriptural and prudent way for us both as ministers and as people, to take, is wholly to refrain from this agitating subject, . . . as alike destructive to the peace of the Church, and to the happiness of the slave himself.

The [1836] bishops then proceeded to enforce their solemn conviction at the annual conferences, refusing to hear conference committee reports on slavery or to hear reports or motions on slavery. The Methodist Episcopal history of the General Conferences written in 1900, summed up the effects of this policy thus:

> *[T]he efforts of the bishops to stop agitation by assuming powers which were never committed to them, only added fuel to the fire, until it set the whole Church ablaze.*[4]

Although the gatekeepers had failed to stifle discussion at General Conference 2008, floor debates and plenary votes fell short of policy change. By a vote of 501 to 417 (55 percent to 45 percent), the majority report of the Church and Society Legislative Committee was rejected in favor of a minority report that retained the incompatibility clause. The rejected majority report would have replaced the incompatibility clause with less judgmental language: "Faithful, thoughtful people who have grappled with this issue deeply disagree with one another; yet all seek a faithful witness" that urged Methodists "to refrain from judgment regarding homosexual persons and practices as the Spirit leads us to a new insight."[5]

Based upon the relatively narrow vote margins, in light of the increased strength of the international bloc, it appeared likely that a majority of U.S. delegates favored removal of the odious incompatibility clause.

Once again, the LGBT-friendly coalition staged floor demonstrations and protests. A lesbian couple, Susan Laurie and Julie Bruno, celebrated their relationship with a marriage ceremony in the public square across from the convention center. Although numerous clergy expressed willingness to preside, the couple preferred that their ceremony be "less about upsetting people and more about being role models," demonstrating that "ceremonies are going on regardless" of Methodist policies.[6]

How long, O Lord?

———

In 1994, the year that Amy DeLong was accepted into seminary, she also fell in love with Val. During her years of pastoral ministry, she was conflicted because her life and her love, which she knew to be good and true, was rejected by her church.

> I naively thought that I could balance and be fully present in both of these relationships. I was wrong. I was in pastoral ministry for 8 years—and in each of those years I felt pulled, almost in two— torn between the Church that I love and the Val that I love.

I tried to keep this core part of my identity hidden, and in so doing, I distanced myself from parishioners and my colleagues—afraid they might ask me questions about my life that I was forbidden from answering. I dreaded sitting down with new congregants because I knew they would ask me if I were married. I am, but I was supposed to say I wasn't—and every time I did that, I felt I was betraying Val.

I dreaded clergy gatherings for the same reasons. I remember one gathering, in particular, when we were supposed to introduce ourselves to the person next to us and ask a couple questions about each others' lives—so already I was terrified and having a minor panic attack.

As I turned to my conversation partner he immediately said to me, "Amy, tell me about the most important thing in your life." I wanted to tell him about Val, but I couldn't. I wanted to tell him about her children whom we were raising together, but I couldn't. So I talked about my cat. Now aside from looking profoundly superficial—the most pathetic part was that I didn't have a cat at the time. My life and my loves had been reduced to telling make-believe stories about a cat I didn't have.

So many of us, clergy and laity alike, have been strangled by various versions of "don't ask, don't tell." Such silence dis-integrates us, divides us—flesh from spirit, the truth we know from the truth we tell, our being from our doing—and it leaves us spiritual schizophrenics.

The church was requiring me to mask my truth and to act on the outside in a way that contradicted the truth I held most deeply on the inside. I realized . . . that the duplicitous policies and practices of the church, coupled with the amount of lying I had to do in order to preserve my job, were damaging my soul and psyche in a way I was afraid I would never be able to repair. My fear of telling the truth was supplanted by my fear of losing myself.[7]

She came out. Initially, there were no repercussions; many colleagues in the Wisconsin Annual Conference, even within the bishop's office, would greet her with "how's Val?" That all changed in 2009 when she and Val registered under Wisconsin's Domestic Partnership law and Amy filed her annual extension ministry report of activities that included her acknowledgement that she had presided at the "holy union" ceremony of a lesbian couple.

The report didn't go unnoticed, and Pastor Amy was called into the assistant to the bishop's office accompanied by her lawyer, who said at the outset, "We're not here for repentance or reformation." When asked to explain her report, Pastor Amy said, "I need to be honest about their love and their relationship. To fail to acknowledge the full truth would diminish them and me."[8]

Reluctantly, Bishop Linda Lee pressed disciplinary charges, and the Committee on Investigation certified the matter for trial, stating, "Rev. Amy Delong has shown extraordinary courage to step forward and freely acknowledge her sexual orientation, and her commitment to be in ministry to all persons, regardless of their sexual orientation."[9] Several trial prosecutors were appointed and subsequently resigned, and the trial process barely moved forward until the seasoned inquisitor of the gatekeepers, Thomas Lambrecht, by then a leader of Good News, became trial prosecutor.

In February 2011, as her trial was pending, she received an implicit statement of support from thirty-three of eighty-five retired UMC bishops. The statement was circulated by two retired bishops, Sharon Z. Rader and Donald A. Ott, with prior connections to the Wisconsin Annual Conference. The statement was entitled "Statement of Counsel to the Church." The statement urged the repeal of the "incompatibility clause" and offered the following bullet points as rationale:

- Laity and clergy, gay and straight, withdrawing membership or absenting themselves from the support of congregational and denominational Church life in order to maintain personal integrity.

- Young adults, especially, embarrassed to invite friends and expressing dismay at the unwillingness of our United Methodist Church to alter its 39-year exclusionary stance.

- Closeted pastors, currently called and ordained in our church, living divided lives while offering effective appreciated ministry.

- Bishops being drained of energy by upholding Church Discipline while regarding it as contrary to their convictions.

- Bishops caught between care for the Church by reappointing an effective gay or lesbian pastor and care for the Discipline by charging them under current legislation.

- Seminary leaders desiring greater flexibility and openness from the church in order to advance their mission of identifying, recruiting, enrolling, educating and spiritually forming Christian leaders.

- Christian gay men and women understanding themselves called of God to seek ministry opportunities within their United Methodist family Church home, but having to decide between:
  * leaving to go to accepting denominations, or
  * staying and praying for change, or
  * challenging Church law and accepting punitive actions.[10]

Finally, in June 2011, the trial convened in a small church in Kaukauna, halfway between Green Bay and Oshkosh in East-central Wisconsin. Despite the isolation, the national press followed the trial closely.

There were two charges against her: that she was a "self-avowed, practicing homosexual" and that she had performed a holy union ceremony.

Church Counsel Lambrecht was unable to prove the first charge. When he asked Pastor DeLong to describe her relationship with Val, she testified, "I am a lesbian. Val is the love of my life; I can't imagine my life without her," DeLong said. "I have committed myself to her, and she has committed to me. We make a lot of our heterosexual friends jealous because they would like a marriage as fine as ours."

General Conference had never defined "practicing," but the Judicial Council did so in a 2001 decision. In that case, the Judicial Council had mandated that a question must be asked during an investigation—whether the accused is engaged in genital sexual acts with a person of the same gender.[11] Because this question had not been asked by anyone leading up to the Amy DeLong trial, Church Counsel Lambrecht pressed further. He repeatedly asked about genital contact, but Amy refused to answer, and he was stymied.

"My answer is still I will never, to anybody who is trying to do me harm, talk about the intimate, private behavior of my partner and me."[12]

Pastor DeLong readily admitted the second charge; indeed, the lesbian couple, Carrie Johnson and Carolyn Larson, testified on her behalf. Johnson testified that she approached DeLong about performing the ceremony because she believed in God and wanted to have a sign of that presence at the service.

"The second reason was why not?" Johnson said. "Why can't we be treated as human beings like everybody else? It was about fairness."[13]

Pastor DeLong was convicted of the same charge that had resulted in Pastor Jimmy Creech's defrocking and Pastor Greg Dell's suspension a little more than a decade earlier. But then something radical happened during the penalty deliberations of the jury. She was not defrocked, like Rev. Jimmy Creech, and she was not indefinitely suspended, like Rev. Gregory Dell. Pastor DeLong was merely to spend a purposeful twenty-day suspension discerning whether or not she would develop recommendations for the church on how better to deal with clergy conflict.

After the trial, *Time* magazine published a feature story, quoting Rev. DeLong: "My hope is that this is the very last time that somebody is put on trial for acts of conscience. Most people hope to be first; I hope this to be last."[14]

The paper was a year in process and resulted from collaborative meetings (four of them) between Pastor DeLong, Bishop Lee, District Superintendent and complainant Rev. Jorge Luis Mayorga, Board of Ordained Ministry chair Rev. Richard Strait, and Pastor Wesley White, who served at Pastor DeLong's request. It was presented to the Wisconsin Annual Conference in June 2012.

Her eleven-page document is a tour de force for the cause of LGBT inclusion that indicts the church, its leaders, and its membership for a lack of courage. Her argumentation is summarized in the words of Dr. King, "In the end, we will remember not the words of our enemies, but the silence of our friends," and the concept of "weeping executioners" that "describe those who express concern for the oppressed, but will not leave their place in the hierarchy of oppression."[15]

Pastor DeLong's paper concluded with an invitation to her colleagues, the ordained clergy of the Wisconsin Annual Conference, to enter into holy conferencing to revisit, reform, and rededicate themselves to a clergy covenant, "not for everyone, always—but for *us, now*. If there truly is a yearning for a restored and new relationship among clergy—beyond charging one another and having winners and losers, beyond perceived purity and false unity—then a new and intentional process and supporting structure are needed."

The invitation to dialogue was accepted by the clergy session of the annual conference, and transparent procedures implemented.

———

As General Conference 2012 approached, Methodist gays, lesbians, and their allies believed momentum was on their side. Since the last General Conference, the Episcopalians, Lutherans, and Presbyterians had all adopted momentous policy reversals, and the gates of exclusion had not only opened but had been smashed down and trampled underfoot. Secular jurisdictions were rapidly joining the march toward marriage equality. President Obama and the U.S. military had ended "don't ask, don't tell" for armed forces personnel. Nearly 40 percent of retired bishops had signed on to the statement urging a change in church policy. The results of the ecclesiastical trial of Rev. Amy Delong in 2011 suggested a softening in attitudes. More than a thousand clergy had promised to perform covenant ceremonies by signing onto a document originating in the Minnesota Annual Conference in 2011. In January of 2012, Pastor Bonnie Beckonchrist, the Reconciling Ministries Board Chairperson, suggested that it might take 60 percent of U.S. delegates to offset the solid bloc of nays expected from the international delegates, but she believed that 60 percent was attainable.[16]

The Conference opened with a pair of seemingly positive developments.

Amory Peck, the Pacific Northwest Conference lay leader, was one of three who delivered the traditional laity address, and she was an out lesbian, though few knew that during the address:

> Only a handful of people knew that, and I feel like I let a lot of people down in not saying it [during the address]. I was sad that I could not say that openly. But the Laity Address is about bring-

ing people together. Of course gays and lesbians are active in the church, but there is fearfulness in being open about it. I wish we could lift the silence because the silence is crushing.[17]

Second, sessions for face-to-face discussions between gays, lesbians, and delegates, a "holy conferencing," were written into the schedule during an early day of the Conference.

Unfortunately, these well-intentioned plans backfired. The discussion sessions were short to begin with and became shorter when other scheduled events spilled over. What was worse, in a few of the sessions, conversations turned into gay-bashing. "There were a number of people who felt abused in what we believed was intended to be a truly holy conversation space," said one participant. "But, for whatever reason, in many, many of the rooms, that was not borne out, and delegates and observers were bullied and . . . (some were) met with derision and scorn."[18]

The next day, an attempt at healing turned into further rejection. Mark Miller, a delegate, a Conference music leader, and a gay man, approached a microphone during the plenary session, accompanied by other gays and lesbians. He attempted to raise a moment of personal privilege to express the hurt of the holy conferencing. The presiding bishop recognized him, but after he began to speak, he was cut off, ruling that he was "out of order."

Four months earlier when Pastor Beckonchrist had said that she hoped that the vote by U.S. delegates would be sufficient to offset the negativity of the international delegates, she hadn't anticipated that the percentage of international delegates would once again surge. In 2008, it had been 28 percent; in 2012, it would be 38 percent. Even though hearts and minds were rapidly changing across many U.S. annual conferences, the solid bloc of conservative international delegates was growing even faster. The target had moved beyond reach. The plenary vote on the recurring attempt to remove the "incompatibility" clause from the *Book of Discipline* failed by 61 percent to 39 percent, worse than four years earlier (55 percent to 45 percent in 2008). Another telling vote, laughable really, was that the foundational Christian doctrine of "grace," expressed in a resolution stating "God's grace is available to all," barely passed this Conference by a vote of 56 percent to 44 percent.

Methodists and Episcopalians share this: not only is there a liberal/ conservative division on these shores, there is a breach between East and West, a culture clash between emerging American values and those of the developing nations. While this dichotomy has not affected Episcopal policy despite continued threats and rants from overseas, the particular polity of the Methodists in which the Central Conference, consisting of international delegates, has voice and vote in denominational policy, has forestalled full Methodist inclusion. If the annual conferences within the United States were free to consider full inclusion apart from international influence, it is likely that the UMC policies would be consistent with those of TEC, the ELCA, and the PC(USA), if not the UCC.

Another floor protest disrupted the plenary session, a subsequent agreement negotiated by Rev. DeLong and certain bishops allowed a gay man to offer the opening prayer for the afternoon session, and the president of the Council of Bishops, Rosemarie Wenner, began the session with an acknowledgement that harm had been done to gay, lesbian, bisexual, and transgender people. While appreciated, the gestures hardly quelled the pain of yet another rejection.

Earlier in the Conference, an "Act of Repentance toward Healing Relationships with Indigenous People" ended the day. Yet Osage Nation member Dr. George Tinker issued this challenge: "It's way too early to talk about reconciliation. It's like asking an abused spouse to live with the abuser without any change. . . . Apologies don't do anything. . . . Repentance is not something done once. It is a way of life."[19]

How long, O Lord?

NOTES

1. "Visitor's Guide," United Methodist Church General Conference 2012, 15.

2. Linda Green, United Methodist News Service, "Doubts Arise Following Gifts of Cell Phones," April 25, 2008.

3. Ibid.

4. Rev. Dr. Jeanne Knepper, "I Don't Wanna Talk about It," *Affirmation Daily*, General Conference 2008, Issue 1, April 23, 2008.

5. Robin Russell, United Methodist News Service, "United Methodists Uphold Homosexuality Stance," April 30, 2008.

6. Ciona D. Rouse, "Same-Sex Couple Says 'I Do' Outside Church Assembly," United Methodist News Service, May 2, 2008.

7. Amy DeLong, "Shattered, Refreshed, and Free," on the website of Love on Trial, accessed September 8, 2012, http://www.loveontrial.org/pages/2-shattered.html.

8. Pastor Amy DeLong, private conversation with the author September 20, 2012.

9. "Trial: Beginning to End," on the website of Love on Trial, accessed September 10, 2012, http://www.loveontrial.org/pages/2-summary.html.

10. Heather Hahn, United Methodist News Service, "33 Retired Bishops Urge End to Gay Clergy Ban," February 2, 2011.

11. United Methodist Church, Judicial Council Decisions, Decision No. 920, October 26, 2001.

12. "2 p.m. EDT DeLong Testifies," United Methodist News Service, *Field Journal*, June 22, 2011.

13. Ibid.

14. Justin Horwath, "The Trial of Pastor Amy DeLong: Methodism and Same-Sex Unions," *Time*, July 1, 2011.

15. Pastor DeLong cited the CommonDreams.org January 2011 article of Presbyterian pastor Rev. Jim Rigby, which expounds upon the concept of the "weeping executioner" of Dr. Walt Herbert, emeritus professor of English at Southwestern University.

16. Pastor Bonnie Beckonchrist, private conversation with the author, January 10, 2012.

17. Neill Caldwell, United Methodist News Service, "Surprise Announcement," April 25, 2012.

18. Tim Tanton, United Methodist News Service, "GC2012: Holy Conversations Have Unintended Effect," April 27, 2012.

19. "Love Prevails at General Conference 2012," on the website of Love on Trial, accessed September 7, 2012, http://www.loveontrial.org/gc_reports/lp-at-gc2012.pdf.

☀ 54 ☀

It Is Time to Cross Over

We encountered Steve Webster back in Madison, Wisconsin, near the start of our Methodist journey. He was the young graduate, eager for ministry, who had been rejected for seminary because he was out. Instead of ordination, his ministry became a life-long advocacy for LGBT inclusion, starting with organizing the first gathering of Methodist gays and lesbians in Wheadon church near Northwestern University in 1975. Later, he would meet and marry his partner, Jim Dietrich.

At the 2012 UMC General Convention in Tampa, Jim said, "We've been together for over twenty years, and I have only seen Steve cry once. This week, when it became clear that our church was going backwards, not forward, I saw him cry again." Jim's own eyes misted. "At a worship service of our gay community, Steve said 'I won't see it happen in my lifetime,' and then he bawled like I've never seen."[1]

Why go on? Why suffer more frustration? Why dare hope only to have hopes dashed again? For too long, that has been the question facing Methodist gays and lesbians.

And yet what of the infants now being baptized? What of the children coming up through our Sunday Schools, Vacation Bible Schools, UMYF that know they're different? That go to the Bible and find frightening words? That hear frightening words from their parents, and their friends, and their youth leaders? From the pulpit on Sunday morning?

Who will speak the words of comfort and reassurance they need to hear? Who will tell them, "Our church has it wrong!"

Who will raise a voice for those who are called to preach God's word, but are told by our Discipline that they're not good enough? Who will object when legislation is put forth saying that they're unstable, not suitable to be preachers of the word?

Who will raise a voice for those with LGBT family members who are afraid to come out about their family for fear they'll lose the support of the church they love? Who will raise a voice for the mother that lost a gay son to AIDS but still suffers in silence? Who will cry "Shame! You have failed as a church!" for her? Who will give voice to her grief? Who will be the church for her?

How many voices have been silenced? How many suffer in silence? How many turn from God because of the spiritual violence of our church? Who will hold the church accountable? Who will tell the church that this is a life and death issue for more people than we'll ever know? Who will tell them that people are dying?

There will be people who say we're insane. We're endlessly repeating the same process and expecting a different result that's just never going to come. We're a bunch of loonies if we expect the outcome to be different this time.

By that definition, yes, [we are] proud to admit insanity. We embrace it . . . we will go from failure to failure, enthusiasm undiminished.[2]

Qoheleth, the teacher of Ecclesiastes, tells us that for everything there is a season, including a time to weep and a time to laugh, a time to keep silence and a time to speak.

Sometimes, Christians are too nice, too quiescent, too willing to accept the status quo. Sometimes, Christians need to challenge authority, to speak the truth about spiritual violence—especially when the church is the oppressor.

At the 2011 Minnesota Annual Conference session in St. Cloud, pastor Bruce Robbins read a statement of personal privilege at the end of the clergy business meeting.

Seventy Minnesota United Methodist clergy members have signed a statement saying they would "offer the grace of the Church's blessing to any prepared couple desiring Christian marriage," including same-sex couples.

"We are convinced by the witness of others and are compelled by Spirit and conscience to act."[3]

Of course, this was open defiance of church law. A year later, by the time of General Conference in Tampa, the movement had spilled over Minnesota borders, and the number of clergy who had signed on had swelled to nearly twelve hundred.

Thursday, May 3, 2012, had been a day for weeping as the LGBT advocates suffered their latest defeat on the plenary floor of General Conference. On Friday, the last day of General Conference, the wounded gays and lesbians gathered in the tent Tabernacle across the street from the Tampa Convention Center. Outside the Tabernacle, the buffoons from Westboro Baptist Church brandished their hate-filled signs and taunted those entering the Tabernacle. "They don't bother me as much as the sugary-sweet claims of Christian love that I hear from our brothers and sisters on the plenary floor," said a voice in the crowd. "At least Fred Phelps is honest about his hatred."

The gathering crowd in the Tabernacle swelled. Bishops, active and retired, filtered forward and lined up in front of the dais to show their solidarity. Elderly Bishop Jack Tuell struggled to move through the mass to take his place. Friday was a time for speaking.

Pastor Robbins from Minneapolis, who had initiated the clergy petition a year earlier, fired up the crowd. "Biblical obedience demands ecclesiastical disobedience," he said, and repeated it again. And again. "Biblical obedience demands ecclesiastical disobedience."

Retired Bishop Melvin Talbert, who had demonstrated a stiff spine of his own a decade earlier when he had squelched the ecclesiastical trials of the "Sacramento 68," was the last to speak. Bishop Talbert is a large black man with a commanding presence, and he spoke in biblical metaphors reminiscent of the civil rights movement.

When Moses confronted Pharaoh, sharing God's word, saying "let my people go," Pharaoh hardened his heart. In the case of this general church it has hardened its heart to GLBT people.

I stand before you here this afternoon and I declare that God has already settled his matter: all human beings are created in the image of God. There are no exceptions, no exclusions. We belong to the family of God.

At the same time, I declare to you that the derogatory language and restrictive laws in the Book of Discipline are immoral, and unjust and no longer deserve our loyalty and obedience.

[The] time has come for those of us who are faithful to the Gospel of Jesus Christ to do what is required of us . . . In light of the actions taken by the General Conference, the time has come to act and to invite others to join what I'm calling an act of biblical obedience.

I call on the clergy who have signed the pledge to stand firm in their resolve to perform marriages among same-sex couples and to do so in the normal course of their pastoral duties. Encourage your congregations to support you by taking actions to support you in your efforts to be faithful to the Gospel by taking action [to use] your local church facilities for such marriages.

I could say that his ringing call to action received a standing ovation, but that wouldn't be quite true since most of the crowd was already on its feet. But the applause, the "amens," and the cheers were long and heart-felt. This was a crowd that wouldn't accept injustice. Steve Webster and Jim Dietrich will fight on. Amy DeLong will fight on. Bishops Jack Tuell and Melvin Talbert will fight on. Twelve hundred clergy and more will fight on.

———

A well-known authority on Christian ethics, retired dean of Yale Divinity School and ordained UMC minister Thomas W. Ogletree, was one of 208 clergy from the New York Conference who signed the petition, promising to perform same-sex marriages, if asked. Like many of his peers, he was asked, and he followed through by officiating at the wedding of his gay son and his partner on October 20, 2012, at the New York City Yale Club.

"What I realized is this was an opportunity for me to make a public witness in support of gay rights,"[Ogletree] said. "Just as I had committed civil disobedience in the civil rights movement, so I committed ecclesial disobedience in the movement for change in our policies toward gay and lesbian persons."[4]

An untold number of UMC clergy have been performing covenant services without fanfare or repercussion, but Professor Ogletree's stature has prompted the gatekeepers to take notice and file charges. Once again, the familiar Methodist gatekeeper, Thomas Lambrecht, has jumped into the fray, even though his Good News organization has not pursued charges against other lesser-known UMC clergy who officiated at lesser-publicized same-sex weddings.

"It's not like we're out beating the bushes looking for cases to file," [Lambrecht] said. "You could spend all day looking at different newspapers around the country trying to find people who violated the Discipline. That's just not our main objective. But when a case becomes public . . . that's when we want to take action."[5]

Whether the case against Ogletree proceeds to trial and what the eventual outcome will be remain unclear. Matthew Berryman, the recently appointed executive director of Reconciling Ministries Network, shall have the last word:

"Public church trials are ultimately, any way you slice it, an expression of the brokenness of our world and the brokenness of Christ's church," Berryman told United Methodist News Service.

"But, as with many things in this paradoxical human life we live under grace, from sad and broken moments flow beauty, goodness and life. In this particular case, there will no doubt be pain involved, but I am certain that the ultimate effects of a potential church trial will be beneficial to the entire church and redemptive to Ogletree and his family."

He added that "any time truth-telling occurs in spite of the church-sanctioned policies of secrecy, silence and shame, a moral victory has been won."[6]

There are sixty-six annual conferences in the United States. Which one will be the first to ordain and appoint an out lesbian or an out gay man? Which one will test the historic Methodist connectionalism in an act of gospel-inspired ecclesiastical disobedience? Which one will hear the exhortation that biblical obedience demands ecclesiastical disobedience? It will not happen in the whole church until voices rise up from below. It is happening in congregations and with individual clergy. Now it is time for the collective voice of an annual conference to speak.

It is time for a bishop to dare to do the right thing. We return to our journey's beginning, and the ringing words of Dr. Charles Willie, whose challenge to Episcopal bishops in 1974 was heeded, the Philadelphia Eleven were irregularly ordained, and the arc of history bent toward justice.

> And so it is meet and right that a bishop, who believes that in Christ there is neither Greek nor Jew, male nor female, ought to ordain any . . . person who is qualified for the Holy Orders. A bishop who, on his own authority, ordains a woman deacon to the priesthood will be vilified, and talked about, but probably not crucified. Such a bishop would be following the path of the Suffering Servant, which is the path Jesus followed. It requires both courage and humility to disobey an unjust law.
>
> The church is in need of such a bishop today.[7]

The prophetic voices of Gene Leggett, Rick Huskey, Steve Webster, Rose Mary Denman, Mark Bowman, Jimmy Creech, Greg Dell, Karen Dammann, Beth Stroud, Amy DeLong, and countless others have led the church to these shores. Now, it is time to stand on their shoulders to gaze upon the promised land, to see what their prophetic eyes have seen, and then it is time to climb down and cross over to the other side.

Will this be the generation of Joshua? "Tomorrow the Lord will do wonders among you . . . then the people crossed over." (Joshua 3:5, 16)

NOTES

1. This account is paraphrased, and the description of the events of May 6, 2012, are based on my own observations.

2. Gary Shepherd, "Our Prophetic Witness," *Drops of Water*, the daily General Conference newsletter of Affirmation, GC 2004, issue #1, April 28, 2004.

3. Victoria Rebeck, United Methodist News Service, "Update: 70 Minn. Clergy OK Same-Sex Unions," June 2, 2011.

4. Heather Hahn, United Methodist News Service, "Theologian charged for same-sex wedding," May 6, 2013.

5. Ibid.

6. Ibid.

7. Bozarth, *Womanpriest*, 93.

P o s t s c r i p t

MUSTARD IS BLOOMING IN THE FIELDS

The number "forty" is mentioned nearly 150 times in the Bible. It rained on Noah and his ark for forty days and forty nights; Moses was on Mount Sinai for forty days; the Israelites wandered in the desert for forty years; and Jesus fasted in the wilderness for forty days. The biblical metaphor is clear; forty symbolizes trial and tribulation followed by restoration or renewal.

In June of 2012, the UCC Coalition celebrated the fortieth anniversary of the ordination of Pastor Bill Johnson. From Stonewall in 1969, it was forty years until 2009 and the Episcopal General Convention and the ELCA Churchwide Assembly that each adopted landmark legislation for LGBT inclusion; for the Presbyterians, it was forty years plus one before their General Assembly opened the door and one more before their presbyteries ratified gays in the pulpit in 2011. The Methodists remain on the River Jordan's banks waiting to cross over, but celebration has followed conflict for the ecumenical denominations after journeys of forty years, more or less. Though there are still unchanged hearts and minds, discriminatory policies have given way toward full inclusion.

Rev. J. Bennett Guess is one of the "gay guys" at UCC headquarters in Cleveland, serving as Executive Minister of Local Church Ministries.

He offered the keynote address at the 2012 UCC Coalition banquet, which included these excerpts (emphasis added):

> I'm so grateful for this occasion tonight, for a great Open and Affirming Banquet, no longer a small bench with seating only for a few, but a great feast with more tables and more chairs being added as we make room for more and more of God's people. A movement—not on the run or in the shadows any longer, but now at the very defining center of UCC life. I know that, on the surface, the ONA movement might be defined as broadening and deepening the church's welcome for LGBT people and our families. I get that. *But at its theological heart, for me, Open and Affirming is about challenging, changing—even reversing—the popular definition and understanding of what it means when we say and hear the word "church."* And that for me is the essence of what ONA is about. But, on behalf of the whole United Church of Christ, thanks be to God and thanks be to you for the work and ministry you have undertaken so courageously, so faithfully, for 40-plus years. Our church, indeed the whole church (if I might be so presumptuous), is redefining itself because of you.[1]

Following the Episcopal General Convention in the summer of 2012, Presiding Bishop Schori commented during the closing press conference:

> You have seen the Episcopal Church not only of the future, but of today, in the presence of young adults, a more significant number than we've seen in a long time, people of many nations and tribes and language traditions. The Episcopal Church is healthy, it's becoming healthier, and it's poised for an even more significant impact on the world around us. There's no stopping us. Watch out world. We're coming.[2]

At the 2012 ELCA Youth Gathering in New Orleans, more than thirty-five thousand teens and chaperones screamed and stomped as speakers extolled the church's newfound openness and inclusivity. In Minnesota, where a marriage equality amendment was on the November, 2012, ballot, five of the six Minnesota ELCA synods passed resolutions in favor of marriage equality (opposing the amendment), and the bishop of the Minneapolis Area Synod, Rev. Ann Svennungsen, became spokesperson for a coalition of clergy that offered public support for marriage equality. With significant Lutheran leadership, faith communities of Minnesota were at the core of the coalition that helped defeat the proposed amendment at the polls, and then went on to encourage the 2013 legislature to adopt marriage equality in Minnesota—the twelfth state to do so. At the LC/NA (now ReconcilingWorks) biennial assembly in Washington, D.C., in July 2012, ELCA Presiding Bishop Mark Hanson offered the keynote address. His mere presence served as symbol of the newfound inclusion, and his warm words drew repeated standing ovations, and the bishop and his wife were mobbed by well-wishers as they slowly weaved through the aisles. In May of 2013, a gay bishop was elected to the Southwest California Synod.

The Presbyterian experience of inclusivity is two years younger, but the website of the Covenant Network of Presbyterians has begun to collect personal stories of celebration following the long season of conflict, entitled "A Season of Welcome," two of which follow.[3]

Dan Roth writes of the vote in his own Sacramento Presbytery (emphasis added):

We discussed and debated, and in true Presbyterian fashion, we voted. To be honest, I did not think we were going to prevail, but when the moderator announced the results I think everyone in the room was stunned. The Sacramento Presbytery had flipped and had joined other presbyteries from around the United States to support changing the ordination standards.

I was in shock. After lots of hugging, handshaking, and pure joy, I made the drive back to Sacramento. Spring was just arriving in the Central Valley, and *the mustard was blooming in the fields*. After a long and dark winter, a new spring was arriving in the Presbyterian Church. . . .

But life changes when you do not have to hide anymore. The energy that it takes to hide suddenly can be used to do God's work. When we are honest with each other, it means we can love each other, and the more people who are allowed to participate in the church, the better we do at discerning God's will. The church is still imperfect, and I know it always will be. But with each step towards inclusion—from taking a strong stance against slavery to allowing women to serve our church—our congregations only get stronger.

Katie Ricks writes,

I used to be focused on the goal of ordination, but now I am keenly aware that the most amazing part of becoming approved as an inquirer or candidate or teaching elder was NOT reaching that milestone. Rather, learning to trust God and God's promise; relying upon a community of support; and experiencing grace-filled moments with people—especially those with whom I disagree—have been the most meaningful experiences of this journey.

To be sure, trust, reliance, community, and grace-filled moments were gifts shared by gays and lesbians on the journey. So, too, has the church been blessed—or at least the sliver of Christendom under discussion here: the ecumenical denominations. Presuming to speak for these churches, I can say that we have relearned the meaning of gospel, we have been healed of a grace-killing sickness of the soul, and we have once again encountered Christ on the road to Damascus.

We are not merely accepting of LGBT folk but profoundly thankful because this seemingly narrow issue has widened our scriptural, moral, and theological sensibilities. We have all been given the gift of extravagant welcome. We are reminded that the fatted calf has been prepared for each of us, and together we feast. It has not been LGBT pilgrims alone who have journeyed, and not merely gays, lesbians, and a handful of allies; it has been all of us; and the people of God have once again come out of the wilderness.

The kingdom of God "is like a mustard seed that someone took and sowed in the garden; it grew and became a tree, and the birds of the air made nests in its branches." (Luke 13:19). Mustard is blooming in the fields.

NOTES

1. J. Bennett Guess, Keynote Address, Open and Affirming Banquet, UCC Coalition for LGBT Concerns, Fortieth Anniversary National Gathering, Elmhurst, Illinois, June 27, 2012.

2. Matthew Davies, Episcopal News Service, "Convention Wrap-Up: Re-Envisioning Church for the 21st Century," July 12, 2012.

3. A Season of Welcome's website, accessed September 17, 2012, http://aseasonofwelcome.org/read-a-story-ii/.

Index